Arlene G. Taylor, PhD, MSLS, BA
Barbara B. Tillett, PhD, MLS, BA
Editors

Authority Control in Organizing and Accessing Information: Definition and International Experience

Authority Control in Organizing and Accessing Information: Definition and International Experience has been co-published simultaneously as *Cataloging & Classification Quarterly*, Volume 38, Numbers 3/4 2004 and Volume 39, Numbers 1/2 2004.

Pre-publication REVIEWS, COMMENTARIES, EVALUATIONS . . .

Authority Control in Organizing and Accessing Information: Definition and International Experience

Authority Control in Organizing and Accessing Information: Definition and International Experience has been co-published simultaneously as *Cataloging & Classification Quarterly*, Volume 38, Numbers 3/4 2004 and Volume 39, Numbers 1/2 2004.

For Kathie,
With continuing
gratitude,
Arlene

Cataloging & Classification Quarterly™ Monographic "Separates"

Below is a list of "separates," which in serials librarianship means a special issue simultaneously published as a special journal issue or double-issue *and* as a "separate" hardbound monograph. (This is a format which we also call a "DocuSerial.")

"Separates" are published because specialized libraries or professionals may wish to purchase a specific thematic issue by itself in a format which can be separately cataloged and shelved, as opposed to purchasing the journal on an on-going basis. Faculty members may also more easily consider a "separate" for classroom adoption.

"Separates" are carefully classified separately with the major book jobbers so that the journal tie-in can be noted on new book order slips to avoid duplicate purchasing.

You may wish to visit Haworth's Website at . . .

http://www.HaworthPress.com

. . . to search our online catalog for complete tables of contents of these separates and related publications.

You may also call 1-800-HAWORTH (outside US/Canada: 607-722-5857), or Fax 1-800-895-0582 (outside US/Canada: 607-771-0012), or e-mail at:

docdelivery@haworthpress.com

Authority Control in Organizing and Accessing Information: Definition and International Experience, edited by Arlene G. Taylor, PhD, MSLS, BA, and Barbara B. Tillett, PhD, MLS, BA (Vol. 38, No. 3/4, 2004 and Vol. 39, No. 1/2, 2004). *Presents international perspectives on authority control for names, works, and subject terminology in library, archival, museum, and other systems that provide access to information.*

The Thesaurus: Review, Renaissance, and Revision, edited by Sandra K. Roe, MS, and Alan R. Thomas, MA, FLA (Vol. 37, No. 3/4, 2004). *Examines the historical development of the thesaurus, and the standards employed for thesaurus construction, use, and evaluation.*

Knowledge Organization and Classification in International Information Retrieval, edited by Nancy J. Williamson, PhD, and Clare Beghtol, PhD (Vol. 37, No. 1/2, 2003). *Examines the issues of information retrieval in relation to increased globalization of information and knowledge.*

Electronic Cataloging: AACR2 and Metadata for Serials and Monographs, edited by Sheila S. Intner, DLS, MLS, BA, Sally C. Tseng, MLS, BA, and Mary Lynette Larsgaard, MA, BA (Vol. 36, No. 3/4, 2003). *"The twelve contributing authors represent some of the most important thinkers and practitioners in cataloging." (Peggy Johnson, MBA, MA, Associate University Librarian, University of Minnesota Libraries)*

Historical Aspects of Cataloging and Classification, edited by Martin D. Joachim, MA (classical languages and literatures), MA (library science) (Vol. 35, No. 1/2, 2002 and Vol. 35, No. 3/4, 2003). *Traces the development of cataloging and classification in countries and institutions around the world.*

Education for Cataloging and the Organization of Information: Pitfalls and the Pendulum, edited by Janet Swan Hill, BA, MA (Vol. 34, No. 1/2/3, 2002). *Examines the history, context, present, and future of education for cataloging and bibliographic control.*

Works as Entities for Information Retrieval, edited by Richard P. Smiraglia, PhD (Vol. 33, No. 3/4, 2002). *Examines domain-specific research about works and the problems inherent in their representation for information storage and retrieval.*

The Audiovisual Cataloging Current, edited by Sandra K. Roe, MS (Vol. 31, No. 2/3/4, 2001). *"All the great writers, teachers, and lecturers are here: Olson, Fox, Intner, Weihs, Weitz, and Yee. This eclectic collection is sure to find a permanent place on many catalogers' bookshelves. . . . Something for everyone. . . . Explicit cataloging guidelines and AACR2R interpretations galore." (Verna Urbanski, MA, MLS, Chief Media Cataloger, University of North Florida, Jacksonville)*

Managing Cataloging and the Organization of Information: Philosophies, Practices and Challenges at the Onset of the 21st Century, edited by Ruth C. Carter, PhD, MS, MA (Vol. 30, No. 1/2/3, 2000). *"A fascinating series of practical, forthright accounts of national, academic, and special library cataloging operations in action. . . . Yields an abundance of practical solutions for shared problems, now and for the future. Highly recommended." (Laurel Jizba, Head Cataloger, Portland State University Library, Oregon)*

The LCSH Century: One Hundred Years with the Library of Congress Subject Headings System, edited by Alva T. Stone, MLS (Vol. 29, No. 1/2, 2000). *Traces the 100-year history of the Library of Congress Subject Headings, from its beginning with the implementation of a dictionary catalog in 1898 to the present day, exploring the most significant changes in LCSH policies and practices, including a summary of other contributions celebrating the centennial of the world's most popular library subject heading language.*

Maps and Related Cartographic Materials: Cataloging, Classification, and Bibliographic Control, edited by Paige G. Andrew, MLS, and Mary Lynette Larsgaard, MA, BA (Vol. 27, No. 1/2/3/4, 1999). *Discover how to catalog the major formats of cartographic materials, including sheet maps, early and contemporary atlases, remote-sensed images (i.e., aerial photographs and satellite images), globes, geologic sections, digital material, and items on CD-ROM.*

Portraits in Cataloging and Classification: Theorists, Educators, and Practitioners of the Late Twentieth Century, edited by Carolynne Myall, MS, CAS, and Ruth C. Carter, PhD (Vol. 25, No. 2/3/4, 1998). *"This delightful tome introduces us to a side of our profession that we rarely see: the human beings behind the philosophy, rules, and interpretations that have guided our professional lives over the past half century. No collection on cataloging would be complete without a copy of this work." (Walter M. High, PhD, Automation Librarian, North Carolina Supreme Court Library; Assistant Law Librarian for Technical Services, North Carolina University, Chapel Hill)*

Cataloging and Classification: Trends, Transformations, Teaching, and Training, edited by James R. Shearer, MA, ALA, and Alan R. Thomas, MA, FLA (Vol. 24, No. 1/2, 1997). *"Offers a comprehensive retrospective and innovative projection for the future." (The Catholic Library Association)*

Electronic Resources: Selection and Bibliographic Control, edited by Ling-yuh W. (Miko) Pattie, MSLS, and Bonnie Jean Cox, MSLS (Vol. 22, No. 3/4, 1996). *"Recommended for any reader who is searching for a thorough, well-rounded, inclusive compendium on the subject." (The Journal of Academic Librarianship)*

Cataloging and Classification Standards and Rules, edited by John J. Riemer, MLS (Vol. 21, No. 3/4, 1996). *"Includes chapters by a number of experts on many of our best loved library standards. . . . Recommended to those who want to understand the history and development of our library standards and to understand the issues at play in the development of new standards." (LASIE)*

Classification: Options and Opportunities, edited by Alan R. Thomas, MA, FLA (Vol. 19, No. 3/4, 1995). *"There is much new and valuable insight to be found in all the chapters. . . . Timely in refreshing our confidence in the value of well-designed and applied classification in providing the best of service to the end-users." (Catalogue and Index)*

Cataloging Government Publications Online, edited by Carolyn C. Sherayko, MLS (Vol. 18, No. 3/4, 1994). *"Presents a wealth of detailed information in a clear and digestible form, and reveals many of the practicalities involved in getting government publications collections onto online cataloging systems." (The Law Librarian)*

Cooperative Cataloging: Past, Present and Future, edited by Barry B. Baker, MLS (Vol. 17, No. 3/4, 1994). *"The value of this collection lies in its historical perspective and analysis of past and present approaches to shared cataloging. . . . Recommended to library schools and large general collections needing materials on the history of library and information science." (Library Journal)*

Languages of the World: Cataloging Issues and Problems, edited by Martin D. Joachim (Vol. 17, No. 1/2, 1993). *"An excellent introduction to the problems libraries must face when cataloging materials not written in English. . . . should be read by every cataloger having to work with international materials, and it is recommended for all library schools. Nicely indexed." (Academic Library Book Review)*

Retrospective Conversion Now in Paperback: History, Approaches, Considerations, edited by Brian Schottlaender, MLS (Vol. 14, No. 3/4, 1992). *"Fascinating insight into the ways and means of converting and updating manual catalogs to machine-readable format." (Library Association Record)*

Enhancing Access to Information: Designing Catalogs for the 21st Century, edited by David A. Tyckoson (Vol. 13, No. 3/4, 1992). *"Its down-to-earth, nontechnical orientation should appeal to practitioners including administrators and public service librarians." (Library Resources & Technical Services)*

Describing Archival Materials: The Use of the MARC AMC Format, edited by Richard P. Smiraglia, MLS (Vol. 11, No. 3/4, 1991). *"A valuable introduction to the use of the MARC AMC format and the principles of archival cataloging itself." (Library Resources & Technical Services)*

Subject Control in Online Catalogs, edited by Robert P. Holley, PhD, MLS (Vol. 10, No. 1/2, 1990). *"The authors demonstrate the reasons underlying some of the problems and how solutions may be sought. . . . Also included are some fine research studies where the researchers have sought to test the interaction of users with the catalogue, as well as looking at use by library practitioners." (Library Association Record)*

Library of Congress Subject Headings: Philosophy, Practice, and Prospects, by William E. Studwell, MSLS (Supp. #2, 1990). *"Plays an important role in any debate on subject cataloging and succeeds in focusing the reader on the possibilities and problems of using Library of Congress Subject Headings and of subject cataloging in the future." (Australian Academic & Research Libraries)*

Authority Control in the Online Environment: Considerations and Practices, edited by Barbara B. Tillett, PhD (Vol. 9, No. 3, 1989). *"Marks an excellent addition to the field. . . . [It] is intended, as stated in the introduction, to 'offer background and inspiration for future thinking.' In achieving this goal, it has certainly succeeded." (Information Technology & Libraries)*

National and International Bibliographic Databases: Trends and Prospects, edited by Michael Carpenter, PhD, MBA, MLS (Vol. 8, No. 3/4, 1988). *"A fascinating work, containing much of concern both to the general cataloger and to the language or area specialist as well. It is also highly recommended reading for all those interested in bibliographic databases, their development, or their history." (Library Resources & Technical Services)*

Cataloging Sound Recordings: A Manual with Examples, by Deanne Holzberlein, PhD, MLS (Supp. #1, 1988). *"A valuable, easy to read working tool which should be part of the standard equipment of all catalogers who handle sound recordings." (ALR)*

Education and Training for Catalogers and Classifiers, edited by Ruth C. Carter, PhD (Vol. 7, No. 4, 1987). *"Recommended for all students and members of the profession who possess an interest in cataloging." (RQ-Reference and Adult Services Division)*

The United States Newspaper Program: Cataloging Aspects, edited by Ruth C. Carter, PhD (Vol. 6, No. 4, 1986). *"Required reading for all who use newspapers for research (historians and librarians in particular), newspaper cataloguers, administrators of newspaper collections, and–most important–those who control the preservation pursestrings." (Australian Academic & Research Libraries)*

Computer Software Cataloging: Techniques and Examples, edited by Deanne Holzberlein, PhD, MLS (Vol. 6, No. 2, 1986). *"Detailed explanations of each of the essential fields in a cataloging record. Will help any librarian who is grappling with the complicated responsibility of cataloging computer software." (Public Libraries)*

AACR2 and Serials: The American View, edited by Neal L. Edgar (Vol. 3, No. 2/3, 1983). *"This book will help any librarian or serials user concerned with the pitfalls and accomplishments of modern serials cataloging." (American Reference Books Annual)*

The Future of the Union Catalogue: Proceedings of the International Symposium on the Future of the Union Catalogue, edited by C. Donald Cook (Vol. 2, No. 1/2, 1982). *Experts explore the current concepts and future prospects of the union catalogue.*

Authority Control in Organizing and Accessing Information: Definition and International Experience

Arlene G. Taylor, PhD, MSLS, BA
Barbara B. Tillett, PhD, MLS, BA
Editors

With the assistance of
Mauro Guerrini
Murtha Baca

Authority Control in Organizing and Accessing Information: Definition and International Experience has been co-published simultaneously as *Cataloging & Classification Quarterly*, Volume 38, Numbers 3/4 2004 and Volume 39, Numbers 1/2 2004.

The Haworth Information Press®
An Imprint of The Haworth Press, Inc.

New York • London • Victoria (AU)
www.HaworthPress.com

Published by

The Haworth Information Press®, 10 Alice Street, Binghamton, NY 13904-1580 USA

The Haworth Information Press® is an imprint of The Haworth Press, Inc., 10 Alice Street, Binghamton, NY 13904-1580 USA.

Authority Control in Organizing and Accessing Information: Definition and International Experience has been co-published simultaneously as *Cataloging & Classification Quarterly*™, Volume 38, Numbers 3/4 2004 and Volume 39, Numbers 1/2 2004.

The development, preparation, and publication of this work has been undertaken with great care. However, the publisher, employees, editors, and agents of The Haworth Press and all imprints of The Haworth Press, Inc., including The Haworth Medical Press® and Pharmaceutical Products Press®, are not responsible for any errors contained herein or for consequences that may ensue from use of materials or information contained in this work. Opinions expressed by the author(s) are not necessarily those of The Haworth Press, Inc. With regard to case studies, identities and circumstances of individuals discussed herein have been changed to protect confidentiality. Any resemblance to actual persons, living or dead, is entirely coincidental.

Cover design by Kerry E. Mack.

Library of Congress Cataloging-in-Publication Data

Authority control in organizing and accessing information : definition and international experience / Arlene G. Taylor, Barbara B. Tillett, editors; with the assistance of Mauro Guerrini, Murtha Baca.
  p. cm.
  Proceedings of the international conference "Authority control: definition and international experiences" held in Florence, Italy, February 10-12, 2003.
  "Co-published simultaneously as Cataloging & classification quarterly, volume 38, numbers 3/4 2004 and volume 39, numbers 1/2 2004."
  Includes bibliographical references and index.
  ISBN 0-7890-2715-1 (alk. paper) – ISBN 0-7890-2716-X (pbk. : alk. paper)
  1. Authority files (Information retrieval)–Congresses. I. Taylor, Arlene G., 1941- II. Tillett, Barbara B. III. Guerrini, Mauro. IV. Baca, Murtha. V. Cataloging & classification quarterly.
Z693.3.A88 A858 2004
025.3'222–dc22
                                                                                            2004016717

Indexing, Abstracting & Website/Internet Coverage

This section provides you with a list of major indexing & abstracting services and other tools for bibliographic access. That is to say, each service began covering this periodical during the year noted in the right column. Most Websites which are listed below have indicated that they will either post, disseminate, compile, archive, cite or alert their own Website users with research-based content from this work. (This list is as current as the copyright date of this publication.)

Abstracting, Website/Indexing Coverage . . . . Year When Coverage Began

- *Computer and Information Systems Abstracts <http://www.csa.com>* **2004**
- *Current Cites [Digital Libraries] [Electronic Publishing]*
  [Multimedia & Hypermedia] [Networks & Networking]
  [General] <http://sunsite.berkeley.edu/CurrentCites/> **2000**
- *Current Index to Journals in Education* **1986**
- *FRANCIS. INIST/CNRS <http://www.inist.fr>* **1999**
- *IBZ International Bibliography of Periodical Literature*
  <http://www.saur.de> **1995**
- *Index Guide to College Journals (core list compiled by integrating*
  48 indexes frequently used to support undergraduate programs
  in small to medium sized libraries) **1999**
- *Index to Periodical Articles Related to Law <http://www.law.utexas.edu>* . . . **1989**
- *Information Science & Technology Abstracts: indexes journal articles*
  from more than 450 publications as well as books, research reports,
  and conference proceedings; EBSCO Publishing
  <http://www.epnet.com> **1980**
- *Informed Librarian, The <http://www.informedlibrarian.com>* **1993**
- *INSPEC is the leading English-language bibliographic information*
  service providing access to the world's scientific & technical literature
  in physics, electrical engineering, electronics, communications,
  control engineering, computers & computing, and information
  technology <http://www.iee.org.uk/publish/> **1982**
- *Internationale Bibliographie der geistes- und sozialwissenschaftlichen*
  Zeitschriftenliteratur . . . See IBZ **1995**

(continued)

Special Bibliographic Notes related to special journal issues (separates) and indexing/abstracting:

- indexing/abstracting services in this list will also cover material in any "separate" that is co-published simultaneously with Haworth's special thematic journal issue or DocuSerial. Indexing/abstracting usually covers material at the article/chapter level.
- monographic co-editions are intended for either non-subscribers or libraries which intend to purchase a second copy for their circulating collections.
- monographic co-editions are reported to all jobbers/wholesalers/approval plans. The source journal is listed as the "series" to assist the prevention of duplicate purchasing in the same manner utilized for books-in-series.
- to facilitate user/access services all indexing/abstracting services are encouraged to utilize the co-indexing entry note indicated at the bottom of the first page of each article/chapter/contribution.
- this is intended to assist a library user of any reference tool (whether print, electronic, online, or CD-ROM) to locate the monographic version if the library has purchased this version but not a subscription to the source journal.
- individual articles/chapters in any Haworth publication are also available through the Haworth Document Delivery Service (HDDS).

Authority Control
in Organizing
and Accessing Information:
Definition and International
Experience

Authority Control in Organizing and Accessing Information: Definition and International Experience has been co-published simultaneously as *Cataloging & Classification Quarterly*, Volume 38, Numbers 3/4 2004 and Volume 39, Numbers 1/2 2004.

Authority Control in Organizing and Accessing Information: Definition and International Experience

AUTHORITY CONTROL EXPERIENCES AND PROJECTS

ABOUT THE EDITORS

Arlene G. Taylor, PhD, MSLS, BA, is Professor Emerita, Department of Library and Information Science, School of Information Sciences, University of Pittsburgh. She has held professional positions in three libraries (Library of Congress, Christopher Newport College, and Iowa State University) and has taught part-time or full-time for several schools of library and information science. She holds a PhD from the University of North Carolina at Chapel Hill, an MSLS from the University of Illinois at Urbana/Champaign, and a BA from Oklahoma Baptist University. Dr. Taylor is author of several books including *The Organization of Information*, 2nd ed. (Libraries Unlimited, 2004) and *Wynar's Introduction to Cataloging and Classification*, 9th ed. (Libraries Unlimited, 2000). Recent articles include: "Teaching Authority Control" (published in these proceedings of the International Authority Control Conference, Florence, Italy, February 10-12, 2003), "Introduction: From Catalog to Gateway to . . ." (to be published by the Association for Library Collections and Technical Services, 2004), "On Teaching Subject Cataloging" (with Daniel N. Joudrey) in *Cataloging & Classification Quarterly* 34, no. 1/2 (2002): 223-232; and "Teaching Seriality: A Major Educational Challenge," in *The Serials Librarian* 41, nos. 3/4 (2002): 73-80.

Dr. Taylor is the recipient of two Fulbright Senior Specialist Program Grants, including posts at Suranarec University of Technology in Thailand and at Bar Ilan University in Israel. She has also been the recipient of the 2000 ALA/Highsmith Library Literature Award, the 1999 Profile in Excellence Award (given by Oklahoma Baptist University in recognition of outstanding accomplishments in the lives and careers of alumni), and the 1996 Margaret Mann Citation, among other honors. She has served on numerous committees in the Association for Library and Information Science Education (ALISE) and the American Library Association (ALA). International activity includes, in addition to the Fulbright grants already mentioned, serving as consultant on Web page organization for the Bodleian Library, Oxford University; serving as consultant on use of the MARC format for the library of Universidade Federal de Goiás (Brazil), and presenting papers in Brazil, Italy, and Japan.

Barbara B. Tillett, PhD, MLS, BA, is Chief of the Cataloging Policy and Support Office (CPSO) at the Library of Congress. That division of about 50 people is responsible for various authoritative cataloging tools, including *LC Rule Interpretations*, *LC Classification* schedules, *LC Subject Headings*, and other cataloging documentation, such as the *Cataloging Service Bulletin, Descriptive Cataloging Manual, Subject Cataloging Manual*, etc. She currently serves as the Library of Congress representative on the Joint Steering Committee for Revision of the *Anglo-American Cataloguing Rules,* chairs the IFLA (International Federation of Library Associations and Institutions) Division IV on Bibliographic Control (former chair of the IFLA Cataloguing Section), and co-chairs the Metadata Policy Group for the Library of Congress as part of the Library's digital strategic planning.

She served along with Tom Delsey, Elaine Svenonius, and Beth Dulabahn, as a consultant on conceptual modeling to the IFLA Study Group on the Functional Requirements for Bibliographic Records, helping to produce the FRBR report. She currently serves as a member of the IFLA Working Group on FRANAR (Functional Requirements for Authority Numbers and Records), which extends the FRBR model to the realm of authority control.

Dr. Tillett has been active in the American Library Association throughout her 34 years as a librarian, including founding the Authority Control Interest Group in 1984 and chairing the ALCTS Cataloging and Classification Section. She also was the first OCLC coordinator for the University of California's southern campuses in the mid-1970s, and has been instrumental in implementations of library automation throughout her career at the University of Hawaii, the University of California-San Diego, and the Library of Congress, where she earned the Library of Congress's highest award as well as the prestigious federal Fleming Award for implementing their ILS on time and under budget before the year 2000. She is also the 2004 recipient of the Margaret Mann Citation.

Preface

The International Conference on Authority Control: Definition and International Experiences was held at the Convitto della Calza in Florence, Italy, February 10-12, 2003. The primary organizer was Professor Mauro Guerrini of the University of Florence. He and his colleagues ran an efficient and enjoyable gathering of many of the world's experts on authority control issues for an unexpectedly large audience, totaling 502 persons. Participants were from Italy, Austria, Belgium, Croatia, Denmark, France, Germany, Hong Kong (China), Japan, Korea, Portugal, Slovenia, Spain, Sweden, Switzerland, the United Kingdom, and the United States.

Sponsors included the University of Florence Faculty of Arts, Middle Ages and Renaissance Studies Department and Library System Coordination Office, the Italian Ministry of Cultural Assets (Head Office for Book and Cultural Institutions, the Tuscany Region), and the Italian Library Association (AIB), plus the financial contribution of several leading library agencies: Burioni, Casalini Libri, Elldiemme, Licosa, Nexus, Pizzo Etichette, and Swets Blackwell. In addition, it was under the auspices of the Istituto Centrale per il Catalogo Unico (ICCU), the Biblioteca Nazionale Centrale di Firenze, and IFLA. With such credentials, it was off to an excellent start.

Professor Guerrini began the conference declaring, "the aim of the meeting is to offer an occasion for rethinking and comparing experiences about a critical aspect of the cataloguing process, and to confirm the attention paid by Italian professionals to the issues most frequently debated at the international level." The international nature of the meeting assured attention well beyond Italy.

The three days of the conference were organized into five sessions as follows:

[Haworth indexing entry note]: "Preface." Taylor, Arlene G., and Barbara B. Tillett. Published in *Authority Control in Organizing and Accessing Information: Definition and International Experience* (ed: Arlene G. Taylor, and Barbara B. Tillett) The Haworth Information Press, an imprint of The Haworth Press, Inc., 2004, pp. xix-xxv. Single or multiple copies of this article are available for a fee from The Haworth Document Delivery Service [1-800-HAWORTH, 9:00 a.m. - 5:00 p.m. (EST). E-mail address: docdelivery@haworthpress.com].

xix

Session I, *State of the Art and New Theoretical Perspectives*
Session II, *Standards, Exchange Formats, Metadata*
Session III, *Authority Control for Names*
Session IV, *Authority Control for Subjects*
Session V, *Authority Control Experiences and Projects*.

The languages of the papers were English or Italian, with most papers provided in both languages to help the audience follow along. The papers were also made available on the Conference Web site. An Italian version of the proceedings, edited by Mauro Guerrini and Barbara Tillett with the assistance of Lucia Sardo, was published in 2003.[1] The English version of the proceedings is published here with some additional papers solicited by the co-editors. The special papers appear in places where they provide useful additional information to the section in which they have been inserted.

A consistent theme of several papers during the Florence conference was the importance of controlling access to names of persons, corporate bodies, works, and subjects–yet acknowledging that this could be done without the necessity for the former Universal Bibliographic Control (UBC) requirement for a single form of the heading to be used by everyone in the world. Indeed, the new view of UBC acknowledges that the user comes first, and that through authority control, the language and scripts that can be read by users and the cultural conventions best understood within a given community can be accommodated. Authority control lends precision to searching and enables collocation or clustering of bibliographic records under names of authors, titles, or subjects.

The first day of the Florence conference began with initial welcoming remarks from officials and a paper setting the stage on authority control in the electronic environment, which appear as the introductory section here. Igino Poggiali and Mauro Guerrini welcome participants to the conference and set the tone of a meeting intended for increasing understanding and knowledge of the important concept of authority control in a world of international communication through global technological connections. Michael Gorman defines authority control and vocabulary control and their place in modern cataloging. He contrasts simplistic metadata schemes with the more complex MARC family of standards and relates the concepts of *precision* and *recall* to authority control in catalogs.

The conference introductory papers were followed by Session I, *State of the Art and New Theoretical Perspectives* that included three papers. In the corresponding section here, Barbara Tillett reports on the state of the art of authority control and new perspectives, including a proof of concept project jointly conducted by the Library of Congress, Die Deutsche Bibliothek, and OCLC for a virtual international authority file (VIAF). This VIAF system is seen as a building block for the future Semantic Web. Arlene Taylor reports that in a survey she conducted of teachers of information organization, respondents emphasized the importance of teaching the concept of authority control despite difficulties in conveying to students such a difficult concept in the face of non-understanding from colleagues, lack of enough course time, and competition from technology courses. Cristina Magliano describes Italy's national effort to build a shared online authority file and describes the implications of maintaining such a resource.

Session II of the conference, *Standards, Exchange Formats, Metadata,* included papers about control of access points, IFLA activities, metadata, and historical reviews. This section begins with Gloria Cerbai Ammannati's description of Italy's Bibliografia Nazionale Italiana UNIMARC database, which has been created using authority control principles. Two papers present activities of the International Federation of Library Associations and Institutions (IFLA): Marie-France Plassard presents a history of IFLA's efforts toward achieving international authority control since the 1970s, and Glenn Patton describes the focus of IFLA's Working Group on Functional Requirements and Numbering of Authority Records (FRANAR) and identifies next steps towards the conceptual model, *Functional Requirements for Authority Records.*[2]

The papers then move on to a digital focus, standards, and computer systems. Metadata standards as means for accomplishing authority control in digital libraries is discussed by José Borbinha. We are given an overview of traditional international library standards for bibliographic control and authority control since the 1960s by Pino Buizza. Alberto Petrucciani gives consideration to the prospect of relieving a bibliographic record of the necessity for including all information needed to describe a manifestation of a work and also all of its relationships to other entities. Instead, he suggests, some of these functions might be taken over by access systems or by links to images or texts of the publications themselves.

The final two papers of this section were solicited by the editors for this publication. Murtha Baca traces the evolution and current status of authority control tools for art and material culture information, a field that did not have authority control or controlled vocabularies until the 1980s. Mirna Willer describes the UNIMARC authorities format.

The second day of the conference began with Session III, *Authority Control for Names,* and included papers on archival perspectives, on NACO, on fact-finding about authority control in Japan, China, and Korea, and on authority control of publishers and printers. We include it here as the section titled, "Authority Control for Names and Works." This section begins with Stefano

Vitali describing the *International Standard Archival Authority Record (Corporate Bodies, Persons, Families)* [ISAAR(CPF)], concentrating particularly on the changes in the second edition to be issued in August 2004. Daniel Pitti, in turn, describes the Encoded Archival Context (EAC), an initiative in the international archival community to design and implement a standard using XML for encoding descriptions of record creators–especially the descriptive data prescribed in ISAAR(CPF). Jutta Weber describes a project to develop a model architecture for collecting, harvesting, linking, and providing access to name authority information regardless of its creation in libraries, archives, museums, or other institutions, called LEAF (Linking and Exploring Authority Files). LEAF is initially linking information about the writers of letters that are harvested by the MALVINE network. It will lead to establishment of a Central European Name Authority File.

Continuing the discussion of authority control of names, John Byrum describes the Name Authority Cooperative (NACO), whose membership includes institutions in 16 countries in Europe, Africa, Oceania, Asia, and Latin America, as well as institutions in most of the states of the United States; the program can be used as a model for other national programs while working toward an eventual global approach to authority control. Eisuke Naito reviews national bibliographic control in China, Japan, and Korea, and he describes workshops on name authority control that were held in the region to set a framework for regional authority control. Lorenzo Baldacchini points out that publishers, printers, and booksellers in the years of hand printing were the entities responsible for the existence of what is called *manifestation* in *Functional Requirements for Bibliographic Records* (FRBR). He suggests that just as national agencies are responsible for authority control of authors, so should they provide authority control of printers, publishers, and booksellers.

Two papers not presented at the conference have been added to this section by the editors. Qiang Jin writes about authority control of corporate names. After observing how much modern users may rely on the Web for the form of names that they search for, she presents three case studies as examples of corporate name authority records that could be improved by addition of current information from the Internet. After pointing out that authority control of works is essentially non-existent, Richard Smiraglia discusses a study of linkages that would be required for authority control of a sample of works. His analysis shows that only a very small proportion have Library of Congress authority records. He points out that collocation can provide implicit linkage if titles of manifestations are the same, but this does not work for title changes, translations, and containing relations.

The second day of the conference ended with Session IV, *Authority Control for Subjects*. In the first paper in this section, Ana Cristán discusses the Program for Cooperative Cataloging's SACO Program, attempting to fit it into the context of subject gateways. She concludes that while SACO is a "gateway" into Library of Congress Subject Headings (LCSH), it is not a subject gateway in the sense of an online service that provides a browsable subject catalog of Internet resources. Genevieve Clavel-Merrin describes MACS (Multilingual Access to Subjects), a system that allows users to carry out searches in major national library collections in Europe using subject headings in their own languages. Rebecca Dean describes OCLC's FAST project, which is an attempt to retain the very rich vocabulary of LCSH while making the schema easier to understand, control, apply, and use. The *Soggettario* (Subject Headings for Italian Library Catalogs) is described by Anna Lucarelli as a thesaurus that will facilitate the transfer of controlled terminology to lists or authority files and archives. Stefano Tartaglia suggests that subject indexing languages should be more concerned with the semantics of subjects than with the syntax in order not to impede its function as a unifying element between the different cataloguing languages. And, finally, Maria Lucia Di Geso describes the work of the Italian network of bibliographic services, Servizio Bibliotecario Nazionale (SBN), and its recent work toward the goal of building a new, consistent vocabulary for documentation of subject matter.

The third day of the conference contained Session V, *Authority Control Experiences and Projects*, a very full day of reports on numerous projects taking place in various countries that have been working on many different aspects of improvement of authority control. Many of these papers have been translated from their original Italian (as were a number of the earlier papers) in order to share the information with the English-speaking world. Claudia Leoncini and Rosaria Maria Servello present experiences with authority control within the project *Census of Italian 16th Century Editions* (EDIT16) carried on by ICCU (Istituto Centrale per il Catalogo Unico) with the cooperation of 1,200 library institutions all over Italy. Massimo Gentili-Tedeschi and Federica Riva discuss issues in the control of music names and titles. Claudia Fabian describes the Consortium of European Research Libraries (CERL) thesaurus file, which particularly serves the interests of early printing, which in the context of the activities of CERL means printing of the handpress book era. Gabriele Messmer gives an overview of the library situation in the Bavarian Library Network and the authority files used in German libraries, after which she discusses experiences in implementing and using the German Name Authority File (PND).

Continuing with the section on experiences and projects, Andrew MacEwan describes Project InterParty, a project that aims to develop a mechanism that will enable the interoperation of identifiers for "parties" or persons (authors, publishers, etc.) across multiple domains, including the book industry, rights management, libraries, and identifier and technology communities. Sherry Vellucci presents some of the issues that are faced when using commercial services for providing authority control, and comments on the challenge of getting vendors to participate in international authority control. Lucia Sardo explains the problems of persons and corporate bodies using multiple names, examines their treatment in library catalogs, and gives a preliminary analysis of the multiple names using FRBR attributes. Lily Hu, Owen Tam, and Patrick Lo provide an overview on the latest developments of Chinese authority control work implemented in Mainland China, Taiwan, Japan, and Hong Kong, concentrating on the Hong Kong Chinese Authority for Names (HKCAN). Maurizio Savoja and Paul Weston's paper reports on the Progetto Lombardo Archivi in INternet (PLAIN), which enables easy public access to the wide heritage of descriptions, already existing in electronic format, of historical archives preserved in the Lombard region. Françoise Bourdon presents work going on at the Association française de normalisation (AFNOR) to model authority data for libraries, archives, and museums. Fausto Ruggeri writes about *Autori cattolici e opere liturgiche in italiano* (ACOLIT), a project for authority control of religious entities for the Catholic Church. Nadine Boddaert discusses two research programs at the Bibliothèque nationale de France aimed at creating authority records for specific fields–specific, but very important for access to the national bibliographic heritage. These two programs are respectively named COFAR (particularly concerned with official corporate bodies of the Ancient Regime) and CORELI (for religious corporate bodies). Claudia Parmeggiani's paper deals with the project *Authority File* which aims at the creation of an experimental aid for reference and bibliographic control addressed to librarians, keepers of archives, and historians interested in the study of the Perugian (Italy) area in the period prior to the nineteenth century.

Luciana Sabini writes on authority control at the University of Florence. Guido Badalamenti presents a case study of a shared authority control system in Tuscany, Italy, involving academic libraries, the Central National Library of Florence, and civic and provincial libraries. Annarita Sansò writes on a project to create an authoritative list of ancient Italian states and the related problems in, first of all, agreeing on a definition, as the concept of state has changed over time. Maria Teresa Donati describes the project to create an authority file of Medieval Latin authors and works for the Biblioteca di Cultura Medievale, that delves into the complexities of historical analysis to discover the true identity for attribution of anonymous works. The project BISLAM described by Roberto Gamberini results from a census of authors of the Medieval Age with the purpose of offering a program useful both to scholars of medieval Latin literature and to specialists in bibliographic catalogs and repertories. The project developed a program entitled *Authors in "Medioevo latino,"* available both in print and on CD-ROM.

The final speaker at the conference was one of Italy's famous librarians, Luigi Crocetti, past President of the Italian Library Association (AIB). His paper speaks eloquently about the importance of this topic and this meeting for libraries in Italy and everywhere.

The final paper in this section was added by the editors as another case study. Lihong Zhu writes about the authority control procedures she and her colleagues developed in order to use the OCLC MARC Record Service (MARS) in conjunction with Innovative Millennium, their local automated system.

Arlene G. Taylor
Barbara B. Tillett

NOTES

1. *Authority Control: Definizione ed esperienze internazionali: atti del convegno internazionale, Firenze, 10-12 febbraio 2003, a cura di Mauro Guerrini e Barbara B. Tillett con la collaborazione di Lucia Sardo (Firenze, Italy: Firenze University Press; Associazione italiana biblioteche, 2003).*

2. Since the conference, the draft *Functional Requirements for Authority Records* was distributed by IFLA for worldwide review as a conceptual model extending the *Functional Requirements for Bibliographic Records (FRBR)* into the realm of authority control for names. It is expected to serve as another fundamental concept in the foundations of cataloging theory.

Welcome to Participants

Igino Poggiali

Authorities, dear colleagues,

First of all I wish to address my deep thanks to the Councillor of Tuscany
Region, Dr. Mariella Zoppi, to Professor Augusto Marinelli, Rector of the
University of Florence, to Professor Paolo Marrassini, Dean of the Faculty of
Humanities of the same University, to Professor Francesco Sicilia, General
Director for Book Patrimony and Cultural Institutions of the Ministry for Cultural Heritage and Activities as well as to Dr. Luciano Scala, Director of ICCU
and Dr. Antonia Ida Fontana, Director of the Central National Library of Florence, for organizing this extremely important international conference together with the Italian Library Association, and its Tuscany Branch.

Next, I would like to thank Professor Mauro Guerrini for the determination
and far-sightedness to carry on, in these years, the debate on professional
themes which are of strategic value for the development of library service in
Italy and in the world, by organizing prestigious events like the one we are going to open.

I wish to thank, together with him, all those who have collaborated in the
organization of the conference, and clearly, the renowned guests and delegates
who will make Florence in these days a place for reflection and a laboratory
for innovation in the management of our institutions. By going through the
programme we can see the level of the contributions of scholars and foreign

Igino Poggiali is National President of the Italian Library Association.

[Haworth co-indexing entry note]: "Welcome to Participants." Poggiali, Igino. Co-published simultaneously in *Cataloging & Classification Quarterly* (The Haworth Information Press, an imprint of The
Haworth Press, Inc.) Vol. 38, No. 3/4, 2004, pp. 1-3; and: *Authority Control in Organizing and Accessing Information: Definition and International Experience* (ed: Arlene G. Taylor, and Barbara B. Tillett) The
Haworth Information Press, an imprint of The Haworth Press, Inc., 2004, pp. 1-3. Single or multiple copies of
this article are available for a fee from The Haworth Document Delivery Service [1-800-HAWORTH, 9:00
a.m. - 5:00 p.m. (EST). E-mail address: docdelivery@haworthpress.com].

http://www.haworthpress.com/web/CCQ
© 2004 by The Haworth Press, Inc. All rights reserved.
Digital Object Identifier: 10.1300/J104v38n03_01

and Italian colleagues, and by the list of registered people we can evaluate the international importance of these conference days in which some 500 librarians and scholars from various European countries, and from very far countries like China, Korea, and Japan will participate.

I would finally like to thank Mme Christine Deschamps, IFLA President, for taking this event under its prestigious auspices.

As for the contents of this meeting, beyond the technical aspects which will be brilliantly illustrated by delegates, I would like to underline the value of elaborations and strategies that will be discussed here on a political, ethical, and professional level.

The overcoming of a hierarchical view of authority entries, and the renunciation of searching a unique entry in favour of a "cluster" entry in which all related headings have equal importance, are possibilities that completely change the perspective of library work. It takes the auspices of openness and ability of inclusion that lie at the basis of our values and that libraries have learned to practice on a logistical level in document selection, and their ability to support free circulation of ideas and knowledge to the level of the management of information. Giving equal dignity to languages and cultures, in which differences of access to data arise, contributes to that globalization based on the dignity of the human being which is the real alternative to the collision of civilizations that darkly hangs over our horizon in these days.

All of that is clearly possible thanks to the help of new technologies. But without the theoretical elaboration that will have a relevant stage of development here, those opportunities would have been totally or partially unusable.

Two developments, I think, could be largely favoured by this research: co-operation among libraries and industrialization of external supports to our activity.

Many papers will discuss cooperative experiences that already exist among library systems implementing national and international authority files, and I believe we can say that the phenomenon is well on its way towards concrete results whose benefits are already visible, beginning in the university environment.

Also, I think that the best way for these processes to become concrete is for the single library to outsource work which is certainly of great value but so complex and costly that it would simply not be possible to realize. To outsource is not necessarily a synonym for privatisation. Much could be done, for example, with national bibliographic services specializing in these duties, possibly separated by the present administrative and bureaucratic setting. The ideal choice would be to use the most suitable solution according to the activity in order to pursue the purposes of quality, cost-saving, and timeliness. This is obvious, but never actually happens!

Whether the work is done inside the library or the task is outsourced, the real problem is the availability of a really professional staff able to face the complexity of these new challenges. The series of problems in which treatment of authority control is set requires a high cultural level of preparation of operators, and a great openness to cultures and ways of thinking that are different and remote. How many of us are really prepared at this level?

During the last ten years the University has been able to take charge in an increasingly timely manner, though in varying degrees, of the problem of training librarians. However, the level of complexity now requires a jump in quality that leads to a preference for training a fewer number of learners who are really interested and qualified and who are able to start working by making a contribution to innovation and efficiency, rather than young people, certainly enthusiastic but having a generic preparation and requiring strong interventions of training for work.

The creation of the two-year Master's in Cataloguing at the University of Florence seems an important answer in this direction. It is of essential importance to have continuous communication between the academic and professional worlds so that these moments of learning hit the center of the desired goals. With regard to this, I believe that, in Italy, quite differently from the Anglo-Saxon context, greater importance than is given today should be addressed to training in the workplace and to its evaluation in the curriculum and profile of future colleagues.

Thanks to all again and good work.

Introduction to the Conference

Mauro Guerrini

The International Conference "Authority Control: Definition and International Experiences" is promoted by the University of Florence (Middle Ages and Renaissance Studies Department and Library System Coordination Office), the Ministry of Cultural Assets (Head Office for Book and Cultural Institutions, through ICCU and the National Central Library in Florence), Tuscany Region, and the Italian Library Association (AIB), under the IFLA auspices. It is sponsored by seven library service agencies, acknowledged professionals in the field: Burioni, Casalini Libri, Ellediemme, Licosa, Nexus, Pizzoetichette, and Swets Blackwell.

The aim of the meeting is to offer an occasion for rethinking and comparing experiences about a critical aspect of the cataloguing process, and to confirm the attention paid by Italian professionals to the issues most frequently debated at the international level. We may cite some examples: the *Seminar on FRBR*, Florence, 27-28 January 2000, the International Conference "Electronic Resources: Definition, Selection, and Cataloguing" Rome, 26-28 November 2001 (with Proceedings published by Editrice Bibliografica), the presentation of the feasibility study for the new *Soggettario delle biblioteche italiane* (subject headings in Italian libraries), Florence, 13 June 2002 and the International Conference on Dublin Core, Florence, 14-17 October 2002. The conference proves how well and profitably its promoters–University of Flor-

Mauro Guerrini is affiliated with Università di Firenze (E-mail: mguerrini@leonet.it).

[Haworth co-indexing entry note]: "Introduction to the Conference." Guerrini, Mauro. Co-published simultaneously in *Cataloging & Classification Quarterly* (The Haworth Information Press, an imprint of The Haworth Press, Inc.) Vol. 38, No. 3/4, 2004, pp. 5-9; and: *Authority Control in Organizing and Accessing Information: Definition and International Experience* (ed: Arlene G. Taylor, and Barbara B. Tillett) The Haworth Information Press, an imprint of The Haworth Press, Inc., 2004, pp. 5-9. Single or multiple copies of this article are available for a fee from The Haworth Document Delivery Service [1-800-HAWORTH, 9:00 a.m. - 5:00 p.m. (EST). E-mail address: docdelivery@haworthpress.com].

Digital Object Identifier: 10.1300/J104v38n03_02

ence, ICCU, National Central Library in Florence, Tuscany Region, and AIB–cooperate.

Effective cataloguing requires controlling the consistency of the form of access points to information so that users can *find, identify, select, and obtain* the information available in a bibliography or catalogue–as stressed by FRBR. *Authority control* is the process that should ensure homogeneity of form in each entity–author, title, body, or descriptor–chosen as an access point; a process that integrates the architecture of the catalogue, not to be separated from its conceptual foundations. Without *authority control* the linking and syndetic structures of the catalogue have feet of clay. Control of form and structure helps eliminate conflicts with other headings already present or likely to be present in the catalogue, increases the precision of searches, and enables appropriate collocation of bibliographic records in OPAC displays.

Authority control is a technique with contents determined by the cataloguer, who is both a child of the times and a member of a real world and a cultural community already defined but at the same time, developing and changing. In short, *authority control* is the process of identifying the various manifestations of a name or title that will guarantee the stability of a default, "authorized," or standard form of heading. The standard form originates from cataloguing conventions based on well-established, accepted cultural traditions; therefore, it is the preferred or predominant, most frequently used form, not necessarily one at a higher level in the hierarchy.

The catalogue allows users to access records of an author's works or a subject from any linked variant form present in the authority record, as well as from any element in the access point. That's why we talk of a *cluster heading*, a term that evokes freeing the concept from the connotations we associate with 'authority,' enabling the display of any of the associated variant forms controlled by an authority record. *Authority control* ensures the quality of indexes and contributes to the overall quality of the catalogue.

The catalogue gets richer thanks to the linguistic realities implied in its compilation. Linguistic pluralism, freed from hierarchies, is a wealth, not a new tower of Babel. Plurality of languages requires a will to cooperate in a homogeneous, non-monolithic cataloguing project, a strong point neither to be wasted nor to be turned into chaos or a liability for smaller cultural communities. "Plurality is not only linguistic but cultural. Humankind, like language, exists only in the plural," the French philosopher Paul Ricouer reminds us.

The Conference logo draws on the theme of the negative aspect of linguistic chaos (i.e., the tower of Babel) in favour of control of access points, a strict but not enforced control, respectful of the information needs of the communities the libraries work for.

As we said (Pino Buizza and I), at the Conference on *Cataloguing and Authority Control* promoted by ICCU, and as was also concluded by the IFLA UBCIM Working Group on Minimal Level Authority Records and ISADN, the former UBC (Universal Bibliographic Control) objective of worldwide adoption of the same form of authorized headings by all is not tenable. The 2001 GARR (*Guidelines for Authority Records and References*) deemed outdated the "uniformity" principle of univocal headings, in favour of one or more "authorized" headings related to the same entity, equal to each other but each suitable to different cultural environments and compiled according to different rules–a new view of UBC. Their equivalence at the international level corresponds to the authority record of the single agency that links its authorized form and references to the "parallel" authorized forms and set of references compiled according to other rules and to other languages or scripts. The objective of linguistic uniformity is bypassed at the international level: we pursue neither the unique language, nor place languages side by side. Thus, work on access point control becomes the work of an interpreter who must no longer pronounce the right name (authority), but must link together the various names used (authorized). The searcher, too, must no longer guess the right name in its precise form but has the interpreter at his disposal who translates his query to the catalogue.

The conference wants to be an occasion for both theoretical exchange among leading experts in the field and to provide information on major international and Italian experiences in creating national authority lists and authority files. Another aim is to make a contribution to the current debate on the revision of national cataloguing codes and their possible harmonization.

During the last few months the Conference was preceded by a series of preliminary meetings promoted by libraries. Among them I would like to mention the one promoted by the Provincial Library in Foggia on *Authority Control and Catalographic Mediation* 27-28 November 2002 and, most of all, the two-day workshop organized by ICCU on *Cataloguing and Authority Control*, Rome, 21-22 November 2002, that was an important occasion for a debate among professional and academic experts who are all engaged in achieving a quality product.

A brief presentation of the sessions of this conference:

Session I, *State of the Art and New Theoretical Perspectives*, will discuss how the concept of authority control has evolved and, to present the new theoretical perspectives enhanced by the evolution of informatics applied to cataloguing practice, it also offers an overview of IFLA's role in the field.

Session II, *Standards, Exchange Formats, Metadata*, will present international standards in the field of authority control, projects linked to the implementation of exchange formats for authority data and the creation of metadata schemes for the control of the form of access to digital documents.

Session III, *Authority Control for Names*, will offer an overview of activities and practices related to the creation of name authority files, in a context ever more characterized by the need for exchange and sharing of authority data across cultural, linguistic, and formal boundaries.

Session IV, *Authority Control for Subjects*, offers an overview of the wide and complex nature of subject authority control in one-language and in multi-language contexts at both national and international levels, presenting the most relevant and innovative developments in the field.

Session V, *Authority Control Experiences and Projects*, provides an opportunity for updating and exchanging opinions in the Italian and international community, presenting some experiences that took place in libraries and similar institutions, and the projects, presently in progress, to make authority control easier and more effective. It pays special attention to implementations by national cataloguing agencies who are most responsible for the creation, maintenance and dissemination of authority data.

ACKNOWLEDGEMENTS

I wish to thank Barbara Tillett, who has contributed to the outline of the program with helpful suggestions, a contribution that continued during the course of a year. I thank the Library System Coordination Office of the University of Florence: Giulia Maraviglia has contributed enthusiastically to the project, forming a group of librarians who worked on the organization: Patrizia Cotoneschi, Margherita Loconsolo, Carla Milloschi, Luciana Sabini, Giuseppe Stroppa, Floriana Tagliabue, Manola Tagliabue, Laura Vannucci; Margherita Loconsolo, with Cristian Contini from Harno, who edited the logo graphics, and Manola Tagliabue, who professionally and speedily edited the planning and updating of the web site. Sandra Torre and Antonella Marinaro took care of the secretarial work at the Middle Ages and Renaissance Studies Department.

I thank Carlo Bianchini, Pino Buizza and Stefano Gambari, for their suggestions, Massimo Pistacchi, from the Ministry for Cultural Assets, Head Office for Book and Cultural Institutions, Massimo Rolle, President of AIB, Tuscany Section, who followed with competence all the organization phases; Lucia Sardo, who collaborated in the scientific organization with devotion and competence–a decisive contribution–and coordinated the editing, in its last phase with the help of Elena Franchini.

I thank the numerous translators: Gabriella Berardi, Carlo Bianchini, Francesco dell'Orso, Grazia di Bartolomeo, Enzo Fugaldi, Agnese Galeffi,

Stefano Gambari, Rossana Morriello, Antonella Novelli, Veronica Park, Barbara Patui; particularly, Maria Letizia Fabbrini, a really helpful person who gave much of her time to translating and revising texts. Eugenie Greig's help was most valuable, as she translated some papers and reviewed various translations into English.

I also want to thank the many foreign participants who have come from Canada, the United States, the Netherlands, Sweden, France, Germany, Japan, Hong Kong, and Iran, as well as the Italian participants coming from all types of libraries, plus a warm welcome to students attending academic courses in Library Science at Pavia, Pisa, and Florence, to doctoral students in Bibliographic Sciences at the universities of Udine, Rome La Sapienza and Milan, and to the students attending the two-year Master's in Archival Science, Library Science, and Codicology at the University of Florence, just inaugurated on the 30th of January.

A final thanks to the FASI Congress, particularly Annarita Pazzaglini and Nicoletta Rambelli, who contributed the necessary logistic support.

We hope this Conference may be a further step towards a future IFLA Conference taking place in Italy.

Have a good working session.

Authority Control in the Context of Bibliographic Control in the Electronic Environment

Michael Gorman

SUMMARY. Defines authority control and vocabulary control and their place and utility in modern cataloguing. Discusses authority records and authority files and the use and purposes of each. Describes the creation of authority records and the sources from which authority data are collected. Discusses "metadata" schemes and their manifold and manifest inadequacies; points out the relationship of the Dublin Core to the MARC family of standards and the fact that both are framework standards–the first, simplistic and naïve; the second, complex and nuanced. Defines *precision* and *recall* as desiderata in indexing and retrieval schemes and relates them to authority control in catalogues. Discusses the problems involved in cataloguing electronic documents and resources, and proposes an international program under the Universal Bibliographic Control (UBC) umbrella, using an international code of descriptive cataloguing, and based on an international name authority file. Calls for urgent action on these proposals. *[Article copies available for a fee from The Haworth Document Delivery Service: 1-800-HAWORTH. E-mail address: <docdelivery@haworthpress.com> Website: <http://www.HaworthPress.com> © 2004 by The Haworth Press, Inc. All rights reserved.]*

Michael Gorman is affiliated with California State University, Fresno.

[Haworth co-indexing entry note]: "Authority Control in the Context of Bibliographic Control in the Electronic Environment." Gorman, Michael. Co-published simultaneously in *Cataloging & Classification Quarterly* (The Haworth Information Press, an imprint of The Haworth Press, Inc.) Vol. 38, No. 3/4, 2004, pp. 11-22; and: *Authority Control in Organizing and Accessing Information: Definition and International Experience* (ed: Arlene G. Taylor, and Barbara B. Tillett) The Haworth Information Press, an imprint of The Haworth Press, Inc., 2004, pp. 11-22. Single or multiple copies of this article are available for a fee from The Haworth Document Delivery Service [1-800-HAWORTH, 9:00 a.m. - 5:00 p.m. (EST). E-mail address: docdelivery@haworthpress.com].

http://www.haworthpress.com/web/CCQ
© 2004 by The Haworth Press, Inc. All rights reserved.
Digital Object Identifier: 10.1300/J104v38n03_03

KEYWORDS. Authority files, cataloguing, descriptive cataloguing, Dublin Core, MARC records, metadata, vocabulary control

There is a sense in which authority control and bibliographic control are co-terminous–two sides of the same coin. At the very least, bibliographic control is literally impossible without authority control. Cataloguing cannot exist without standardized access points, and authority control is the mechanism by which we achieve the necessary degree of standardization. Cataloguing deals with order, logic, objectivity, precise denotation, and consistency, and must have mechanisms to ensure these attributes. The same name, title, or subject should always have the same denotation (in natural language or the artificial languages of classification) each time it occurs in a bibliographic record, no matter how many times that may be. Unless there are careful records of each authorized denotation, the variants of that denotation, and citations of precedents and the rules on which that denotation is based (i.e., authority control), the desired and necessary standardization cannot be achieved.

Let us begin by looking at the fundamentals of cataloguing. A catalogue record consists of three parts:

- An access point
- A bibliographic description
- A location or (nowadays) the document itself[1]

The access point leads the user to the record; the description enables the user to decide whether the item desired is the one sought; and the location takes the user to the desired document. This is a simple and profound formulation and is the basis of all cataloguing. Even the wretched Dublin Core, of which more later, contains access points, descriptive elements, and locational information. Each element of a catalogue entry is standardized. The description and the location are presented in standardized form (or they could not be understood). The standards that govern the description (principally, the International Standard Bibliographic Description standards) and the local standards for location designations are not part of authority control. Therefore, authority control and the related vocabulary control are concerned with access points and their standardization. The access point has two basic functions. It enables the catalogue user to find the record and it groups together records sharing a common characteristic.[2] In order to carry out the first function it must be standardized (obviously the user should always find *Il gattopardo* under **Tomasi di Lampedusa, Giuseppe [Gattopardo]**, and not sometimes under that access point and sometimes under **Lampedusa, Giuseppe Tomasi di** and/or translations and variations of the title). This is what is known as vocabulary control–the presentation of every name (personal or corporate), uniform title, series, and subject denotation in a single, standardized form. The reason why we have cataloguing rules is that any cataloguer following those rules should, theoretically, achieve the same, standardized result in each case.

AUTHORITY RECORDS

Vocabulary control is vital to authority control but it is only the first, if most important, aspect of authority work. Robert Burger discusses the concept of the authority record–the vehicle that contains the results of authority work.[3] In summary, he writes that the role of the authority record has five components:

- To record the standardized form of each access point
- To ensure the gathering together of all records with the same access point
- To enable standardized catalogue records
- To document the decisions taken, and sources of, the access point
- To record all forms of the access point other than the one chosen as the normative form (i.e., forms from which reference is made).

To which I would add:

- To record precedents and other uses of the standardized access point for the guidance of cataloguers.

In many card and other pre-OPAC catalogues, the authority record existed only implicitly–in the evidence of the catalogue entries themselves. Online catalogues demand the explicit formulation of authority records, linked to catalogue entries and containing at least the elements demanded by the roles listed above. That is, they must contain:

- The standardized access point
- All forms from which *See* reference is made
- A connection (a *See also* reference) to all linked authority records
- The sources from which the standardized access point has been derived
- Lists of precedents and other uses of the standardized form.

In addition, in developed machine records, the authority record will itself be linked to all the bibliographic records to which it pertains.[4] The database made by assembling all the authority records used in a catalogue is called an authority file or, looked at another way, a thesaurus.

FROM WHENCE DOES THE CONTENT
OF AUTHORITY RECORDS COME?

The content of authority records (the authoritative form, variant forms, links, and notes of various kinds) is obviously of the greatest importance. In cases in which there are variants, there is always a reason for choosing one form over the others and, crucially, one source of information over the others. The primary agent in such choices is the code of cataloguing rules in force in the area in which the cataloguing is done. Because we have no global cataloguing code (though the *Anglo-American Cataloguing Rules, Second Edition*–AACR2–has a global reach), global lists of subject headings, or global classification systems, cataloguers in different areas may reach completely different conclusions, even when they are proceeding from exactly the same evidence. That evidence is a mixture of the objective (the evidence presented in the materials themselves and in reference sources) and the subjective (the cataloguer's interpretation of the cataloguing rules or subject matter of the document being catalogued).

Here are some of the sources that have to be taken into consideration in constructing catalogue records:

* Existing national and local authority files
* The applicable cataloguing code, subject heading list, etc.
* The document being catalogued
* Reference sources (using the broadest definition of the term–any source providing useful data).

Each of these has to be weighed against the others and, even within each category, some sources have more authority than others. No source can be regarded as always dominant. For example, the evidence presented in the document itself may be superseded by the evidence found in reference sources when the cataloguing code's rules tell the cataloguer to do so. Again, a national authority file may be more authoritative in one case, but a local authority file more authoritative (because of special local knowledge) in another. Within the document itself, information found in one part may conflict with information found in another. Lastly, there is an obvious hierarchy of reference sources. Some publishers produce works of higher quality than others, and most printed sources are more authoritative than most electronic sources.

The result of all of this is the need for the cataloguer to be able to negotiate these ambiguities by exercising skill, good judgement, and the fruits of experience. The *skill* lies in knowledge of the type of material being catalogued; knowledge of the rules that govern cataloguing; knowledge of the interpretations of those rules in the past; and knowledge of applicable reference sources and their strengths and weaknesses. The good *judgment* lies in the ability to weigh all of these factors and to decide based on the spirit of the rules when the letter of those rules is ambiguous. The *fruits of experience* lie in the cumulation of knowledge of rules, policies, and precedents gained from cataloguing many materials over the years. Given these three attributes, a cataloguer can produce records that are truly authoritative and that will benefit cataloguers and library users across the world.

METADATA AND AUTHORITY CONTROL

Metadata–literally, "data about data" (a definition that would include real cataloguing if taken literally)–arose from the desire of non-librarians to improve the retrievability of Web pages and other Internet documents. The basic concept of metadata is that one can achieve a sufficiency of recall and precision (see later for a discussion of these criteria) in searching databases without the time-consuming and expensive processes of standardized cataloguing. In other words, something between the free-text searching of search engines (which is quick, cheap, and ineffective) and full cataloguing (which is sometimes slow, labor-intensive, expensive, and highly effective). Like all such efforts to split the difference, metadata ends up being neither one thing nor the other and, consequently, has failed to show success on any scale, which is the touchstone by which all indexing and retrieval systems must be judged. Any system can be effective if the database is small. The real test is how the system handles databases in the millions. Catalogues, even vast global catalogues such as the OCLC database, have been shown to be effective. Search engines, even the supposedly advanced systems such as Google, are demonstrably ineffective in dealing with vast databases.

After many papers and numerous conferences (a process in which renegade librarians joined), a quasi-standard promoted by OCLC and called the Dublin Core emerged as the shining example of metadata and what it could achieve. The Dublin Core (DC) consists of 15 denotations, each of which has a more or less exact equivalent in the MARC record. As any true cataloguer knows, MARC contains far more than 15 fields and sub-fields, in addition to the information contained in coded fixed fields. In addition, there are MARC formats for a variety of different kinds of publication, from books and serials to electronic resources, which adds to the variety of denotations. Those who advocate metadata and, implicitly or explicitly, believe that the whole range of bibliographic data can be contained in 15 categories ignore the fact that the MARC formats are not the result of whimsy and the baroque impulses of cataloguers, but have evolved to meet the real characteristics of complex documents of all kinds. What we have is a simplistic (in many ways naïve) short list of categories that is expected to substitute for cataloguing when put in the hands of non-cataloguers.

The literature of metadata is littered with references to "MARC cataloguing," an ignorant phrase that betrays the hollowness of the metadata concept.[5] MARC, as any cataloguer knows, is a framework standard for holding bibliographic data. It does not dictate the content of its fields–leaving that to content standards such as AACR2, LCSH, etc. People who talk of "MARC cataloguing" clearly think of cataloguing as being a matter of identifying the elements of a bibliographic record without specifying the content of those elements. It is, therefore, clear that those people do not understand what cataloguing is all about. The most important thing about bibliographic control is the *content* and the controlled nature of that content, not the denotations of that content. So, when all of the tumult and shouting are over and the metadata captains and kings have spoken, we are left with the absurd proposition that a 15-field subset of the MARC record, with no specification of how those fields are to be filled by non-cataloguers, is some kind of substitute for real cataloguing. The fact that metadata and the Dublin Core have been discussed *ad nauseam* for about five years with very few people pointing out this obvious flaw in the argument is reminiscent of the story of the little boy and the naked Emperor. In this case, however, the Emperor keeps strolling around *sans* clothes (controlled content), at least so far.

AUTHORITY CONTROL
AND THE CONTENT OF BIBLIOGRAPHIC RECORDS

Even if one leaves aside the limited number and nature of the categories proposed for the Dublin Core and other metadata schemes, they lack the concepts of controlled vocabularies and authority work–the means by which controlled vocabularies are implemented and maintained. Given the complex structures of bibliographic records and the need to standardize their content, it is evident that the Dublin Core cannot succeed in databases of any size. Random subject, name, title, and series denotations that are not subject to any kind of standardization–vocabulary control–will lead to progressively inchoate results as databases grow and, when a Dublin Core database is of a sufficient size, the results will be no more satisfactory than those using free-text searching on the Web.

PRECISION AND RECALL

All retrieval systems depend on two crucial measurements–*precision* and *recall*. In a perfectly efficient system, all records retrieved would relate exactly to the search terms (100% precision) and all relevant records would be retrieved (100% recall). To take a simple example, both measurements would be perfect if a user approached a catalogue searching for works by Oscar Wilde and found all the works by that author the library possessed and no other works. In real life, a library will possess a number of works by Oscar Wilde that are not retrieved by a search in the catalogue (poems in anthologies, essays in collections by many writers), but one might expect to find all of the books, plays, collected letters and poetry collections by Wilde. One might also expect the precision to be high in that a search for Wilde in a well-organized library catalogue will yield no, or very few, materials unrelated to that author. Compare that to the results of free-text searching using search engines. Even a simple author search for someone with a relatively uncommon name will yield aberrant results. For example, for the purposes of this paper, I did a search on "Michael Gorman" on Google. It yielded "about 7,710" results. Three in the first 10 (supposedly the most relevant) related to me. The other references were to a philosopher of that name in Washington, DC; a historian at Stanford; an Irish folk musician; and a consulting engineer in Denver, Colorado. The remaining 7,700 entries are in no discernable order and some do not even relate to anyone called Michael Gorman. This is what results from the absence of authority control. Were each entry on Google to be catalogued, it would be assigned standardized name, title, and subject access points, so that the more than 7,700 entries would appear in a rational order–each entry relating to each Michael Gorman being grouped together and differentiated from the entries relating to other Michael Gormans. In other words, the searcher would have a reasonable chance of identifying those entries relating to the Michael Gorman she or he is searching for (precision) and identifying all the entries with that characteristic (recall).

Two things are obvious. The system with authority control is clearly superior to the system without. In fact, the latter can hardly be said to be a system as the results of the search are almost completely useless. What is a searcher to do with thousands of records in no order and with no differentiation? The second obvious thing is that supplying the vocabulary and authority control necessary to make searching with the Google system successful would be prohibitively time-consuming and expensive. These two factors are at the core of the dilemma concerning the "cataloguing of the Web" and bringing the world of the Internet and the Web under bibliographic control. If we are to ensure precision and recall in searches, we must have controlled vocabularies, but we cannot afford to extend that control to the vast mass of marginal, temporarily useful, and useless Web documents. What shall we do?

SOLUTIONS

First, I believe that we should either abandon the whole idea of metadata as something that will ever be of utility in large databases used by librarians and library users or we should invest metadata schemes with the attributes of traditional bibliographic records. The idea of giving up on metadata is attractive, if only because it is patently obvious that such schemes as currently practiced cannot possibly succeed except in small niche databases of specialized materials. However, the idea of enriching metadata to bring it up to the standards of cataloguing may be more psychologically and politically palatable. After all, a number of influential people and organizations are involved in, or supporting, metadata schemes and programs, and it is hard to imagine them facing the reality and declaring metadata dead as far as libraries are concerned. The dilemma with which such organizations are faced is neatly encapsulated in the report of the library at Cornell University on their participation in the Cooperative Research Cataloging project (CORC)–one of the largest metadata projects:

> Many staff members are dissatisfied with the paper-based selection form we are using now to pass along selection information to acquisitions and cataloging, and having technical services staff start from scratch with each Internet resource description is wasteful. But if selectors and reference staff begin creating preliminary records, how much would be expected of them, in terms of record content? Should students and acquisitions staff be taught to use CORC and DC to obtain preliminary records?
>
> Related to the issue above–we are not sure how to implement the Dublin Core element set. Should there be guidelines? Would it make sense to agree on some basic guidelines for the content of a CUL DC [Cornell Dublin Core] record from CORC (like the University of Minnesota library has done)? We are sure we don't want using DC to be tedious, time-consuming or complicated, so if we have guidelines, they must be simple and straightforward to teach and use.[6]

The fact is that the use of people without the skills and experience of cataloguers to complete metadata templates will lead, inevitably, to incoherent, unusable databases. Another indisputable reality is that real cataloguing is, equally inevitably, "time-consuming" and "complicated." The world of recorded knowledge and information is complicated, and the number of complications tends to the infinite. It is impossible to conceive of a system that allows for consistent retrieval of relevant information while lacking "guidelines" (i.e., rules dictating the nature and form of the content of the records). Eventually the fact that you cannot have high quality cataloguing on the cheap will dawn on those involved in metadata schemes but not, I fear, before we have gone through a long and costly process of education and re-education and experienced the failure of databases containing records without standards and authority control.

The second solution lies in a rigorous and thorough examination of the nature of electronic documents and resources. We cannot and should not catalogue the majority of electronic documents, any more than we catalogued the millions of sub-documents and ephemera found in the print world. The problems are how to identify those electronic documents of lasting worth and, once they are catalogued, how to preserve them. These are profound and complex questions, not easily answered, but they are vital to our progress in making electronic documents and resources available to all library users. [7]

TOWARD UBC

The ideal behind Universal Bibliographic Control (UBC) is that each document would be catalogued once only in its country of origin and that the results of that cataloguing would be made available throughout the world. That ideal, though it is nearer to being realized than ever before, still lacks two vital elements–a universally accepted cataloguing code (and subject heading list) and an international authority file. There is only one way to provide these missing elements and, thus, achieve UBC.

First, we must have a cataloguing code for access points with identical wording in each language (we already have international agreement on descriptive elements in the form of the *ISBD* standards). Such a code must, of necessity, consist of only the broad generally accepted rules that transcend linguistic and cultural differences. For example, we could all agree that the form of heading for a person should be based on the form most commonly found in that person's publications, in some stated cases, and the form most commonly found in reference sources, in other stated cases. Equally, we could agree that direct entry of the names of corporate bodies is preferable and agree on the cases in which corporate bodies can be considered "authors" of their publications. As a practical matter we could use the general rules in *AACR2* Part 2 as the basis for discussions on the universal code rather than attempting to start from scratch.

Second, we should establish a global authority file in which each person, corporate body, uniform title, and subject is identified by a number (based on the ideas behind the ISBN)–that number identifying a record in which can be found the standardized form of the name or title in each linguistic and cultural context *identified as such.* To take a simple example, the Roman poet **Quintus Horatius Flaccus** is known by that name and as **Horace** in English-speaking countries and as **Quinto Orazio Flacco** and as **Orazio** in Italy. The global authority file record for the poet would contain all four forms (as well as the forms by which he is known in all other languages) with indications of which is the preferred form in English, Italian, German, French, etc. (see Appendix).

In transmitting records, only the neutral numerical indicator for the name or title would be included in the relevant field of the MARC record. For example, a MARC record for the complete works of Horace published in Florence would contain the following:

100 #a 32170-99

230 #a 97288-73

which, upon being matched to the global authority file, would be displayed in a British, American, Canadian, etc., library as:

Horace

[Works]

and in an Italian library as:

Orazio

[Opere]

In this way, the global cataloguing code would prescribe the heading as being based on the form of name most commonly found in reference sources within the language or cultural grouping and the uniform title as "Works" in the appropriate language. The global authority file would permit transmission of records that both conform to the cataloguing code and make provision for linguistic or cultural differences in a neutral manner.

CONCLUSION

Authority control is central and vital to the activities we call cataloguing. Cataloguing–the logical assembling of bibliographic data into retrievable and usable records–is the one activity that enables the library to pursue its central missions of service and free and open access to all recorded knowledge and information. We cannot have real library service without a bibliographic architecture and we cannot have that bibliographic architecture without authority control. It is as simple and as profound as that.

NOTES

1. In the case of many systems giving access to electronic documents and resources, the "location" is a URL or something similar that, upon being clicked, takes the user to the document or resource itself.

2. Schmierer, Helen F. "The Relationship of Authority Control to the Library Catalog." *Illinois Libraries* 62:599-603 (September 1980).

3. Burger, Robert H. *Authority Work*. Littleton, Colo.: Libraries Unlimited, 1985. p. 5.

4. I have been advocating this developed system for more than a quarter of a century. See, for instance: Gorman, Michael. "Authority Files in a Developed Machine System." In *What's in a Name* / ed. and comp. by Natsuko Y. Furuya. Toronto: University of Toronto Press, 1978. pp. 179-202.

5. See, for example among many such: Weibel, Stuart. "CORC and the Dublin Core." *OCLC Newsletter*, no.239 (May/June 1999).

6. CORC at Cornell; final report. http://campusgw.library.cornell.edu/corc/.

7. For an extended exploration of this topic, see: Gorman, Michael. *The Enduring Library*. Chicago: ALA, 2003. Chapter 7.

APPENDIX. Extract from the Library of Congress Authority File

100 0_	**a** Horace
400 1_ |**w** nna |**a** Horatius Flaccus, Quintus
400 0_	**a** Horaz
400 0_	**a** Orazio
400 1_	**a** Goratsii Flakk, Kvint
400 0_	**a** Horacjusz
400 0_	**a** Horacy
400 0_	**a** Horats
400 0_	**a** Horatiyus
400 0_	**a** Horatiyos
400 0_	**a** Gorats⁻ii
400 1_	**a** Horacjusz Flakkus, Kwintus
400 1_	**a** Khoratsii Flak, Kvint
400 0_	**a** Khoratsii
400 1_	**a** Orazio Flacco, Quinto
400 0_	**a** Horacij

STATE OF THE ART
AND NEW THEORETICAL PERSPECTIVES

Authority Control:
State of the Art
and New Perspectives

Barbara B. Tillett

SUMMARY. Authority control is necessary for meeting the catalog's objectives of enabling users to find the works of an author and to collocate all works of a person or corporate body. This article looks at the current state of authority control as compared to the visions of the 1979 LITA (Library Information and Technology Association) Institutes and the 1984 Authority Control Interest Group. It explores a new view of IFLA's Universal Bibliographic Control (UBC) and a future vision of a virtual international authority file as a building block for the Semantic Web, and reinforces the importance of authority control to improve the precision of searches of large databases or the Internet.

KEYWORDS. Authority control, access control, universal bibliographic control, virtual international authority file, cataloging objectives, precision of searching

Barbara B. Tillett, PhD, MLS, BA, is Chief, Cataloging Policy and Support Office, Library of Congress, 101 Independence Avenue, SE, Washington, DC 20504-4305 (E-mail: btil@loc.gov).

[Haworth co-indexing entry note]: "Authority Control: State of the Art and New Perspectives." Tillett, Barbara B. Co-published simultaneously in *Cataloging & Classification Quarterly* (The Haworth Information Press, an imprint of The Haworth Press, Inc.) Vol. 38, No. 3/4, 2004, pp. 23-41; and: *Authority Control in Organizing and Accessing Information: Definition and International Experience* (ed: Arlene G. Taylor, and Barbara B. Tillett) The Haworth Information Press, an imprint of The Haworth Press, Inc., 2004, pp. 23-41.

http://www.haworthpress.com/web/CCQ
Digital Object Identifier: 10.1300/J104v38n03_04

The virtues of authority control have been debated and restated for decades. Catalogers for at least a century and a half have documented their decisions on how the single, authorized form of name for each entity should be represented in their catalog. They traced the various forms of names given to an entity to record the cross references they provided to users of their catalogs. They brought together their notes to further identify the entity for themselves and other catalogers building the catalog, documenting their research in the process of authority work. Some said it was unnecessary, most said it was essential to fulfill the objectives of the catalog to find and collocate the records for bibliographic resources. Still others said, stop debating and just get on with it, and we have, but ever mindful of the costs.

Since the 1970s people have claimed that authority work is the most expensive part of cataloging, and we still seek ways to automate and simplify the work to reduce costs. A giant step in that direction has been the move to share the work and share a resource authority file among many libraries. Examples have been the now famous cooperative program, NACO, the Name Authority Cooperative project involving the Library of Congress and other partners. There are also numerous examples of regionally and nationally shared authority files, like the Hong Kong Chinese Authority Name, known as HKCAN. Today's technology opens up opportunities for us to now link these many authority files and build on their strengths, to improve those resources, and to open new doors for service to users.

When we apply authority control in today's Web environment, we are reminded how authority control brings precision to searches, how the syndetic structure of references enables navigation and provides the end user with explanations for variations and inconsistencies, and how the controlled forms of names and titles and subjects help collocate (group together) works in displays. Even more today, we can envision using authority records to actually link to the authorized forms of names, titles, and subjects beyond the catalog for which they were originally intended to various online-accessible reference tools and resources, like directories, biographical dictionaries, abstracting and indexing services, and so on. Library catalogues can now be found in the mix of various tools that are available on the Web.

In 1979 LITA (Library and Information Technology Association) held a series of institutes entitled, "Authority Control: The Key to Tomorrow's Catalog" reminding us that the syndetic structure of catalogs in North America owes its origins to Charles Ammi Cutter. In his *Rules for a Printed Dictionary Catalog* in 1876, Cutter stated that controlling the forms of names was one of the "means" for meeting the objectives (he called them "objects") of the catalog. The objectives were "to enable a person to find a book of which either the author, title, or subject is known" (this is often called the finding objective), "to show what the library has by a given author, on a given subject, in a given kind of literature" (this is called the collocating objective), and "to assist in the choice of a book as to its edition (bibliographically), as to its character (literary or topical)" (this is part of an identifying objective).[1] He stressed the importance of the syndetic structure of cross references in a catalog to get the user to the authorized form used to collocate the works of an author.

Seymour Lubetzky in his *Principles of Cataloging* in 1969 noted that one could accomplish the collocation objective by enabling an inquiry under any variant form to retrieve the works of an author under any of the names he/she used–even a citation from a bibliography, and thus eliminate the problem of choice of name by which to identify an author in the catalog.[2]

During the 1979 LITA Institutes, Ritvars Bregzis also made the case that we don't need the extra work of devising an authorized form of name or uniform title, as long as we can make the associations, the relationships among related works. He wrote that "the computer technology has given us an opportunity to return to the record syndetic structure of the catalog, the structure in which the authentic form of the identificatory information describing the publication, being also the most frequently cited form, is given its own identity as a component of the catalog."[3] We do this using references to direct the user to where the collection of records are filed that collocate the works of an author. This collection of records can be accomplished on a screen on a computer terminal, which the computer can manage without actually storing the records in any particular order in the database–but instead indexing them for displays as needed. As Ritvars Bregzis noted, the inclusion of an authorized form of heading is not a requirement for the bibliographic record, as long as we can link it in the computer to the related works of the author. Although he did not foresee the use of ISADN's or work/expression level citations, such tools are available to use today to meet the same objectives. Michael Gorman also spoke at those institutes. He and others have suggested how to accomplish the linking,[4] using a structure where there were unique records for each physical item linked to records for the related persons, corporate bodies, works, subject, and other records for physical items. There would be an authority record for each work with more than one bibliographic description and identified by more than one title. Gorman also said there would be no composite author/title authority records. This view would fit very well in today's FRBR conceptual model of the bibliographic universe.

When I started the Authority Control Interest Group (ACIG) in ALA in 1984, I conducted an opinion poll to get discussion started. At that time 18% of the respondents had online catalogs and 90.4% were using some bibliographic utility for shared cataloging. I compared the results of the ACIG opinion poll with two other surveys conducted earlier, and found that somewhere between 13 to 28% of the libraries had no authority files, but instead relied on the records from other libraries. However, of the at least 72% that did maintain their own in-house authority files, we know it was at great expense when aggregated nationally. We also recognized the value of the NACO project in helping reduce the overall cost to the nation's libraries. Some of the desired capabilities were a comprehensive, internationally shared resource authority file with the ability for any library to add to the file. Catalogers wanted keyword access to the files in addition to the search keys and direct text string searches. The respondents wanted browsable files, especially for author/title uniform titles and links to the bibliographic file, as well as ways to easily navigate among parts of hierarchies and earlier/later names. As for maintenance, it was recognized that names change and the respondents wanted a way to automatically identify those changes that should be reflected in their local catalogs, with a fast, easy method to update and resolve conflicts. More identifying information was wanted—more dates, and there were pleas to bring back the history and scope notes. It was also clear that local libraries felt it was important for their catalogs to be customized to meet the needs of their target user groups.[5]

SO ARE WE THERE YET?

The dreams of the 1979 LITA Institutes are still with us, and the hopes of ALA's Authority Control Interest Group of the mid-1980s remain unfulfilled.[6] Some have blamed our MARC formatted records and the online library systems built around these records. Is that what is holding us back? Or can we use the MARC Format and make it do what we want? Do we expand MARC to encode the links and relationships or come up with a new mechanism? In the Anglo-American cataloging world using the MARC Format, we used to specify the relationships or roles of persons and corporate bodies by adding a "relator" term to access points in bibliographic records (as prescribed in AACR2 rules) and sometimes the corresponding MARC code (and this is still done for some music and rare book areas), but generally the practice was abandoned as being too expensive to continue in our shortsighted efforts to cut near-term costs. We find that now inhibits our fully implementing FRBR, where such roles are essential to clear identification, so it may be time to revisit that administrative policy decision.

We've recently seen a renewed focus on user needs and the tasks users perform when using a catalog, stated again in the IFLA *Functional Requirements for Bibliographic Records*[7] (FRBR). FRBR lists four "user tasks"–things we feel a user wants to do relative to the bibliographic universe:

Find an entity or entities in a database using attributes or relationships (Elaine Svenonius has suggested this should actually be in two parts–to locate and to collocate entities.[8])

Identify–to confirm that the entity found corresponds to the entity sought

Select –to choose an entity meeting the user requirements for content, physical format, etc.

Obtain–to acquire an entity or to access an item

and we could add a task (as Elaine Svenonius does):

Navigate–that is, the catalog should enable a user to navigate through related materials that may be in the collection or indeed in the entire bibliographic universe.

FRBR is an evolving model and is currently being extended in the realm of authority control through the work of IFLA's Working Group on the Functional Requirements for Authority Numbers and Records (FRANAR), chaired by Glenn Patton, who will be speaking at this conference. We may find that this FRBR conceptual model enables us to meet the objectives of a catalog in new ways.

OBJECTIVES OF AUTHORITY WORK

And what about the objectives of authority work? Through authority records, catalogers in the days of book and card catalogs maintained a record of their decisions for the authorized form of a heading and the variant forms for which cross reference entries (in book catalogs) or cards (in card catalogs) were made. These records were mainly needed for larger catalogs and cataloging units to maintain consistency among multiple catalogers. The use of a consistent form of heading enabled libraries to help avoid the costly unintentional ordering or cataloging of materials already held in the library's collection. It enabled a user to save time and effort by showing the user the references to the authorized forms for headings and collocating works under a single form with references to related entities when appropriate.

The authority record documented the references made to the authorized heading and that enabled maintenance of the catalog. When a heading changed or was to be deleted (for example, when material was withdrawn from the collection and the heading no longer was needed), the "tracings" of the references were used to pull the associated reference cards or remove the references from book catalogs.

The authority records also documented the cataloger's authority work. Notes about sources that were checked to establish the authorized form were added to the authority record, sometimes both the sources where information was found as well as sources that were checked but no information was found. Other notes for catalogers were added as needed to further explain the identity of the entity covered by that heading, distinguishing it from others with similar names.

OBJECTIVES FOR AUTHORITY RECORDS

The Web environment opens up new uses for authority records and new objectives to augment the traditional objectives. For example, as we have found through sharing the authority records from the Library of Congress online and particularly now on the Web, the sharing of the workload reduces cataloguing costs.

Our community has expanded, especially in Europe these days, where libraries are viewed with archives, museums, and rights management agencies as cultural "memory institutions." We are moving from the stand-alone authority files of a single institution, or even from the shared online files towards a goal of sharing authority files among all communities. Shared authority information has the added benefit of reducing the global costs of doing authority work while enabling controlled access and better precision of searching.

Other objectives for authority control are:

- to simplify the creation and maintenance of authority records internationally when we can all access the authority records
- to enable users to access information in the language, scripts, and form they prefer or that their local library provides for them.

The existence of authority records for an entity also opens up new possibilities for links to other resources, like the home page for the entity described and links to digital resources such as biographical dictionaries, abstracting and indexing services, telephone directories, and other references sources on the Web. More about these objectives later.

As integrated library systems were created in the 1970s and 80s and new generations were developed in the late 1990s, we realized some of the promises of automated authority control. Even some of the early systems provided direct links between the bibliographic records and the authority files. This structure often placed a code in the bibliographic record for the authorized name found in the associated authority record and the system could pull up the authorized form for displays of the full bibliographic record. This structure also made maintenance of the headings and references much easier, as the correction needed to be made only once in the authority record and all associated bibliographic records would display properly. Other systems without linked bibliographic and authority records also developed global update capabilities, and some still do not have it, so there is a wide variety on the market today.

Most systems display reference information to direct the user to the authorized forms of headings, but some systems do not use the authority records at all.

Many systems also offer validation of the form of the heading, matching the form entered by the cataloger in a bibliographic record to the forms in authority records and reporting back whether an authority record exists or not. These capabilities are a great help in automating authority work, but still have not gone far enough.

Web catalogs and associated integrated library systems provide the traditional authority control functions of creating and updating authority records and displaying the cross references but have primarily been seen as a tool for catalogers. As we open our authority files for access through the Internet, we find the authority file becoming a useful tool for other librarians and information professionals and even for end-users.

Catalogers and others can use the authority file as another reference tool for name variations and information to identify entities, as well as a channel for reaching bibliographic records, and from there, reaching directly to digitized resources. The records in these automated files also enable navigation to related entities.

The concept of record may disappear, but it is not yet clear what will emerge in its place. It's still easier for us to use the record construct than to make the larger mental leap to totally new structures; but they will come. We can think of a small step where the records would serve to control the various forms of names for an entity rather than having any single heading be the only authorized form (back to the 1979 LITA Institutes). We've talked about this for decades, and the Getty does it in several of its controlled vocabulary tools. For example, in the *Union List of Artist Names*[9] there is a listing of the forms of name for an entity that have been found in various resources, brought together to use for searching and displays. The entry indicates the reference source where that form of name is used. In their search and retrieval systems, the system uses all the variant forms when generating a Web search, but there is a downside to this. The users are not yet told why they are getting all the variant forms that are retrieved–they do not realize it is the same entity.

When we control all the possible variations for the names of an entity, and we associate them with the bibliographic records for the bibliographic resources that they have some role in creating, producing, or owning, we need to explain that to the user.

Let's say I searched under Lewis Carroll, the author of *Alice's Adventures in Wonderland.* Why am I getting back information about this mathematician, Charles Lutwidge Dodgson, 1832-1898? In fact, it's the same person with two separate bibliographic identities and not a case of variant names.

You need to tell the user about variant names used for the same person or corporate body or work, or somehow convey the relationship of the variant names to the entity and related entities. Yes, we want to collocate the works of the person or corporate body, but we also want the user to understand what is going on.

STANDARD NUMBERS

Another way to enable collocation when there are several variant forms of name used by an entity, and this is a method that has been suggested many times over the years,[10] is the use of standard numbers. Why not just store the language-neutral number for the entity in the bibliographic record and link that to the authority record where the display form would reside? Or, as some authors have suggested, let the user choose the form he/she wants to see. Several early integrated library systems offered and still use this technique.

In 1980 IFLA also proposed using an ISADN, International Standard Authority Data Number. There have also been suggestions for an ISAN, International Standard Authority Number, as well as the ISO International Standard Text Code (ISTC to identify works and expressions). Still another suggestion has been to just use the authority record control numbers, such as Library of Congress Control Numbers, as this unique, persistent identifier.[11] I personally would like to test using the unique, persistent record control numbers and to see if that works.[12] Or we might use the number assigned to an information package (i.e., a future version of what we now call a "record") for an entity under OAI (Open Archive Initiative) protocols that I will mention in a moment. That would avoid having to set up an expensive international organization to manage the distribution and maintenance of such numbers. The organizational overhead and costs are partially why the original IFLA suggestion never came to fruition.

The future prospects are tempting us to believe that we might reach some of those futuristic goals of the 1979 LITA Institutes and beyond–to allow the user to choose the displayed form, to automatically generate many of the variant forms (permuted, direct order, abbreviated, etc.–in fact some systems now offer this capability), and to link to other Internet resources, including digital objects (some systems can do this now, too), reference tools, as well as other tools in a future semantic Web.

CHALLENGES AT THE GLOBAL LEVEL

As we know there are many challenges to accomplishing authority control or even sharing authority records on a global scale. There are different cataloging rules that rightly focus on the needs of their users. There are systems we might wish to link to that have no rules at all. Clearly there is a great challenge with different languages and scripts, and there is the technical challenge of accessing and displaying records that are encapsulated in different communication formats, particularly the various "MARCs"–MARC 21, UNIMARC, RUSMARC, etc., and XML.

In the digital library world and libraries in general, there is increased recent focus on the need for interoperability. This is being proposed in many ways, including the fact that we can now map different communication formats with Z39.50 protocols (in fact the LEAF Project explores this model).

We have developed crosswalks to the "MARCs," including crosswalks from MARC 21 to and from ONIX, and others. We have also mapped MARC 21 into an XML format. These crosswalks and mapping strategies can help us to search and retrieve library resources effectively with publishers' databases, abstracting and indexing services, and other resources on the Web.

Over the past few years there have been several projects that help us get closer to providing authority control on a global scale. There are several sponsored by the European Union, such as the AUTHOR Project that converted a sampling of authority records from the seven participating countries to the same communication format, UNIMARC.[13] The LEAF project that I just mentioned is looking at linking authority files for archival purposes using Z39.50 protocols and OAI (Open Archive Initiative) protocols. The <indecs> and INTERPARTY projects were looking for cooperative work among libraries, museums, archives, and rights management communities in sharing authority information. HKCAN is the Hong Kong Chinese Authority for names that provides a successful shared authority file among the libraries in the consortium, enabling romanized forms of headings and Chinese traditional and simplified character forms.

Within the International Federation of Library Associations and Institutions the *Guidelines for Authority Records and References*[14] (GARR) was issued in 2001. In 1998, the IFLA MLAR (Minimal Level Authority Records) Working Group identified essential data elements needed in authority records (today we'd call these metadata).[15] This work continues through the IFLA Working Group on FRANAR (Functional Requirements for Authority Numbers and Records). They are reviewing and updating the MLAR findings and recently enlisted the help of Tom Delsey in extending the FRBR model to authority records.

Within the digital metadata community, there is a Dublin Core "Agents" working group that continues to explore recommendations for dealing with authority information in the digital environment, as does the DELOS/NSF Working Group on "Actors/Roles." The Archival community also is developing an Encoded Archival Context for authority metadata using XML.

At OCLC, discussions continue about authority records in CORC (now known as Connexion). This is a potential OCLC project that looks towards global expansion to build an authority file. Connexion now provides simultaneous creation of both MARC 21 and Dublin Core bibliographic records.

Another development over the past few years has been the acceptance of Unicode within Microsoft tools, such as the Windows operating system, that facilitates more global compatibility with multi-script capabilities. And the worldwide expansion of NACO and SACO to users of the *Anglo-American Cataloguing Rules* and *Library of Congress Subject Headings* also promotes authority control on a global scale. We will hear more about these various projects and initiatives later in this conference.

The availability of millions of authority records worldwide, multiple automated national and regional authority files, and the technological capabilities of the Internet and protocols are all coming together now, and we are really at the brink of making a virtual international authority file a reality.

NEW VIEW OF UBC

We're also making an historic change to how we view Universal Bibliographic Control (UBC). The IFLA UBC principles for authority control are parallel to those for bibliographic control, namely that:

- each country is responsible for the authorized headings for its own personal and corporate authors (they didn't mention uniform titles, series, or subjects), and
- the authority records created by each national bibliographic agency would be available to all other countries needing authority records for those same authors. Even more, that the same headings would be used worldwide.

In the 1960s and 1970s when this was really catching on, technology had not yet advanced to make such sharing practical on an international level. Plus, the lack of funding for an international center to manage such a program prevented that visionary concept from becoming reality. As for the same form being acceptable worldwide, the IFLA developers at that time were primarily from North America and Europe and apparently did not acknowledge the necessity for multiple scripts when dealing with users worldwide.

For the past couple of years a *new* view of Universal Bibliographic Control has been emerging from several working groups within IFLA. This new perspective reinforces the importance of authority control, yet puts the user first. It's a practical approach that recognizes users in China may not want to see the heading for Confucius in a Latinized form, but in their own script. Similarly users in Japan or Korea would want to see the heading in *their* own script and language. National bibliographic agencies still need to have their own authority records for their own bibliographic control, but we can link them globally to create a virtual international authority file that will enable sharing of authority information and enable future displays that show a user's preferred form.

We can link the authorized forms of names, titles, and even subjects from the authority files of national bibliographic agencies and other regional agencies through a virtual international authority file. There are several models for how this might work, and we need to do more pilot projects of prototypes of these models to test which would be best to pursue.

In order to be of most use to the library users in each country, the scripts should be the scripts they can read! Figure 1 shows that the names we give to an entity can be expressed in many languages and in many scripts. For example, we could write a name in English or German with a roman script, in Russian in Cyrillic scripts, or in Japanese (in any of three scripts!) and in many other languages and scripts.

Transliteration may serve as a way for some users to be able to decipher records, but much better is the accuracy of using original scripts. In fact, we should eventually be able to display the script and form of a heading that the user expects and wants.

I believe that many catalogers within IFLA realize the value of preserving parallel authority records for the same entity. This allows us to reflect the national and cultural needs of our individual users, and at the same time allows us to set up the syndetic structure of cross references and authorized forms of headings to be used in our catalogues intended for a specific audience following our own cataloging rules. It also allows us to include variants in alternate scripts, at least as cross references for now.

As we look at linking we must recognize that different cataloguing rules have differences in what they consider entities–AACR2's choices are not universal. For example, German rules (*Regeln für die alphabetische Katalogisierung*–RAK) do not recognize that a ship's logs can be under an entry for the name of the ship, so they would not have an authority record for the name of the ship. Similarly for events, for example, the meetings of corporate bodies, AACR2 creates a hierarchically subordinate heading for a meeting

FIGURE 1. Names in Many Languages and Scripts

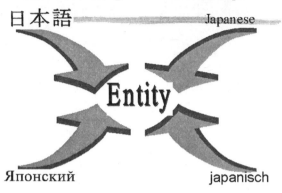

under the name of the corporate body. The German rules would not create a heading for the "meeting." There are also different practices for undifferentiated names–the Germans recently changed their rules to differentiate more names–they more commonly used undifferentiated forms for personal names using just initials for forenames.

However, even under the same cataloguing rules, say AACR2, when we get more information to differentiate a person, we can make a new authority record to differentiate that person from others grouped together under an undifferentiated form of name. As a result, the record for the undifferentiated name can reflect different associated entities over time.

If we agree that sharing authority information on a global scale is worthwhile, how do we get there? Several major authority files exist, built according to their own cataloguing rules and rule interpretations. We need a one-time project to link the existing records for the same entity–a retrospective matching project. One suggestion has been to use matching algorithms, such as those developed by Ed O'Neill and others at OCLC, building on bibliographic clues for machine matching at a fairly high level of accuracy. A "proof of concept" project to test this approach is underway between OCLC, the Library of Congress, and the Deutsche Bibliothek (German National Library) in Frankfurt, Germany. We would still have manual matching and checking to do, but we expect machine matching will be a great help. We could also have the computer add linking text strings and record control numbers or an entity identification number to facilitate later links and pathways to preferred forms for displays. Or we may find we do not need to specifically record these links, if our future systems are smart enough to make the links for us.

Some local systems already provide us with computer-assisted mechanisms for automatic checking of headings against an existing authority file, and we could see this expanded to launch a search against a virtual international authority file, if no match was found locally. We can also envision the capability of displaying the found matches from the virtual file for a cataloguer to edit or to merge information, if desired, into the local authority record, including capturing the information for future linking.

We can also envision extending authority control to users through display of public notes and references (as most systems do today) and through links to related resources, such as official Web sites for the entity, authoritative biographical dictionaries, and other identifying resources.

We could soon realize future switching capabilities to display forms the user wants. Some systems now provide community specific retrievals to concentrate on the subject needs of a community in selecting resources for online searches, and other systems like "my library" or "my opac" even go beyond that to specific retrievals customized for individual users. Those systems could build in the authority preferences for user preferred scripts and displays for controlled vocabularies.

We want to have the authorized form preferred by a library as the default offered to most users, but we can also envision offering user-selected preferences through client software, or "cookies" that let the users specify once what their preferred language, script, or cultural preference is–for example, spelling preferences when cultures have variations, like American English and spelling preferences in the United Kingdom (e.g., labor and labour).

Also, for example, when a Russian-speaking user comes along, the local system or the "cookies" on the user's system, could specify he/she wants to see the Cyrillic form of headings and we could display it for them. You can also imagine displaying any script or a Braille keyboard output, or we could provide voice recognition response, built on users' profiles or their "cookies." This might be accomplished by putting variant forms in variant scripts all in one authority record, or it may be better to link parallel authority records that each reflect the needed syndetic structure of the cataloging rules upon which they are each based.

Within a single authority system, we might incorporate the references appropriate to those cataloging rules governing the catalog for which the authority record was intended. Let me show you how this might look applied to a Library of Congress authority record for Confucius.

Figure 2 is an example of what a Library of Congress authority record might look like with Unicode capability to include original scripts as cross references in a library's catalog. Actually with Unicode the roman script

FIGURE 2. Authority Record for Confucius

Tag	I1	I2	Subfield Data
010			‡a n 80050515
035			‡a (DLC)n 80050515
040			‡a DLC ‡c DLC ‡d DLC ‡d NIC
100	0		‡a Confucius
400	0		‡a Konfuzius
400	0		‡a K'ung Fu-tzu
400	0		‡a Kongzi
400	1		‡a Kong, Qiu
400	0		‡a K'ung-tzu
400	1		‡a K'ung, Ch'iu
400	0		‡a K'oshi
400	0		‡a Konfu t si i
400	0		‡a Kongja
400	0		‡a Kung Fu
400	1		‡a K'ung, Fu-tzu
400	0		‡a Confucio
400	0		‡a Конфуций
400	0		‡a 孔夫子
400	0		‡a 孔子
400	0		‡a 孔丘
400	0		‡a こうし
400	0		‡a コウシ
400	0		‡a 공자
670			‡a Jakobs, P. M. Kritik an Lin Piao und Konfuzius, c1983: ‡b t.p. (Konfuzius)
670			‡a Konfu t si i, 1993: ‡b t.p. verso (551-479 B.C.)
670			‡a His Gespr ache (Lun y u), 1910: ‡b t.p. (Kungfutse)
670			‡a Web connection ‡u http://www.friesian.com/confuci.htm
700	0		‡a 孔夫子 ‡5 HKCAN

diacritics would appear after the letter rather than before the letter shown here, but this just gives you an idea of what it would be like.

There is no particular order to the arrangement of the references, except to place the non-roman scripts following the roman scripts, but even that ordering is not necessary for the computer–it just makes the record easier for the cataloger to follow. This model shows English, Italian, German, Chinese, Japanese, Korean, Russian, and transliterations (including Wade-Giles and pinyin for the Chinese, since the Library of Congress just switched to use pinyin).

Notice also the new MARC 21 capability to include the URL for a Web page in the last 670 note field. This also shows the use of a linking 700 field to show that an authority record was located at the National Library of China and shows the form of authorized heading according to their rules. In Hong Kong they have a regional name authority file, known as HKCAN, that uses the 7XX fields for the authorized form in the traditional Chinese script. They use Innovative Interfaces INNOPAC system and are able to use this information in OPAC displays to direct users to additional material cataloged under that alternate form. That enables bibliographic control for collocation under the name of the person or corporate body.

VIAF MODELS

So, what models might we explore for this international authority file? We currently have a *distributed model*, where a searcher would use a standard protocol like Z39.50 or soon "ZING," the next generation of Z39.50. A recently agreed-upon extension to the Bath profile for Z39.50 will enable searching and retrieval of authority records. Through this protocol we can search the *independent authority files* of participating National Bibliographic Agencies and regional authorities.

Another model is to have one *central authority file with links to all others*. This model requires the central agency to match entities and make the links while the other participants continue to maintain their own file. A cataloger would then get access to all of the authority records for that entity worldwide by a single search of the central file.

Yet another model is to have a centralized agency coordinate the work of many participants with the centralized agency maintaining a centralized *union authority file* and libraries could contribute to it as they wished. NACO uses this model in a controlled way. It might also be a model for a more open system where any library could contribute authority records, such as has frequently been proposed for OCLC. However, such an open model also lends itself to less consistent information, unless the contributors adhere to mutually agreed upon standards and there are checks to avoid unintentional duplication of records for the same entity. In this model the user or the users' local system would just search the single file.

A variation on this centralized union authority file model, instead of linking to one authority file, would be to link them all to a centralized server or "*virtual*" *union authority file*. It is "virtual" because the full authority records remain in the national and regional authority files with only minimal data harvested by the server. We may find that this model is the best approach in terms of record maintenance. It might employ the Open Archives Initiative (OAI) protocols with a central server that harvests metadata from the national or regional authority files. The records for the same entity would be linked at the central server. That information would be refreshed in the server whenever there are changes in the national files. This means the day-to-day record maintenance activities continue to be managed as they are now by the National Bibliographic Agency (or regional authority).

There are many other models we could imagine. I am sure you can think of others, and we need to try them out to see which will work best in today's Internet environment.

The German National Library (Die Deutsche Bibliothek) and the Library of Congress together with OCLC have started a proof of concept project to test the centralized union authority file model using OAI protocols. We envision this project in at least four stages.

The first stage of this project began in 2002 to link our existing authority records for personal names. OCLC has matching algorithms they are testing to compare the LCNAF (Library of Congress Name Authority Files–about five million records) and the DDB's Personal Name Authority File (PND–about one million records). They use the bibliographic records and information in authority records to do this matching. We want to see how much the machine can match and how much human work will be needed. It is hoped that if this proves successful, it can be the basis for a true Virtual International Authority File.

In Stage 2, as we make the links we will be building one or more servers with this "metadata"–one will be housed at OCLC, probably another at the OCLC European office (PICA), and another at the DDB. We were not planning on having a separate server at the Library of Congress for this project.

As we continue to populate the OAI server with matched records, the user (at this stage the user would be a cataloger) would be able to check the system (probably using SiteSearch or a similar software) to see if the authority record already exists for the entity the cataloger is trying to establish.

We would hope, later on, that vendors would build in software to automatically launch a search of the VIAF if the entity was *not* found in the local authority file.

For Stage 3 of the proof of concept project, we also want to test using the OAI protocols to do the ongoing maintenance of updating the information in the server by harvesting metadata for new and updated or deleted information in the home authority files.

A possible last stage, Stage 4, would be to test the end-user-display capabilities to switch the preferred form of language displayed on his/her machine. This stage is in the future, but it reminds us of the opportunities that libraries have now to contribute to the infrastructure of the future Internet environment.

We can envision a shared international authority file being an integral part of a future "Semantic Web." You may have heard about this in the *Scientific American* article by Tim Berners-Lee, founder of the Internet.[16] The idea is to make the Internet more intelligent for machine navigation rather than human navigation of the Web. It involves creating an infrastructure of linked resources and the use of controlled vocabularies called "ontologies." These ontologies could be used to enable displays in the user's own language and script.

Here's where libraries have an opportunity to contribute to the infrastructure of the future Web–we already have controlled vocabularies in our various authority files. Those would be linked with other controlled vocabularies of abstracting and indexing services, of biographical dictionaries, of telephone directories, and many other reference tools and resources, to help users navigate and to improve the precision of searches, so users could find what they're looking for.

All of these tools would also link to their respective databases for bibliographic and other resources. For example, Library of Congress authority files would link to the bibliographic and holdings databases of the Library of Congress, and even to our digital repositories for the linked digital objects themselves.

You can see that we would also build in the search engines and future tools that as a collective resource would connect us to the entire digital world.

All of this, of course, would have built-in, appropriate security and privacy assurances, and ways to identify and acknowledge resources that we can trust and rely on, and somehow, miraculously, all of the copyright issues will be resolved. It's great to think about the possibilities and opportunities for testing this out and to think about how we can improve upon our dreams. The Internet has brought us a new way to convey information and has opened up possibilities and opportunities that we never dreamt of even a few years ago. Catalogers can build authority records using the Web and all communities (publishers, rights management agencies, archives, museums, and other libraries) can use this information and reduce costs worldwide. Authority control will help users of the Web to benefit from collocation and search precision that authority control enables. And, very importantly, it also means we can do it in ways that are meaningful to users in their preferred language and script.

We can open up the valuable information within our authority records to users worldwide and use the authority records as tools to connect, not only to bibliographic data, but to biographical dictionaries, telephone directories, abstracting and indexing services, official Web sites for the entity, and more. The authority records can be a key part, a building block for the infrastructure of the Semantic Web and beyond.

We still need more research and testing, but we also have a lot to offer the world, and this wonderful resource, created and maintained by libraries worldwide, can offer us a fresh perspective for talking with other communities and moving together to the future.

NOTES

1. Cutter, Charles A. *Rules for a Printed Dictionary Catalogue*. [Washington, D.C., Government Printing Office, 1876] p, 10.

2. Lubetzky, Seymour. *Principles of Cataloging*. Los Angeles, Calif.: Institute of Library Research, University of California, 1969, p. 94.

3. Bregzis, Ritvars. "The Syndetic Structure of the Catalog," *Authority Control: The Key to Tomorrow's Catalog*; proceedings of the 1979 Library and Information Technology Association Institutes, edited by Mary W. Ghikas. [Phoenix, AZ], 1982, p. 24.

4. Gorman, Michael. "Authority Control in the Prospective Catalog," *Authority Control: The Key to Tomorrow's Catalog*; proceedings of the 1979 Library and Information Technology Association Institutes, edited by Mary W. Ghikas. [Phoenix, AZ], 1982, p. 166-177.

5. Tillett, Barbara B. "1984 Automated Authority Control Opinion Poll," *Information Technology and Libraries*, v. 4, no. 2 (June 1985), p. 171-178.

6. Arlene Taylor also recently discussed this point: Taylor, Arlene G. "Authority Control: Where It's Been and Where It's Going," presentation at the NELINET sponsored conference *Authority Control: Why It Matters*. Worcester, MA, 1999. Also available online at: http://www.nelinet.net/edserv/conf/cataloging/cts/1999/taylor.htm.

7. *Functional Requirements for Bibliographic Records: Final Report*, IFLA Study Group on the Functional Requirements for Bibliographic Records. (Consultants: Tom Delsey, Elizabeth Dulabahn, Elaine Svenonius, Barbara Tillett). München: K.G. Saur, 1998. Available as: www.ifla.org/VII/s13/frbr/frbr.pdf or as html: www.ifla.org/VII/s13/frbr/frbr.htm.

8. Svenonius, Elaine. *The Intellectual Foundation of Information Organization*. Cambridge, Mass.: MIT Press, 2000, p. 17-18.

9. From its web site, the Getty says, "The Union List of Artist Names (ULAN)–is a structured vocabulary containing more than 220,000 names and biographical and bibliographic information about artists and architects, including a wealth of variant names, pseudonyms, and language variants." See online at: http://www.getty.edu/research/conducting_research/vocabularies/ulan/ (formerly: http://www.getty.edu/research/tools/vocabulary/ulan/).

10. Poncet, J. "Authority Files in Machine Systems," in *The Interchange of Bibliographic Information in Machine Readable Form*: papers given at the Western European Seminar on the Interchange of Bibliographic Information in Machine Readable Form held at Banbury, England, 12-16 May 1974, sponsored by the British Council, the British Library and the Library Association, R. E. Coward and M. Yelland, eds.–London: Library Association, 1975, p. 96-98. Malinconico, S. Michael. "Bibliographic Data Base Organization and Authority File Control," *Authority Control: The Key to Tomorrow's Catalog*; proceedings of the 1979 Library and Information Technology Association Institutes, edited by Mary W. Ghikas. [Phoenix, AZ], 1982, p. 1-15. Also in *Wilson Library Bulletin* (Sept. 1979).

11. For example, in the recommendations of the IFLA UBCIM Working Group on Minimal Level Authority Records and ISADN. *Mandatory Data Elements for Internationally Shared Resource Authority Records*. IFLA, UBCIM, 1998, p. 1. Also available online at: http://ifla.org/VI/3/p1996-2/mlar.htm.

12. I realize that Library of Congress Control Numbers occasionally do change for the same entity, but by and large they can be considered "persistent."

13. For example, see Danskin, Alan. 1998. "International Initiatives in Authority Control." *Library Review* 47, no. 4: 200-205.

14. *Guidelines for Authority Records and References.* 2nd ed., revised by the IFLA Working Group on GARE Revision. München: K.G. Saur, 2001. 46 p.

15. *Mandatory Data Elements for Internationally Shared Resource Authority Records*: Report of the IFLA UBCIM Working Group on Minimal Level Authority Records and ISADN, chair Barbara B. Tillett, Françoise Bourdon, Alan Danskin, Andrew MacEwan, Eeva Murtomaa, Mirna Willer. International Federation of Library Associations and Institutions, Universal Bibliographic Control and International MARC Programme, 1998. 95 p. Also available online at: http://ifla.org/VI/3/p1996-2/mlar.htm.

16. Berners-Lee, Tim, James Hendler and Ora Lassila. "The Semantic Web: A New Form of Web Content That Is Meaningful to Computers Will Unleash a Revolution of New Possibilities," *Scientific American*, May 17, 2001. Also available online at: http://www.sciam.com/article.cfm?articleID=00048144-10D2-1C70-84A9809EC588EF21.

Teaching Authority Control

Arlene G. Taylor

SUMMARY. The teaching of authority control in schools of library and information science has been given little attention until recently. A 2002 article reported that only a little over a third of respondents to a questionnaire believed they had learned about authority control in school. This paper reports on a survey of teachers to determine how much authority control is taught in school. Respondents all emphasized the importance of trying to teach authority control to all students of library science and enthusiastically shared their methodologies, while admitting that it is a difficult concept to get across to students. Teachers also face non-understanding from colleagues, lack of course time, and competition from technology courses. *[Article copies available for a fee from The Haworth Document Delivery Service: 1-800-HAWORTH. E-mail address: <docdelivery@haworthpress.com> Website: <http://www.HaworthPress.com> © 2004 by The Haworth Press, Inc. All rights reserved.]*

KEYWORDS. Authority control education, library school courses, cataloging faculty, name authority control, subject headings, MARC authority records

Arlene G. Taylor is Professor, School of Information Sciences, University of Pittsburgh (E-mail: ataylor@mail.sis.pitt.edu).

The author wishes to thank Daniel N. Joudrey for his assistance in formulating the set of questions sent to those who teach in the area of organizing information. She also is grateful to A. Wayne Benson and Daniel N. Joudrey for reading and commenting on the manuscript. Their suggestions were invaluable.

[Haworth co-indexing entry note]: "Teaching Authority Control." Taylor, Arlene G. Co-published simultaneously in *Cataloging & Classification Quarterly* (The Haworth Information Press, an imprint of The Haworth Press, Inc.) Vol. 38, No. 3/4, 2004, pp. 43-57; and: *Authority Control in Organizing and Accessing Information: Definition and International Experience* (ed: Arlene G. Taylor, and Barbara B. Tillett) The Haworth Information Press, an imprint of The Haworth Press, Inc., 2004, pp. 43-57. Single or multiple copies of this article are available for a fee from The Haworth Document Delivery Service [1-800-HAWORTH, 9:00 a.m. - 5:00 p.m. (EST). E-mail address: docdelivery@haworthpress.com].

Digital Object Identifier: 10.1300/J104v38n03_05

Little has been written about the teaching of authority control in programs of library and information science. Perhaps this is because it has been assumed to be an inseparable part of the teaching of cataloging, and it was not considered necessary, or even possible, to single out this part of the process when discussing education for cataloging. In an article about changes in cataloging education between the mid-1960s and the early 1990s, I wrote, "There was [in the mid-1960s] considerable concentration on the aspect of cataloging that we now call authority work, although it was not called that, and the process did not seem to have a name then."[1] Lynn Connaway, in writing about the development of a model curriculum for cataloging education at the University of Denver, wrote about the integration of theory and practice in the teaching of the organization of information.[2] She specifically mentioned the inclusion of "controlled language systems" and the introduction of AACR2, but did not mention authority control per se. Eloise Vondruska, advocating continuing education, stated that "Graduate library school teaches a core of theories and facts," but went on to say that because many students have little library work experience, continuing education should be used to synthesize those facts with experience.[3] In an earlier article Vondruska had specifically mentioned "the use of authority files" in a list of concerns for which catalogers needed continuing education.[4]

In a recent book detailing research on the needs for library and information science education in the developing world, Sajjad ur Rehman addressed competencies wanted in graduates of both graduate and undergraduate programs in library and information science.[5] Managers in academic, public, and special libraries rated specific cataloging knowledge and skill competencies wanted in new professionals. That list did not include mention of authority control specifically. However, in his comparison of graduate and undergraduate competencies wanted, one item was "Developing authority files of cataloging."[6] Respondents were asked to rate the importance of teaching the competency in graduate programs versus undergraduate programs. In Rehman's study, the respondents were evenly split on whether developing authority files ought to be taught in undergraduate or graduate education. I believe this finding points up a major difficulty for those believing in the importance of authority control education: it is considered by many to be a less-than-professional skill that does not require professional attention.

The first serious attention to education for authority control is reported in an article recently published in *Cataloging & Classification Quarterly*.[7] Rebecca Mugridge and Kevin Furniss asked on Autocat (an international discussion list for catalogers) for responses to a survey. Their first question asked how the respondent had learned about authority control, giving a list of possibilities that included "Library school course" as one of the options (of which respondents could choose as many as applied). Only 18 of the 49 respondents (37%) believed they had learned about authority control in library school, and some of these 18 hedged with statements like "in general terms" or "vaguely." The second question asked what would make authority control easier to learn, and 10 respondents stated that it should be taught in library school. Another 10 respondents seemed also to be talking about library school courses by indicating that it would be easier to learn if it were studied in a systematic way. The third question asked what responsibilities for the teaching/learning of authority control should be assumed by: (a) the library school, (b) the employer, (c) the individual. Thirty-two respondents indicated that "the responsibility of the library school lies in teaching the fundamental theory and concepts of authority control," while 6 respondents indicated that some hands-on practice should be included. Three respondents indicated that they thought that library schools are hopeless in teaching authority control because either they have given up, or they barely teach even cataloging, or they never have taught it and so probably will not teach it in the future. Mugridge and Furniss concluded that "most librarians learn about authority work and authority control on the job. Those that are exposed to it in library school often receive only a cursory or basic examination of the subject. There is a perceived lack of hands-on practice available in library school."[8]

STUDY OF TEACHING AUTHORITY CONTROL IN NORTH AMERICA

In an effort to learn something about how the teaching of authority control is approached in library schools in North America, I sent a list of questions to 114 people that I was able to identify who seemed to teach in the area of organization of information in schools of library and information science in the United States and Canada. I explained that I was looking for qualitative data, not quantitative data; so it was not necessary to answer questions in a certain way or even to answer every question. I received replies from 42 people, of whom 5 stated that they do not teach in this area or have not done so for several years. Of the remaining 37 replies, 4 were from four schools in Canada. The remaining 33 people teach in 24 schools in the United States. The distribution by rank is: Professor–11; Associate Professor–7; Assistant Professor–7; Adjunct–11; Doctoral student–1.

The courses identified as being courses in which the respondents cover authority control at some level are, for the most part, either introductory (usually required) Organization of Information/Knowledge courses or Cataloging courses (at various levels). Other courses mentioned in which authority control is addressed are: Indexing and Abstracting, Information Retrieval, Subject Analysis, Technical Services, Metadata [in various manifestations], Design and Construction of Bibliographic Databases, Thesaurus Construction, Systems Operation/Analysis, Library Automation, Comparative Bibliography, and Foundations of Library Research.

The questions I asked my colleagues were:

- What do you consider to be the basic principles and/or basic components of authority control that need to be understood by all students before they receive the MLIS?
- Do you teach authority control (name/title and/or subject) in any of the classes you teach? (If not, thank you for your time. You don't need to look at the remaining questions.)
- If so, in which courses is it covered?
- How much time is spent on it in each course?

[In the following questions, if you could give separate answers for beginning and advanced courses, it would be helpful.]

- Do you approach authority control from a purely theoretical point of view, or do you go into the nuts and bolts of creating authority records, or something in between?
- Do you have a hands-on approach using a system like OCLC Connexion? Do you use paper exercises? Do you discuss it as an idea?
- If you have discussion, how detailed is the discussion?
- Briefly describe methodologies you use to get authority control concepts across.
- Do you cover authority control for personal names? Corporate bodies? Conferences? Geographic names? Subject headings?
- Do you teach the MARC authority format?
- Do you teach AACR2 rules for heading creation?
- Do you teach MARC records as created by LC for LCSH?
- Do you teach how systems incorporate authority control? Do you go into any technical aspects? If so, please describe briefly.
- Are there other aspects not covered in these questions that you could comment on?

Two of the respondents stated their unequivocal belief in the importance of teaching authority control, but stated that they no longer teach in this area and therefore would not answer the remaining questions. The other 35 people responded to my questions, some in much more detail than others, but all provided useful information. I refer to the latter responses in the presentation that follows.[9] (Permission was obtained for the quotations that are attributed to their writers.)

BASIC AUTHORITY CONTROL CONCEPTS REQUIRED FOR ALL STUDENTS

The basic principles and components that need to be understood by all MLIS students, regardless of kind of work they will do, according to my respondents are:

- What authority control is
- Why authority control is important
- Why authority control is important to users in information retrieval
- How authority control is accomplished
- How the standard tools for authority control function
- Systems issues that are involved in implementing authority control
- How authority control enhances cooperation and sharing.

These issues were identified in many different ways, of course, but content analysis of the statements that were made in response to the first question yielded these seven categories. The first category, "What authority control is," was mentioned in some way by 20 respondents (57%). They said such things as: "the function of authority control," "what IS authority control?," "the objectives of authority control (what it is and why it is important)," "fundamental principles underlying authority control," and "that access points do not arrange themselves." Two people mentioned here that students need to understand the different kinds of authority control, and four people specifically mentioned Cutter's objectives (in particular the finding function and the collocation function) as being essential for understanding by all students.

Some respondents to my survey mentioned the difficulty of getting "what it is" across to students. Hope Olson stated that "authority control always takes longer to click than I can imagine it should. Hence, I tell the students that I can't remember not understanding it and so they'll have to be patient with me and keep asking questions." Susan Hayes wrote that "students with any real interest in cataloging 'get' authority control immediately, but students who have no interest in cataloging often find it hard to grasp."

I have found in my own teaching that the "What is it?" question is very difficult to get across. The words themselves are quite off-putting. The concepts of "authority" and "control" in American culture, with its emphasis on individu-

alism, are not readily welcomed, and the words have negative connotations for
many people. Barbara Tillett, Linda Barnhart, and I corresponded a few years
ago about using "access control" instead of "authority control." But "access
control" has come to mean an operating system feature that controls the access
that certain categories of users have to files and to functions. In traveling
through Brussels recently, I was required to enter the airport through a door-
way labeled "Access Control." Perhaps Mauro Guerrini's suggested concept
of "cluster heading" will become useful here. In my teaching and in my book,
The Organization of Information, I continue to introduce "access control" as
"the results of the process of doing authority work, but without the necessity of
choosing one form of name or title and one subject term to be the 'authorized'
selection. In access control every variant name, title, or term is given equal status, with one form chosen for default display; however, a searcher may use any
of the forms to gain access to information packages related to the name, title,
or subject."[10] I find in my teaching that students react much more positively to
"access control," seeing very quickly the international implications of giving
access to a name or subject using whatever form is best known to the particular
user who is seeking it, without figuratively punishing the user with some kind
of statement that they looked for the wrong form, and they'll have to search for
the "right" one in order to get what they seek.

   Returning to the categorized list of what every MLIS student should be
taught about authority control, the second category, "Why authority control is
important," was mentioned by 16 people (46%). They made statements such
as: "the purpose of authority control," "the idea of quality control of a database," "the impact of authority control in the organization of bibliographic
data," "the governing role that authority control has in any information system, whether that system is electronic or print-based," and "problems if it's
not done or [is] done badly." Here, as with the "What is it?" question, there is
difficulty getting the concept across. Lee Shiflett commented: "One of the major problems is simply getting across the idea that it is important and that there
are rules or conventions for it that must be mastered if you are to function."

   The third category, "Why authority control is important to users in information retrieval," is very closely related to the second, and it could perhaps be
considered a subset of the concept of understanding the purpose of authority
control. However, it seemed to be a separate category in the minds of several
respondents, and so I kept it separate. Fifteen people (43%) specifically mentioned the importance of authority control in searching. Respondents wrote,
for example: "the role of controlled vocabularies in information retrieval,"
"vocabulary control increases precision in searching," "vital importance of
authority control to end-user searching and information retrieval," and, "importance of [authority control] to improve precision of searches." Larry

Osborne spoke of the consequences of *not* teaching authority control: "I think it's especially important that reference librarians and [computer] geeks understand its necessity so that we don't produce a crop of people who believe keyword searching of full text [is satisfactory] in a big database."

The fourth category of basic authority control concepts needed by all students is "How authority control is accomplished." Twenty-seven respondents (77%) made statements that fall into this category when they answered the first question. Example statements supporting this concept as being essential for all students to understand were: "how?" "the basics of how it works," "how it works," and "how to create and maintain authority records, reference structures, and authority files." That we need to teach how to distinguish representations of names and subjects from representations of information packages was well expressed by Grant Campbell, who wrote: "how authority work is based on the principle of establishing database entities for people, corporate bodies, places, and subject concepts, and that these entities are distinct from, but related to, the bibliographic entities that populate the bibliographic universe."

Two subcategories of this group emerged that I might call "Uniqueness and consistency of headings" and "Syndetic structure." Some statements about uniqueness and consistency of headings were: "that authority control serves the collocating function of the catalog by ensuring that a uniform and consistent heading is established to represent entities in the catalog," "principle of uniform heading and principle of unique heading," and "a foundation for applying the basic principles of uniqueness and consistency." Statements about syndetic structure included: "cross reference structure," "importance of authority control in creating the syndetic structure of the catalog," "the function of links (see/see also) in bibliographic databases," "understanding of syndetic structure and its purpose in searching," "the use of references/equivalence relationships between authorized and unauthorized forms of entry," and "the syndetic structure of cross references." Several respondents noted the need for syndetic structure so that users do not have to search under several variants for names, titles, or subjects, and still wonder whether they have found everything for which they might be looking.

The fifth category of basic authority control concepts, "How the standard tools for authority control function," was mentioned by 15 respondents (43%). Specific tools mentioned were: *Library of Congress Subject Headings* (LCSH), *Sears List of Subject Headings* (Sears), Library of Congress Name Authority File (LCNAF), *Anglo-American Cataloguing Rules, Second Edition* (AACR2), and Machine Readable Cataloging (MARC) records and files. Some of the statements were: "existing standards or schedules, e.g., LCSH," "the various tools of authority control," "they need to understand that we use basic authority control tools like Sears, LC subject headings, and such things as the LC authority control file," "follow a standard, e.g., AACR2," "how to 'read' and use MARC authorities," "familiarity with standard tools, e.g., AACR2, part II; LCSH," and "LC Name Authority Files; bibliographic networks and authority control."

The sixth category that my colleagues believe to be important for all students is that of "Systems issues that are involved in implementing authority control." Eleven people (31%) specifically mentioned these. Example statements are: "how authority control is reflected in information systems," "it is presented hand in hand with the concept of data dictionary in database construction," "how authority work works 'behind the scenes,'" and "transferability of authority control principles to database and other information management contexts." The need for comprehending the transferability of authority control to the Web was expressed by Grant Campbell, who stated that students need to understand "that authority control is desperately important, and that current developments in the W3C around the semantic web are reinventing the authority control concept to enhance web use."

Finally the seventh category of basic authority control concepts, "How authority control enhances cooperation and sharing," was mentioned by only three respondents, but these three seemed to feel strongly about this: "shared authority files allow the work to be done once, for all users of the system, thus increasing efficiency over all," "importance of authority control to cataloguing context (creating; exchanging records)," and "it serves catalogers' needs as well, by recording other catalogers' decisions about established headings so that we can be consistent and do not have to reinvent the wheel every time we create a heading." I suspect that this idea of cooperation is not one that comes to mind immediately in association with the words "authority control," but that upon reflection, many of the respondents would say that this is, indeed, an important understanding for everyone to have. In fact, I suspect that if I were to have done this as a Delphi study[11] and had sent this list of seven categories back to my 35 respondents for ratings, all seven of these categories would have been rated highly.

THE "HOW" OF TEACHING AUTHORITY CONTROL

Response to my question about how much time is spent on authority control in each course was quite varied. Responses ran from "about 30 minutes" to "in reality, the whole course is about that." Most people found it difficult to estimate any amount of time because "it's integrated into different units." Statements were made that indicated that there is an attempt at a formal introduction to authority control early in the term, but then it comes up again and again, e.g., in discussion of AACR2, in discussion of controlled vocabulary, in discussion of integrated systems, in discussion of encoding standards (e.g., XML DTD), and in discussion of implementing a name authority file or a subject authority file in a relational database. Ellen Crosby wrote, "It's been useful to me to go back . . . to see what I have taught. Not enough! But I am comforted by the thought (correct or not) that because I consider authority control and authority work to be essential parts of original cataloging, it comes out of my mouth as I speak."

In response to my question about teaching theory versus practice, no one was willing to admit to not approaching authority control from a theoretical point of view. While a couple of folks claimed to use only theory, most responded that they use a mixed approach, introducing the theoretical concept(s) followed by practical application. About 60% of respondents said they have the students use a real system, such as OCLC Connexion, to learn about authority records. They also use paper exercises; although only 6 said that they have students actually create authority records.

In response to my question, "If you have discussion, how detailed is the discussion?" only 3 respondents stated that they do not have discussion of the issue, and 3 people did not say anything about discussion. The others (about 80%) use discussion. Often, though, discussion consists of students asking the teacher questions and getting answers. I have found in my own experience, however, that there are questions the professor can ask that elicit quite animated discussion. For example: How does authority control affect collocation? How can all manifestations of the same work be brought together, even though they may have different titles and formats? How can persons or entities with the same name be distinguished from each other? Why is authority control important for public services? Can keyword searching and artificial intelligence ever replace controlled vocabulary assigned by human indexers? How can natural language (i.e., keywords) and controlled vocabulary be used together advantageously? What are the problems of using multiple controlled vocabularies in the same system? Can the latter be merged? Can ontologies take the place of thesauri and subject heading lists? Such questions placed on an online "discussion board" (where students are required to contribute a certain number of "postings") can provoke very thoughtful answers from students, and as they react to each other's responses, one can see them grow in their understanding.

The question asking for description of methodologies used to get authority control concepts across evoked some unique responses along with some more traditional ones. Most respondents mentioned use of searching of various kinds to get students to see the difference that authority control makes. It seems that experiencing the user's frustration of knowing that a name/subject you want is there (because the professor told you it is), but not being able to find it (or finding it only with great difficulty) because of poor or no authority control, is a good way to get the point across. After such an exercise, students can be shown how authority control can alleviate the situation. Some professors use famous names (e.g., Dr. Seuss, John Gardner, the current pope, the wife of John F. Kennedy) and ask students to search for these in various tools (e.g., Web search engine, OCLC or RLIN, bibliographic index, US OPAC, non-US OPAC, back-of-the-book index) and then discuss their findings. For topical subject terminology, comparison of searching by keyword with searching by controlled vocabulary is often used to demonstrate the value of authority control.

Experimentation with various online tools that exist is a methodology used by some. There are a number of online authority files, controlled vocabularies, ontologies, and, of course, online catalogs with varying degrees of authority control. Anita Coleman has constructed a Web page with links to many of these tools for her students. She calls it a "toolbox" which she uses as a "playground" for student discovery.[12]

Another methodology mentioned was having students read and interpret MARC authority records. For example, they might look at authority records for the authors of the readings they have for the course. Sometimes there are students in the class for whom authority records have been created because they have other advanced degrees for which they wrote theses. Such authority records can be useful teaching tools. And the realization that they often can learn a professor's age from her/his authority record can bring a break-through for some students!

Some teachers (usually using the MARC authority format only in advanced classes) have students create authority records showing authorized form of name along with cross references. If there are students in class who have had name changes due to marriage or other circumstance, their names can make good examples. One unique suggestion from Hope Olson was to create authority records for some of the cats in T. S. Eliot's "The Naming of Cats."

A difficulty that was mentioned by several respondents is getting across the difference between cross references and added entries. I also have this difficulty. In my introductory class I have students create ISBD descriptions of themselves as "information packages." (This works well for most students, as it allows them to concentrate on the *kind* of information that goes into each area rather than having to figure out from an item in hand what is the *right* information to go into each area. Unfortunately, a few students lack the imagination to really appreciate this and complain that it has no "practical" value.)

Then I have them make simple authority records for themselves (i.e., the "subject") and their family members (i.e., "contributors" to the existence of the "information package"). In these simple records, they use "x" to indicate references, as I find that trying to introduce MARC authority tagging at this level is much too complicated. Then they are asked to add the authorized forms of the names to their ISBD descriptions as "added entries." Inevitably, some students include references as well as authorized forms or use references instead of authorized forms. (It can be rather depressing.)

Some additional methodologies specifically for getting across subject and classification authority control concepts were reported. Almost everyone who addressed subject authority control has students use subject heading lists and/or thesauri to index some sample information packages. Several professors have students construct a thesaurus–the complexity of such an assignment depends upon the level of the class being taught. Another idea is to diagram the syndetic structure of a subject heading from a subject heading list or thesaurus.

Finally, a methodology used by a few respondents involves building in-house "live" databases into which students enter bibliographic records complete with authority control. These are often used in conjunction with the teaching of relational database concepts.

In response to my question as to whether respondents covered authority control of personal names, corporate names, conferences, geographic names, and/or subject headings, 60% responded that they cover all of these, and a few people added that they also cover authority control for works, uniform titles, and monographic series. The remaining respondents, for the most part, cover personal names and subject headings, with about half of these also covering corporate names. All but four respondents use AACR2 to deal with name authorities, and they use LCSH or Sears to deal with subject headings.

When asked whether they teach the MARC authority format, 60% of respondents said they teach the MARC name authority format, although only 2 respondents specifically mentioned teaching students to *create* MARC authority records. Another 20% show students the MARC name authority format, and 20% do not introduce it at all. LCSH records in MARC format are taught by half the respondents, another 10% only show it to students, and 30% do not cover it at all. This seems to be a matter of time. With fewer than 45 classroom hours in which to introduce all the basics of all matters of concern in organizing information, something often has to be omitted, and the details of MARC authority records seem to be less essential than other things.

In response to my asking if respondents teach how systems incorporate authority control, 29% responded that they do try to cover this, with another 23% saying that they do it in a very general way. Almost half (46%) do not cover it at all. This seems to be at least partly a factor of knowledge on the part of the teacher. One person mentioned that it comes up in class when the university's head of cataloging does a demo of cataloging in an integrated system. On the other hand, Larry Osborne, who teaches a systems operations class in addition to a cataloging class stated that he can purposely corrupt the in-house database while demonstrating it so that students can see what disasters can happen. He said that at least one student usually advances the idea that we do not need authority control in an automated environment, and that "sets me up for a rant!" A negative implication of system design that should be pointed out, according to Pauline Cochrane, is to "deplore what the ILS [Integrated Library System] has done to local authority control for multiple vocabularies."

My last question was "Are there other aspects not covered in these questions that you could comment on?" I mention here four of the responses to this question: Pauline Cochrane suggested the inclusion of authority control measures for website metadata and commented: "As ontologies are invading our authority file space to a great degree, not to mention classification schemes and taxonomies, I would hope these would be asked about, too." Lynne Howarth wrote about the usefulness of authority control applications in situations other than the traditional cataloging environment: "E.g., when one needs to create and maintain standards for structured data in an enterprise portal, consider the principles of authority control as documented in/supported by AACR and MARC." Sheila Intner mentioned international standardization of name authorities and the merging of LC's and other national library files. Richard Smiraglia commented that "authority control for works, FRBR [Functional Requirements for Bibliographic Records] notwithstanding, still is pretty bad."

PERCEPTIONS OF FORMER STUDENTS
vs. PERCEPTIONS OF TEACHERS

There seems to be a considerable disconnect between the perceptions of respondents to my study and perceptions of the Mugridge/Furniss respondents. The people who responded to me are passionate about the teaching of authority control. Just sample some of their comments: John Leide: "Authority work is integral to the effective organization of information. Syndetic structure is fundamental to the purposes of librarianship." Lee Shiflett: "Authority control is so basic to this whole business that it is ubiquitous." Larry Osborne: "I think authority control is the most important thing we teach in cataloging. . . . It's appalling that people create data retrieval systems without authority control. I think it was Martha Manheimer who told me that if you don't have authority control you don't have a catalog; you only have a big list."

Among the librarians who responded to Mugridge and Furniss, however, several of the few who said they had learned about authority control in library school included some qualifying statements: "such as, 'in general terms,' 'it was mentioned in my cataloging class, but we did not study it in any detail,' 'small part of cataloging core course,' 'was probably mentioned, but did not sink in,' and 'vaguely.'"[13] It would be interesting to know if any of the 49 librarians responding to the Mugridge/Furniss questions had studied with any of the 37 teachers responding to my questions. Probably there is little, if any, overlap. Even so, does that imply that the teachers who did not respond to me do not teach authority control? I know that is not true, because I know a number of the non-responders personally, and I know that they care about teaching authority control even though they did not have time to respond to my questions.

I think that perhaps the librarian who wrote that authority control "was probably mentioned, but did not sink in" was highly representative. I know that the concept is a difficult one. Anything that one learns about for the first time often needs repetition in various circumstances before it really "sinks in." I have had the experience several times of hearing a former student say that s/he had never been taught "x," when I knew for certain that I had covered "x" in class with that student.

Another point to make about librarians' perceptions of whether they learned about authority control in library school is that in a one-year program, which is the length of most programs in the U.S., most students have time to take only one course in organizing information, and that one is crammed in with, usually, three other courses on different topics in the same semester. The mind can only absorb so much new information at once. It was clear from the responses I received from the teachers in Canadian programs, which are two-year programs, that they have more courses in this area and have more time for the inclusion in their courses of practical exercises on authority control.

In addition, great emphasis is being placed on information technology in schools of library and information science. Rehman found in his study that "Effective and intelligent application of information technology is obviously the foremost priority. . . . Capabilities related to automation, database skills, development of information systems and utilities, and effective application of new technology were considered the hard-core content for the preparation of professionals."[14] As a result, courses in basic library competencies are squeezed out.

CONCLUSION

I believe we can say that the teaching of authority control in schools of library and information science is alive and well, even though it is not perceived this way by some former students. Many professors are fervently attempting to imbue the next generation of librarians with an understanding of the necessity for authority control. Unfortunately, they have to fight the non-understanding of colleagues, the lack of course time to be as thorough as desired, and the perception that information technology is uppermost in importance among courses to be taught. However, because the chaotic environment of the Web has brought attention to the need for authority control (e.g., the "semantic web"), we have a new opportunity to teach these concepts to a new generation of information professionals.

NOTES

1. Arlene G. Taylor, "A Quarter Century of Cataloging Education," (in *Technical Services Management, 1965-1990: A Quarter Century of Change and a Look to the Future: Festschrift for Kathryn Luther Henderson*, Linda C. Smith and Ruth C. Carter, eds. New York: The Haworth Press, Inc., c1996), p. 300.

2. Lynn Silipigni Connaway, "A Model Curriculum for Cataloging Education: The Library and Information Services Program at the University of Denver," *Technical Services Quarterly* 15, no. 1/2 (1997): 35.

3. Eloise M. Vondruska, "Continuing Education and Technical Services Librarians: Learning for 1965-1990 and the Future" (in *Technical Services Management, 1965-1990: A Quarter Century of Change and a Look to the Future: Festschrift for Kathryn Luther Henderson*, Linda C. Smith and Ruth C. Carter, eds. New York: The Haworth Press, Inc., c1996), p. 310.

4. Eloise M. Vondruska, "Education for Cataloging: An Open Entry," *Illinois Libraries* 67 (May 1985): 443.

5. Sajjad ur Rehman, *Preparing the Information Professional: An Agenda for the Future* (Westport, Conn: Greenwood Press, 2000).

6. Ibid., p. 124.

7. Rebecca L. Mugridge and Kevin A. Furniss, "Education for Authority Control: Whose Responsibility Is It?" *Cataloging & Classification Quarterly* 34, nos. 1/2 (2002): 233-243.

8. Ibid., p. 242.

9. The author wishes to acknowledge and thank the respondents (each name is followed in parentheses by the name of the university in which the person teaches): Jim Anderson (Rutgers University), Linda La Puma Bial (University of Illinois at Urbana), Rick Block (Long Island University), Cameron Campbell (Dominican University), Grant Campbell (University of Western Ontario), Lois Chan (University of Kentucky), Allyson Carlyle (University of Washington), Pauline Cochrane (University of Illinois at Urbana), Anita Coleman (University of Arizona), Ellen Crosby (Indiana University, IUPUI), Bruce Ford (Pratt Institute), Vania Goodwin (Indiana Univer-

sity, IUPUI), Rebecca Green (University of Maryland), Vicki Gregory (University of South Florida), Susan Hayes (Long Island University), Elizabeth Haynes (University of Southern Mississippi), Kathryn Henderson (University of Illinois at Urbana), Lynne Howarth (University of Toronto), Ingrid Hsieh-Yee (Catholic University of America), Sheila Intner (Simmons College), Long Hwey Jeng (University of Kentucky, Lexington), Frank Kellerman (University of Rhode Island), Jim Kelly (University of Rhode Island and Simmons College), Kathryn LaBarre (Indiana University), John Leide (McGill University), Yan Ma (University of Rhode Island), Shawne Miksa (University of North Texas), Kwong Bor Ng (Queens College), Hope Olson (University of Alberta), Larry Osborne (University of Hawaii), Taemin Park (Indiana University), Betsy Schoeller (University of Wisconsin, Milwaukee), Candy Schwartz (Simmons College), Lee Shifflett (University of North Carolina at Greensboro), Richard Smiraglia (Long Island University), Carol Truett (Appalachian State University), Yin Zhang (Kent State University).

10. Arlene G. Taylor, *The Organization of Information*, 2nd ed. (Westport, Conn.: Libraries Unlimited, 2004), p. 353.

11. The Delphi method allows geographically dispersed experts to deal systematically with a complex problem by responding to a questionnaire, the answers to which are collected for a second round questionnaire. In the second round (and sometimes a third round) statements made in the first round are evaluated and/or rated by the experts. See http://www.iit.edu/~it/delphi.html.

12. Anita Sundaram Coleman, "KS Toolbox: IRLS 401/501—Knowledge Structures I, Fall 2002," School of Information Resources & Library Science, University of Arizona, available: http://www.sir.arizona.edu/faculty/coleman/501/kbox.html.

13. Mugridge and Furniss, "Education for Authority Control," p. 237.

14. Rehman, *Preparing the Information Professional*, p. 57.

Guidelines and Methodology
for the Creation of the SBN Authority File

Cristina Magliano

SUMMARY. Italy's ICCU (Istituto Centrale per il Catalogo Unico) is coordinating a national effort to build a shared online authority file through the National Library Service (SBN). The status of that project and the implications of maintaining such a resource are described. *[Article copies available for a fee from The Haworth Document Delivery Service: 1-800-HAWORTH. E-mail address: <docdelivery@haworthpress.com> Website: <http://www.HaworthPress.com> © 2004 by The Haworth Press, Inc. All rights reserved.]*

KEYWORDS. ICCU, SBN, Italian National Authority File Project, authority control, cooperative programs, database maintenance

INTRODUCTION

This conference follows the "Study Days on Cataloguing and Authority Control" devoted to the future evolution of RICA (the Italian cataloguing code) and to authority control in SBN (Servizio bibiotecario nazionale or

---

Cristina Magliano is affiliated with ICCU.

[Haworth co-indexing entry note]: "Guidelines and Methodology for the Creation of the SBN Authority File." Magliano, Cristina. Co-published simultaneously in *Cataloging & Classification Quarterly* (The Haworth Information Press, an imprint of The Haworth Press, Inc.) Vol. 38, No. 3/4, 2004, pp. 59-69; and: *Authority Control in Organizing and Accessing Information: Definition and International Experience* (ed: Arlene G. Taylor, and Barbara B. Tillett) The Haworth Information Press, an imprint of The Haworth Press, Inc., 2004, pp. 59-69. Single or multiple copies of this article are available for a fee from The Haworth Document Delivery Service [1-800-HAWORTH, 9:00 a.m. - 5:00 p.m. (EST). E-mail address: docdelivery@haworthpress.com].

"National Library Service"), which were conducted by the ICCU (Istituto Centrale per il Catalogo Unico delle biblioteche Italiane e per le informazioni bibliografiche) on November 21 and 22, 2002 in Rome. Among the participants were Barbara Tillett and Françoise Bourdon and also Professor Mauro Guerrini. These study days also provided an opportunity for reflection and study in anticipation of today's international seminar, which has also been sponsored by the Libraries Directorate of the MBAC (Ministero per i Beni e le Attività Culturali).

I would like to outline the context in which the Italian National Authority File project developed. First of all, the birth and development of the SBN and the formation of the SBN Index has led rapidly to the growth of the national database and of the database of authors (personal and corporate). The SBN Index is a collective catalogue of considerable proportions, formed and enlarged through online shared cataloguing activity. In November 2002, the database consisted of 1,893,403 records for authors' names (personal and corporate) and 6,266,074 records for titles (5,346,993 monographs and 237,672 serials). In all there were 17,240,313 locations, the results of shared cataloguing by the libraries with SBN *Poli* and the loading of several Italian retrospective bibliographies, in addition to retrospective conversion projects mounted by libraries participating in the SBN cooperative network (such as the *Bibliografia nazionale italiana* 1958-1984, the *Bollettino delle opere moderne straniere acquisite dalle biblioteche statali* 1958-1980, retrospectively converted data relating to the *Fondi meridionalistici*, the *CUBI* 1886-1957).

From the beginning, the ICCU has been committed to the dissemination of standards for cooperative cataloguing. This it has done by publicizing the national application of standards for description and also by giving authoritative interpretations of our cataloguing code (RICA, *Regole italiane di catalogazione per autori*. Roma: ICCU, 1979), especially the part concerning forms of name, so that all additions to the catalogue will be accurate and consistent, particularly with regard to access points. Following these standards and rule interpretations will also facilitate comparing records added to the database and help guard against the duplication of bibliographic records.

Furthermore, given the different types of materials and differing timeframes that co-exist in online catalogues, one comes across inconsistencies that are the result of years of cataloguing practices in a non-sharing environment. Thus, there is a need to provide criteria and methods for ensuring uniformity of treatment, which seemed particularly necessary with regard to elements affecting access and the grouping of records.

Work on the standardization of access points was conducted to compare the major foreign catalogues and bibliographies. For instance there was the formalization of punctuation in personal and corporate names, which was absent from our cataloguing code, but practical for the automatic processing of data and especially for an arrangement that is acceptable and clear to the user.

MAINTENANCE STRUCTURE OF THE SBN ARCHIVE

In March 1994, a Working Group was created for essential regular maintenance activities, coordinated by ICCU. This was made up of expert librarians from the parties cooperating in SBN: librarians who–through institutional expertise, geographic distribution, representation of particular SBN software packages, or special nature of functions and usage–could bring to the cooperative context the professionalism and commitment that are indispensable for their difficult and onerous assignment.

At present 14 library institutions are taking part in the activity having to do with "Structure," and are described as "nodes" or "Poli" (poles) for the system. Those institutions are: the Regional Polo of Piemonte at the National University Library, Torino; Polo of the Universities of Lombardia–CILEA, University Library of Pavia; Polo MBCA at the Marciana National Library, Venice; Polo of the National Central Library, Florence; Polo of the National Central Library Vittorio Emanuele II, Rome; Regional Polo of Sicily, Central Library of the Region of Sicily, Palermo; Polo of the Library Network of Romagna, Ravenna; Joint Polo of Bologna–the University Library and the Library of the Archiginnasio, Bologna; the SBN University Polo of the Veneto, Padova; the MBCA Polo at the National Central Library Vittorio Emanuele III, Naples; Polo of the Cultural Institutes of Rome–IEI, Rome.

The first phase of data maintenance and control involved eliminating duplications among both titles and authors, as well as removing inconsistent and incorrect headings and adjusting them to agree with the dictates of our national rules. As part of that phase, the ICCU published a *Guide to Cataloguing in Accordance with SBN Procedures* that incorporates the ISBD standards that are not explicitly present in our cataloguing code (RICA) and the coded data of the SBN format. The *Guide* has gone through two revised editions in order to incorporate directions and some general procedures for shared cataloguing practice, as these became consolidated and as different institutions became involved.

The need for precise instructions on the treatment of access points involved the group on "Structure." They monitored the cooperative contributions and developed a series of instructions, which together form a guide to acceptable practice in the performance of cooperative activity–a sort of code of ethics in relation to the work of cataloguing, having regard also to the needs of the end-user. In particular regarding authors, to avoid linking a title with the wrong author or duplicating a record for an author already present in the Index, a great deal of emphasis was placed on the need for care in searching and preventive identification, by checking for the presence of a record for another person with the same name to which it is obvious that the record should not be connected, or for the presence of the author's name in a form other than the one used in the search. Specific rule interpretations were established to cover these situations.

Such rules also cover indications of a general organizational character, methods of work, and especially, directions for the cataloguing, capture, and correction of data. Over the years we have helped to maintain control over all data that the "Structure" group regards as priority, and also involved cataloguers in the *Poli*. Intervention has mainly been concerned with elimination of author/title duplications and with corrections. The experience gained has made it clear that the SBN Index requires a permanent body for maintenance, working full-time on quality control and conformity of data for authors and titles.

THE SBN PROTOTYPE AUTHORITY FILE (AF)

The issues regarding an archive authority file (AFArchive) began to be examined back in 1989 by an ICCU-BNCF study group. Analyzing the international standards edited by IFLA available at the time (GARE, *Guidelines for Authority and Reference Entries*, published in 1984 and UNIMARC/A of 1991), the group identified the elements necessary for the formation of such an authority file and assessed its feasibility, particularly comparing international standards and national rules. The group concluded its work in 1991 with the production of a technical document of functional specifications and guidelines, among which a structure for technical cooperation between libraries was outlined at an operational level.

The aim was to create an instrument for control within the cooperative environment, following SBN usage, so that across the riches of bibliographic data that were being accumulated, it would be possible to guarantee uniformity and consistency among access points and to derive the National Authority File from them. Unfortunately, from the analysis and study of the creation of such a model until its reality, several years were to pass, partly because of inadequate funding, partly because of the difficulty of testing a new and complex tool in a broad context such as that of SBN.

Beginning in 1992, under resolution CIPE 12/8/1992 published in the G.U. S.g. N.222 21/9/92, the Institute (ICCU) obtained an initial financial allocation to launch a study in collaboration with the National Central Library of Florence on the 'Reorganization of bibliographic services in Italy.' This study provided for the development of the SBN network through primary services in support of cataloguing and with assistance for research. From all of this arose the requirement to build a National Authority File within the SBN environment. The original project provided for the whole undertaking to be divided into different segments, the execution of which then had to be subdivided into two stages.

In the first stage, the following principal functions came into effect:

- formation of a single database of authorities for authors and for uniform titles (gathering titles);
- procedures for loading of author records from the SBN author archive file, and of title records from the title archives for ancient and modern material, respectively;
- functional capabilities in the Authorities archive for online creation, cancellation, and correction/merging of records;
- procedures for periodic downloading in batch mode of data, validated or directly produced, from the Authorities archive into the SBN author archive; and, for uniform titles, into the Index archive files for modern and ancient titles, respectively. Also the necessary control functions to guard against possible duplications or unwarranted suppressions during the loading and merging of "validated" data, in the Index, with an authority level higher than that of cataloguing.

The format for entry took into account international standards and the past experience of the ICCU in the course of work carried out as a participant in the Working Groups of the IFLA Section on Cataloguing.

In particular, we applied the rules regarding forms of heading contained in our code, while at the international level reference was made to the first *GARE*, published by IFLA in 1984, translated into Italian in 1993, and subsequently to *GARR (Guidelines for Authority Records and References)* of 2001. A uniform structure was adopted for each type of entry in the archive file (authority record, reference, explanatory reference), with the aim of facilitating the international communication of bibliographic records. The GARR standard recognizes the importance of maintaining national rules in determining "authorised forms for headings," in order to facilitate consultation and understanding on the part of users; and those related to the display of authority and reference information for all types of heading, including uniform titles of legal and religious works, musical compositions, and publications in series. In this sense this requirement has been met by providing for a type of heading for titles and by adopting the method of making separate records for an authorized heading and for reference headings.

From the phase of experimentation and testing of the model it then became possible to move to an experimental operation of the system, thanks to new funding.

THE SBN INDEX ENHANCEMENT PROJECT

With the project for enhancement of the SBN Index–L. 662.96–"Services of de-duplication of the modern SBN Index and augmentation of the SBN and National Authority File," which lasted for 18 months and was completed in November 2002, significant development occurred in the work of maintenance and quality control of the bibliographic data in the national Index. Above all, however, we achieved a consolidation of the gains made to that point in the prototype National Authority File project in SBN. The two immediate goals were: (a) to eliminate records for authors and titles that were duplicated in the modern SBN Index; and (b) to get the National Authority File up and running.

Point (a) concerned the action launched in November 2000, to eliminate duplicate records in the modern SBN Index database, and clearly also foreshadowed de-duplication of authors' names as an activity consequent upon the work on titles.

The second point (b) concerned the fuelling and start-up of the authority file operation. The file had its origins in the SBN database, and so it has the dual purpose of being a support and control mechanism for national union catalogue activities, and at the same time, of serving as a point of reference for organizations not in SBN. The working file resides on the central system, but it is a file separate from the Index database, with which it interacts at present in batch mode; however, with the new Index Evolution project/program it will be totally integrated with the bibliographic database operation and will be able to be updated online.

The creation/correction/augmentation of authority records, references, and general explanatory records are carried out in the SBN database. The structure of these authority records follows the data provided for by GARR, in particular, for notes containing biographical or historical information and cataloguers' notes showing sources consulted. In anticipation of international instructions, each authority record has been assigned an identifying number, with 13 alphanumeric characters, in place of the eventual international ISADN number.

This activity requires complex and dedicated work by expert staff. Determining the authorized form of the name of a person or body or of a title, requires careful verification based on the code of rules and on inventory and other kinds of sources from which to extract the various pieces of information that will justify the choices made. Furthermore, besides agreeing with the rules, those choices must take into account different requirements of usage that apply to contexts that differ according to type of institution (local government libraries, state or university libraries, etc.).

PARTICIPANTS: SBN-AF ENHANCEMENT PROJECT

Together with the ICCU, which was in charge and coordinated the SBN-AF Enhancement project, other participants were the BNCF (National Central Library of Florence), the BNCR (National Central Library of Rome), the Biblioteca Nazionale Braidense (Milan) with the CILEA university consortium and the University Library of Bologna. One member of staff worked on the project at each institution, under the supervision of a designated librarian.

In our situation, the production, management, and distribution of a National Authority File of necessity has several kinds of institutional involvement. ICCU serves as project coordinator and is also responsible for the National Library Service; and the National Central Library of Florence is responsible for the Italian National Bibliography. The two central institutions have assumed a special role in this project, in that both are responsible for the creation of national tools and services and also for international exchange and the maintenance of international formats. It is interesting to observe that, also at an international level (see the introduction to the 2nd edition of *GARR*, 2001), IFLA emphasized how in different countries all bibliographic activities, including those relating to bibliographic control, are increasingly taking effect within a cooperative environment.

Starting from the assumption that each country is responsible for its national authors, work began with the names of Italian personal authors. In all, 34,388 records have been examined and approximately 9,900 personal author headings processed, i.e., raised to authority record status complete with reference apparatus, biographical notes, and notes of sources. In many cases this work also involved the systematic arrangement of the bibliographic records linked to the name.

METHODS OF WORK AND SELECTION CRITERIA

The first stages of the work for the SBN-AF Enhancement project were slow and included experimentation to determine the most productive methods for work that had never before been implemented on a cooperative basis.

ICCU arranged training courses for the operators, conducted by the librarians who were trainers for the project. Later, a series of instructions was issued, in particular specifying the qualifications to be used in author entries for the purpose of differentiating between like headings, in the following order of priority: (a) qualifications which usually accompany the name; (b) in the absence of such a usual qualification, chronological details are to be used; (c) in the absence of both (a) and (b), a phrase may be formulated by the cataloguer, in Italian where possible. It was emphasized that qualifications in the form of a word or phrase had to be drawn from reference works, since they were to agree with the principle of preferring the form "commonly used." There were instructions for forenames in the form of initials, in particular when it is necessary for them to be spelled out, and a series of instructions for forms of reference and for notices grouping several undifferentiated authors. Such notices and the related procedures were published on the ICCU's website in order to communicate the choices made to cooperating institutions.

A procedures manual also was produced, and a file commenced for bibliographic reference works. This file is available for consultation online and is updated centrally, similarly to the one already produced by the Laboratory for Retrospective Bibliography. On the basis of the workflow developed, operators are made aware of the steps to be followed, for example, to always check the Index first for consistency and then work on the authority file database.

The authority file database includes the network of references and all information pertaining to any notes that are necessary to identify a person who is connected to the bibliographic entities present in the SBN Index. This work, in some cases, has extended to the systematic arrangement of records relating to linked titles, working on both files in succession.

The greatest difficulties encountered concerned: (1) the stages of controlling the batch return of authority file data into the SBN Index database, which had never been previously tested in an online cataloguing environment, and (2) methods relating to the selection criteria for the entities on which to work. The practice of exhaustive preliminary research proved from the beginning to be a lengthy business and not useful, especially for modern authors who were not cited in reference works and with few associated titles. Selecting entities based on subject and/or timeframe was a choice made by the ICCU that brought to a conclusion the work on Italian literary authors of the 20th century (approximately 1,800 headings). The success of this work demonstrated the validity of that selection, even with the difficulties associated with the numerous cases of identical names encountered.

THE NATIONAL AUTHORITY FILE PROJECT
AND THE COMMITTEE FOR THE REVISION OF RICA

It is important to bear in mind that the National Authority File project was proceeding at the same time as code revision was being undertaken by the Ministerial Committee on RICA. Given this situation, it was often problematic, where the code was controversial or unclear, to tackle cases which over the years had produced customary interpretations and practices that were not always uniform. Furthermore, some rather impractical solutions had emerged in the light of the retrieval potential of online catalogues, in which strategies can be adopted that, in some cases, disregard the standards traditionally followed.

The section of RICA regarding forms of name received the most attention from the Committee, for the simple fact that, more than others, it is in need of updating and simplification.

Cataloguing in SBN, however, has never departed from RICA standards: an example of this is the choice of using dates to qualify only those authors with identical names. Some others declare more widespread use of dates to be obligatory in the archive authority file.

FUTURE DEVELOPMENT

In the project for the evolution of the national SBN Index there is envisaged a complete integration of the authority file database following an extension of the present procedures active in version 3270 of the SBN system, in order to supply services independently of the Polo software. In addition, the present authority file archive will be extended to other entities, including uniform titles of music, edited collections, subject headings, classification, place names, and printers' marks for ancient materials.

The main aim of the project is to restructure the complex architecture of the National Library Service (SBN), reviewing both the technological and organizational aspects of cooperation, for the purpose of opening up the system to collaboration with other networks and public and private structures–with special mention of other library management systems–allowing a major expansion of the services offered to users. The new protocol, besides guaranteeing continuity of operation of the present SBN Polo software, within an architecture and on a database both completely different, is meant to build architectural, organizational, and technological tools to achieve the fundamental objectives of growth and evolution of the SBN system.

The plan for the database includes eventually having the potential to process records coming from databases external to SBN. This will set in motion the supply of new services. Such an "opening-up" through a new SBN-MARC communications protocol must, of necessity, bring with it tighter controls against duplication of data, but must also allow for integration of data with eventual local solutions that will be able to enrich the network of links referring to authorities.

The model has been designed so as to be able to take in the variety of materials currently being processed by Italian libraries and present in databases now managed by ICCU that must be absorbed into the new database, namely, ancient books, modern books, and music.

The system preparing for the management of authority files integrated in the database, will facilitate the standardization of the form of access points for cataloguing descriptions.

The archive file of national work thus conceived must yield–as a result of the choices made and the corrections and checking carried out–a reliable product, consistent and uniform in the criteria applied, valid for all authors and titles, whatever the source of the data, with regard to the various databases external or present on the SBN Index system (Ancient and Modern Indexes, Music database, Manuscripts, Census data).

This is a sizeable undertaking, an enormous amount of checking and management that will require cooperation on a national scale, which, of necessity, must involve various structures at various levels and must provide for them to be taken in gradually.

From the moment of cataloguing, all biographical and bibliographical information must be provided for new authors entered by all cataloguers sharing the work on SBN. The ICCU has commissioned a study on the organization of such a service and an organizational model has already been identified.

A system with a strong, central coordinating facility is planned, to which are connected other facilities that are specialized and local, also with particular subject expertise. The operators of the authority file will receive information from all sources and will also be open to proposed corrections. The central facility will have responsibility for training the cooperating facilities in matters regarding standards, rule interpretations, and advisable checks on the work carried out.

The need also to relate to Italian non-library systems (museums and archives) will serve to harmonize differing requirements and tend towards a sharing and definition of data that they have in common, and specification of that which is separate, providing for use of differentiated displays in their respective OPACs, for the differing usage requirements of the various types of institution, also in the light of future interoperability.

Finally, the process of analysis and gradual evolution must take into account the models already existing within international projects (VIAF, LEAF, NACO) and of IFLA's new study, FRANAR (Functional Requirements and Numbering of Authority Records), which is under development. Furthermore, national application is planned of the *UNIMARC/Authorities, Universal format for authorities*, published by IFLA in 2001, of which the Institute is about to publish the Italian translation.

I should like to conclude by remembering that, in this international and cooperative context, the idea has also been advanced of a harmonization of cataloguing rules and interoperability between different sectors, which is also one of the priorities and objectives of the IFLA Section on Cataloguing, as we heard from Dr. Barbara Tillett. The library community is therefore hopeful for the advancement of standards that are more widely accepted and are applicable in different contexts and areas.

STANDARDS, EXCHANGE FORMATS, METADATA

The Bibliografia Nazionale Italiana and Control of Access Points

Gloria Cerbai Ammannati

SUMMARY. In its role as a national bibliographic agency, the Bibliografia Nazionale Italiana (BNI) has never been in a position to fulfill what should be one of its main functions: authority control. Despite the creation of various committees, studies, and projects, and the close relationship between the BNI and the Servizio Bibliotecario Nazionale (SBN), no plan of action with regard to authority control, whether shared or developed in consultation, has been produced to date. Recently, a significant result was achicved: the specification of the new BNI/UNIMARC database, structured according to authority control principles. And in collaboration with the Region of Tuscany, a project for control of access points destined for the users and librarians of that

Gloria Cerbai Ammannati is affiliated with BNI.

[Haworth co-indexing entry note]: "The Bibliografia Nazionale Italiana and Control of Access Points." Ammannati, Gloria Cerbai. Co-published simultaneously in *Cataloging & Classification Quarterly* (The Haworth Information Press, an imprint of The Haworth Press, Inc.) Vol. 38, No. 3/4, 2004, pp. 71-81; and: *Authority Control in Organizing and Accessing Information: Definition and International Experience* (ed: Arlene G. Taylor, and Barbara B. Tillett) The Haworth Information Press, an imprint of The Haworth Press, Inc., 2004, pp. 71-81. Single or multiple copies of this article are available for a fee from The Haworth Document Delivery Service [1-800-HAWORTH, 9:00 a.m. - 5:00 p.m. (EST). E-mail address: docdelivery@haworthpress.com].

Digital Object Identifier: 10.1300/J104v38n03_07

region is in progress, providing the opportunity to initiate the systematic control of BNI access points. The BNI is now in a position to begin to realize the first objective recommended by the IFLA Working Group on an International Authority System more than twenty years ago: to establish authority headings, including cross-references, for its bibliographic records. *[Article copies available for a fee from The Haworth Document Delivery Service: 1-800-HAWORTH. E-mail address: <docdelivery@haworthpress.com> Website: <http://www.HaworthPress.com> © 2004 by The Haworth Press, Inc. All rights reserved.]*

KEYWORDS. Authority control, access points, RICA, ISBD, Biblioteca Nazionale Centrale di Firenze (BNCF), Bibliografia Nazionale Italiana (BNI), Servizio Bibliotecario Nazionale (SBN), UNIMARC, OPAC, SBN Index

In its role as a national bibliographic agency, the Bibliografia Nazionale Italiana (BNI) has never been in a position–and still is not today–to fulfill one of the functions that are peculiarly its own: authority control. The main reason for the lack of planning for this activity is the chronic shortage of staff available for it. This is a serious situation, one that is embarrassing to admit and certainly too serious to be allowed to continue.

Following recommendations emerging from the National Conference of Libraries held in Rome in January 1979, which proposed the creation of a national bibliographic service, the Servizio Bibliotecario Nazionale (SBN), the Ministero per i Beni Culturali e Ambientali established the Commissione Ministeriale per l'Automazione delle Biblioteche. This commission had envisioned a national bibliographic file, expert responsibility for which would rest with the BNI. There was an implicit understanding from the beginning that the SBN and the BNI would have their own separate goals and operations, and it was stated that the BNI was "aimed at ensuring the quality, completeness, and consistency of bibliographic description entered into the file, within the dynamics of national bibliographic control."

Documenting national publishing output institutionally is essentially a scholarly operation, different from the essentially practical one required of any given catalog, whether individual or collective. In this sense the position of the BNI was not within the SBN, but alongside it. To date, not even this close relationship between the BNI and the SBN has produced, or substantially provided for, any plan of action with regard to authority control, whether shared or developed in consultation. In fact, the two Italian bibliographic agencies, each with its own area of expertise, would have been able to collaborate–and should have done so–in order to guarantee services, separately and/or in common, geared to the control of access points for bibliographic records.

The feasibility study on the reorganization of national bibliographic services in Italy (financed jointly in 1990 by the Ufficio Centrale per i Beni Librari e gli Istituti Culturali and the European Economic Community) began in 1991. In 1992, after six months of work, it concluded with a proposal to establish the *Centro per il Coordinamento dei Servizi Bibliografici Italiani* (CECOSBI), which provided for a whole range of roles and tasks to be undertaken in order to meet users' needs.

The study identified two primary directives for the BNI: to create a bibliography dedicated to monographs that was current, timely, and exhaustive in coverage; and, in tandem with it, to provide a series of bibliographic services dedicated to particular types of documents, to ensure coverage of the national publishing output.[1] The study brought out all of the difficulties and shortcomings of the BNI, and how users' expectations had been frustrated over time; in its turn, the concluding report signaled a salutary moment of crisis, if only for having provided documentary evidence of heavy costs and unacceptable delays.

As usual, after the 1991 feasibility study, there was no further talk about an issue that would have involved the Ufficio Centrale per i Beni Librari, the Biblioteca Nazionale Centrale di Firenze (BNCF), and the Istituto Centrale per il Catalogo Unico delle Biblioteche Italiane (ICCU), and so all the hard work, suggested solutions, and opportunities that had arisen were in vain.

The EDIFICARE project took shape during the following years.[2] This project had its origins in the 1991 feasibility study and was financed by a 1992 resolution of the Comitato Interministeriale per la Programmazione Economica (CIPE). EDIFICARE was intended to be an attempt to begin the reorganization of national bibliographic services on the basis of the results of the feasibility study.

The BNI acknowledged that, in order to provide new services, it would be necessary to review some of the SBN Index procedures; it proposed to devote one third of its total anticipated funding allocation to improve the cataloging functionality of the system. As a result, it was logical to hope–or indeed, to claim–that the BNI was making progress in relation to the SBN. Its own clearly defined position would be that of an autonomous bibliographic service alongside a library service, with the awareness that a bibliographic service is indispensable for an effective library service, and all the more so when both utilize the same technology and the same specifications for their work.

The EDIFICARE project was the opportunity to plan for a new BNI subdivided into different series. The BNCF, having to produce diversified BNI services as part of its responsibility for the national bibliography, at that point adopted the thinking of Luigi Crocetti, for whom "the determining factor is the coverage that the bibliography strives to provide, whatever the means it adopts to achieve it."[3] This is a view analogous to the one expressed in other words by Diego Maltese: "Whether or not the items upon which [the bibliography] is based are owned by the library that produces it, is of itself of no consequence. What makes the publications described relevant to the purpose of the national bibliography is simply the fact that they provide documentary evidence of the national bibliographic output."[4]

The problem is also this: at present no library in Italy can claim to represent the sole existing bibliographic service, much less a comprehensive one. CECOSBI sought to ensure that a variety of well-defined, interconnected services, made possible through collaboration between public and private information producers, would be provided at the national level and as an official public commitment. The BNI was, and remains, lacking in outside contributors, in that there have been no proposals for collaboration or dealing with this problem, and the six series of which the BNI is presently composed (Monographs, Periodicals, Children's Books, Musical Scores, Doctoral Theses, and Textbooks) are produced by it alone, also making use of databases that differ from the SBN ("Doctoral Theses" does not describe national editions), or collaborating with external partners (the children's book list *Libri per ragazzi* is produced with the TINLIB software). However, even for these two series, the obligation to guarantee quality of service cannot be disregarded.

On the occasion of the first release (October 1993) of the new BNI, I maintained that an essential condition for the BNI was "the guarantee of a new organizational and professional structure, with regard to both the resources and the services that a national bibliography is under an obligation to deliver: one need only mention the problem of authority files." Almost ten years later, the problem has yet to be faced, much less solved.

Looking at the control of access points, it is plausible that the two Italian agencies could agree, perhaps even in the short term, to start making joint plans for dealing with this problem and also, hopefully, for sharing the tasks associated with it. On the other hand, we shouldn't forget that the first, and almost the only, reason that nothing has been done to address this problem–funding–is always a central, driving force in projects of this type. Nevertheless, whatever the actual situation may be, the BNI must propose and pursue a phased plan, minimal but sustainable, for controlling author and title access points–a plan that will permit at least the first, indispensable step in authority control to be achieved and maintained: the definition of an authority record. An authority record that is such not only because it is from the BNI, but also because it has been established in accordance with national and international rules. What can be done to keep up the momentum in this regard?

It is both urgent and necessary to arrive at a definition of work protocols in the SBN, since it is neither acceptable nor opportune nor economical that the BNI's role should be simply that of an equal partner. To concede to the BNI its natural role would also be advantageous for the SBN as a whole; it would underscore the principle that libraries have a right to be able to count on data that is certain and reliable, and that has been verified and guaranteed by others.

This should not be taken as a criticism of the SBN, but only as confirmation of the facts surrounding the intertwined paths of two complex organizations, the SBN and the BNI, both of which require guarantees and structures that are carefully defined in order to arrive at an appropriate and productive working relationship.

THE BNI TODAY AND ITS ACTIVITY
WITH REGARD TO CONTROL OF ACCESS POINTS

Internal Activity to Control BNI/SBN Data

The administration of the BNCF, in anticipation of the start of the SBN Index and the EDIFICARE project, had only itself to rely on; and so, by agreement with the BNI and in the spirit of service that has always characterized both, beginning in 1993 it decided to redesign the internal flow of its cataloging procedures. It adopted the recommendations of the 1991 feasibility study and, given the limited staff available, looked at new workflows. The administration proceeded to structure the BNI by control areas, delegating the problem of descriptive cataloging to another section. The BNI therefore has special, though small, areas of responsibility as a bibliographic agency: control of the description of monographs, control of the file of Italian collections (including those not relevant to the BNI), control of the author files, and control of serial titles. The publication of some series of the BNI, in particular those produced outside of the SBN, is entrusted to staff of other sections of the library.

The control structure, comprising only 10 staff members in all, carries out continuous checking. These checks, however, are sporadic and ephemeral, in the sense that they are performed on headings within individual issues, since it is impossible to plan the work on a larger scale. Hence this control is the result of an operation arising from immediate and specific needs, not from any ongoing or dedicated activity.

The forms of names and titles of collections recorded prior to the introduction of RICA (*Regole italiane di catalogazione per autori*) and ISBD (*International Standard Bibliographic Description*) in Italy remain unaltered in the SBN Index, unless they have been entered since the introduction of RICA and

ISBD. It is reasonable to regard this kind of formal inconsistency as tolerable in the SBN Index, but not in the BNI CD, where records display headings in both the original form–and thus not in keeping with the changed rules–and in the updated version, if the data has been used, and yet again, in the variants about which Mauro Guerrini complains in *Il catalogo di qualità*.[5] For instance, the BNI CD displays both "Beatles" and "Beatles (musical group)" as headings. This shows what can happen in the absence of a dedicated electronic file, and this is the story behind it: when the BNI CD was planned, the BNI's UNIMARC database, derived from the SBN, was only a temporary working file that did not preserve any data beyond the end of the production phase of the issues or the annual printed cumulation. In addition, records from 1958 to 1984 had, through the so-called "Cultural Deposits" program (1987-1990), been recovered one by one and successively loaded into the SBN; and finally, the tapes of BNI work from the SBN from 1985 became available. In short, when the BNI CD was designed in 1995, with the intention of cumulating data from 1958 on, it was necessary to take into account this complex situation, obviously no longer agreeing with the BNI's "historical" data, such as it was.

In addition, the BNI had adopted RICA *in toto* in 1981 and ISBD in 1984; as a result, headings or series titles could differ from the earlier situation, for instance, if they had been re-used in the SBN. Returning to the above-mentioned example "Beatles," the explanation is this: the heading in the printed BNI for 1973, "Beatles (The)," was corrected in 1979 to "Beatles, pseud. (corporate)" in accordance with the earlier rules, and was changed in the SBN beginning in 1994 to "Beatles (musical group)" on the basis of RICA 70.1, a form used by the BNI in 1997. The simple form "Beatles," which the BNI adopted in 1984 in its printed list and in 1993 (in the SBN and the printed list), is derived in the CD from the data taken from the UNIMARC tapes. The early days of library automation and the results offered by its products are a long, involved story.

Oddly enough, the activity of standardization and maintenance performed by the BNI for pre-1985 data was of greater benefit to the SBN than to the BNI itself. The BNI CD was, as one can see, simply a cumulative file, generated by additions. It was not a true inventory, and certainly not a fully processed, organized file. Paradoxically, on the other hand, the OPAC database and the CD of the BNCF have always been aligned in that both are updated periodically by the UNIMARC conversion program since they are both derived from the SBN and not from the UNIMARC tapes.

At this point, I would like to thank Mauro Guerrini for bringing these problems out into the open. I sincerely hope that this conference can help to achieve the desired changes.

In its current activity, the BNI continues to carry out the customary procedures practiced from the time of the print-only bibliography, with records rich in information, in indications of coverage, and in history. Thus control of the Italian collections, whether processed by the BNI or not, is regular; it is an opportunity for the insertion of cataloging notes that are useful for collaborating catalogers, or even for a simple indication to the effect that a collection is not described by the BNI. The BNI also takes care to insert details required by the SBN: the language code or absence thereof (cited as a function of the principal object of the publication), and the type of publication code (frequently ignored, but relevant for research: catalogs, conference proceedings, exhibition catalogs, dictionaries, etc.). For names of new authors, all useful preparatory work is done to assist with authority control: date of birth and other relevant information found in the publication itself are always recorded in a note. These are small details that reflect both an awareness of the fundamental importance of authority control and the labor necessary for an activity that in itself constitutes only a part of the task.

Particular attention is given to titles, as they are increasingly coming to represent users' alternative access point, if not their preferred one, after the author's name. Verifying and accurately recording what is presumed to be the principal title of a publication, as required by ISBD, becomes a form of authority control done "in advance." One can say the same for original titles, which often, in translations of modern works, create difficulties when checked against foreign databases, being almost contemporary editions; and it is not uncommon in certain types of publications for the original titles to be incorrectly cited if not, at times, modified.

Likewise, a title within a bibliographic record can also be an access point; for example, one title that is given prominence among others, or that is included in the official name of a conference. Another essential link should be made between titles of periodicals that succeed one another, or are in some way connected. The form of series titles found in the chief source is always linked by means of a reference to a variant form present in another part of the document and, obviously, to the titles of its subsections. Series titles, finally, are always linked back to the responsible body by means of an added entry; this treatment is considered by the BNI to be an indispensable type of access in its own right, one essential for research purposes.

A considerable amount of research is done for uniform titles of translated modern books. Sometimes this research is unsuccessful, which causes the BNI to exercise caution and, in such a case, to use these as original titles placed in the note field, rather than making them into cluster or filing titles. A separate issue is the decision not to use uniform titles in the BNI Children's Books series, which is produced outside of the SBN, given the particular requirements of its users.

Regular control is exercised over publications not entered in the SBN Index (the above-mentioned Doctoral Theses and Children's Books), and over other material described by the BNCF within the SBN (publications not belonging to the BNI), or described in particular databases (the so-called Groups). So much activity, so much checking, in the SBN and in the BNI, separately and jointly–all of which is of more benefit to cooperative cataloging than to the BNI itself, which is left in the uncomfortable situation of being unable to do more. A thankless, disagreeable, and costly task: this is a jeremiad that underlines the difficulties of the BNCF and of the BNI, but that also reveals the enthusiasm and dedication of the staff involved in this work.

After more than seventeen years of work on the SBN, a significant result was achieved in recent months: the specification of the new BNI/UNIMARC database. While still derived from the SBN, it will be able to independently maintain its own file of authors and titles, including those of series produced outside of the SBN. The file is structured according to authority control principles, and thus can be organized and maintained; it is no longer just a temporary working file for the production of issues of the BNI and the annual printed cumulation. I should make it clear that we will not be in a position to construct a true BNI authority file in the UNIMARC database for quite some time; but we certainly can establish its indispensable essentials: authority headings and cross-references for personal and corporate authors, which can always be added to, and the insertion, as appropriate, of informational notes and notes for the cataloger. The same will be done for uniform titles and titles of collections. The result may well be that authoritative reference file of which Diego Maltese always used to remind not only the BNI catalogers, but everyone at the BNI.[6] Furthermore, the new file will make it possible to transfer information to the CD from the file itself rather than from the SBN Index. The resultant records in UNIMARC format will naturally be shared with the SBN partners, as is to be expected of a "senior partner."

An interesting enhancement to the BNI was initiated in 2000 with the ARSBNI[7] program, which permits the OPAC display of some digitized pages (cover, half-title, title page, table of contents, preface, etc.) of publications described beginning with 1994, the year of the latest upgrade. The file at present consists of approximately 560,000 images relating to 70,000 volumes. The intention is to continue to implement this program regularly, but it will depend on the availability of funding. The availability of images has nothing to do with the problem of control of access points, but it is certainly a further service that facilitates utilization of the BNI and demonstrates the commitment and inventiveness that have always been present and nurtured by the BNCF in order to offer a BNI that is responsive to users' needs. It is a direct commitment on the part of the director of the BNCF, who in her additional role as director of the BNI is required not only to supervise its production and distribution in accordance with international standards and programs, but also to explore and test techniques aimed at the improvement of national bibliographic and library services, to increase the consistency of the databases available on the Web, and to enable access beyond the records, to the images as well, and so to promote the creation of an Italian digital library.

Cooperation Beyond the SBN

From what I have outlined above, it is clear what will be the new challenges for those responsible for ensuring the production of the Italian national bibliography. It is a considerable task that in its intentions would justify, once again, expectations of new possibilities for the BNI.

Returning to the control of access points, it is clear that the BNI has obligations outside of and beyond the SBN, obligations that cannot be denied or delegated: the establishment of authority headings being a case in point. The BNI is ready to act on these obligations with any organization that declares its willingness to collaborate, to offer or facilitate favorable opportunities for users and for cooperative arrangements.

Antonia Ida Fontana, the present director of the BNCF, who is also director of the BNI with its new and expanded charge, has warmly welcomed a proposal for cooperation by the Region of Tuscany, resulting from a joint state-region declaration on the occasion of the signing of the agreement for a framework for the program. Under this agreement, "the common purpose of improving the bibliographic and library services of the territory must act as a stimulus to the integration of the library networks present within the regional territory and the national network formed by the SBN." As a result, the BNCF is working together with the Region of Tuscany, the University of Siena, and the Biblioteca Forteguerriana di Pistoia on a project for control of access points destined for the users and librarians of Tuscany. This will be a lengthy, labor-intensive project, with results to be reached in phases. BNCF management accepted the proposal, recognizing that it alone offered the opportunity for revising BNI authors and titles from 1958 onwards. These headings, as already noted, require rechecking, if only for changes in the form of names introduced by RICA and for new ISBD elements in the recording of titles.

In order for collaboration within the region of Tuscany to be as effective as possible, the following factors must be in place:

- a core metadata schema in accordance with IFLA recommendations;
- the acceptance of RICA as the standard for forms of headings;
- the coding of authors in the UNIMARC/A format;
- the updating of the controlled list with the addition of new headings and/or cross-references;
- the possibility of increasing the number of participating partners.

The project hinges on the guarantee that all partners will be able to continue to use the forms of authors' names that they require, whether those authors are unique to them or not, provided that all are linked back to the controlled list. The goal is to achieve concrete results within a short time, making the data available–with controlled modalities–even during the phase when the shared file is under revision. Thus the BNCF has been presented with an extraordinary and propitious opportunity to initiate the systematic control of BNI access points.

In all honesty, the BNI, even with its chronically slender staffing resources, seriously intends to take on projects that are manageable and useful, rather than undertaking projects that are ambitious, but without a realistic likelihood of success. It wishes to be able to benefit both users and librarians, in particular the so-called end users, a category that often seems ill-defined and inaccessible, but that is, after all, the focus of library activity.

In conclusion, the BNI is now in a position to adopt the first objective recommended by the IFLA Working Group on an International Authority System more than twenty years ago (1980): to establish authority headings, including cross-references. The structure of these headings, however, will not always be able to be guaranteed as required by the Gruppo per l'Armonizzazione delle Reti della Ricerca (GARR), and the plan will accommodate whatever comes up in the course of the work. In other words, minimum provisions for authority control will be pursued: the forms of names of authors as required by RICA, accompanied by appropriate cross-references, and the forms of titles of monographs, works, series, and uniform titles.

NOTES

1. Carla Guiducci Bonanni and Giuseppe Vitiello, "Servizi bibliografici nazionali: dalla diagnosi al progetto," *Accademie e biblioteche d'Italia*, (July/Sept. 1992): 55-70.
2. EDIFICARE stands for Esperienza di Immediata Catalogazione con Fiduciaria Attivazione di un Rapporto Diretto con gli Editori (Experiment in Immediate Cataloging with Fiduciary Activation of a Direct Relationship with Publishers).
3. Antonella Agnoli (ed.), *Bibliografia del libro per ragazzi 1988-1992* (Palermo: Regione Siciliana, Assessorato dei Beni Culturali e Ambientali e della Pubblica Istruzione, 1992): 3-4.

4. Diego Maltese, *La biblioteca come linguaggio e come sistema* (Milan: Editrice Bibliografica, 1985): 121.

5. Mauro Guerrini, *Il catalogo di qualità* (Florence: Regione Toscana, Pagnini e Martinelli, 2002).

6. Maltese, *La biblioteca come linguaggio*; see the chapters entitled "Lo schedario di controllo delle intestazioni"and "Le schede di rinvio."

7. ARSBNI stands for ARricchimento Servizi Bibliografia Nazionale Italiana (Enrichment Services in the Italian National Bibliography).

IFLA and Authority Control

Marie-France Plassard

SUMMARY. Since the 1970s the International Federation of Library Associations and Institutions (IFLA) has worked toward establishing an international system of authority control. It has concentrated on two main areas: publication of international authority lists, and formulation of international rules for the structure of authority forms. The work of IFLA in these areas is described in this paper. *[Article copies available for a fee from The Haworth Document Delivery Service: 1-800-HAWORTH. E-mail address: <docdelivery@haworthpress.com> Website: <http://www.HaworthPress.com> © 2004 by The Haworth Press, Inc. All rights reserved.]*

KEYWORDS. Authority control, IFLA, UBC, UNIMARC format for authorities

In 1974, at the UNESCO Intergovernmental Conference, one of the key recommendations put forward for long-term policy for UBC was the confirmation that each national bibliographic agency is responsible for establishing the authoritative form of the name of its country's authors, both personal and corporate, as well as authoritative lists of these.[1] And in 1977, one of the recommendations issued at the end of the International Congress on National

---

Marie-France Plassard is affiliated with IFLA UBCIM Programme.

[Haworth co-indexing entry note]: "IFLA and Authority Control." Plassard, Marie-France. Co-published simultaneously in *Cataloging & Classification Quarterly* (The Haworth Information Press, an imprint of The Haworth Press, Inc.) Vol. 38, No. 3/4, 2004, pp. 83-89; and: *Authority Control in Organizing and Accessing Information: Definition and International Experience* (ed: Arlene G. Taylor, and Barbara B. Tillett) The Haworth Information Press, an imprint of The Haworth Press, Inc., 2004, pp. 83-89. Single or multiple copies of this article are available for a fee from The Haworth Document Delivery Service [1-800-HAWORTH, 9:00 a.m. - 5:00 p.m. (EST). E-mail address: docdelivery@haworthpress.com].

http://www.haworthpress.com/web/CCQ
© 2004 by The Haworth Press, Inc. All rights reserved.
Digital Object Identifier: 10.1300/J104v38n03_08

Bibliographies organized by IFLA and UNESCO, stated that "each national bibliographic agency should maintain an authority control system for national names, personal and corporate, and uniform titles in accordance with international guidelines."[2]

Also in the late 1970s, IFLA initiated and sponsored many studies with a view toward establishing an international system of authority control. Its work on standardization concentrated on two main areas: publication of international authority lists, and formulation of international rules for the structure of authority forms.

INTERNATIONAL AUTHORITY LISTS

Anonymous Classics (1978),[3] based on *The International List of Uniform Headings*, lists uniform headings for European literatures. The publication is being revised by the IFLA Cataloguing Section and will be enlarged to cover other continents. *A List of Uniform Headings for Higher Legislative and Ministerial Bodies in European Countries* first appeared in 1975 and was revised in 1979.[4]

The *List of Uniform Titles for Liturgical Works of the Latin Rites of the Catholic Church* provides titles from the Council of Trent (1546-1563) to 1980.[5] *Names of States* (1981) is an authority list of language forms for cataloguing entries.[6] The national equivalent standards of original names are given in English, French, German, Russian, and Spanish, now the official languages of IFLA (Spanish was not an official language at the time).

INTERNATIONAL RULES

International rules were aimed at ensuring that the author's name is found in bibliographies and catalogued worldwide in a consistent way. *Names of Persons*, first published in 1977, lists national practices for entry in catalogues. A major revision led to the publication of the 4th revised enlarged edition in 1996.[7] *Form and Structure of Corporate Headings*, published in 1980,[8] aimed to promote uniformity in headings appearing in bibliographic records produced for international exchange within the framework of UBC. The IFLA Cataloguing Section began to update it in the 1990s, but then the focus shifted to the promotion of international sharing of corporate name headings in (national) authority files. The new publication, titled *Structures of Corporate Name Headings*,[9] was posted on the IFLANET in January 2001.

TOWARDS AN INTERNATIONAL AUTHORITY SYSTEM

It was decided in 1978 to develop an international authority system, and a working group was established for that purpose during the IFLA Conference in Strbské Pleso in former Czechoslovakia. Its terms of reference were the following:

- to discuss and formulate the specifications for an international authority system to satisfy the bibliographic needs of libraries
- to develop the UNIMARC format for authorities
- to develop methods for the efficient and effective exchange of authority data.

The first objective implied the elaboration of standards to stipulate the elements of the entry, give the order of these elements and specify a system of punctuation. It was achieved with the publication of the *Guidelines for Authority and Reference Entries (GARE)* in 1984.[10] Nearly ten years later, in 1993, *Guidelines for Subject Authority and Reference Entries (GSARE)* was published.[11]

The GARE were designed for print and microprint only. Developments in new technology, as well as other considerations, dictated a revision of the guidelines. Although the concept of UBC was still present in the 1990s, there was a growing perception of the need to preserve cultural traditions. Since new technologies are supplying automated devices for linking all authority records created by various national bibliographic agencies, it seems no longer mandatory to use the same form of headings in all countries. I shall come back to this shift later on. The new edition, published by K. G. Saur in 2001, and titled *Guidelines for Authority Records and References (GARR)*,[12] covers, of course, a wider range of media. It provides the specifications for authority and reference entries for names and uniform titles to be shared in print, microprint, and machine-readable form. They have been updated to govern the display of authority information and references for all types of material, including legal and religious works, musical compositions and performances, manifestations/works by individual and multiple authors known under one or more titles, as well as serial publications. *GARR*, like the previous guidelines, deals only with the broader structure of entries and does not prescribe the actual form of headings, references, or URLs, since this information is considered the territory of national bibliographic agencies and those responsible for cataloguing rules.

To go back to the working group on an international authority system, its second objective, to develop the UNIMARC format for authorities, was entrusted to a Steering Group created in 1984 comprising members from the IFLA Cataloguing and Information Technology sections. This goal was achieved with the publication in 1991 of the first edition of *UNIMARC/Authorities* (in the Saur UBCIM New Series),[13] which started with this introductory statement: "The primary purpose of *UNIMARC/Authorities* is to facilitate the international exchange of authority data in machine-readable form among national bibliographic agencies."

The third objective was to develop methods for the efficient and effective exchange of authority data. In a report sponsored by a Robert Vosper Fellowship and published by Saur in 1993, *International Cooperation in the Field of Authority Data*,[14] Françoise Bourdon, from the Bibliothèque nationale de France, made a detailed analysis of the situation and gave recommendations. She insisted on the need to have proper terminology when defining the data suitable for international exchange or identifying the organizations equipped to produce these data. "If we are to ensure that the great diversity of computer systems used to run automated names authority files becomes a source of richness rather than confusion, we must be able to refer to their contents unambiguously."[15] Indeed terminology has been a source of concern for many years within IFLA. The translation of the word "authority" into Russian, for example, was the theme of a lively discussion during an International Seminar on Authority Files held at the National Library of Russia in St. Petersburg in 1995. The working group on the revision of *GARE* had taken this need for unambiguity into consideration when reviewing and enlarging the "definitions" for the new edition. A working group within the Section on Cataloguing is addressing this problem in a more general way since it works on a "Multilingual Dictionary of Cataloging Terms and Concepts." It is chaired by Monika Münnich (from the University Library in Heidelberg), who presented the project at the IFLA Conference in Boston.[16]

Françoise Bourdon had also examined the role of the ISADN, the International Standard Authority Data Number, which should make it possible to indicate an identity unambiguously on an international level, unimpeded by language barriers.

At the end of the International Seminar on Authority Files (1995) already mentioned, several recommendations were addressed to UBCIM, including "that it resume work to facilitate the international exchange." A UBCIM working group launched in 1996 and chaired by Barbara Tillett was charged with reconsideration of this international system and creation of the ISADN. However, this Working Group on Minimal Level Authority Records (MLAR) and the ISADN started to discuss issues in a different light. I have already mentioned the shift from the traditional approach to a new perception dictated by the fact that new technologies are able to supply automated devices for linking all authority records, making it seem not mandatory any more to use a single authorized form of heading everywhere in the world. In fact, this new approach to UBC recognizes the needs of users who can display the script/language of their own countries while the National Bibliographic Agencies (NBAs) are still responsible for control in their own regions.

The Working Group remained informed of similar developments, for example, the European Project Author which developed remote access to multiple authority files. Five participating national libraries were involved (Belgium, France, Portugal, Spain, and the UK), whose names authority files (names of persons and corporate bodies) were made available in UNIMARC.

The Working Group's final report[17] suggested that the international sharing of authority information would greatly assist libraries and national bibliographic agencies in reducing the costs of cataloguing and insisted on the usefulness of facilitating the international sharing of data. It recognized, however, that it was unrealistic to require that everyone use the same form of headings and that it was important to allow the preservation of differences in authorized forms of headings, which should best meet the language and cultural needs of the users. The report listed data elements which are mandatory when applicable for an internationally shared authority record. They are the following:

record status
type of record
entity category
encoding level
record identifier/ record control number
International Standard Authority Data Number (ISADN)
date entered into the file
version identifier
language of cataloguing
character set/s
script of cataloguing
description rules
source agency for the record
differentiated and undifferentiated personal name
authorized heading
nationality of entity (can be "undetermined")
variant forms of the authorized heading ("see" references)
related authorized heading ("see also" references)
source citation note.

Highly recommended are:

bibliographical, historical, or other information about the entity
source data not found
general notes.

The members of the Working Group proposed that each National Biblio-graphic Agency (NBA) make its authority files available on the Internet using the IFLA homepage to register current information about what is available and what restrictions are in force. Access to the files should be "Read only." The exercise is limited to authority records for names of persons, corporate bodies, conferences, and for uniform titles. It omits series, subject headings, and classi-fication authorities.

The Group made recommendations to various other working groups in-cluding the one working on the revision of *GARE*, and to the Permanent UNIMARC Committee (PUC) preparing the second edition of the UNIMARC format for authorities which was published in 2001.[18] The revisions reflect de-velopments in telecommunications and information technology. The new edi-tion incorporates the recommendations of the MLAR Working Group on the definition of data which should be mandatory in all authority records in order to facilitate exchange and re-use of authority records. "Appendix 0: Format Changes" mentions this consistency with the recommendations of the MLAR Working Group and extension of the format to facilitate links to electronic ma-terial, thus promoting international exchange of authority data.

Concerning the ISADN, the members of the MLAR Working Group had decided that the concept should be reviewed later on. They had concerns about the cost and about the infrastructure needed to maintain such a system (the cre-ation of a new registration authority). They thought that technological devel-opments should be watched and that IFLA should cooperate with the archival community, with other professional associations and with publishers. A new Working Group was created in 1999, Functional Requirements and Number-ing of Authority Records (FRANAR). A description of the work of this group follows in the paper by Glenn Patton.

NOTES

1. Anderson, Dorothy. Universal Bibliographic Control: A Long-Term Policy, a Plan for Action. Pullach bei München: Verlag Dokumentation, 1974.

2. *Guidelines for the National Bibliographic Agency and the National Bibliogra-phy*. Prepared by the IFLA International Office for UBC. Appendix B, page 4. Paris: Unesco, PG1/79/WS/18.

3. *Anonymous Classics: A List of Uniform Headings for European Literatures*. Compiled by the IFLA International Office for UBC, edited by Rosemary C. Hewett.

Based on: International List of Uniform Headings for Anonymous Classics compiled by Roger Pierrot. London: IFLA International Office for UBC, 1978.

4. *List of Uniform Headings for Higher Legislative and Ministerial Bodies in European Countries.* Compiled by the USSR Cataloguing Committee (for the IFLA Section on Cataloguing). 2nd ed. Revised. London: IFLA International Office for UBC, 1979.

5. *List of Uniform Titles for Liturgical Works of the Latin Rites of the Catholic Church.* Recommended by the Working Group on Uniform Headings for Liturgical Works. 2nd ed. Revised. London: IFLA International Office for UBC, 1981.

6. *Names of States: An Authority List of Language Forms for Catalogue Entities.* Compiled by the IFLA International Office for UBC. London: IFLA International Office for UBC, 1981.

7. *Names of Persons: National Usages for Entry in Catalogues.* 4th revised and enlarged ed. München: K.G. Saur, 1996 (UBCIM Publications–New Series, v. 16).

8. *Form and Structure of Corporate Headings.* Recommendations of the Working Group on Corporate Headings, approved by the Standing Committees of the IFLA Section on Cataloguing and the IFLA Section on Official Publications. London: IFLA International Office for UBC, 1980.

9. *Structure of Corporate Name Headings.* Final Report, November 2000. Compiled and Introduced by Ton Heijligers. International Federation of Library Associations and Institutions, Universal Bibliographic Control and International MARC, 2001. http://www.ifla.org/VII/s13/scatn.final2000.htm.

10. *Guidelines for Authority and Reference Entries.* Recommended by the Working Group on an International Authority System, approved by the Standing Committees of the IFLA Section on Information Technology. London: IFLA International Office for UBC, 1984.

11. *Guidelines for Subject Authority and Reference Entries.* Working Group on Guidelines for Subject Authority Files of the Section on Classification and Indexing of the IFLA Division of Bibliographic Control. München: K.G. Saur, 1993 (UBCIM Publications–New Series, v. 12).

12. *Guidelines for Authority Records and References.* Revised by the IFLA Working Group on GARE Revision. Formerly Guidelines for Authority and Reference Entries. München: K.G. Saur, 2001 (UBCIM Publications–New Series, v. 23).

13. *UNIMARC/Authorities. Universal Format for Authorities.* Recommended by the IFLA Steering Group on a UNIMARC Format for Authorities. Approved by the Standing Committees of the IFLA Sections on Cataloguing and Information Technology. München: K.G. Saur, 1991 (UBCIM Publications–New Series, v. 2).

14. Bourdon, Françoise. *International Cooperation in the Field of Authority Data: An Analytical Study with Recommendations.* Translation from the French by Ruth Webb. München: K.G. Saur, 1993 (UBCIM Publications–New Series, v. 11).

15. Ibid., p. 33.

16. Münnich, Monika. "Progress on the Multilingual Dictionary of Cataloging Terms and Concepts." *International Cataloguing and Bibliographic Control*, 31(2), pp. 31-33.

17. *Mandatory Data Elements for Internationally Shared Resource Authority Records.* Report of the IFLA UBCIM Working Group on Minimal Level Authority Records and the ISADN, 1998. http://www.ifla.org/VI/3/p1996-2/mlar.htm.

18. *UNIMARC Manual–Authorities Format.* 2nd revised and enlarged edition. München: K.G. Saur, 2001 (UBCIM Publications–New Series, v. 22).

FRANAR:
A Conceptual Model for Authority Data

Glenn E. Patton

SUMMARY. Discusses the work of the IFLA Working Group on Functional Requirements and Numbering of Authority Records. Describes the activities of the group to build liaison relationships with other sectors of the information community that create and maintain data which are similar to library authority files. Provides a description of the entity-relationship model being developed by the Working Group to extend the FRBR model to cover authority data. *[Article copies available for a fee from The Haworth Document Delivery Service: 1-800-HAWORTH. E-mail address: <docdelivery@haworthpress.com> Website: <http://www.HaworthPress.com> © 2004 by The Haworth Press, Inc. All rights reserved.]*

KEYWORDS. Authority records, conceptual models, entity-relationship models, FRANAR, FRBR

BACKGROUND

Looking back from the admittedly short-term perspective of five years, the publication of the IFLA *Functional Requirements for Bibliographic Records* in 1998 stands out as a defining moment in the history of cataloging as the li-

---

Glenn E. Patton is affiliated with OCLC.
Note: Readers should be aware that the Working Group's entity-relationship model has changed considerably since this paper was written in December 2002.

[Haworth co-indexing entry note]: "FRANAR: A Conceptual Model for Authority Data." Patton, Glenn E. Co-published simultaneously in *Cataloging & Classification Quarterly* (The Haworth Information Press, an imprint of The Haworth Press, Inc.) Vol. 38, No. 3/4, 2004, pp. 91-104; and: *Authority Control in Organizing and Accessing Information: Definition and International Experience* (ed: Arlene G. Taylor, and Barbara B. Tillett) The Haworth Information Press, an imprint of The Haworth Press, Inc., 2004, pp. 91-104. Single or multiple copies of this article are available for a fee from The Haworth Document Delivery Service [1-800-HAWORTH, 9:00 a.m. - 5:00 p.m. (EST). E-mail address: docdelivery@haworthpress.com].

http://www.haworthpress.com/web/CCQ
© 2004 by The Haworth Press, Inc. All rights reserved.
Digital Object Identifier: 10.1300/J104v38n03_09

brary world approached the 21st century. The model developed by the FRBR Study Group focuses on the entities associated with bibliographic records and on the various types of relationships between those entities and the bibliographic record. The introduction to the report notes that the model "does not analyse the additional data that are normally recorded in an authority record, nor does it analyse the relationships between and among those entities that are generally reflected in the syndetic apparatus of the catalogue" and then goes on to say, "the study group recognizes the need to extend the model at some future date to cover authority data."[1]

Another group, the IFLA UBCIM Working Group on Minimal Level Authority Records and ISADN, was addressing for authority data part of what FRBR does for bibliographic data–the specification of a basic level of data to be included in records that are shared. The group's report, *Mandatory Data Elements for Internationally Shared Resource Authority Records,* issued in 1998,[2] also raised the possibility of a virtual shared resource authority file under the auspices IFLA.

In response to these two suggested activities as well as to recommendations from the International Conference on National Bibliographic Services, held in Copenhagen in November 1998,[3] and at various other international meetings, the Coordinating Board of the IFLA Division of Bibliographic Control agreed at its April 1999 meeting to set up a new Working Group under the joint auspices of the Division and the Universal Bibliographic Control and International MARC Programme (UBCIM).

THE WORKING GROUP AND ITS TERMS OF REFERENCE

Members of the Working Group on Functional Requirements and Numbering of Authority Records (FRANAR), as originally appointed, were Françoise Bourdon (Bibliothèque nationale de France); Olga Lavrenova (Russian State Library); Andrew McEwan (The British Library); Eeva Murtomaa (Helsinki University Library, Finland); Glenn Patton (OCLC, USA); Reinhard Rinn (Die Deutsche Bibliothek, Germany); Henry Snyder (University of California, Riverside, USA); Barbara Tillett (Library of Congress, USA); Hartmut Walravens (International ISBN Agency, Germany); and, Mirna Willer (National and University Library, Croatia). Mme Bourdon served as the initial chair of the group with Glenn Patton taking over that role in January 2002. Reinhard Rinn was replaced following his retirement by Christina Hengel-Dittrich, also of Die Deutsche Bibliothek. Throughout its work, the group has been assisted by Marie-France Plassard, UBCIM Programme Director. In October 2001, Tom Delsey (retired from the National

Library of Canada) agreed to join the Working Group as a consultant. His long experience (including serving as a consultant to the IFLA Study Group on the Functional Requirements for Bibliographic Records) has proved invaluable.

The FRANAR Working Group agreed to three terms of reference proposed by Françoise Bourdon during discussions with the IFLA Coordinating Board:

1. to define functional requirements of authority records, continuing the work that the "Functional requirements of bibliographic records" for bibliographic systems initiated.
2. to study the feasibility of an International Standard Authority Data Number (ISADN), to define possible use and users, to determine for what types of authority records such an ISADN is necessary, to examine the possible structure of the number and the type of management that would be necessary.
3. to serve as the official IFLA liaison to, and work with, other interested groups concerning authority files: INDECS (Interoperability of Data in E-Commerce Systems), ICA/CDS (International Council on Archives/ Committee on Descriptive Standards), ISO/TC46 for international numbering and descriptive standards, CERL (Consortium of European Research Libraries), etc.

In the remainder of this paper, I would like to review the Working Group's activities in each of these areas and then comment on the next steps for the group.

LIAISON ACTIVITIES

The liaison aspect of the Working Group's activity has proved to be the easiest to achieve. Some relationships, such as the suggested one to ISO/TC46 and to CERL, were easy because of group members' activities in those groups. In particular, the Working Group has spent considerable time commenting on the activity of ISO/TC46/SC9 Working Group 3 and the evolving International Standard Text Code (ISTC).[4] In the case of the ICA Committee on Descriptive Standards, a joint meeting of IFLA and ICA members in Beijing in 1995 had laid the groundwork for a mutual liaison relationship, which has continued during that group's work on revisions to the *International Standard Archival Authority Record for Corporate Bodies, Persons, and Families*.

At the time that FRANAR was initiated, the <indecs> Project (Interoperability of Data in E-Commerce Systems)[5] was well underway and it was already clear that this effort "focused on the practical interoperability of digital content identification systems and related rights metadata within multi-media e-commerce"[6] was related to the potential scope of FRANAR. IFLA was an affiliate organization in this European Commission-funded project. The work of the <indecs> project is currently carried on by INTERPARTY.[7] IFLA is a project partner in INTERPARTY as is the British Library, with the Library of Congress and OCLC acting as "unfounded" partners, so Working Group members have many opportunities to keep up with INTERPARTY activity as well as to share news of FRANAR work.

In addition, other authorities-related projects have come to the Working Group's attention during the course of our activities. Recent meeting agendas and postings on the group's electronic discussion list have also included reports of the activities of the MALVINE (Manuscripts and Letters via Integrated Letters in Europe)[8] and LEAF (Linking and Exploring Authority Files)[9] Projects, the DELOS/NSF Actors and Roles Working Group,[10] the Dublin Core Agents Working Group,[11] the HKCAN (Hong Kong Chinese Authority Name Work Group),[12] the HKUST XML Name Access Control Repository,[13] the MACS (Multilingual ACcess to Subjects) Project,[14] METAPERS,[15] the AFNOR Working Group on Authority Metadata, and the Virtual International Authority File (VIAF) Proof of Concept Project,[16] many of which are topics for this conference.

THE FEASIBILITY OF AN ISADN

In a paper prepared for the IFLA Conference in Boston in 2001,[17] Françoise Bourdon laid out the conundrum that the International Standard Authority Data Number has posed for the Working Group. The potential for the ISADN has a long history going back to the publication of the *Guidelines for Authority and Reference Entries (GARE)* in 1984. When the UNIMARC Authorities Format was first published as the universal exchange format for authority data, a field was reserved for the ISADN even though no structure for the number had yet been defined. Mme Bourdon laid out a structure for the ISADN in her report, *International Cooperation in the Field of Authority Data*[18] and, at the same time, attempted to lay to rest previous uncertainty about whether the ISADN as a number was to be assigned to an authority heading or an authority record by specifying that the number should apply to the record as a whole. Later in the decade of the 1990s, an IFLA Seminar held in Vilnius and the International Conference on National Bibliographic Services held in Copenhagen continued to call for international exchange of authority data and to look for a standard number to help in the exchange process.

The ISADN also shows up in the work of the IFLA Working Group on Minimal Level Authority Records and ISADN, which was active from 1996 through 1998. During the work of that group, however, we begin to see a shift from the traditional goal of Universal Bibliographic Control–requiring everyone to use the same form of heading globally–toward a more user-centered view of using headings that meet the user's needs and expectations. That shift has brought with it the idea of linking together authority records that document headings established by different bibliographic agencies that represent the same entity. At the same time, it also became clear, because of the IFLA involvements with <indecs> (and with the successor project, INTERPARTY) and with the International Council on Archives, that there were other players emerging that had interests in the names used to identify persons, corporate bodies, and the other entities in the bibliographic world.

Mme Bourdon goes on to describe that the initial meetings of FRANAR concentrated on attempts to bring some conclusion to this multi-year (even multi-decade) discussion of a standard number. The Working Group set forth a basic principle that we would not create a new standard number; rather, we would look toward the use of existing numbers such as the numbers already assigned automatically by systems in which authority records are created or the rapidly growing set of ISO standard numbers such as the ISAN, the ISWC, the ISRC, etc. Throughout these discussions, there remained the nagging question of "what exactly were we attempting to number?" Was it the entity regardless of the form of the heading used for that entity? Was it each different authorized heading for that entity? Was it the authority record itself to which the number applied?

That led the group to the conclusion that we needed to put aside the question of the ISADN for the moment and concentrate our efforts on the third of our charges, the definition of functional requirements for authority records. The group approached that effort with the hope that a clearer understanding of the functions of data in authority records would clarify the questions surrounding the number, especially in an environment that places more importance on the potential sharing of the intellectual aspects of authority data rather than the exchange of physical authority records.

Since we are still in the process of refining an entity-relationship model for authority data, it is too soon to know for certain whether that "clearer understanding" will emerge. It is clear, however, that ongoing work in other projects, such as INTERPARTY and VIAF, will inform our discussions.

FUNCTIONAL REQUIREMENTS
AND THE EVOLVING CONCEPTUAL MODEL

After some examination of the entities recorded in authority records and the uses that authority records serve, the Working Group's real consideration of the functional requirements began with discussion of a "straw man" document prepared for the group by Tom Delsey in January 2002. This initial draft was designed to provide a first cut at laying out functional requirements. It was focused on authority records for name headings used for persons, families, and corporate bodies and for name-title and title headings associated with FRBR works and expressions, and with series. Authority data for subject headings or thesauri terms, for geographic names and for series were excluded from this initial version of the model. Figure 1 shows this first model.

The group discussed this model (and associated definitions of the entities and their attributes along with a draft set of user tasks) electronically over the following months and at a meeting in May 2002. During the face-to-face meeting, members quickly came to the realization that, while this model is an accurate representation of the traditional relationships among bibliographic entities, the headings that represent those entities and the records that embody those headings, it did not incorporate any of the concepts that the group had encountered through our liaison activities. Our consultant, Tom Delsey, was quickly able to sketch out a new model that built on the traditional model while making relationships to the broader world of entities. Needless to say, the graphic representation of this new model is much more complex.

Since the May 2002 meeting, the model has continued to evolve as Working Group members have made comments on both the diagrams and the draft text. The version of the diagram used in this paper is currently being evaluated and may be further revised.[19]

> The conceptual model for authority records is presented graphically in Figures 2A and 2B. The entity definitions have been derived largely from three sources: *Functional Requirements for Bibliographic Records* (FRBR); *Guidelines for Authority Records and References*[20] (GARR), and *The <indecs> Metadata Framework*[21] (<indecs>).

> The first entity-relationship diagram (Figure 2A) focuses on the entities associated with the *names* and *identifiers* that are registered in authority files. The center column of the diagram incorporates the ten entities defined in FRBR (*work, expression, manifestation, item, person, corporate body, concept, object, event*, and *place*), plus the additional entity *family*, which the Working Group believes to be an essential addition based on our liaison activity with the archival community.

> The second diagram (Figure 2B) focuses on the formal or structural entities that come into play when a *name* or *identifier* is used to formulate an *access point* and the access point is subsequently registered in an author-

ity file as an *authorized heading*, or *variant heading* in an *authority record* or *reference record*, or when an *explanatory heading* is registered in a *general explanatory record*. The diagram also highlights two entities that are instrumental in determining the content and form of authority records (*rules* and *agency*).

The entities depicted in the center column of Figure 2A (the *FRBR entities* with the addition of *family*) are "bibliographic" entities. They reflect intellectual constructs or concepts that are integral to the rules used to create library catalogues.

The entities depicted to the left portion of Figure 2A are the five "primitive" entities defined in the <in*decs*> model: BEING, THING, CONCEPT, EVENT, and SITUATION. These entities are defined as follows in the <in*decs*> model:

- BEING: An entity which has the characteristics of animate life; anything which lives and dies.
- THING: An entity without the characteristics of animate life.
- CONCEPT: An entity which cannot be perceived directly through the mode of one of the five senses; an abstract entity, a notion or idea; an unobservable proposition which exists independently of time and space.
- EVENT: A dynamic relation involving two or more entities; something that happens; a relation through which an attribute of an entity is changed, added, or removed.
- SITUATION: A static relation involving two or more entities; something that continues to be the case; a relation in which the attributes of entities remain unchanged.

These "primitive" entities have been included in the model for two purposes. The first purpose is to highlight the fact that the bibliographic entities defined in FRBR represent complex classes or types that are derived from and are specific to bibliographic practice in a library context. The mapping of the FRBR entities to the <in*decs*> "primitive" entities serves to illustrate the fact that any one FRBR entity may comprise a mix of generic entity types (e.g., a specific instance of the entity PERSON, as defined in FRBR, may be either a "real" human being, a "fictional" character, or possibly even an inanimate object).

The second purpose for including the "primitive" entities is to show how the "bibliographic" entities associated with the names and identifiers regis-

FIGURE 1. Name and Title Authorities—Entity-Relationship Diagram (2002-01-18 Version)

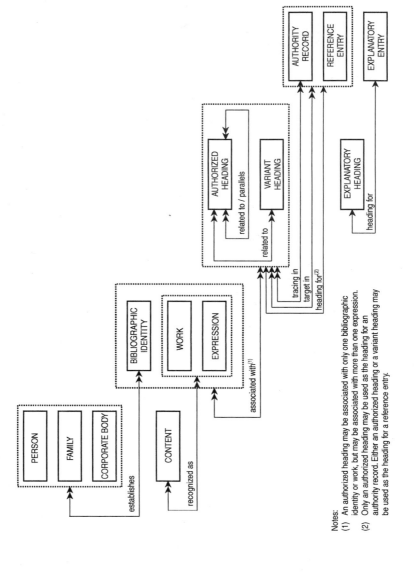

Notes:

(1) An authorized heading may be associated with only one bibliographic identity or work, but may be associated with more than one expression.

(2) Only an authorized heading may be used as the heading for an authority record. Either an authorized heading or a variant heading may be used as the heading for a reference entry.

FIGURE 2A. Entity Names and Identifiers (2002-12-10 Version)

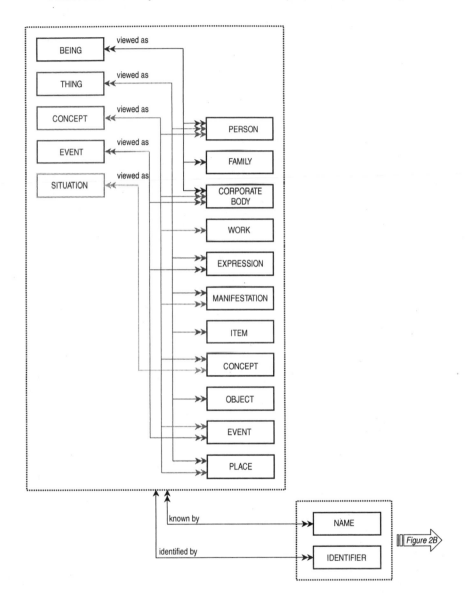

FIGURE 2B. Access Points and Authority Records (2002-12-10 Version)

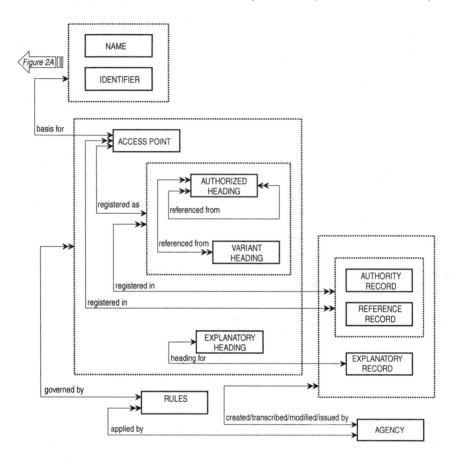

tered in library authority files map to a more generic set of entities that might be used as a common point of reference by other communities that also create files that serve a similar, though not necessarily identical, purpose in other sectors (archives, museums, rights administration organizations, etc.).

The entities depicted in the center of Figure 2B (*authorized heading, variant heading, explanatory heading, authority record, reference record,* and *general explanatory record*) reflect the logical groupings of data that make up an authority file. In the FRBR model, the record and individual parts of the record (headings, areas of the description, etc.) were not represented as separate entities. The reason for that was that the FRBR model was designed simply to highlight the kind of information contained in a typical bibliographic record. Its focus was on providing a clearer understanding of the "external" entities that are the center of interest to users of bibliographic records. This model for authorities is similar in that it also reflects the "external" entities that are of interest to users of authority records (both the "real world" entities and the "bibliographic" entities noted above). However, the model for authorities has been developed not only to assist in clarifying the relationship of the information contained in authority files to those "external" entities, but also to address a number of critical issues related to the management of authority data *per se*. It is essential, therefore, that the model reflect the key logical groupings of authority data (i.e., headings and records) as entities in their own right.

> The kinds of relationships depicted in Figure 2A also differ somewhat from those depicted in the FRBR model. The entity-relationship diagram in FRBR reflected the high-level relationships between entity types (e.g., a *work* is realized through *expression*). Although those same relationships are conceptually valid for the FRBR entities that are represented in the conceptual model for authorities, they have not been shown explicitly in the entity-relationship diagram, largely because they have no direct functional relevance in the context of authority files. The relationships reflected in the entity-relationship diagram for authorities are those that have a direct bearing on the construction and compilation of authority records.

In addition to the relationships shown in Figures 2A and 2B, the Working Group recognizes that there are also other types of relationships. Elsewhere in the description of the model are descriptions of the relationships between and among entities that are reflected in the reference structures in authority records. Examples of these include earlier name/later name relationships between corporate bodies, real name/pseudonym relationships, whole/part and adaptation relationships between works, and relationships between individuals and groups of which they are a part. Also described are "linking" relationships such as those which exist between headings that are parallel language forms of heading for the same entity or those that are alternate script forms of heading for the same entity.

Finally the conceptual model defines user tasks and maps the entity attributes and relationships to those user tasks. In considering the user tasks, Working Group members first defined three groups of users:

• cataloguers and reference librarians who use authority files directly

- library patrons who use authority information either through direct access to authority files or indirectly through the headings and references in library catalogues, national bibliographies, etc.
- database management and applications software designed to support the creation, maintenance, search and retrieval of data contained in bibliographic and authority files.

User tasks fall into two broad categories: those that are associated with resource discovery and those associated with data management. Working group members currently have defined a total of eight tasks as follows:

Resource Discovery

Search   Search for an entity corresponding to stated criteria (i.e., to search either a single entity or a set of entities using an attribute or relationship of the entity as the search criteria).

Identify   Identify an entity (i.e., to confirm that the entity represented corresponds to the entity sought, or to distinguish between two or more entities with similar characteristics).

Control   Control the form of heading used for entries in a catalogue, bibliography, list, etc. (i.e., to ensure that the form of heading representing a particular entity is used consistently in order to support collocation).

Relate   Establish or clarify the relationship between one entity and another (i.e., to establish the relationship between two or more authorized headings or between variant headings and the authorized heading, or to clarify the relationship between two or more corporate bodies, works, etc.).

Data Management

Process   Process a record or heading (i.e., to add, delete, replace, output, etc., a logical data component).

Sort   Sort a heading or record for purposes of alphabetic or numeric arrangement.

Display   Display an entry, heading, or data field (i.e., to display data or generate a print constant in a form appropriate for the user, or to suppress a display).

Integrate   Integrate a record, entry, or heading into an existing authority file (i.e., to import data from an external source for purposes of adding to or updating an existing file in a manner
that is consistent with the rules and conventions reflected in
that file).

WHAT'S NEXT?

The next goal for the Working Group is to complete work on the draft functional requirements document so that it can be made available for an initial
worldwide review. It is my hope that we can accomplish that before the end of
2003. Following that initial review, the group must respond to comments received and, then, we must return to the issue of numbering before we can complete our work.

It has also become clear during the Working Group's discussions that, as a
result of the analysis that we have undertaken, revisions to some existing IFLA
publications may be necessary. We have identified *Guidelines for Authority
Records and References, Mandatory Data Elements for Internationally
Shared Resource Authority Records,* and the *UNIMARC Manual–Authorities
Format* and there may be others. Working Group members have agreed to recommend changes.

I encourage you to watch for announcements of future reviews and to help
us complete these important tasks. I noted at the beginning of this paper that
the FRBR Study Group recognized the need to extend their model to cover authority data. Just as their work has changed how we think about bibliographic
data, we hope that our work will bring a clearer understanding of authority
data and its relationships to the catalog.

NOTES

1. *Functional requirements for bibliographic records: final report.* München:
K. G. Saur, 1998, p. 5. Also available online <http://www.ifla.org/VII/s13/frbr/frbr.
pdf>.
2. *Mandatory data elements for internationally shared resource authority records.*
Frankfurt-am-Main: IFLA UBCIM, 1998. Also available online <http://www.ifla.org/
VI/3/p1996-2/mlar.htm>.
3. http://www.ifla.org/VI/3/icnbs/fina.htm.
4. http://www.nlc-bnc.ca/iso/tc46sc9/wg3.htm.
5. http://www.indecs.org.
6. <indecs>. *Summary final report.* August 2002, p. 3. Available online <http://
www.indecs.org/pdf/SummaryReport.pdf>.

7. http://www.interparty.org/.

8. http://www.malvine.org.

9. http://www.leaf-eu.org.

10. http://www.delos-nsf.actorswg.cdlib.org/.

11. http://dublincore.org/groups/agents/.

12. http://hkcan.ln.edu.hk/.

13. http://library.ust.hk/info/reports/xmlnac.html.

14. http://infolab.kub.nl/prj/macs/.

15. http://deposit.ddb.de/meta_pers.htm.

16. http://www.oclc.org/research/projects/viaf/index.shtm.

17. Bourdon, Françoise. Functional requirements and numbering of authority records (FRANAR): to what extent can authority control be supported by technical means? In: *67th IFLA General Conference and Council, August 16th-25th, 2001, Boston, USA* [on line]. The Hague: International Federation of Library Associations and Institutions, 2001. Available from World Wide Web: http://www.ifla.org/IV/ifla67/papers/096-152ae.pdf.

18. Bourdon, Françoise. *International cooperation in the field of authority data: an analytical study with recommendations*. München: K. G. Saur, 1993, p. 79-80.

19. This description of the current version of the model is adapted from text prepared for the Working Group by Tom Delsey.

20. *Guidelines for authority records and references*. 2d edition. München : K.G. Saur, 2001.

21. Rust, Godfrey, and Mark Bide. *The <indecs> metadata framework: principles, model and data dictionary*. June 2000. <http://www.indecs.org/pdf/framework.pdf>.

Authority Control in the World of Metadata

José Borbinha

SUMMARY. This paper discusses the concept of "metadata" in the scope of the "digital library," two terms recently used in a great diversity of perspectives. It is not the intent to promote privilege of any particular view, but rather to help provide a better understanding of these multiple perspectives. The paper starts with a discussion of the concept of digital library, followed by an analysis of the concept of metadata. It continues with a discussion about the relationship of this concept with technology, services, and scenarios of application. The concluding remarks stress the three main arguments assumed for the relevance of the concept of metadata: the growing number of heterogeneous genres of information resources, the new emerging scenarios for interoperability, and issues related to the cost and complexity of current technology. *[Article copies available for a fee from The Haworth Document Delivery Service: 1-800-HAWORTH. E-mail address: <docdelivery@haworthpress.com> Website: <http://www.HaworthPress.com> © 2004 by The Haworth Press, Inc. All rights reserved.]*

KEYWORDS. Digital libraries, metadata, interoperability, authority control

---

José Borbinha is affiliated with Biblioteca Nacional de Portugal.
The author wishes to thank Barbara Tillett for her valuable comments.

[Haworth co-indexing entry note]: "Authority Control in the World of Metadata." Borbinha, José. Co-published simultaneously in *Cataloging & Classification Quarterly* (The Haworth Information Press, an imprint of The Haworth Press, Inc.) Vol. 38, No. 3/4, 2004, pp. 105-116; and: *Authority Control in Organizing and Accessing Information: Definition and International Experience* (ed: Arlene G. Taylor, and Barbara B. Tillett) The Haworth Information Press, an imprint of The Haworth Press, Inc., 2004, pp. 105-116. Single or multiple copies of this article are available for a fee from The Haworth Document Delivery Service [1-800-HAWORTH, 9:00 a.m. - 5:00 p.m. (EST). E-mail address: docdelivery@haworthpress.com].

DIGITAL LIBRARIES

"Metadata" became a recent buzzword related to the explosion of the Internet and the emerging of new contents and services in some way associated with libraries, archives, museums, and related organisations. A name given to this new paradigm has been "Digital Libraries."

Figure 1 illustrates an evolutionary view of the problem, taken from the perspective of the traditional library. Here we see the Internet as the most recent relevant factor in the evolution of the "library," following a series of other factors. From those, we stress the generic introduction of the computer in the library, which had an impact in the digital catalogue and in the definition of recent standards for bibliographic description. That was followed by the first data communication services (X.25, TELNET, BBS–Bulletin Board Systems, etc.), providing remote access to the catalogue and to other common library services. In the late 1980s, we had the emerging of the personal computer and the CD-ROM, which brought the digitized library now providing access also to the contents. Finally, we had the Internet and the World Wide Web, with which we are working today.

This evolution brought us to the problem of the definition of the "virtual library," or in a more common term, the "digital library." This became a recent hot topic of discussion, with some demagogy but also with lots of real serious work, both conceptual and technical. It also attracted professionals and communities from outside the traditional library world, especially from Computer Science and Engineering.

From a generic technical perspective, those communities have understood the "digital library" as a case of a specific class of "information systems," as proposed early in the classification system of the ACM–Association for Computer Machinery, shown in Figure 2 [2]. A similar view resulted from a brainstorming meeting reported by DELOS, as illustrated also in Figure 2 [11], which addresses the problem from a wider perspective. For those interested in developing a complete view of those activities, discussions and visions, two important resources are the D-Lib Forum [15] and the DELOS Network [12].[1]

In spite of all the thinking and developments in recent years, we have to accept that there is not a unique and global definition for the "Digital Library." The perception of it depends too much on the perspective taken (this might not sound very good to traditional libraries, but we should remember that this fuzziness of concepts is not so strange to, for example, archives or museums). That is a fact that we assume, and it is not the purpose of this paper to discuss it. Nevertheless, it is very important to recognise it, especially if our next steps are going to be the definition of common models, procedures, and standards that everyone associates with the term "Authority Control."

FIGURE 1. Libraries and Technology Among the Times

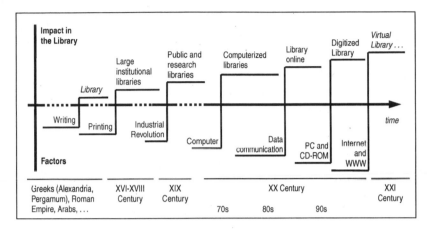

FIGURE 2. The "Digital Library" According to ACM and DELOS

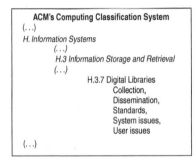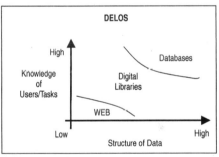

Nevertheless, and for the purpose of our discussion here, let us propose a simple definition for Digital Library as "a free or controlled group of services, maintained by an identified entity, making possible the discovery and access to documents, multimedia or any other possible classes of digital information resource artefacts."

METADATA AND DIGITAL LIBRARIES

Metadata was a term coined by computer scientists and engineers from the database world to refer to structured information that describes database schemas (e.g., the way in a database the data is organized).[2] This is not how the term has been used in digital libraries, and it is very important to be aware of this detail. In digital libraries, we usually have defined metadata as simply "data about data" (which once stored in a database would mean, for the previous perspective, just the data inside a database, while metadata would be the information needed to describe the organisation of that database). In this way, the "Internet community" took the term after the emerging of the World Wide Web, and now the most common usage for it is really in this area. Moreover, we should prefer for it the definition of "structured information about other information or resources."

However, even in this scope there are a few common misunderstandings around this term. For example, we must be very careful and stress that metadata is supposed to refer to information coded according to a specific schema, and not the technology that handles it nor the conceptual spaces to control the values of the information elements. In this sense, MARCXML [25] or DCMES [10] are not metadata, but metadata schemas, i.e., definitions of how to express metadata as structured information about other information or resources. In the same sense, XML [38] in itself is just a generic language, and not metadata or even a metadata schema. With XML, we can define an application context by using a DTD–Document Type Definition, or more recently by using the more powerful XML Schema language [42]. In addition, authoritative spaces, such as indexing languages, classification systems, etc., are also not metadata in themselves, but values or rules to find the right values to assign to metadata elements.

In recent digital libraries' activities and literature, we can find several examples of different classes of metadata, namely (the classes listed below are just illustrative, covering overlapping areas in some cases, so without any intention to represent any formal typology for metadata):

- Bibliographic metadata (also called descriptive metadata): Bibliographic description and identification of the resources, such as titles, authors, indexing terms, classification codes, abstracts, surrogates, etc.;
- Administrative metadata: Administrative information about the resource, such as information about acquisition process and costs, rights, etc.;
- Preservation metadata: Technical or management information and requirements for long-term preservation of the resources;
- Technical and structural metadata: Technical information and requirements to manipulate the resource (systems and tools), etc.;
- Access, usage and reproduction metadata: Information about how to access the resources (addresses, passwords, etc.), terms and conditions for access and reproduction, etc.;

- Metadata for the administration of metadata: Information about other metadata classes, such as date of creation, origin, authenticity, etc.

The bibliographic description of resources is a common issue in traditional libraries and archives, where respectively the MARC family of schemas [20][25] and the EAD schema [23] are widely used. The world outside these traditional scopes is also moving, creating description models that, once in place, might be reused at a low cost. One interesting example of that is the ONIX metadata descriptive format, defined by a publishers' consortium [16].

More recently, additional requirements were identified for metadata beyond those for basic bibliographic description, for example, for technical description of the resources [40], for new approaches for the classification and relationships between resources [39][37], for preservation [5][31][35], for rights management [8], etc.

Other relevant actions have been the development of generic frameworks aiming at covering several classes of metadata. One interesting example is the definition by the Library of Congress, in the United States, of the METS schema, aiming to cover mainly structural metadata and administrative requirements for that same metadata, but focusing also on bibliographic and administrative metadata [26]. Another interesting example is that of the MPEG–Moving Picture Expert Group [30], especially the MPEG-7 standard [9] and more generically MPEG-21 initiative [4], which give special attention to the scopes of "Digital Item Declaration" (a generic metadata package), "Digital Item Identification and Description" (identifiers, bibliographic and technical description) and "Intellectual Property Management and Protection" (administration, access and usage of resources).

At this high level, in some sense similar to MPEG-21, are also the reference models of CIDOC [6]. This intends to be a mediation framework to promote interoperability in museums using heterogeneous descriptive metadata, model requirements for the management of archiving electronic records, MoReq [18], and the well-known principles of FRBR–Functional Requirements for Bibliographic Records [19], promoted by IFLA. These are not specific metadata schemas, but very important guidelines for their definition, in the same sense as the AACR has been important until now to the development of bibliographic standards, systems and services in libraries [1].

METADATA AND TECHNOLOGY

Another important issue that we must take into account when we discuss metadata is the relationship of the concept with the technology. In a general sense, a conceptual model or a metadata schema should be independent of any technological implementation. That is not always true, however, since sometimes we see examples where, especially for the sake of illustration and a better understanding (and to help its immediate application), models are accompanied by specific technological solutions. That is what happened with MARC and ISO2709 [21], which did not obstruct the actual definition of MARCXML.

To proceed with this discussion we will propose a reference model of four principal perspectives: conceptual, context, service and technology. Figure 3 illustrates that model.

The Conceptual Perspective is where the generic reference models are considered. Here, we do not yet have records, databases or data files, but only concepts and models about how things can or should be done. We can subdivide this perspective into three areas: generic reference models, which are supposed to define objective top-down models; metadata schemas, which must be related with a specific issue or area of application (but that should still be independent of the technology); and metadata implementations, where finally technological issues are addressed (especially for coding).

The Context Perspective means the instantiation of the Conceptual Perspective. The ways those instantiations are done depend on technological options or constraints, as also on the nature and characteristics of the local services. For example, in one specific context we can decide to transport and explore a set of UNIMARC records coded in ISO2709, while in other context we might decide to achieve the same results but using MARCXML. The objective value and meaning of the information processed in both these solutions is the same, only the technical implementations are different. That might be dictated by the technology to be used in the final service, or by the legacy or new systems with which the new solution is expecting to interact.

This drives us to the last level, the Service Perspective. Here we deal mostly with interfaces, for humans or for other systems (protocols). Usually, for a protocol, the coding format of the metadata to be transported is not irrelevant, but the tendency has been to make that as flexible as possible. One example of that is the protocol OAI-PMH [33], which specified Dublin Core as its default format, but that has been evolving in order to support any other format able to be expressed in XML. It is expected that a broader generalization of this approach be achieved by the concept of Web Services [41], of which ZING, the next generation of Z39.50, is potentially a very interesting example [28].

FIGURE 3. Multiple Perspectives for the "Metadata" Problem

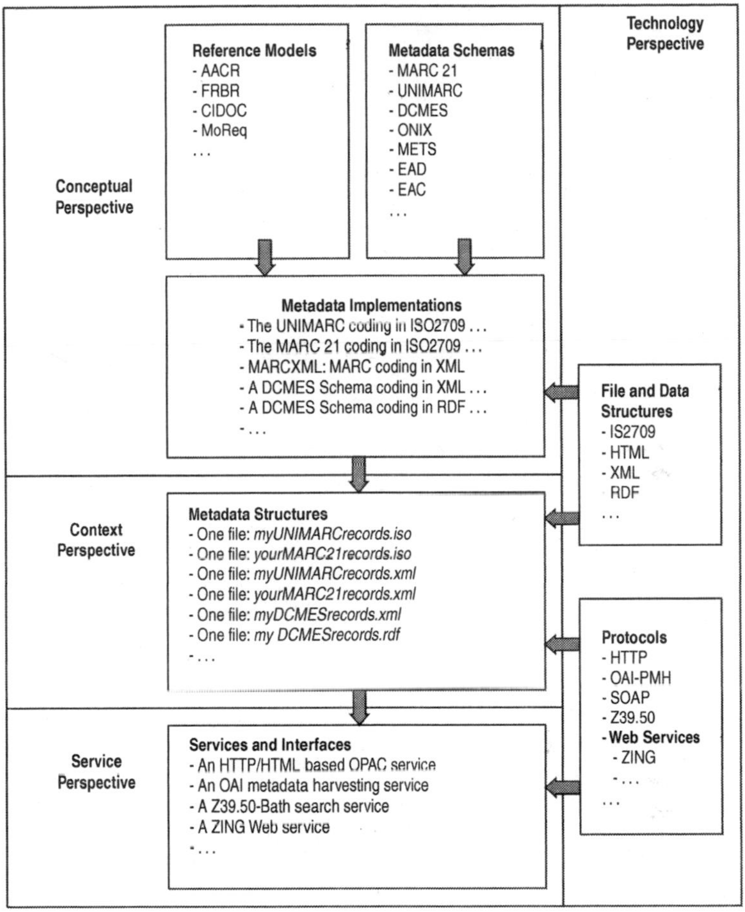

METADATA IN THE INFORMATION SOCIETY

It is time to ask a fundamental question: if metadata is an answer, what is, after all, the question? What are the fundamental requirements of the digital library to which a concept like "metadata" is supposed to provide a solution? We will find those requirements in three major classes:

- Heterogeneity of genres: The new information artifacts are not simple and stable genres, as are printed books, magazines or newspapers. A large heterogeneity and dynamism of new objects have characterized "digital publishing." To deal with this in a technical and cost-effective way, the digital library must expect and understand clearly each class of objects and models. Media, data formats, versioning, type, etc., are examples of characteristics that can define new genres of resources. Genres are important for the definition of selection criteria for licensing, acquisition, and deposit, independent of their subject, intellectual, or artistic contents. To help the library to deal with those problems, we have, for example, the concepts of structural and technical metadata.

- Interoperability: The digital library is part of the World Wide Web. In that scope, it has not only evolved beyond the traditional library but also offers a conceptually higher level of service. In this scenario, the users expect not only to reach the library from anywhere, but also to reach anything. This means that users might not understand (and not accept it at all) if they are told that they cannot use a single service to search a library and a film archive at the same time and to access books and movies created by and about, for example, Federico Fellini. In order to be able to offer services of this kind, the digital library needs to be designed as a distributed service or as an aggregation of heterogeneous services (Figure 4). This requires cooperation among generic and specialized libraries and archives, museums, and other classes of organizations and people. Once again, the ability to automate this interoperability is crucial for its cost and technical effectiveness, bringing requirements for new classes of interfaces and metadata, defined or simply adopted by those actors. That has been done traditionally by means like Z39.50 [27], complemented recently by new models and solutions involving bibliographic records in XML [25], taking advantage of simple structures such as Dublin Core [10], or by providing bulk records for harvesting by OAI-PMH [32][33]. This is technology that was especially conceived by digital library communities, but, for the future, we might start thinking in scenarios reusing more generic solutions.

- Technology: As the Semantic Web develops, and its technology becomes more generic and ubiquitous, many of the components and products applied in digital libraries will be generic, especially for user interfaces, database technology, protocols and Web Services. In this scenario, metadata will be not a concept specific only to digital libraries, but a general concept in any information system (in fact, a "digital library" is just a type of information system). Accordingly, digital library communities must be effective not only in assuring that their requirements are in the definition of those components (working together, for example, with the World Wide Web Consortium, the International Standardization Organization, etc.), but also must be open to reuse solutions that might have been defined and become standards elsewhere. A well-accepted factor in the actual world of information technology is that it can be very expensive to provide the first new development for a specific problem, but after that, the cost of generalization of that solution can be very low. Libraries, museums, and archives, which are always struggling with investment constraints, must consider this.

THE CHALLENGES

We can conclude that the "digital library" has evolved from managing very well defined entities, with established interfaces, to a new less-defined concept, required by a more dynamic environment. This will have important implications in some of the fundamental thinking in libraries, museums, and archives, where authority control is just one of the issues.

Traditional libraries are used to recognizing several actors relevant to bibliographic and object descriptions, such as ownership, copyright, access control and authority control in general [24]. The new paradigm makes it necessary not only to keep those concepts, but also to extend the analysis to broader scopes, reconsidering new key issues related, for example, with authentication of objects, rights management in multimedia and cross-media environments, etc.

Several international projects have been analyzing those problems, namely the INTERPARTY project [16], the DC-Agent activity [10], and more the generic DELOS/NSF Working Group on Actors in Digital Libraries [13]. In the

FIGURE 4. Interoperability in a Networked World

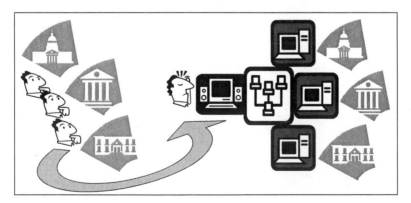

specific context of the archives, the EAC–Encoded Archiving Context [17][7] is an interesting work in authority description that should be followed with attention by everyone. That has been done, for example, in the LEAF project [22], a follow-up of MALVINE [29]. These projects, where the National Library of Portugal is an active partner, are interesting demonstrations of how heterogeneous schemas and sources of metadata can be combined in common services, with relevant benefit. In LEAF, we expect to demonstrate that having to deal with heterogeneous descriptions of authorities must not always be a problem. In fact, we will even take advantage of that to improve other rich descriptions, and to improve the recall in resource discovery tasks in MALVINE and in another project, TEL [36].

Finally, I think that an important lesson to be learned from this discussion and to be transmitted to any discussion more centered on authority control issues is this: deal with heterogeneity. The digital library cannot ignore the new centers of gravity, including popular providers of resources, such as the online bookstore Amazon, gateways like Yahoo, and generic resource discovery services such as Google. I don't think that libraries should ignore these and other similar new actors entering the Information Society, because some might represent very important potential new partners, bringing valuable new resources or services. In scenarios like this, the key word for libraries has to be "adaptation," meaning the capability to interface and interoperate in order to take the best from each partner without imposing strict rules that would be too costly for the other partner (keeping them away). The technology is powerful enough to deal with that. This assumption, when applied to scenarios of authority control, means that the problem might no longer be how to conceive and put in place processes that follow unique rules, descriptions and formats, but instead be able to understand the rules, description and formats used by the others and take from them the best we can for our purposes, while also being able to give the best from us to our partners.

NOTES

1. More information and discussion about this, taken from the perspective of a deposit library, is also present in [3].
2. An example of this perspective is [34].

REFERENCES

[1] AACR. Joint Steering Committee for Revision of Anglo-American Cataloguing Rules. http://www.nlc-bnc.ca/jsc/.
[2] ACM. ACM's Computing Classification System. http://www.acm.org/class/.

[3] Borbinha, José. The Digital Library–Taking in Account Also the Traditional Library. Elpub2002 Proceedings, VWF Berlin, 2002, pp. 70-80.

[4] Bormans, Jan; Hill, Keith. MPEG-21 Overview. ISO/IEC working group JTC1/SC29/WG11/N4318. Version 0.2, July 2001.

[5] CEDARS. Curl exemplars in digital archives. http://www.leeds.ac.uk/cedars/.

[6] CIDOC. CIDOC Conceptual Reference Model. http://cidoc.ics.forth.gr/.

[7] Cover Pages. Encoded Archival Context Initiative (EAC). http://xml.coverpages.org/eac.html.

[8] Creative Commons. http://creativecommons.org/.

[9] Day, Neil; Martínez, José M. Introduction to MPEG-7. ISO/IEC working group JTC1/SC29/WG11/N4325. Version 3.0, July 2001.

[10] DCMI. Dublin Core Metadata Initiative. http://www.dublincore.org.

[11] DELOS. Digital Libraries: Future Directions for a European Research Programme. Brainstorming Report. San Cassiano, Alta Badia–Italy. June 13-15, 2001. htpp://www.iei.pi.it/DELOS/delo2/International/brainstorming.htm.

[12] DELOS. Network of Excellence on Digital Libraries. http://www.ercim.org/delos/.

[13] DELOS. Reference Models for Digital Libraries: Actors and Roles. http://www.delos-nsf.actorswg.cdlib.org/.

[14] DiTeD. Digital Thesis and Dissertations. http://dited.bn.pt.

[15] D-Lib Forum. http://www.dlib.org.

[16] EDItEUR. http://www.editeur.org.

[17] Encoded Archival Context (EAC). http://www.library.yale.edu/eac/.

[18] IDA. Model Requirements for the Management of Electronic Records (MoReq) http://www.cornwell.co.uk/moreq.

[19] IFLA. Functional Requirements for Bibliographic Records. www.ifla.org/VII/s13/frbr/frbr.htm.

[20] IFLA. IFLA Universal Bibliographic Control and International MARC Core Activity (UBCIM). http://www.ifla.org/VI/3/ubcim.htm.

[21] ISO. ISO 2709: Documentation format for bibliographic information interchange for magnetic tape. ISO 1981.

[22] LEAF. Linking and Exploring Authority Files. http://www.leaf-eu.org/.

[23] LOC. Encoded Archival Description (EAD). http://www.loc.gov/ead/.

[24] LOC. MARC Code Lists for Relators, Sources, Description and Conventions. http://www.loc.gov/marc/relators/.

[25] LOC. MARC Standards. http://www.loc.gov/marc/.

[26] LOC. METS–Metadata Encoding & Transmission Standard. http://www.loc.gov/standards/mets/.

[27] LOC. Z39.50 Maintenance Agency. http://www.loc.gov/z3950/agency/.

[28] LOC. ZING, Z39.50-International: Next Generation. http://www.loc.gov/z3950/agency/zing/.

[29] MALVINE. Manuscripts and Letters via Integrated Networks in Europe. http://www.cordis.lu/libraries/en/projects/malvine.html.

[30] MPEG. Moving Picture Expert Group. http://www.cselt.it/mpeg.

[31] NEDLIB. http://www.konbib.nl/nedlib.

[32] OAF. Open Archives Forum. http://www.oaforum.org/.

[33] OAI. Open Archives Initiative. http://www.openarchives.org/.

[34] OMG. Catalog of OMG Specifications. http://www.omg.org/technology/documents/spec_catalog.htm.

[35] PANDORA. Preserving and Accessing Networked Documentary Resources of Australia. http://pandora.nla.gov.au/.

[36] TEL. The European Library. http://www.europeanlibrary.org/.

[37] Topic Maps. Topic Maps Consortium. http://www.topicmaps.org/.

[38] W3C. Extensible Markup Language (XML). http://www.w3c.org/XML/.

[39] W3C. Resource Description Framework (RDF). http://www.w3.org/RDF/.

[40] W3C. Synchronized Multimedia Integration Language. http://www.w3.org/TR/REC-smil/.

[41] W3C. Web Services Activities. http://www.w3c.org/2002/ws/.

[42] W3C. XML Schema. http://www.w3.org/XML/Schema.

Bibliographic Control and Authority Control from Paris Principles to the Present

Pino Buizza

SUMMARY. Forty years ago, the ICCP in Paris laid the foundations of international co-operation in descriptive cataloging without explicitly speaking of authority control. Some of the factors in the evolution of authority control are the development of catalogs (from card catalog to local automation, to today's OPAC on the Web) and services provided by libraries (from individual service to local users to system networks, to the World Wide Web), as well as international agreements on cataloging (from Paris Principles to the UBC programme, to the report on *Mandatory Data Elements for Internationally Shared Resource Authority Records*). This evolution progressed from the principle of uniform heading to the definition of authority entries and records, and from the responsibility of national bibliographic agencies for the form of the names of their own authors to be shared internationally to the concept of authorized equivalent heading. Some issues of the present state are the persisting differences among national rules and the aim of respecting both local culture and language and international readability. *[Article copies available for a fee from The Haworth Document Delivery Service: 1-800-HAWORTH. E-mail address: <docdelivery@haworthpress.com> Website: <http://www.HaworthPress.com> © 2004 by The Haworth Press, Inc. All rights reserved.]*

Pino Buizza is affiliated with Biblioteca Queriniana, Brescia.

[Haworth co-indexing entry note]: "Bibliographic Control and Authority Control from Paris Principles to the Present." Buizza, Pino. Co-published simultaneously in *Cataloging & Classification Quarterly* (The Haworth Information Press, an imprint of The Haworth Press, Inc.) Vol. 38, No. 3/4, 2004, pp. 117-133; and: *Authority Control in Organizing and Accessing Information: Definition and International Experience* (ed: Arlene G. Taylor, and Barbara B. Tillett) The Haworth Information Press, an imprint of The Haworth Press, Inc., 2004, pp. 117-133. Single or multiple copies of this article are available for a fee from The Haworth Document Delivery Service [1-800-HAWORTH, 9:00 a.m. - 5:00 p.m. (EST). E-mail address: docdelivery@haworthpress.com].

Digital Object Identifier: 10.1300/J104v38n03_11

KEYWORDS. Bibliographic control, authority control history, ICCP, International Conference on Cataloguing Principles, internationally shared authority records, Paris Principles

The relationship between standards, objectives, and the environment [whether it be physical, cultural, or technological] is reciprocal and dynamic, where changes in one component inevitably have an effect on another, and often necessitate modification or realignment of the relationships between each.

–Tom Delsey[1]

Bibliographic control is the context within which authority control develops and distinguishes itself. Within the limits of this paper I will present a concise outline of the evolution of authority control over the past 40 years in its various aspects: theory, rules and standards, and applications, with reference to technological innovation in the catalogue and the changing environment of library work.[2] I will refer mainly to personal authors, but my remarks are intended to cover corporate bodies and titles also, making the appropriate allowances.

I have identified three phases: the initial phase (the 1960s), development (1970s and 80s) and a change of direction (1990s).

THE ICCP, THE LIBRARY LOOKING OUT ONTO THE WORLD, THE CARD CATALOGUE, UNIFORM HEADINGS

The goal of the 1961 International Conference on Cataloguing Principles was international convergence on the fundamentals of the author and title catalogue, with a view to the future uniformity of rules furthering the exchange of bibliographic data; authority control was not under discussion. The *Statement of principles*[3] describes the following aspects of the catalogue:

- finding and collocating functions (the latter twice over: for checking which works of an author and which editions of a work are in the library),
- structure (at least one main entry per book, with added entries and references),
- devices (uniform headings, both main and added),

- some general rules for choice of main and added entry headings, in situations other than that of a book containing only one work by a single personal author (e.g., works by two or more authors, anonymous works, works catalogued under the name of a corporate body, collections . . .) and for forms of name and title in headings (the form commonly used in the original, with few exceptions).

The cataloguing tool adopted was in keeping with the technology available at the time: individual typewritten catalogue cards. Only the main entry was a complete bibliographic entry with tracings; added entries could be reduced for reasons of economy, and lacked tracings.

The second function of the Paris Principles, the collocating function (Section 2: "The catalogue should be an effective instrument for ascertaining . . . 2.2 (a) which works by a particular author . . . are in the library") was "most effectively discharged . . . 5.2 when variant forms of the author's name or of the title occur, [by] an entry for each book under a uniform heading," so that entries for the same author, given their identical headings, were located together at one point in the catalogue (or rather, in a sequence of consecutive points); variant forms converging on that point through use of reference cards. [4]

The issues for the form of heading at this stage are:

- recognizing the identity of the author of different works and of different editions of the same work under the various names and forms of name by which that author is represented (a bibliographical and philological issue, pertaining to branches of learning and their literary history), [5]
- choosing from among variants, the form to be used as uniform heading (a cataloguing problem, pertaining to rules, cultural environment and biography).

The recommendations of the *Statement of principles* regarding form of heading (sections 7, 8, 9.4 and 11.3) offer criteria for checking in turn: the name used in original editions, whether another name has since become established in general usage, and whether the name is in a language not normally used in the catalogue.[6] Reference to different national and linguistic situations is explicit in section 12, dealing with entry-words for personal authors, which are to be determined by the national bibliographic agencies. In accordance with the ICCP spirit of international cooperation, the expression of, and mutual respect for, national peculiarities in names should guarantee consistent choices and should make for easier comprehension and exchange of data. The heading is to be uniform in the individual catalogue (under pain of ineffectiveness), in the national environment (through adherence to the same code) and intentionally also at an international level. Libraries are called on to investigate, beyond their own collections, the names used in original editions and variant forms and to follow the linguistic usage of other nationalities–tasks requiring additional bibliographic resources. In Paris there was keen awareness of these difficulties, and of the importance of careful and culturally accurate references to be shared for agreement on consistent, uniform headings.

Among the preliminary working papers, one was devoted to authors with name variations, one to the question of compound surnames and surnames with prefixes, and four to forms of name for authors from particular geographic areas or using particular languages.[7] Of the working groups on particular topics held during the conference, five were dedicated to the examination of forms of name for authors from particular areas or language groups,[8] and three others to problems of considerable relevance to the form of heading: bilingualism, liturgical texts and transliteration. ICCP resolution no. IV proposed publication of the following: a statement of the practice approved in each country for the entry of the personal names of its nationals (in accordance with section 12 of the *Statement of principles*);[9] lists of headings for states and other territorial authorities; uniform titles for the anonymous classics of each country; and some tentative lists of headings for Greek and Roman classical authors, and the major corporate bodies of each country and of international organizations.

Yet one cannot say that, because of this, the ICCP was actually concerned with *authority control*. There was no consideration of methods of working on uniform headings, or the actual construction and management of a reference list: solutions were of interest, not the means of achieving them. Authority control was purely an operational aspect of cataloguing activity; not codified or discussed–nor, often, put into practice by libraries other than empirically, with varying degrees of care and accuracy. The catalogue, in which non-preferred headings are inserted as references, simply presents all forms of all names in alphabetical order. The practice of adding tracings of references to the main entry makes it into a kind of knot, gathering together all the variant forms of the heading. This method becomes redundant if applied to every main entry of an author, and is inadequate for authors appearing only in added entry headings. In the *Norme per il catalogo degli stampati* of the Vatican Library, an "identity entry" assembles all references from variant forms[10] without these disadvantages; but it is a spurious catalogue entry, since it does not refer to any publication, either directly or indirectly, and contains information about the author and reasons for the choice of heading based on bibliographical sources. In other cases at this time, references are recorded in the "official" catalogue, if the library has one. In *Rules for a dictionary catalogue*, to avoid duplication of work, Charles A. Cutter had provided for a list of authors for the cataloguer's use, in which to record the preferred forms of name, with a note of the authorities consulted and variants found.[11] In Italian rules and manuals the issue was not dealt with; nor, so far as I know, was the identity entry adopted in our libraries.[12] On the other hand, testifying to the more progressive Anglo-American approach to cataloguing, the Library of Congress had been maintaining its own *authority cards* for each new author at least since 1899, recording the preferred form of name, variants, the full form, sources and the book which occasioned the heading.[13] The presence of these instructions in successive U.S. manuals does not seem to have made authority cards a current practice, the majority of American libraries perhaps feeling exempted from authority work because of that performed by the Library of Congress.

Outcomes of the ICCP resolutions appeared in some IFLA publications over the following years, some of them also in revised editions, mainly because of expanded coverage.

- *National usage for the entry of names of persons,* published in 1963, with definitive edition *Names of persons* in 1967, 3rd edition in 1977, supplement in 1980, 4th edition in 1996.
- *Liste internationale de formes approuvées pour le catalogage des noms d'Etats = International list of approved forms for catalogue entries for names of states*, provisional edition in 1964, new edition *Names of states* in 1981.
- *Liste internationale de vedettes uniformes pour les classiques anonymes = International list of uniform headings for anonymous classics* in 1964, new edition *Anonymous classics* in 1978.
- *List of uniform headings for higher legislative and ministerial bodies in European countries* in 1975, revision in 1979.
- *List of uniform titles for liturgical works of the Latin rites of the Catholic Church* in 1975, 2nd edition in 1978.[14]

Leaving aside the delay with which these publications appeared, they are clearly at the same time both useful and yet inadequate: they are concerned with a limited number of countries, and with only some of the kinds of heading about which knowledge of original usage and forms of heading recommended at international level are necessary. There is no longer a great deal produced or available in terms of national lists of headings for personal or corporate authors, although the need for these is also there.[15]

The problem is made worse by differences in the choice of form of heading in cataloguing codes published after ICCP. Taking full advantage of the exceptions allowed, and in some cases making them stretch even further, they resisted the trend towards internationalization. The International Meeting of Cataloguing Experts (IMCE) in Copenhagen, 1969, intervened to correct some misleading interpretations of the Paris Principles, setting a decisively international course with a preference for original forms rather than the vernacular choices designed to meet the needs of the local library public more than emphasizing the international exchange of bibliographic data.[16]

THE UBC PROGRAMME, LIBRARY SYSTEMS, THE AUTOMATED CATALOGUE, THE AUTHORITY ENTRY

From the IMCE there emerged the standardization of bibliographic description with ISBD and the UBC programme for Universal Bibliographic Control, confirming and giving new impetus to the role of national bibliographic agencies.

Technological development brought catalogue automation, its first phase applied to traditional procedures without transforming them. New tools offered the distribution and exchange of authority lists by magnetic tape, among other services. Increasingly the availability of telecommunications links permitted cataloguing in cooperation, with savings and with issues of consistency within the expanded catalogue.

This combination of factors broadened the scope of international cooperation, increasing both the quantity and variety of contacts between different cultures and languages (mainly non-European, given the centrality of Western culture already in these catalogues). With this, came major difficulties in recognizing foreign linguistic and cultural patterns and the need for deeper and more precise knowledge. Control over forms of name and references between variants was, in practice, left up to individual libraries. In order to fill the gap left by national bibliographies, the Library of Congress began publishing *Library of Congress name headings with references* in 1974.[17]

Growing needs, together with the cogent logical analysis of procedures and products that had to be carried out in order to program automated systems, brought on a greater awareness of the clear, logical distinction between bibliographic records and authority records, and between the differing functions of the catalogue and the authority file, which began to be seen as needing to be separate files with links between their records.

As description with ISBD had acquired a precise role within the record, so, too, the heading acquired independence, and could no longer be considered a mere appendix placed at the head of the entry, like a "handle" with which to extract the card from the catalogue (to use "la metafora [. . .] ardita e forse volgare, benché calzatissima" [the audacious and maybe a little vulgar, although extremely apt metaphor] by Giuseppe Fumagalli).[18] The heading was the name of an entity (personal author or corporate body or work) which, along with all other entities of the same kind and their names, must be processed in a file (choosing the preferred form, permanent or updated over time or in different situations, to be linked with other forms, and distinguished from the names of other entities): all of which was independent of a work or book to which it might be applied from time to time. The difference was profound but the effect appeared identical: in the card catalogue, the entries for the works of an author were kept together because they had the same heading and the alphabetical arrangement brought them together; in the electronic catalogue, works by an author were brought together because they were all linked to the one single heading or record in the authority file. As a consequence, to give an example, a correction to the form of a heading involved: in the first instance, one correction for every entry and every reference; in the second, a single correction to the authority record; that is, the variation is made to that which actually changes: the form representing the entity–not the heading in the catalogue, where the links between that entity and the works for which it is responsible remain unaltered. A prototype of the latter more sophisticated approach was realized with the automation of the New York Public Library in the 1970s. [19]

In the ferment of innovation, cooperative projects sprang up (in Germany, the combining of the authority files of the larger libraries, commencing with corporate bodies;[20] and overseas, NACO, the Name Authority Cooperative project, launched by the Library of Congress in 1977).[21] High-level experiments such as that at the Bibliothèque Nationale in Paris came to fruition and the desire for standardization grew stronger. IFLA undertook the study of an authority system on an international scale, to clarify the logical issues and to propose a standard format for authority entries.[22]

After surveys of existing files and formats and more intensive analyses, the *Guidelines for authority and reference entries*[23] were published in 1984, dealing with three types of entry (authority, reference and general explanatory entry) in headings for personal names, corporate bodies, and titles of anonymous classics. GARE authority entries contained headings, information notes, tracings, sources and the International Standard Authority Data Number (ISADN), a new number paralleling the existing standard numbers, for the identification of individual headings. Forms of heading were not considered there, although preliminary surveys had revealed differences in the styles in which they were recorded.

Just as ISBD had provided a formal structure for the exchange of bibliographic data, so GARE provided one for the authority record, creating a language that was comprehensible and communicable over and above linguistic barriers.

GARE permitted the recording of non-cataloguing data for cataloguing purposes: notes concerning the author's identity and sources used. The syndetic structure and the collocating function were also moved outside of the catalogue. A new kind of catalogue began to take shape: the *corpus* of an author's works was no longer presented at one, single point in the alphabetical sequence, as ensured by the repetition of the identical uniform heading on every card. Instead it was shown in the contextual display of all the bibliographic records linked to the one authority record; here were gathered also the variants, that is, access points corresponding to references that were dispersed in the card catalogue. The process was made possible by the direct search of headings (uniform or variant, in exact wording or truncated, or via one or more words or roots of words contained in them), independently of alphabetical order, thanks to the computer's vocabulary. In the catalogue there was still a need to provide access from all variants when lists were displayed for consultation; whether in *browse* or in *search* mode, the reply gives the works directly, without requiring the catalogue user to go via the uniform heading.[24] One limit of the *Guidelines*: an indication needs to be provided as to which headings are to be considered authoritative because they are published by the national bibliographic agency responsible, and which are not.[25]

A machine-readable format, *Authorities: a MARC format*, had been prepared in the meantime (1981), while the *UNIMARC/Authorities*[26] format did not appear until 1991.

MLAR RESEARCH, THE LIBRARY WITHOUT WALLS, THE CATALOGUE ON THE NETWORK, AUTHORIZED EQUIVALENT HEADINGS

The innovation of computerized networks (especially the development of communications protocols such as FTP and Z39.50 and the spread of the Internet and the World Wide Web), the recent widening and intensification of exchanges, and data sharing at an international level, are increasingly highlighting the adverse effects of differences in headings and the lack of authoritative reference tools. The path leading towards an international language mapped out in Paris seems to have reached an impasse, just when OPACs on the Web are turning every library into a world library, hence one with a potentially universal readership. As an example of the problem, the name of an ancient Roman author recorded in the local language of the library makes sense to the local user; but not necessarily to one who is online, if besides searching under the original form, he must search for and identify as equivalents, the variants accepted in different languages.

Projects and studies to share authority files and their control systems have had various outcomes: positive, if national in scope and when there is a leading file with which other institutions cooperate within a common structure (e.g., NACO); more difficult when files from different countries and languages are being brought under one umbrella (among others, the AUTHOR project, between five European national libraries;[27] and also the Anglo-American Authority File, AAAF,[28] an experiment of the British Library and the Library of Congress–which of course refers to the same cataloguing code and the same language).

All of the difficulties, demands and possibilities of the 1990s, and the pressing need for institutions to contain their costs, provided the stimulus and the conditions for re-examining authority control in relation to studies of minimum levels of descriptive cataloguing. The IFLA UBCIM Working Group on Minimal Level Authority Records (MLAR) and ISADN was formed to identify obstacles to the exchange of authority data. It produced a report, *Mandatory data elements for internationally shared resource authority records.*[29] In this report, the UBC objective of a single form of heading, recognised by all, is abandoned in favour of a plurality of equivalent headings authorized by different codes, no one form being given preference over others. However they have to be headings authorized by a code, as opposed to variants not adopted by any code.

The report of the MLAR had special relevance for this change in direction and because, despite its seemingly modest title, the recommended mandatory elements were not derived by narrowing down a selection from an abundant whole, but, rather, by the "exercise of identifying basic elements, providing a definition for each, recognizing which ones already exist in communications formats and suggesting those that should be added in order to implement the formats." In it, elements pertaining to the communications format are considered, as well as those related to "cataloguing" content. Innovative terminology is used, as the examination of the concepts and entities concerned is new and more analytical. For instance, the heading with qualifier is broken down into *entity identifier* and *qualifying data* to form, in the case of persons, a *differentiated personal name*–or an *undifferentiated personal name,* when it is recognized that qualification is necessary, but the appropriate attribution data is not available; and, to speak of "entry identifier" means not only dealing with the question of form, but that the reality beneath the form is being investigated–the entities involved in authority work; the concept of bibliographic identity is introduced as derived from the Anglo-American tradition. The report is the basis and represents a call for GARE and UNIMARC/ Authorities to be renewed. In 2001 the second revised and enlarged edition of the *UNIMARC Manual: Authorities Format* acknowledged these innovations, in part.[30]

The new edition of GARE, published in 2001 with the title *Guidelines for authority records and references,*[31] GARR, recognizes the equivalence of headings formulated according to different codes. The *authority record* compiled by a bibliographic agency can sit side by side with an authority record compiled for the same entity in accordance with other rules, in other languages and scripts, with authorized headings and indications of provenance; and the links established in the authority system between authorized equivalents ensure that a request for an entity, from whatever form of heading, will produce a uniform response (equal and complete in every case). The syndetic network that holds equivalent authorized records together is fundamental and has now been completely transferred from the catalogue to the authority file.

To improve the communication and effectiveness of links between records, a study was made with a view to the adoption of a standard identification number, ISADN, for entities (person, body, work), in addition to the identifying numbers of records in their files of origin. The structure of headings (type, component elements, their arrangement, punctuation . . .) is also relevant for data exchange, whether in planning for internationally valid headings, or for equivalent headings. For corporate bodies in particular, the revision of *Form and structure of corporate headings*[32] (which in 1980 had signalled an attempt to bring conformity through common rules, to names treated differently in various codes) adopts the new viewpoint of authorizing headings considered more convenient locally. *Structures of corporate name headings,*[33] the final report issued in 2001, presents the survey with commentary on the types and structures of corporate headings in use by some national bibliographic agencies, with the aim of facilitating the formation of a virtual database of authority records.

There is still a need for a greater availability of authoritative lists resulting from choices based on cultural considerations as well as on cataloguing, both for international exchanges and for internal use. Now national authority files are becoming available on the Web (for some months now free access has been available to Library of Congress Authorities). While on that point, one should keep in mind some printed publications of great value that have developed and continue to provide invaluable sources of supply, beginning with the lists included in the German rules for names of persons from antiquity: *Personennamen der Antike: PAN*[34] and from the Middle Ages: *Personennamen des Mittelalters: PMA,*[35] right through to private projects such as *DOC: Dizionario delle opere classiche* by Vittorio Volpi[36] and *ACOLIT: Autori cattolici e opere liturgiche* by the Associazione dei bibliotecari ecclesiastici italiani (Association of Italian Ecclesiastical Librarians).[37]

Once again, technological innovation and skilful analysis of the objects treated permit a significant improvement in quality. Because of its flexibility the electronic catalogue, unlike manual formats, can keep data and its structure distinct from the outputs that are produced by manipulating it. With appropriate coding of data and suitable systems, the possibility now arises of tailoring the search and display system to the profile of the individual user, who can choose to search and receive responses according to a certain code and in a particular language. This takes to the extreme the distinction between the entity and its nominal representation, which is interchangeable and temporary, like clothing put on by an individual, who remains the same person upon taking it off again. Thus, a move to new terminology can be justified. *Authority control* has always been the concern of the cataloguer, for more speedy and precise work aimed at consistency in the catalogue–a service from which the user gains an advantage as a consequence; now it is still organized by the cataloguer and invisible to the user, for whom it shortens the searching time; but in the structure now being advanced, it has a more precise goal, that of meeting personal requirements with an active possibility of choice. Therefore, one can remove the emphasis on authority inherent in the traditional expression and propose the expression *access point control*, which better underscores the possibility of an effective catalogue-user interface.[38]

The equivalence of various forms of heading does not alter the fact that in a catalogue, the same authorized form must always appear as the heading, whilst those forms present in publications appear in the bibliographic description; even in brief displays it is advisable that the uniform heading appear without the graphic ambiguities arising from the word order and the typical marks of the statement of responsibility. In browse displays, however, all recorded variants must appear, whether authorized or not.

With this new approach, some of the cataloguing agency's tasks already mentioned remain unchanged:

- recognizing identities between different names and different forms of the same name,
- recording all significant variations,
- applying consistent criteria to the choice of uniform or authorized heading, as an identifying element in single-entry displays,
- discovering and distinguishing between the same name referring to different entities (a phenomenon ever increasing with the growth and enlarged sources of data, e.g., those responsible for works and expressions in non-print formats).

Preoccupation with the international value of headings can give way, so long as the codes still provide for it, to research into forms tied to local requirements, gaining the capacity for local communication without losing the international approach.

A GLIMPSE BETWEEN PAST AND FUTURE

Today's most discussed and most interesting topics (such as the study of functional requirements for authority records, FRANAR[39] and the project for a virtual international authority file, VIAF),[40] have been expertly covered by the speakers of these days.

Looking back at past events I note that the ICCP model of the catalogue did not succeed in combining

- the adopted tool: the uniform heading, and
- the chosen method: original forms and national expertise,

to achieve

- the stated objective: international sharing.

Now, by means of the measures outlined and taking full advantage of the available technology, that has become possible, because the new tool, the system of controlling access points, can manage both local entities and foreign ones, with names that are local, original or foreign at the same time, and it can offer information as to which works of an author are available, in a variety of presentations that are different but internally consistent, the choice being up to the user.

The model of access point control would succeed in combining:

- the adopted tool: the authority record, and
- the chosen method: links between equivalent records in the authority file,

to achieve

- the stated objective: complete international intelligibility of all author names, for all readers.

Respect for the culture and language of origin was and is intellectually correct; maintaining it has required considerable efforts of adjustment by the cultures and languages of destination in order to pass through the bottleneck of the single authority form. The "translation" effected by access point control can now make this passage a lot smoother.

Progress in the field of authority control brings precision, speed, economy and greater coverage for sharing and exchange, but it has not led to any increment or enhancement of the catalogue as defined in Paris. In reality, whatever has been developed has happened through infiltrations/inclusions of new elements, or elements that do not conform to the Paris Principles. These initially grew out of current practices and were then used in the context of more complex problems, without being specifically compared to the Paris Principles and without an explicit approval process. In addition to the other historical differences, it will be difficult (or at least it may be a source of confusion) to put together headings of a completely different structure involving problems in the choice of heading for:

- multiple bibliographical identities (which is valid: the personal or the bibliographic identity?)
- corporate body with subheading for a person (instead of the choice between heading for the body and heading for the holder of the office)
- corporate body with conference subheading (instead of the distinction between permanent and temporary corporate bodies).

Thinking of the future without too great a stretch of the imagination, and recalling the foundations of the past, makes me think of one task from the Paris Principles that is still incomplete. It concerns the third function of the catalogue, that which brings together the editions of works, both anonymous and by known authors. For the latter, the addition of a uniform title following the author heading ensured the coming together of entries for editions of the same work at one point in the catalogue, but this practice was seldom followed. The uniform title is, logically, an additional collocating device, closely associated with the author heading, that should likewise be placed under authority control. Now, in GARR, provision is made for the authorized heading for the title of a work preceded by the name of the author; in the authority record there can follow the title variants from which reference has been made, always preceded by the author's name. A link with the author record in the authority file should keep the authority records for that author's works together, a constellation to be systematically reviewed with regard to the identity of the works, and occasionally, as to the titles with which they are displayed; their respective divisions may also be added, if there is literary warrant.

In a display of search results, uniform titles can serve as the first display of works, with the bibliographic records of editions (expressions and manifestations) of the works selected by the searcher being reserved for the next display. The parallel with the relationship between work and person or body in the FRBR model is obvious (section 3.1.2; the FRBR report is taken into account in GARR). Basically, there is also a parallel with the method reserved by the great printed catalogues (Paris and London) for "voluminous" authors; even earlier, this was the practice in compiling book catalogues, adding in one line for brevity and economy of space, only data essential for showing the difference between a new edition and the preceding ones. Once the threshold of authority control is crossed, it becomes clear that it is possible to control access by going further into the second conjunction of relationships (the work), instead of limiting oneself to the first entity (person or body as author). The third function can thus be fulfilled, if only the task is taken on.

Experience has shown how many difficulties can arise in the course of a project, and investigation of works presents an even greater challenge culturally. This latest goal may appear premature, given that after forty years, there is still some work remaining to be done on the second function . . . but now time is rushing by apace and as we run, before one foot touches the ground, the other is already off again.

NOTES

1. Tom Delsey, "Standards and standardization," *Cataloging & Classification Quarterly* (1982), v. 2 no.1/2, p. 69-81, cit. p. 69; report at the International Symposium The Future of the Union Catalogue, Toronto, 1981.

2. I discussed cataloguing in the same period with reference to codes and other normative works in *La catalogazione dopo Parigi: attività normative e strumenti per il controllo bibliografico universale, 1961-1997.* Udine: Forum, 1998 and with reference to theory in *Dai Principi di Parigi a FRBR*, paper read at meeting: La teoria catalografica alla ricerca di nuovi requisiti funzionali: il modello FRBR, Modena, 14 dicembre 2001, now in *Bibliotime*, (2002), v. 5, n. 1, URL: http://www.spbo.unibo.it/bibliotime/num-v-1/buizza.htm.

3. In *Report* / International Conference on Cataloguing Principles, Paris, 9th-18th October, 1961. London: International Federation of Library Associations, 1963, p. 91-96; published also with commentary as: *Statement of principles adopted at the International Conference on Cataloguing Principles, Paris, October, 1961.* Annotated ed. with commentary and examples by Eva Verona, assisted by Franz Georg Kaltwasser, P. R. Lewis, Roger Pierrot. London: ILFA Committee on Cataloguing, 1971.

4. On the other hand, entries dispersed under different names fragment the *corpus* of an author's works (an inefficient method) and require more references ($n(n-1)$ instead of $n-1$, a less economic method). To obtain a result it is enough to recognize the identity of the single author (identical entity). For efficiency a particular form of name is chosen, on which all information converges at a single point in the catalogue.

5. The Paris Principles do not give guidance in this regard: verification of anonymous publications (3.22) and of works of multiple attribution (3.24) is presumed to result from research into bibliography and literary history.

6. For an analysis of the topic see Pino Buizza–Mauro Guerrini. *Il controllo del punto di accesso alla registrazione per autore e titolo: riflessioni sul comportamento delle principali agenzie bibliografiche nazionali a quarant'anni dai Principi di Parigi*, a report to the Giornate di studio Catalogazione e controllo di autorità, Roma, 21-22 novembre 2002, URL: http://www.iccu.sbn.it/BuizzaGuerrini.doc. An English translation has been published as background paper for the First IFLA Meeting of Experts on an International Cataloguing Code, Frankfurt am Main, July 28-30, 2003: *Author and title access point control: on the way national bibliographic agencies face the issue forty years after the Paris Principles*, URL: http://www.ddb.de/news/pdf/ papers_ buizza.pdf.

7. These are: Pavle Kalan, "Choice of entry for authors whose names vary," p. 219-227; Fernanda Ascarelli, "Compound surnames and surnames with prefixes," p. 229-241; Maria Luisa Monteiro da Cunha, "Treatment of Brazilian and Portuguese names: problems and solutions," p. 243-254; Benoyendra Sengupta, "Rendering of Indic names-of-person in catalogue entries," p. 255-265; Mahmud Sheniti, "Treatment of Arabic names," p. 267-276; R. Edelmann, "The treatment of names in Hebrew characters and title entry for Hebrew books," p. 277-279, in *Report*, cit.

8. These were meetings on: "Arabian, Indonesian and Malayan names, Hebrew names, Indic names-of-persons (non-Muslim), Iranian names, Muslim names in India and Pakistan," with notes in *Report*, cit., p. 99-109.

9. Agreements between countries sharing a language are recommended in Resolution V.

10. Biblioteca apostolica Vaticana. *Norme per il catalogo degli stampati*. 3. ed. Città del Vaticano: Biblioteca apostolica Vaticana, 1949, p. 4-5 e § 141, p. 100-101. In the first edition, 1931, it is called an "identification entry" and is provided only for societies, § 141, p. 119-120. The identity entry is taken up by Maltese in the project to revise the Italian cataloguing rules, in: Diego Maltese. *Principi di catalogazione e regole italiane*. Firenze: Olschki, 1965, p. 66.

11. Charles Ammi Cutter. *Rules for a dictionary catalogue*. 4th ed. rewritten. Washington: Government printing office, 1904, p. 133.

12. Cf. Diego Maltese. "Lo schedario di controllo delle intestazioni," *Giornale della libreria*, (1981), 94, 2, p. 60; later in: Diego Maltese. *La biblioteca come linguaggio e come sistema*. Milano: Editrice bibliografica, 1985, p. 40-45.

13. Cf. Barbara B. Tillett. "Bibliographic structures: the evolution of catalog entries, references and tracings." In: *The conceptual foundations of descriptive cataloging*, edited by Elaine Svenonius. San Diego: Academic Press, 1989, p. 149-165.

14. Complete citation in *La catalogazione dopo Parigi*, cit., p. 160-161. For IFLA activity *cf.* report by Marie-France Plassard in the present proceedings.

15. In the report published in *La catalogazione dopo Parigi*, cit., publicly available lists of some kind are mentioned for only about fifteen countries (Saudi Arabia, Brazil, Egypt, Ethiopia, the Philippines, Germany, Japan, India, Indonesia, Iran, Malta, Singapore, United States of America, Soviet Union); with summary, p. 130-132.

16. "Report of the International Meeting of Cataloguing Experts, Copenhagen, 1969," *Libri*, (1970), v. 20, no. 1, p. 105-132.

17. *Cf.* "Name headings," *International cataloguing*, (1975), v. 4, no. 1, p. 3.

18. Giuseppe Fumagalli. *Cataloghi di biblioteche e indici bibliografici*. Firenze: Sansoni, 1887, p. 102.

19. *Cf.* S. Michael Malinconico. "The role of a machine based authority file in an automated bibliographic system." In: *Automation in libraries: papers presented at the CACUL workshop on library automation, Winnipeg, June 22-23, 1974*. Ottawa: Canadian Library Association, 1975, and later in: *Foundations of cataloging: a sourcebook*, edited by Michael Carpenter and Elaine Svenonius. Littleton: Libraries Unlimited, 1985, p. 211-233.

20. Annelise Budach. "The joint authority file for corporate bodies of the Staatsbibliothek Preussicher Kulturbesitz, Berlin, the Deutsche Bibliothek Frankfurt, and the Bayerische Staatsbibliothek, Munich," *International cataloguing*, (1980), v. 8, no. 4, p. 34-36.

21. Judith G. Fenly, Sarah D. Irvine. "*The Name Authority Co-op (NACO) project at the Library of Congress: present and future,*" *Cataloging & Classification Quarterly*, (1986), v. 7, no. 2, p. 7-18. Renamed in 1987 National Coordinated Cataloging Operations Project (NCCP), NACO is now part of the PCC, Project for Cooperative Cataloging. *Cf.* the paper by John D. Byrum in these proceedings.

22. The Working Group on an International Authority System, was formed under the chairmanship of Tom Delsey. *Cf.* "Authority system," *International cataloguing*, (1978), v. 7, no. 4, p. 1.

23. *Guidelines for authority and reference entries*, recommended by the Working Group on an International Authority System; approved by the Standing Committees of the IFLA Section on Cataloguing and the IFLA Section on Information Technology. London: IFLA International Programme for UBC, 1984.

24. At least in the better installations. In reality, how many OPACs still do not give access from non-preferred forms?

25. Françoise Bourdon. *International cooperation in the field of authority data: an analytical study with recommendations*, translated from the French by Ruth Webb. München: Saur, 1993.

26. *UNIMARC/Authorities: Universal format for authorities*, recommended by the IFLA Steering Group on a UNIMARC Format for Authorities, approved by the Standing Committees of the IFLA Sections on Cataloguing and Information Technology. München: Saur, 1991.

27. Françoise Bourdon–Sonia Zillhardt. "AUTHOR: vers une base européenne de notices d'autorité auteurs," *International Cataloguing and Bibliographic Control*, (1997), v. 26, no. 2, p. 34-37.

28. Alan Danskin. "The Anglo-American Authority File: an idea whose time has come?" *International cataloguing and bibliographic control*, (1996), v. 25, no. 3, p. 57-59.

29. *Mandatory data elements for internationally shared resource authority records*, Report of the IFLA UBCIM Working Group on Minimal Level Authority Records and ISADN, 1998, URL: http://www.ifla.org/VI/3/p1996-2/mlar.htm.

30. *UNIMARC manual: authorities format*. 2nd rev. and enl. ed. München: K. G. Saur, 2001.

31. *Guidelines for authority records and references*. 2nd ed., revised by the IFLA Working Group on GARE Revision. München: K. G. Saur, 2001.

32. International Federation of Library Associations and Institutions. *Form and structure of corporate headings*. London: IFLA international office for UBC, 1980.

33. IFLA Section on Cataloguing, Working Group on the Revision of FSCH. *Structures of corporate name headings*, final report, November 2002, compiled and introduced by Ton Heijligers, URL: http://www.ifla.org/VII/s13/scatn/final2000.htm.

34. *Personennamen der Antike: PAN*, Ansetzungs- und Verweisungsformen gemäß den RAK, erarbeitet von der Bayerischen Staatsbibliothek. Wiesbaden: Reichert, 1993.

35. *Personennamen des Mittelalters: PMA*, Ansetzungs- und Verweisungsformen gemäß den RAK, erarbeitet von der Bayerischen Staatsbibliothek. Wiesbaden: Reichert, 1989, 2 v. and *Supplement*, 1992; and *Personnennamen des Mittelalters: PMA: Namensformen für 13000 Personen gemäß den Regeln für die Alphabetische Katalogisierung (RAK)*, redaktionelle Bearbeitung Claudia Fabian. 2. erw. Ausg. München: K. G. Saur, 2000.

36. Vittorio Volpi. *DOC: Dizionario delle opere classiche*. Milano: Editrice bibliografica, 1994, 3 v.

37. *ACOLIT: Autori cattolici e opere liturgiche*, diretto da Mauro Guerrini. Milano: Editrice bibliografica, 1998- . *Cf.* the paper by Fausto Ruggeri in these proceedings.

38. The idea and expression are not new, but now have become shared and applicable. *Cf.* Barbara B. Tillett. "Considerations for authority control in the online environment," *Cataloging & Classification Quarterly*, (1989), v. 9, no. 3, p. 1-11 (also published as *Authority control in the online environment: considerations and practices*, Barbara B. Tillett editor. New York; London: The Haworth Press, Inc., 1989).

39. Françoise Bourdon. "Functional Requirements and Numbering of Authority Records (FRANAR): to what extent can authority control be supported by technical means?" *International cataloguing and bibliographic control*, (2002), v. 31, no. 1, p. 6-9. *Cf.* the paper by Glenn Patton in these proceedings.

40. Barbara B. Tillett. *The Virtual International Authority File*, report at the 67th IFLA Council and General Conference, Boston, 2001, URL: http://www.ifla.org/IV/ifla67/papers/094-152ae.pdf.

The Other Half of Cataloguing:
New Models and Perspectives
for the Control of Authors and Works

Alberto Petrucciani

SUMMARY. Today's electronic catalogue makes retrieval of specific records very simple and quick in most (not all) cases, but searches aimed at the reliable retrieval of all material answering a well-defined need (author, work, theme, form, etc.) are still long and tiring, and sometimes impossible, in crowded bibliographic databases. In spite of its great relevance, authority control has been, and still is, the "poor relative" of cataloguing, the often neglected or overlooked "other half" if we compare it to the creation of bibliographic records. The *FRBR* study and the new authority control standards (*GARR* and *UNIMARC Authorities*) are important steps towards future perspectives. Even today, cataloguing codes do not make clear the difference between the access points for bibliographic records and the relationships (work-to-work, author-to-work, etc.) that are independent from specific publications. With the development of richer authority records and relationships, the bibliographic record might be relieved of information related to entities different from publications, and of all functions more suitably worked out upstream

Alberto Petrucciani is affiliated with Università di Pisa.

[Haworth co-indexing entry note]: "The Other Half of Cataloguing: New Models and Perspectives for the Control of Authors and Works." Petrucciani, Alberto. Co-published simultaneously in *Cataloging & Classification Quarterly* (The Haworth Information Press, an imprint of The Haworth Press, Inc.) Vol. 38, No. 3/4, 2004, pp. 135-141; and: *Authority Control in Organizing and Accessing Information: Definition and International Experience* (ed: Arlene G. Taylor, and Barbara B. Tillett) The Haworth Information Press, an imprint of The Haworth Press, Inc., 2004, pp. 135-141. Single or multiple copies of this article are available for a fee from The Haworth Document Delivery Service [1-800-HAWORTH, 9:00 a.m. - 5:00 p.m. (EST). E-mail address: docdelivery@haworthpress.com].

or downstream in access systems or by links to the images and/or the texts of the publications themselves. A "light" bibliographic record would no longer be the paramount component of library information systems; it would keep its central role rather as a nimble, swift turntable between access and content organization systems, and systems for management and display of digital resources themselves. *[Article copies available for a fee from The Haworth Document Delivery Service: 1-800-HAWORTH. E-mail address: <docdelivery@haworthpress.com> Website: <http://www.HaworthPress.com> © 2004 by The Haworth Press, Inc. All rights reserved.]*

KEYWORDS. Bibliographic relationships, authority control, access points, bibliographic records

The title of this paper recalls the one of an article published exactly 30 years ago (1973) in *Library Resources & Technical Services* that aroused considerable interest at the time; in it two librarians from Florida analysed, with great clearness and wealth of examples, the complex set of activities required for a correct and functional integration of the new cards into the catalogue.[1] It was the time of the card catalogue but also of the spread of OCLC automated services essentially based on the Library of Congress MARC records. In fact, the described procedures included the retrieval of the Library of Congress MARC records on the OCLC terminal, their control and adaptation, for the following arrangement of the printed cards to be inserted by hand. The authors wrote:

> Catalog building consists of two phases: (1) the creation of cataloging copy representing the works being added to the collection; and (2) the integration of that copy into the existing catalog. Phase One simply involves the creation of a record; Phase Two determines whether or not the reader will be able to retrieve that record once it has been dropped below the rod among a million others.

This warning should be rewritten today in slightly different terms, but its relevance is unaltered.

More exactly, today's electronic catalogue makes retrieval of specific records very simple and quick in most (but not all) cases. We may use many different elements, combined or truncated. Difficulties arise in two cases: when the information used in a search is not exact or when the available clues are not sufficiently distinguishing, that is, they are all elements very frequently occurring in the database. What is easy is *only* the retrieval of one or more records including certain elements, that, in a card catalogue, would have implied very long, tiring, or even impossible searches. However, searches aimed at the full, reliable retrieval of material answering a well defined research need (author, work, theme, form, etc.) are still long and tiring, and sometimes not feasible–particularly in ever richer and crowded bibliographic databases. Therefore, the activity usually included under the label of *authority control* or *control of access points* is essential, or even, in many ways, more and more important.

In spite of its great relevance, both for the catalogues of the past and today, authority control has been and still is the "poor relative" of cataloguing, the often neglected or overlooked "other half," if we compare it to the more striking one: the creation of bibliographic records by document description.

The study on *Functional Requirements for Bibliographic Records* (FRBR), as well as the new versions of authority control standards, including *Guidelines for Authority Records and References* (GARR) and the *UNIMARC Manual: Authorities Format*, are important steps towards a thorough consideration of access points, a not merely instrumental and managerial consideration but one stimulating us to think about future perspectives.

The analysis model for *entities* and *relationships*, cannot be regarded as new, because it has already been applied widely not only on a theoretical level but also for links among bibliographic records in large databases (e.g., on a particularly ample scale in the Italian National Bibliographic Service). Yet, the relational model has not had a deep impact on author cataloguing; on the contrary, the logical schemes we are accustomed to, the traditional ones of twentieth century codes, are flat, based on a stiff, mono-dimensional approach. An example: in the present cataloguing rules, from RICA (§ 17) to AACR2 (§ 21.9 and following), the treatment of works based on other works is still seen as the addition of another access point to the same bibliographic record (the main entry of the original work used as an added entry). This is an intricate as well as unsatisfactory solution, because the user searching under access points other than the main entry of the original work will not get any information about the related work.

Not making clear the differentiation between relationships among works, irrespective of specific publications, and the access points related to elements in the publication is equivalent to the lack of actual development of a catalogue beyond "two-dimensions": the one dimension of access points to the documents' records and the other dimension of the network of relationships among records of entities that are not publications (works, expressions).

Analogically, this lack of a clear differentiation, reminds us of the "prehistory" of alphabetic subject cataloguing, a time when it was not yet clear and accepted–even as obvious as it was later–that references link subjects, not books. It follows that access points to specific documents, though multiplied and manipulated, cannot perform the linking function among subjects. In subject indexing, then, the basic feature of the distinction between paradigmatic or *a priori* relationships, independent from specific documents, and *a posteriori* ones, implying more concepts being present in one subject (distinct from the still diverse case, of more subjects being present in the same document), is universally accepted.

I believe that in this phase, when we are basically reassessing the catalogue structures, and developing logical, simple, powerful searching models to help us control extremely rich archives, the continuous comparison between the author and title cataloguing tradition and modern semantic indexing is really helpful and necessary. These two traditions have lived almost completely isolated one from the other, developing fully disconnected conceptual tools and even vocabularies, while, at the same time, the physically separate catalogues of the past were becoming an electronic catalogue that is converging more and more with bibliographic databases.

The author and title cataloguing tradition offers various hints for a new assessment, provided we look from an "estranged" viewpoint not taking the traditional methods for granted. For example, we take for granted that a bibliographic record must include proper headings under persons and corporate bodies, represented by *only one* form of their name (not by all the variants). It would be even better, when represented by an automatic link to a single authority record, so that the form of name can be easily controlled and, if needed, changed. But we take equally for granted an opposite treatment for titles (proper title, original title, uniform title, etc.), and we consider them access points to a single record instead of different forms to refer to the same, single entity. It certainly isn't the same situation, but we have here situations similar enough to raise at least a doubt about the advisability of treating them in the same way, instead of an opposite way.

Following *FRBR* we might take this analogy much further. As we consider it obvious that the issue of the form of heading for Dante Alighieri is not an issue to be dealt with in the description of a single publication but at the authority file level, couldn't it be equally obvious–to those who come after us–that the issue of whether or not Dante is the author of the *Divina commedia* or of the *Fiore* has equally nothing to do with the compilation of the bibliographic record, but must be dealt with in an archive treating the relationships between *authors* and *works* (not *publications*)? For the document description, the only pertinent element is whether or not it is an edition of the *Divina commedia*, or of the *Fiore*. We would consider primitive or amateur any person who might consider enumerating on the same level *Dante* and *Alighieri, Dante* among the headings of a bibliographic record. Those who come after us might give the same judgement on our practice of repeating the original title and the names of the two authors of, let us say, the *Manifesto of the communist party* in Italian in the record for each single edition; three elements among which, obvious *a priori*, are in a constant relationship, independent from the single document, an indexer would say. It looks as if the control of authors and works might usefully be distinguished, much more than it presently is, from the bibliographic description of publications and developed autonomously from the necessary–essential–relationships with bibliographic records.

If these are, as I believe, the insights and trends that *FRBR* and related works arouse, what relationships can we perceive in them with the most relevant features of the recent evolution of standards for authority control? I think the most innovative elements in the standards for authority files are two:

- the development of authority records in order to include *information about the entity* itself (e.g., for a person: sex, nationality, language, dates of birth and death, bio-bibliographical data), together with elements of a more technical and housekeeping relevance (institution creating the record, adopted cataloguing rules, used sources),
- the tendency to consider equivalent the original forms of names and the translated or adapted forms, preferring the latter ones–when they exist–in the various linguistic and national contexts.

This second trend has, I think, both immediate and future drawbacks on which we should reflect more, but upon which I cannot touch now. I deem the first one, instead, very interesting and stimulating, although not free from risks. It is easy but perhaps necessary to reassert that, basically, libraries have responsibilities of a bibliographic nature, related to the control and availability of publications; whereas, responsibilities for taking the census of persons and corporate bodies, except for their being authors of publications and within the limits of elements functional to a bibliographic search, is not one of a library's specific tasks. Today, authority control is carried on in a deeply changed context, in which other considerations are against the above reassertion. On the one hand, activities for access point control in more and more comprehensive and wide cooperative databases involve an enormous amount of work and imply vast information and competence. Considering this investment only as a "housekeeping" function, strictly confined to cataloguing technicalities, seems reductive, while its potential for a wider information function is clear.

We must not forget that, while the traditional library catalogue covered a modest fraction of the bibliographic universe and usually played its role only for on-site users, today's great bibliographic databases are even bigger than the major bibliographic reference works of the past and tend to surpass them also in exhaustivity. At the same time, they are within reach of a very vast on-site and distant public, much more so than the large reference (or biographic, encyclopaedic, etc,) works actually to be perused–in most cases–only in the reference rooms of great libraries. Even more, today's large databases are within reach of a public not limited to the library's users and, with greater reasons, to strictly bibliographic search objectives.

Therefore, the wider information objectives that authority files may take on must be carefully–bravely too–defined and assessed, starting from the realization that these objectives exceed the proper and exclusive field of libraries–the one of bibliographic control–and must, therefore, be pursued in cooperation with a wider range of partners, starting with cultural and research institutions. Libraries can bring into these new forms of cooperation a considerable wealth of competence and resources, a wealth of concepts and methods developed in their long cataloguing and indexing experience and applied in huge, structurally complex information databases.

In order to plan effective, wide-ranging information initiatives, shared with other partners, the clarification prompted by entity-relationship analysis is greatly valuable. It shows how to avoid duplicating information, and conversely, how to share it, for different applications too, provided it has been isolated (i.e., from our viewpoint, separated from the bibliographic records).

Very interesting insights come, for example, from comparison with the field of archives that shows us a formulation opposite, under certain aspects, to the one typical in a library environment. In the archival field, description of documentary material is often brief and "light," while information on creators, in other words, according to *FRBR* terms, information related to "Group 2 entities" rather then to the "Group 1 entities," tends to be rich and elaborate. The information function of this "other half" of archival treatment (for the history of institutions, families, etc.) is not marginal. On the contrary, it is obviously a primary, basic function.

I do not want in the least to sustain that these differences reflect simple habits, indeed I am convinced that basic functional differences exist (and persist) between archives and libraries. But, in spite of differences, it is useful to look carefully at analogies and stimuli aroused by these same differences, not in order to make them the same or level, but to positively cross-fertilize diverse methodologies and experiences.

In order to try and outline possible future perspectives, it is always useful to look back, to measure and assess the road already covered. The last quarter of the 20th century, from the cataloguing point of view, was characterized by the standardization of bibliographic records, particularly in their descriptive elements, with the development of MARC formats and ISBDs. The modern, better organized and more structured bibliographic record has become the basic element, the *building block*, for the application of computer systems in libraries. Then, with the development of cooperation and the Internet, bibliographic records further are the building blocks for today's huge bibliographic databases. These databases are basically made up of proper bibliographic records, records of the features of specific documents, while other elements, if not absent, are definitely on a secondary level.

On the contrary, the new signals of interest and attention that we perceive in recent years urge us to look "upstream" and "downstream" of the bibliographic record in the strictest sense. On the one hand, we start from the already classical authority control functions and move towards the development of information systems and relationship networks related to entities which are not strictly bibliographic (works and authors, organizations, events, concepts, etc.). On the other hand, we move towards the enrichment of the traditional function of document description and identification with further information on contents or digital reproductions of documents parts, down to the access of the full text. The bibliographic record, then, might be relieved of information not in its province (being related to entities different from publications) and of all the functions more suitably worked out upstream or downstream (in access systems or, when needed, as links to the images and/or the texts of the publications themselves).

A "light" bibliographic record would no longer be, as is the case today, the paramount component of library information systems; instead, it would keep its central role–probably permanently linked to the library function– rather as a "joint": a nimble, swift passage or interconnection point between intelligent systems for access and content organization, and intelligent systems for remote use of digital resources.

NOTE

1. Ohmes, Frances and J.F. Jones. "The other half of cataloging," *Library Resources and Technical Services*, v. 17, no. 3 (summer 1973), p. 320-329.

Fear of Authority?
Authority Control and Thesaurus Building for Art and Material Culture Information

Murtha Baca

SUMMARY. Until the 1980s, concepts like authority control, controlled vocabularies, and metadata and schemas were all but unknown in the world of art and material culture information. This paper traces the evolution and current status of tools and resources for authority control of art information, and gives examples of how the lack of authority control can impede end-user access. Collection-specific thesauri and subject indexes, and vocabulary-assisted searching and query expansion are also discussed. *[Article copies available for a fee from The Haworth Document Delivery Service: 1-800-HAWORTH. E-mail address: <docdelivery@haworthpress.com> Website: <http://www.HaworthPress.com> © 2004 by The Haworth Press, Inc. All rights reserved.]*

KEYWORDS. Authority control, art museum information, thesauri, thesaurus building, local thesauri, vocabulary-assisted searching, query expansion, LCNAF, LCSH, TGM, AAT, ULAN, TGN, ICONCLASS, access points, controlled vocabularies, subject access, metadata schemas, CDWA, VRA Core Categories, *Cataloguing Cultural Objects*

Murtha Baca is affiliated with the Getty Research Institute.

[Haworth co-indexing entry note]: "Fear of Authority? Authority Control and Thesaurus Building for Art and Material Culture Information." Baca, Murtha. Co-published simultaneously in *Cataloging & Classification Quarterly* (The Haworth Information Press, an imprint of The Haworth Press, Inc.) Vol. 38, No. 3/4, 2004, pp. 143-151; and: *Authority Control in Organizing and Accessing Information: Definition and International Experience* (ed: Arlene G. Taylor, and Barbara B. Tillett) The Haworth Information Press, an imprint of The Haworth Press, Inc., 2004, pp. 143-151. Single or multiple copies of this article are available for a fee from The Haworth Document Delivery Service [1-800-HAWORTH, 9:00 a.m. - 5:00 p.m. (EST). E-mail address: docdelivery@haworthpress.com].

http://www.haworthpress.com/web/CCQ
© 2004 by The Haworth Press, Inc. All rights reserved.
Digital Object Identifier: 10.1300/J104v38n03_13

My first job at the Getty, in the late 1980s, was as a name authority editor in what was then called the Vocabulary Coordination Group (now the Getty Vocabulary Program). With a joint doctorate in art history and Italian language and literature, and having up to that point devoted myself to teaching and translation work, I was immersed in visual culture and well aware of the power of language, but had never heard of "authority control." Unlike the library world, where cataloging and authority control have long been viewed as essential for providing access to information, the art and cultural heritage communities have only relatively recently become aware of the importance of managing information and using standards and authority files in order to provide access to their collections.

Although the art library and visual resource communities were aware of tools like LCSH, LCNAF, and the *Thesaurus for Graphic Materials* (TGM),[1] few if any art museums were even aware of the need for such tools, much less the existence of the specific tools themselves until the last decade or so. In the mid- and late 1980s, when TGM I (Subject Terms) and TGM II (Genre and Physical Characteristics Terms) were being developed, most art museums didn't have anything that could be called a collections information system. Many still don't, even though they may have purchased collection management software.

In 1980, the Getty began work on the *Art & Architecture Thesaurus* (AAT),[2] seeking to build a tool that would be useful as an authority file for those whose job it was to catalog and describe not only bibliographic materials about art and material culture, but also visual surrogates of works of art, architecture, and material culture (in the case of slide libraries, photographic archives, and similar repositories), as well as the objects themselves (in the case of museums, archives, and other holding institutions). In those now distant days before the advent of the World Wide Web and the creation of millions of uncataloged, largely unstructured Web resources, little did we know how potentially powerful authority files and thesauri could be; the variant terms and broader and narrower terms can increase both precision and recall in the online environment, as we shall see in the examples given below.

In the mid-1980s, the Getty began developing its second vocabulary tool: the *Union List of Artist Names* (ULAN),[3] a database of preferred and variant names, biographical information, and bibliographic citations for artists, architects, and other creators in the field of visual arts and architecture. Once again, the goal was to create an authority file (in this case, a personal name authority) for catalogers and indexers in the visual arts and architecture. Another reason for the development of the ULAN was the fact that multiple Getty projects built and maintained their own local name authorities; by creating a union resource, we could both enhance the scope and depth of our name authority work, and eliminate redundant work on different projects. In the late 1980s, work began on the third vocabulary database: the *Getty Thesaurus of Geographic Names* (TGN),[4] with the data first published on the Web in 1997 (yes, it can take that long to build a good thesaurus, particularly when it has more than a million names in it).

Building our three vocabularies has been, and continues to be, a time- and labor-intensive undertaking. Perhaps an even greater challenge is getting museums to use these and other tools for authority control and end-user access. Curators and other museum professionals tend to be horrified by an expression like "authority control." The mere idea of an art historian who considers him- or herself to be an "authority" on a particular artist, school, or art form being told the exact name to use for a particular artist, or what an object in the collections under his or her care should be called, is abhorrent. Thus, a period of "consciousness raising" and education began as museums made the first attempts to control their collections information, and the effort is still going on as of this writing. Museums, or rather the decision-makers and those who allocate resources (financial and human) at museums, need to understand that simply purchasing computers, a scanner, and collection management software will not provide good access to their collections information for the wide range of potential users of that information, from in-house users (registar's office, curatorial departments, education department, security staff, etc.) to external users (from advanced researchers to first-time museum visitors and casual Web visitors). The skills, tools, and methods long known to the library community, including cataloging and controlled vocabularies, are essential for organizing and publishing information on any collection. And curators and other art experts need to understand that authority files do include a preferred form or heading, but also accommodate variant names and forms, which are clustered together with the preferred or display form. The philosophy of the Getty Vocabulary Program is that all names or terms in a cluster are equally valid as both access points and descriptive metadata; one is not "better" than the others.

Let's take a look at what happens when there is no authority control for art databases. AMICO,[5] one of the first large-scale image repositories for the study of art history, "federates" information and images from the many member museums that contribute to it. The idea is to provide access to high-quality, high-resolution images (and the images in the AMICO library are certainly beautiful) and information, for educational and research purposes.

The AMICO library (a misnomer, considering that the word "library" implies organization and classification) is built by taking contributed records from participating institutions. Although the AMICO data dictionary is loosely based on *Categories for the Description of Works of Art* (CDWA),[6] and there is a required format for contribution of data to AMICO, this is not the same as contributing MARC records to a bibliographic utility. Many, if not most, of the institutions that contribute to AMICO don't appear to consistently follow a standard metadata schema in their local collection management systems, nor do they appear to have authority control on their artist names; the AMICO library certainly doesn't. So, if a user enters a search for "creator= van gogh" from the Simple Search screen, he is taken directly to an alphabetical list, in which the name "van Gogh" does not appear. At this point, many users would simply assume that the AMICO library contains no images of works by Vincent van Gogh. If the user persists, however, and tries the strategy of simply entering the single keyword "gogh" in the "creator" field, he or she is presented with another alphabetical display, in which there are 48 hits for "Gogh, Vincent Van" and 3 hits for "Gogh, Vincent Willem Van." This is because the Philadelphia Museum of Art, which is one of the AMICO contributors, uses the form "Gogh, Vincent Willem Van," while all of the other contributing museums use "Gogh, Vincent Van" (incidentally, the preferred LCNAF form is "Gogh, Vincent van;" inexplicably, AMICO chose to capitalize the prefix "van," even though its contributing museums, and of course LCNAF, which follows AACR, do not). At least two things are happening here: (1) there is no authority control, so the variant form used by the Philadelphia Museum of Art is not clustered with the preferred form used by all of the other contributing museums; and (2) the search engine is not doing keyword searching, but phrase searching, so the direct form "van Gogh" is not retrieved because the records in the AMICO repository only have the inverted form "Gogh, Vincent Van" in the "Creator" field.

As anyone who has worked with art-historical materials knows, pre-modern artist names can be particularly problematic. A search for "gherardo delle notti," or even the single keyword "notti" on the Web site of the Hermitage Museum,[7] retrieves no results, because the Hermitage lists this Dutch artist who spent much of his career in Italy under the Dutch form of his name, "Gerrit van Honthorst." The same thing occurs on the Web site of the National Gallery of Art, London; the National Gallery of Art, Washington, DC; the National Portrait Gallery; the Louvre; and even in the databases of commercial image collections such as the Bridgeman Art Library.[8] And, as within an AMICO search, a search on the Hermitage site for "Gerrit van Honthorst" retrieves zero results, while a search on the single keywords "gerrit" or "honthorst" does. Why? Because the search engine is doing a phrase search, and the name is given only in inverted form ("Honthorst, Gerrit van"). Once again, there are at least two barriers to end-user access. The Uffizi in Florence, instead, uses only the nickname by which Gerrit van Honthorst became famous during his stay in Italy, "Gherardo delle Notti," which appears in virtually all of the scholarly literature in the Italian language on this particular artist. The LCNAF record for this artist (which was contributed by the Getty through the Library of Congress's Program for Cooperative Cataloging, NACO) has eight variant forms in addition to the preferred form "Honthorst, Gerrit van" (Figure 1); the ULAN record for the same artist (Figure 2) has 26 variant names in addition to the preferred name (which is identical to the LCNAF preferred name) and the display name "Gerrit van Honthorst"; this is because the ULAN allows "variants of variants," and also includes a "display name" in natural order, both for purposes of display and to accommodate phrase searches. All of these names, which have appeared in scholarly literature, in primary documents, or on art objects, are valid access points that can lead users to the information they are seeking.[9]

In addition to variant forms, of course, the hierarchical structure of authority files that take the form of thesauri can make them potentially very powerful as retrieval tools. Thus, to use an example from the AAT, a non-expert user will retrieve a *cartonnier* even if he or she doesn't know the specific name and has searched on "cabinet," provided that the object has been indexed using the broader term. A searcher who is looking for the town in Tuscany with many medieval towers, but can only remember that it's near Siena and begins with "San," can find the name San Gimignano by searching on "Siena" in the TGN and expanding the hierarchy below Siena province.

In addition to searching by personal and geographic names and object types, users seeking information and/or images of works of art often search by what is depicted in or on those works–their subject matter.[10] "Subject matter" can range from ordinary objects depicted in or on a work of art, to complex narrative and iconographic themes. For searchers looking for depictions of particular objects, tools like LC's *Thesaurus for Graphic Materials* and the AAT can be very helpful. The *Thesaurus for Graphic Materials* offers the broader term "bathing suits" (and its variant "swimsuits") for the search term "bikini." The AAT also distinguishes between "bikinis (bathing suits)" and "bikinis (underwear)."

For users searching for the narrative content or iconographic themes of works of art, a powerful if misunderstood (and mis-marketed) tool that specifically classifies the narrative content of figurative works of art (particularly western European art) is ICONCLASS.[11] This tool can assist users with variant terms (e.g., "Heracles" for "Hercules"; "Hera" for Juno), but it also uses a hierarchical structure to help users identify specific narrative episodes that are "children" of broad concepts (e.g., "Hercules in love with Deianira, daughter of Oeneus," which is a child of the broader concept "Love-affairs of Hercules," in its turn a child of "Story of Hercules," which is a child of "Greek heroic legends"). Another potentially powerful functionality of the ICONCLASS

FIGURE 1. Library of Congress Name Authority File (LCNAF) Record for Gerrit van Honthorst

LC Control Number: nr 96007892

HEADING: Honthorst, Gerrit van, 1590-1656

Used For/See From: Honthorst, Gerard von, 1590-1656
Van Honthorst, Gerrit, 1590-1656
Della Notte, Gherardo, 1590-1656
Fiammingo, Gherardo, 1590-1656
Notte, Gherardo della, 1590-1656
Notti, Gherardo delle, 1590-1656
Delle Notti, Gherardo, 1590-1656
Honthorst, Gerrit, 1590-1656

Found In: Thieme-Becker: v. 17, pp. 447-450 (Honthorst, Gerrit (Gerard) van or Gherardo della Notte (also Gherardo Fiammingo); portraitist, painter of genre and historical scenes, advocate of naturalism à la Caravaggio, pupil of Abraham Bloemart; due to his passion for night scenes and candlelights he gained the nickname "Gherardo della Notte," his work had an impact on the young Rembrandt; also portraitist in his later years; b. Utrecht 11/04/1590, d. Utrecht 04/27/1656)
Benezit, 1976: v. 5, pp. 607-608 (Honthorst, Gerrit van, called Gherardo della Notte; painter of historical motifs, portraitist and engraver)
Müller-Singer, 1921: v. 2, p. 482 (Honthorst, Gerard von; Dutch painter)
Bryan's dict. of painters and engravers: v. 3, pp. 70-71 (Honthorst, Gerard van)
Biographical dict. of artists, 1995: p. 257 (Honthorst, Gerrit van)
Neues allgemeines Künstlerlexikon, 1838: v. 6, pp. 285-86 (Honthorst, Gerhardt)
A biographical dict. of artists, 1995: p. 297 (Honthorst, Gerrit van)
Union list of artist names, 1994: (Honthorst, Gerrit or Gerard van (Gherardo della Notte or delle Notti, or Gherardo Fiammingo))
RLIN database, 03/06/96 (hdg.: Honthorst, Gerrit van, 1590-1656; usage: Gerrit van Honthorst; Gherardo delle Notti)
Gerrit van Honthorst 1592-1656, 1999: p. xxxiii (born Nov. 4, 1592 in Utrecht; died Utrecht April 27, 1656)
Gerard und Willem van Honthorst, 1966: p. 15 (Gerard van Honthorst; born 1592 and not 1590 as previously assumed)
Gherardo delle Notti, c1999: t.p. (Gherardo delle Notti; Gerrit Honthorst) p. 11 (b. Nov. 4, 1592) p. 7 (d. Utrecht, 1656)

system are the keywords that it associates with specific notations.[12] Thus the notation 94A332 ("Hercules searching for Hylas") comes "pre-packaged" with keywords like "mythology," "Greek legend," "hero," "searching," "sailing," "Mysia" (the place where Hercules' beloved companion Hylas was abducted by a nymph), and so on. The power of these keywords can make it possible to identify the iconographic or narrative content of images and/or to retrieve images that have been indexed with these keywords. For example, if the ICONCLASS description and accompanying keywords had been used to index the images, a search on "hair cutting" would retrieve images of Samson having his hair cut off by either Delilah and/or a Philistine (the perpetrator varies, especially in depictions from the Baroque period).

In order to exploit the power of the hierarchical structure of a thesaurus, the broader term(s) must be entered either manually or automatically at the point of cataloging. Thus the cataloger who is describing a "bonnetière" will also enter the term "cabinet" and even "furniture" to assist searchers who do not know the specific name of the object for which they are searching; it may even be useful (if heretical, at least in the traditional library world) to enter a wrong broader term, or "false parent" such as "desk," because that may be how the user has interpreted the object. Of course this kind of cataloging can be labor-

FIGURE 2. *Union List of Artist Names* (ULAN) Record for Gerrit van Honthorst

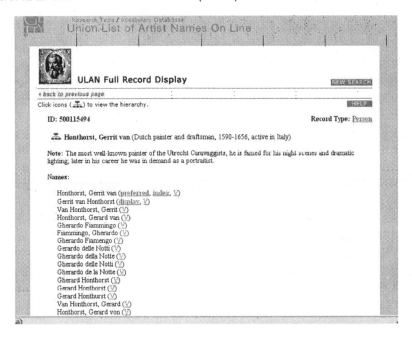

and hence time-intensive. A "mechanized" solution is to write a computer program that will automatically include the broader term or terms from the thesaurus. Thus, if a user enters the word "desk" on the search page of the Getty Web site,[13] the results will include a page for a "secrétaire à abbattant" on which the word "desk" does not appear; unbeknownst to the end-user (and this in itself could be a source of usability problems), a program has inserted that term into the Keyword META tag in the source of the HTML page, because that is the parent term in the local thesaurus.

Another machine solution is to interpose an authority file between the searching and the resources being searched. If a visitor to the Getty Web site enters the name "Carucci" on the search page, Web pages relating to the artist known as Pontormo (the name of his birthplace), whose given name was Jacopo Carucci, will be retrieved. This is because the user's search statement is being run against a copy of the ULAN data, and when a match is found, all of the name forms, preferred and variant, from that record are submitted to the search engine. Of course, a computer program can't make the decision to include a misnomer or false parent because that's what some users may be likely to use in their search for a particular item. (I am convinced that in my lifetime, no computer program will be able to catalog better than an appropriately trained human cataloger.)

Simply adopting or interposing a published authority file or classification system such as LCSH or the ULAN or ICONCLASS is not, however, the most efficient way of enhancing end-user access to art information (or information in any other field of study or interest, for that matter). Large authority files like the Library of Congress authorities or the AAT or TGN (which has more than 1 million names referring to circa 900,000 places) are not only unwieldy as "searching assistants," they probably aren't the right tools to use to enhance precision and recall in searching specific collections. Many museums and other cultural heritage collections (and the vendors who build the systems they use for collection management, many of which now include thesaurus modules) are coming to realize that the best way to enhance end-user access by means of vocabularies is to build collection-specific thesauri and indexes, taking terms and names from standard published authorities such as LCSH (and recording the source of such terms), but also adding additional variants from curators, educators, and even "wrong" terms (e.g., "pot" as a broader term for "lekythos," or "jar" as an alternate term for "hydria"). Again, some of this can be automated (e.g., by writing a program that takes the broader terms and variant terms from the local thesaurus and uses them to populate the Keywords META tag on a Web page for a museum object, as in the example from the Getty Museum given on the preceding page); but at some point (in this case, when the local thesaurus or subject index is being constructed, or when the object is originally being cataloged), a human being who both understands the collections and understands thesaurus construction and authority control has to do the work–that is, a person with skill, good judgment, experience, and knowledge of the material being described, to echo Michael Gorman in his essay "Authority Control in the Context of Bibliographic Control in the Electronic Environment" in the present collection of essays.

In the museum world as in the library world, cataloging and authority control are (or should be) essential for organizing, documenting, and providing good end-user access to information on our collections–in short, they are part of the indispensable set of tools we need to fulfill our basic mission of preserving and providing access to our collections. Metadata schemas like *Categories for the Description of Works of Art*, MARC VIM, and the VRA Core Categories[14] that are specifically designed for cataloging works of art and visual materials exist, as do a range of vocabulary tools that are appropriate for populating metadata element sets for art and material culture. As of this writing, an editorial team of members of the Visual Resources Association, with an advisory group of leading experts on cataloging works of art from the museum, library, and archival communities, is nearing completion of the first version of *Cataloguing Cultural Objects: A Guide to Describing Cultural Works and Their Images*, which one hopes will become an essential part of the art and image cataloger's "desktop."[15]

Still missing at many museums are an awareness of these tools and methods, and the skilled people to implement them, in order to ensure that what we have all rushed to make available on the World Wide Web can be found, identified, selected, and eventually obtained[16] (or at least viewed) by our huge audience of end-users.

NOTES

1. "[D]eveloped to support the cataloging and retrieval needs of the Library of Congress Prints and Photographs Division." See www.loc.gov/rr/print/tgm1/.

2. Available at www.getty.edu/research/conducting_research/vocabularies/aat.

3. Available at www.getty.edu/research/conducting_research/vocabularies/ulan.

4. Available at www.getty.edu/research/conducting_research/vocabularies/tgn.

5. See www.amico.org. The AMICO library is available by subscription from the Research Libraries Group.

6. A metadata element set developed by a task force that was modeled after NISTF, sponsored by the College Art Association and what was formerly know as the Getty Art History Information Program. See www.getty.edu/research/conducting_ research/datastandards/cdwa/.

7. See www.hermitagemuseum.org/. All of the Web searches in this article were conducted in late August, 2003.

8. On the Web at www.bridgeman.co.uk.

9. N.B. The full ULAN record does not appear in this figure; it also includes roles, events, related persons, sources for all names, and bibliographic citations.

10. See M. Baca, ed., *Introduction to Art Image Access* (Los Angeles: Getty Publications, 2002), especially the essays by Sara Shatford Layne and Colum Hourihane.

11. See http://www.iconclass.nl/.

12. One of the weaknesses of the ICONCLASS system are the alphanumerical notations that it employs, which are quite forbidding and user-unfriendly. These are, I believe, a vestige of the very early, paper-based days of this system (which dates from the 1950s).

13. At www.getty.edu/search/.

14. Available at http://www.vraweb.org/vracore3.htm.

15. Available as of this writing in draft form at http://www.vraweb.org/CCOweb/.

16. These are the four generic user tasks identified by IFLA's *Functional Requirements for Bibliographic Records* final report, which is available at http://www.ifla.org/VII/s13/frbr/frbr.htm.

UNIMARC Format for Authority Records:
Its Scope and Issues for Authority Control

Mirna Willer

SUMMARY. The IFLA standard for authority data, UNIMARC author-itics format, is described in the light of developments of IFLA standards in the field of authority files, IFLA's activities in promoting the exchange of name authority records within the program of Universal Bibliographic Control and the design of the UNIMARC format for bibliographic records that established principles for its structure and design. The second revised and enlarged edition, *UNIMARC Manual: Authorities Format*, is described. Particular attention is paid to the methods for expressing relationships between different forms of headings, and relationships between different languages and scripts of headings. The maintenance of the format and sources for its revision are described. *[Article copies available for a fee from The Haworth Document Delivery Service: 1-800-HAWORTH. E-mail address: <docdelivery@haworthpress.com> Website: <http://www.HaworthPress.com> © 2004 by The Haworth Press, Inc. All rights reserved.]*

Mirna Willer, PhD in LIS, MA, is Consultant for Library Automation and Standards Officer, Croatian Institute for Librarianship, National and University Library, Croatia. She is also a standing member of the IFLA Permanent UNIMARC Committtee since 1991, and its chair since 1997, member of the WG on MLAR and the ISADN, member of the FRANAR Working Group, and chair of the CERL Advisory Task Group.

[Haworth co-indexing entry note]: "UNIMARC Format for Authority Records: Its Scope and Issues for Authority Control." Willer, Mirna. Co-published simultaneously in *Cataloging & Classification Quarterly* (The Haworth Information Press, an imprint of The Haworth Press, Inc.) Vol. 38, No. 3/4, 2004, pp. 153-184; and: *Authority Control in Organizing and Accessing Information: Definition and International Experience* (ed: Arlene G. Taylor, and Barbara B. Tillett) The Haworth Information Press, an imprint of The Haworth Press, Inc., 2004, pp. 153-184. Single or multiple copies of this article are available for a fee from The Haworth Document Delivery Service [1-800-HAWORTH, 9:00 a.m. - 5:00 p.m. (EST). E-mail address: docdelivery@haworthpress.com].

http://www.haworthpress.com/web/CCQ
© 2004 by The Haworth Press, Inc. All rights reserved.
Digital Object Identifier: 10.1300/J104v38n03_14

KEYWORDS. Universal Bibliographic Control (UBC), authority control, UNIMARC authorities format, IFLA standards for authority files

INTRODUCTION

UNIMARC/Authorities: Universal Format for Authorities[1] was published in 1991 as the IFLA standard machine-readable format for the exchange of authority records. It was recommended by the IFLA Steering Group on a UNIMARC Format for Authorities, and approved by the Standing Committees of the IFLA Sections on Cataloguing and Information Technology. In 2001, *UNIMARC Manual: Authorities Format*, the 2nd revised and enlarged edition,[2] was published under the responsibility of the Permanent UNIMARC Committee (PUC) within the IFLA UBCIM Programme (Universal Bibliographic Control and International MARC Programme).

Its second edition most probably will not hold the stability of the first edition of the UNIMARC format. The reasons for this are found in the impact of the Internet on the means of creating, publishing, communicating and organising information; the change in paradigm from the concept of the Universal Bibliographic Control (UBC) regarding the bilateral exchange of bibliographic and authority records to the concept of a shared environment; the design and use of systems that enable the building of co-operative authority files; the rising number of libraries using library systems with linked bibliographic and authorities files; and users' requirements. The challenging test for the format, which is also expected to influence the direction of its further development, will be the application to the format of the entity relationship model that is being developed by the IFLA Functional Requirements and Numbering of Authority Records (FRANAR) Working Group. The model is being developed for authority records created in different linguistic environments and by different cataloguing rules defined for different publishing conditions for an entity that has to be uniquely identified in the process of retrieval in multiple catalogues. But as MARC format is only a vehicle for the content which is defined by cataloguing rules, it is expected that additional requirements for the development of the format will come from the recommendations and agreements reached at the IFLA Meeting of Experts on an International Cataloguing Code held in Frankfurt am Main, Germany, in July 2003. This meeting is the first in a series of regional meetings of cataloguing experts with the aim "to increase the ability to share cataloguing information worldwide by promoting standards for the content of bibliographic and authority records used in library catalogues."[3]

BACKGROUND TO THE DEVELOPMENT
OF THE UNIMARC FORMAT FOR AUTHORITIES

The background of the UNIMARC format for authority records briefly traced here is the development of IFLA standards and guidelines for name and subject authority records on which the format is based, IFLA's activities during the 1990s to promote international co-operation in the field of name authority files which influenced its development, and the design of the UNIMARC format for bibliographic records which established the principles for its design.

IFLA Standards in the Field of Authority Files

The beginning of standardisation in the field of authority files goes back to the 20th IFLA Conference held in Zagreb in 1954 when "Mr. Frances reported that the Committee on Cataloguing Principles had been requested by the International Advisory Committee on Bibliography of UNESCO to make a study on the standardisation of cataloguing rules." Subsequently, the resolution was passed to accept the invitation "to examine and report on the co-ordination of cataloguing principles," and the working group was constituted with its first task being "the examination of the possibility of reaching agreement on principles to be observed in establishing main entries for anonyma and works of corporate authorship, the latter with special reference to government publications."[4] Following the resolution, the International Conference on Cataloguing Principles, organised by the IFLA Committee on Cataloguing with the support of the Council on Library Resources and UNESCO was held in Paris in 1961.[5] The aim of the Conference was to define principles on which international as well as national cataloguing rules could be based. The Paris Principles were concerned with the choice and form of headings in main and added entries, and cross-references in catalogues, while in sections 7 and 12 they explicitly stipulate the choice of uniform heading and the entry word for personal names:

> Section 7: Choice of uniform heading–The uniform heading should normally be the most frequently used name (or form of name) or title appearing in editions of the works catalogued or in reference to them by accepted authorities.

> Section 12: Entry word for personal names–When the name of a personal author consists of several words, the choice of entry word is determined so far as possible by agreed usage in the country of which the

author is a citizen, or, if it is not possible, by agreed usage in the language, which he generally uses.

The adoption of the Paris Principles in national cataloguing rules designed after 1961 showed varied interpretations of the above-mentioned stipulations. That fact led to the need for their reconsideration, which was done during the first part of the International Meeting of Cataloguing Experts, Copenhagen, 1969.[6] The task to lead the discussion and prepare the annotated edition of the Statements of Principles with commentary and examples was entrusted to Eva Verona. It was, however, decided that the commentary should encourage the use "wherever possible of the original forms of names and titles, rather than the forms used in the language of the country in which the library is located" in order to advance international uniformity in relation to the choice of uniform heading.[7]

The annotated edition, *Statement of Principles Adopted at the International Conference on Cataloguing Principles, Paris, October, 1961* published in 1971, recognised that different interpretations and therefore different approaches towards the choice of uniform heading were basically due to differences in definition of the term "individual author" which Paris Principles did not define, and also to the areas that needed further elaboration. The latter are the treatment of an author who wrote under different names for different types of material; change of name by a living author; works issued by dignitaries which, although appearing under their personal names, carried a collective authority; original forms of names of cities and states, nature of entries for laws, constitutions, etc.; works produced by several authors; and transliteration according to a standard international system.[8]

It was the international uniformity of headings for names and titles recorded in their original form that was considered a way to the exchange of authority data with the view of effective and cost-saving cataloguing of library material and users' access to libraries catalogues. The concept and principles of Universal Bibliographic Control, prepared by Dorothy Anderson and published in 1974 under the title *Universal Bibliographic Control: A Long Term Policy, a Plan for Action*,[9] established the framework for that endeavour within the total system of UBC defined as depending "upon universal recognition and acceptance that each national bibliographic agency is the organisation responsible for creating the authoritative bibliographic record of the publication of its own country and of international standards in creating the bibliographic record." In this context the national bibliographic agencies should accept "responsibility for establishing the authoritative form of names for its country's authors, both personal and corporate, and authoritative lists of its country's authors, personal and corporate."[10] This seminal IFLA document was supported at the UNESCO Intergovernmental Conference on Planning National Overall Documentation Library and Archives Infrastructures in 1974, confirming the responsibilities of national libraries.[11] The International Conference on Bibliographies held in Paris in 1977, in its thirteenth recommendation stipulated that a national bibliographic agency "should maintain an authority control system for national names, personal and corporate, and uniform titles, in accordance with international guidelines."[12] Twenty-one years later, the International Conference on National Bibliographic Services, held in Copenhagen in 1998, revisited and reaffirmed the recommendations from the 1977 Conference.[13]

In order to achieve the wished for uniformity, IFLA published a series of international rules for structuring authority forms and authority lists in order to help cataloguers in creating uniform headings for names and titles emanating from different countries, belonging to different language and cultural traditions, and embodied in different national cataloguing rules.[14]

The efficient exchange of authority data between and among national bibliographic agencies was recognised as critical, and, during the IFLA World Congress in Brussels, 1977, the Steering and Advisory Committees of the IFLA International Office for UBC approved a "new project to establish principles for the creation of authority files and facilitate the international exchange of authority information." The IFLA Working Group on an International Authority System was set up during the IFLA General Conference in Strbske Pleso in 1978, with the following terms of reference: (1) to discuss and formulate the specifications for an international authority system to satisfy bibliographic needs of the libraries, (2) to develop the UNIMARC format for the exchange of authority data, and (3) to develop the methods for the efficient and effective exchange of authority data.[15]

Guidelines for Authority and Reference Entries[16] were published in 1984. They define a set of elements to be included in the authority entry, reference entry, and general explanatory entry, assign an order to the elements, and specify a system of punctuation for the entry in print and micro-print form. Three types of authorities are defined: headings for personal names, headings for corporate bodies, including conferences and territorial authorities, and uniform titles for anonymous classics. The Working Group decided to exclude from the scope of the Guidelines subject headings and series.[17] The specifications of the Guidelines, however, are confined to the overall structure of the entry, they "make no attempt to specify the form or structure of uniform headings or references *per se*, nor do they prescribe punctuation to be used within the defined element." The specifications pertaining to the form of heading should be made, where applicable, according to other IFLA standards and guidelines, and national cataloguing rules.[18]

Another purpose the Guidelines served that was "equally if not more important for the international authorities program as a whole in that they provided a base for developing an international format for authorities. [IFLA recognised] that the development of a format for authorities to parallel the UNIMARC format for bibliographic records was key to the realization of even the most basic form of automated authority control on an international scale."[19] The Steering Group was set up in 1984, and *UNIMARC/Authorities: Universal Format for Authorities* was published in 1991. It was approved by the Standing Committees of the IFLA Sections on Cataloguing and Information Technology. The major difficulties encountered in developing the format, wrote Tom Delsey, were similar to those that had challenged the Working Group in developing the Guidelines. These were the questions of structure, that is, the "complexities of the relationships between authority headings, references, and tracings" in the context where a machine-readable record "can be structured in such a way as to support more than one form of display, thus obviating the need for redundancy of data that so often occurs in printed entries." Thus, "one of the fundamental issues that had to be dealt with [was] the question of how far the format should go in accommodating variant approaches to the structuring of the authority and reference data it is designed to convey." Being conscious of the experience with UNIMARC bibliographic format, which allows multiple options and therefore multiple implementations, thus complicating conversion to national formats, the Steering Group made "a conscious effort . . . to minimize structural options." This made the task of developing format more difficult but "ultimately the effort should yield significant benefits for the users of the format and should help to ensure that data encoded in the format can be processed with equal efficiency regardless of its source."[20]

The format follows the Guidelines in defining data elements and structure of authority and reference entries and general explanatory entry, but expands on its types of headings for name authorities, and adds tagging for subject authority control. Content designators (tags, indicators and subfield identifiers) are defined for headings for names (personal, corporate, including conferences and territorial or geographic authorities) with the addition of heading for family name, uniform titles for works not entered under specific authors which are not restricted to anonymous classics only as in the Guidelines, and for the additional headings for uniform titles for works by individual authors (name/title and name/collective title headings) and topical subjects. The entities thus defined are normally used on bibliographic records as primary, alternative and secondary entries whether for author or title, and as subject entries. Although one can read in the introduction to the format that authority records for series entries are limited to heading information and that it does not accommodate series treatment data that is included in authority records by some agencies, the possibility of recording series title is restricted to uniform title heading. As already mentioned, the compilers of GARE excluded authorities for series pending further discussion with representatives of the IFLA Section on Serial Publications and the International Serials Data System (ISDS).[21] Obviously, no decisions were made on this issue during the ten years that elapsed between publishing of the two standards.[22] The *Guidelines for Subject Authority and Reference Entries*[23] were not yet published at the time of the development of the format, so the fields for those entities were defined in accordance with corresponding fields in UNIMARC bibliographic format. The format, as well as the Guidelines, does not define the content of authority and reference records but delegates this issue to standards and rules prescribed by IFLA and national cataloguing rules.

However, the first objective set before the Working Group on an International Authority System was not yet achieved. The model for the establishment of an international authority system was not defined and the task was still to be carried out. At the time of developing UNIMARC/Authorities, Delsey perceived that in spite of the fact that with the finalisation of UNIMARC/Authorities and its implementation a major milestone in the IFLA programme for international authority control had been reached, and bilateral exchange of authority data on an international scale had been standardised, "when one looks more closely at the complexities of authority control on an international scale, one soon realises that an infrastructure more sophisticated than that supporting simple bilateral exchange is required."[24] This is the situation for which we still lack a solution. One can read in the Foreword to the format: "When a model for an international authority system is worked out by IFLA, targets for data element requirements may be set out so that records exchanged internationally will have more consistency. Such a model may also indicate the need to add data elements to UNIMARC/Authorities in order to accommodate and facilitate exchange in a world-wide environment."[25]

IFLA's Activities in Promoting the Exchange of Authority Records

Concerned with furthering developments in authority control and to meet the third objective of developing methods for the efficient and effective exchange of authority data, IFLA commissioned two studies. The first one was *Management and Use of Name Authority Files (Personal Names, Corporate Bodies and Uniform Titles): Evaluation and Prospects* conducted by Marcelle Beaudiquez and Françoise Bourdon.[26] It was presented during the meeting of the Section on Bibliography during the 55th IFLA Conference in Paris in 1989 and published in 1991. The authors of the study observed that (1) authority lists were more numerous than expected, although often lacking obligatory elements of a record that would comprise a true authority file, (2) although the automated authority files are almost all in MARC format, very few countries declared their willingness to adopt UNIMARC/Authorities and GARE, and the exchange of magnetic tape is not common, (3) IFLA recommendations (*Names of Persons, Anonymous Classics, Names of States*) are used relatively little–only if they are compatible with national cataloguing rules, and (4) existing authority files do not serve to identify the authors of a particular country, and "this no doubt explains why the various countries have not arranged to share the work amongst themselves in accordance with the principles of UBC and why there is less desire to exchange authority files with more or less identical contents than had been previously thought."[27]

The second study was *International Cooperation in the Field of Authority Data: An Analytical Study with Recommendations* conducted by Françoise Bourdon and published in 1993.[28] Its aim was to "identify the current obstacles to the international exchange of authority data, whether in manual or automated form, and to submit recommendations to IFLA to be ratified and thus to contribute to international cooperation in this area." The analysis of international standards showed that there was a lack of clarity in the aims of international standardisation, which was visible in the gaps in available standards in regard to the definition of the typical content of authority records that were intended to be reusable outside the context in which they were created. This failure resulted from the lack of identification of the different functions of an authority file in an automated environment. Bourdon identifies two types of authority files according to their function. The first one is a management name authority file designed to ensure the formal management of name access points in a given catalogue and therefore not suitable for the exchange of authority data. The second one is identification name authority file, which identifies the entity that is the subject of the authority record. The presence of different types of notes in addition to management functions in authority records makes this type of authority file independent from the catalogue, and therefore applicable for re-use in a new context. These files are most suitable for international exchange. The specific information Bourdon calls attention to can be summarised as information on the choice of authorised form and on the relationship between the rejected forms, information explaining the structure of the name, such as the nationality of the author or the work, the language usually used in the author's works, biographical information, background information on the organisation usually explaining the changes in names, information on the problems involved in attributing the work to a particular author, details concerning the genre, the dating of the text, the manuscripts preserved, instructions to users on the use of headings in the bibliographic file, and information on the sources used to establish the authority record, and those consulted without success. She warns that all these elements were not properly considered in the process of defining GARE, and consequently in UNIMARC/Authorities. An additional problem is that national cataloguing rules do not address these questions, since in general they do not even mention such files.[29]

In answer to the growing interest in the international exchange and re-use of authority records, IFLA organised a series of seminars all of which stressed the importance of resuming work in the field: Seminar on Bibliographic Records (organised by IFLA Division of Bibliographic Control and UBCIM Programme) held during the 56th IFLA General Conference, Stockholm, 1990,[30] the UNIMARC/CCF Workshop (organised by UNESCO and IFLA UBCIM Programme), Florence, 1991,[31] IFLA UBC/UNIMARC Seminar, Vilnius, 1994,[32] and IFLA International Seminar on the Creation and Use of Authority Files, St Petersburg, 1995.[33]

The direct outcome of the last mentioned seminar's recommendations was the setting up of the Working Group on Minimal Level Authority Records (MLAR) and the International Standard Authority Data Number (ISADN). It was established in 1996 by the IFLA UBCIM with the aim to reconsider the way for international exchange of authority data and provide recommendations for the additions to UNIMARC and GARE. The final report was published in 1998.[34] The Working Group once again recognised that national libraries, due to various historical and cultural reasons, to their users' needs and habits, and to technological constraints, variously follow IFLA recommendations published within the programme for the UBC. It therefore concluded that it is not realistic nor practical to impose the same form for headings globally, that it is important to allow the preservation of national differences in authorised forms of headings which should best meet the language and cultural needs of the users, and that some other mechanism should be set up for their re-use. The Group accepted the concept of shared authority records, where each National Bibliographic Agency would make their authority files available over the Internet, preferably using the IFLA home page to register current information on their files and conditions of use. This would enable searching single national or multinational authority files online in a shared environment and exchanging them in electronic form in ISO 2709 format. The Group did not, however, consider the development of a mechanism for the creation and maintenance of the ISADN as a link among authority records created for the same entity in a multinational context but concluded that due to organisational and financial constraints for maintenance of such a system, its realisation should be postponed, and the concept should be reviewed again in the future. It recommended waiting to see how the emerging electronic environment and advances in developing technologies impact the linking of records.[35]

Based on the comparison of data elements of UNIMARC/Authorities with nine MARC formats for authorities[36] limited to name authorities, i.e., authority records for names of persons, corporate bodies, conferences and uniform titles, and excluding series, subject headings and classification authorities, the Working Group made recommendations to the Permanent UNIMARC Committee for additions to UNIMARC/Authorities. These recommendations included the addition of the category for the entity (e.g., person, corporate body and work) and the coding for differentiated and undifferentiated personal name, the extension of codes to distinguish among types of series, the addition of a new coding structure for the language of the base heading because it often differs from the language of the catalogue in which the additional qualifying data that form part of the heading and notes are recorded, the allowance of the use of $7 Script within all heading fields, new subfields for transliteration scheme and direction of the script to be used within all heading fields, new data element for recording nationality of entity as mandatory, the use of biographical notes, i.e., biographical, historical or other information about the entity notes, to be made highly desirable for the inclusion into the records, and that the ISADN should be made a mandatory element when developed. The Working Group endorsed the provision of UNIMARC/Authorities for recording parallel language forms of headings in separate records.

The Working Group recommended the following mandatory elements for an authority record: record status, type of record, entity category, encoding level, record identifier, International Standard Authority Data Number (ISADN), date entered into the file, version identifier, language of cataloguing, character set/s, script of cataloguing, description rules, source agency for the record, differentiated or undifferentiated personal name, authorised heading, nationality of entity (can be "undetermined"), variant forms of the authorised heading ("see" references), related authorised heading ("see also references"), and source citation note. Highly recommended are biographical, historical or other information about the entity, source data not found, and general notes. All these recommendations were built into the 2nd edition of UNIMARC/Authorities format published in 2001.

The Working Group's recommendations to the Working Group on the Revision of Guidelines for Authority and Reference Entries (GARE), established in 1997 during the IFLA Conference in Copenhagen, were: GARE, which is standard for print and microprint forms, should be revised in light of online catalogues and new media, definition of required elements for a record to be complete or minimal, to revise glossary, to give instruction on recording parallel data, to give broader scope of notes, to revise punctuation requirements, provide more information on the structure and relationships of headings and references, to include new categories of entities, like publishers, to review whether all types of authority records were represented, e.g., publishers names, and to add examples.

Guidelines for Authority Records and References (GARR)[37] were published also in 2001. The specifications for authority and reference entries for names and titles are provided not only for print and microprint form, as in GARE, but also for machine-readable form. This is visible in the vocabulary change (e.g., authority entry to authority record) and in definitions (e.g., authority record, authority file, general explanatory record, but reference entry). The extension of the types of materials covered by the Guidelines is made by adding examples for legal and religious works, musical compositions and performances, works by individual and multiple authors known under one or more titles, and serial publications (addition of "designation of part of work" in Title sub-elements, 1.1.1.4). Of particular interest to UNIMARC authorities format is, however, the definition of the parallel heading which extends the concept of a parallel heading from "an alternate form of the authority heading based on another language form of the name or title" (GARE) to "an alternative, authorised form of the authorised heading for the same entity, formulated according to different rules or alternative languages (when there are two or more official languages)" (GARR). Thus a parallel heading is the term covering:

1. An alternative, authorised form of the authorised heading: GARR narrows down the concept of parallel heading of GARE, which is an "alternate form" of the "authority heading" (i.e., uniform heading), and whether the parallel form is treated as a variant or related heading depending on the rules of a particular national cataloguing code, to related heading only, which is the authorised heading (the reference to the related heading only in the definition of parallel heading shows that explicitly);
2. The form formulated according to different cataloguing rules: this is an important new attribute of the heading whether in its use as a variant or related heading;
3. The form in alternative languages (when there are two or more official languages): GARE's concept of "another" language is changed into "alternative official language." This implies that "another" language of the entity is recorded only in the official languages of a country, which is in line with the treatment of a parallel heading as an authorised heading, and not in all the languages found on the publication regardless whether they are treated as variant or related headings.

Regardless of the fact that the form of heading formulated according to different cataloguing rules could have been named "different rules heading" and treated as a distinct type of heading in GARR, UNIMARC could have accommodated such a requirement. That could have been done by extending the definition of the subfield $2 Subject System Code that is used with 7-- Linking Heading Block fields to "system code" covering both subject and descriptive cataloguing rules.[38] However, the renaming of a control subfield cannot be enough. The need for coding such information is particularly important in co-operative international authority files for recording national cataloguing rules, but also for recording rules that are no longer used or are used for particular user groups in national authority files. Joan M. Aliprand calls the relationship in authority records in which the two fields are the same with respect to *meaning*, the "semantic equivalence."[39] Aliprand elaborates this concept in her analysis of linkage in bibliographic records in which she states that "semantic equivalence is a key concept in the discussion of field association and linkage in bibliographic records . . . Another way to say this is that a singular *identity* is the target of all different names. The concept of identity should be familiar to catalogers from another context: when new cataloguing rules are adopted, the authorized name of an entity may change, but the item being named does not change–it retains its identity. The old form of name and the new form of name are semantically equivalent."[40] However, how do different cataloguing rules treat such a relationship, i.e., do they stipulate what procedure to take with the "old" forms of names? Do they prescribe creating a new authority record with a link to the old one, or subsuming (e.g., see reference tracing) the old form into the record for a new form? How can one code it in MARC formats? What is the general principle for the construction of a catalogue when new cataloguing rules are adopted taking into consideration linked bibliographic and authority files?[41] It is appropriate that GARR has brought out these questions, for they beg for solutions in everyday practice.

GARR includes a new type of note in the Information Note Area to record "information to identify the entity." This element corresponds to the UNIMARC new field 340 Biography and Activity Note, the much-needed note particularly for use with headings for personal and family names. Namely, in the first editions of both GARE and *UNIMARC/Authorities Format* this information was provided only for corporate bodies.

IFLA's work in pursuing the efficient international flow of authority records, however, did not stop with the publication of the two mentioned revisions of its standards. Besides, there was still no solution to the creation, functionality, maintenance and use of the ISADN in view. On the other hand, IFLA's study on the Functional Requirements for Bibliographic Records (FRBR), published in 1998, stopped short of defining requirements for authority records: the FRBR model "does not analyse the additional data that are normally recorded in an authority record, nor does it analyse the relationships between and among those entities that are generally reflected in the syndetic apparatus of the catalogue . . . the study group recognises the need to extend the model at some future date to cover authority data."[42] The need to wrap up IFLA's efforts, link them to the various international and national projects in the field of authority data within library[43] and archives,[44] as well as rights management communities and participants in e-commerce[45] became obvious. Not to lose momentum, the IFLA Division on Bibliographic Control with the UBCIM set up the Working Group on the Functional Requirements And Numbering of Authority Records (FRANAR) in 1999. Its tasks were defined as follows: (1) to define functional requirements of authority records (FRBR), (2) to study the feasibility of an International Standard Authority Data Number (ISADN): to define possible use and users, to determine for what type of authority records such an ISADN is necessary, to examine the possible structure of the number and the type of management that would be necessary, and (3) to serve as the official liaison to, and work with, other interested groups concerning authority files such as ICA/CDS (International Committee on Archives/Committee on Descriptive Standards), ISO TC46, CERL (Consortium of European Research Libraries), etc.[46]

It is expected that the entity relationship model developed for authority records and the requirements for data elements that should uniquely identify an entity to which an ISADN would be assigned will have direct and immediate influence on the future development of the UNIMARC format for authorities.

UNIMARC Format for Bibliographic Records

The first edition of the UNIMARC format for bibliographic records was published in 1977. Its subsequent editions were published in 1980, 1983 (*UNIMARC Handbook*[47]), and in 1987 (*UNIMARC Manual: Bibliographic Format*[48]). The *Manual*'s 2nd edition[49] was published as the responsibility of the Permanent UNIMARC Committee in 1994, and its regular updates are issued every second year. The format defines content designators for bibliographic data grouped in the so-called functional blocks. These are:

0-- Identification Block: contains numbers that identify the record and the item recorded in it.
1-- Coded Information Block: contains coded fixed length data elements.
2-- Descriptive Information Block: contains areas covered by the ISBD with the exception of notes and standard numbers.
3-- Notes Block: contains notes.
4-- Linking Entry Block: contains links to the item(s) not described in the main body of the record; the linking field can contain the identifier of the

record for the item being linked to, or, if there is no record, to identify the item itself.

5-- Related Title Block: contains titles other than the title proper related to the item being catalogued and generally appearing on the item.

6-- Subject Analysis Block: contains subject data constructed according to various systems, both verbal and notational.

7-- Intellectual Responsibility Block: contains names of persons, corporate bodies, families and trademark having some kind of intellectual responsibility for the creation of the item described.

8-- International Use Block: contains internationally agreed fields, e.g., originating source, ISSN centre, and general cataloguer's note.

9-- National Use Block: reserved for national use by agencies where UNIMARC is the basis of the domestic format.

Of interest to the authorities format are the heading fields, which include the $3 Authority Record Number subfield defined as a link to the authority record. The necessity to functionally structure and link segments of bibliographic information depending on users requirements[50] was already present in theoretical thinking,[51] as well as in the design of MARC authority formats for library systems with linked bibliographic and authority files in the 1970s.[52] The creators of both UNIMARC formats must have drawn from those considerations and experiences, as well as from those in the design of USMARC, UKMARC, INTERMARC and MAB (Maschinelles Austauschformat für Bibliotheken) formats for other of its features.

The heading fields for which the link to the authority record is defined are: 500 Uniform Title, 7-- intellectual responsibility fields, 60- fields for subject analysis and 620 for recording Place Access. As a UNIMARC bibliographic record is designed to carry a link to another entry, e.g., name and title of other edition of a work described in the main body of a record, embedded fields for uniform title and author's name (primary responsibility) also carry a link to the authority record. The same tagging is used, i.e., 500 and 700 fields. The heading fields can carry either authority record number only, and/or data fields, depending on the implementation of the format in a library system and the design of maintenance of the authority control over the catalogue (e.g., global change). However, the option chosen should be described in the documentation to accompany the exchange of records.

At this point a question can be raised as to which records? Of course, bibliographic, but those records have pointers to another type of record–authority records, which should accompany them, as they carry supplementary information without which bibliographic records are incomplete. UNIMARC does not say anything on that issue: both formats treat respective records as separate entities encapsulated into the ISO 2709 exchange format. However, how is it possible to transport the functionally designed modular structure of the inter-linked bibliographic and authority records? Several scenarios can be described, as in fact the first two of them in various combinations have been in practice for decades. (1) A "traditional" one in which separate packages of bibliographic records and authority records are exchanged or broadcast. (2) A "working" scenario in which one by one, a separately identified record, either authority or bibliographic, is dragged or downloaded from the target into the source catalogue. And (3) a "composite" scenario in which a particular bibliographic record with its corresponding authority records are dragged or downloaded from the target into the source catalogue. (UNI)MARC, as defined in ISO 2709 format, does not have a clue for the third option. Even ISO 23950 (or Z39.50) as specified in the Bath Profile separately defines functional requirements for bibliographic and authority record search and retrieval between library catalogues,[53] i.e., transmission of bibliographic and authority records between and among open systems. A solution could be sought in the direction of development into which both MARC 21[54] and UNIMARC[55] are heading. This direction is the replacement of their ISO 2709 physical layer for the XML platform, and the subsequent structuring of MARC-XML bibliographic and authority records within the RDF (Resource Description Framework) record. The complexity, effectiveness and efficiency of creating such a record, as well as real life needs for its implementation and use could be a decisive drive towards exploring this territory.

UNIMARC FORMAT FOR AUTHORITIES, 2ND EDITION

The Maintenance of the Format and Sources for Its Revision

The 2nd edition of the UNIMARC authorities format, as already mentioned, is the first revision since it was published in 1991. The responsibility for the development and maintenance of this format, as of other formats in the UNIMARC family, rests with the Permanent UNIMARC Committee (PUC) set up in 1991 under the umbrella of the IFLA UBCIM Programme (which later changed its name to IFLA UBCIM Core Activity) following the recommendation of the Seminar on Bibliographic Records held during the IFLA General Conference in Stockholm, 1990.[56] Since March 2003, the PUC works within the newly organised IFLA programme–UNIMARC Programme hosted by the National Library of Portugal, one of the successors of the UBCIM Core Activity.[57] Additions and changes to the UNIMARC formats[58] are made only through the PUC during its annual meetings (regular meeting in March and Ad

Hoc meeting during IFLA General Conference). Proposals are usually submitted by UNIMARC users or creators of UNIMARC records, and also by PUC members who monitor the developments in IFLA's sections, particularly in the Division on Bibliographic Control, MARBI, ISO TC46, ISBN, ISSN, IAML, ICA/CDS, international projects, and national UNIMARC users groups,[59] either through direct participation or indirectly through members of their respective institutions. UNIMARC formats and documentation, annual reports of the meetings, as well as any other developments and description of formats' implementation and use are announced and/or published in the IFLA journal *International Cataloguing and Bibliographic Control* and on the IFLANET.

The decision to publish the format's 2nd edition was made by the PUC at its meeting in Zagreb in 1997. The reasons for it were multiple: IFLA's general policy about the regular revisions of its standards, intensive activities within IFLA in the evaluation and possible evolution of the UBC programme concerning authorities with the aim to promote efficient exchange and reuse of authority data to better meet users' requirements, implementation of UNIMARC in national systems and consequent user requirements, additions to UNIMARC bibliographic format and the need for format consistency, results of international projects and co-operative work on maintaining international databases, and developments in telecommunications and information technologies which not only influenced librarians' reassessment of the bibliographic universe but also opened the possibilities for realisation of setup tasks that could not have been fulfilled by the preceding technology. The meeting also decided that the layout of the revised edition would be the same as in the *UNIMARC Manual: Bibliographic Format*, which means that a detailed description of the use of fields, subfields and codes would be given. Therefore, the title of the 2nd revised and enlarged edition is *UNIMARC Manual: Authorities Format*.

During the revision process, the PUC worked together with the Working Group on the Revision of GARE, and closely monitored for possible impact on the format design the work by the IFLA Working Group on Form and Structure of Corporate Headings that was established in Istanbul, 1995.[60] No requirement was received from the latter. The IFLA Standing Committee of the Section on Classification and Indexing was approached for their comments on possible additions, especially in the light of the GSARE and newly published *Principles Underlying Subject Heading Languages*.[61] A general feeling of the members reported to the PUC was that detailed changes in relationship codes in subfield $5 Tracing Control, suggested by a UNIMARC user, would create unnecessary complications and were therefore rejected. The Committee did not report on any requirements.

It is important to briefly mention one project and one organisation that had particularly proactive influence on the development and the revision of the format: the European Commission (EC) project AUTHOR and the Consortium of European Research Libraries (CERL). The Project AUTHOR,[62] funded through the European Commission's COBRA Programme (Coordinated Bibliographic Record Actions) as a partnership between the national libraries of UK, France, Belgium, Portugal and Spain, had the objective of demonstrating the utility of UNIMARC/Authorities as a medium of communication of authority data that originated in different national environments and exploring means of their sharing. The project's recommendations on the improvement of the format partly coincided with the recommendations that the PUC received from the MLAR Working Group, as to the need to code nationality, category of the entity, and richer biographical information either in notes or coded data fields. Other proposals were:

- adaptation of the content in respect to the definition of a minimum content of the record including: biographic dates, nationality information, titles of masterpieces, language of fields, and the definition and choice of using a code of good practice in order to guarantee that the minimum content will be available in every case;
- additional information on the type of authors recorded in each authority file: authors of printed books, of series, of audio-visual materials, of electronic resources, etc.
- code for language used by the author different from the language used for variant headings and from language of cataloguing;
- develop fixed length coded fields for the possibility of coding characteristics of the entities that are not language dependent;
- develop in more detail the information note block;
- enable recording parallel language headings in one authority (multilingual) record;
- add to the authorities format the standard subfielding technique in 7-- Linking Heading Block in order to conform to the same, newly adopted technique in the bibliographic format in 4-- Linking Entry Block;
- correct incompatibilities between bibliographic and authorities formats for author/title fields.[63]

Some of the recommendations were built into the new edition, but some were left for further consideration. The requirements for additions to the format are indicative of the type of authority data European national libraries either record in their national authorities formats or consider indispensable for recording of national authors. New fields according to the recommendations are 101 Language and 102 Nationality of the entity, 120 Coded Data Field: Personal Name to record gender of the entity and the distinction between differentiated and undifferentiated personal name, 340 Biography and Activity Note, 356 Geographical Note, while standard subfielding techniques are included in name/title and name/collective title fields. The recording of parallel language headings in one multilingual record is allowed in the format only if such a heading is considered a variant heading, i.e., as a see reference tracing, which concept has been confirmed by the new edition.

The Consortium of European Research Libraries (CERL) is the organisation which has developed and is maintaining a multinational database of the Hand Press Book (HPB) in Europe and which is hosted by the RLG.[64] For the moment, it comprises eighteen files (1.2 million records) from different national, research and special libraries, showing different cataloguing traditions and practices in recording rare books. CERL's communication format is UNIMARC, although it also accepts MARC21 and UKMARC formats, and therefore, was and still is one of the major sources for proposals for additions to the format.[65] Its proposals for additions to the UNIMARC bibliographic format had indirect impact on the authorities format. The 2nd edition includes new fields that were suggested by its members' rare book librarians: 260 Place Access and 280 Form, Genre or Physical Characteristics, as well as the coded data field for recording co-ordinates for territorial or geographic name, 123 Coded Data Field–Territorial or Geographic Name. Authority control over the headings in such a database is considered one of the priorities set up for the Consortium's Advisory Task Group. The ATG is developing a series of thesaurus files that would each comprise place, printers, authors, and precedents names. A "thesaurus," rather than "authority" file, is being developed because the ATG reasoned that only in the environment that would provide an equal status to authorised and variant forms, the national differences in authorised forms of names of historical places, persons and bodies could be preserved.[66] In such a context, the ATG has also been urging the development of the ISADN. The ATG liaises with the PUC, and it is expected that it will continue to take an active part in the future developments of the authorities format by reporting on its work and findings in the development of the CERL thesauri.

Format's Design and Basic Features

As an interdependent format, UNIMARC/Authorities adheres to the same standards as UNIMARC format for bibliographic records on the three levels of the machine-readable record format. These are: (1) the structure of the record, which is the physical representation and layout of the information standardised by ISO 2709, (2) the content designators for the record, which identify and supply information about data elements and which correspond to UNIMARC bibliographic format tagging, and (3) the data content of the record which is subject to standardisation by national cataloguing agencies.

Functional Blocks are the following:

0-- Identification Block: contains numbers that identify the record or the authority.

1-- Coded Information Block: contains fixed length data elements describing various aspects of the record or data.

2-- Heading Block: contains the authority, reference, or general explanatory heading for which the record has been created.

3-- Information Note Block: contains notes, intended for public display.

4-- See Reference Tracing Block: contains variant headings from which a reference is to be made to see the heading for the record.

5-- See Also Reference Tracing Block: contains related uniform headings from which a reference is to be made to see also the heading of the record.

6-- Classification Number Block: contains classification numbers that are related to the heading of the record.

7-- Linking Heading Block: contains a form of the record heading (2--) in another language or script and links to another record in which that form is the 2-- headings.

8-- Source Information Block: contains the source of the record, and cataloguer's notes about the data not intended for public display.

9-- National Use Block: contains data local to the originator of the record. Field tags will not be defined in UNIMARC/Authorities for intersystem exchange.

The correspondence between UNIMARC format for authority records and UNIMARC format for bibliographic records at the field level is described in Table 1, while correspondence at the subfield level is described in Table 2. The correspondence of UNIMARC and GARE is described in Table 3.

The correspondence between the two formats can be illustrated by the personal name heading. The UNIMARC authorities 200 Heading–Personal Name field corresponds to 70- primary, alternative and secondary intellectual responsibility fields, 70- fields embedded in 4-- Linking Entry Block fields, 600 Personal Name Used as Subject field and 70- fields embedded in 604 Name/Title Used as Subject field in UNIMARC bibliographic format. In such a way, the consistency of the uniform form of a heading is being secured.

The role of the control subfields in the format is twofold. The already mentioned subfield $2 Subject System Code is excluded from this categorisation.

TABLE 1. Correspondence Between UNIMARC/Authorities and UNIMARC/Bibliographic Formats

UNIMARC/Authorities Heading Fields	Heading Usage in UNIMARC Bibliographic Fields
200 Personal name	700, 701, 702 4-- with embedded 700, 701, 702 600 604 with embedded 700, 701, 702
210 Corporate or meeting name	710, 711, 712 4-- with embedded 710, 711, 712 601 604 with embedded 710, 711, 712
215 Territorial or geographic name	710, 711, 712 4-- with embedded 710, 711, 712 601, 607 604 with embedded 710, 711, 712
216 Trademark	716 Trademark
220 Family name	720, 721, 722 4-- with embedded 720, 721, 722 602 604 with embedded 720, 721, 722
230 Uniform Title	500 4-- with embedded 500 605
240 Name and title (embedded 200, 210, 215, or 220 and 230)	4-- with embedded 7-- and 500 7-- 604 with embedded 7-- and 500 500
245 Name and collective title (embedded 200, 210, 215, or 220 and 230)	4-- with embedded 7-- and 501 604 with embedded 7-- and 501 7-- 501
250 Topical subject	606
260 Place access	620
280 Form, genre or physical characteristics	608

The subfields control relationships between different forms of headings and relationships between different language and script of headings.

Control subfields are the following:[67]

$0   Instruction phase
$2   Subject System Code
$3   Authority Entry Record Number
$5   Tracing Control
$6   Interfield Linking Data
$7   Script of Cataloguing and Script of the base of the heading
$8   Language of cataloguing and language of the base heading

TABLE 2. Example of the Correspondence at the Subfield Level

UNIMARC/Bibliographic

700   PERSONAL NAME – PRIMARY
        INTELLECTUAL
RESPONSIBILITY

First indicator: #
Second indicator : 0
                                    1

$a Entry Element
$b Part of Name Other than
      Entry Element
$c Additions to Names Other
      than Dates
$d Roman Numerals
$f Dates
$g Expansion of Initials
      of Forename
$3 Authority Record Number
$4 Relator Code

UNIMARC/Authorities

200 HEADING– PERSONAL NAME

First indicator: #
Second indicator : 0
                                    1

$a Entry Element
$b Part of Name Other than
      Entry Element
$c Additions to Names Other
      than Dates
$d Roman Numerals
$f Dates
$g Expansion of Initials
      of Forename
$4 Relator Code
$j Form subdivision
$x Topical Subdivision
$y Geographical Subdivision
$z Chronological Subdivision

Relationships Between Different Forms of Headings

The methods used to express relationships between different forms of headings in the display of reference and authority entries are the following:

1. The tagging of tracing fields: tracings are divided into 4-- fields for see
   reference tracings and 5-- fields for see also reference tracings.
2. The use of standard relationship code in the tracing control subfield $5,
   Tracing Control: the subfield is used to express standard relationships
   that the 4-- and 5-- tracings may have with the 2-- record heading. Since
   the relationship is coded, the specific relationship may be displayed in
   the language choice of the recipient in addition to, not in lieu of, the
   symbols >, >> and <, << . There are two data elements defined for the
   subfield: relationship code and reference suppression code. The relationship code values are the following:

$5 Tracing Control

a = earlier heading	f = real name	j = married name
b = later heading	g = broader term	k = name before marriage
d = acronym	h = narrower term	l = shared pseudonym
e = pseudonym	i = name in religion	m = secular name
		z = other

Reference suppression code indicates that a reference entry should not be automatically generated from a heading in a tracing because a 305, Textual See Also Reference Note exists in the authority record for the heading or a separate reference record for the heading exists with the 310, Textual See Reference Note. In both cases, only the reference note should be displayed.

3. The use of instruction in textual form in the tracing control subfield $0, Instruction Phrase: the control subfield is used when the relationship between the heading and the tracing cannot be expressed by one of the standard relationship codes in $5, but the relationship is still a one-to-one relationship. The instruction in the control subfield is language dependent; so the receiving agency that may have no use for it can display the relationship using symbols derived from the 4-- and 5-- tracing fields value. Since the control subfield can occur in addition to the $5, its coded value can be displayed in such a case also.

4. The use of information notes: 3-- information notes[68] are used when a relationship between the reference and the referred to heading is several-to-one or has other complexities that make it desirable to transmit the reference as an information note in addition to tracings. The receiving agency that may have no use for information notes because of the language differences can display the relationship using symbols derived from the 4-- and 5-- tracing fields value.

Relationships Between Different Language and Script of Headings

A general principle for the construction of the record in UNIMARC authorities is that one language form of one heading is being described and that heading is appropriate for a catalogue in the language designated by the 100, General Processing Data field. The reference tracings, instruction phrases and information notes constitute the reference structure for that heading in that catalogue.

The subfields used in coding those types of relationships are $3 Authority Entry Record Number, $6 Interfield Linking Data, $7 Script of Cataloguing and Script of the Base Heading, and $8 Language of Cataloguing and Language of the Base Heading. Subfield $6 is used to link fields in the record for processing purposes. One of the two linking explanation codes used in the field specifies that the reason for the interfield linkage is alternate script. (The value of the other code is "Other.") The subfield can be used in 3-- information note and 4-- and 5-- tracing fields.

TABLE 3. Correspondence of UNIMARC/Authorities and GARE

UNIMARC/Authorities	Areas Specified in GARE
Content Record	
Present in *all* types of records:	
0-- Identification Block	ISADN area (where applicable)
1-- Information Block	
8-- Source Information Block	Cataloguer's note area, Source area
Authority entry record: (Type of record = x)	
2-- Heading block (uniform heading)	Authority heading area
300 Information note	Information note area
305 Textual see also reference note	Information note area
4-- See reference tracing block	See reference tracing area
5-- See also reference tracing block	See also reference tracing area
7-- Linking heading block	Authority heading area
Reference entry record: (Type of record = y)	
2-- Heading block (variant heading)	Reference heading area
300 Information note	Information note area
310 Textual see reference note	Uniform heading area
7-- Linking heading block	Reference heading area
General explanatory entry record: (Type of record = z)	
2-- Heading block (explanatory heading)	Explanatory heading area
320 General explanatory reference note	Information note area
7-- Linking heading block	Explanatory heading area

If a cataloguing agency needs to construct a parallel catalogue(s) based on another language(s), parallel language forms of the 2-- headings and the phrases, notes and tracings appropriate to the parallel headings are recorded in a separate authority entry record(s). If these parallel language headings are in a different script, in addition to being in a different language, they are still encoded following the rules for parallel data. However, if the headings are in a different script but in the *same* language as their corresponding fields then the rules for alternative script, described below, are followed. Headings in separate authority entry records may be linked through 7-- linking fields and the use of $3, Authority Entry Record Number subfield. Subfields $7 and $8 are used to code script and language respectively.

If a cataloguing agency treats parallel forms of the 2-- heading as simple variants or references, 4-- or 5-- reference tracings are used with or without specifying language. The reference structures for parallel forms are *not* needed and are not included in the record.

The script of cataloguing, i.e., heading, notes, tracings, etc., is identified in the 100 field of the record. If an agency needs to record heading and reference structure in more than one script form because of transliteration and alternative script orthographies used for a language, alternative script representations may be co-resident in an authority record or may reside in separate linked records. However, if the alternative script representations differ in language from their corresponding headings, then the rules for parallel data apply.

The second edition of UNIMARC authorities format, following the recommendation of the MLAR Working Group, makes distinction between the language and script of cataloguing and the language and script of the base heading. The language/script of cataloguing is the language/script defined in the 100 field and defined as being used for qualifiers in the headings (2--), see reference tracings (4--), see also reference tracings (5--), linking headings (7--), and for notes (3--) and instruction phrases ($0). The base heading is defined as "the part of the heading that identifies the entity excluding any qualifying data." For example: in the heading 200#0$aIohannes Paulus$dII$cpapa, the base heading is *Iohannes Paulus*, the form of the name constructed according to the cataloguing rules defined in 152$a which stipulate that the original, Latin language form is used for the heading. The language of cataloguing being Croatian, the qualifier is expressed in Croatian, i.e., $c*papa*. Thus, the appropriate coding for the language of cataloguing (*scr*) and the language of the base heading (*lat*) in this field would be: 200#0$8scrlat$aIohannes PaulusdIIcpapa. The same technique can be used for the script of cataloguing and the base heading, as well as for various combinations of languages and scripts. To meet the requirements of recording different scripts, the second edition extends the system of codes for the script, from one coded data element, which identifies the script of the data in the field in the first edition to six data elements. These are the script of cataloguing, direction of the script of cataloguing, transliteration scheme for the script of cataloguing, and the same system of codes for the script of the base heading.

The use of the described coding technique, however, should be monitored. If we look at the distinction between the language/script of cataloguing and the language/script of the base of the heading, what can be defined as a qualifier in different types of headings? In a personal name heading, it can be $c, Additions to Name Other than Dates; however, $d, Roman Numerals poses a problem. The $d subfield definition states that "if an epithet (or a further forename) is associated with the numeration, this too should be included." Can it then be defined as a qualifier in addition to $c which itself includes "titles, epithets or indication of office," apart from "any additions to names"? Field 260, Heading–Place Access contains subfields for country, state, county and city as access points. What is the basc heading and what is a qualifier in this case? The example to 260 field 260##$aItalia$dVenezia would be 260##$aItalija$dVcnczia in which Croatian and Italian language forms would bc used according to cataloguing rules that are different from those used in the first example and that are intended for a different language public. Obviously, the PUC should analyze these issues in greater detail.

For structural and implementation issues in the use of USMARC, i.e., MARC 21 and UNIMARC for multiple languages and scripts in authority control, one should turn to Joan M. Aliprand's articles on *Linkage in USMARC Bibliographic Records*[69] and *Linking of Alternate Graphic Representation in USMARC Authority Records*,[70] and to her article co-authored with Bella Hass Weinberg *Closing the Circle: Automated Authority Control and the Multiscript YIVO Catalog*,[71] the most thorough analysis of UNIMARC authorities format on this issue. The basic argument in Weinberg and Aliprand's article is that "because names may differ across languages *even when the script used for writing the name is the same*, authority files should be language-based, not script-based." They pose the question: "Where multiple sources of authority are used to create preferred forms in several languages (and possibly scripts), why can't all the preferred headings for one entity be contained in a single composite record?" IFLA has decided against a single record basing the decision on the argument that one must choose a preferred form of name for each language, while ALA's MARBI committee has not yet made a decision. However, Weinberg and Aliprand find that one impediment to the single-record approach is that only one source of authority for a name is allowed in a UNIMARC as well as MARC 21 authority record. This limitation is enforced by non-repeatable data elements.

Another argument, they infer, "against a single composite record with multiple syndetic structures is that its structural complexity makes it harder to process and update. One source of complexity is the one-to-many and many-to-one data relationships that can occur in authority records, particularly in a multiscript environment." Therefore "the complex relationships that occur when a name is represented in different script environments is an argument *against* a single composite authority record, and *for* the IFLA model of complementary records in linked language-based authority files."[72]

In identifying multiscript issues, the authors found that the limitation of the UNIMARC authorities format is in permitting only one alternative script per field, when a heading may contain more than one script. Their comment, written before the second edition was published, should be reviewed in the context of the newly defined coding technique for the script of cataloguing and the base heading, under the condition that UNIMARC defines what data elements make a "qualification" for a particular type of heading.[73] Another call for improvement lies in the authors' objection that the traditional and simplified written forms cannot be indicated in UNIMARC, because it specifies a single script code for Chinese.[74]

Weinberg and Aliprand's basic requirements for multilingual authority control are:

1. The ability to include diacritics and non-Roman scripts in authority records. Inability to do so leads to loss of differentiation among headings as a result of romanization.
2. A common data model for authority records, to facilitate retrieval and data exchange. We believe that the IFLA model of multiple authority records for a single entity is correct.
3. The capability to link separate authority records, to facilitate comprehensive retrieval of the works of a single author, whatever the language and scripts of publication.[75]

CONCLUSION

UNIMARC authorities format is based on international standards developed and maintained by IFLA bodies within the framework of Universal Bibliographic Control, being itself such a standard. Its development has depended on but will have to continue to depend on the requirements put forward by its users from multinational and multilingual environments, its ability to "talk" to other MARC authorities formats, particularly MARC 21,[76] the possibilities of exchange or sharing of authority records enabled by the developments in information technology, and, especially, on the development of national cataloguing rules which, in fulfilling the objectives of the catalogue, have a certain user in view.

NOTES

1. *UNIMARC/Authorities: Universal Format for Authorities* / recommended by the IFLA Steering Group on a UNIMARC Format for Authorities; approved by the Standing Committees of the IFLA Section on Cataloguing and Information Technology. München, [etc]: K. G. Saur, 1991.

2. *UNIMARC Manual: Authorities Format.* 2nd revised and enlarged ed. München: K. G. Saur, 2001.

3. First IFLA Meeting of Experts on an International Cataloguing Code, July 28-30, 2003, Frankfurt am Main, Germany. At: http://www.ddb.de/news/ifla_conf_index.htm.

4. Actes du Conseil de la FIAB 20me Session, Zagreb, 27 septembre-1er octobre 1954. La Haye: Martinus Nijhoff, 1955. pp. 65-66.

5. International Conference on Cataloguing Principles, Paris, 9th-18th October, 1961. *Report*. London: Clive Bingley, 1969.

6. International Meeting of Cataloguing Experts, Copenhagen, 1969. *Report*. // IFLA Annual 1969.

7. *Report of the International Meeting of Cataloguing Experts*, Copenhagen, 1969. In: *Libri* 20(1970), 110.

8. *Statement of Principles Adopted at the International Conference on Cataloguing Principles*, Paris, October, 1961. Annotated ed. with commentary and examples by Eva Verona assisted by Franz Georg Kaltwasser, P. R. Lewis, Roger Pierrot. London: IFLA Committee on Cataloguing, 1971. For Verona's elaboration of the problem of the definition of the author see p. 1.

9. Anderson, Dorothy. *Universal Bibliographic Control: A Long Term Policy, A Plan for Action*. Pullach, München: K. G. Saur, 1974.

10. Ibid., p. 47.

11. Anderson, Dorothy. "IFLA's Programme of Universal Bibliographic Control: Origins and Early Years." In: *International Cataloguing and Bibliographic Control* 29(2000) 2, 23-26. p. 23.

12. International Conference on National Bibliographies, Paris, 1977: Final Report. Paris: UNESCO, 1978.

13. ICNBS, Copenhagen, 25-27 November, 1998: *Proceedings of the International Conference on National Bibliographic Services* / IFLA. Copenhagen: The Royal Library, 2001. pp. 118-119. The recommendations are available at: http://www.ifla.org/VI/3/icnbs/fina.htm.

14. These are: *Names of Persons: National Usages for Entry in Catalogues, Form and Structure of Corporate Headings, Corporate Headings: Their Use in Library Catalogues and National Bibliographies, Anonymous Classics: A List of Uniform Headings for European Literatures, List of Uniform Titles for Liturgical Works of the Latin Rites of the Catholic Church, Names of States: An Authority List of Language Forms for Catalogue Entries*, and *List of Uniform Headings for Higher Legislative and Ministerial Bodies in European Countries*.

15. Delsey, Tom. IFLA Working Group on an International Authority System: A Progress Report. In: *International Cataloguing* 9(1980)1, 10-12. P. 10. Besides describing setting up the scene and tasks put forward for the Working Group, the article delineates the framework for the "definition of the functions, bibliographic activities, and medium of exchange that an international authority system would support." The issue is particularly interesting today, twenty and some years later, when the possibilities

of available technological infrastructure, the recognition of complexities of authority record content in multinational and multilingual environment, and high motivation to crack the problem driven by economics and the need to efficiently serve users are converging to the critical point which could make its realisation possible.

16. *Guidelines for Authority and Reference Entries* / recommended by the Working Group on an International Authority System; approved by the Standing Committees of the IFLA Section on Cataloguing and the IFLA Section on Information Technology. London: IFLA International Programme for UBC, 1984.

17. Ibid., pp. ix-x.

18. Ibid., p. 1.

19. Delsey, Tom. "Authority Control in an International Context." In: *Cataloguing & Classification Quarterly* 9(1989)3, 21.

20. Ibid., pp. 22-23.

21. *Guidelines*. Ibid., p. ix.

22. The issue is still unresolved. See Ingrid Parent's presentation of the problem in "Key title/Uniform title as benchmark to determine major changes" in: Parent, Ingrid. "From ISBD(S) to ISBD(CR): A Voyage of Discovery and Alignment" In: *The Serials Librarian* 43(2003)4.

23. *Guidelines for Subject Authority and Reference Entries* / Working Group on "Guidelines for Subject Authority and Reference Entries" of the Section on Classification and Indexing of the IFLA Division of Bibliographic Control. München [etc.]: K. G. Saur, 1993.

24. Delsey, Tom. Authority Control in an International Context. Ibid., p. 23.

25. *UNIMARC/Authorities*. Ibid., p. 8.

26. Beaudiquez, Marcelle and Françoise Bourdon. *Management and Use of Name Authority Files (Personal Names, Corporate Bodies and Uniform Titles): Evaluation and Prospects*. München [etc.]: K. G. Saur, 1991.

27. Ibid., p. 28.

28. Bourdon, Françoise. *International Cooperation in the Field of Authority Data: An Analytical Study with Recommendations*. München [etc.]: K. G. Saur, 1991.

29. For detailed analysis of the problem further elaborated by the author, see: Bourdon, Françoise. Name Authority Control in an International Context and the Role of the National Bibliographic Agency. In: *International Cataloguing and Bibliographic Control* 23(1994)4, 71-77.

30. *Seminar on Bibliographic Records: Proceedings of the Seminar Held in Stockholm, 15-16 August 1990* / ed. Ross Bourne. München: K. G.: Saur, 1992.

31. *UNIMARC/CCF: Proceedings of the Workshop held in Florence, 5-7 June 1991* / IFLA/Unesco; edited by Marie-France Plassard and Diana McLean Brooking. München: K. G. Saur, 1993.

32. See the Report by Ross Bourne and a selection of papers in: *International Cataloguing and Bibliographic Control* 23(1994)4.

33. See Summary Report by Alan Danskin. In: *International Cataloguing and Bibliographic Control* 25(1996)2, 27-28, and a selection of papers in: *International Cataloguing and Bibliographic Control* 25(1996)3 and 4.

34. *Mandatory Data Elements for Internationally Shared Resource Authority Records: Report of the IFLA UBCIM Working Group on Minimal Level Authority Records and the ISADN*. 1998. At: http://www.ifla.org/VI/3/p1966-2/mlar.htm.

35. Ibid., pp. 1-2.

36. The analysed formats were AAAFMARC (Anglo-American Authority File MARC), BLMARC, Belgian KBR MARC, CANMARC, Croatian UNIMARC, FINMARC, INTERMARC, MAB and USMARC.

37. *Guidelines for Authority Records and References*. 2nd ed. revised by the IFLA Working Group on GARE Revision. München: K. G. Saur, 2001.

38. In its present edition, UNIMARC bibliographic format defines subfield $2 as Systems Code for recording subject thesauri and classification schemes in appropriate subject heading fields, but also for recording cataloguing rules and formats codes in 801 Originating Source and 886 Data not Converted from Source Format fields.

39. Aliprand, Joan M. Linking of Alternate Graphic Representation in USMARC Authority Records. In: *Cataloguing & Classification Quarterly* 18(1993)1, 27-62. p. 29.

40. Aliprand, Joan M. Linkage in USMARC Bibliographic Records. In: *Cataloguing & Classification Quarterly* 16(1993)1, 5-37.

41. This issue is particularly sensitive from the historical perspective: if a particular form of a name warranted by the then valid cataloging rules is linked to bibliographic records, can one certify that if one changes the name according to the new rule the link would be authentic for the context? The change of a personal name, under the same rules, poses a similar *historical* probem. It is interesting that with the change of corporate body name there is no conflict in this latter respect. On the contrary: the rule is to collocate all works under the paricular form of the corporate body name that is considered to be the same *identity*.

42. *Functional Requirements for Bibliographic Records: Final Report* / IFLA Study Group on the Functional Requirements for Bibliographic Records; Approved by the Standing Committee of the IFLA Section on Cataloguing. München: K. G. Saur, 1998. Available at: http://www.ifla.org/VII/s13/frbr/frbr.pdf p. 5.

43. For detailed listing of projects see: Patton, Glenn. FRANAR: A Conceptual Model for Authority Data (International Conference Authority Control: Definition and International Experiences, Florence, Italy, February 10-12, 2003. At: http://www.unifi.it/biblioteche/ac/en/home.htm) At: http://www.unifi.it/universita/biblioteche/ac/relazioni/patton_eng.pdf also published in this volume.

44. The WG on MLAR and the ISADN had already established close working relations with ICA, Committee on Descriptive Standards which reviewed and commented upon its report from the aspect of their work on the International Standard Archival Authority Record for Corporate Bodies, Persons, and Families: ISAAR(CPF). See: *The Internal Standard Archival Authority Record for Corporate Bodies, Persons and Families (ICA) and the Essential Data Elements for Internationally Shared Resources Authority Records (IFLA): A Comparison and Report* / prepared by Dagmar Parer (with Adrian Cunningham) and Michael Fox of The International Council on Archives Committee on Descriptive Standards (ICA/CDS). Released and distributed electronically to the members of the ICA/CDS and the IFLA Working Group on Minimal Level Authority Records and the ISADN, 30 July 1998.

45. See the <indecs> project at: http://www.indecs.org/project.htm. Its follow up is the INTERPARTY project at: http://www.interparty.org: InterParty is an EC-funded project (2001-2003) to design and specify a network to support interoperability of party identification (both natural and corporate names) across different domains. It developed the blueprint of a network that will provide participating agencies with a means of online, on-demand, checking of identities–a virtual Directory of Parties–and will enable party identifiers to be mapped automatically between domains. The Euro-

pean partners were EDItEUR, BL, The Royal Swedish Library, IFLA, BookData, KOPIOSTO, and U.S. partners were LC, OCLC, IDF and CNRI.

46. Bourdon, Françoise. Functional Requirements and Numbering of Authority Records (FRANAR): To What Extent Can Authority Control be Supported by Technical Means? In: *International Cataloguing and Bibliographic Control* 3(2002)1, 6-9. For detailed description of the work in progress see: Patton, Glenn. FRANAR: A Conceptual Model for Authority Data. Ibid.

47. *UNIMARC Handbook* / compiled and edited by Alan Hopkinson; with the assistance of Sally H. McCallum and Stephen P. Davis. London: IFLA International Office for UBC, 1983.

48. *UNIMARC Manual: Bibliographic Format* / compiled and edited by Brian P. Holt; with the assistance of Sally H. McCallum and A. B. Long. London: IFLA Universal Bibliographic Control and International MARC Programme, British Library Bibliographic Services, 1987.

49. *UNIMARC Manual: Bibliographic Format* / IFLA; IFLA UBCIM. 2nd ed. München [etc.]: K. G. Saur, 1994.

50. See, for example, Willer, Mirna. Formats and Cataloguing Rules: Developments for Cataloguing Electronic Resources. In: *Program* 33(1999)1, 41-55. pp. 47-49.

51. See, for example, Malinconico, S. Michael. The Library Catalog in a Computerized Environment. In: M. J. Freedman, and S. M. Malinconico (eds). *The Nature and Future of the Catalog*. Phoenix, AZ: Oryx Press, 1979, pp. 46-68; and the discussion, pp. 68-71; Gorman, Michael. Cataloging and the New Technologies. In: M. J. Freedman, and S. M. Malinconico (eds). *The Nature and Future of the Catalog*. Phoenix, AZ: Oryx Press, 1979, pp. 127-136; and the discussion, pp. 137-152.

52. See, for example, Malinconico and Buchinski's description of linked bibliographic and authority files and their design of the authority format for the New York Public Library and the National Library of Canada's systems correspondingly. Malinconico, S. Michael. The Role of a Machine Based Authority File in an Automate Bibliographic System. In: *Automation in Libraries: Papers presented at the CACUL Workshop on Library Automation, Winnipeg, June 22-23, 1974*. Ottawa: Canadian Library Association, 1975. Cited from: Carpenter, Michael and Elaine Svenonius (eds). *Foundations in Cataloging: A Sourcebook*. Littleton, CO: Libraries Unlimited, 1985, pp. 211-233. Buchinski, Edwin J. Authorities: A Look into the Future. In: *What's in a Name? Control of Catalog Records Through Authority Files*. Vancouver; Toronto: University of Toronto Library Automation System, 1978, pp. 203-224. Buchinski, Edwin J.; William L. Newman and Mary Joan Dunn. The Automated Authority Subsystem at the National Library of Canada. In: *Journal of Library Automation* 9(1976) 4, 279-298.

53. The Bath Profile: An International Z39.50 Specification for Library Applications and Resource Discovery. Release 2.0. At: http://www.nlc-bnc.ca/bath/tp-bath2-e.htm.

54. MARC in XML. At: http://www.loc.gov/marc/marcxml.html.

55. BiblioML: An XML Application for Bibliographic Records, based on the UNIMARC Bibliographic Format, and for Authority Records, based on UNIMARC / Authorities // Une application XML pour des références bibliographiques, basée sur le Format Bibliographique Unimarc, et pour des notices d'autoritésn, basée sur Unimarc / Autorités. At: http://www.culture.fr/BiblioML. For general approach to the UNIMARC in XML see: Carvalho, Joaquim de. XML and Bibliographic Data: the TVS (Transport, Validation and Services) Model presented at the 68th IFLA Council and General Con-

ference, Glasgow, August 18-24, 2002 at: http://www.ifla.org/IV/ifla68/papers/075-095e.pdf. Carvalho, Joaquim Ramos de. UNIMARC Next Generation (NG)–A Technological Roadmap: Reflection Notes. In: *International Cataloguing and Bibliographic Control* 32(2003)1, 3.

56. The Permanent UNIMARC Committee (PUC) was formed in 1991, under the aegis of the IFLA UBCIM Programme and in accordance with resolution No. 5 issued at the end of the Seminar on Bibliographic Records held in Stockholm before the IFLA General Conference, August 1990. The main objective of the PUC is to control the UNIMARC format in accordance with the principles of Universal Bibliographic Control. At: http://www.ifla.org/VI/3/puc.htm.

57. IFLA Universal Bibliographic Control and International MARC (UBCIM) Core Activity. At: http://www.ifla.org/VI/3/ubcim.htm. For information on «Closure of IFLA/UBCIM Core Activity and Office» see: *International Cataloguing and Bibliographic Control* 32(2003)1, 2. E-mail of the UNIMARC Programme: unimarc@bn.pt.

58. Besides maintaining UNIMARC bibliographic and authorities formats, the PUC has developed *UNIMARC/Classification Format*, which final draft has passed world-wide review and is in the revision process, and *UNIMARC/Holdings Format*, which final draft is posted on IFLANET for world-wide review until October 2003.

59. For example, French, Russian and Portuguese UNIMARC user groups.

60. IFLA Section on Cataloguing Working Group on the Revision of FSCH. *Structures of Corporate Name Headings: Final Report, November 2000* / compiled and introduced by Ton Heijligers. IFLA UBCIM Programme, 2001. At: http://www.ifla.org/VII/s13/scatn/final2000.htm.

61. *Principles Underlying Subject Heading Languages (SHLs)* / edited by Maria Inês Lopes and Julianne Beall; Working Group on Principles Underlying Subject Heading Languages; approved by the Standing Committee of the IFLA Section on Classifiaction and Indexing. München: K. G. Saur, 1999.

62. AUTHOR Project: Transnational Application of National Name Authority Files. Libraries Project PROLIB/COBRA-AUTHOR 101174: Final report. Version 1, 11 June 1998. Author Sonia Zillhardt, Françoise Bourdon. http://www.bl.uk/gabriel/projects/pages/cobra/author.pdf. See also: Bourdon, Françoise et Sonia Zillhardt. AUTHOR: Vers une base européenne de notices d'autorité auteurs. In: *International Cataloguing and Bibliographic Control* 26(1997)2, 34-37.

63. Recommendations from the AUTHOR project were presented to the PUC in the form of proposals by the PUC standing member and representative of the Bibliothèque nationale de France. For the interim report on the revision of the format see: Willer, Mirna. UNIMARC/Authorities. In: *International Cataloguing and Bibliographic Control* 28(1999) 2, 48-50; for AUTHOR's proposals see p. 49.

64. Consortium of European Research Libraries. At: http://www.cerl.org.

65. Application of UNIMARC to Multinational Databases: Feasibility Study / Bayerische Staatsbibliothek, Consortium of European Research Libraries; [study] coordinated by Claudia Fabian; report compiled by Anthony G. Curwen and Chris Kirk. München: K. G. Saur, 1999.

66. CERL Thesaurus. At: http://www.cerl.org/Thesaurus/thesaurus.htm. See also: Fabian, Claudia. CERL Thesaurus File. (International Conference Authority Control: Definition and International Experiences, Florence, Italy, February 10-12, 2003), published in this volume.

67. Subfield $4 Relator Code is not described in the section on Control Subfields but is listed in personal name, corporate body name and family name fields (200, 210

and 220). This type of information is normally held in a bibliographic record heading as the relationship between the person, etc., named in the field and the bibliographic item described in the record, and as specific to that particular instance.

68. As already mentioned, the information notes are also used to provide historical information about the heading.

69. Aliprand, Joan M. Linkage in USMARC Bibliographic Records.

70. Aliprand, Joan M. Linking of Alternate Graphic Representation in USMARC Authority Records.

71. Weinberg, Bella Hass and Joan M. Aliprand. Closing the Circle: Automated Authority Control and the Multiscript YIVO Catalog. In: *International Cataloguing and Bibliographic Control* 31(2002)3, 44-48.

72. Ibid., pp. 45-46.

73. Weinberg and Aliprand's example for this issue gives two subject headings with personal name in Latin and Chinese scripts each, and the subject subdivisions in Latin script in both headings. How can this be treated in a UNIMARC authority record? If one wants to use the available method for coding different languages and scripts in one field, can the personal name be treated as the "base heading" and subject subdivisions as the «qualifier»? Certainly not.

74. See, for the application of UNIMARC/Authorities in the CJK languages: Record of Workshop on Authority Control among Chinese, Korean and Japanese Languages held at National Institute of Informatics (NII) in cooperation with National Diet Library, January 10-11, 2001. At: http://www.nii.ac.jp/publications/CJK-WS/.

75. Ibid., p. 47.

76. For the most systematic analysis of USMARC and UNIMARC authorities formats known so far to me, see Marc Truitt's article published in 1992. Truitt, Marc. USMARC to UNIMARC/Authorities: A Qualitative Evaluation of USMARC Data Elements. In: *Library Resources and Technical Services* 36(1992)1, 37-58.

AUTHORITY CONTROL
FOR NAMES AND WORKS

Authority Control of Creators and the Second Edition of ISAAR(CPF), International Standard Archival Authority Record for Corporate Bodies, Persons, and Families

Stefano Vitali

SUMMARY. The International Standard Archival Authority Record (Corporate Bodies, Persons, Families), ISAAR(CPF), is a standard developed by the International Council on Archives for the management of creators of archives in archival descriptive systems. Since 2001, ISAAR(CPF) has been undergoing a revision process which will conclude at the next International Congress of Archives in Vienna in August

Stefano Vitali is affiliated with Archivio di Stato, Firenze.

[Haworth co-indexing entry note]: "Authority Control of Creators and the Second Edition of ISAAR (CPF), International Standard Archival Authority Record for Corporate Bodies, Persons, and Families." Vitali, Stefano. Co-published simultaneously in *Cataloging & Classification Quarterly* (The Haworth Information Press, an imprint of The Haworth Press, Inc.) Vol. 38, No. 3/4, 2004, pp. 185-199; and: *Authority Control in Organizing and Accessing Information: Definition and International Experience* (ed: Arlene G. Taylor, and Barbara B. Tillett) The Haworth Information Press, an imprint of The Haworth Press, Inc., 2004, pp. 185-199. Single or multiple copies of this article are available for a fee from The Haworth Document Delivery Service [1-800-HAWORTH, 9:00 a.m. - 5:00 p.m. (EST). E-mail address: docdelivery@haworthpress.com].

Digital Object Identifier: 10.1300/J104v38n03_15

2004 when a second edition of the standard will be issued. The draft of the new edition of the standard, prepared by the Committee on Descriptive Standards, contains various changes in comparison with the first edition. The paper describes these changes, discussing their theoretical relevance, methodological implications, and practical consequences in archival descriptive systems. It focuses in particular on the new features of ISAAR(CPF) which enhance the possibility of establishing relationships between archival description systems and bibliographic catalogues, sharing or exchanging authority data on corporate bodies, persons, and families which are creators of archives or responsible for the creation or edition of books. *[Article copies available for a fee from The Haworth Document Delivery Service: 1-800-HAWORTH. E-mail address: <docdelivery@haworthpress.com> Website: <http://www.HaworthPress.com> © 2004 by The Haworth Press, Inc. All rights reserved.]*

KEYWORDS. Archival authority records, archival descriptive systems, authority data exchange, International Standard Archival Authority Record (Corporate Bodies, Persons, Families), ISAAR(CPF)

FOREWORD

The process of developing standards for archival description started, at the end of the eighties, on the initiative of the International Archives Council that appointed an *ad hoc* Commission for descriptive standards in 1989. During the first half of the nineties, the Commission produced the two final documents that are the basic cornerstones of the above process.

The first document, the International Standard of Archival Description (General) (ISAD[G]) showed the basic principles of archival description starting from the statement of its articulation according to a hierarchy of levels proceeding from the general (fonds) to the particular (item), thus reflecting the typical organization of fonds internally structured into series, sub-series, archival items and documentary items. ISAD(G) also identified the descriptive elements appropriate for archival description independent from medium or characteristics of documents, fonds structure and level of description.

ISAD(G) underwent a revision process between 1997 and 2000, and at the July 2000 Seville International Congress on archives, a second edition was issued that may presently be regarded as the authoritative version of the international standard for archival description. It is also the reference source for the implementation of the national standards that are being developed–with different schedules and features–within the various archival communities in many countries, often in relation to the accomplishment of shared projects of online description of archives.

The second document, or rather the second standard, produced by the *ad hoc* commission was the International Standard Archival Authority Record (Corporate Bodies, Persons, Families), the standard for the implementation of authority files for creators of archives. This standard is presently under a revision process that started in 2001, it will be completed on the occasion of the International Archives Conference to be held in Vienna, Austria in 2004, where its final second edition will be issued.

In these months, this process is at a crucial point because during the last meeting of the Commission for Descriptive Standards, held in Rio de Janeiro from 19th to 22nd November, 2002, a first draft of the new version of the standard was agreed upon. The archival community has been asked to voice comments and observations, previous to its final approval at the next meeting of the Commission. In this paper, I will try to relate the new features in the latest edition of ISAAR(CPF); before that, I will expound what ISAAR(CPF) has meant and means for the international archival community.

WHY ISAAR(CPF) IS IMPORTANT

I believe we are not far from the truth when we say that ISAAR(CPF) has been and is–probably even more than ISAD(G)–a real turning point in the theory and practice of archival description. Furthermore, this standard appears, in many ways, a tool by which we may overcome some theoretical doubts the archival profession has been involved with for a long time and on which there was much thinking and discussing in the last decades of the 20th century, particularly in some national settings, like Italy, the one I obviously know best and the one I will often refer to in this paper.

Creators of archives have always been at the core of archival description and have always been held as the basic access point to them, that is, the primary way to access an archive. The person who enters an archive–Francesco Bonaini, founder of the State Archives in Florence, declared 150 years ago–must look for institutions (i.e., creators), not for subjects, thus distancing himself from previous attempts at arranging and presenting archival documents on the basis of topical classification systems that, in view of collocating apparently similar documents regardless of their origin, cut their links with the context they originated from.

Today these statements sound obvious and granted. Archives are a by-product of a body's, institution's, person's, or family's activities and business and of the record keeping systems they implemented. This is an accepted datum, as well as the fact that these individual and corporate entities' nature, structure, historical, and biographical events are a basic key to understand and evaluate the documents preserved in the archives they created.

Therefore, describing archives means, first of all, providing information about their creators and about the historical context of their creation. By tradition, information about the context of creation ended up in the introductions to finding aids, such as inventories, representing, as a rule, their most relevant component part, particularly in the Italian tradition, deeply influenced by Giorgio Cencetti's lesson. Nevertheless, the creators' administrative and historical or biographical sketches have not always acquired an autonomous and well-defined dimension, being interspersed among information of a different nature in those introductions.

We find the same approach in the building of the first computerized systems for archival description in the eighties and nineties, when, as a general rule, information on the context of creation was considered and treated as an integral part of the description of single archival fonds. ISAD(G), too, is based on a similar model, although it does not rule out different modes of structuring information "on context."

These are choices–the ones about integrating the description of the creator within the description of archival documents–perfectly in line with the traditional methodological trends of archival description and its theoretical foundations. An approach adequately and effectively reflecting an idea of the relationship between fonds and creators as linear, mono-dimensional, and static (in some interpretations, like the ones prevailing in Italy in the middle decades of the last century, a little mechanical too), an idea that sees a creator as corresponding (or due to correspond) to one and only one archival fonds and conversely, each archival fonds comprising (or likely to comprise) the documents of one and only one creator. In the past, this type of approach had consequences of a practical nature, when, in the presence of archives that did not fit the model of direct match between fonds and creators, there was a meddling "with the papers" (or, more cleverly, "on the paper" as was the case with *Guida generale degli archivi di Stato italiani*), creating such a match where there was none or there was none left–without even asking why it had been lost or whether it had ever really existed. Thus, sometimes separate fonds created by the same creator were unified in a larger fonds, or fonds made up by documents created by various creators were separated.

More recently, archivists have become more aware of the inadequacy of the model of one-to-one relationship between archives and creators. This was due both to the remarkable complexity of the structure, functions, and record keeping systems of contemporary institutions (including the large firms) and to a better comprehension of the processes of transmission of archival materials in the past centuries. These processes, at a closer examination, proved to be less linear than the archival theory had stated and envisaged.

In the course of these processes, it often happened that archives were either divided or assembled, scattered or merged one into the other, according to modes and courses, often unpredictable, due to binding political-institutional, or bureaucratic-administrative reasons, or, sometimes, to cultural choices and influences.

A model of relationship between creators and archives like the traditional one seems inadequate to give an effective account of the ways in which both the vicissitudes of the transmission of archives and the interrelations of functions and structures in modern organizations affect the forms of accumulation of contemporary documents. In the language of one of the most widespread tools for creating representation models adopted by computer scientists, the entity-relationship model, such a situation does not imply at all a one-to-one relationship between fonds and creators, rather a many-to-many relationship. This means that, when we represent the relationships taking place between archives and their creators, we must build up a model envisaging the possibility that more than one creator can be linked to one archive and, conversely, that more than one archival fonds can be linked to one creator. The result is a model envisaging a multilinear, multidimensional, dynamic relation in a diachronic perspective.

Now, one of ISAAR(CPF)'s main merits–the one that most influenced not only the forms of organization of archival description, but the very ways of assessing archives–was the fact that it offered a model for separate and linked description of creators and archives. This model was apt to represent more effectively the complex and multidimensional relationship between fonds and creators that has been recognized with ever-greater awareness in the last decades.

Describing creators autonomously, linking them to the documentation they really produced, independent from the institution preserving it or its place in the hierarchy of levels by which the fonds is divided, actually means, on one side, virtually bringing back to unity the whole archive produced by a given creator; on the other side, respecting the modes of organization and transmission of documents which are always rich in meanings and have manifold implications. But, founding archival description on such a model implies recognition of the possibility–and the opportunity–of sharing the descriptions of entities among archival institutions (and not only such institutions), which might keep documents created by the same creator. This sharing might have international scope. We cannot rule it out. These are some of the main needs that ISAAR(CPF) was created to address.

As the introduction to the new edition of the standard states, recalling concepts already voiced in the first edition:

> There are many reasons why separate capture and maintenance (. . . .) of contextual information is valuable. The practice enables the linking of descriptions of provenance entities to descriptions of records from the same creator(s) that may be held by more than one repository and to descriptions of other resources such as library and museum materials that relate to the entity in question. (1.5)

> Where a number of repositories hold records from a given source they can more easily share or link contextual information about this source if it has been maintained in a standardized manner. Such standardization is of international concern when the sharing or linking of contextual information is likely to cross national boundaries. The multinational character of past and present record keeping creates the incentive for international standardization that will support the exchange of contextual information. For example, processes such as colonialization, immigration, and trade have contributed to the multinational character of record keeping. (1.6)

So, sharing of information–first of all information on creators of archives–is pivotal to the new way of describing archives, a sharing certainly materialized and spurred by the spread of informatics, and mostly by the networks. I believe we are not exaggerating if we stress the decisive role played by the advent of informatics in the repositioning of the objectives and, most of all, the tools of archival description. If the advent of the Internet has generally contributed to bringing to the fore the dimension of communication as a non-detachable component part of any intellectual activity, as regards precisely archival institutions, it has been a powerful picklock to break down the self-referential quality so common in archival institutions and in the cultural behaviour of single archivists, stressing vigorously the need to single out tools that make possible the capture and linking of archival descriptions at the local, national, and international level.

THE CONTINUITY ASPECTS BETWEEN THE FIRST AND THE SECOND EDITION OF ISAAR(CPF)

The theoretical principles guiding ISAAR(CPF) and the objectives, just outlined above, are aspects of deep continuity between the first and the second edition, in spite of the notable changes made in the standard in its new edition.

Then, ISAAR(CPF) is mainly a tool for the authority control of the names of creators of archives, and therefore a tool to standardize what in the new edition is defined as an "authorised form of name." ISAAR(CPF), as an international standard, does not define any specific rule for the creation of the "authorised form of names," it simply refers to the national rules, to the national and international conventions, and points to the general processes supervising its creation.[1] The single national agencies will only have to adopt "codes" of rules on the subject already in existence (first of all the rules on author cataloguing in libraries), or to create them *ex novo*, obviously with an eye to well-established experiences in close subject fields. As regards Italy, for example, the archivists have been following this second course for about one year, thanks to the activity of an *ad hoc* work-group formed on the initiative of the Italian Archival Administration and of the Italian National Archives Association, entrusted to work out rules for the establishment of authority records of creating entities within local, regional and national archival systems.

Clearly, as a tool to optimize access and search in archival description systems, the model offered by ISAAR(CPF) has remarkable similarities and concurrencies with authority control of authors' names in library catalogues. This is a point stressed in the introduction to new edition of ISAAR(CPF):

> Archival authority records are similar to library authority records in as much as both forms of authority record need to support the creation of standardized access points in descriptions. The name of the creator of the unit of description is one of the most important of such access points. (1.7)

The differentiating elements start with the chief aspects that the authority records for creating entities take in archival description systems, because of the basic role given to the context of production within the archival description. We cite again from the introduction to the new ISAAR:

> Archival authority records, however, need to support a much wider set of requirements than is the case with library authority records. These additional requirements are associated with the importance of documenting the context of records creation in archival description and control systems. As such, archival authority records go much further and usually will contain much more information than library authority records. (1.8)

The authority records of creators are meant to include a much more complex set of information than traditional bibliographic authority records, exactly because they are devoted to implementing the model of separate description of archives and creators on which we have expatiated above. Thus, we find in the "Description area" those elements crucial for the description of creators of archives as: the dates of existence (5.2.1); the creator's history and geography (5.2.2); the geographical areas in which he has worked (5.1.3); the legal status (5.1.4); the functions, occupations and activities (5.1.5); the mandate or sources of authority (5.1.6); the internal structure (5.1.7); the information on the political, social, cultural context in which the creator worked (5.1.8); other possibly significant information not included in the previous elements (5.1.9).

We notice that like the first edition, the second, too, openly admits–and more clearly–a plurality of forms to organize and present the descriptive information: unstructured prose, text structured into fields, links to external electronic resources or an ensemble, changeable according to the features of the specific systems of implementation, of the three forms together.

THE MOST RELEVANT NEW FEATURES
IN THE SECOND EDITION OF ISAAR(CPF)

In spite of the certain continuity of the basic features in the first and second edition of ISAAR(CPF), there are many relevant new features in the new version of the standard. We have already hinted at some, as the different organization of the descriptive elements. But it is on the ones with, so to say, a conceptual character, that it is worth lingering longer, stating beforehand that one of the factors that have driven towards a substantial rewriting of the standard was the initiative for the implementation of a XML DTD for the management of context information (the Encoded Archival Context, which is the object of a relevant paper at this conference), started at the same time as the revision of ISAAR(CPF) by a group of American and European archivists.

Very interesting theoretical and practical considerations and contributions issued from this experience. They could but flow back into the process of revision of the international standard for authority control of creators of archives and the need for the greatest possible concurrence of ISAAR(CPF) and EAC.

The first aspect of theoretical relevance, implied in the whole framework of the second edition of ISAAR(CPF), is certainly the greater emphasis on its feature as a tool for managing the description of entities, rather than for establishing authority names. As we said above, both the first and the second edition intend both objectives but their relevance and the modes to pursue them have undoubtedly changed. While in the first edition the aim was to manage first of all, standardised headings of creators, providing, in addition, information on their structure and history, today the framework looks overturned. The aim of ISAAR(CPF) 2nd ed. is to describe those entities (institutions, corporate bodies in general, persons, and families) who happen to be creators of archives and form the context of archival material. The formulation of an "authorised form of name" is consequent on this objective, and aims first of all at univocally identifying those entities rather than making unambiguous similar names, as in the first edition of ISAAR. In short, the stress is on the thing (the real entity), rather than on the name of the thing (the authorised heading).

This difference in the framework can be seen mostly in the way the issue of the relationships among different entities (that is among the various creators) is faced in the new edition of the standard.

While in the first version they were managed mainly as relationships among authority entries, by "see" and "see also" references, in the second edition there is a special area whose purpose is to present the relationships of a given creator with other corporate bodies, persons, families,[2] pointing to: name and identifier of the related entity (5.3.1); category of relationship (hierarchical, chronological, associative) (5.3.2); specific nature of the relationship and its description (5.3.3); dates of relationship (5.3.4). We sense, in this attention to relationships among different entities, the design to implement systems that are not limited to managing the fonds/creators relationship but that, putting the latter at the centre, can represent the complex links existing among the various creators, links that can be important traces from which a researcher can get information on relevant search courses to be verified and followed also inside archives and documents produced by the various creators. But we also sense something more in this model for managing relationships, that is the design to make possible for archival systems to get–so to say–out of themselves, in the direction of prefiguring the sharing of archival authority records in wider environments than the merely institutional ones, pointing out links between local and national archival systems, but also between archival systems and descriptive systems or cataloguing ones of a different nature (obviously I am thinking mostly of the ones of libraries and museums and, in general, of cultural assets). These connections might take place also by means of linking different entities that are described in specific authority records in diverse systems: for example, linking a political party, that is the creator of archival fonds, to one of its leaders who, on the contrary, is the author of essays, lectures and so on, recorded in a library catalogue.

Also, other component parts of the new ISAAR(CPF) pursue to break what I have previously defined the self-referential quality of archival systems and to envisage the possibility of sharing and linking data and information with catalogues and descriptive systems existing outside of the archival domain. First of all, the descriptive element 5.1.4. ("Standardized forms of name according to other rules") points to this direction.[3] Its main aim is just to record authorised forms of names constructed according to different rules from the ones followed by the archival institution compiling the authority record, for example, giving an account of how the record for the same body can be represented according to Regole Italiane di Catalogazione per autore (RICA) or AACR2. I do not think I need to expatiate on the greatly innovative purport of this element. It gives the possibility of establishing authority records to which we can get access through archival descriptive systems by a given heading and that we can retrieve at the same time within search systems shared by archives and libraries, by access to a heading built according to different rules. This is a point that it would be worth thinking upon and discussing again, because it is but a first limited step towards the design of systems that can talk to each other thanks exactly to the fact that they share and exchange authority records.

Anyway, it must be stressed that in the new version of ISAAR(CPF) there are other steps in the same direction. A section completely devoted to the modes for linking authority records, archival descriptions, and information resources of a different nature has been introduced. As stated in the brief introduction to chapter 6 of the new edition of ISAAR(CPF):

> Archival authority records are created primarily for the purpose of supporting the linking of descriptions of records creators to descriptions of the records they created. Archival authority records can also be linked to other relevant information resources that are related to the records creator. This Section provides guidance on how such linkages can be created in the context of an archival descriptive control system. (6)

The aim of this section is clear. On one hand, it confirms the model of separate description for creators and archival material within an archival descriptive systems and explains their mechanism (also by an attached diagram to the purpose). On the other hand, it shows the possible extension of the same model towards the linkage between personal bodies and families and other information resources. Here, too, we have an instance of the courses leading towards archives getting out of themselves, as I hinted above. Computer technology, first and foremost the development of the Internet, has enabled implementing linkages between archival descriptive systems and resources of a different nature: bibliographical resources, descriptions of museum collections, texts, images, and so on.

The tools for the authority control of creators look like the most profitable ground for carrying out such a linking objective. In the same way by which they are linked to the descriptions of archival documents produced, the authority records of persons, families, and institutions can be easily linked to information resources related to them and can be found in databases different from the archival ones or in web sites accessible through the Internet.

Thus, we witness a perspective encouraging the linkage of archival systems to other resources retrievable on the Internet, so as to allow, for example, to find, by means of the same authority record of a given person, the descriptive record of the archival fonds created by him, the catalogue records of the books he authored, but also, if present in digital format, their texts and so on.

ARCHIVAL DESCRIPTION SYSTEMS ON THE INTERNET AND ISAAR(CPF)

Summing up, archivists are more and more convinced that the new technologies can but greatly change many features of archival descriptions. Creating archival descriptions in a digital environment and communicating them through the Internet is not the same as doing it on paper, as was traditional. In this case, too, as in other cases, the medium greatly influences the structure and contents of information and leads to reassess the forms of organizing knowledge and the modes to acquire it.

It is not by chance then, given the central position that the context of production has in archival description, that the strongest impulses to change methods and practice of archival description originate from the new models that ISAAR(CPF) suggests in an implicit or explicit way.

The separate and related description of archives and creating entities on one side, and the central position of the authority records of the latter as linking aids to various information resources on the other side, are the basic features of some of the most interesting archival systems on the Web.

In the first case, suffice it to point at the *National Register of Archives* of the *Historical Manuscripts Commission* of the United Kingdom,[4] a database containing thousands of records with brief information on the nature and location of manuscripts and fonds concerning the history of Great Britain, preserved in mainly, but not only, British public and private institutions. In this database the access point is only the creator of the archival material (mainly persons and families, but also corporate bodies and institutions), which is often scattered in libraries and archives in Great Britain and in other countries which were dominated or influenced by it.

Bright Sparcs has a similar framework, but it is even more willing to include non-archival resources. It is a database implemented by the Australian Science and Technology Heritage Centre, containing over four thousand biographies of persons who have played a role in the most diverse branches of science, technology, and medicine in Australia during the two last centuries. The biographies are linked to descriptions of the archival materials produced by them or related to them, as well as to bibliographic resources of diverse nature.[5]

As regards the Italian situation, the online guide to the State Archive of Florence represents the most significant example of this reshaping of the archival finding aids in a digital environment. The model of separate and linked description of archival material and creators has been adopted and developed there, too, so that research can be done starting from the bodies, institutions, persons, or families who created the archival material. One can follow the network of connections and synchronic relationships (for example, the correlations of hierarchical subordination among various institutions or the kinship, association, or clientele relationships between persons and families) and diachronic ones (for example, the transfer of jurisdiction from one institution to another over time), connections and relationships that can point to as many searching routes and that often influence the organization modes, as well as the presence/absence of specific documentary units inside archival fonds. The online guide of the Archivio di Stato in Florence is something more than what its name implies. In fact, it is not a simple, sheer transposition of a traditional archival guide, based upon descriptions of fonds, series and, at the most, creators. Actually, it is a complex information system that widens the boundaries of traditional guides, including the description of a large number of entities beyond the ones usually included in the latter. It implies, for example, a wider idea of the production context of documents than the one referring only to the creator's history and structure. We find in the system the outlines of each politico-institutional phase of the Florentine, Tuscan, and national history, in which the producing institutions acted, coalescing inside the various "constitutional" systems in each phase. The link between these wider institutional contexts and the single institutions becomes in itself an extremely relevant historical datum and a crucial tool for critical guidance when, for instance, it highlights the considerable stickiness of the administrative and bureaucratic machinery when passing from one "constitutional" system to the other, providing further context data that may prove significant for both a right setting of search strategies among fonds that show very strong connections and references and for evaluating the relevance and overall meaning of the archival documents to be consulted.

Besides, the Florentine system does not look like a database "closed" within itself. Quite the reverse, it can be considered a starting point (or only a transit point) inside searching routes that see the Internet as their own general horizon. The descriptions of fonds and of creators included in it are linked to archival and non-archival resources present on the site of the Archivio di Stato in Florence or on other sites. Thus, links are provided to qualified, reliable sites that study in depth and develop themes referred to in the descriptions both of the fonds and of their creators, or to archival, bibliographic, or other resources retrievable on the Internet and strictly related to the fonds preserved in the Florentine archives or to their creators. I'm thinking of the catalogues and inventories of archival fragmentary sections, or library personal and family fonds displaced to other institutions, even foreign ones, that are subsidiary to material in our Institute, like–just to give an example–Guido Mazzoni's library–whose papers are preserved in the Florentine Archives–a collection preserved at Duke University,[6] or the *Spinelli Archive*, part of which is presently owned by Yale University.[7]

These are only examples, not to make a general statement from. Yet some of their peculiar aspects–for instance, the central position of creators as preferred access point to archival descriptions–even though with diverse modes and at different levels, are rapidly spreading in many archival finding aids on the Internet and contribute to changing the styles, the methods, and most of all, the structures and the language of archival description. All this implies, and will imply ever more in the future, an inevitable reorientation in the way we consider and do research in archives and in the way users evaluate the results. A change for better we may foretell, or at least hope, also thanks to the international descriptive standards that have been developed for over a decade.

NOTES

1. "Record the standardized form of name for the entity being described in accordance with any relevant national or international conventions or rules applied by the agency that created the authority record. Use dates, place, jurisdiction, occupation, epithet and other qualifiers as appropriate to distinguish the authorized form of name from those of other entities with similar names. Specify separately in the Rules and/or conventions element (5.5.3) which rules have been applied for this element" (5.1.2).

2. "The purpose of this area is to describe relationships with other corporate bodies, persons and families. In the case of complex hierarchies or administrative changes, refer to national rules for guidance on when to create separate authority records. Where it is decided to describe such complexity in the context of a single authority record, record relevant information in the Internal structure element (5.2.7)" (5.3).

3. "To record standardized forms of name for the corporate body, person or family that have been constructed according to rules other than those applied by the agency that has created the authority record" (5.1.4).

4. The database of the National Register of Archives is available at the URL: http://www.hmc.gov.uk/nra/nra2.htm.

5. *Bright Sparcs* can be consulted at the URL: http://www.asap.unimelb.edu.au/bsparcs/bsparcshome.htm. For further details on the project see Gavan McCarthy, "Utilizing the Web to build a network of archival authority records," in *Janus*, XVII (1999), 1, pp. 96-107; Id., "The Structuring of Context: New Possibilities in an XML Enabled World Wide Web," in *Journal of the Association for History and Comput-*

ing, III (2000), 1, at the URL: <http://mcel.pacificu.edu/JAHC/JAHcIII1/ARTICLES/ McCarthy/index.html.

6. The inventory can be seen at the URL: http://scriptorium.lib.duke.edu/mazzoni/.

7. The *Spinelli Archive* is described at the URL: http://webtext.library.yale.edu/ sgml2html/beinecke.spinell.sgm.html.

APPENDIX

ISAAR(CPF)

International Standard Archival Authority Record For Corporate Bodies, Persons and Families

Draft Second Edition

Prepared by the Committee on Descriptive Standards Rio de Janeiro, Brazil, 19-22 November 2002

TABLE OF CONTENTS

Creator Description:
Encoded Archival Context

Daniel V. Pitti

SUMMARY. Encoded Archival Context (EAC) is an ongoing initiative within the international archival community to design and implement a prototype standard based on Extensible Markup Language (XML) for encoding descriptions of record creators: individuals, families, and organizations that create records. EAC is intended to represent the descriptive data prescribed in the International Council for Archives' International Standard Archival Authority Record for Corporate Bodies, Persons, and Families (ISAAR(CPF)). Description of record creators is an essential component of the preservation of the documentary evidence of human activity. A standard for creator description has many professional as well as economic benefits. EAC promises to enhance access and understanding of records as well as provide an important resource independent of record description. EAC also promises to enable repositories to share creator description. Given the costs of authority control and description, such sharing potentially will be an important economic benefit. As an XML-based standard, EAC specifies the semantic and structural features of creator description. The developers of EAC hope that the archival

Daniel V. Pitti is affiliated with the Institute for Advanced Technology in the Humanities, University of Virginia.

[Haworth co-indexing entry note]: "Creator Description: Encoded Archival Context." Pitti, Daniel V. Co-published simultaneously in *Cataloging & Classification Quarterly* (The Haworth Information Press, an imprint of The Haworth Press, Inc.) Vol. 38, No. 3/4, 2004, pp. 201-226; and: *Authority Control in Organizing and Accessing Information: Definition and International Experience* (ed: Arlene G. Taylor, and Barbara B. Tillett) The Haworth Information Press, an imprint of The Haworth Press, Inc., 2004, pp. 201-226. Single or multiple copies of this article are available for a fee from The Haworth Document Delivery Service [1-800-HAWORTH, 9:00 a.m. - 5:00 p.m. (EST). E-mail address: docdelivery@haworthpress.com].

community will be able to collaborate with similar efforts in other cultural heritage communities. *[Article copies available for a fee from The Haworth Document Delivery Service: 1-800-HAWORTH. E-mail address: <docdelivery@haworthpress.com> Website: <http://www.HaworthPress.com> © 2004 by The Haworth Press, Inc. All rights reserved.]*

KEYWORDS. Encoded Archival Context, EAC, authority control, biography, administrative history, archival description, descriptive standards, International Standard Archival Authority Record for Corporate Bodies, Persons, and Families, ISAAR(CPF)

INTRODUCTION

Encoded Archival Context (EAC) is an ongoing initiative within the international archival community to design and implement a prototype standard based on Extensible Markup Language (XML) for encoding descriptions of record creators. The primary developers of this prototype standard are members of the international archival community. The description of individuals, families, and organizations that create records is an essential component of the preservation of the documentary evidence of human activity. Identifying record creating entities; recording the names or designations used by and for them; and describing their essential functions, activities, and characteristics, and the dates and places they were active is an essential component of the management of archival records. Creator description facilitates both access to and interpretation of records.

Description of creators is also essential in bibliographic systems, and in museum documentation, and thus EAC may be of interest to other cultural heritage communities as well. As custodians of the records upon which biographies and organizational histories are based, and with an ongoing need to create biographies and histories as an essential component of record description, archivists are well-placed to develop a standard that will assist in the fulfillment of their professional responsibilities, and at the same time lay the foundation for building international biographical and organizational history reference resources.

RECORDS

Archival records are the evidence of people acting individually, in families, or in formally organized and named groups. From a strictly archival perspective, records are the byproducts of people living their lives, or carrying out official duties or responsibilities. Archival records are the results of human functions and activities. Records document the conduct of business and as evidence of activities and official functions, they frequently have legal and historical value. Records, broadly speaking, encompass both the narrower archival definition, but also all artifacts, whether created as byproducts, or as intentional products. "Anything made by human art and workmanship"[1] is thus a record: books, articles, movies, sound recordings, paintings, sculptures, collections of natural objects, and so on.

CREATOR AND RECORD DESCRIPTION

Most standards development work to date has focused on the description of records or resources. While there are notable exceptions, this is true of the archival community, such as in the development of Encoded Archival Description (EAD), as well as standards development efforts in other communities. The best-known example is the Dublin Core initiative, which has concentrated on basic description of resources to facilitate their discovery. The Dublin Core community recognized the value of creator description as a complement to resource description, but the effort to develop a standard for describing creators (or agents) is still in its infancy.[2] The library community has long had standards for both the description of bibliographic entities as well as for uniquely identifying the individuals, corporate bodies, and conferences responsible for their creation and dissemination. The library community, though, traditionally has concentrated on controlling names, and not on detailed description of the people and organizations bearing the names. In other words, library authority control standards serve bibliographic or resource description by controlling the headings or entries used therein. Archival control differs from library control in the need for not only authority or heading control, but also detailed biographical and historical description of named entities.

Archival records function as both legal and historical evidence, so documentation of the context of record creation is essential. In order to evaluate, understand, and interpret records, users need to know the circumstances that surrounded their creation and use. Recording information about individuals, families, and organizations responsible for the creation of records is essential in the documentation of context. In particular, such creator description needs to document the name or names used, biographical or historical information about the creator, and information concerning activities and responsibilities.

Archivists are in a unique position for developing a standard for describing creators. While libraries, museums, and archives are all responsible for the preservation of records generated by and through human activities, archives in particular are responsible for the official records and personal papers that are considered the primary evidence on which biographical and historical description is based. As the custodians of the unique documentary evidence on which biographies and histories are based and with a professional obligation to describe creators, archivists are uniquely placed to play a major role in developing a standard for creator description.

BACKGROUND

The effort to develop a standard for creator description is taking place within the context of related initiatives within the international archival community. In 1996, the International Council on Archives (ICA) published *International Standard Archival Authority Record for Corporate Bodies, Persons and Families* (ISAAR(CPF)).[3] Under the auspices of ICA's Ad Hoc Commission on Descriptive Standards, work on this structural standard was initiated in 1993. While ISAAR has served as the point of departure for the EAC efforts, the initial design of EAC has not been constrained by it. ISAAR is currently undergoing revision. Draft of a second edition was released for comment in February 2003, and comments were considered at a meeting in Canberra, Australia in October 2003.[4] Several members of the ICA committee reviewing ISAAR are represented in the EAC initiative. Through them, the EAC initiative is informing the review of ISAAR.

At the same time that ICA was developing ISAAR, there was an American effort to develop an SGML-based prototype standard for archival records description (or finding aids). This initiative eventually developed into an international effort, and resulted in the release of version 1.0 of Encoded Archival Description (EAD) in 1998.[5] EAC is intended to extend and complement EAD. EAC will support the descriptive needs of the archival community, specifically in the creation, maintenance, and publication of creator description.

Wendy Duff (University of Toronto) and Richard Szary (Yale University) first proposed an effort to develop an encoding standard for creator or context description in 1998. With the assistance of the author, and with funding from the Digital Library Federation in the United States, they organized a meeting held at Yale University in 1999. The effort was slow until 2000, when, with the encouragement and assistance of Anne Van Camp of the RLG, funding was secured from the Gladys Krieble Delmas Foundation. Two meetings were organized and convened in 2001, at the University of Toronto in March and the University of Virginia in June. Following the meeting at the University of Virginia, an alpha version of EAC was released for testing. In September 2003, Dick Sargent (Public Records Office, UK), Per-Gunnar

Ottosson (Riksarkivet, Sweden), and the author met in Stockholm to revise EAC based on input and suggestions from those experimenting with the alpha version. With the completion of a tag library, EAC *beta* is scheduled for release in early 2004.

The organizers of the initial meetings attempted to identify and select internationally recognized archival description experts and supporting technologists as participants. In addition to selecting recognized experts, the organizers also sought participants with experience in working collaboratively and cooperatively in the development of standards and best practices. When the working group met in Toronto, its initial efforts were devoted to developing a general methodological framework as well as a detailed list of principles and objectives to guide the design.[6]

The working group explicitly acknowledged that standards are intellectual and technical products as well as inherently political products. Cooperation and consensus are absolutely essential, and thus participants would have to be able and willing to collectively create and shape ideas. A successful standard would need to embody agreement sufficient to be useful in developing national and institutional systems and exchanging data between systems. At the same time, the standard would have to accommodate national, institutional, and cultural differences. A successful standard would have to identify and delicately balance shared and individual interests. Such a process is necessarily iterative. Each set of objectives needs to be provisionally implemented and the prototype standard evaluated with respect to both shared and individual objectives. In general, institutions and individuals are willing to develop and adopt standards if the benefits of using them outweigh the sacrifices required to use them.

ECONOMIC AND PROFESSIONAL BENEFITS

Standardization of creator description offers economic benefits. Anyone familiar with authority control and creator description knows that it is an expensive undertaking. Description of individuals, families, and organizations frequently involves detailed and challenging research, followed by careful composition of the description. This expense is in addition to the description of records and other resources. It is quite frequently more time-consuming than the description of the records themselves. Records with a common provenance are frequently dispersed within or shared by more than one repository. In such instances, the creator research and description done by one archive, if based on a standard, could be shared and enhanced by other repositories, thereby distributing the costs. A standard also offers the potential for importing descriptive information from sources outside of the archival community, and adapting and enhancing such information to meet descriptive objectives.

In addition to economic benefits, a standard for creator description will provide professional benefits. A semantic and structure standard will facilitate an accurate representation of creator description that enables effective access to and description of archival records. A vexing and ongoing challenge is that individuals, families, and organizations frequently conduct business under different names. Both archivists and public users frequently have difficulty in locating records simply because the name used to document the provenance of records is not the same as or significantly differs from the name with which they are familiar. A creator description standard will provide a means to uniquely identify creating entities and to document all of the names used by the entity. Further, a creator description standard will facilitate effective documentation of the critical characteristics of creator entities. Indexing the characteristic information can further enhance access.

In addition to more effectively achieving long-held professional description and access objectives, a standard for creator description will facilitate building international, national, regional, and institutional biographical and historical databases that can serve as resources. Through links to record descriptions, creator descriptions can serve as a gateway to records. Creator descriptions can also function as an independent resource for users seeking information about individuals, families, and organizations. As important as these benefits are, perhaps of more appeal to archivists is the opportunity presented by digital technologies to describe and control archival records more effectively and accurately than is possible in the print medium.

While there are notable exceptions, traditionally, most archival description has been based on provenance. All of the records originating from one individual, family, or organization are preserved as a unit, and described collectively. When record arrangement and description is based on provenance, there is a one-to-one correspondence between the archival descriptive unit and the creating entity. Such a one-to-one correspondence makes it logical to document both the creator and the records created in the same descriptive apparatus. Thus creator description has traditionally been an integral component of archival description.

The opportunities for improving archival practices and services presented by computers and network technology have inspired archivists to engage in a new analysis of archival description. The challenge of effectively and economically representing description in computers has forced a rigorous analysis of the logic and structure of the description. This analysis is leading to increasing differentiation and formal definition of the components of description and the relations between components.

While traditional archival description documents creators, records, and functions in a single, provenance-based descriptive apparatus, markup and relational database technologies are inspiring archivists to envision new systems that use a distinct apparatus for each component and then dynamically interrelate them to form a complete archival descriptive system. Archivists increasingly recognize that the single apparatus represented in the traditional printed finding aid is inflexible and inefficient when dealing with complex, interrelated records.

While it is possible to establish the provenance of most records, it is common for records to be of mixed provenance, or records of the same provenance to be dispersed. Providing creator or context information in such common situations using traditional finding aids requires repeating information in more than description or finding aid. When records with a common provenance are dispersed in different repositories, it frequently means that expensive creator research and description is duplicated.

The relations between functions, creators, and records also present problems. Within groups of records with a common provenance, it is frequently possible to identify groups of records that document or reflect the same function or activity. But functions and activities are not fixed in one organization or person. They frequently are shared by two or more creators, or transferred from one creator to another. In a descriptive system based on provenance, sharing or transferring functions leads to the descriptive separation of records documenting the same function or activity.

Relations between records, creators, and functions and activities are dynamic and complex, and not fixed and simple. Creators are related to other creators. Records are related to other records. Functions and activities are related to other functions and activities. And each of these is interrelated with the others. Markup and relational database technologies enable the development of flexible and dynamic descriptive systems. By developing dedicated semantics and structures for describing each descriptive component and its complex interrelations, we can build descriptive systems that are far more efficient and effective than those we have realized in print.

Developing a descriptive system for creators related to systems for describing records and functions and activities will enable the creator description to do more than provide context for the origination of records, as essential and central as this role is for archival description. Creator descriptions can function as a first and important step in the discovery of records, as well as discovery of related creating entities and functions and activities. Pursuing any relation will reveal new constellations of relations, and so on. Independent of relations to other entities, creator descriptions can function as biographical and historical resources. Relational and markup technologies thus offer us the opportunity to develop flexible, dynamic, sustainable descriptive systems that are far more useful than traditional print-based finding aids.

STRUCTURE AND SEMANTICS

While development of EAC is still in the early stages, the developers have made significant progress in defining the structure and semantics of the prototype standard, and have begun evaluating its effectiveness in addressing archival descriptive needs. Therefore, the following description of EAC structure and semantics is provisional. While the overall structure has achieved a measure of stability, many of the details need additional analysis, elaboration, and testing.

Each EAC document begins with the <eac>. <eac> has a mandatory TYPE attribute that specifies the type of entity described: corporate body, person, or family. The <eac> contains two mandatory elements, the <eacheader> and the <condesc>-context description. The <eacheader> contains data used in the control of the creator description, and to provide the context of the description. The <condesc>-context description encompasses the description of the creator. Both <eacheader> and <condesc> contain specific elements that support the functional intentions of the parent or containing element.

The <eacheader> contains the following subelements:

- **<eacid>–eac identifier.** Contains a unique identifier for the descriptive document within the owning system. Accommodates both machine- and human-readable[7] versions of the identifier. Required.
- **<mainhist>–maintenance history.** Contains one or more <mainevent>-maintenance events that document creating, importing, updating, and deletion of the description. Each maintenance event contains the name of the person or system responsible for the event, date, and description of the event. Each <mainevent> has a MAINTYPE attribute to accommodate one of four possible values: create, update, import, or delete. <date> and MAINTYPE are machine-readable. Required.
- **<languagedecl>–language declaration.** Contains one or more machine- or human-readable declarations of the language of the description. Optional.
- **<ruledecl>–rules declaration.** Contains one or more machine- or human-readable declarations of the content rules used in the creation of the description. Optional.
- **<sourcedecl>–source declaration.** Contains one or more machine- or human-readable declarations of the sources for the information used in the description. Optional.

- **\<authdecl\>–authority declaration.** Contains one or more machine- or human-readable declarations of authorities from which either descriptive categories or values are taken. Optional.

In addition to the subelements, the \<eacheader\> element also contains several attributes. The STATUS attribute is used to designate the editorial status of the description–draft, edited, or deleted. The ENCODINGANALOGSYS is used to designate the system in which there are semantic analogs for descriptive values used in the EAC document. This attribute is used in conjunction with the EA-encoding analog attribute, available on EAC descriptive elements. The value given in an EA attribute is the analog designation for the containing element used in the system identified in the ENCODINGANALOGSYS.

Four other attributes associated with the \<eacheader\> are used to designate authorities for values used in the description or rules for formulating such values. These have default values:

- **LANGENCODING** Code values for language of description. Defaults to ISO 639-2b
- **SCRIPTENCODING** Code values for script used. Defaults to ISO 15924
- **DATEENCODING** Rules for formulating normalized date values: Defaults to ISO 8601
- **COUNTRYENCODING** Code values for designating countries. Defaults to ISO 3166-1
- **OWNERENCODING** Code value rules for repository or owner codes. Defaults to ISO 11551

The \<condesc\>-context description comprises the description of the creating entity. Similar to the \<eacheader\>, \<condesc\> has several complex subelements used to describe different features of the entity:

- **\<identity\>** Complex structure containing the name or name used by the entity over the course of his, her, or its existence. Required.
- **\<eacrels\>** Contains references to descriptions of related individuals, families, or organizations. Optional.
- **\<resourcerels\>** Contains references to descriptions of related archival, bibliographic, or museum resources or records. Optional.
- **\<funactrels\>** Contains references to descriptions of related functions or activities. Optional.

- **<desc>** Contains formal description of entity characteristics as well as prose or a chronological list of biographies and histories. Optional.

The most complex element in the EAC DTD is the <identity>. In addition to needing to accommodate one or more names used for or by the entity, <identity> must accommodate two or more parallel names in different languages or scripts. In countries where there is more than one official language, such as Canada, names of corporate bodies are frequently provided in more than one language.

The <identity> contains the following elements:

- **<legalid>** Legal identifier for the individual, family, or organization. Optional.

followed by one or more from each of the following pairs of elements. Within each pair, the <*grp> can be intermixed with the <*head>, but the pairs are exclusive:[8]

- **<persgrp>** or **<pershead>** One or more personal name-groups, for containing one or more parallel personal name headings; or one or more personal name headings.
- **<corpgrp>** or **<corphead>** One or more corporate name-groups, for containing one or more parallel corporate name headings; or one or more corporate name headings.
- **<famgrp>** or **<famhead>** One or more family name-groups, for containing one or more parallel family name headings; or one or more family name headings.

followed optionally by one or more of the following:

- **<nameadds>** Name-additions contains subelements for distinguishing additions to the base heading. While additions can be made directly within the <*grp> and <*head> elements when they are used uniquely within the <*grp> or <*head> to qualify names, they can, when shared by all of the headings, be contained here and shared in indexing, sorting, and display of the headings.
- **<didentifier>** Digital-identifier contains a machine-readable reference to an Internet accessible digital portrait or other non-textual digital identifiers of the described entity.

The <pershead>, <corphead>, and <famhead> elements each contain the same subelements:

- **<part>** Contains a part of the name. A TYPE attribute may be used to provide a precise designation of the name component, "forename," "surname," "parent body," and so on. Repeatable.

followed by:

- **<existdate>** Contains the life dates of individuals, or the active dates of families and organizations. It should not be confused with the <usedate>, which contains the date or date range when the name was used by or for the entity. Optional.
- **<place>** Contains the name of a place associated with the heading. A TYPE attribute may be used to provide a precise designation of the role of the place name in relation to the heading (for example, "Birthplace"). Optional.
- **<nameadd>** Contains additions made to the base name to distinguish it from the same name used for another entity, or to enhance the base name's intelligibility. A TYPE attribute may be used to specify a precise designation for the addition, for example, "expansion" for expansion of initials used in the name. Repeatable.
- **<usedate>** Contains the date or date range when the name was used by or for the entity. It should not be confused with <date>, which contains the life or active dates of the entity. Optional.

The <persgrp>, <famgrp>, and <corpgrp> elements each contain two or more <*head> elements of the same entity type as the parent element. In each <*grp>, each <*head> contains a parallel heading. After the <*head> elements, the following may be used: <nameadds>, <sourceref> or <sourcerefs>, or <descnote> or <descnotes>.

The following elements are available directly inside <identity>, the <*grp> elements, and the <*head> elements.

- **<sourcerefs>** or **<sourceref>** <sourcerefs> contains two or more <sourceref>; <sourceref> contains a reference to the resource used in composing a heading or headings that is declared in the <eadheader> using the <sourcedecl>. The <sourceref> also contains a <sourceinfo> subelement for containing a transcription of the source information used in composing one or more headings.
- **<descnotes>** or **<descnote>** <descnotes> contains two or more <descnote> elements; <descnote> contains the editor's description of judgments and decisions not otherwise documented in the declarations

made in the <eacheader>, evaluations of the evidence when there are contradictions or suspected or known inaccuracies, and so on.

Because <nameadds> is a grouping element for <nameadd> that facilitates economic reuse of name additions, it is directly available in <identity> and the <*grp> elements. The <nameadd> element is available directly inside the <*head> elements because some additions are specific to an individual heading.

Similarly, the <sourcerefs>, <sourceref>, <descnotes> and <descnote> elements available directly inside a <*head> element are intended to apply only to the specific heading, while those available inside <identity> and the <*grp> elements are intended to apply to all sibling <*head> elements.

The <identity> element is intended to facilitate control of the names used by and for an entity. Unlike traditional authority control, the notion of "authorized heading" and "variant heading" is not explicitly privileged in the naming of the elements. Instead, there is an AUTHORIZED attribute. To privilege one heading over the others for indexing, sorting, or display, users enter their owner or repository code in the AUTHORIZED attribute. Where more than one heading is authorized within the context of a descriptive system, or different headings are authorized for different contexts, there are additional attributes available: RULE, the descriptive rules used in the composition of the heading; LANGUAGECODE, the language of the heading; and SCRIPTCODE, for the script of the heading. For example, within the context of the Archive of Ontario, parallel French and English headings can be designated by placing the repository code of the Archive in two parallel <corphead> elements using the AUTHORIZED attribute, with the two different headings being distinguished by the values in the LANGUAGECODE.

RELATIONS

As a component of archival description, creator description must be brought into relation with the other descriptive components. Creator descriptions must be dynamically related to the record descriptions for which they provide context, and the functions and activities in which the creators engage and that the records document. With the exception of unique relations, it is the nature of relations that they take place between entities and not within them. Creators are related to other creators, to activities and functions, and to records. Similarly, activities and functions are related to other functions and activities, creators, and records; and records are related to other records, to creators, and to functions and activities. Each creator, record, or function/activity description can thus function as a node in a set of relations.

Because relations are *between* the descriptive nodes, they are most efficiently created and maintained outside of each node.[9] A person, for example, can be related to one or more persons, organizations or families; to one or more archival records, books, journals, and museum objects; and to various occupations and activities. Each of the related entities can be related to one or more other entities. To record all of these relations in the description of each node is inefficient, as correction of an error would require updating two or more descriptions.[10]

While maintaining relations independent of descriptions is efficient, when communicating descriptions between systems or to users it will be necessary to assemble or gather and represent the related descriptions using descriptive surrogates. Each surrogate for a related description will optimally include both human- and machine-readable information. The human-readable information provides succinct descriptions of the related entity, creator, records, or function/activity sufficient to enable identification and a relevancy judgment. The machine-readable information supports a traversable link to the related description.

There are three elements for describing EAC relations with other descriptive entities: <eacrels> (EAC to EAC relations), <resourcerels> (EAC to resource relations), and <funactrels> (EAC to function and activity relations). The <eacrels> contains one or more <eacrel> as well as <sourcerefs>, <sourceref>, <descnotes> or <descnote> for documenting the source or sources of information documenting the relation, and descriptive notes. The <resourcerels> and <funactrels> are similarly structured, though the principal contained element is <resourcerel> and <funactrel> respectively. The <*rel> elements have attributes to facilitate traversable links to resources described in contained descriptive surrogates.

Each <*rel> has a RELTYPE-relationship type attribute, with a closed list of primitive values.

<eacrel> has the following RELTYPE values available:

- superior
- subordinate
- earlier
- later
- parent
- child
- associative
- identity

<resourcerel> has the following RELTYPE values available:

- origination
- destruction
- control
- causa
- subject
- other

Since there has been no attempt at this time to design and implement function and activity description, preliminary decisions concerning the typing of EAC to function and activity relations have been deferred.

There are two principal rationales behind the primitive or basic typing of relations. First, there is general interest in enabling coherent expression and navigation of relations as well as creation of graphic displays of organizational charts, family trees, and timelines. The primitives are an experimental attempt to provide the data necessary to construct such displays. At this point, there has been no attempt to test the utility of the structures with graphic displays. Second, basic information about the nature of relations is necessary in order to make the relation intelligible to users. Given cultural and institutional differences, the number of possible relation types is, in principle, unlimited. EAC designers decided, though, that to achieve a minimum level of functionality there needed to be consensus on a set of basic or primitive relation types.

Each <*rel> element has one or more subelements available for representing surrogate description of a related entity. Because <eacrel> is self-referential, the surrogate description presents no major semantic and structural difficulties: <eacrel> simply contains <persname>, <famname>, and <corpname>, which accommodate the heading subelements in <pershead>, <famhead>, and <corphead>. The designers chose to provide a minimally structured element, <funact>, to accommodate surrogate representation of function and activity description, pending development of a descriptive structural standard for function and activity description.[11] In essence, the <funact> element is merely a placeholder.

The representation of surrogate information for records presents difficult technical challenges because any EAC entity can, in principle, be related to records (broadly defined) outside the control of archivists and therefore outside the scope of archival standards. For example, EAC documents may be related to archival records as well as books and journals, for which librarians have responsibility, and museum artifacts and collected natural objects, for which museum catalogers have responsibility.

EAC to EAD relations can be addressed by negotiations within the archival community to reconcile EAC and EAD semantics and structure. Bibliographic descriptions and museum descriptions must be accommodated with a different strategy. Since the primary function of the information is to make a surrogate intellectual description that provides context for the presence of a traversable link to a related resource, the elements need only accommodate a minimal semantics and structure. The surrogate need not support detailed, sophisticated searching, as this is addressed in the referenced description. It need only facilitate a coherent display of the description of the resource that will be sufficient for the user to decide whether or not to pursue the link. An alternative approach would use XML Namespace, which supports incorporating different semantic and structural XML standards into one document.[12]

Assuming and pending more robust implementation of XML Namespace, the designers of EAC have chosen to provide minimally defined surrogate elements inside <resourcerel> for bibliographic and museum description: <bibunit>-bibliographic description and <musunit>-museum description. The <archunit>-archival description elements contain all of the EAD <did>-descriptive identification subelements, though at this stage of development, it is not entirely compatible with the EAD <did>. The <bibunit> contains a minimal set of elements to support a basic bibliographic citation. Assuming and pending the emergence of one or more museum description encoding standards, <musunit> element has the same structure and semantics as <bib>.

DESCRIPTION

The <desc>-description element accommodates a variety of both controlled and prose description of creators. Three elements are available for grouping controlled or element specific description of each entity type: <persdesc>, <famdesc>, and <corpdesc>.

<persdesc> contains the following:

- **<existdesc>** dates of existence and associated places
- **<legalstatus>** legal status
- **<sex>** sex
- **<location>** location
- **<descentry>** descriptive entry

followed optionally by any of the following:

- **<funactdesc>** function or activity description
- **<character>** personal characteristics
- **<env>** environment
- **<ocd>** other context description

<corpdesc> contains the following elements:

- **<existdesc>** dates of existence and associated places
- **<corptype>** corporate body or organization type
- **<legalstatus>** legal status
- **<location>** location
- **<descentry>** descriptive entry

followed by:

- **<causa>** mandates and warrants
- **<funactdesc>** function or activity description
- **<assetstruct>** assets and administrative structure
- **<env>** environment
- **<ocd>** other context description

<famdesc> contains the following elements:

- **<existdesc>** dates of existence and associated places
- **<legalstatus>** legal status
- **<location>** location
- **<descentry>** descriptive entry

followed by:

- **<funactdesc>** function or activity description
- **<assetstruct>** assets and administrative structure
- **<env>** environment
- **<ocd>** other context description

There are two structurally distinct classes of <*desc> subelements. The first class, represented by the elements in the above lists that precede the phrase "followed by," are intended to provide controlled vocabulary description of important characteristics of the described entity. Each of these elements represents a particular descriptive category and has the same subelements: <value>-value, optionally followed by <date>, <place>, <descnote>, and <sourceref>. The <descentry> element is used as a repeatable means of expanding the descriptive categories, and thus has a TYPE attribute for specifying the category.

The second class of <desc> elements is similar to the first, except that it allows using one or more category-value pairs for representing aspects of the parent descriptive category, followed optionally by prose description. The <descentry> is used for representing the category-value pairs. <ocd>-other context description is a generic element used when no other element of this structural type is appropriate. Like <descentry>, <ocd> has a TYPE attribute for designating the descriptive category.

The <bioghist>-biography/history element, borrowed from EAD, can be used for prose description of any entity type. It enables simple or complex, brief or lengthy biographies and organization histories. Particularly noteworthy among its subelements is the <chronlist>-chronological list, which enables a succession of two- or three-part entries <date>, <event>, or <date>, <place>, <event>.

TYPE ATTRIBUTE: THE ONE AND THE MANY

As an international effort, the designers of EAC are attempting to agree on as much as possible while accommodating cultural and institutional differences. The semantics and structure described above represents the current semantic and structural consensus.

In addition to the elements <descentry> and <ocd>, described above, several descriptive elements also have the TYPE attribute that accommodates arbitrary textual content to facilitate national, regional, and local extensions to the EAC semantics. <date> and <place> are widely available and thus may be used to qualify other descriptive information in a variety of ways. Other elements, in particular elements representing an abstraction of several suggested and more specific alternatives, also bear the TYPE attribute.

It is widely recognized that such extensions can undermine communication and collaboration objectives. To ameliorate this danger, each TYPE attribute is accompanied by two related attributes, TYPEAUTH, and TYPEKEY. The TYPEAUTH provides a means to reference an authority declared in the <eacheader> using <auth>, and through <auth> to reference the authority when it is Internet-accessible. The TYPEKEY attribute provides the unique identifier for the particular term or phrase in the authority. A similar set of attributes is used to specify the values used in the <value> element: VALUEAUTH and VALUEKEY.

CONCLUSION

The effort to develop an archival encoding standard for authority control and detailed description of individuals, families, and corporate bodies is in the initial stages. There are many difficult intellectual, technical, cultural, linguistic, and political challenges to be addressed in order for the effort to be successful. While all of the challenges are significant, the political challenges stand out as particularly difficult.

Traditionally, authority control has been imposed on a system-by-system basis. Within each system, identifying, recording names, describing, and interrelating individuals, families, and corporate entities is recorded and carefully maintained. Essential to the success of descriptive systems has been unilateral administrative control of the technology, the intellectual infrastructure, and the professionals maintaining the information. As economically and professionally desirable as cooperative, shared authority control, and biographical and historical description is, successful realization will require standards and systems that are collaboratively developed, administered, and maintained. These standards and systems will have to serve both individual and shared interests. Successfully balancing competing interests will require a great deal of patience, goodwill, and intelligence.

Concurrent with the EAC effort are related initiatives in other cultural heritage communities. Many of the efforts within the library and museum communities are inspired by economic and professional objectives that are the same or similar to those motivating the archival community. While the visions behind these efforts are compelling, it is much too early in the process to know whether all or any of these efforts will be successful. Collaboratively developed and maintained standards and systems across the cultural heritage communities is clearly a desirable goal, as the artifacts and resources collected by libraries, archives and museums are historically and intellectually interrelated. At a minimum, the cultural heritage communities need to share information and experiences, successes as well as failures, and begin building a mutual understanding and trust that will enable us to balance our individual needs and shared interests in a quest to realize integrated access to our shared heritage.

NOTES

1. This is the lead definition of "artifact" (or in British spelling, "artefact") in the *Oxford English Dictionary Online* (3rd ed.): http://dictionary.oed.com/.
2. The Dublin Core community uses the term "agents" for creating entities. For information on the Dublin Core Metadata Initiative Working Group and its ongoing work see http://dublincore.org/groups/agents/.
3. International Council on Archives (ICA) published *International Standard Archival Authority Record for Corporate Bodies, Persons and Families*: http://www.ica.org/isaarf.html.

4. The draft second edition of ISAAR is available at http://www.hmc.gov.uk/icacds/eng/ISAAR(CPF)2.pdf.

5. Version 2002 of EAD was released in December 2002.

6. A complete list of participants is provided in Appendix A, and the detailed EAC design objectives and principles, the *Toronto Tenets*, can be found in Appendix B.

7. In the description of the elements, machine-readable means that the information can be used to provide a traversable link to a resource or resources, or can be used to link related information within the <eac> through attributes of type ID and IDREF. All of the declarations in the <eacheader> play both roles: lead to resources, and are (or can be) associated with descriptive information in the <condesc>. Human-readable means that the same or related information is supplied in a form that is intelligible to a human being.

8. The asterisk in the tag is used here and elsewhere as a wildcard to indicate all elements that end with the name component following the asterisk.

9. This is a cardinal principle of both relational database and hypermedia theory.

10. In order to assist in the design of EAC, a provisional, related DTD, called Encoded Archival Relations (EAR), was developed to document relations.

11. EAC designers assume that the international archival community will, in the near future, undertake an attempt to develop a standard for function and activity description. The <funact> element and related elements would necessarily need to be modified for compatibility if and when a standard emerges. A similar strategy was adopted in the development of EAD with respect to elements now being more rigorously defined in EAC.

12. For more information on Namespace, see http://www.w3.org/TR/REC-xml-names/.

APPENDIX A

Linking and Exploring Authority Files (LEAF, an EU-funded project)

Tone Merete Bruvik (University of Bergen; EU LEAF)

Adrian Cunningham (National Archives of Australia; ISAAR)

Wendy Duff (University of Toronto)

Joanne Evans (Australian Science and Technology Centre, University of Melbourne)

Margaret Hedstrom (University of Michigan)

Hans Hofman (Information Policy Department, Ministry of the Interior, The Netherlands)

Gunnar Karlsen (University of Bergen; EU LEAF)

Bob Krawczyk (Archives of Ontario)

Michelle Light (Northeastern University)

Gavan McCarthy (Australian Science and Technology Centre, University of Melbourne)

Per-Gunnar Ottosson (Riksarkivet, Sweden; EU LEAF; ISAAR)

Daniel Pitti (Institute for Advanced Technology in the Humanities, University of Virginia)

Kathleen Roe (New York State Archives)

Dick Sargent (Public Records Office, U.K.; ISAAR)

Richard Szary (Yale University)

Anne Van Camp (RLG)

Stefano Vitali (Archivio di Stato di Firenze; ISAAR)

Stephen Yearl (Yale University)

APPENDIX B

Toronto Tenets
Principles and Criteria for a Model for Archival Context Information

March 2001

This document defines principles and criteria for designing, developing, and maintaining a representational scheme and communication structure for archival context information.

A description of archival records sufficient to support the accurate interpretation of the records must include a description of the circumstances that surrounded their creation and use. Primary among these circumstances is a recording of information about the creative responsibility for the records, usually vested in an organization or person(s). With this information, users can understand the records more completely since they will know the context within which the organization or person operated and created records.

This model primarily addresses the description of creating entities, a central component to the description of archival records, and clearly an archival responsibility. It recognizes the existence of other information, such as functions and business processes, geographic places, events, concepts, and topics, that are crucial to archival description, which are also important, but which may be defined more fully by other agencies and not included in this model.

While traditional heading control functions may be accommodated by this model, its primary purpose is to standardize descriptions about records creators so that they can be discovered and displayed in an electronic environment, linked to each other to show/discover the relationships amongst record-creating entities, and linked to descriptions of records.

Definitions and Uses

1. Archival context information consists of information describing the circumstances under which records (defined broadly here to include personal papers and records of organizations) have been created and used. This context includes the identification and characteristics of the persons, organizations, and families who have been the creators,

users, or subjects of records, as well as the relationships amongst them.

2. Context information is not metadata that describes other information resources, but information that describes entities that are part of the environment in which information resources (i.e., records) have existed.

3. The recording of context information in archival information systems directly supports a more complete description and understanding of records as well as the provenance approach to retrieval of these records across time and domains.

4. Context information also can have value as an independent information resource, separate from its use in supporting the description, retrieval, and interpretation of records.

5. This model is also intended to support the exchange and sharing of context information, especially in those instances where repositories have holdings or interests that have context information in common, especially about creators or subjects of records.

Structure and Content

6. Context information has traditionally been embedded in catalog records, finding aids, and other archival descriptive tools. This model can be used either as a component of existing descriptive approaches that fully integrate contextual information into descriptive products or as an independent system that is linked to descriptive systems and products.

7. Each instance of context information describes a single entity.

8. The model provides a framework within which the full range and depth of context information can be recorded and suggests a minimum set of elements for describing an entity, but defers recommendations for appropriate use of other elements to application guidelines developed for specific implementations.

9. The model defines a universe of elements used to describe entities and the structure of interrelationships amongst those elements. These elements and structure support the discovery, navigation, and presentation of context information and the linking of that information to descriptions of records, especially those encoded according to EAD, MARC, and similar standards.

10. The model supports the linking of descriptions of contextual entities to digital or other surrogate representations of those entities.

Technical Issues

11. The model is expressed as an XML-compliant document type definition to encourage platform independence and portability of information. The model may also be implemented using other approaches.

Components, Relationship to ISAAR(CPF), and Ownership

12. Two parts: dtd and guidelines.
13. The model was designed as an implementation of the International Standard for Archival Authority Record for Corporate Bodies, Persons, and Families–ISAAR(CPF). ISAAR(CPF) was under review at the time the model was being developed and the model may incorporate different approaches than that defined in the original ISAAR(CPF) standard. Principles and approaches adopted for the model will be submitted to the International Council on Archives Committee on Descriptive Standards to inform their review of ISAAR(CPF). It is expected that the model will fully conform to the revised ISAAR(CPF).
14. Responsibility for control and maintenance will be carried out by Yale for some period of time and the original working group will continue to develop the model until it is appropriate to be opened to a wider community for further discussion and verification and testing.

APPENDIX C

EAC Example

Entity Description

Identity Section

Used:

Rostovzeff, Michael I. (Michael Ivanovitch), 1870-1952.

Not used:

Rostovzeff, Michael Ivanovitch
Rostovtzeff, Michael I. (Michael Ivanovitch)
Rostovtzeff, Michael (Michael)
Rostovtzeff, Michael Ivanovitch
Rostowzew, M. (Michael)
Rostowzew, Michael
Rostovtsev, Mikhail Ivanovich

Resources

Archival Records:

Creator:	Rostovzeff, Michael I. (Michael Ivanovitch), 1870-1952.
Title:	Papers of Michael Ivanovitch Rostovzeff, (1897-1968)
Extent:	Linear ft. of shelf space occupied: 4.5; Number of items: ca. 2,500
Repository:	Duke University. Special Collections Library.
Abstract:	The Michael I. Rostovzeff Papers span the years 1897 to 1968 with the bulk dated 1926 to 1954. The collection chiefly consists of the correspondence of Michael Rostovzeff and C. Bradford Welles, a colleague of Rostovzeff's at Yale University, with other scholars in the fields of ancient history, archaeology, and philology. Other materials include autobiographical writings by Rostovzeff, photographs, financial papers, and clippings. The papers primarily reflect Michael Rostovzeff's tenure as a faculty member of the Classics Department at Yale University.

Description

Biographical Note

Date	Event
1870, Nov. 10	Born, Zhitomir (the Ukraine), Russia
1888	Graduated from the First Classical Gymnasium, Kiev, Russia
1892	B.A., University of St. Petersburg
1899	Master of Latin Literature, University of St. Petersburg
1901	Married Sophie M. Kulczycki
1903	Doctor of Latin Literature, University of St. Petersburg
1905-1918	Member, Constitutional Democratic Party
1916-1919	Member, Russian Academy of Sciences
1918	Emigrated to Great Britain
1918-1920	Lecturer, Queen's College
1920-1925	Professor of Ancient History, University of Wisconsin, Madison, Wis.
1925-1939	Sterling Professor of Ancient History, Yale University
1926-1927	Published *A History of the Ancient World*
1926	Published *The Social and Economic History of the Roman Empire*
1928-1937	Director of the Yale University Expedition at Dura-Europos
1938	Published *Dura-Europos and Its Art*
1939	Appointed Director of Archaeological Studies, Yale University
1941	Published *The Social and Economic History of the Hellenistic World*
1944	Appointed as the Sterling Professor of Ancient History and Classical Archaeology, Emeritus
1952, Oct. 20	Died, New Haven, Conn.

Professor Rostovzeff received honorary degrees from the University of Leipzig (1909), Oxford University (1919), University of Wisconsin (1924), Cambridge University (1934), Harvard University (1936), Athens University (1937), and the University of Chicago (1941). He was also a member of numerous national academies and learned societies, both in the United States and Europe. Included among these are Phi Beta Kappa, the American Academy of Arts and Sciences, the American Philological Society, La Pontificia Accademia Romana di Archeologia, Academie des Inscriptions et Belles Lettres, and the Polish Academy of Science.

Record Control Information

Record type: personal name

Editorial status: draft

Language encoding standard: ISO 639-2B

Script encoding standard: ISO 15924

Date encoding standard: ISO 8601

Country encoding standard: ISO 3166-1 a2

Owner encoding standard: ISO 11551

Record identifier: US::VaU::Example06

Maintenance history:

Name	Date	Event
Daniel Pitti	3 September 2001	Record created using <bioghist> element in rostov.xml and LCNAF record.

Language/Script of description: English in Latin Script.

Descriptive rules: Anglo-American Cataloging Rules, Second Edition.

Sources:

Guide to the Papers of Michael Ivanovitch Rostovzeff
Michael Ivanovitch Rostovzeff, 1870-1952

Library of Congress Name Authority File, record id:
His *Istoriia gosudarstvennago otkupa*, 1899.
nuc89-43423: His *Iranians & Greeks in south Russia* [MI] 1922 (hdg. on MH rept.: Rostovtsev, Mikhail Ivanovich, 1870-1952; usage: M. Rostovtzeff) *Römische Bleitesserae*, 1979: t.p. (Michael Rostowzew)

LEAF:
Linking and Exploring Authority Files

Jutta Weber

SUMMARY. LEAF tries to enhance search and retrieval facilities by providing high quality access to international authority information for everyone. For this purpose LEAF is developing a model architecture for collecting, harvesting, linking of, and providing access to existing local or national name authority data, independent from their creation in libraries, archives, museums or other institutions and independent from national differences. When a user searches for a name string, LEAF will search the records of all LEAF Data Providers and combine these records to one single LEAF authority record. This record will automatically be stored in a "Central Name Authority File" which will thus contain international name information of high quality and high user relevance, as it will only contain records for which searches were actually done. *[Article copies available for a fee from The Haworth Document Delivery Service: 1-800-HAWORTH. E-mail address: <docdelivery@haworthpress.com> Website: <http://www.HaworthPress.com> © 2004 by The Haworth Press, Inc. All rights reserved.]*

KEYWORDS. Authority information, names of persons, libraries, archives, museums, user relevance, harvesting, linking, international authority file, authority control

---

Jutta Weber is affiliated with Staatsbibliothek zu Berlin–Preussischer Kulturbesitz.

[Haworth co-indexing entry note]: "LEAF: Linking and Exploring Authority Files." Weber, Jutta. Co-published simultaneously in *Cataloging & Classification Quarterly* (The Haworth Information Press, an imprint of The Haworth Press, Inc.) Vol. 38, No. 3/4, 2004, pp. 227-236; and: *Authority Control in Organizing and Accessing Information: Definition and International Experience* (ed: Arlene G. Taylor, and Barbara B. Tillett) The Haworth Information Press, an imprint of The Haworth Press, Inc., 2004, pp. 227-236. Single or multiple copies of this article are available for a fee from The Haworth Document Delivery Service [1-800-HAWORTH, 9:00 a.m. - 5:00 p.m. (EST). E-mail address: docdelivery@haworthpress.com].

Digital Object Identifier: 10.1300/J104v38n03_17

227

The LEAF project[1] is funded by the European Union (EU) under the 5th framework (IST program). It started in March 2001 and will run for three years.

The scope of LEAF reflects the important role that the creation and the use of authority data has in libraries, archives, and museums:

- in cataloguing work the quality of the data is dependent on the quality of the authority data used–co-operation on the national level between libraries worldwide is very much based upon national authority files for person names, names of institutions, and subject terms
- the communication in information networks is much more effective when common authority data are created and used–a standard once established in libraries finds more and more interest also in archival networks and co-operation between museums
- the higher the quality of authority data, the better the access to information–the more we find information contained in one authority record, the higher is the expectation that this information will match with a search term.

In other words, today not only libraries, archives, and museums share a high interest in the use of high-quality authority data for their proper work, but there is an increasing interest in authority data on the part of end users, who want to have access to the results of cataloguing work–worldwide, without limitations concerning languages to be used or special knowledge of access rules. Whatever work will be done in the sector of authority control, it will have to reflect these facts. But there are millions of authority data records originating from very different sources (archives, libraries, museums, reference works, research institutions, biographical indexes, or just individual scholarly work), which have existed for a long time and which all have their own user community and are only known there.

It is not only economical reasons that encourage institutions to leave those disparate, local, or material-specific solutions. Authority information should be usable by everybody (librarian, archivist, museologist, public user) in a way that

- all effort put into the creation of specific authority data remains visible,
- all complementary information is preserved,
- the quality of the accumulated authority information is as high or even higher than it was on the local level,

- the accumulation work is done automatically,
- actual user needs are defined where additional work has to be done to enhance the quality of the common and international authority data offerings.

LEAF will try to enhance search and retrieval facilities by providing high-quality access to international authority information for everybody. For this purpose LEAF is developing a model architecture for collecting, harvesting, linking, and providing access to existing local or national name authority information, independent from their creation in libraries, archives, museums or other institutions and independent from national differences. The scenario will be built using authority files of personal names and integrating the user directly into the establishment of a Central European Name Authority File.

The LEAF consortium, working to find answers to these needs, consists of:

- The Coordinator: Staatsbibliothek zu Berlin, Berlin
- The Manager: Crossnet Systems Ltd., Newbury
- The System developer: JOANNEUM RESEARCH, Graz

and Biblioteca Nacional de Portugal, Lisbon; Biblioteca de Universidad Complutense, Madrid; British Library, London; Deutsches Literaturarchiv, Marbach; Forschungsstelle und Dokumentationszentrum für Österreichische Philosophie, Graz; Goethe- und Schiller-Archiv, Weimar; Institut Mémoires de l'édition contemporaine, Paris; Österreichische Nationalbibliothek, Vienna; University of Bergen, Bergen; Swiss National Library, Bern; National and University Library, Ljubljana and Riksarkivet, Stockholm.

There are a large number of observing partners which do not get any funding, but which want to participate in the project as institutions working in the same field and interested in sharing preliminary results and giving advice when needed. These are: Archives de France pour les technologies de l'information et de la communication, Paris; Det Arnamagnæanske Institut, Copenhagen; Biblioteca Nacional de España, Madrid; Biblioteca Nazionale Centrale di Roma (National Central Library of Rome), Rome; Jagiellonian Library, Krakow; Warsaw Public Library, Warsaw; Torun University Library, Torun; Warsaw University Library, Warsaw; Bibliothèque Nationale de France, Paris; CIMI consortium, Chicago; Constantijn Huygens Instituut foor Tekstedities en Intellectuele Geschiedenis, 's-Gravenhage; Dansk Biblioteks Center, Copenhagen; Die Deutsche Bibliothek, Frankfurt am Main; Dokimas

Group Holdings Ltd., Nottingham; EKT (National Documentation Centre), Athens; Franz-Michael-Felder-Archiv der Vorarlberger Landesbibliothek, Bregenz; GTAA, Grupo de Trabajo de Autoridades de Aragón, Zaragoza; Interparty, Boston Spa, Wetherby; Istituto Centrale per il Catalogo Unico delle Biblioteche Italiane e per le Informazioni Bibliografiche, (ICCU), Rome; Jewish National & University Library, Jerusalem; Det Kongelige Bibliotek, Copenhagen; Koninklijke Bibliotheek, The Hague; Library of Congress, Washington, D.C.; Magyar Tudományos Akadémia, Budapest; Onderzoekssteunpunt en Databank Intermedaire Structuren in Vlaanderen; Online Computer Library Center (OCLC), Dublin, Ohio; Research Libraries Group (RLG), Mountain View, California; Tartu University, Tartu; University of Virginia, Charlottesville, Virginia; and Wiener Stadt- und Landesbibliothek, Vienna. There are also sponsoring partners that agree to provide test data when needed: K. G. Saur Verlag, Munich; J. A. Stargardt, manuscript dealer, Berlin; Library of Congress, Washington, D.C.

It is from experience in the network MALVINE that the idea of LEAF was born: MALVINE (www.malvine.org) is a search engine that harvests databases which provide information about letters written by famous persons that are kept in very different institutions in Europe. Due to the lack of better information provided by the participating institutions, only names, not individuals, can be searched for. Scholars working in the sector of handwritten resources of our cultural heritage and searching in MALVINE are happy with the results as long as the names they are searching for are used only by one single person. Whenever two or more persons use the same name, however, scholars want to distinguish them. This term of distinction may consist of a different date of birth, profession, etc.; in other words, all of the information that national authority files try to provide. The problem is that small institutions normally don't have access to these national authority files. So it will not be surprising that only very few MALVINE participants are able to provide this sort of authority information.

The LEAF model will be based on a very simple idea: data from different providers are stored in a central server, and this server will be uploaded regularly, or a harvesting mechanism will add new data every time a user is doing a search in LEAF. The following table illustrates how very different information about one person might be. Data from three institutions in German-speaking countries provide such complementary information concerning one person that it is very tempting to combine them by a linking mechanism and create one single virtual authority record.

LEAF element	FDÖP	SBB	ONB
Leaf.Local_ID_number	FDÖP-NrAutor: 130	ZKA-Nummer 00038680	
National Authority Record ID		PND-Nummer 118529277	
Leaf.Main_heading	Ehrenfels, Christian Freiherr von	Ehrenfels, Christian von	Ehrenfels, Christian von
Leaf.Other_Name (See-Reference)		Ehrenfels, Maria Christian Julius Leopold Karl von	
Leaf.Other_Name		Ehrenfels, Christian	
Leaf.Date_of_birth	20.06.1859	1859	20.06.1859
Leaf.Date_of_death	08.09.1932	1932	08.09.1932
Leaf.Place of_birth	Rodaun (Wien)		Rodaun (Wien)
Leaf.Place of_death	Lichtenau		Lichtenau (NÖ)
Leaf.Place_of_flourishing	Wien, Prag		
Leaf.Nationality		AT	
Leaf.Profession		Philosoph	
Leaf.Profession, non standardized	Philosoph	Freiherr, Professor; Prag, Wien-Rodaun, Lichtenau/NÖ (Wirkungsorte) Österr. Philosoph, Psychologe und Dramatiker; Begründer der Gestaltpsychologie, auch Philosophie der Mathematik	Philosoph, Schriftsteller Freiherr
Leaf.Curriculum	Curriculum: Sohn des Leopold von Ehrenfels und der Klothilde von Coith; besuchte von 1870 - 1876 die Realschule in Krems a. d. Donau; 1877: Studium an der Hochschule für Boderkultur in Wien; inskribierte im WS 1879/80 an der Philosophischen Fakultät der Universität Wien Philosophie, Germanistik und Geschichte, daneben auch juridische Studien; ....; Emeritierung: er hielt aber weiterhin Vorlesungen ab bis zum WS 1931/32.		

LEAF will link all records that obviously (i.e., according to the LEAF linking rules that compare name, first name, dates of birth and death) contain information about one and the same person automatically. In order to have a network where those linked records may be of interest for users, the LEAF demonstrator will be integrated into the MALVINE search engine. Every time an end user submits a query concerning a person name in MALVINE, he/she will be able to verify the correctness of the links he/she will find, and in case they are mistaken, an annotation can be made. This annotation concerning the incorrect linking done by the user shall automatically be sent to the providers of the records linked, and they will have to react and, if need be, correct the linking.

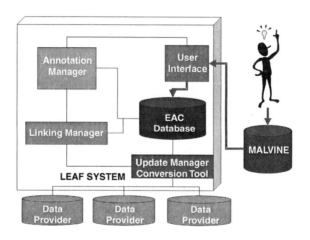

The following features of the LEAF central system are planned:[2]

"1. **Local authority records** (LAR) will be uploaded by the **Update Manager** from the local servers of the participating organisations to the central LEAF system. Regular updates of the uploaded data will ensure that data in the central LEAF system is as up-to-date as possible. The update process will be possible in different ways depending from the institutions' facilities. There will be upload and download facilities via ftp, search and retrieval access with Z39.50, harvesting by the use of OAI and message exchange by the use of SOAP.

2. After having converted the data in the **LEAF conversion tool** via XSLT in the currently emerging EAC (Encoded Archival Context) format, the data will be stored in the central LEAF EAC Database in the EAC format as Local Authority Files (**LAF**).

3. With the help of **automated linking rules** defined within the project, those authority records which refer to the same entity are linked together. Of course, it will be possible to check these automatically created links and overrule them manually if necessary. Whenever a user queries the LEAF system using a name string as search argument, this name string will thus represent an entity–or, in LEAF's jargon, various local authority records representing the same entity will be aggregated to form a "Shared Name Authority Record" (SLAR) which themselves will form the "Shared Name Authority File" (**SLAF**). It is crucial to note that local name authority records will not be merged into one definitive "corporate" record, but grouped or linked in recognition that, despite whatever local differences might exist, they refer to the same entity. In this way, maintaining local authority traditions (which has many practical advantages) may be seen to be compatible with a desire for greater accuracy and consistency for the end user. The **Linking Manager** will process the automatic linking of records referring to the same entity.

4. All **registered users** of the LEAF system will be able to post annotations to particular data records in the LEAF system. This functionality is mainly geared towards the improvement of local authority records and is expected to require some negotiation between the annotating user and the owner of the data record in question. LEAF will provide a framework in which such negotiation processes can be easily carried out. Further to this, it will be possible to attach additional information to a specific data record, e.g., small institutions without an electronic data offer of their own can thus inform users of LEAF that manuscripts related to a specific entity can be found in that particular institution. Furthermore, manuscript dealers can indicate that manuscripts of a particular person are on sale, etc. The Annotation Manager will deal with the processing and administration of annotations to records that were posted by users of LEAF.

5. Existing Internet applications could, in many cases, clearly benefit from the integration of authority information. Since names represent the

most common access point to bibliographic databases and networks, on-line retrieval will be greatly improved by the linking of authority name records to bibliographic records. To demonstrate this, LEAF will be **integrated into the existing MALVINE Service** (www.malvine.org).

6. Information which is retrieved as a result of a query submitted to LEAF will be stored in a pan-European "**Central Name Authority File**" (CNAF). Since every new query will generate a new record to be saved, this "Central Name Authority File" will grow with each query and at the same time will reflect precisely which data records the users of LEAF were interested in. Libraries and archives wanting to improve authority information will thus be able to prioritise their editing work.

7. A **LEAF Maintenance Suite** will automate, as much as possible, the process of integrating new partners' data into LEAF."

The following diagram of the simplified LEAF System Architecture illustrates the main technical components of the LEAF system:

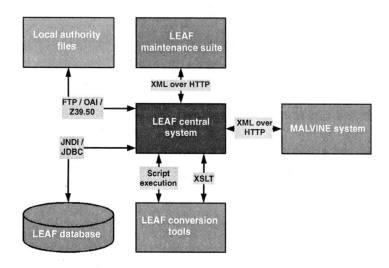

One example may illustrate the LEAF idea: A user searches for " Smith, John." The local LEAF Data Provider Servers contain a number of authority records referring to "Smith, John." Via the Linking Manager these records are grouped in a way that may look like this:

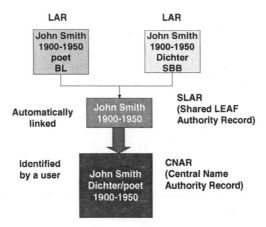

As all local authority files will, in addition to the Central Name Authority Record (to be shown in the LEAF presentation format), be preserved independently from LEAF as they were (or, sometimes in an enhanced quality), there is a great variety of possible uses of the LEAF results:

1. All local information concerning one person will be visible together.
2. All information concerning one person can be compared.
3. The core information concerning one person will be internationally standardised in the LEAF presentation format.
4. One institution may profit from the knowledge of another one.
5. The chance to retrieve the person searched for grows with every additional name form provided by one of the participating institutions.
6. Institutions that do not have the resources for putting much effort into the elaboration of detailed authority data may profit from the high quality information about a person provided by a specialised institution.
7. Small institutions can provide their data as well as big ones.
8. Existing information is of use for others.
9. New and additional information may also be added by a public user.
10. The use of LEAF will be free of charge and registration for everybody.
11. Additionally user workspaces will allow for storing "private" annotations and for specific re-use of LEAF results by registered users.
12. The enhancement of authority data as a result of LEAF will influence the quality of national authority files.

The technical implications are multiple; a prototype of the LEAF demonstrator has been developed upon this draft. Please visit www.leaf-eu.org to get up-to-date information.

NOTES

1. LEAF may be found at: www.leaf-eu.org.
2. This text is based on: Lieder, Hans-Jörg, "LEAF in a nutshell," *LEAF Newsletter*, issue no. 1 (March 2002).

NACO:
A Cooperative Model
for Building and Maintaining
a Shared Name Authority Database

John D. Byrum, Jr.

SUMMARY. The Name Authority Cooperative (NACO), founded in 1976, now encompasses some 395 institutions that have collectively developed and maintained a database of more than 2,000,000 authority records in addition to the more than 3,500,000 records created by Library of Congress staff. The NACO family of libraries is expanding at a rate of about 50 new members annually. The membership includes institutions from all but four of the 50 U.S. states and 43 institutions in 16 countries within Europe, Africa, Oceania, Asia, and Latin America. The NACO model has changed over time to create more cost-effective and user-friendly policies and procedures to meet participants' needs. Increased recognition, especially by library administrators, of the value of authority control also encouraged NACO to flourish. This presentation explains membership requirements, benefits to the participants, as well as the role of the Library of Congress which serves as secretariat to NACO and oversees a variety of training and documentation activities to support program operations. One of NACO's unique features–the opportunity to participate via a "Funnel Project" in which a group of institutions band together–is also described. Internationally, as the trend

John D. Byrum, Jr., is Chief, Regional and Cooperative Cataloging Division, Library of Congress, Washington, DC 20544.

[Haworth co-indexing entry note]: "NACO: A Cooperative Model for Building and Maintaining a Shared Name Authority Database." Byrum, John D., Jr. Co-published simultaneously in *Cataloging & Classification Quarterly* (The Haworth Information Press, an imprint of The Haworth Press, Inc.) Vol. 38, No. 3/4, 2004, pp. 237-249; and: *Authority Control in Organizing and Accessing Information: Definition and International Experience* (ed: Arlene G. Taylor, and Barbara B. Tillett) The Haworth Information Press, an imprint of The Haworth Press, Inc., 2004, pp. 237-249.

http://www.haworthpress.com/web/CCQ
Digital Object Identifier: 10.1300/J104v38n03_18

towards adopting AACR and MARC 21 increases, the number of
NACO partners outside the U.S. also increases. For countries where
other standards prevail or where English is not the official language,
NACO can serve as a model framework for a national program to consider while awaiting longer-term development of a more global approach to authority control.

KEYWORDS. NACO, name authority records, catalogers' training,
catalogers' documentation, Program for Cooperative Cataloging, Library of Congress, authority control, international aspects

More than 25 years have passed since the Name Authority Cooperative
(NACO) was conceived.[1] Although not the most senior of cooperative cataloguing initiatives hosted by the Library of Congress–that distinction is
held by the Cooperative Online Serials program (CONSER) dating from
1972–NACO has nevertheless emerged in terms of size of membership and
extent of production as the largest endeavor of its nature in the history of bibliographic control.

NACO, which began with an agreement with but a single institution in
1976, now encompasses some 395 institutions that have collectively developed and maintained a database of more than 2,000,000 authority records in
addition to the more than 3,500,000 records created by Library of Congress
staff. The NACO family of libraries is expanding at a rate of about 50 new
members annually. The number of new and updated name and series authority
records is currently growing by nearly 220,000 records each year.[2] The strategic goal established for NACO is to increase production by a minimum of 10%
annually from 2003 to 2006. Indeed, with a membership now including institutions from all but four of the 50 states comprising the U.S., and including 43
institutions in 16 countries within Europe, Africa, Oceania, Asia, and Latin
America, we no longer are actively recruiting new members.

How does one explain the popularity of, and commitment to, this partnership focused on promoting the concept and reality of authority control?

First and foremost was the *gradual* recognition that the utility of the catalogue–any catalogue–depends on uniform and unique headings as access
points to bibliographic data, and that the national library by itself could not
provide controlled headings for all materials of interest to the library community as a whole. I say "gradual" because, when NACO was first offered as a cooperative vehicle to achieve increased authority control, there was, frankly,
some resistance to joining on the part of many libraries. Administrators, in
particular, often felt that creating authority records at the local level was a lux-

ury that their cataloguing departments could not afford. And, at that time, the minority of libraries that did undertake to produce authority records often would limit them to cases of name headings that required cross references. In addition, to further reduce the expense of authority records when created, cataloguers were often instructed to limit research to materials in hand whenever possible, and to omit mention of citations or other data now routinely provided.

The generally skeptical attitude about the cost-effectiveness of name authority work that prevailed in the1970s and into the 1980s put a great deal of pressure on NACO management to streamline process and procedures. As a result, the original model for this cooperative program has changed considerably. For example, when NACO first began to recruit members, an interested institution was required to send a staff member to the Library of Congress for two weeks of training, at the institutions's own expense, and with that person in turn providing training to others back at the local institution. Today, NACO training has been condensed to a five-day session. Prospective members usually can reduce start-up expenses by selecting from among a cadre of 20 regional trainers scattered throughout the U.S. and arranging for local onsite training of up to 12 cataloguers. In addition, NACO documentation was rewritten to make it more "user-friendly," and some of the standards were relaxed to encourage "cataloguer judgement"–for example, when the specifications for information recorded in the "sources found" note were better defined and simplified regarding form and style.[3]

Mark Watson summarized the case for library management support of cooperative programs such as NACO in his paper "Top Five Reasons Why Library Administrators Should Support Participation in the Program for Cooperative Cataloging."[4] Here in short are the arguments that he put forth in advocating cooperation:

- First, he points out that "the very act of considering membership is an excellent opportunity for cataloguers, their public services colleagues, and library administrators to . . . set aside some time to consider the big picture, to think about why cataloging is performed, what makes it valuable, what is essential and what is not, and whether it makes sense to approach it in a cooperative environment. . . ."
- Next, he argues that "that the act of participation imposes a greater discipline . . . that can pave the way for better original and upgraded copy cataloging, higher morale, and potentially higher production and productivity. . . ."
- Thirdly, Watson contends that "an investment in the overhead necessary for participation pays dividends that, in a short period of time, more than

exceed the costs," a point that most library managers have come to appreciate.

- A closely related argument follows: "cataloging in general is labor-intensive to begin with and, when the effort is shared according to mutually agreed-upon standards, [it] becomes less so for everyone."
- And, finally, pointing out that those who help others in fact help themselves, he concludes: ". . . it's too expensive **not** to participate–the more participants, the lower the overall cost for everyone."

In his recent and comprehensive treatise, *Maxwell's Guide to Authority Work*, Robert Maxwell addresses this latter point in particular, pointing out that the lack of authority work transfers the cost of using the catalogue to the end-user, who would have to bear the burden of thinking of all possible forms a cataloguer might have used to provide access in the catalogue to a particular author.[5]

In short, NACO not only survived initial resistance to its goals, but ultimately succeeded in becoming accepted as the most cost-effective means of adding more authority records to distributed national and international databases, and to accomplish more dependable, timely, and efficient cataloguing, with better problem-solving through networking and access to expert training. As Brian Schottlaender, then Associate University Librarian at the University of California, Los Angeles, wrote to me: "Our attempting to create the same level of authority control we (and our patrons!) currently enjoy in our local database without benefit of the [NACO] file would be so cost-prohibitive as to be virtually unthinkable."[6]

While efforts to make NACO participation an affordable activity were unfolding, other forces were also reinforcing a new view about the value of authority control and the need to invest staff resources in achieving it. As large bibliographic utilities such as OCLC and RLG flourished, users more fully appreciated the structure of controlled access to information. Reflecting the "explosion" of publications in a wide variety of languages, scripts, and formats, these databases have grown at such a pace it became increasingly obvious that controlled access would entail creation of authority records far beyond what any national library by itself might produce. The NACO program proved to be the logical mechanism to meet the need for an organized and coherent response to the proliferation of bibliographic information.

As a result of the successful efforts to make NACO membership an affordable venture and of the increasing acceptance of the necessity of authority work, this program has experienced dramatic growth during the past decade. Last year, NACO libraries contributed 64% of all the total name authority production distributed by the Library of Congress, while LC staff contributed 36%. About the same ratio applies to the output of authority records for series, where last year NACO libraries created/updated about 12,000 such records in comparison to 8,000 produced by LC staff. These ratios are a complete reversal of the situation barely 10 years previously, at which time LC cataloguers were the major suppliers of name and series authority data.

To become a partner in NACO, an institution must be selected for membership in the Program for Cooperative Cataloging (PCC), since NACO operates within the PCC as one of its four core activities.[7] Any kind of institution may join the PCC, as the Program's membership is comprised of libraries of various sizes and types. About half of the PCC's current participants are academic libraries, with the remainder coming from public, governmental, and special libraries. Utilities and vendors may also participate.

Since this is an international conference, it might be of interest to identify those institutions outside the U. S. that are current NACO members: British Library; Cambridge University Library; El Colegio de Mèxico; English Short Title Catalogue; Hong Kong University of Science and Technology; Memorial University of Newfoundland; National Art Library (Great Britain); National Library of Canada; National Library of New Zealand; National Library of Scotland; National Library of South Africa; National Library of Wales; Oxford University Library (The Bodleian); Singapore Integrated Library Automated Services (SILAS); Trinity College (University of Dublin); Universidade de San Andrès (Argentina); Universidade de São Paulo (Brazil); University of Regina; University of South Africa; University of Strathclyde (Scotland); University of Toronto-Hebraica Project (Canada); and Wellcome Library (London). In addition, there are 17 South African libraries, one from Hong Kong, two from Canada, and one from Italy (Unione romana biblioteche) participating in one of the NACO's various funnel projects (to be described later).

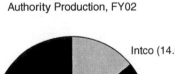

International Name
Authority Production, FY02

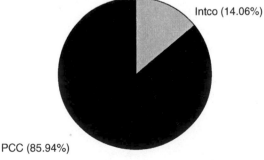

Intco (14.06%)

PCC (85.94%)

Last year, these international partners (sometimes referred to as "IntCo" libraries) contributed 14.1% of NACO's total contribution. International NACO members have also been responsible for a relatively high percentage of updates to established headings. Thus, last year the IntCo partners contributed 21,386 new name authority records and revised 7,513 existing records.[8] To facilitate further international expansion, the Program for Cooperative Cataloging recently established a Task Group on International Participation in the PCC. This group will examine all discoverable obstacles that hamper participation of libraries outside the U.S. in order to devise strategies for overcoming them.[9]

The benefits of membership help to explain the popularity of the PCC, whether domestic or abroad, and all of them potentially apply to NACO contributors:

- Members participate in the programs of the largest cooperative name authority conglomerate in the world and thereby help to shape the future of cataloguing practice.
- Members participate in the development and review of national and international standards designed to create more reliable and cost-efficient authority control.
- Members enjoy reduction in the cost of their cataloguing operations by increasing the number of authority records that can be used with little or no local editing.
- Members also benefit from a reduction in the amount of authority creation and maintenance that must be done locally by increasing the number of authority records contributed through NACO.
- Members are empowered to update authority records, including those created by national libraries, without needing to secure their permission to do so.
- Members receive staff training by experienced NACO trainers at minimal cost, and are eligible to participate in a variety of seminars and workshops developed for program partners.
- Staff of member institutions interact with colleagues at national libraries and other libraries through numerous meetings and electronic discussion networks.
- Members receive free-of-charge training and cataloguing documentation.
- Members benefit from a reduction in the cataloguing burden on a local scale through collective efforts on a global scale. And, finally,

- Members directly influence the objectives, policies, and standards applicable to name and series authority work by serving on committees and task forces created to improve NACO effectiveness.

To enjoy these benefits, libraries seeking NACO membership must be able to meet certain requirements. Firstly, and most important, they must follow the standards established for the formation of headings and cross-references and supply other data as required. Essentially, the standards stipulated are AACR2 and MARC21, both widely applied within the Anglo-American community and by an increasing number of cataloguers elsewhere.

Secondly, they need to belong to a bibliographic utility for record contribution. Today, RLIN and OCLC provide the technical means by which NACO cataloguers can search the bibliographic and authority files as well as contribute completed name authority records. Once received by the bibliographic utility, the new or updated authority records are transmitted immediately to the Library of Congress, which maintains the master database. Through nightly file exchanges with the copyholders, the file is recreated from the work of the previous day's contributions, and then redistributed to OCLC and RLIN. (The British Library is also a partner in this contribution/distribution queue.) Since the membership of these two utilities are increasingly international in scope, it has proved possible for institutions located in countries outside of the U.S. to meet this particular requirement. And, as the utilities extend operations in Europe, Latin America, Asia, and the Middle East, prospects for increased international partnerships in the NACO program appear bright.

Thirdly, it is expected that NACO institutions will commit staff to work actively in performing authority work as a part of their cataloguing activities. Full integration of NACO contributions into the local library's workflow has proved most effective. However, NACO libraries themselves determine which name authority records they will contribute, and some select only a sub-set of headings to submit in order to contain costs.

Nevertheless, there is a clear expectation that all NACO members will meet established thresholds for contributions: for a small library, the minimum rate of new and updated records combined has been set at 100 records per year, and for a large library, the minimum rises to 200 records annually.

Established in November 2002 as the principal provision in a policy of "managed growth," these modest quantitative goals are needed in order to justify the costs of processing records contributed–the fewer the records submitted, the more likely they will need review by higher graded (and therefore more costly) staff–and to justify the expense of providing subscriptions and other documentation for the membership.

Not only are these requirements being applied to new NACO libraries, but existing members are being held accountable for meeting them as well. This is because a study revealed that the 16% of the NACO membership currently contributing at the required level only produce 1% of the total number of authorities; in addition, they incur 14% of the total annual cost for operating the NACO program. It is gratifying that when presented with the need to increase output, most of these low-producing libraries decided to commit to meeting the new requirements, although one decided to join a funnel instead, and only three withdrew from the membership.

Related to these expectations are two additional requirements, also components of the policy of managed program growth. First, new NACO members need to achieve independence within one year after joining the program. Independent status is granted by trainers to institutions whose staff have proved reliable in formulating records according to standards, based on a review of records created following training. Independence may be granted in stages, for example, initially for personal names and later for corporate and/or geographic names. For most institutions, this requirement is not a problem, and most are freed from review within a few months after having received training.

The other newly adopted expectation is that every NACO institution will designate a second person to serve as back-up to an individual primarily appointed to be responsible for the library's day-to-day NACO activities. The need for a back-up became apparent over the years due to some situations where a NACO library's principal contact comprised the sole source of authority control expertise within the institution. When that person left for another job or for whatever reason, the library found itself without any staff qualified to continue its NACO participation and had to begin anew.

Should a library wish to join NACO but is unable to produce the minimum number of records required, there is still an opportunity for participation. This option is available to libraries that wish to partner with others in one of NACO's "funnel projects." Indeed, these funnel projects have become a major feature of the NACO program–currently, there are 223 libraries participating in 19 funnels. A NACO funnel project results when a group of libraries join together to contribute name authority records to the master database. Funnel members which create records in modest numbers are able to consolidate their efforts to make a larger contribution as a group. These joint endeavors are typically based on a shared interest among the participating libraries: some funnels are subject- or language-based, such as the Arabic, Hebraica, Art, Music and Law funnels. Some reflect geographic proximity among the funnel members (such as the Detroit Area funnel). And, a few occur from common membership in a consortium (such as the GAELIC South Africa funnel). Thus, funnel projects serve two needs: (1) to enable smaller libraries with modest resources and contributions to participate in NACO; and (2) to provide a means for cataloguers with special interests to interact and collaborate with colleagues who share their expertise. In 2002, contributions from funnel projects accounted for 17.5% of new name records (28,396 such records) and 15% of updated name records (6,650), providing clear evidence that the funnel projects are quite productive.

Crucial to the success of a funnel project are the interest and dedication of the person who volunteers to organize it and serve as its coordinator. This person recruits participants and generally hosts training sessions; disseminates information about NACO policy and practice to funnel members; receives documents distributed by NACO subscription and distributes copies of them to funnel members; and may serve as trainer and reviewer for members, with help from other funnel members when needed. In short, the funnel coordinator is the individual soley responsible for administration of the funnel entire activities. The coordinators are held accountable for conforming to NACO policy and practice on behalf of the whole funnel membership. As a result, a great deal of authority is delegated to them, and they are largely autonomous in their administration of funnel operations. Funnel coordinators are granted authority to determine whether to admit a library to the funnel, whether to grant independent status to individual members, and whether to retain those that are very low producers.[10]

On several occasions, this presentation has referred to NACO training and documentation. Together they are the two most important ingredients to the program's success. The basic training is provided in the course of a five-day workshop taught by a certified trainer which covers the basic cataloguing rules for personal, corporate, and geographic names, as well as uniform titles and cross-references. Also included are related topics such as MARC format issues, searching requirements, and administrative matters. The format divides each day into instruction in the morning and hands-on practice sessions in the afternoon, with trainees expected to bring to the classroom examples from their daily work for discussion or input and contribution.[11]

A considerable amount of work has been devoted to ensuring that these training sessions are as easy to conduct, uniform in content, and user-friendly to the trainees as possible. A Web page has been mounted for trainers providing a document to use to prepare for the training assignment, as well as training manuals, PowerPoint slide shows, tips by way of lists of "things to remember," and the answers to exercises developed to reinforce each topic covered by the course. There is another Web page for the trainees. This page accesses material which provides the actual documentation that they will need for participation, including the relevant Library of Congress rule interpretations, appropriate LC Descriptive Cataloging Manual sections and excerpts from the MARC format regarding the topics covered during training.

Beyond the basic introduction to policies and procedures given to staff of all new NACO member libraries are other training sessions intended to provide on-the-job learning opportunities. Many of these take the form of workshops held in conjunction with the semiannual meetings of the American Library Association which attract large numbers of cataloguers. In addition, the program periodically offers the NACO Series Institute open to experienced NACO cataloguers at independent NACO libraries. This three-day course covers searching techniques for series as well as the various complexities of series, including sub-series, series-like phrases, qualifiers, multi-part items, cross-references, and successive entries. This Institute is considered to have generally helped to improve the general level of cataloguer expertise in this rather complicated area of bibliographic control. Also drawing strong interest among cataloguers have been the NACO Training-the-Trainer courses offered to assist NACO trainers in building their teaching abilities.

Documentation is another major strength of the NACO program. A high priority is given to the creation and maintenance of technical and administrative guidelines and written instructions in order to enable participants to create and update records in a standardized way. This material is also intended to help them resolve problems more independently. The NACO Participants Manual, now undergoing its third revision, is perhaps the most substantial document produced for the membership, but many other shorter documents are produced and shared. In addition, all NACO members receive, at no cost, the MARC 21 Authorities Format, parts of the Library of Congress Rule Interpretations and updates to both.

Throughout most of the 1990s, NACO documentation was published mostly in print and distributed by mail. However, recently a decision was implemented utilizing the Web in order to make NACO material universally available as quickly as possible. As a result, the Program is now realizing annual savings in excess of $20,000 (U.S.) in the costs of printing, assembling, and posting material.

What is the role of the Library of Congress in helping to operate NACO? By way of a general reply, I can say that we view our role as one of leadership through collaboration. We provide the impetus to bring the NACO partners together to set goals and standards, and we coordinate the work of NACO expansion. We serve as Secretariat and thereby provide the infrastructure for the day-to-day business by which the members pursue their NACO work. We are responsible for maintaining effective communications among the NACO partners and with other interested parties. Through the Cataloging Distribution Service, the Library widely shares the fruits of the contributed records with utilities, libraries and many others throughout the world. In short, LC is fully wedded to the NACO program and accepts an ongoing and major role for furthering its goals and contributing to its accomplishments.

More specifically, the Library dedicates staff resources to the work that is needed to support operations and realize expansion of the NACO program. Within LC's Cataloging Directorate is a team of a dozen cataloguing specialists whose full-time work is devoted to cooperative cataloguing. They contribute to the preparation of documentation and training materials. These staff diligently maintain the Program's Web site by posting new documents, summaries of meetings, announcements, FAQs about various programs and cataloguing policy questions. They update calendars, rosters, and other documents that are also available on the Web site. In the past five years, nearly 95,000 visits were recorded to the PCC home page which provides access to all of the NACO Program information generated. The cooperative cataloguing specialists also answer a steady stream of queries regarding related LC cataloguing policics and practices that come in from around the world.

The investment that LC makes in supporting and promoting NACO is more than repaid–most directly in the reduction of the costs of our cataloguing operations. For example, a study undertaken in the late 1990s focused on the re-use of headings established by the British Library as part of its NACO contribution. This study found that "Library of Congress catalogers had used two-thirds of these headings to support copy cataloging of the same bibliographic titles for which the British Library had created authority records."[12] Clearly, such evidence makes clear that NACO has made it possible for LC to decrease the amount of staff resources needed to perform authority work, which is considered one of the most time-consuming and expensive portions of cataloguing activities overall. Other important benefits accrue to the Library through closer relationships between the Cataloging Directorate and many of its numerous constituents, as a result of this cooperative program bringing our staff into direct relationships with staff of other libraries. We learn from hearing the concerns and problems of others in performing authority works, and they from our responses. We also benefit from the support and endorsement that these partners dependably lend to supporting the activities and programs that require approval and funding from the national legislature.

In conclusion, NACO offers a viable cooperative model for building and maintaining a shared name authority database. NACO is a real-time program that has proven itself through rapid growth, as more and more libraries decide to participate as partners in building and maintaining a shared database for the benefit of all members. Internationally, as the trend towards adopting AACR and MARC 21 increases, we expect the number of partners outside the U.S. also to increase.

Nevertheless, we fully appreciate that bibliographic agencies that catalogue in languages other than English will want to pursue an alternative. For them, the principles that NACO embodies offers a model by which they, too, might replicate NACO successes, whether their model is set up within a single nation or across national boundaries on the basis of a shared language and common cataloguing tradition. As Mauro Guerrini made clear in his introductory remarks to this Conference, much professional interest in now focused on finding a way by which authority data can be effectively shared across linguistic and cultural boundaries, a theme elaborated by Michael Gorman at the conclusion of his keynote presentation; several other papers have set forth possible pathways to achieve such a goal. Thus, NACO is a model to consider while we await the long-term research and development of a more global approach to authority control.

Such cooperative projects might incorporate the basic principles upon which NACO has been built. In summary, these principles are:

- Seek to minimize the cost of participation to the members by avoiding over-exacting requirements and excessive quality control.
- Follow standards that allow participants to determine themselves the level of their contribution.
- Recruit a broadly based membership so that libraries of all types and sizes can join.
- Involve the membership in interpreting the standards to be followed, in providing the training needed for program expansion, and in deciding program goals, administrative policies, and governance.
- Invest in efforts to increase efficiency of operations through rapidly advancing and increasingly affordable automation.
- Develop a clear statement of benefits to accrue from participation, so that all staff of member institutions buy into the cost of the work required for participation, and pursue public relations initiatives that will share the values of cooperative name authority control with the information community at large.

I would like to leave you with a thought that was expressed by the University Librarian of Cornell University, Sarah E. Thomas, on the occasion of NACO's 20th anniversary in 1997. She said:

> As I reflect on NACO's accomplishment, I find NACO is a model of successful partnership between the Library of Congress and an international community of cataloguers. Working together, LC and hundreds of other institutions have cut the cost of cataloguing, and even more impor-

tantly, have increased the reliability of access to bibliographic records through the provision of authoritative headings. . . . Truly, NACO demonstrates the power of collaboration and the importance of common standards. May its achievements continue to grow and benefit many more generations of library users."[13]

ENDNOTES

1. An excellent overview of NACO's history for the period 1976-1992 is provided by: Reimer, John J. and Morgenroth, Karen, "Hang Together or Hang Separately: The Cooperative Authority Work Component of NACO," *Cataloging & Classification Quarterly*, v. 17, no. 3/4 (1993), pp. 127-161.

2. These figures do not include authority records created or updated by Library of Congress staff.

3. In her unpublished paper "Advances in Authority Control" given at the June 1993 meeting of the LITA/ACLTS Authority Control in the Online Environment Group, Sarah Thomas identifies the major changes to improve NACO as: (1) developing a single generic NACO manual; (2) basing authority work on a shared database (not just the LC file as was previously the case); (3) adopting a "whole book" approach to NACO work; (4) nurturing a participant-oriented training program, as described in this paper; (5) modifying Library of Congress Rule Interpretations to reflect the shared cataloguing environment enabled by technological developments.

4. Available at: <http://www.loc.gov/catdir/pcc/topfive.html> [Jan. 2003].

5. Maxwell, Robert L., *Maxwell's Guide to Authority Work*, Chicago: American Library Association, 2002, p. 6-8.

6. Letter from Brian E. C. Schottlaender to John Byrum, 30 Oct. 1997.

7. For further information regarding the PCC, visit its Web site at: <http://lcweb.loc.gov/catdir/pcc/> [Jan. 2003].

8. For a discussion of the PCC's international activities, see: Franks, Anthony R. D., "International Participation in the Program for Cooperative Cataloging: Present Status," *International Cataloguing and Bibliographic Control*, v. 30, no. 2, pp. 23-26.

9. For further information regarding the charge, timeline and membership of the Joint Task Group on International Participation on the PCC, see its Web page at: <www.loc.gov/catdir/pcc/tgip.html> [Jan. 2003].

10. For further information regarding the duties of the funnel coordinators, see: <http://www.loc.gov/catdir/pcc/naco/funres.htm> [Jan. 2003].

11. The outline of the 5-day basic course is available at: <http://www.loc.gov/catdir/pcc/naco/outline.html> [Jan. 2003].

12. Franks, *ibid.*

13. Letter from Sarah E. Thomas to John D. Byrum, Oct. 27, 1997.

Names of the Far East:
Japanese, Chinese, and Korean
Authority Control

Eisuke Naito

SUMMARY. Personal names in Chinese, Japanese, and Korean appear not only in domestic publications but also in publications of foreign regions in original, transcribed, and transliterated forms, and produce misleading searches and confusion among information users. National bibliographic control in China, Japan, and Korea is reviewed to determine the status and common tasks. Three workshops were held discussing name authority control in the region in 2001 and 2002. IFLA's work on UBC/IM as well as FRBR and VIAF were introduced in the workshops to set a framework for regional development. Future regional cooperation was pursued among national bibliographic agencies in East Asia. *[Article copies available for a fee from The Haworth Document Delivery Service: 1-800-HAWORTH. E-mail address: <docdelivery@haworthpress.com> Website: <http://www.HaworthPress.com> © 2004 by The Haworth Press, Inc. All rights reserved.]*

KEYWORDS. Chinese personal names, Japanese personal names, Korean personal names, Japan MARC, KOR MARC, China MARC, regional cooperation, national bibliographic control

Eisuke Naito is Professor, Faculty of Sociology, Toyo University, Japan.

[Haworth co-indexing entry note]: "Names of the Far East: Japanese, Chinese, and Korean Authority Control." Naito, Eisuke. Co-published simultaneously in *Cataloging & Classification Quarterly* (The Haworth Information Press, an imprint of The Haworth Press, Inc.) Vol. 38, No. 3/4, 2004, pp. 251-268; and: *Authority Control in Organizing and Accessing Information: Definition and International Experience* (ed: Arlene G. Taylor, and Barbara B. Tillett) The Haworth Information Press, an imprint of The Haworth Press, Inc., 2004, pp. 251-268. Single or multiple copies of this article are available for a fee from The Haworth Document Delivery Service [1-800-HAWORTH, 9:00 a.m. - 5:00 p.m. (EST). E-mail address: docdelivery@haworthpress.com].

BACKGROUND

Chinese Characters

Diffusion of Chinese Characters

Writing systems of East Asia have been based on Chinese characters (scripts) formed around 3rd century BC, and became the basis of writing systems in the region. Each Chinese logographic (ideographic) character has meanings and readings that evolved through the ages and through geographic variations. The languages of China, Korea, and Japan are different, but all use Chinese characters under their own language conventions. The Chinese character is so robust in its logographic and semantic features that written materials can be commonly assimilated in the region. However, over time and space, Chinese characters have evolved in China, Korea, Japan, and Vietnam with variations in shapes and meanings tailored to local language conventions.

Movable type printing was invented in 1234 AD in Korea. Hangul, the Korean phonetic alphabet, originally with 28 characters, was established by Sejong the Great of the Yi Dynasty in 1443 AD. Hangul became the national characters of Korea after World War II. There are differences in Hangul between South and North Korea.

It is believed that Dr. Wang In, a Korean monk, brought the *Analects of Confucius* and the *Thousand Characters Text–A Primer of Chinese Characters* into Japan in 285 AD. Local developments were made to derive phonetic symbols of 48 Kana, based on the Japanese pronunciation of Chinese characters, and they became the basic components, together with Chinese characters, of the Japanese writing system over time.

In China, the Government introduced simplified Chinese characters in 1956 for the national literacy policy. This created a major impact on the conventions of use of characters in neighboring countries. The shapes of simplified characters maintain the original forms of radicals; therefore, people in both Korea and Japan are able to assume the original characters.

The total number of Chinese characters is thought to be about 100,000. Variant shapes of Chinese characters exist in each language. New Chinese characters are constantly created by combining radicals for personal names, especially in Hong Kong. However, the number of domestic creations of Chinese characters in Korea and Japan remains less than 100 in each language after 1,700 years. Learning Chinese characters, even to master newspaper reading (3,000 characters in the case of the Japanese language), takes a long time.

Chinese Characters on Computers

Computer diffusion in East Asia has been phenomenal, especially since 1995.[1] Computer development work started in the 1950s in each country. Until around the mid 1970s, language support was unavailable in each country because of multiple scripts and the large number of characters in the East Asian languages. Character codes/sets for local languages were necessary for national (natural) language processing. In terms of software applications, the Western products were localized in the early stage. It should be noted that Chinese characters are commonly used in three languages but the language and conventions are different from one another. The fundamental characteristic of Chinese characters is the open-ended nature, i.e., new characters can emerge by government policy, by voluntary addition, or by mistake. Thus, it is theoretically impossible to get a complete set of Chinese characters in each language.

In the last 30 years of the 20th century, efforts were made to establish standard character codes/sets in three languages. During the 1970s, all three countries established national standards for computer character sets in one byte based on ASCII, followed by the development of national standards of domestic Chinese characters in two bytes. They are Japanese JIS C 6226 in 1978, Chinese GB 2312 in 1980, Chinese (Taipei) CNS 11643 in 1986, and Korean KS C 5601 in 1987. CCCII code created in Taiwan in 1980 became the East Asian Common Character (EACC) used by the U.S. Research Libraries Group (RLG) and others, and then became ANSI Z39.64: 1989.

In the computer industry, de facto standards are common practice. The Big 5 was developed in Taiwan in 1984 for Chinese characters, and the Shift JIS code was developed for Japanese PCs during the 1970s. Both de facto standards are widely used.

The publication of the Unicode 1st edition in 1991 and UCS (Universal Character Set: ISO 10646) in 1993 impacted the computer industry, consumers, the governments in the East Asia, and worldwide users of Chinese characters (or East Asian languages).[2] Industry and governments made a tremendous effort to harmonize the development of Unicode, ISO/UCS and national standards of computer character sets. In the beginning of the 21st century, it seems that technical harmonization has been achieved among the Unicode, UCS and the national standards. The next step is the changeover to the Unicode/UCS environment among users. It is estimated that a company-wide changeover of the character codes in big companies needs investment on a scale of several million U.S. dollars.

National Bibliography Databases and Library Networks

National MARCs

Computer capabilities of national (natural) language processing made possible the creation and maintenance of national bibliographic databases (MARC) in East Asian national languages. They are the China MARC, the Japan MARC and the KOR MARC. Housekeeping processing, typically circulation control function, was started during 1970s.

The National Diet Library (NDL),[3] Tokyo, founded in 1948, is the national parliamentary library under the management of the legislature. It started to computerize its operations in 1970. Prior to the Japan MARC distribution in 1981, the cataloging system for Japanese materials (1977), and weekly list printing (1978) were implemented in NDL. Japan MARC is IFLA UNIMARC-compatible and covers 2.7 million catalog records since 1864. Web OPAC of NDL holdings is one of the most popular Web sites. The second NDL, the new Kansai-Kan was opened in 2002 in Nara near Osaka.

The National Library of China (the Beijing Library),[4] established in 1909, which now holds 23 million items, started computer utilization in the middle of 1980s and established China MARC production in 1990. The China MARC format is IFLA UNIMARC-compatible, and was established as a cultural professional standard (WH/T 0503-96) in 1996. The China MARC database covers 1.1 million bibliographic records of Chinese books published since 1979.

The National Library of Korea (NLK),[5] Seoul, established in 1945, started computerization of bibliographic services in 1976, backed by a government plan of computer application for administration; and KOR MARC printed card distribution was started in 1983. The total for KOR MARC was 4.1 million records in 2001. Its format is a national standard (KS X 6006-2) that is US MARC-compatible; it covers 1.8 million bibliographic records, and is being operated on the KOrean Library System (KOLIS) based on the Windows system. NLK has run the Korean Library Information Network (KOLIS-NET) since 1991. The Digital Library Program was started in 1998 and holds 59 million pages of scanned images.

National MARC Authority Files

The National Diet Library, Tokyo, started the Japan MARC Authority file distribution service in 1997, and began distribution of CD-ROMs in January 2001 with 60,000 records. NDL studied the IFLA UNIMARC (A) in detail and added data elements to meet their own needs, such as the Notes for Dates (birth/death, establishment/abolition) as 301, and the Notes for Kanji (character) as 831.

The National Library of China established the China MARC (CN MARC) Format based on the UNIMARC Handbook 1983, and the "China MARC Format / Authority 1990" was established in 1990 based on UNIMARC Authority 1991. Both formats were revised in 1998. The number of distributed name authority records was 300,000 by 2001.

The National Library of Korea established a name authority format in 1999 based on the US MARC Authority, and started input in 2000. The number of KOR MARC Authority records is 60,000. Authority files exist among universities and large public library systems in Korea because computer application was started in the 1980s. The total number of these authority records exceeds 1.15 million. Harmonization between KOR MARC Authority and these existing authority records will be a task for the immediate future.

National MARC Authority Files

National MARC	Name Authority File Creation	No. of Records in 2001
Japan MARC	1997	60,000
China MARC	1998 ?	300,000
KOR MARC	2000	60,000

Library Networks

Bibliographic utilities were developed in the region during the 1980s and 1990s. They are NII/NACSIS (Japan),[6] KERIS (Korea)[7] and CALIS (China)[8] among others. The common feature is that these three organizations were established primarily for academia, are maintained by government funding, and are non-profit. Also, the academia or higher education institutions in each country are being subjected to a reformation process by the governments. And the reformation affects the future development of these bibliographic utilities.

In 1984, a shared cataloging system was installed in Japan, which became NACSIS-CAT. It was designed on a relational database system based on the entity-relationship model. As of 2001, 1,200 libraries of 900 universities among 1,200 higher education institutions in Japan are participating in NACSIS-CAT, which has 6.1 million bibliographic records and 58.6 million holding records. The annual growth is slowly decreasing as the total amount of the database system becomes larger. A few hundred thousand records are expected to be added to the name authority file annually. Reference MARCs are also offered, such as US MARC Authority (3.4 million) as well as Japan

MARC Authority (320,000). NACSIS/NII offers an online shared cataloging system, ILL requests transfer, an online journal (scanned journal articles), and Web-Cat. NACSIS was changed to the National Institute of Informatics (NII) in 2000.

In 1994, the Korea Research Information Center was established by the Ministry of Education and changed to the Korea Education and Research Information Services (KERIS) in 1999. The mission of KERIS is development, management, and provision of education and research information on a national level, such as (1) management of the Research Information Sharing Union, (2) management of the integrated retrieval system, (3) digital thesis collection and service, (4) development of research information meta DB, and (5) management of the inter-library loan system (L2L). KERIS has not developed any original authority control function yet, and continues surveys on authority databases of its core participating universities among the 155 member libraries. As a result of 20 years of development of individual library systems, there exists variation of format, description rules, and data contents. The 155 university libraries are participating in the KERIS system in 2001 with a total of 5.4 million bibliographic records. It seems that the KERIS system needs some time until it establishes an integrated authority system.

In 1998, the China Academic Library and Information System (CALIS) was established by funding from the government with 70 participating university libraries and core subject-centers at Beijing University, Tsinghua University, China Agriculture University, and Beijing Medical University, as well as seven regional sub-centers covering the whole country. CALIS' missions are shared cataloging, ILL, document delivery, document digitization, the Internet portal, and an online journal licensing consortium, among others.

International Use of National MARC Databases

Use of US MARC in the Far East was started in the middle of the 1980s by the National Diet Library and NACSIS/NII. Mutual utilization of the source MARCs of the Far East countries just started in the beginning of 2000 because of slow development processes of the national bibliographic databases, as well as the development speed of domestic national networks for bibliographic information, together with the progress of computer processing of national (natural) languages among these countries. For example, NACSIS/NII installed China MARC in January 2000, and KOR MARC in February 2002 as reference source MARCs in its system. It took 5 years to start the service after setting up a feasibility study committee in 1995.

How Personal Names Are Displayed in Neighboring Countries[9]

Translation is common practice for paper publications. Author names appear in different languages, or one person appears in newspapers in various countries in different forms of local languages. This presents a task for bibliographic control. The name of a person is transcribed into different script systems. A typical example is a Chinese poet–most probably his name was written in the old Chinese script. His name appears in the art column of newspapers, magazines, or scholarly publications in foreign languages, in translated form, transcription, Romanization, as well as in modern Chinese scripts of domestic conventions.

Form	Script systems
芥川　竜之介	Authorized form as he writes
あくたがわ　りゅうのすけ	Phonetic transcription in Hiragana
アクタガワ　リュウノスケ	Phonetic transcription in Katakana
ｱｸﾀｶﾞﾜ ﾘｭｳﾉｽｹ	Phonetic transcription in half-width Katakana for computer use
Akutagawa Ryūnosuke	Romanization in authentic form
Akutagawa Ryunosuke	Romanization in simple form (no macron)
Ａ ｋ ｕ ｔ ａ ｇ ａ ｗ ａ Ｒ ｙ ｕ ｎ ｏ ｓ ｕ ｋ ｅ	Romanization in 2 bytes full-width Latin alphabet

One author, however, would appear in the three databases of China, Japan and Korea. For example, the name of a Japanese novelist, AKUTAGAWA Ryunosuke, appears in three languages because of his original and translated works. In Japanese bibliographic databases, his name is assigned a variety of data strings.

The similar example of "KUROSAWA Akira" is shown in Appendix 1. If his work is translated into the Chinese language, then a record could be added with data for Chinese users:

- Chinese characters used commonly in China
- Romanization in the standard Chinese (Pinyin)
- Chinese characters in Japanese original way, if available
- Original Japanese data (additional).

The same happens in Korea. For Korean uses, this record is assigned Korean script of Hangul and Korean readings of foreign names, etc. Chinese and Korean authors appear in foreign language databases in a similar manner, without standard rules and conventions. An example of a Korean name appearing in the Japanese language is shown in Appendix 2. Other examples, prepared by YONEZAWA Makoto are shown in Appendix 3.[10] These variant forms or variations are drastically increasing, and creating a lack of integrity for retrieval precision.

THREE WORKSHOPS

The National Institute of Informatics hosted three workshops held in Tokyo entitled "Authority Control among Chinese, Korean and Japanese Scripts (CJK Authority)." They were supported by the National Diet Library (NDL), Japan. The 1st and 2nd workshops were part of an international research program entitled "International Sharing of Japanese Information," funded as grant-in-aid by the Japanese Ministry of Education, Culture, Sports and Technology for fiscal year 1998 through 2000. The third workshop in March 2002 was supported by NII initiative as part of the leadership program.

Aims, Scope, and Project Target

The aim of this project is to pursue a standardised or harmonised cumulation of the name authority data in Chinese, Korean and Japanese languages in other countries.

The focus of the workshop is "Name." Names are, in the first instance, "Author Name." In the future, if the project factors allow, there will be coverage of proper nouns used locally in other countries.

The target of this project is a "CJK Interchange Format of Authority Data" that conforms to the IFLA UNIMARC Authorities Concept incorporating the FRBR model.

Time and Reports

Time and reports of the three workshops are listed below:

Time	Date	Report
1st	January 10-11, 2001	Record of Workshop . . . compiled by YONEZAWA Makoto (ISBN 4-924600-97-0) http://www.nii.ac.jp/publications/CJK-WS/mokuji.html
2nd	March 28-29, 2001	
3rd	March 14-18, 2002	Record of Workshop . . . compiled by YONEZAWA Makoto [and OGIWARA Hiroshi] (ISBN 4-86049-002-9) http://www.nii.ac.jp/publications/CJK-WS3/mokuji.html

Participants

Five East Asian national libraries and national bibliographic utilities explored the way for sharing bibliographic information throughout the region. For more than the last two decades, these institutions have been creating national bibliography and national union catalogs through computer networks, with similar situations and demands: a large number of characters, different shapes of the same character, font problems, pronunciation, and semantic variations. The invited participants were as follows:

- National Library of China, Beijing
- National Library of Korea, Seoul
- Korean Education and Research Information Services (KERIS), Seoul
- National Diet Library, Tokyo
- National Institute of Informatics (NII), Tokyo.

Ms. Marie-France Plassard (IFLA UBCIM) was invited to the 2nd Workshop, and Dr. Barbara B. Tillett of the U.S. Library of Congress was invited to the 3rd Workshop.

Development

The target of the project is a CJK Interchange Format that conforms to the IFLA UNIMARC Authorities Format. However, domestic conditions are all so different among these three countries that it is not so simple and easy a task to design a common format for meeting the demands that exist in three countries. The primary task of the workshop was to find and understand facts about one another.

In the first meeting (January 10 and 11, 2001), the participants carried out fact-finding about institutional operations of authority control. However, the status of computer applications, the degree of domestic networking, and the development of shared cataloging systems among three countries were so different that the fact-finding was not as simple as expected. This also characterized the keen importance of this kind of professional meeting among neighboring countries, to maintain expert knowledge and professional discussion among staff with the responsibility to maintain the authority control systems. The first meeting was also characterized by the fact that not all participants shared a common methodology or common work target. By the end of the first meeting, as there was a possibility of holding the second workshop, homework was proposed: to collect authority records of 10 authors from each language (total of 30 authors) in the database of the participating institutions for comparison in the second meeting.

In the second meeting (March 28-29, 2001), a comparative study was carried out for the 30 authors. Participants were the same as in the first meeting. Ms. Marie-France Plassard of IFLA UBC/IM was invited to give a presentation about the current status of IFLA's promotion of authority control activities.

In 2001, after the two workshops, there was a difficult situation in and outside of NII for holding Workshop 3. However, with the strong support by Dr. Yasuharu Suematsu, Director General of NII, NII managed to host the third workshop in March 2002, only a year after Workshop 2. Therefore, it is too early to expect possible outcomes of the cooperative activity. In Workshop 3, the participants prepared a "Situational Report" of their organizations. As the workshop recognized the implication of IFLA activities, Dr. Barabara B. Tillett of the U.S. Library of Congress was invited to give a presentation on IFLA's direction.

These are the development processes of the three workshops held in January, March 2001 and March 2002. So far, it was the first time for these institutions to get together at the expert staff level, as well as to exchange facts and practices about how to share the common national task of bibliographic data integration. At least common ideas were shared about the responsibility, functions, future directions and the reality of counterparts. Standardization of this practice shall be the future task, but the time factor presses very hard because database creation in these three countries is so rapid that tremendous variations in data description are being created without coordination and control.

FUTURE TASKS

Organizational Establishment

The expert meeting may not have been the first of this sort; however, it was the first time for holding a regional meeting of staff in charge of authority control. There are organizational principles and conventions for each country in the Far East, and there was a fear of creating organizational derangement. Also, there are historical memories of the 19th and 20th centuries. There was an anxiety of political danger in meeting for discussing names, which are one of the core elements of cultural and political significance; although, in reality, names are being used and exchanged in the region.

Furthermore, an expert meeting does not produce an immediate result. It depends intensively on organizational ecology. But the three expert meetings may have introduced a step towards the evolution of awareness. The meetings can be recognized as opportunities to share knowledge such as technical contents, administrative elements, international and regional status, and can also be recognized as touchstones for modernizing and internationalizing organization management among the institutions concerned.

Mutual Understanding by Staff

National libraries in the Far East, as those in any other region, have national responsibilities that should be administered in domestic orientation. At the same time, a national library carries out national responsibility by having international views, perceptions, and opinions. This also applies to national bibliographic utilities. National institutions can bear national responsibilities by executing international roles.

It is assumed that the Internet revealed that domestic responsibility synchronize with the international role. This means that it is necessary for staff to sharpen consciousness on international trends for carrying out national responsibility. In this regard, it is a basic task for the staff to get acquainted with the counterparts in neighboring countries and maintain mutual understanding.

Possible Solutions in the Near Future

Directions of authority control are diverse, and greatly depend on technological foundations and financial conditions. The following possibilities can be listed from a professional viewpoint:

- An author name authority file is a unique database that is created by a national bibliographic agency or by a national bibliographic utility.
- The primary purpose of an author name authority file is, currently, to maintain the integrity of bibliographic information, i.e., to maintain integrity among national bibliographies and national union catalogs.
- Potential of the author name authority file is high for secondary use, i.e., the application/usage of the file may be increased by linking with other databases such as those for journal articles, and biographical directories. This possible linking device would increase social responsibility of the profession.
- Technical direction of author name authority control may depend on adjustments to the Internet application, the entity-relationship model, and the object-oriented model.
- The experience of creating and maintaining author name authority is unique to the profession, and it forms a basic skill for management of re-

corded knowledge. The skill can be applied to the construction and linking work of quality knowledge bases.

- Name Authority Control requires a universal approach not limited to one language, and it is being pursued in many cases. The profession shall watch the policies and practices of data-producing agencies in other countries.

List of Presentations

January 10-11, 2001

NAITO Eisuke (NII)	Why Have Authority Control Among Chinese, Korean and Japanese Languages?
MIYAZAWA Akira (NII)	Basic Concept of Authority Control in NACSIS-CAT
SAKAI Kiyohiko & KYOTO Toru (NII)	NACSIS-CAT Author Name Authority Record: Its Function and Processing
YOKOYAMA Yukio (NDL)	The Current Status of Authority Control of Author Names in the National Diet Library: NDL
ZHOU Shengheng (NLC)	Chinese Name Authority in China
LEE Chi-Ju & LEE Jae-Sun (NLK)	Author Name Authority Control in KORMARC
PARK Hong-Seok & LEE Ji-Won (KERIS)	The Current Status of the Authority DB in Korea and a Development Plan

2nd Workshop: March 28-29, 2001

Marie-France PLASSARD (IFLA UBCIM)	Authority Control in an International Environment: The UNIMARC Format for Authorities
MATSUI Sachiko (Ulis)	NACO Activity: A Literature survey
MIYAZAWA Akira (NII)	Towards Cooperative Authority Control
ASOSHINA Masumi (NDL)	Description Rule for the JAPAN/MARC Authors' Name Authorities
SAKAI Kiyohiko & KYOTO Toru (NII)	The Description Rules for Author Name Authority Data in NACSIS-CAT
KI Min-Do & LEE Jae-Sun (NLK)	Name Authority Data by KORMARC
PARK Hong-Seok (KERIS)	Comparative Analysis of Author Name Authority Records of Seoul National University and Yonsei University (Part 1)
ZHOU Shengheng (NLC)	Description Rules for Name Authority Data
OZAWA Nobuko (NDL)	Comparison of Authority Data: NDL
SAKAI Kiyohiko & KYOTO Toru (NII)	Comparative Analysis of Author Name Authority Data
KI Min-Do & LEE Lea-Sun (NLK)	Comparative Analysis of Authority Data
PARK Hong-Seok (KERIS)	Comparative Analysis of Author Name Authority Records of Seoul National University and Yonsei University (Part 2)
ZHOU Shengheng (NLC)	Union Heading for Personal Names

3rd Workshop: March 14-18, 2002

MIYAZAWA Akira (NII)	Network of East Asian Library Networks: Feasibility
SAKAI Kiyohiko & KYOTO Toru (NII)	Current Situation of NACSIS-CAT as of FY 2001
YOKOYAMA Yukio & MOTOHASHI Osamu (NDL)	Cataloging in the National Diet Library: Centering on the Outline from April 2002 and the Relationship with the NII
SUN Beixin (NLC)	The Development of Authority Database in National Library of China
LEE Jae-Sun (NLK)	Authority Files in the National Library of Korea
PARK Hong-Seok (KERIS)	The Revision of the Cataloging Rule (KCR4) and Authority Control under the New Rule
Barbara B. TILLETT (LC)	The FRBR Model (Functional Requirements for Bibliographic Records)
Barbara B. TILLETT (LC)	A Virtual International Authority File
Barbara B. TILLETT (LC)	AACR2's Updates for Electronic Resources: Response of a Multinational Cataloguing Code (presented at the Japan Library Association)

NOTES

1. Windows 95 was released in 1995. It can be recognized as the preceding background, that national information policies arrived around 1995 at a certain stage that has passed the initial phase in the Far East countries.

2. http://www.cicc.or.jp/homepage/english/library/in_af.htm.

3. http://www.ndl.go.jp/.

4. http://nlc.nlc.gov.cn/english.htm.

5. http://www.nl.go.kr/.

6. http://www.nii.ac.jp/.

7. http://www.keris.or.kr/eng/eng.html.

8. http://www.calis.edu.cn/.

9. This part was delivered at AFSIT-15 November 7-8, 2001, Katmandu, Nepal in "Identification, Integration and Links for Recorded Knowledge: Standards, Standard Frameworks for Accessing."

10. YONEZAWA Makoto, (Tohoku University Library, E-mail: yonezawa@library.tohoku.ac.jp). Entries are included in the main report. YONEZAWA Makoto [and OGIWARA Hiroshi] ed., "Record of Workshop on Authority Control among Chinese, Korean and Japanese Languages." NII. April 2001, 326 p. ISBN 4-924600-97-0.

APPENDIX 1. Japanese Personal Name

黒澤明	Form he used
黒沢明	Simplified character of "澤"
くろさわ　あきら	Phonetic description in Hiragana
クロサワ　アキラ	Phonetic description in Katakana
ｸﾛｻﾜ ｱｷﾗ	Phonetic description in Katakana by computer half-width character still in use
Kurosawa Akira KUROSAWA Akira	Romanized form Family name + Given name
Akira Kurosawa Akira KUROSAWA	English form (?) Given name + Family name

APPENDIX 2. Korean Personal Name in Japanese Usage

金大中	Korean name in Chinese Character
[Korean Hangul description]	Official form in Korean language *<not available in my PC>*
きん　だい　ちゅう キン　ダイ　チュウ ｷﾝﾀﾞｲ ﾁｭｳ	Japanese phonetic transcription in Hiragana, Katakana, and half-width Katakana
Kin Dai Chû	Romanization of Japanese reading
Kim Dae Jun	Korean Romanization
Dae Jun, Kim	Korean Romanization (English form)
きむ　で　じゅん キム　デ　ジュン ｷﾑ ﾃﾞ ｼﾞｭﾝ	Japanese phonetic transcription from Korean sound in Hiragana, Katakana, and half-width Katakana

APPENDIX 3. Sample of Name Authority Records from East Asia

Sources of Appendix 3 Examples

No.	Source
3-1	Japan MARC created by the National Diet Library, Tokyo
3-2	NACSIS Union Catalog Database Record, NII, Tokyo
3-3	KORMARC created by the National Library of Korea, Seoul
3-4	Name Authority Record created by the Seoul National University Library, held at KERIS, Seoul
3-5	Name Authority Record created by the Yonsei University Library, held at KERIS, Seoul
3-6	China MARC Name Authority Record created by the National Library of China, Beijing

APPENDIX 3-1. Japan MARC Created by the National Diet Library, Tokyo

```
001  00001509
005  20000107150300.0
100     $a19790401ajpny0112      da
152     $aNCR
200  1$6a01$a芥川$b竜之介
200  1$6a01$7dc$aアクタガワ,$bリュウノスケ
200  1$6a01$7ba$aAkutagawa,$bRy^unosuke
300  0 $a号:澄江堂主人
300  0 $a号:寿陵余子
300  0 $a俳号:我鬼
301     $a1892—1927
400  1$6a02$aあくたがわ$bりゅうのすけ
400  1$6a02$7dc$aアクタガワ,$bリュウノスケ
400  1$6a02$7ba$aAkutagawa,$bRy^unosuke
400  1$6a03$a芥川$b龍之介
400  1$6a03$7dc$aアクタガワ,$bリュウノスケ
400  1$6a03$7ba$aAkutagawa,$bRy^unosuke
400  0$6a04$a澄江堂主人
400  0$6a05$a寿陵余子
400  0$6a06$a我鬼
801  0$aJP$bNDL$c20001122
810     $a生きることへの懐疑
810     $a根拠:大人名事典
830     $a作家
911     $ap$ba
```

APPENDIX 3-2. NACSIS Union Catalog Database Record, NII, Tokyo

ID = DA00187353
CRTDT = 19860624
SOUCE = JP
MARCID = IN0000384X
RNWDT = 19911212
HEADG = 芥川, 龍之介(1892-1927)
HEADGR = アクタガワ, リュウノスケ
TYP = p
TIM = 1892-1927
SEEFM = 芥川, 竜之介(1892-1927)
SEEFM = *Akutagawa, Ryunosuke, 1892-1927
SEEFM = Akutagava, R., 1892-1927
SEEFM = Актагава, Р., 1892-1927
SEEFMR = アクタガワ, リュウノスケ
SEEFMR =
SEEFMR =
SEEFMR =
NT = 大正時代の文学者

APPENDIX 3-3. KORMARC Created by the National Library of Korea, Seoul

001	KAC199631100
005	20001228101355
008	960908 n aznnnabbn a a a a
040	▼a011001▼c011001
100	1	▼a아쿠타가와 류노스케,▼d1892-1927
400	1	▼a개천용지개=▼h芥川龍之介,▼d1892-1927
400	1	▼aAkutagawa, Ryunosuke,▼d1892-1927
678	▼a일본작가

APPENDIX 3-4. Name Authority Record Created by the Seoul National University Library, Held at KERIS, Seoul

004	0000102392
010	▼a n 79091265
040	▼a DLC ▼c DLC
090	▼5 211032 ▼y 01 ▼a 895.6X4 ▼b Ak87
100 1	▼a Akutagawa, Ryu^nosuke, ▼d 1892-1927
400 1	▼a Riunoske, Akutakava, ▼d 1892-1927
400 1	▼a Akutakava, Riunoske, ▼d 1892-1927
400 1	▼a Riunoske, Akutagava, ▼d 1892-1927
400 1	▼a Akutagava, Riunoske, ▼d 1892-1927
400 1	▼a芥川龍之介, ▼d 1892-1927
400 1	▼a개천용지개, ▼d 1892-1927
400 1	▼a아쿠타가와, 류노스케, ▼d 1892-1927
400 1	▼a니하라, 도시조, ▼d 1892-1927
400 1	▼a新原敏三, ▼d 1892-1927
400 1	▼a신원민상, ▼d 1892-1927
400 1	▼a Niihara, Toshizo^, ▼d 1892-1927
670	▼a Takeuchi, M. ▼b Akutagawa Ryu^nosuke ... 1934.
670	▼a Grivnin, V. S. Akutagava Riunoske, 1980: ▼b t.p. (Akutagava Riunoske)
670	▼a라쇼몽: ▼b겉표지 (본명은 니하라 도시조)
670	▼a國立國會圖書館著者名典據錄: 生きることへの懷疑
678	▼a作家
999	▼a 01SOLARSBATCH ▼c 6806012025915

APPENDIX 3-5. Name Authority Record Created by the Yonsei University Library, Held at KERIS, Seoul

100 1	▼a개천용지개 ▼h芥川龍之介
400 1	▼aアクタガワ, リュウノスケ
400 1	▼aAkutagawa, Ryu^nosuke
400 1	▼a아쿠타가와, 류노스케
400 1	▼a아꾸다가와, 류노스께

APPENDIX 3-6. China MARC Name Authority Record Created by the National Library of China, Beijing

```
00564nx###2200181a##45##
001        A9801495
005   ##   19971201120120.0
100   ##   $a19971201achiy0110####ea
200   #0   $c(日)$a芥川龙之介
           $f(1892~1927)
200   #0   $7ba$ajie chuan gui zhi jie
300   0#   $a小说家。别号柳川隆之介、寿
           陵余子、我鬼等。著有《地域
           变》、《玄鹤山房》等，出版《芥
           川龟之介全集》凡20卷。
400   #0   $6a01$a柳川隆之介
400   #0   $6a01$7ba$aliu chuan long zhi
           jie
400   #0   $6a02$a寿陵余子
400   #0   $6a02$7ba$ashou ling yu zi
810   ##   $a日本人物辞典
```

Authority Control
of Printers, Publishers, and Booksellers

Lorenzo Baldacchini

SUMMARY. The functions of publishers, printers, and booksellers in the years of hand printing and their connection with the concept of *manifestation* in FRBR are quite interesting, and the form given to their denotations becomes important when this element turns into a stable and fundamental access point to bibliographic information. The normal access point for the entity responsible for the *manifestation* must cease to be a mere indexing element and must become part of a *thesaurus*–that is, the terms it contains must be subject to *authority control*, as only this will allow the user not only to access an item, but also to relate it correctly with other items that share certain features with it, such as, for instance, the responsibility for the *manifestation*. Data about those in charge of the publication of early printed books is often inconsistent, unreliable, and sometimes even misleading, and authority files for such names will of necessity be very complicated.

This paper traces the evolution of access points for printers, publishers, and booksellers from the annals of the eighteenth century to modern bibliographical databases and catalogs of early printed materials, and discusses the recent suggestion that an authority file should be designed by each national agency for their printers, publishers,

Lorenzo Baldacchini is affiliated with Università di Bologna.

[Haworth co-indexing entry note]: "Authority Control of Printers, Publishers, and Booksellers." Baldacchini, Lorenzo. Co-published simultaneously in *Cataloging & Classification Quarterly* (The Haworth Information Press, an imprint of The Haworth Press, Inc.) Vol. 38, No. 3/4, 2004, pp. 269-280; and: *Authority Control in Organizing and Accessing Information: Definition and International Experience* (ed: Arlene G. Taylor, and Barbara B. Tillett) The Haworth Information Press, an imprint of The Haworth Press, Inc., 2004, pp. 269-280. Single or multiple copies of this article are available for a fee from The Haworth Document Delivery Service [1-800-HAWORTH, 9:00 a.m. - 5:00 p.m. (EST). E-mail address: docdelivery@haworthpress.com].

Digital Object Identifier: 10.1300/J104v38n03_20

and booksellers–just as happens for authors–to create a Virtual International Authority File. *[Article copies available for a fee from The Haworth Document Delivery Service: 1-800-HAWORTH. E-mail address: <docdelivery@haworthpress.com> Website: <http://www.HaworthPress.com> © 2004 by The Haworth Press, Inc. All rights reserved.]*

KEYWORDS. Authority control, name authority file, personal names, corporate names, printers, publishers, booksellers, antiquarian booksellers, hand printing, early printed books, access points, annals, indexes, inventories, thesauri, Consortium of European Research Libraries (CERL), EDIT16, FRBR manifestation

The whole structure of the FRBR document [20] and, in particular, the concept of *manifestation* as stated and developed in sections 3.2.3 (Manifestation) and 4.4 (Attributes of a Manifestation), seems to have been influenced by the observations on works, texts, and authors made during the 1980s, in particular by Donald F. McKenzie's comments on bibliography and the sociology of texts (think of assertions such as "form affects meaning" and "new readers of course *make new texts*, and their new meanings are a function of their new forms") [27], and Gérard Genette's [12] considerations on the paratext and editorial peritext.

Particularly interesting in this regard are the function of publishers, printers, and booksellers in the years of hand printing (circa 1450-circa 1830) and their connection with the *manifestation*. Some years ago, during a workshop organized by the Tuscan division of the AIB (Associazione Italiana Biblioteche), it was brought out that FRBR places particular emphasis on the *manifestation*, as this represents a traditional access point in bibliographic information on early printed books [35]. On the other hand, it has often been argued that the problem of the standardization of access points in the cataloging of early printed books is far more complex than in modern cataloging. I agree with Mauro Guerrini [14], who some years ago complained about the lack of authority files in Italy, including those for the people responsible for the publication, who are so fundamentally connected to the *manifestation*–in other words, to use more modern language, publishers, printers, and booksellers. It follows that the form given to their denotations becomes important when this element turns into a stable and fundamental access point to bibliographic information. It is indeed a very useful feature for the identification of a particular *manifestation*, an entity based on data that is often more objective (because in large part "material") than the other access points (author, title, additional contributors, and so on). The person responsible for the publication and therefore for the *manifestation*–who is often identified by a *personal name* and by a *corporate body name* as well–is as important as the author or the translator, and sometimes even more important. If he is a printer, he leaves a "fingerprint" on the book; and typeface and type size are considered to be attributes of a *manifestation* in the FRBR Final Report. But the publishing world is often in a state of flux; it is an environment in which economic and commercial developments intertwine with family, institutional, and political events. Changes of location, personal names, corporate names, and signatures, as well as alliances, partnerships, inheritances, marriages and widowhoods, and frequent cases of homonyms and semi-homonyms (not to mention anonymous attributions) make data about those responsible for the *manifestation*–especially (though not only) in the days of hand printing–inconsistent, unreliable, and sometimes even misleading, albeit still very rich in information and always fascinating. To say nothing of the instances of counterfeits, fakes, and even censorship. Therefore an authority file for such names will of necessity be very complicated, because it not only has to record a personal name, such as *Francesco Fusi, Giovanni Resnati*, or *Anton Fortunato Stella*, or a corporate body name such as *Società tipografica dei classici italiani*; it must also create a connection between the two. By the way, we have not only a first *Società tipografica dei classici italiani* (April 1802-December 1818), founded by Giovanni Angelo Borsa, Innocenzo Domenico Giusti, and Giulio Ferrario, but also a second (Fusi, Stella & Co., January 1819-December 1824) and even a third (directed by Francesco Fusi beginning in January 1825) [2].

These facts are of interest not only to historians; they are rightly part of an essential body of information that the cataloging process (and not only cataloging related to early printed books) must provide. It is for this reason that the normal access point for the person responsible for the *manifestation* must cease to be a mere indexing element and must become part of a *thesaurus*–that is, the terms it contains must be subject to *authority control*, as only this will allow the user not only to access an item, but also to relate it correctly with other items that share certain features with it, such as, for instance, the responsibility for the *manifestation*.

But when in the past did the access point for publisher/printer/bookseller begin to be considered useful for the retrieval of bibliographic information, and in what form? It would appear to have been in the eighteenth century, initially in the form of an index. We can reasonably think that annals–a bibliographic genre *tout court*–were what produced this effect in the cataloging field. This is where the trend of creating chronological lists giving prominence to the place of publication and those who produced a particular *manifestation* began.

There is considerable evidence testifying to the importance of indexes within this new bibliographic genre that began to become popular in the first half of the eighteenth century. For example, in 1773, in the preface to the first supplementary volume of his famous *Annales typographici ab artis inventae origine ad annum MD*, defined as "the first attempt to chronologically and alphabetically inventory European printing production, from the origins of printing up to 1664" [37], Michael Mattaire gave the following definition of the nature and composition of the alphabetical index: *"Index,* quem molior, non nuda tantum librorum authorumque nomina complectetur; sed *titulos,* quantum ad brevem notitiam sufficiat, declarabit; & quo *loco annoque,* per quem *typographum,* necnon qua voluminis *forma* libri prodierint, indigitabit" [26]. Although not all the entities indicated in italics in the previous passage become access points, we have in incipient form the function of an access point for the "person in charge of publishing, printing and distribution." This was confirmed some years later by the homonymous work *Annales typographici,* written by Georg Wolfgang Panzer (1793-1803) [32]. Even so, no mention of an access point for the printer is to be found in the two masterpieces of bibliography of early printed books: Jacques Charles Brunet's *Manuel du libraire et de l'amateur de livres*[10], first published in Paris in 1810, and the *Trésor de livres rares et précieux ou nouveau dictionnaire bibliographique contenant plus de cent mille articles de livres rares, curieux et recherchés,* written by Georg Theodor Graesse and published in Dresden between 1859 and 1869 [13]. And yet, the world of antiquarian booksellers has long influenced bibliographic practices concerning rare and early books. As for Italy, a particular emphasis on the *manifestation* is to be found in Pellegrino Orlandi's *Origine e progressi della stampa o sia dell'arte impressoria e notizie dell'opere stampate dall'anno M.CCCC.LVII. sino all'anno M.D.* [30], published in Bologna in 1772 and belonging to the "annals of printing" genre. On an international level, 1891 represented a turning point; Konrad Burger [11] published the *Indices uberrimi* of Ludwig Hain's *Repertorium bibliographicum* (1826) [15], which are, in fact, a series of indexes of the printers, publishers, and booksellers of the incunabula described in Hain's *Repertorium.* But it was the first of the *Short-title Catalogues* published by the British Museum before and after the Second World War that marked the definitive turning point. From that time on, no printed catalog of early books would ever be deemed acceptable if it lacked an index of printers, publishers, and booksellers. We are referring, obviously, to the period beginning with the works of Pollard and Redgrave up to those of Katharine Pantzer [34, 6, 7, 8, 9, 38, 31].

And today? Naturally, we have gone from paper to electronic publications, and thus from traditional indexes in printed catalogs (or the headings on card catalogs) to access points in online systems. Publishers and printers usually represent an *entry* in the electronic catalogs of early printed books. Nevertheless, a certain inconsistency remains, despite the various attempts to create authority files, especially on a national level. We will now examine some examples of databases: that of the Bibliothèque Nationale de France [3], the "SBN Antico" in Italy [18], EDIT16 [16], and, on an international level, the Consortium of European Research Libraries' Hand Press Book database [17], the British Library's Incunabula Short-title Catalogue, and so on.

Let us examine the criteria of several printed bibliographies. In fact, some of these printed catalogs were generated from databases, such as the one produced in France by Jean-Dominique Mellot and Elisabeth Queval, the *Répertoire d'imprimeurs/libraires XVIe-XVIIe siècle. État en 1995 (4000 notices)* [28]. Mellot himself described the genesis of this catalog in one of the "CERL Papers" (no. 11) [29]. It emerged in response to two main needs–bibliographic and research. The bibliographic need was to refine cataloging and make indexing richer, thanks to the authority files made possible by the electronic environment; the research need was to obtain a reference resource for a growing number of scholars and researchers interested in the history of books, editions, and bibliographies. It is worth remembering that most major catalogs only quote the place of publication, the initial of the first name, and the surname of the publisher, printer, or bookseller–data that is proving more and more crucial for retrospective bibliographies. We must also emphasize the importance of the indexes of retrospective catalogs, especially the British Museum's Short-title Catalogues, as well as the compilations of card files organized according to printers and places of publication that has occurred in French libraries since the 1970s. But there was a time when the same thing happened in Italian libraries. Here I can recall Alberto Tinto's printed catalog of sixteenth-century editions in the Biblioteca Nazionale Centrale di Roma and Fernnada Ascarelli's catalog for the Biblioteca Alessandrina, also in Rome, confining myself to the two catalogs I have used most.

The *Guide pour la rédaction des notices d'autorité imprimeurs/libraires en format Intermarc* was compiled in 1987 [4]. Starting in 1988, with the first publication of the *Guide*, this huge amount of data became available to the public. And it has grown by leaps and bounds: 1,000 entries in 1988, 2,000 in 1991, 4,000 in 1997, and around 5,200 entries in 1999. As María Luisa López Vidriero rightly points out, this is a task for national libraries [24]. Naturally, the database does not have broad coverage, because, from a geographic point of view the *Guide* privileges French editions, and from a chronological point of view it features eighteenth-century editions. As a more imposing mass of bibliographic data becomes available every day, thanks also to the retrospective conversion of card catalogs, it would be unthinkable–again, according to Mellot–to not attempt to provide users with the specific tools for accessing it. The *Répertoire d'imprimeurs/libraires* is one of these new research tools: it is more specialized than the indexes, less comprehensive, but richer and more flexible than the national thesauri. Another of these national thesauri is the one used in the EDIT16 database (a census of sixteenth-century Italian editions) produced by the ICCU (Istituto Centrale per il Catalogo Unico delle Biblioteche Italiane). And one can well say that it has benefitted from the brilliant work carried out by Gedeon Borsa in his *Clavis typographorum librariorumque Italiae*, 1465-1600 [5]. Since its very beginning in the early 1980s, EDIT16 has been improving and refining Borsa's work, initially publishing printed volumes and eventually creating a database that has been online for three years. This database cites the standard entry with all the variants appearing in the different editions (e.g., under the entry *Compagnia Minima* there is a reference to *Minima Societas*, and so on.). The EDIT16 record (Figure 1) for the publisher Nicolò Zoppino (perhaps he was also a printer, but in any case he was a sort of middleman), with all the variants of his name (in the "Nome su edizioni" field), is a clear example of the importance of authority control for printers, publishers, and booksellers [16].

It hardly seems necessary to stress the importance of the definition of a standard heading; it promotes the adoption of homogeneous forms, also by scholars in essays dealing with the history of printed books, in bibliographies, and in quotations, and this permits a more rapid and accurate circulation of information. The archive of pre-1831 books of the Servizio Bibliotecario Nazionale (SBN) provides access through publisher and printer names, but has not yet achieved anything that could be called an authority file; users' search expressions must match the SBN headings character-for-character. For example, a search for *Società tipografica dei classici* retrieves no results, but if we add *italiani* to the end of the search string, we retrieve 290 records!

I would like to conclude by relating the experience of a European database, the Hand Press Book of the Consortium of European Research Libraries (CERL) [17]. Italy is taking part in this project along with 28 other major European institutions and libraries. The aim is to build a central European database for early printed materials.

The Consortium will use a "cluster" system for the bibliographic records contributed by member countries, with one selected record for a given edition and all the other records for the same edition linked to that record, thus facilitating user navigation. The Consortium has now started to test a "thesaurus file," which chooses as a heading the form of the name linked to the bibliographic record, but also enables linking to all the other forms. Such forms are considered "authorized forms," as they have been established in compliance with the different national rules of the participating countries. As Werner Schwartz stated in his presentation at the CERL meeting held in Padua in November of 1999: "As a principle CERL shall not impose the authoritative form of a name" [36].

FIGURE 1. EDIT16 Record for the Publisher Niccolò Zoppino

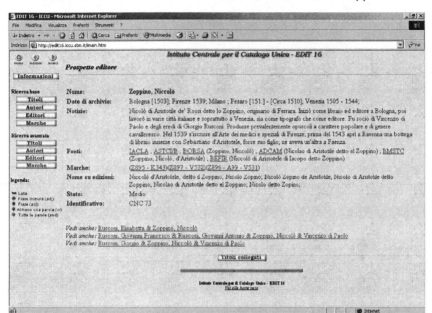

The following examples illustrate this point. If we search for *Società tipografica* in the Hand Press Books database, under "imprint" we find different printers or publishers, dates, and places of publications (see Figures 2, 3, 4).

The system was explained by Schwartz in his presentation on the CERL Thesaurus at the 1999 meeting in Padua, and was confirmed by Cristina Magliano in the Bologna conference on archives and authority headings the following year [25].

But the whole world of networked information, with both its huge potential and the disheartening inaccuracy of search engines, can be affected by the introduction of viruses. As far as the chaos of the Internet is concerned, during a conference on authority control in archives that took place in 2002, it was stated that: "We can rely on nothing but our traditional deontology to face this problem, preserving our cultural heritage and disseminating it via the new technologies. This implies the adoption of univocal descriptive formats, at least for recording data about individual objects and series. This doesn't mean that we should give up the specific modalities of connotation and contextualization of such objects, which do and must retain their own characteristics,

FIGURE 2. Search Results List for "Societa Tipografica" in the Hand Press Books Database

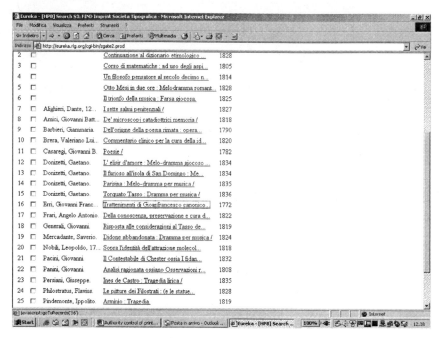

depending upon the category to which they belong. But all the apparatus that we might apply to each of our paintings, manuscripts or records would turn out to be completely useless unless we have devised headings and keywords capable of making our treasures available on the Web" [22].

This is the origin of the proposal that each of the national agency create its own authority file for its printers, publishers, and booksellers–as they do for authors–in order to create a Virtual International Authority File of the persons responsible for publication, distribution, and printing of the manifestation, based on the model for authors that Barbara Tillett has shown in her paper for this conference. Such a file would eventually be used in all national and international contexts, as CERL does, if only indirectly. The point of reference obviously will be the *Guidelines for Authority Records and References* [21], although very useful information can also be drawn from the world of archives and in particular from the document *International Standard for Archival Authority Records (Corporate Bodies, Persons, Families)* [19], which includes guidelines for constructing authority files for the creators of archives. The

FIGURE 3. Full Record Display from Hand Press Books Database

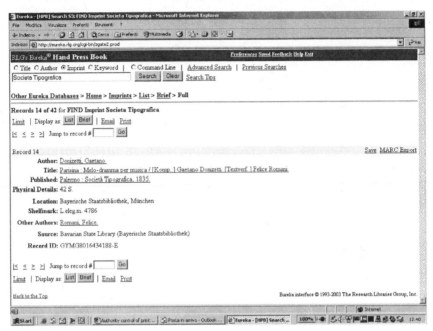

world of art history might supply other useful information, for example, from the experience of the application of authority control to Italian art history databases [22, 23].

We should bear in mind the *Osservazioni* [1] on FRBR, made by the Gruppo di Studio sulla Catalogazione of the Associazione Italiana Biblioteche: "The catalog would no longer be presented as a list, but as the universe of this network, navigable by contiguous phases from any starting point; a bibliographic list would be a sort of a journey through this network of related information." In the end, bibliographers would realize one of their dreams: a thesaurus of the "annals of printing" of the *ancien régime*. This will be possible only if bibliographers, book historians, and catalogers in libraries and in bibliographic agencies cooperate as completely as possible. This collaboration concerns not only authority files of printers, publishers, and booksellers, but all aspects of cataloging the products of hand printing, such as, for example, the entity, the copy, and data relative to a particular item, which have recently attracted notable interest, and to which the *FRBR Final Report* alludes in section 4.5 (Attributes of an Item) [20].

FIGURE 4. Full Record Display from Hand Press Books Database

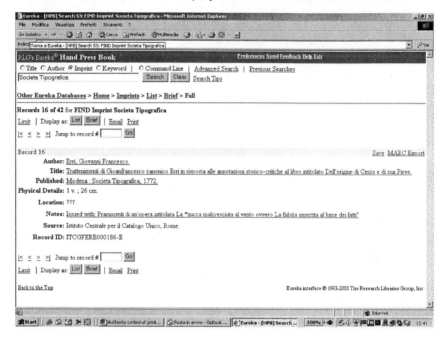

REFERENCES

1. Associazione Italiana Biblioteche, Gruppo di studio sulla catalogazione. "Osservazioni su: Functional Requirements for Bibliographic Records: Final Report," in *Bollettino AIB*, vol. 39 no. 3, (Sept. 1999): 303-311. Also available online at http://www.aib.it/aib/commiss/catal/frbrit.htm.

2. Berengo, M. *Intellettuali e librai nella Milano della Restaurazione*. Turin: Einaudi, 1980, 9-22, 61-62, 168-169.

3. Bibliothèque Nationale de France. *Catalogue général : imprimés des origines à 1970*. Paris: Éditions Bibliòtheque nationale de France, 1996 (on CD-ROM).

4. Bibliothèque Nationale de France. Département des Livres Imprimés. *Imprimeurs/libraires 16.-18. Siècles: guide pour la rédaction des notices d'autorité imprimeurs/libraires en format INTERMARC*. Paris: Bibliothèque nationale, 1987.

5. Borsa, G. *Clavis typographorum librariorumque Italiae, 1465-1600*. Baden-Baden: V. Koerner, 1980.

6. British Museum Department of Printed Books. *Short-title Catalogue of Books Printed in Italy and of Italian Books Printed in Other Countries from 1465 to 1600 Now in the British Museum*. London: The British Museum, 1958.

7. British Museum Department of Printed Books. *Short-title Catalogue of Books Printed in France and of French Books Printed in Other Countries from 1470 to 1600 Now in the British Museum*. London: The British Museum, 1966.

8. British Museum Department of Printed Books. *Short-title Catalogue of Books Printed in the German-Speaking Countries and German Books Printed in Other Countries from 1455 to 1600 Now in the British Museum.* London: Trustees of the British Museum, 1962.

9. British Museum Department of Printed Books. *Short-title Catalogue of Books Printed in The Netherlands and Belgium and of Dutch and Flemish Books Printed in Other Countries from 1470 to 1600 Now in the British Museum.* London: Trustees of the British Museum, 1965.

10. Brunet, J. C. *Manuel du libraire et de l'amateur de livres.* Paris: chez Brunet, 1810.

11. Burger, K. *Ludwig Hain's Repertorium Bibliographicum: Register die Drucker des 15. Jahrhunderts.* Leipzig: O. Harrassowitz, 1891.

12. Genette, G. *Seuils.* Paris: Éditions du Seuil, 1987.

13. Graesse, J. G. T. *Trésor de livres rares et précieux ou nouveau dictionnaire bibliographique contenant plus de cent mille articles de livres rares, curieux et recherchés.* Dresden: Rudolf Kuntze, 1859-1869.

14. Guerrini, M. "Le cinquecentine empolesi: un tassello di un mosaico," in Biblioteca Comunale Renato Fucini, *Catalogo delle edizioni del Cinquecento,* Eleonora Gargiulo, ed. Empoli: Comune di Empoli; Regione Toscana, 1999 (on CD-ROM). See http://www.comune.empoli.fi.it/biblioteca/cdrom.htm.

15. Hain, L. *Repertorium bibliographicum in quo libri ab arte typographica inventa usque ad annum 1500.* Stuttgartiae: J.G. Cotta, 1826-38.

16. http://edit16.iccu.sbn.it/iccu.htm (Censimento delle edizioni italiane del XVI secolo).

17. http://www.rlg.org/hpb.html (Consortium of European Research Libraries' Hand Press Book database).

18. http://opac.sbn.it ("SBN Antico" in Italy).

19. ICA Committee on Descriptive Standards. *International Standard Archival Authority Record for Corporate Bodies, Persons, and Families.* Available online at http://www.ica.org/biblio.php?pdocid=2.

20. IFLA Study Group on the FRBR. *Functional Requirements for Bibliographic Records. Final Report.* München: Saur, 1998 (UBCIM Publications, New Series Vol. 19). Available online at http://www.ifla.org/VII/s13/frbr/frbr.htm.

21. IFLA Working Group on GARE Revision. *Guidelines for Authority Records and References (GARR),* 2nd ed., revised by the IFLA Working Group on GARE Revision. München: K. G. Saur, 2001. (UBCIM publications, New Series Vol. 23). Available online at http://www.ifla.org/VII/s13/garr/garr.pdf.

22. Lattanzi, M. "L'Archivio di controllo Autore e il Catalogo Generale dei beni: storia, analisi e prospettive," in *Catalogazione e controllo di autorità,* [a workshop organized by the Istituto Centrale per il Catalogo Unico], Rome, 21-22 November 2002. Available online at http://www.iccu.sbn.it/ricaaf.html.

23. Lattanzi, M. "La normalizzazione del linguaggio nelle basi dati dei beni architettonici, archeologici e storico-artistici: i vocabolari di controllo e gli authority file Autore e Bibliografia," in *Archivi e voci d'autorità: Metodologie ed esperienze a confronto per i beni archivistici, librari e storico-artistici.* Seminar, Bologna, 3 October 2000. Available online at http://www.ibc.regione.emilia-romagna.it/soprintendenza/htm/arcaut/lattanzi.html.

24. López Vidriero, M. L. "Face aux attents des chercheurs: réflexions sur les bases données rétrospectives," in *The Scholar and the Database: Papers Presented on 4 No-*

vember 1999 at the CERL Conference Hosted by the Royal Library, Brussels, edited by Lotte Hellinga. London: Consortium of European Research Libraries, 2001, 28-37.

25. Magliano, C., "Orientamenti e standard a livello internazionale," in *Archivi e voci d'autorità: Metodologie ed esperienze a confronto per i beni archivistici, librari e storico-artistici*, Seminar, Bologna, 3 October 2000. Available online at http://www. ibc.regione.emilia-romagna.it/soprintendenza/htm/arcaut/magliano.html.

26. Maittaire, M. *Annales typographici ab artis inventae origine ad annum MD [-MDLVII–Appendix ad annum MDCLXIV]*. Hagae Comitum [Londini]: 1719-1741: IV . . . ad annum MDCLXIV . . . Amstelodami: P. Humbert, 1733.

27. McKenzie, D. F. *Bibliography and the Sociology of Texts*. London: The British Library, 1986.

28. Mellot, J.-D. and Queval, E., *Répertoire d'imprimeurs/libraires XVIe-XVIIe siècle. État en 1995 (4000 notices)*, Paris : Bibliothèque Nationale de France, 1997.

29. Mellot, J.-D. "Le Répertoire d'imprimeurs/libraires de la Bibliothèque Nationale de France (v. 1500-v.1810): premiers enseignements quantitatifs et qualitatifs," in *The Scholar and the Database: Papers Presented on 4 November 1999 at the CERL Conference Hosted by the Royal Library, Brussels*, edited by Lotte Hellinga. London: Consortium of European Research Libraries, 2001, 66-78.

30. Orlandi, P. *Origine e progressi della stampa o sia dell'arte impressoria e notizie dell'opere stampate dall'anno M.CCCC.LVII. sino all'anno M.D.*. Bononia: Costantino Pisarri, 1722.

31. Pantzer, K. F. *A Printers' and Publishers' Index, Other Indexes & Appendices, Cumulative Addenda & Corrigenda; with a Chronological Index by Philip R. Rider*. London: Bibliographical Society, 1991 (3rd vol. of Pollard and Redgrave's *Short-title Catalogue of Books Printed in England*).

32. Panzer, G. W. *Annales typographici ab artis inventae origine ad annum 1500 post Maittairi Denisii aliorumque doctissimorum virorum curas in ordinem redacti . . . volumen primum [-undecimum]*. Norimbergae: Joannis Eberhardi Zeh, 1793-1803.

33. Pisauri, N. *Archivi e voci d'autorità Metodologie ed esperienze a confronto per i beni archivistici, librari e storico-artistici*. Seminar, Bologna, 3 October 2000. Available online at http://www.ibc.regione.emilia-romagna.it/soprintendenza/htm/arcaut/ pisauri.html.

34. Pollard, A. W. and G. R. Redgrave. *A Short-title Catalogue of Books Printed in England, Scotland, and Ireland, and of English Books Printed Abroad: 1475-1640*; with the help of G. F. Barwick . . . [et al.] London: Bibliographical Society, 1926.

35. Rossi, M. "Presupposti e attribuzioni della catalogazione del libro antico," in *Associazione Italiana Biblioteche. Sezione Toscana, Seminario su FRBR*, Florence, 27-28 January 2000. Available online at http://www.aib.it/aib/sezioni/toscana/conf/ frbr/rossi.htm.

36. Schwartz, W. "The CERL Thesaurus. Present State and Future Development," presentation from CERL meeting held in Padua, 10 November 1999; available online at http://www.cerl.org/thesaur/thesaur.ppt. The CERL Thesaurus is available at http:// www.cerl.org/thesaur/.

37. Serrai, A. *Storia della bibliografia*, Rome: Bulzoni, 1991-1999. Vol. VII: *Storia e critica della catalogazione bibliografica*, 1997, 352.

38. Thomas, H. *Short-title Catalogue of Books Printed in Spain and of Spanish Books Printed Elsewhere in Europe before 1601 Now in the British Museum*. London: British Museum, 1940.

Creating Up-To-Date Corporate Name Authority Records by Using Official Corporate Home Web Pages

SUMMARY. The Internet has changed the way users access information for their research needs. According to recent surveys, we have a generation of Google users who search for information for their research needs in Web search engines before they search the OPAC. Catalogers are faced with the issue of how to help users improve access to the bibliographic world in the Internet environment. This article presents three case studies as examples of corporate name authority records that could be greatly improved by using or adding current information from the Internet. Strategies for searching official corporate body Web pages, adding references, and updating local catalogs are discussed. *[Article copies available for a fee from The Haworth Document Delivery Service: 1-800-HAWORTH. E-mail address: <docdelivery@haworthpress.com> Website: <http://www.HaworthPress.com> © 2004 by The Haworth Press, Inc. All rights reserved.]*

Qiang Jin, MLS, is Original Cataloging Librarian and Assistant Professor of Library Administration, University of Illinois at Urbana-Champaign, Urbana, IL 61801.

[Haworth co-indexing entry note]: "Creating Up-To-Date Corporate Name Authority Records by Using Official Corporate Home Web Pages." Jin, Qiang. Co-published simultaneously in *Cataloging & Classification Quarterly* (The Haworth Information Press, an imprint of The Haworth Press, Inc.) Vol. 38, No. 3/4, 2004, pp. 281-290; and: *Authority Control in Organizing and Accessing Information: Definition and International Experience* (ed: Arlene G. Taylor, and Barbara B. Tillett) The Haworth Information Press, an imprint of The Haworth Press, Inc., 2004, pp. 281-290. Single or multiple copies of this article are available for a fee from The Haworth Document Delivery Service [1-800-HAWORTH, 9:00 a.m. - 5:00 p.m. (EST). E-mail address: docdelivery@haworthpress.com].

KEYWORDS. AACR2, authority control, corporate names, LC NAF, NACO, NPM, OCLC, Internet, Web

The Internet has completely changed the way users search for information. A survey by the Pew Internet Project Survey Analysis in 2002, "The Internet Goes to College: How students are living with today's technology," revealed that 80% of students are likely to use information found on search engines and various Web sites as research materials.[1] Another survey by the Digital Library Federation and Council on Library and Information Resources indicated that most college students search the Internet first before they search the OPAC for their research needs.[2] This gives rise to the name "Google generation."

The convenience of the Web certainly contributes to this prevalent practice. But according to these same recent surveys mentioned above, users still trust library materials more than the information they find on the Web.[3] Given that users are obtaining more current corporate names from Web sites and using those names for searching OPACs, the challenge for the cataloger is to provide access to current, unestablished forms of corporate headings.[4] This is why authority control is so important.

What is authority control? Barbara Tillett in her recent paper, *Authority Control: State of the Art and New Perspectives* states that "the Web environment opens up new uses for authority records and new objectives to augment the traditional objectives . . . We are moving from the stand-alone authority files of a single institution, or even from the shared online files towards a goal of sharing authority files among all communities. Shared authority information has the added benefit of reducing the global costs of doing authority work while enabling controlled access and better precision of searching."[5] How will authority control in this new Web environment enhance the Google generation's discovery and access to information?

PREVIOUS RESEARCH

The author's previous paper presented the results of a sample that compared one hundred corporate names listed in the Library of Congress Name Authority File (LC NAF) as viewed on OCLC to the corporate names listed on official corporate home Web pages.[6] The results of the research indicated that the forms of 25% of corporate names were different in the LC NAF and on official corporate home Web pages. This will affect users' searching for materials by corporate bodies in the OPAC. What can catalogers do to help users in this Internet environment? A search in the library literature reveals that no previous research has been done on this problem.

This study aims to provide catalogers with some suggestions on how to create up-to-date corporate authority records by using or adding current information from the Internet. In this way, the Google generation will be able to find materials by corporate bodies in the OPAC.

HISTORY OF CORPORATE AUTHORITY RECORDS

Before addressing this problem, it is important to review the history of why corporate authority headings are the way they are now. Between 9th-18th October, 1961, an international conference on cataloguing principles organized by the International Federation of Library Associations under the sponsorship of the Council on Library Resources was held in Paris. Representatives from 55 nations around the world reached the agreement that "the standard heading for works entered under a corporate body is the official name of the body in the form most frequently used on the title-pages of its publications."[7] The reason for this was that "behind the form of heading for corporate authors was the form to be adopted for corporate headings aiming at following as closely as possible the same principles as those which regulated the choice of heading of personal authors."[8]

Anglo-American Cataloging Rules (AACR1), prepared under the direction of the American Library Association, the Library of Congress, the Library Association and the Canadian Library Association, was published in 1967. AACR1 rule 60 stated, "Enter a corporate body directly under its name."[9] Rule 61 said: "When the name of a corporate body found in reference sources varies from that used by the body on the publications of which it is author, publisher, or sponsor, the latter form is preferred."[10] Rule 62 added: "If variant forms of the name are found in the body's own publications, use the name as it appears in formal presentations (as at the head of the title, in the imprint, and in formal author statements) as opposed to forms found in running text or in titles."[11] In this way, AACR1 followed the Paris Principles on the standard form of heading for corporate bodies.

In 1978, AACR2 modified the rule for corporate headings for corporate bodies. They were still entered directly under their names. AACR2 24.1 specifies, "Enter a corporate body directly under the name by which it is predominantly identified. Determine the name by which a corporate body is commonly identified from items issued by that body in its language. If variant forms of the name are found in items issued by the body, use the name as it appears in the chief sources of information as opposed to the forms found elsewhere in the items."[12] AACR2 extended the idea of Paris Principles and AACR1 that the form of corporate heading should be that which is found predominantly on items issued by the body itself. In the case of variant forms, the chief source of information is preferred. In the case of printed monographs, title pages are the chief sources of information.

Since 1978, the rules for determining the authorized corporate headings have not changed a great deal. During this time, especially since the mid-1990s, the Internet has come to dominate users' way of searching for information.

METHODOLOGY

This study examines examples of corporate names in order to describe and analyze the forms of corporate names that appear on the title pages of publications and on official corporate body Web pages. What follows is a qualitative analysis of the selected cases. The main objective of the study is to find ways for catalogers to create up-to-date authority records to facilitate retrieval for users in today's Internet Age by using official corporate home Web pages as sources for references, and to raise a crucial question regarding evidentiary sources for official forms of corporate names.

For many years, catalogers have been relying on the Library of Congress Name Authority File for authority work. Since the NACO project is responsible for LC NAF, it is important to check the *NACO Participants' Manual* (NPM, the name authority program component of the Program for Cooperative Cataloging). The NPM provides guidance for catalogers who wish to cite Web home pages in the 670 field (Source data found).

The *NACO Participants' Manual* 1996 states: "Give the name of the home page, gopher, etc., and the date it was consulted. In subfield $b, give a location, if appropriate, and the information found. Generally, don't include the URL (Uniform Resource Locator) since the address often changes."[13] NACO rules do allow catalogers to add references from corporate body home Web pages. The author has recently observed that more references to Web sites are appearing in 670s, generally given in the form of:

670 Its Web site, Aug. 29, 2002 . . .

670 Internet, GBV Gesamtkatalog, Nov. 25, 2002 . . .

If the form of a corporate name on a corporate home page differs from the form of a corporate name on the title page, does NACO require catalogers to look in other resources for variant forms? In the section for the Frequently Asked Questions (FAQ) on the 670 (Sources found) in name authority records (NARs) for NACO (http://www.loc.gov/catdir/pcc/naco/670faq.html), one question asks: when do NACO procedures require catalogers to look in other sources (beyond the item-in-hand and the database in which one is cataloging) for variants, fuller forms of the heading or dates, etc.? The answer is "Generally, only when the heading conflicts with another in the NAF and the item-in-hand does not provide enough information to break the conflict." This tells us that if the form on the title page matches the form in the LC NAF, catalogers are not required to check corporate body home Web pages to see if there is a different form of the corporate name.

Examples are found in the following records:

The first example shows variations in usage between Arabic numerals and Roman numerals. The LC NAF record:

```
010    n  90697321
040    DLC ǂc DLC ǂd DLC
005    19990615092824.1
110 2  Universit´e Charles de Gaulle-Lille III
410 2  UL3
410 2  Universit´e de Lille III, Charles de Gaulle
410 2  University Charles de Gaulle Lille III
510 2  Universit´e de Lille III ǂw a
```

Here is the corporate body Web page:

URL: http://www.univ-lille3.fr/ (viewed on April 30, 2003)

In the LC NAF, "Universit'e Charles de Gaulle-Lille III" was found as the authorized corporate heading since it was on the title page of its publications when the heading was established in 1990. However, this differs from "Universit'e Charles de Gaulle-Lille 3" on its official corporate body Web page. Recently the author cataloged a book entitled: "La Réception du Roman

Francais Contemporain dans l'Europe de l'Entre-Deux-Guerres," published in 2002 and edited by Anne-Rachel Hermetet. "Université Charles-de-Gaulle Lille 3" was on the title page. In some integrated library systems searching the Arabic numeral would not bring up the roman numeral, thus the need for the reference.

The second example reflects a change of name on a corporate body's official Web page. It is difficult to take into account because LC NAF still has its old form.

LC NAF corporate authority record:

```
010      no 93033087
040      MH ǂc MH
005      19931115121714.8
110  2   National Foundation for Women Business Owners
410  2   NFWBO
670      NFWBO news, spring 1993: ǂb t.p. (National Foundation for Women Business Owners; NFWBO)
```

The official corporate body Web site starts:

Center for Women's Business Research, founded as the National Foundation for Women Business Owners, is the premier source of knowledge about women business owners and their enterprises worldwide.

URL: http://www.nfwbo.org/ (viewed on March 25, 2003)

This is an example of a completely new form of a corporate name appearing on its official corporate body Web page while the old form of corporate name remains on the title page of its publication issued by the body in its own language. "National Foundation for Women Business Owners" on the title page matches the form in the LC NAF. On the official corporate body Web page, it states that "Center for Women's Business Research" was founded as "National Foundation for Women Business Owners." If users search under "Center for Women's Business Research" in the OPAC, they will not find anything by the corporate body. Several questions arise with this example. When did the name change? Has the body issued publications since the change? If it hasn't, what should catalogers do with the old form? The author's suggestion is that catalogers should add the new name in the 510 field of the authority record and create a new authority record for the new corporate heading with a 510 reference back to the older form. In the future, we might find "Center for Women's Business Research" on the title pages of its print publications, but in the meantime, users are not able to find anything by the form of corporate name on its official corporate body home Web page.

The third example shows that the official Web page sometimes omits words from the corporate name.

LC NAF authorized corporate heading:

```
▶010     n  81126866
▶040     DLC ǂc DLC ǂd DLC
▶005     19961202170347.6
▶110 2   Council of Europe. ǂb Council for Cultural Co-operation
▶410 2   Council for Cultural Co-operation
▶410 2   Conseil de la coop´eration culturelle
▶410 2   Council of Europe. ǂb Conseil de la coop´eration culturelle
▶410 2   Council of Europe. ǂb Consejo de la Cooperaci´on Cultural
▶410 2   Consejo de la Cooperaci´on Cultural
▶410 2   Rat f¨ur Kulturelle Zusammenarbeit
▶410 2   Council of Europe. ǂb Rat f¨ur Kulturelle Zusammenarbeit
```

The corporate body web page:

URL: http://www.coe.int/T/E/Cultural_Co-operation/ (viewed on May 16, 2003)

Even though the corporate body home page does make "Cultural Co-operation" look like nothing more than a subject term or a title (it is off on the left margin in a small font), users who have seen the Web page might search under this term in the OPAC, and they will not be able to find materials by "Council of Europe. Council for Cultural Co-operation." When the official corporate Web page omits words from the corporate name above, it may be useful to add the form on the official corporate body Web page to the authority record as a "see" reference. Access is the most important issue for catalogers. Further research is needed on the forms that this corporate body uses in its publications.

What should catalogers do to solve these problems in order to help users find materials by corporate bodies in the OPAC? Should they search the Web for a different form of corporate heading even if the heading on the title page they are working with matches the form in the LC NAF? If a different form of corporate name appears on official corporate body Web pages, and since users might use that form to find materials by the corporate body in the OPAC, this may be useful.

A PROPOSAL

Catalogers could use current information on official corporate home Web pages to create up-to-date corporate authority records even if the form of corporate names on the title pages of the publications match the form in the LC NAF. What are the advantages and disadvantages of this proposal? The advantage is that catalogers could create up-to-date corporate authority records to aid users in finding materials issued by those corporate bodies in the OPAC. One of NACO's goals is "to increase the timeliness of cataloging copy" and the Web has definitely provided catalogers with this opportunity. The disadvantage might be that there could be a lot of work involved in creating new authority records and linking the old and new authorized names where the corporate body home Web pages have indicated name changes. Because of the instability of the Web, pointing to a resource that could easily change seems risky; in addition, Web design changes may be misleading as far as headings are concerned. To justify the extra work to look up every corporate home Web page, catalogers need to do further research on how stable corporate changed names are. How often do those changed corporate names end up being used on publications of the body? How often would a keyword search of the name (old and new) result in a failed search for the users?

According to the author's sample of one hundred corporate names, 70% of the forms of corporate names match exactly in the LC NAF and on official corporate body home Web pages. This searching could save catalogers a lot of time not having to check print reference sources to determine the authorized corporate headings. Due to budget constraints, the library may not even have the print sources needed. The corporate body Web page usually provides its corporate history, contact information, and additional information that could be used in the 670 field. Since almost all catalogers have unlimited access to Internet resources, searching the Web by various search engines could be quick and easy.

CONCLUSION

In 1961, representatives around the world met together in Paris and made decisions on how to establish corporate authority headings. They were only dealing with print monographs and serials at that time. AACR1 and AACR2 followed and modified the Paris Principles on the standard form of heading for corporate bodies. The world has changed greatly since then. Print still dominates, but the Web has introduced a new, online Internet source of evidence. We have a generation of Google users who search for information for their research needs in various search engines before they search the OPAC. This paper is the first step to deal with the issue.

This study examines how catalogers could use the form of corporate names on official corporate home Web pages to create up-to-date corporate authority records. Should catalogers make a general practice of looking up the official corporate Web sites even if NAF records are available? Should electronic publications such as Web sites be considered publications emanating from the bodies in the terms used in AACR2? Should they be considered differently from other publications of the bodies? Do some of the non-matching headings need to be *see also* references rather than *see* references in the case where the name changes? Since more and more users are searching the Web first for information, catalogers need to have an open mind to keep learning and adjusting to the changes in the Internet environment in order to keep the OPAC the most relevant place for users to meet their research needs now and in the future.

REFERENCES

1. Pew Internet Project Survey Analysis in 2002, "The Internet Goes to College: How Students Are Living in the Future with Today's Technology," http://www.pewinternet.org/reports/toc.asp?Report=71.

2. Digital Library Federation (DLF) and Council on Library and Information Resources (CLIR) in 2002, "Dimension and Use of the Scholarly Information Environment: Introduction to a Data Set Assembled," http://www.clir.org/pubs/abstract/pub110abst.html.

3. Ibid.

4. Ibid.

5. Barbara Tillett, "Authority Control: State of the Art and New Perspectives," presented at the International Conference, Authority Control: Definition and International Experiences, Florence, Italy, February 10-12, 2003 (published in this volume, pp. 23-41).

6. Qiang Jin, "Comparing and Evaluating Corporate Names in the Library of Congress Name Authority File as viewed on OCLC and on Corporate Body Web Pages," *Cataloging & Classification Quarterly* 36(2) (2003): 21.

7. See International Federation of Library Association, *International Conference on Cataloguing Principles, Paris, 9th-18th October, 1961: Report,* p. 51, (Published by the Organizing Committee of the International Conference on Cataloguing Principles, c/o National Central Library, Malet Place, London, W.C.1).

8. Ibid., 52.

9. American Library Association, *Anglo-American Cataloging Rules,* (Chicago: American Library Association, 1967), p. 106.

10. Ibid., p. 106.

11. Ibid., p. 106-107.

12. American Library Association, *Anglo-American Cataloguing Rules,* 2nd ed., (Chicago: American Library Association, 1978), p. 402-405.

13. *NACO Participant's Manual.* 2nd ed. (Washington, D.C.: Library of Congress, Cataloging Distribution Service, 1996), p. 61.

Authority Control of Works: Cataloging's Chimera?

Richard P. Smiraglia

SUMMARY. Explicit authority control of works is essentially non-existent. Our catalogs are built on a principle of controlling headings, and primarily headings for names of authors. Our syndetic structure creates a spider's web of networked relationships among forms of headings, but it ends there, despite the potential richness of depth among bibliographic entities. Effective authority control of works could yield richness in the catalog that would enhance retrieval capabilities. Works are considered to constitute the intellectual content of informative artifacts that may be collected and ordered for retrieval. In a 1992 study, the author examined a random sample of works drawn from the catalog of the Georgetown University Library. For each progenitor work, an instantiation network (also referred to as a bibliographic family) was constituted. A detailed analysis of the linkages that would be required for authority control of these networks is reviewed here. A new study is also presented, in which Library of Congress authority records for the works in this sample are sought and analyzed. Results demonstrate a near total lack of control, with only 5.6% of works for which authority records were found. From a sample of 410 works, of which nearly half have instantiation networks,

Richard P. Smiraglia is Professor, Palmer School of Library and Information Science, Long Island University, Brookville, NY 11548.

[Haworth co-indexing entry note]: "Authority Control of Works: Cataloging's Chimera?" Smiraglia, Richard P. Co-published simultaneously in *Cataloging & Classification Quarterly* (The Haworth Information Press, an imprint of The Haworth Press, Inc.) Vol. 38, No. 3/4, 2004, pp. 291-308; and: *Authority Control in Organizing and Accessing Information: Definition and International Experience* (ed: Arlene G. Taylor, and Barbara B. Tillett) The Haworth Information Press, an imprint of The Haworth Press, Inc., 2004, pp. 291-308. Single or multiple copies of this article are available for a fee from The Haworth Document Delivery Service [1-800-HAWORTH, 9:00 a.m. - 5:00 p.m. (EST). E-mail address: docdelivery@haworthpress.com].

291

only 23 works could be said to have implicit authority control. However, many instantiation networks are made up of successive derivations that can be implicitly linked through collocation. The difficult work of explicitly linking instantiations comes with title changes, translations, and containing relations. The empirical evidence in the present study suggests that explicit control of expressions will provide the best control over instantiation networks because it is instantiations such as translations, abridgments, and adaptations that require explicit linking. *[Article copies available for a fee from The Haworth Document Delivery Service: 1-800-HAWORTH. E-mail address: <docdelivery@haworthpress.com> Website: <http://www.HaworthPress.com> © 2004 by The Haworth Press, Inc. All rights reserved.]*

KEYWORDS. Works, instantiation networks, expressions, authority control, linkages, syndetic depth

Authority control of works is one of cataloging's chimeras. It is powerful and intoxicating, and yet so elusive as to be non-existent. At least, explicit authority control of works is essentially non-existent. Our catalogs are built on a principle of controlling headings, and primarily headings for names of authors. There has not been a similar conception of the catalog as a file of controlled access points for works. Instead we have relied on the implicit control afforded by the concatenation of controlled name headings and unique title statements. But this implicit system relies on a faulty assumption, that the title of a given document (e.g., a book) is likely to be the authoritative title of the work contained therein. In this paper, I summarize these issues and present empirical evidence about both the potential for authority control of works, and the near total lack of explicit control over works that exists at present.

BACKGROUND: SYNDETIC DEPTH

Access to works is the fundamental purpose of bibliographic control. Yes, there are secondary purposes–such as inventory of collections to support acquisition, circulation, and preservation. But in the end, our intention is to make available the world's store of recorded knowledge to help people solve problems. And this is made possible by providing access to works. Authority control is not universally employed in indexing services but library catalogs have found it essential, primarily to assist the public in efficient retrieval.

However well we have done at creating huge inventories of bibliographic records, we have until recently been building primarily linear files of names and titles. One can skim alphabetically across this file; with hyperlinks one can move about in a sea of references, but in the end there is very little depth in the catalog. Our syndetic structure creates a spider's web of networked relationships among forms of headings, but it ends there, despite the potential richness of depth among bibliographic entities. One approach to increasing syndetic depth is to make more sophisticated networks of relationships explicit in catalogs so that users might effectively follow them. Effective authority control of works could yield richness in the catalog that would enhance retrieval capabilities.

Authority control, of course, is the series of processes associated with establishing unique headings, maintaining consistency in their usage in a bibliographic file, and creating a syndetic structure–a network of links among variant and related forms of the headings. A form of vocabulary control, this seminal process facilitates query transformation in the retrieval process. Traditionally authority control has embraced two kinds of links in the catalog. Perhaps most common are the links among variant forms of a controlled heading that are created using "see from" (or "used for") references. Also common are links among related headings that are created using "see also from" references. Together, these kinds of links form a syndetic structure, which Bregzis (1982, 19) referred to as "entry syndetic structure."

Links that involve references are termed *explicit* links. Explicit links direct the user deliberately to move from one point to another in a file. *Implicit* links, which require inference, also are used in the catalog. For instance, when two bibliographic records are collocated–found side by side–an implicit link exists between them. Related works (e.g., the musical score of an opera, the printed libretto of its text) are linked implicitly in the catalog through collocation. Implicit links of this sort require the user to examine the collocated bibliographic records and infer the relationship between the two works described. For example, a search for Charles Dickens' *Oliver Twist* might yield both a bibliographic record for an edition of the novel, and adjacent to it a bibliographic record for Lionel Bart's musical *Oliver!* These two bibliographic records collocate because each bears an access point for Dickens' work. But the works represented are quite different; it will be up to the user to read both bibliographic records to discover both what they have in common (Dickens' original conception) and why they differ.

In many other cases, the links are even less explicit. For instance, the anthology *Culture Gulch* by art critic John Canaday contains reprints of some of his articles from the *New York Times*. An implicit link exists between the *New York Times* and *Culture Gulch* by virtue of a note in the catalog record for *Culture Gulch*. However, it would require some detective work on a users' part to trace the contents of Canaday's anthology to the loci of the original columns in *The New York Times*.

For some time now, authors have been suggesting the catalog's syndetic structure should be enhanced by providing links among related bibliographic records. Bregzis (1982, 20) wrote:

> Cutter's . . . conceptualization [of] 'entry' is equivalent to our current concept of record, and . . . syndetic structure refers to record relationships and not to relationships of entries . . . which are the backbone of our current catalog structure.

In other words, the network of relationships mapped in the catalog that constitutes its current syndetic structure consists entirely of references among synonyms and among related headings, but includes no references among more complex entities. In particular, bibliographic relationships are haphazardly expressed in the catalog, and rarely accommodated by the catalog's syndetic structure. Referring to Lubetzky, Bregzis points out that references should include sufficient contextual information to allow the user to find one work in the context of other, related works. He goes on to suggest (1982, 23):

> The syndetic depth, however, cannot be expected to be increased through the automation of the entry syndetic structure. The objective of bibliographic correlation is to attain increased scope and depth of relating variants of bibliographic description, i.e., records, as they are anticipated by the seeker, rather than relating variant entry forms dissociated from the bibliographic descriptions.

Online catalogs employ an automated entry syndetic structure. Increased syndetic depth, however, will only come when many more kinds of bibliographic relationships are incorporated into the catalog's syndetic structure. Perreault (1982) suggested that relationships exist not only among works but also among the forms of names associated with those works. Perreault rejected the premise of headings that are divorced from bibliographic descriptions and offered a formalization that would allow author-name-title variants to be made equivalent to each other at any level. In 1990, Ayres suggested that a uniform title should be required for any given work, to serve as flags (or locating devices), to signal the presence of collocated related works and to provide implicit links among the collocated records for related works. The use of uniform titles for all works would require the presence of authority records for all works.

Carlyle has written about users' experiences seeking works in online catalogs, presenting research results from several studies about what sorts of grouped displays users might find helpful. Of course, she reported that online catalogs did not collocate work records very well (1996, 546). Works, she discovered, were collocated less well than authors, and grouped displays of works are often interrupted by the display of irrelevant records (1996, 553). In a subsequent study conducted among potential searchers, she had fifty participants sort items related to Dickens' *A Christmas carol*, then describe the attributes they used for grouping the items. Physical format, audience, content description, pictorial elements, usage, and language were the elements used most frequently for grouping the items. Carlyle suggests that many of these attributes exist in current bibliographic records and could be used to cluster records in work displays.

This overview is admittedly incomplete–many of these authors wrote some time ago in the early days of online catalogs. Much work has been done to define explicit bibliographic relationships that might help to increase syndetic depth in the catalog. Yet, even with the introduction of hyperlinks in web-based catalogs, we still are working with catalogs that are not designed to control works. Rather, they primarily are designed to control bibliographic entities or titles. Thus, there are no explicit means for controlling relationships among works in the catalog. Likewise, there are no explicit means for controlling access to the grouped displays of works.

Definition of "A Work"

So, what exactly is it we mean when we talk about "a work?" Works are deliberate intellectual creations. Works are considered to constitute the intellectual content of informative artifacts (usually referred to as documents) that may be collected and ordered for retrieval. Works have two properties, which I have defined as ideational and semantic (Smiraglia 2001, 54). The ideas, or propositions, expressed in a work constitute the ideational content; the words, texts, images, etc., which express ideational content, constitute the semantic content. In groups of *versions* of works, the members differ from each other in either or both ideational and semantic content.

Libraries are, of course, collections of works (among other things). The importance of works has always been understood yet it is only of late that the work-phenomenon–that is, the complexity and extent of instantiation of individual works–has begun to be well and fully comprehended. In the catalog we have focused primarily on the description of artifacts (i.e., documents)–the packages that contain and may deliver one or more creative, communicative conceptions. Both the package (the document or artifact), and its content (which might be a work) are joined variously. A bibliographic record represents a bibliographic entity–both the physical characteristics of the artifact or document and headings that represent the intellectual content or work. As Wilson pointed out ([1987] and 1989), we have taken Cutter's objectives too literally and have designed catalogs of documents rather than catalogs of works. However, when it comes to retrieval, in many cases it is the work that is sought rather than the document. Once a gathering of instantiations of a work has been located, a searcher then makes a choice among the documentary formats available.

In my dissertation (Smiraglia 1992), I reported an investigation of the derivative bibliographic relationship, which holds among all versions of a work. Using a taxonomy derived from cataloging rules, I was able to refine the definition to include several different categories of derivation. Subsequent epistemological analysis (Smiraglia 2002b) has demonstrated that there are, in fact, two ways in which works can be seen to change over time–derivation and mutation. The derivation categories are:

- simultaneous derivations–such as editions published in two places at the same time;
- successive derivations–such as second, third, revised, etc., editions;
- translations;
- amplifications–such as text with commentary, etc.;
- extractions–such as a song from a musical issued separately on a recording;
- adaptations–wholly rewritten versions, such as a children's version or a digested portion; and,
- performances.

Simultaneous, successive, amplifications, and extractions are derivative. That is, their instantiations differ in various ways, but the ideational and semantic content do not change dramatically. Translations, adaptations, and performances, on the other hand, are mutants. In these cases there has been real change in ideational and semantic content. Another category was used in the original study–predecessor. This category was assigned whenever it was discovered that a progenitor had itself been descended from another work. Obviously, if the change in ideational and semantic content has been sufficient to constitute what is clearly seen as a new work, the predecessor relation can also be categorized as a mutation.

These changes can be observed empirically (see Smiraglia 2001) and have been attributed in large part to the concept of canonicity. Works that become part of a canon–that is, works that are accepted in some culture–become in some way the property of the culture, deriving and mutating over time to satisfy cultural demands (Smiraglia 2002b). This is the source of the library's need for authority control over works. If a variety of culturally divergent instantiations of a work exist, should not the library catalog offer a user a choice among them?

AUTHORITY CONTROL OF WORKS: ONE IDEA

Of course, it is possible that a degree of control over the relationships among works is exercised by the authority control that already exists over headings for works. That is, while we know there is no such thing as an authority record for a work, we can rely to some extent on authority records for uniform title headings that include references from alternative titles, variant titles (such as the title of a translation), or titles of excerpted portions of a work. Such authority records can provide explicit control of some of the relationships among works that have different headings–usually different uniform titles. Likewise, cataloging codes require the use of added entries for related derivations in many cases. For instance, the bibliographic record for the motion picture of a novel should include an author-title added entry for the original (or, progenitor) work (*AACR2R* 21.30G). These added entries cause the bibliographic records for the motion picture and the novel to collocate, thus providing an implicit linkage among the related works. Finally–perhaps obviously–the bibliographic records for most successive derivations (i.e., subsequent editions) will collocate because they will all bear the same heading. This too is a means of implicit linkage.

1992 Redux

For the aforementioned dissertation, I examined a random sample of works drawn from the catalog of the Georgetown University Library. For each progenitor work, an instantiation network (also referred to as a bibliographic family) was constituted. This was accomplished by locating bibliographic records for all extant instantiations. The bibliographic records were then examined in detail, and a record was made of every instance in which an explicit linkage would be required to collocate the instantiations. Thus, if a work had been translated once, a translated title was recorded. Every instance in which a related work might require either an explicit reference via an authority record or an implicit link via collocation achieved through the use of added entries was recorded. Each such instance was considered to constitute a *node of control*–that is, a point at which a user might reasonably expect a catalog to provide explicit control over the relationship. These nodes of control fell into six categories as follows (Smiraglia 1992, 104 ff.):

- Translated Titles: Titles proper of translations were recorded when they differed from the title proper of the progenitor (e.g., *The light in the piazza* was translated into Spanish *Luz en la plaza*; however, *Pnin* retained the title *Pnin* even when translated).
- Title Change: The title of a work that had changed over time was recorded. In some instances these changes reflect semantic or ideational changes in a work (e.g., *Nelson's English course* became *The new Nelson English course*). In other instances alternative titles become better associated with the work (e.g., *The fallen idol* became known as *The basement room*).
- Extraction Relations: The title of a segment of a work that is published separately was recorded.
- Containing Relations: The title of a work that was published in a larger bibliographic entity (e.g., in an anthology) was recorded.
- Performance Derivations: The title of a motion picture, radio play, or other recorded performance of a work was recorded.
- Successive Derivations: All other members of bibliographic families will be linked implicitly through collocating identical entries.

One hundred eighty-two nodes of control were recorded among the 205 instantiation networks, for a mean total of .88 nodes per family. Explicit control is provided through references in authority records for translated titles, title changes, and extraction derivations. One hundred forty-six nodes required explicit control. The categorical breakdown is given in the following table (Smiraglia 1992, 245):

Node	Implicit	Explicit	
Translation		107	
Title changes		20	
Containing	23		
Extraction		19	
Performance	13		
Total	36	146	182

Additionally, for each instantiation network a categorical variable was assigned for the presence of each category of derivation or mutation (i.e., simultaneous, successive, predecessor, translation, amplification, extraction, performance) to test the hypothesis that certain types of instantiations might be associated with the need for explicit authority control. Cross tabulations were constructed and χ^2 was calculated. Statistically significant values of χ^2 were found for instantiation networks that include mutations–translations, amplifications, and performances.

Implicit authority control can be said to be provided through added entries for containing relations and for performances and through collocating identical headings for successive derivations. There were 734 instances of implicit control. These included 36 instances of containing relations and performance derivations, and 698 instances of successive derivations. Again the associative hypothesis was tested to see whether certain types of instantiation could be associated with the need for implicit authority control. Statistically significant values of χ^2 were found for instantiation networks that include predecessors, and translations (Smiraglia 1992, 246-248). Clearly, instantiations that can be classified as mutations, perhaps because they involve substantial change in ideational or semantic content, are more likely to have headings that differ from the headings for the progenitor work. Thus, they are more likely to require authority control.

About a third (32.5% $\pm$ 4%) of the works in the sample required no explicit or implicit control other than collocating headings. For these works, the relatively small instantiation networks (mean = 5) were constituted primarily of successive derivations. About two-thirds (66.5% $\pm$ 4%) of works require other techniques, in part because they have larger instantiation networks (mean = 15), which means there is more room for the introduction of variation over time. Analysis demonstrated that this difference was statistically significant (Smiraglia 1992, 248). That is, a statistically significant difference exists and is predictable between small groups of second and third editions, which require no explicit authority control, and larger groups of translations, which do require explicit authority control.

For example, we can look specifically at one work from this study to see the dimensions of the problem of authority control over instantiation networks. Elizabeth Spencer's *Light in the piazza*, was a popular romantic novel that first appeared in New York in 1960 published by McGraw-Hill. It was included that same year in *Reader's Digest Condensed Books*. A London, Heinemann edition appeared in 1961, as did a Spanish translation in Buenos Aires. A New York Pocket Books edition appeared in 1962. In 1966, it was contained in two anthologies: *Great Modern Short Novels* and *Best-in-Books*. The first McGraw-Hill paperback edition appeared in New York in 1972, the same year that a Japanese translation appeared in Tokyo (with an English-language title page). Penguin Books editions appeared simultaneously in Ontario and New York in 1986. There also was a Finnish translation in 1967, a film version released in 1961, the soundtrack from the film released on LP disc in 1962, and a score of the theme song from the soundtrack, issued the same year.

The nodes of control for this work include the original title and the two translated titles (*Kohtans firenzessa* and *Luz en la Plaza*), the three containing anthologies (*Reader's Digest Condensed Books*, *Great Modern Short Novels*, and *Best in Books*), the film, and the music. The existing syndetic mechanism yielded the following added entries and references:

Added Entries:

> Spencer, Elizabeth.
>> Light in the piazza
>
> Best-in-books

> Spencer, Elizabeth.
>> Light in the piazza
>
> Great modern short novels

> Spencer, Elizabeth.
>> Light in the piazza
>
> Readers Digest condensed books

> Spencer, Elizabeth.
>> Light in the piazza
>
> Light in the piazza (Motion Picture)

> Light in the piazza (Motion Picture)
>
> Light, Enoch.
>> Theme from Light in the piazza

Authority Record Generated References:

> Spencer, Elizabeth. Kohtanz firenzessa
>> search under
>
> Spencer, Elizabeth. Light in the piazza. Finnish

> Spencer, Elizabeth. Luz en la plaza
>> search under
> Spencer, Elizabeth. Light in the piazza. Spanish

In this case, most of the nodes of control represent members of the instantiation network that will collocate through the use of added entries–implicit authority control has been exercised. But the translations represent nodes of control that require explicit authority control to cause them to collocate through the use of uniform titles.

In contemporary library catalogs, the nodes of control would be covered by the use of at least three different syndetic mechanisms: (1) an authority record for the author-title heading for the progenitor work with cross references for translations or other related works with differing titles; (2) another authority record for the heading for the excerpt with cross references for extraction derivations; and (3) added entries for all other related works in the bibliographic records for the variant related works. At the time, I suggested (Smiraglia 1992, 115) that a simpler mechanism for control could exist were the authority record for the heading for any work to be reconceived as an authority record for the node of control. In such a conception, few authority records would be needed for each instantiation network–one for each substantial node with differing titles or attribution–and all derivative relations could be mapped among the authority records. Using such a schema would not have been burdensome for libraries or bibliographic utilities because, although instantiation networks are in many cases quite complex in their node structure, few contain variant identifying features (such as titles), and fewer still are contained in a local library's catalog.

AUTHORITY CONTROL OF WORKS TODAY: AN EMPIRICAL ANALYSIS

The 1992 study gave us evidence from a decade ago that increasing authority control over works could be accomplished fairly easily. Given that, it seemed appropriate to subject the questions of how much and what kind of authority control actually exists for works to empirical study. To do so can provide statistical parameters that will help us better understand the dimensions of the problem as well as to glimpse potential approaches to a solution. Remember, there is *no* authority control of works at present–the standard by which we can undertake this research relates to the presence of authority control for the *headings* for works or their creators.

Research Questions

Therefore, the following specific research questions were formulated to guide this study:

1. What proportion of works can be considered implicitly controlled with name-title or uniform title authority records?
    a. What proportion have any coverage in the LC Name Authority File?
    b. What proportion of works with implicit control are works in instantiation networks?
    c. What are the bibliographic characteristics of works with implicit control–i.e., what kinds of works have records in the LC Name Authority File? What kinds have no records in the LC Name Authority File?

2. What proportion of works have partial coverage through name-only authority records?
    a. What proportion of works with name-coverage are works in instantiation networks? What proportion are not?
    b. What are the bibliographic characteristics of works with name-coverage?

3. Do the data exist in the LC Name Authority File to generate authority records?
    a. What proportion of works would be covered if the 670 field in the name authority records were converted automatically to a name-title authority record?
    b. What proportion of such works have instantiation networks? What proportion do not?
    c. What proportion of works with no authority records at all have LC assigned name headings on MARC records?

Methodology

A sample of works was the first requirement, and because my datafiles include several samples of works it made sense to return to one of those samples. In fact, it seemed to me best to return to the original sample of works from the catalog of Georgetown University. The sample of 411 works was sufficient to make statements with 95% confidence about the characteristics of works in the catalog at Georgetown. An important point, therefore, and a limitation of this study is, that statements made here are directly generalizable only to the collection at Georgetown. However, we know from prior research that U.S. academic library collections tend to have common characteristics. We know that they differ from the characteristics of special libraries and from those of the bibliographic utilities. Specifically, an academic research library will tend to hold more progenitor works from the western liberal arts and sciences canon, and thus will have more demand for authority control of instantiation networks for those works with many editions, translations, adaptations, and so forth (see Smiraglia 2002a).

For the present study, the original sample was reemployed. To operationalize the research questions it was necessary to assume that a work might be authority-controlled if a Library of Congress Name-Authority File (LCNAF) record existed for its name-title entry. Alternatively, and realistically, it was also assumed that one might credit the current structure in the event that the work itself was not controlled but the heading for its creator entity (an author, a corporation, a government, etc.) was.

Thus, for each work in the sample the LC Name Authority File was searched to find any applicable authority record (for the work, usually a name-title authority record). Next, all main entry headings (mostly personal names of authors but some corporate entities) were also searched in the LCNAF. The idea here was, even if the work itself is not controlled, if the name of the creator is controlled, that provides some partial control over instantiations of the work (because they will at least all collocate under that same unique heading). During the searching, it became apparent that a significant number of works were actually listed as source documents in the 670 (source data found) fields of LC authority records for their creators' name headings. So the next step was to search all authority records to determine the proportion of works that might easily be controlled were those notes shifted into heading position (yes, regardless of the *form* of heading that might result). Finally, for all works or creators for whom no LCNAF records existed, a search of the bibliographic files was conducted to see whether the name or name-title heading existed in an LC-authorized form in a MARC record.

Results

The first research question asked what proportion of works in the sample could be considered implicitly controlled by name-title or uniform title authority records. A search of the LC Name Authority File (LCNAF) revealed, as was expected, a near total lack of control. Authority records had been created for 5.6% of works. Looked at the other way, a whopping 94.4% of works have no authority records. The works for which there were authority records were mostly in western European languages (over half in English, French or

German), published in Germany, Britain, France, and the UK, in LC classes B, D, P, and Q, and had a mean age of 41.13 years. (Throughout this report, 95% confidence intervals were negligible, ranging from .0001 to .0006.)

Of the works in the sample, 49.8% were progenitors of instantiation networks, so it is logical to ask what proportion of the works that were discovered to have authority control are among those works. Of the works with LC authority records, 10.8% were works with instantiation networks. In fact, 23 works in the sample had LC authority records for their name-title headings, 22 works with name-title heading authority records had instantiation networks. Small comfort perhaps to know that what little authority control exists is at least going to good use. Because all but one of the works with authority records were works with instantiation networks, there is no difference in the bibliographic characteristics reported, except for a slight rise in the mean age of the progenitor to 42.5 years.

The second research question asked what proportion of works might have partial authority control. For instance, one could consider a work partially authority-controlled if an authority record exists for the heading for the creator (author) of the work. Results were much better–87.1% of headings for creator's names are controlled by authority records (and thus 12.9% were not). These works represent the majority of the sample and thus the collection at Georgetown itself. Most are in English (71.1%), published in the U.S. or U.K. (64.7%), range across the entire LC classification, and the progenitors have a mean age of 31.8 years. Again I checked to see whether the works with instantiation networks were among those controlled with name-heading authority records. The result was encouraging, 92.2% of the works in instantiation networks have author name-heading authority records. The bibliographic characteristics do not change greatly; 68.1% are in English and published in the U.S. or U.K. (62.7%), the majority of works in this category fall into LC classes B, D, H, or P, and the mean age of the progenitor is 40.7 years.

The third research question asked about the potential to create controlling authority records for these works. In other words, if there is an authority record for the author's name heading, and the progenitor work is cited in a 670 "source data found" note, then it is conceivable that a simple algorithm could be written to create authority records that could control the works. The title in the 670 field could be "flipped" to a subfield $t in the 100 field to create a name-title authority record. Unfortunately, the results were not as encouraging as had been hoped for. Of the works (82 works) in the sample, 20% are cited in 670 fields of the authority records for the headings for their authors. The bibliographic characteristics of these works are similar to those already described–the only slight change noted was the preponderance of works in LC classes D, H, and P, and the mean age was quite lower, 24 years. Another 7.6% (31 works) were recorded in heading position on LC catalog records, meaning LC had the data necessary to create name-title authority records. Of the works with instantiation networks, 17.6% (36 works) can be found cited in authority records for their authors' name headings; another 4.9% (10 works) can be found in LC bibliographic records. The bibliographic characteristics are the same as before; the mean age of the progenitor in this group is 34 years.

Of the works with instantiation networks, 89.2% have no authority records, 10.8% have an authority record. Of the works with instantiation networks for which there are no authority records, 91.8% have authority records for authors' name headings, 19.8% of the titles appear in 670 fields, and 5.5% appear on an LC bibliographic record. Automatic creation of name-title authority records would raise the proportion to 36.1%, or would triple the amount of control over works.

Analysis of Works Controlled

From a sample of 410 works, of which nearly half have instantiation networks, only 23 works could be said to have implicit authority control. These works are identified in the table below. Seven are works of fiction, 1 is a motion picture, 1 is a liturgical document, and the rest are non-fiction. Because there are so few works in the group, it is impossible to make useful statistical statements about this, or any other, breakdown. Thus, there is little rationale to connect them, which is to say, there seems no rhyme or reason about why one work might have authority control and another does not. Most likely it is purely a matter of LC's own internal priorities at a given point in time.

	Main entry heading	Title	LCNAF Coverage
1		*Eneas, a twelfth-century French romance*	*work with refs. from variant titles*
2	Akutagawa, Ryuonosuke.	*Kappa*	*author and 2 translations*
3	Ames, Roger T.	*The art of rulership*	*author and 1 translation*
4	Broszat, Martin.	*Der staat Hitlers*	*author and 1 translation*
5		*Trouble in mind (motion picture)*	*serial control of motion picture heading*
6	Capitani, Francois de.	*Die Gesellschaft im Wandel*	*author work with pseud. heading*
7	Carroll, Lewis.	*Phantasmagoria*	*bibliographic identity and work (containing relation)*
8	Cassirer, Ernst.	*The question of Jean-Jacques Rousseau*	*author and 2 translations*
9	Dario, Ruben.	*Azul*	*author and work (containing relation)*

	Main entry heading	Title	LCNAF Coverage
10	Demianov, V.F. and V.N. Malozemov.	*Introduction to minimax*	*author and 1 translation*
11	Falckenberg, Richard.	*Geschichte der neueren Philosophie von Nikolaus von Kues bis zur Gegenwart*	*author and 1 translation*
12	Galsworthy, John.	*The Forsyte saga*	*author and 2 translations*
13	Hadwiger, Hugo.	*Combinatorial geometry in the plane*	*author and 1 translation*
14	Hijab, Nadia.	*Womanpower*	*author and 1 translation*
15	Horne, Alistair.	*Macmillan*	*author and work (variant title proper)*
16	Izaguirre, Bernadino.	*Historia de la misiones franciscanas ...*	*author and 1 translation*
17	Machado de Asis.	*Yaya Garcia*	*author and work (variant title proper)*
18	Maupassant, Guy de.	*Pierre et Jean*	*author and 2 translations*
19	Orthodox Eastern Church. Liturgy and ritual. Molityoslov. English.	*Euchology ...*	*corporate body and 2 translations*
20	Sollers, Philippe.	*L'ecriture et l'experience*	*author and 1 translation*
21	Stalin, Joseph.	*Marxism and problems of linguistics*	*author and 1 translation*
22	Tanin, O.	*When Japan goes to war*	*author and 1 translation*
23	World Meteorological Organization.	*International meteorological vocabulary*	*corporate body and 1 translation*

However, of these 23 works, all have authority control over the heading for the author (or main entry), and the clear majority control headings for translations. Three control variant titles and two control containing relations. A qualitative conclusion, then, is that authority control is more likely when variant titles proper exist, or when works are nested within multi-work items. However likely a conclusion this might seem, our evidence is too slight to make a statistically significant statement about these phenomena.

CONCLUSIONS

The mythical chimera was a frightful fire-breathing beast with the head of a lion, the body of a goat, and the tail of a dragon. The term is sometimes used to describe an organism that has mutant components–not entirely unlike the large instantiation network that arises from a progenitor work over time. For a busy scholar seeking a specific instantiation, working through the maze of today's online catalogs can certainly seem like doing battle with a chimera. Metaphorically, the chimera has come to be used to describe vain, foolish fantasies, which is why I chose the term to describe authority control of works. Eleven years ago my analysis of the works in the library at Georgetown University suggested that, though at least half of the works had instantiation networks, authority control could be improved dramatically with the explicit control of work nodes. Today, we see that virtually no authority control exists (at least over this collection of works), and that what does exist is unpredictable at best.

But the news is not all bad. Even from the cursory examination presented here we can see that many instantiation networks (in this academic research library's collection) are made up of successive derivations that can be implicitly linked through collocation. The difficult work of explicitly linking instantiations comes with title changes, translations, and containing relations. The majority of works with instantiation networks–92.2%–have authority control established for their creator's name headings. Data exist either in authority records or in bibliographic records already established that could be used to provide work records for approximately 36.1% of the works encountered here. As I suggested before, it would be possible for work titles found in 670 notes in name authority records to be flipped into the title position in a name-title record. Obviously, post-verification of such automatically generated records would be required, but such a maneuver could improve authority control of works substantially.

The library world is currently working hard to comprehend and incorporate IFLA's entity-relationship model for the bibliographic record. Known as FRBR (for Functional Requirements for Bibliographic Records), this model has the potential to unmask our chimera and help us move from fantasy to reality in the explicit control of work nodes. The model sees the work relationship as a hierarchy of entities: works, expressions, manifestations, and items. A work is a distinct intellectual or artistic creation, an expression is the intellectual or artistic realization of a work. The entities work and expression reflect intellectual content, a manifestation embodies an expression of a work, and a physical carrier–an item–embodies a manifestation. A work may be realized through one or more expressions, which may be embodied in one or more manifestations, which may in turn be exemplified in one or more items (IFLA 1998, 12-13).

The empirical evidence in the present study suggests that explicit control of expressions will provide the best control over instantiation networks because it is instantiations such as translations, abridgments, and adaptations that require explicit linking. The line between what constitutes an expression and what constitutes a manifestation in the IFLA model is unclear. Data in my earlier analyses of works (Smiraglia 2001) suggest the line between work and expression must be placed at a point where ideational or semantic content change (as is the case with translations and adaptations). A statistical analysis of the OCLC WorldCat suggests this as well (Bennett, Lavoie, O'Neill 2003), demonstrating that most manifestations are unique but the smaller corpus of expressions can be explicitly controlled. It remains unclear at present how we will get from here to there. That is, how will we move from our present muddle of online catalogs with entry-level syndetic structure to a FRBR-like model with syndetic depth and explicit control of works? Nonetheless, it is clear we must now turn our attention to the authority control of works.

WORKS CITED

Anglo-American cataloguing rules. 2003. 2nd ed., 2002 rev. Chicago: American Library Association.

Ayres, F. H. 1990. Duplicates and other manifestations: a new approach to the presentation of bibliographic information. *Journal of Librarianship* 22: 236-251.

Bennett, Rick, Brian F. Lavoie, Edward T. O'Neill. 2003. The concept of a work in WorldCat: An application of FRBR. *Library collections, acquisitions, and technical services* 27n1: 45-59.

Bregzis, Ritvars. 1982. The syndetic structure of the catalog. In *Authority control: The key to tomorrow's catalog*, ed. by Mary W. Ghikas, 19-35. Phoenix: Oryx Press.

Carlyle, Allyson. 1996. Ordering author and work records: An evaluation of collocation in online catalog displays. *Journal of the American Society for Information Science* 47: 538-54.

Carlyle, Allyson. 1999. User categorisation of works: Toward improved organisation of online catalogue displays. *Journal of documentation* 55: 184-208.

International Federation of Library Associations, Study Group on the Functional Requirements for Bibliographic Records. 1998. *Functional requirements for bibliographic records.* München: K.G. Saur.

Perreault, Jean M. 1982. Authority control: old and new. *Libri* 32: 124-48.

Smiraglia, Richard P. 1992. Authority control and the extent of derivative bibliographic relationships. Ph.D. diss., University of Chicago.

Smiraglia, Richard P. 2001. *The nature of a work: Implications for knowledge organization.* Lanham, Md.: Scarecrow Press.

Smiraglia, Richard P. 2002a. Further progress in theory in knowledge organization. *Canadian Journal of Information and Library Science* 26n2/3: 30-49.

Smiraglia, Richard P. 2002b. Works as signs, symbols and canons: The epistemology of the work. *Knowledge organization* 28: 192-202.

Wilson, Patrick. [1987] 1989. The second objective. In *The conceptual foundations of descriptive cataloging*, ed. by Elaine Svenonius, 5-16. San Diego: Academic Press.

Wilson, Patrick. 1989. Interpreting the second objective of the catalog. *Library quarterly* 59: 339-353.

AUTHORITY CONTROL FOR SUBJECTS

SACO and Subject Gateways

Ana L. Cristán

SUMMARY. This presentation attempts to fit the subject contribution mechanism used in the Program for Cooperative Cataloging's SACO Program into the context of subject gateways. The discussion points to several subject gateways and concludes that there is no similarity between the two. Subject gateways are a mechanism for facilitating searching, while the SACO Program is a cooperative venture that provides a "gateway" for the development of LCSH (Library of Congress Subject Heading list) into an international authority file for subject headings.

KEYWORDS. Library of Congress Subject Headings, LCSH, Program for Cooperative Cataloging, PCC, SACO, subject gateways

In researching the topic of my presentation it was my task to determine if the SACO Program component of the Program for Cooperative Cataloging

Ana L. Cristán is Acting Team Leader, Cooperative Cataloging Team, Library of Congress.

[Haworth co-indexing entry note]: "SACO and Subject Gateways." Cristán, Ana L. Co-published simultaneously in *Cataloging & Classification Quarterly* (The Haworth Information Press, an imprint of The Haworth Press, Inc.) Vol. 39, No. 1/2, 2004, pp. 309-322; and: *Authority Control in Organizing and Accessing Information: Definition and International Experience* (ed: Arlene G. Taylor, and Barbara B. Tillett) The Haworth Information Press, an imprint of The Haworth Press, Inc., 2004, pp. 309-322.

http://www.haworthpress.com/web/CCQ
Digital Object Identifier: 10.1300/J104v39n01_01

(PCC) could be related to subject gateways or if it might be considered a subject gateway in its own right.

BRIEF BACKGROUND

SACO is described as the subject component of the Program for Cooperative Cataloging. The PCC is an organization collaboratively led by the Library of Congress and the major cataloging utilities in the United States, OCLC, and RLG, and is dedicated to enabling catalogers to create and make accessible bibliographic and authority records that are formulated and structured according to mutually acceptable standards.

That is to say that PCC catalogers create bibliographic and authority records using a set of rules, guidelines, and documentation which they have all agreed to apply in their cataloging. The user is thereby provided uniformity and predictability when using these records in their cataloging.

Within the PCC framework it is SACO that allows catalogers to submit subject heading proposals for possible inclusion in the list of *Library of Congress Subject Headings* (LCSH) and allows for the modification of existing subject headings and/or modification of the existing subject heading hierarchy. LCSH, in the grand scheme of things, may be called a "boutique" file, particularly when comparing its less than 300,000 authority records with that of the shared NACO Authority File that contains ca. 5 1/2 million records (2 million of which have been contributed by PCC participants), nonetheless it does not lack in popularity and usefulness. Both authority files reside at the Library of Congress where the staff is responsible for the maintenance and the day-to-day oversight of receiving and distributing these records. To reinforce what has been said by my LC colleagues at this conference, there are a total of four component parts to the PCC: NACO the name authority record component, SACO the subject authority record component, BIBCO the bibliographic record component, and CONSER the serial record component.

The Venn diagram in Figure 1 shows the interaction of the component parts with each other and reveals that in some aspects SACO is independent of the others, a characteristic that this presentation will examine later. Information on these programs is available via the World Wide Web on the PCC Home Page at: http://www.loc.gov/catdir/pcc/.

This presentation focuses its attention on the SACO program and grapples with its connection to subject gateways that may be found by searching the World Wide Web.

FIGURE 1. Interrelationship of PCC Programs

SUBJECT GATEWAYS

The definition that appears to be the most straightforward is the one found on the Desire web site which states that: "subject gateways are online services and sites that provide searchable and browseable catalogues of Internet-based resources." The definition goes on to say that "subject gateways will typically focus on a related set of academic subject areas."[1]

The TERENA–Trans-European Research and Education Networking Association focuses attention on librarians or information specialists in the use of subject gateway when stating that: ". . . subject gateways, select, classify and describe quality resources in a specified subject area. They [the subject gateways] effectively fill the role of information broker for information seekers in that [particular discipline] and the people selecting and describing resources are usually subject-specialists, for example librarians. . . . gateways can be relied on to identify useful quality online resources, and to be an important resource for anyone working in a field in which there is a significant mass of online source material."[2]

Further web crawling points to a number of sources, including the site by the National Library of Australia (NLA). NLA has developed an online resource that provides a "Best practice checklist for Australian subject Gateways." The checklist presents a "core set of content, business, and functional characteristics" that is intended "to stimulate further debate on the coherent development of gateways, and to provide Australian gateways with a common framework for participating in the cooperative development of both national and overseas gateways."[3] This site contains a grid that lists subject gateways and their characteristics in addition to a list of standards to be used in order for NLA to accept the site as a gateway. One of the thesauri included in NLA's grid used to map to specific gateways is indeed LCSH. Thus, we begin to see a connection of sorts to SACO.

The levels of the subject gateways vary considerably and certainly the most sophisticated appear to be those developed by the European library community. PINAKES is one of these gateways. This site bills itself as a "subject launch pad" and serves not only a subject gateway but also supplies links to multiple subject gateways.[4]

There is at least one website designed to provide downloadable software for setting up a subject gateway. ROADS, the Resource Organisation and Discovery in Subject-based services is a singular example. It is funded by Joint Information Systems of the UK.[5]

This source offers guidelines for using the software provided by ROADS and provides step-by-step instruction for building a more focused searching mechanism. The site features information regarding the usefulness of gateways and cites among the benefits that subject gateways seek to overcome the problems of retrieving huge numbers of irrelevant results. That is to say that when using search engines such as Yahoo, Google, or Lycos, users will get results that often do not provide meaningful or independent descriptions of the sites; thereby requiring the user to sift through an imprecise mélange. Other factors cited to show the usefulness of subject gateways include the points that most subject gateways provide link checking and that because the search is more focused the results are retrieved and displayed more efficiently.

Suffice it to say that subject gateways run the gamut from simple to sophisticated. The Library of Congress has a site called a "global gateway" that provides links to a list of resources grouped by country via its "portals to the world."[6] While this site does not provide a search engine as used by most subject gateways described earlier this site provides links to resources by country and therein by subject.

For the purposes of my discourse the definition of a "subject gateway" which best describes how the SACO Program might relate is found in the 1998 article authored by John Kirriemuir et al., which states that: "a subject gateway, in the context of network-based resource access, can be defined as some facility that allows easier access to network-based resources in a defined subject area. The simplest types of subject gateways are sets of Web pages containing lists of links to resources."[7]

The SACO Program has on its Home Page a list of resources for use in the creation of subject headings. This Web page has been developed and is maintained by PCC participant, Adam Schiff, Principal Cataloger at the University of Washington. This list of resources is available at: http://www.loc.gov/catdir/pcc/saco/resources.html (see Figure 2).

And much like the "Portals to the World" site, the Web Resources for SACO Proposals is a set of Web pages containing a list of links to resources. Thus, according to the Kirriemuir definition it may be considered a simple subject gateway. For the SACO Program the access that this Web page provides is extremely important.

LCSH uses the MARC 21 communication format as its standard for providing a framework to enable data sharing in machine-readable form. Among the hallmarks of an LCSH authority record is the inclusion of the *MARC 21 Authority Format's* "sources found" field, often better known by its numerical equivalent, the "670 field." This field is a requirement for all subject-heading proposals submitted to the SACO Program. The 670 field allows the cataloger to provide the literary warrant that justifies or authorizes the heading and/or may even be used to justify variant forms of the heading. In a shared environment the 670 field is an indispensable feature. In the case of SACO this field is used by the subject specialists at LC to provide editorial oversight without access to the item being cataloged. The LC subject specialists rely on the information provided by the cataloger in the 670 field for justification of the heading, possibly for justification of the variant forms, and for the determination as to whether or not the heading being created is appropriate to the work being cataloged.

Given the importance of providing evidence of research when constructing a subject-heading proposal for possible inclusion in LCSH it would certainly behoove the SACO Program to investigate building a more sophisticated subject gateway for SACO using this "List of Web resources" as a starting point. However, the ROADS documentation cites "people" as one of the key elements in building and maintaining a subject gateway. Given the current level of staffing of the SACO Program, it would be easier to link from the SACO Web resources page to one of a number of existing subject gateways. Certainly subject gateways are a valuable cataloging tool that catalogers developing subject proposals for contribution to LCSH could benefit from using. Therefore, how does SACO relate to subject gateways? Only if one wishes to use the word "gateway" in its most basic meaning–that is to say that it provides a pas-

FIGURE 2. No Search Engine–Basic Listing of Web Sources

Geographic Names Sources

Worldwide
- Alexandria Digital Library Gazetteer Server
- Finnish Place Names Outside Finland
- A Gazetteer of the Roman World
- GEBCO Names of Undersea Features
- GeoNative
- GEOnet
- Getty Thesaurus of Geographic Names
- Global Gazetteer
- Jerry Hill Presents Names - scroll down to Place Names
- National Geographic Map Machine
- National Parks Worldwide
- Orbis Latinus Online
- Park Search
- A Political World Gazetteer
- The Probert Encyclopaedia Gazetteer
- United Nations List of Protected Areas (1997)
- The World Factbook
- Yahoo! Parks and Public Lands

Antarctica

sageway from one area into another can one say that the SACO Program is a gateway. Indeed SACO is the "gateway" that offers the opportunity to catalogers and institutions that wish to have subject headings become part of the Library of Congress subject headings authority file. LCSH no longer restricts the development of new subject headings to those relevant to materials housed in LC's collection; instead, via the SACO Program, LCSH incorporates subject headings proposed by catalogers from around the world. Thus, while subject gateways provide a transparent searching mechanism for information in specific areas, SACO provides a mechanism for the development of the indexes through which those links may be built.

HISTORY OF SACO

The genesis of the SACO Program began with a letter sent in 1981 from the National Library of Australia to LC's then Director for Cataloging, Henriette Avram, requesting a mechanism for including Australian subject headings for local flora and fauna in LCSH. As it was structured in 1981, LCSH contained only subject headings which had been used to catalog items in LC's collections. Experience was gleaned from other cooperative subject ventures, and with the advance of technology, in 1992 the SACO Program was developed to allow subject headings that are developed in accordance with LCSH guidelines to be added to the LC subject authority file. Consequently, SACO now boasts participation from more than 80 institutions, and at least 15 of these partners are from the international arena. A current list of those international partners who contribute on a regular basis includes the British Library, Trinity College Dublin, the universities of Oxford and Cambridge, as well as the national libraries of Scotland, Canada, Australia, New Zealand, and Singapore.[8]

It is interesting to note that many of the current international NACO partners began PCC participation by first submitting subject heading proposals via the SACO Program. A mainstream workflow for NACO contribution of name authority headings requires membership in one of the bibliographic utilities; however, for SACO there is no such requirement. For membership in the CONSER and/or BIBCO Programs an institution must first become a participating NACO member, yet there is no such requirement for participation in the SACO Program. For membership in NACO, CONSER or BIBCO an institution must first submit an application and agree to undergo training appropriate to each component program, yet there is currently no such requirement for SACO. It may be that lack of these specific program requirements may have encouraged international participation in SACO, but I offer two additional arguments for SACO's universal appeal: (1) the use of the MARC authority format and (2) that English is one of the official languages of the catalogs of those participating institutions.

BARRIERS TO PARTICIPATION

These two common bonds more than anything else, have enhanced the SACO Program's growth. In fiscal year 2002 PCC participants contributed more headings to LCSH than did the staff at the Library of Congress (see Figure 3).

However, this growth has brought increased challenges to the PCC and to LCSH. Many non-English speaking countries are attempting to develop subject headings based on LCSH and find the process of translating LCSH laborious, frustrating, and not cost effective. In a survey conducted by Magda Heiner-Freiling in 2000 for an article in *Cataloging and Classification Quarterly,* on the occasion of LCSH's cenntenial, it was found that there are more than 36 countries in which LCSH is used and that at least 12 of these institutions use "translations or adaptations of LCSH into their own language."[9] Instead of translating the entire LCSH authority file, each institution has developed a mechanism for translating a subset of LCSH when needed for lo-

FIGURE 3. SACO Contributions by PCC Partners, 2002

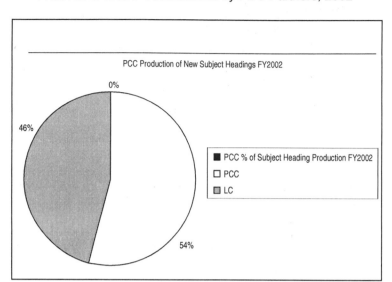

PCC Production of New Subject Headings FY2002

■ PCC % of Subject Heading Production FY2002
☐ PCC
▨ LC

cal use, and there appears not to be a mechanism in place that allows for sharing of these files outside the immediate region.

In spring of 2002 at LC the subject specialists on staff at the Cataloging and Policy Support Office, in concert with the Cooperative Cataloging Team, joined to offer a workshop on LCSH to 17 catalogers from Latin American countries. The objective of this workshop was to lay a foundation for Spanish speaking catalogers to understand the principles and underlying structure of LCSH with the expectation that this would facilitate translation of LCSH into Spanish. I served as the coordinator of that workshop, and it was LC's interest in the development of a Spanish language LCSH and the commitment made to support the work that is being done by El Colegio de México in developing a bi-lingual subject headings list that led to this workshop being held. In March 2001 I attended a seminar on cooperation in authorities in Mexico City, sponsored by El Colegio de México, that sought to bring together Mexican libraries into the systematic development of a shared database of Spanish and English LCSH. LC and the PCC continue to support cooperative efforts in Latin America and have recently reaffirmed the desire to seek solutions to barriers to international participation through the formation of a PCC Task Group on International Participation.[10]

Another effort to facilitate non-English subject headings into LCSH was the workshop presented at a Baltic Conference in September 1997; as a result the National Library of Lithuania has contributed some vernacular subject headings via the SACO process. An example of several of these headings can be seen in Figures 4-7.

Incorporating non-English headings into LCSH is possible, particularly in areas such as geographic and man-made features including rivers, parks, buildings, and/or streets. In other areas the creation of vernacular headings is more problematic or prohibited by rules. If there is a predominance of English language forms of a term or concept found in English language reference sources, the guidelines require that the heading must be established in English. Moreover, the foreign language equivalent term may not be added as a cross-reference unless the item being cataloged is also in English. There is work going on by IFLA committees and others, which you have heard about at this conference, that may help to resolve this issue. As noted earlier, the PCC is aware of the need to play a role in the resolution of these barriers to expanded international participation and cooperation.

CURRENT METHODS OF CONTRIBUTION TO SACO

Improvements in the SACO Program are of concern at LC. Consequently, LC authorized an independent study to determine what steps need to be taken to decrease the amount of time it takes for a proposed subject heading to work its way through the LCSH editorial process. Currently the proposal process of contributing new or changed subject headings for LCSH through SACO continues to take a minimum of 4-6 weeks. As noted earlier, NLA requested the addition of Australian subject headings via a letter in 1981; nonetheless, it was not until the early 1990s that LC began to accept electronic mail submission of proposals. Prior to that time contributors were asked to send forward proposals on LC forms via surface mail and later via fax.

In the late 1990s a Web form was developed and made available for participants to use; however, the SACO workflow remains a manual process. While the need for re-keying has been minimized, it has not disappeared. Catalogers are still required to manipulate the proposals in order for these to be integrated into the process of editorial review. The independent LC study concluded that it is a combination of the integration of a proposed heading into the database and the subject editorial review process that play a role in the time lag for processing subject headings via SACO. Certainly the requisite editorial review will and should continue; I suggest that the SACO Program needs to develop, in concert with the bibliographic utilities, a mechanism for accepting propos-

FIGURE 4. First Step in Subject Heading Authority Record Search

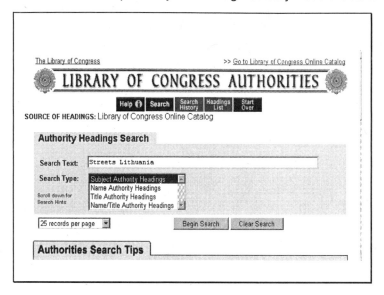

FIGURE 5. Search Results from Figure 4

#	Bib Records	*select icon in first column to...* View Authority Headings/References	Type of Heading
Authorized & References 1	0	Streets Lithuania	LC subject headings
2	2	Streets Lithuania Vilnius.	LC subject headings
3	1	Streets Lithuania Vilnius Pictorial works.	LC subject headings
Authorized Heading 4	0	Streets Living Theater (Musical group)	LC subject headings
5	1	Streets Ljubljana region, Slovenia Directories. [from old catalog]	LC subject headings
Authorized & References 6	0	Streets Louisiana	LC subject headings
7	5	Streets Louisiana New Orleans.	LC subject headings
8	1	Streets Louisiana New Orleans 1850-1860.	Thesaurus for graphic materials: TGM I, sub. terms
9	2	Streets Louisiana New Orleans 1900-1910.	Thesaurus for graphic materials: TGM I, sub.

FIGURE 6. Narrower Term Search Results

SOURCE OF HEADINGS: Library of Congress Online Catalog
INFORMATION FOR: Streets Lithuania

Please note: Broader Terms are not currently available

Select a Link Below to Continue...

Authority Record

Narrower Term: Bernardinu gatve (Vilnius, Lithuania)

Narrower Term: Ausros Vartu gatve (Vilnius, Lithuania)

Narrower Term: Didzioji gatve (Vilnius, Lithuania)

Narrower Term: Pilies gatve (Vilnius, Lithuania)

Narrower Term: Dominikonu gatve (Vilnius, Lithuania)

Narrower Term: Svento Jono gatve (Vilnius, Lithuania)

Narrower Term: Traku gatve (Vilnius, Lithuania)

Narrower Term: R¯udninku gatve (Vilnius, Lithuania)

Help - Search - Search History - *Headings List* - Start Over

FIGURE 7. MARC View of a Subject Heading Authority Record

035 __ |a (DLC)261304

906 __ |t 0034 |u te04 |v 0

010 __ |a sh 00008507

040 __ |a Lit |b eng |c DLC

151 __ |a Svento Jono gatve (Vilnius, Lithuania)

451 __ |a Balio Sruogos gatve (Vilnius, Lithuania)

451 __ |a Sv. Jono gatve (Vilnius, Lithuania)

550 __ |w g |a Streets |z Lithuania

667 __ |a This heading is not valid for use as a geographic subdivision.

670 __ |a Work cat.: 99169704: Caplinskas, A. Vilniaus gatviu istorija : Sv. Jono, Dominikonu, Traku gatves, 1998: |b p. 31 (called Balio Sruogos gatve, 1947-1989; called Sv. Jono gatve from 1989)

670 __ |a Vilnius : miesto gatviu ir aiksciu pavadinimu pakeitimai, naujos gatves ir aikstes iki 1991.

952 __ |a 0 bib. record(s) to be changed

953 __ |a yz00

als on a parallel with that of the NACO Program and its FTP transfer of name authorities to the LC master file. Earlier today John Byrum spoke of the great success of the NACO Program. This success can be attributed to the cooperation forged between the bibliographic utilities (OCLC and RLG), the British Library, and LC to enable a contribution/distribution mechanism for processing name authorities in a timely, cost-effective manner.

The PCC Policy Committee (PoCo) is very aware of the need to meet the challenge of institutionalizing SACO. At their annual meeting in November 2002 PoCo authorized a task force to develop a plan to transform the SACO Program into a full-fledged component of the PCC with guidelines and membership parameters.

This task force is charged with describing a scenario for contribution of subject proposals via the utilities or some other mechanism that would facilitate local review and eliminate re-keying. Parameters for participation, including goals for a minimum number of required proposals per annum will be addressed. The development of courses for beginning, advanced, and continuing subject cataloging education should also become incorporated into the responsibilities of the PCC. Of course, the proposed curriculum would include training and documentation to facilitate the development of subject headings. The report from this task force is due in summer of 2003. Alas, it may be easier to describe and recommend what needs to be done than it is to carry out those tasks.

As mentioned earlier, one of the most challenging workflow issues for the SACO Program will be the need to enable LCSH to handle non-English language subject headings. It is here that the power of the subject gateways may be harnessed or worked to an advantage, given that subject gateways are now attempting to provide the capability of multi-lingual searching. The challenge may be met by the use of a "virtual international authority file" (VIAF) as described by Dr. Barbara Tillett (Chief, CPSO) in her presentations. As envisioned by Dr. Tillett the VIAF is designed to allow the linking of "authorized forms of names, titles, and even subjects" in order to maximize the benefits of shared authority work.[11] Models and prototypes of the VIAF are currently being planned. The MACS (Multilingual Access to Subjects) project under development by the national libraries of France, Germany, Switzerland, and England also provides a glimmer of hope that these linguistic barriers may be surmounted.[12]

In the short term the answer may be as simple as expanding the use of the full range of MARC 7XX fields in subject headings as has been done for name headings in the NACO Program. Although implementation of the use of the 7XX field in subjects would not be the most cost-effective mechanism, it would allow the authorized form of headings for other national bibliographic agencies to be linked or made available via the LCSH subject authority record.

In the meantime while developments on the VIAF, MACS, and other efforts are brewing, the SACO Program continues to provide a mechanism for the development of LCSH that promotes a standardized file structure that can be described and used in a predictable and uniform manner. SACO helps to prevent the duplication of effort by those that use LCSH in their cataloging. By working collaboratively the PCC continues to welcome the inclusion of new participants and seeks to implement new technologies.

In conclusion, it is not the SACO Program that interacts with subject gateways, but it is LCSH that may be used for mapping to its headings from other authority files and/or subject gateways in order to provide more focused searches. Thus, it stands to reason that the more complete and inclusive that LCSH is, the better it can be used as a vehicle for searching a large number of resources, and the easier it will be to fit those files into any new technology. It is via the SACO Program that this development is taking place.

A visit to the SACO Home Page will reveal that currently any institution may participate in SACO by agreeing to follow the current LCSH guidelines and submitting a completed subject Web proposal.[13] To help facilitate the process, sample forms, guidelines, and a subject gateway will enable prospective participants to fulfill the requirements for research and to speed that subject proposal through the process.

The main requirements for creating a subject proposal to submit to SACO are:

1. The use and application of the guidelines found in a current edition of LC's *Subject Cataloging Manual: Subject Headings*. (4 vols. Available from the Cataloging Distribution Services at LC.)[14]
2. The ability to search to a current copy of the LCSH authority file. This is done to assure that a heading is not a duplicate of an established heading or a heading that is in the process of being proposed. Note that a search via the World Wide Web of the LC Web authorities module at: http:// authorities.loc.gov/ will find current valid subject headings as well as any new heading or modifications of existing headings being proposed without the need of an intervening vendor.
3. Access to a current copy of the *Free-Floating Subdivisions: An Alphabetical Index*. This document is necessary, as it will help prevent the proposing of an unnecessary heading that may be constructed by means of a subject–subdivision formulation.
4. Access to a current copy of the *MARC 21 Authority Format*. In order to be able to use LCSH properly it is necessary to recognize the MARC

codes and fields used in subject authority records, especially when checking to see if a heading or its reference structure is valid, etc.

5. A MARC 21 identification code. This code is used in the MARC 21 Cataloging Source (040) field to identify the institution that is submitting a proposal. This field is necessary for statistics kept by the Cooperative Cataloging Team and may be obtained online at the LC's Network Development and MARC Standards Office at: http://www.loc.gov/marc/organizations/orgshome.html#requests.

6. While not a requirement (at this time) attendance at an LCSH workshop is strongly encouraged. LCSH workshops may be provided "on demand" by contacting CPSO@loc.gov, by contacting the Cooperative Cataloging Team at acri@loc.gov, or by attending the SACO workshops held in conjunction with the biannual American Library Association conferences. Note that the workshops are free but that institutions requesting training may be asked to pay for the travel expenses of a trainer.

NOTES

1. Desire http://www.desire.org/html/subjectgateways/subjectgateways.html.

2. Terena Web site http://www.terena.nl/library/gnrt/websearch/gateways.html.

3. National Library of Australia (NLA)Web site http://www.nla.gov.au/initiatives/sg/index.html.

4. PINAKES Web site http://www.hw.ac.uk/libWWW/irn/pinakes/pinakes.html.

5. ROADS Web site http://www.ukoln.ac.uk/metadata/roads/what/.

6. Library of Congress Global Gateway http://international.loc.gov/intldl/intldlhome.html.

7. Kirriemuir, John et al., "Cross-searching subject gateways" *D-Lib Magazine* online at: http://www.dlib.org/dlib/january98/01kirriemuir.html.

8. International PCC Partners. http:// [fill this in!!!].

9. Heiner-Freiling, Magda. Survey on subject heading languages used in national libraries and bibliographies. *Classification and Cataloging Quarterly*, v. 29, no. 1/ 2 (2000): p. 189-198.

10. PCC Task Group on International Participation http://www.loc.gov/catdir/pcc/tgip.html.

11. Tillett, Barbara B. A virtual international authority file (VIAF). In: *Record of a workshop on Authority Control among Chinese Korean and Japanese Languages (CJK Authority 3)*, March 2002, p. 117-139.

12. MACS Web site http://infolab.kub.nl/prj/macs/.

13. SACO Home Page. http://www.loc.gov/catdir/pcc/saco.html.

14. LC Cataloging Distribution Service. http://www.loc.gov/cds/.

MACS (Multilingual Access to Subjects): A Virtual Authority File Across Languages

Genevieve Clavel-Merrin

SUMMARY. Shared authority files and cooperation in the development of national lists, both author and subject, have enabled libraries to share resources and improve access to their collections. As we move from national resource sharing to a more international approach, we face problems accessing catalogues in other languages. By creating links between existing subject heading languages (initially in French, German, and English), MACS (Multilingual Access to Subjects) allows users to carry out searches in major national library collections in Europe using subject headings in their own languages. An operational service will be available in 2004. *[Article copies available for a fee from The Haworth Document Delivery Service: 1-800-HAWORTH. E-mail address: <docdelivery@haworthpress.com> Website: <http://www.HaworthPress.com> © 2004 by The Haworth Press, Inc. All rights reserved.]*

KEYWORDS. MACS, multilingual subject access, national libraries, international cooperation, authority files, linking

---

Genevieve Clavel-Merrin is affiliated with the Swiss National Library.

[Haworth co-indexing entry note]: "MACS (Multilingual Access to Subjects): A Virtual Authority File Across Languages." Clavel-Merrin, Genevieve. Co-published simultaneously in *Cataloging & Classification Quarterly* (The Haworth Information Press, an imprint of The Haworth Press, Inc.) Vol. 39, No. 1/2, 2004, pp. 323-330; and: *Authority Control in Organizing and Accessing Information: Definition and International Experience* (ed: Arlene G. Taylor, and Barbara B. Tillett) The Haworth Information Press, an imprint of The Haworth Press, Inc., 2004, pp. 323-330. Single or multiple copies of this article are available for a fee from The Haworth Document Delivery Service [1-800-HAWORTH, 9:00 a.m. - 5:00 p.m. (EST). E-mail address: docdelivery@haworthpress.com].

http://www.haworthpress.com/web/CCQ
© 2004 by The Haworth Press, Inc. All rights reserved.
Digital Object Identifier: 10.1300/J104v39n01_02

INTRODUCTION:
AUTHORITY CONTROL COMES OF AGE

Shared authority files and cooperation in the development of national lists, both author and subject, have enabled libraries to share resources and improve access to their collections. As we move from national resource sharing to a more international approach (for example with the TEL (The European Library) project (http://www.europeanlibrary.org)) the difficulties of searching across collections have been underlined. Variations in author and corporate author headings across languages and subject headings in different languages have meant that frequently the search option of choice has been keyword. This brings results but its limitations are well-known.

Attempts are now being made to build on the significant work carried out in many countries to build and maintain subject heading languages and authority files. This is possible for a number of reasons, both organisational and technical: the increasing use of standard communication formats, the preparation and maintenance of well-structured manuals, and the development of sophisticated distributed management and updating structures built upon the widespread availability of the networking environment enabling the institutions increased access to the centralised authority control systems developed previously. As a result the application of authority control to collections using the same subject heading language is facilitated as libraries can exchange and copy records and thus improve (monolingual) indexing consistency across collections.

In addition, recognising that many subject heading languages follow similar construction and application principles (see the IFLA *Principles underlying subject heading languages*[1]), the groundwork is laid to allow libraries to build on the solid infrastructure for authority control at a monolingual level in order to extend control and access at a multilingual level.

Whereas, traditionally, bilingual/multilingual access was assured through multiple subject headings coded in the authority records, today many research initiatives seek to provide access through Internet based linking processes. Concepts such as language cross-linking, or interoperability in subject heading languages, which are common in today's research in multilingual access were limited ten years ago to language specialists. MACS (Multilingual Access to Subjects) uses the stable authority control environment and this linking process to extend the use of subject heading languages on an international networked multilingual level.

BACKGROUND TO THE MACS INITIATIVE

MACS was created in 1997 in response to a request by the Conference of European National Librarians (CENL) to find a solution to the problem of multilingual subject access to European databases. As a multilingual country, Switzerland is, of course, particularly interested in finding solutions, but it is significant that other countries were interested in this multilingual approach even if they have traditionally been considered monolingual. This serves to underline the international needs of users and the necessity to co-operate in collection building and access not only on a regional or national level but increasingly within the international sphere.

A working group was set up in order to discuss the issue, and among many approaches discussed, the idea of establishing links between different subject heading languages (SHLs) was, for four of the participating libraries, a promising solution. Four libraries, the Swiss National Library (SNL), the Bibliothèque nationale de France (BnF), the British Library (BL) and the Deutsche Bibliothek (DDB) accepted the task of defining a concept and conducting a study to determine the feasibility of such a concept, details of which are given below. The MACS project was then set up with its main goal: "to provide the means by which library databases can be accessed on a multilingual basis by the use of equivalent headings from subject authority files." The approach taken was to create broad multilingual access that could be used as widely as possible by using indexing languages that are commonly used in most libraries in any given country.

This multilingual access is made possible thanks to the equivalence links established between the three subject heading languages used in these libraries: SWD/RSWK for German, RAMEAU for French and LCSH for English. Each of these subject heading languages is widely used at a national and international level, e.g., the use of SWD is widespread in Germany but also in Austria and Switzerland, RAMEAU is used in university, municipal, and public libraries in France and is being taken up by other francophone countries, while the spread of LCSH in English-speaking countries and in international institutions is well-known.

The decision to use the approach of linking also took into account the fact that the libraries (French, German, English) have invested considerable time and effort in the creation and maintenance of each SHL (LCSH, RAMEAU, and SWD) and which have been used extensively to provide subject access to millions of documents, both in the national libraries but also as noted above, among libraries throughout the countries concerned and elsewhere. Creating a new multilingual vocabulary, based on translation, would have been unrealistic and uneconomical. Using the resources available maintains access to documents already indexed and extends access across linguistic boundaries.

The study took a subset of headings from the three SHLs in the fields of Theatre and Sport, plus the most frequently used headings used to index documents in the Bibliothèque nationale de France. The group studied different mapping methods including the comparison of indexing of the same document in different subject heading languages before establishing links between the headings manually. Methods to solve one-to-many or many-to-many mappings were analysed and principles of co-operative link creation and management were established. The results of the study were encouraging and showed that linking headings was a feasible approach to cross-language access to documents in many though not all cases. A match or link was considered successful when a concept, represented by similar headings in the different SHLs which are matched manually (intellectually) returned almost equivalent results in subject retrieval.

Details of the feasibility study may be found at: http://infolab.kub.nl/ prj/macs. The group recommended that a prototype be developed in order to test the management structure, link creation, and multilingual searching.

PROTOTYPE

Following a restricted tender, the contract to develop the system was awarded to Index Data aps and Infolab Tilburg. The system is available for guest access at http://infolab.kub.nl/prj/macs.

The prototype contains the following data:

- All headings from the subject areas *Sports* and *Theatre* for which terms had been matched in the feasibility study, plus 500 most used headings identified first in the RAMEAU database and their equivalent headings from the other SHLs amounting to around 3000 headings;
- 1200 links created between the concepts;
- Bibliographic records containing these headings extracted from each of the 4 partners' databases in order to allow the system to simulate searches of the library catalogues using the Z39.50 protocol.

The prototype is a standards-based Web application independent of the partners' systems and the SHLs used. It has two modules:

The *Link Management Interface* enables link creation and maintenance, with mechanisms for managing partial or complex links. The system is based on the principle of 'federative management,' i.e., each SHL is autonomous with each partner being responsible for link management in their own SHL (shared responsibility for SWD between DDB and SNL) and no central editor. Partners may make proposals concerning other parts of a link but these must be confirmed by the appropriate partner. An annotation function enables partners to comment on links or proposals or to indicate where problems have occurred. The following principles are observed in link management:

- All SHLs are of equal status; there is no pivot SHL. Instead, the system contains mappings that are considered as conceptual clusters, identified by an abstract (numeric) identifier only;
- Hierarchical structures, thesaural relationships or non-preferred terms are not mapped or reproduced as part of the process of linking individual headings: only headings at the authority level are linked;
- Where an equivalence cannot be found, a proposed heading should stand alone in the system to represent the concept (for possible future mapping).

The *User Search Interface* enables end users to carry out subject searches in the language of their choice simultaneously across target catalogues (currently subsets of the partners' catalogues) using the Z39.50 protocol. The user enters a search term from one of the available Subject Headings Lists (currently LSCH, RAMEAU or SWD), chooses one or more target catalogues then may either launch a search across the targets or choose to browse a list of corresponding headings and their equivalents from which one or more clusters may be chosen before the search is sent out. Tests have shown that this latter approach leads to better results and puts less strain on target resources. From the search result set the user can access individual bibliographic records in any of the libraries by simply clicking on the title. In the prototype options are provided for a brief display or for a full display in the MARC format used by the selected library.

TESTS

MACS has made searching and a read-only access to the Link Management Interface available since 2001. During that time, over 500 people from all over the world have signed up to test the MACS prototype. With comments received and tests conducted by the MACS partners, refinement of the organisational model has resulted in the design of a new version of the MACS system. Despite improvements in the linking mechanisms, the basic task of establishing links will remain very time consuming. Fortunately the partners can build on existing bilingual links in the RAMEAU authority files managed at the Bibliothèque nationale de France and loaded in the MACS system. Approximately 70,000 RAMEAU authorities contain a proposed LCSH heading and have been assigned a subject domain number. Work on adding the SWD headings to these links will start in 2003 and will be divided between partners in Germany and Switzerland according to domains. In the meantime, other methods to facilitate link creation will be studied.

INTEGRATING MACS INTO REAL-LIFE ENVIRONMENTS

The search results have shown that pertinent documents can be retrieved using links across subject headings, and a move from using subsets of data to the partners' own databases is planned. In April 2002 tests began with the catalogue of the Deutsche Bibliothek, in Summer 2002 the Bibliothèque nationale de France carried out successful tests, and the Swiss National Library will carry out a similar test in Winter 2002. Changes in the Search Interface will be necessary to ensure that users can obtain manageable queries and search sets, and of course an increased number of links is essential. The interest of the library community in MACS is underlined by the fact that the national library partners in the TEL project wish to integrate the product in the TEL portal, which, in its prototype phase, aims to offer access to the resources of 8 European national libraries. Portal suppliers will be asked to propose ways in which MACS could be integrated, at the simplest level by a link to the system or perhaps by taking over the MACS data itself.

INCORPORATING TRUE AUTHORITY MANAGEMENT (SEE AND SEE ALSO REFERENCES)

As initially planned, only headings at the authority level are linked. The partners recognise that it is not always easy for users to find the preferred terms for searching without the help of see-and see also-references. The goal is to incorporate an access to the national authority files as an option for users who wish to check headings and refine their search before sending it to the target databases.

In addition, no SHL remains static, headings may be altered in response to linguistic change or new discoveries. It is essential that such changes be carried over into the Link Management System (and also, of course, into the appropriate library catalogues). Where a straightforward replacement occurs, it should be possible to update the Link Management System: this will require the SHL providers to be able to track and extract changed headings and their IDs and will require the Link Management System to load and match these changes. Since the Link Management Interface contains the authority IDs for the headings, the links for navigation and updates when approved headings are modified can be incorporated without the need to duplicate information.

THE FUTURE

The immediate value for users of the Swiss National Library (SNL) is the real possibility that in the near future subject searches will be conducted in more than one language. As a federal institution, the Swiss National Library is committed to serving its users in the three official languages of Switzerland (German, French and Italian). The SNL's decision in 1998 to adopt the SWD as its indexing standard came with the assurance that the French and Italian users would also profit from that indexing though a multilingual search tool. Going beyond national boundaries, other users of the SNL and of other national libraries will also find their searches facilitated by a multilingual gateway to their catalogs. The Deutsche Bibliothek views the project as a way to foster the value of the SWD and will make the MACS results available to its partners in Germany and Austria. The Bibliothèque nationale de France has already undertaken a survey to look into ways of extending the MACS linking work at a national level.

Extending the links to other subject heading languages is a goal, though future partners should be aware that the investment in staff time can be considerable since, at present, linking is still analyzed and carried out manually. Until the operational system is up and running it is still difficult for the partners to estimate the exact time required for link creation and checking, but preliminary estimates show that the time required per link may vary between two and eight minutes depending on the subject area and the complexity. Any potential partner therefore should have an infrastructure similar to those in France or Germany in which the management of the subject heading language is spread across participating institutions.

A VIRTUAL AUTHORITY FILE?

At present MACS is restricted to the authorised headings from the participating subject heading languages, and as Freyre and Naudi[2] have indicated, could be considered in some respects to play the role of a *multilingual dictio-*

nary of subject heading languages, a "bridge between systems that are themselves designed to organise and name concepts." The incorporation of a link to the other elements of the authority records within the partners' national authority files will build on this to create a virtual multilingual authority file.

NOTES

1. Maria Inês Lopes and Julianne Beall, ed., *Principles Underlying Subject Heading Languages (SHLS)*. Working Group on Principles Underlying Subject Heading Languages, IFLA Section on Classification and Indexing (München: K.G. Saur, 1999).

2. Elisabeth Freyre and Max Naudi, "MACS: Subject Access Across Languages and Networks," in *Subject Retrieval in a Networked Environment: Papers Presented at an IFLA Satellite Meeting Sponsored by the IFLA Section on Classification and Indexing & IFLA Section on Information Technology, OCLC, Dublin, Ohio, USA, 14-16 August 2001*. Dublin, OH: OCLC, 2001.

FAST:
Development of Simplified Headings for Metadata

Rebecca J. Dean

SUMMARY. The Library of Congress Subject Headings schema (LCSH) is the most commonly used and widely accepted subject vocabulary for general application. It is the de facto universal controlled vocabulary and has been a model for developing subject heading systems by many countries. However, LCSH's complex syntax and rules for constructing headings restrict its application by requiring highly skilled personnel and limit the effectiveness of automated authority control.

Recent trends, driven to a large extent by the rapid growth of the Web, are forcing changes in bibliographic control systems to make them easier to use, understand, and apply, and subject headings are no exception. The purpose of adapting the LCSH with a simplified syntax to create FAST (Faceted Application of Subject Terminology) headings is to retain the very rich vocabulary of LCSH while making the schema easier

Rebecca J. Dean is affiliated with the OCLC Office of Research.
FAST is an OCLC Office of Research Project. The members of the FAST team are: Edward T. O'Neill, Eric Childress, Rebecca Dean, Kerre Kammerer, Diane Vizine-Goetz, Anya Dyer (OCLC, Dublin, OH USA); Lois Mai Chan (University of Kentucky, Lexington, KY USA); and Lynn El-Hoshy (Library of Congress, Washington, DC USA).

[Haworth co-indexing entry note]: "FAST: Development of Simplified Headings for Metadata." Dean, Rebecca J. Co-published simultaneously in *Cataloging & Classification Quarterly* (The Haworth Information Press, an imprint of The Haworth Press, Inc.) Vol. 39, No. 1/2, 2004, pp. 331-352; and: *Authority Control in Organizing and Accessing Information: Definition and International Experience* (ed: Arlene G. Taylor, and Barbara B. Tillett) The Haworth Information Press, an imprint of The Haworth Press, Inc., 2004, pp. 331-352. Single or multiple copies of this article are available for a fee from The Haworth Document Delivery Service [1-800-HAWORTH, 9:00 a.m. - 5:00 p.m. (EST). E-mail address: docdelivery@haworthpress.com].

http://www.haworthpress.com/web/CCQ
Digital Object Identifier: 10.1300/J104v39n01_03

to understand, control, apply, and use. The schema maintains compatibility with LCSH–any valid Library of Congress subject heading can be converted to FAST headings. *[Article copies available for a fee from The Haworth Document Delivery Service: 1-800-HAWORTH. E-mail address: <docdelivery@haworthpress.com> Website: <http://www.HaworthPress.com> © 2004 by The Haworth Press, Inc. All rights reserved.]*

KEYWORDS. Library of Congress Subject Headings, LCSH, Faceted Application of Subject Terminology, FAST, semantic interoperability, Dublin Core

INTRODUCTION

The enormous volume and rapid growth of resources available on the World Wide Web as well as the emergence of numerous metadata schemas have spurred a re-examination of the way subject data are provided for Web resources. There is broad agreement that a subject schema for metadata must exhibit both simplicity and interoperability. Simplicity refers to the usability by non-catalogers. Interoperability enables users to search across both discipline boundaries and across information retrieval and storage systems. Additional requirements identified by the ALCTS/SAC/Subcommittee (1999) specify that the schema should:

- Be simple and easy to apply and to comprehend,
- Be intuitive so that sophisticated training in subject indexing and classification, while highly desirable, is not required in order to implement,
- Be logical so that it requires the least effort to understand and implement,
- Be scalable for implementation from the simplest to the most sophisticated.

Another central issue involving the syntax revolves around the choice of pre-coordination or post-coordination. Both have precedence in cataloging and indexing practices. Subject vocabularies used in traditional cataloging typically consist of pre-coordinated subject heading strings, while controlled vocabularies used in online databases are mostly single-concept descriptors, relying on post-coordination for complex subjects. For the sake of simplicity and semantic interoperability, the post-coordinate approach is more in line with the basic premises and characteristics of the online environment. Chan et al. (2001) provides additional background on the metadata requirements particularly as they relate to Dublin Core applications.

The ALCTS/SAC/Subcommittee recommended that metadata for subject analysis of Web resources include a mixture of keywords and controlled vocabulary. The potential sources of controlled vocabulary the Subcommittee identified included:

- Using an existing schema(s),
- Adapting or modifying existing schema(s),
- Developing new schema(s).

Each of these options offers clear advantages. The use of an existing schema is certainly the simplest approach if a suitable one can be found. Of the existing schema, LCSH is the most obvious choice, but its complexity greatly limits its use by nonprofessionals. There are many excellent subject specific schemas available but, since the Web is so interdisciplinary, combining diverse schemas is likely to create significant interoperability problems. Obtaining rights to the required schemas could also pose a serious problem.

At first glance, developing an entirely new schema appears to be very attractive. However, the effort required to develop a new subject indexing system appears considerably less attractive upon further examination. The cost would be very high without any guarantee the new schema would necessarily be superior to one of the existing schema. It is quite possible that a new system could trade a set of known problems with its own set of unknown problems. It became quickly clear that attempting to develop a system as comprehensive as LCSH would be very challenging. As was concluded by the ALCTS/SAC/Subcommittee, the options of modifying an existing schema appeared more attractive. As a result, the FAST project team concluded that the most viable option for a general-purpose metadata subject schema was to adapt LCSH.

This new schema, known as FAST (Faceted Application of Subject Terminology), is derived from LCSH but will be applied with a simpler syntax. The objective of the FAST project is to develop a subject-heading schema based on LCSH suitable for metadata that is easy-to-use, understand, and maintain. To achieve this objective, this new schema is being designed to minimize the need to construct new headings and to simplify the syntax while retaining the richness of the LCSH vocabulary. The primary data source used for the research effort was OCLC's WorldCat database, which contains bibliographic records containing approximately eight million unique topical and geographic headings.

LIBRARY OF CONGRESS SUBJECT HEADINGS

LCSH is the most widely used indexing vocabulary and offers many significant advantages:

- Its rich vocabulary covers all subject areas,
- It has the strong institutional support of the Library of Congress,
- It imposes synonym and homograph control,
- It has been extensively used by libraries,
- It is contained in millions of bibliographic records, and
- It has a long and well-documented history.

While LCSH has served libraries and their patrons well for over a century, its complexity greatly restricts its use beyond the traditional cataloging environment. It was designed for card catalogs and excelled in that environment. However, because real estate on a 3 × 5 card is limited and each printed subject heading requires a new card, the number of headings per item that can be assigned was severely restricted. Since the card catalog is incompatible with post-coordination, the pre-coordinated headings were the only option available.

LCSH is not a true thesaurus in the sense that it is not a comprehensive list of all valid subject headings. Rather LCSH combines authorities, now five volumes in their printed form, with a four-volume manual of rules detailing the requirements for creating headings that are not established in the authority file and for the further subdivision of the established headings.

The rules for using free-floating subdivisions controlled by pattern headings illustrate some of these complexities. Under specified conditions, these free-floating subdivisions can be added to established headings. The scope of patterns is limited to particular types (patterns) of headings. For example, **Burns and scalds–Patients–Family relationships** is a valid heading formed by adding two pattern subdivisions to the established heading **Burns and scalds**. The subdivision **Patients** is one of several hundred subdivisions that can be used with headings for diseases and other medical conditions. Therefore, it can be used to subdivide **Burns and scalds**. However, the addition of **Patients** changes the meaning of the heading from a medical condition to a class of persons. Now, since **Family relationships** is authorized under the pattern for classes of persons, it can also be added to complete the heading.

Other examples of some of the complexities are illustrated by a type of authority records known as 'multiples.' Multiples are headings that establish a pattern of use, for example, the subdivision **$x Translating into French [German, etc.]**, indicates that the language 'French' can be replaced with the name of any established language. The 'multiple' heading that actually appears in the 1xx field of an authority record should never be used in its multiple form in a bibliographic record. All the possible headings that can be created using 'multiples' are not included in LCSH.

A third area that illustrates the complexities is music. Some of the complexities involved: determining the group for each solo instrument (e.g., wind instruments), the ordering of instruments within the individual group, and when a heading should and should not be qualified (e.g., Concertos). Overall, music accounted for the largest number of correctly constructed headings represented by the fewest number of authority records.

While the rich vocabulary and semantic relationships in LCSH provide subject access far beyond the capabilities of keywords, its complex syntax presents a stumbling block that limits its application beyond the traditional cataloging environment. Not only are the rules for patterns headings complex, their application requires extensive domain knowledge since there is no explicit coding that identifies which pattern subdivisions are appropriate for particular headings. Although FAST will retain headings authorized under these rules, they will be established in the authority file, effectively hiding the complexity of rules under which they were created.

The LCSH environment has resulted in a complex system requiring skilled professionals for its successful application and has prompted several simplification attempts. Among these, the Subject Subdivisions Conference (The Future of Subdivisions, 1992) attempted to simplify the application of LCSH subdivisions. Recently, the ALCTS/SAC/Subcommittee on Metadata and Subject Analysis (Subject Data in the Metadata Record. . . , 1999) recommended that LCSH strings be broken up [faceted] into topic, place, period, language, etc., particularly in situations where non-catalogers are assigning the headings. The Library of Congress has also embarked on a series of efforts to simplify LCSH.

THE FAST SCHEMA

After reviewing the previous attempts to update LCSH or to provide other subject schema, OCLC decided to develop the FAST schema. While FAST is derived from LCSH, it has been redesigned as a post-coordinated faceted vocabulary for an online environment. Specifically it is designed to:

- Be usable by people with minimal training and experience,
- Enable a broad range of users to assign subject terminology to Web resources,

- Be amenable to automated authority control,
- Be compatible with use as embedded metadata,
- Focus on making use of LCSH as a post-coordinate system in an online environment.

The first phase of the FAST development includes the development of facets based on the vocabulary found in LCSH topical and geographic headings and is limited to six facets: topical, geographic, form, period, with the most recent work focused on faceting personal and corporate names. This will leave headings for conference/meetings, uniform titles, and name-title entries for future phases. With the exception of the period facet, all FAST headings will be fully established in a FAST authority file.

Topical Facet

The topical facet consists of topical main headings and topical subdivisions. FAST topical headings look very similar to the established form of LCSH topical headings with the exception that established headings will include all commonly used (i.e., free-floating) topical subdivisions and each of the common multiple headings will be individually established. FAST topical headings will be created from:

- LCSH main headings from topical headings (650) assigned to MARC records,
- All associated general ($x) subdivisions from any type of LCSH heading,
- Period subdivisions containing topical aspects from any type of LCSH heading.

All topical headings strings will be established in an authority file. Examples of typical FAST topical headings are shown below:

> **Project management $x Data processing**
> **Colombian poetry**
> **Blacksmithing $x Equipment and supplies**
> **Epic literature $x History and criticism**
> **Pets and travel**
> **Quartets (Pianos (2), percussion)**
> **Natural gas pipelines $x Electric equipment**
> **School psychologists**

Blood banks
Loudspeakers $x Design and construction
Burns and scalds $x Patients $x Family relationships

FAST headings retain the hierarchical structure of LCSH, but topical subdivisions can only be subdivided by topical subdivisions, likewise, geographic headings can only be subdivided by geographic headings, etc. For example, in FAST, one would not see headings of the type:

Colombian poetry $v Indexes
Pets and travel $v Guidebooks
Quartets (Pianos (2), percussion) $v Scores and parts
Blood banks $z Italy $z Florence
Italy $x History $y To 476

Geographic Facet

The geographic facet includes all geographic names, and following the practice of the Library of Congress, populated places are the default and are not qualified by type of geographic unit. However, in FAST, these place names will be established and used in indirect order. For example, **Ohio–Columbus** is the established form in FAST rather than the direct order form, **Columbus (Ohio)**. In LCSH, place names used as main headings are entered in direct order, but when they are used as subdivisions, those representing localities appear in indirect order. First level geographic names in FAST will be far more limited than in LCSH. They will be restricted to names from the *Geographic Area Codes* table. Linking the first level entries with the Geographic Area Codes also provides additional specificity and hierarchical structure to the headings. In this way, the Geographic Area Codes can be used to limit a search. As with topical headings, all geographic headings will be established in an authority file.

During the process of linking first level heading entries with Geographic Area Codes, some established geographic headings could only be associated with the code for 'Other.' These include headings associated with geographic locations for the earth, sun, and the planets in its solar system, as well as comets, stars, satellites, and planets in other galaxies. Creating a set of headings with 'Other' as the first level did not meet the goal of providing specificity, and after evaluating the headings that were associated with 'Other,' a proposal for new Geographic Area Codes was submitted to the MARC Standards Office. As a result, a series of new codes were established:

x	Earth
xa	Eastern Hemisphere
xb	Northern Hemisphere
xc	Southern Hemisphere
xd	Western Hemisphere
zd	Deep space
zju	Jupiter
zma	Mars
zme	Mercury
zmo	Moon
zne	Neptune
zo	Outer space
zpl	Pluto
zs	Solar system
zsa	Saturn
zsu	Sun
zur	Uranus
zve	Venus

Second level names will be entered as subdivisions under the name of the smallest first level geographic area in which it is fully contained. For example, the Maya forest, which spans Belize, Guatemala, and Mexico, would be established as North America–Maya Forest instead of simply as Maya Forest. The same geographic names may appear significantly different in their direct and indirect forms. In LCSH, North Carolina as a first level entry or as a subdivision, is spelled out, but, as a qualifier, it is abbreviated as N.C. (e.g., Chapel Hill (N.C.)) To ensure a comprehensive search, users frequently must search for multiple forms of the same name. Some examples of FAST geographic headings and their corresponding Geographic Area Codes are:

> **England $z Coventry** [e-uk-en]
> **Great Lakes** [nl]
> **Great Lakes $z Lake Erie** [nl]
> **Italy** [e-it]
> **Maryland $z Worcester County** [n-us-md]
> **Ohio $z Columbus** [n-us-oh]
> **Deep space $z Milky Way** [zd]
> **Solar system $z Hale-Bopp comet** [zs]

Type qualifiers (County, Lake, Kingdom, Princely State, etc.) will be used when the name is not a unique geographic name. For the United States, county names will be the most common means to identify a particular place name when the name is not unique within the state. For example, there are two Beaver Islands in Michigan; the larger one and better-known island is in Lake Michigan, but another Beaver Island exists in the Isle Royle National Park, located in Lake Superior. To uniquely specify the island in Lake Michigan, Beaver Island would be qualified by the county:

Michigan $z Beaver Island (Charlevoix County) [n-us-mi]

When different type of geographic entities use the same name, the name is qualified to reflect the type of entity. For example, Otsego Lake is both a town and a lake in Michigan–to distinguish between the town and the lake, a qualifier would be added to the heading for the lake, leaving the populated place unqualified.

Michigan $z Otsego Lake [n-us-mi]
Michigan $z Otsego Lake (Lake) [n-us-mi]

In some cases, an LCSH geographic heading for city sections contains more information than can be expressed in two FAST levels. In FAST, headings of this type will be expressed as three levels. For example, headings of the type **Hollywood (Los Angeles, Calif.)** and **German Village (Columbus, Ohio)** would be expressed in FAST as:

California $z Los Angeles $z Hollywood [n-us-ca]
Ohio $z Columbus $z German Village [n-us-oh]

Form Facet

The form facet includes all form subdivisions. The form headings were established by extracting all form subdivisions from LCSH topical and geographic headings. However, because many form subdivisions are currently still coded as $*x* instead of subfield $*v* in LCSH headings, they were algorithmically identified and re-coded as $*v* prior to their extraction. O'Neill et al. provides the details of the algorithm used to identify the form subdivisions for re-coding. Some examples of FAST form subdivisions are:

$v Translations into French
$v Rules

$v Dictionaries $x Swedish
$v Controversial literature $v Early works to 1800
$v Statistics $v Databases
$v Bibliography $v Graded lists
$v Slides
$v Directories
$v Juvenile literature
$v Scores

As with the topical and geographic facets, all form headings will be established in the authority file.

Chronological Facet

The period facet follows the practice recommended by the SAC/ALCTS Subcommittee, and a continuance of the recommendations discussed at the Airlie Conference, specifically, that chronological headings reflect the actual time period of coverage for the resource.

In FAST, all period headings will be expressed as either a single numeric date or as a date range. In cases where the date is expressed in LCSH as a century (e.g., 20th century), in FAST, the date is expressed as a range of dates–1900-1999. Similarly, periods related to pre-history eras would be expressed as dates–Jurassic would be expressed as 190000000-140000000 B.C. The only exception to this practice is for period headings that are represented in the authority file as established topical headings. These will be treated as topical headings, and not as periods (e.g., Twentieth century when found used as a main heading).

Since the only general restriction on periods is that when a date range is used, the second date must be greater than the first, there is no need to routinely create authority records for period headings. For example, no period authority record would be created for the period facet **$y To 1500**.

Complexities on the treatment of period facets in headings of the type *[Geographic] $x History $y [topical descriptor, date range]*. Some examples of these types of headings include: **Argentina $x History $y Peronist Revolt, 1956,** and **Maine $x History $y King William's War, 1689-1697**. In these examples, the chronological subdivision contains additional information than can be expressed in a date or date range (e.g., King William's War). As the research on faceting headings of this type continue, the objective of the FAST project remains, which is to develop a subject-heading schema based on LCSH suitable for metadata that is easy-to-use, understand, and maintain.

Names Facet

The facet for personal and corporate names is the area of most recent re-search. Similar to the topical main facet, FAST headings for personal and corporate names are very similar, and in most cases exact, to the established name heading in the LC authority file. Unlike the approach taken for the topical, geographic, and chronological facets, however, more restrictions were implemented when selecting headings from bibliographic records for inclusion in the FAST scheme. In part, this decision was made simply due to the difference in the number of name authority records versus the number of subject authority records. Currently, there are over 5.4 million name authority records, in constrast to the approximate 270,000 subject authority records.

- Name headings found in bibliographic records must be represented in the LC names file, AND
- Name heading must be used at *least one time* as a subject heading.

Multi-Faceted Phrase Headings

There are a small number of Library of Congress Subject Headings that contain multiple facets presented in a phrase-like structure, and all bounded within a single $a. Examples of these types of headings are:

- Geo. A. Hormel & Company Strike, Austin, Minn., 1985-1986
- War of the Mascates, Brazil, 1710-1714
- Bull Run, 2nd Battle of, Va., 1862

These types of headings are retained as topical headings in Phase I of the FAST project, but they will require more extensive manual review in future phases. Based on the cursory research that has been completed on these types of headings, the faceting could result in the following:

- Geo. A. Hormel & Company Strike, Austin, Minn., 1985-1986
  - ○ 110   Geo. A. Hormel & Company
  - ○ 150   Strikes and lockouts
  - ○ 151   Minnesota $z Austin
  - ○ 148   1985-1986

FAST Headings in Metadata Records

One of the goals of the ALCTS/SAC/Subcommittee was to develop a subject heading scheme compatible with Dublin Core and other metadata schemas. The subcommittee was also specific in regards to endorsing the use of other Dublin Core elements (e.g., coverage) to accommodate different facets. As the MARC 21 format is currently the most heavily used format by libraries in the United States, it was important that FAST be developed in a way that was compliant with both MARC 21 and Dublin Core formats. The following chart shows the faceting of the data extracted from LCSH headings and how it would be expressed in Dublin Core:

Extracted from MARC 21 Bibliographic tag	FAST Facet	Expressed as Dublin Core Qualifier
650, second indicator 0, $a	Topical	Subject
6xx, second indicator 0, $x	Topical	Subject
6xx, second indicator 0, $y	Topical	Subject
6xx, second indicator 0, $y	Chronological	Period
6xx, second indicator 0, $v	Form	Type
651, second indicator 0, $a	Geographic	Coverage.spatial
6xx, second indicator 0, $z	Geographic	Coverage.spatial
600, second indicator 0, $abcdq	Personal name	Creator/namePersonal or Contributor/namePersonal
610, second indicator 0, $abndc	Corporate name	Creator/nameCorporate or Contributor/namePersonal

For example, the LCSH heading:

650 0 Authority files (Information retrieval) $z Italy $z Florence $v Congresses

would be faceted into the following three FAST headings:

- Topical: Authority files (Information retrieval)
- Geographic: Italy $z Florence
- Form: Congresses

And re-expressed in Dublin Core as:

- Subject: Authority files (Information retrieval)
- Coverage.spatial   Italy • Florence
- Type: Congresses

Similarly, the LCSH heading:

651 0 United States $x Civilization $x Italian influences $x History $y 20th century $v Sources would be faceted into the following four FAST headings:

- Geographic: United States
- Topical: Civilization $x Italian influences $x History
- Period: 1900-1999
- Form: Sources

And re-expressed in Dublin Core as:

- Coverage.spatial   United States
- Subject: Civilization • Italian influences • History
- Period: 1900-1999
- Type: Sources

However, to express the same data in MARC 21 format presented problems, as neither the MARC 21 bibliographic or authority formats had defined tags to support the entry of chronological data as a main ($a) subfield. As a result, the team met with staff at the Library of Congress, and later wrote a MARBI proposal to expand the MARC 21 bibliographic and authority formats. In 2002, the proposal was accepted by the MARBI committee, and allows complete mapping of FAST facets to MARC 21 bibliographic tags:

FAST Facet	Expressed as Dublin Core Qualifier	Expressed in MARC 21 Bibliographic tag
Topical	Subject	650, second indicator 7, $a/$x, $2 fast
Chronological	Period	648, second indicator 7, $a, $2 fast
Form	Type	655, second indicator 7, $a, $2 fast
Geographic	Coverage.spatial	651, second indicator 7, $a/$z, $2 fast
Personal name	Creator/namePersonal or Contributor/namePersonal	600, second indicator 7, $abcdq, $2 fast
Corporate name	Creator/nameCorporate or Contributor/namePersonal	610, second indicator 7, $abndc, $2 fast

In authority records, the MARC 21 tags for the FAST facets are:

FAST Facet	Expressed in MARC 21 Authority tag
Topical	150
Chronological	148
Form	155
Geographic	151
Personal name	100
Corporate name	110

Authority Records

The FAST team selected the MARC 21 Authority Format because the format is a well-proven, sophisticated protocol specifically designed to carry controlled vocabulary elements and support a synthetically-structured database. In FAST, the synthetically structured database was expanded to include the retention of obsolete authority records to ensure compatibility within a linked structure. To minimize the number of broken links once a heading has been established and an authority created, that heading and its authority record will be permanently retained in the FAST authority file with its 1XX field unchangeable. FAST authority records containing obsolete headings in the 1XX field headings will contain value 'o' (Obsolete) in the Leader/05 to indicate that the heading is not the preferred term.

The difference between Leader/05 'o' and Leader/05 'd' is purely one of a physical nature: Leader/05 'o' identifies authority records in which the heading is obsolete, but the authority record *physically* remains in the file to support the linked structure of the database. Leader/05 value 'd' indicates the record should be physically deleted from the file.

A second area identified by the FAST team lacking in the MARC 21 Authority Format was one to facilitate systematic maintenance as headings and relationships between headings occur. Below are the four basic types of identifying heading changes and supporting updating that occur in LCSH, and how these would be handled within FAST using current and newly defined MARC elements. All FAST records will be linked back to the LC authority record from which it was derived using 7xx linking fields.

The final component of the MARBI proposal defined a new $w/1 subfield value for the 700-785 fields to support the ability for automatic replacement of headings. Three codes were defined that could be used by systems to automatically update bibliographic records with the replacement heading(s), specifically:

- **a**   **Heading replacement does not require review.**
  Identifies headings that are always used to replace the obsolete heading.

- **b**   **Heading replacement requires review.**
  Identifies headings that may be used as replacement, but requires subject analysis to determine its appropriateness.

- **n**   **Not applicable.**
  The heading is not being replaced; if code n is applicable, $w/1 need not be used.

1. 'One-to-one' changes, for example, the heading **Trade-unions** is replaced by the heading **Labor unions**. The heading for Trade-unions now appears as a 450 heading in the authority record for **Labor unions**.

- The incoming authority record distributed by the Library of Congress containing the 150 heading **Labor unions** would contain the value 'c' (Corrected or revised) in the Leader/05 position.

  <u>LC Authority record</u>
  Leader /05 'c'
  001   2032352
  010   sh 85136516
  040   DLC $c DLC $d DLC
  150   Labor unions
  450   Trade-unions

- In FAST, a new authority record for **Labor unions** would be created, with the value 'n' (New) in the Leader/05 position. A 750 field would be added to the authority record.

  <u>FAST Authority record</u>
  Leader /05 'n'
  001   [OCLC assigned number]
  005   [OCLC assigned date/time stamp]
  040   OCoLC $b eng $c OCoLC $f fast
  150   Labor unions
  450   Trade-unions
  750 0   Labor unions $0(DLC) sh 85136516

- In FAST, the authority record for **Trade-unions** would be retained as a separate record, but would be updated to contain value 'o' in the Leader/05. The 750 linking field in the record showing a relationship to the FAST authority record for Labor unions would remain, with *$w a* added to the 750 linking field indicating that any occurrence the FAST heading **Trade-unions** found in bibliographic records should be replaced by the heading **Labor unions**.

  <u>FAST Authority record</u>
  Leader /05 'o'
  001   [OCLC assigned number]
  005   [OCLC assigned date/time stamp]
  040   OCoLC $b eng $c OCoLC $f fast
  150   Trade-unions

750 0   *Labor unions $0(DLC) sh 85136516*
750 7   *Labor unions $7(fast) [OCLC assigned number] $w a*

2. *'And/Or'* changes, for example, the heading **Alms and almsgiving** is replaced by two or more different headings–in this case, the replacement headings are **Charity** and **Charities**. In this instance, one or the other, and maybe both, of the identified headings would be the appropriate replacement for the obsolete heading.

- The incoming authority record distributed by the Library of Congress containing the 150 heading **Alms and almsgiving** would contain the value 'd' (Deleted) in the Leader/05 position. Two new authority records, with the value 'n' in the Leader/05 position would also be distributed for the headings **Charity** and **Charities**, respectively.

  LC Authority record
  Leader /05 'd'
  001   [OCLC assigned number]
  010   [LC control number]
  040   DLC $c DLC $d DLC
  150   Alms and almsgiving

  LC Authority record
  Leader /05 'n'
  001   2137277
  010   sh 85022672
  040   DLC $c DLC $d DLC
  150   Charity
  450   Alms and almsgiving

  LC Authority record
  Leader /05 'n'
  001   2137212
  010   sh 85022665
  040   DLC $c DLC $d DLC
  150   Charities
  450   Alms and almsgiving

- Using value 'o' in the Leader/05 position of the authority record containing **Alms and almsgiving** and value 'n' (New) in the Leader/05 position of the two new authority records created for **Charity** and **Charities**. The presence of the same text appearing in the 450 field in multiple records would generate $w b$ in the 750 FAST linking fields of the obsolete record, indicating that the one or both headings may be used as a replacement.

FAST Authority record
Leader /05 'o'
001   [OCLC assigned number]
005   [OCLC assigned date/time stamp]
040   OCoLC $b eng $c OCoLC $f fast
150   Alms and almsgiving
750 0 Alms and almsgiving $0(DLC) sh 85136516
750 7 Charity $7(fast)[OCLC assigned number] $w b
750 7 Charities $7(fast)[OCLC assigned number] $w b

FAST Authority record
Leader /05 'n'
001   [OCLC assigned number]
005   [OCLC assigned date/time stamp]
040   OCoLC $b eng $c OCoLC $f fast
150   Charity
450   **Alms and almsgiving**
750 0 Charity $0(DLC) sh 85022672

FAST Authority record
Leader /05 'n'
001   [OCLC assigned number]
005   [OCLC assigned date/time stamp]
040   OCoLC $b eng $c OCoLC $f fast
150   Charities
450   **Alms and almsgiving**
750 0 Charities $0(DLC) sh 85022665

3. *'Or' changes*, for example, the heading **Hotels, taverns, etc.** is replaced by two or more different headings–in this case, the replacement headings are **Bars (Drinking establishments)**, and/or **Hotels**, and/or **Taverns (Inns)**.

- Similar with the *and/or* changes, the incoming authority record distributed by the Library of Congress containing the 150 heading **Hotels, tav-**

erns, etc. would contain the value 'd' in the Leader/05 position. Three new authority records, with the value 'n' in the Leader/05 position would also be distributed for the headings **Bars (Drinking establishments)**, **Hotels**, and **Taverns (Inns)**, respectively.

- Using value 'o' in the Leader/05 position of the authority record containing **Hotels, taverns, etc.** and value 'n' in the Leader/05 position of the three new authority records created for **Bars (Drinking establishments)**, **Hotels**, and **Taverns (Inns)** respectively. The presence of the same text appearing in the 450 field in multiple records would generate $w\ b$ in the 750 FAST linking field of the obsolete record, indicating that the heading may be used as a replacement, but requires subject analysis to determine its appropriateness.

4. 'And' changes such as occur with the faceting of a particular type of FAST heading that occurs when a single LCSH heading contains multiple facets within a single subfield (e.g., $a).

LC Authority record
001   2488003
010   sh 89000691
040   DLC $c DLC $d DLC
150   Geo. A. Hormel & Company Strike, Austin, Minn., 1985-1986

- Value 'o' in the Leader/05 authority record for Geo. A. Hormel & Company Strike, Austin, Minn., 1985-1986. The 7xx FAST linking fields in the record would remain, with $w\ a$ added to indicate that the heading for **Geo. A. Hormel & Company Strike, Austin, Minn., 1985-1986** is replaced by multiple FAST headings.

FAST Authority record
Leader /05 'o'
001   [OCLC assigned number]
005   [OCLC assigned date/time stamp]
040   OCoLC $b eng $c OCoLC $f fast
150   Geo. A. Hormel & Company Strike, Austin, Minn., 1985-1986
710 7   Geo. A. Hormel & Company $7(fast)[OCLC assigned number]
              $w a
750 7   Strikes and lockouts $7(fast)[OCLC assigned number] $w a
751 7   Minnesota $z Austin $7(fast)[OCLC assigned number] $w a
748 7   1985-1986$7(fast)[OCLC assigned number] $w a

750 0 Geo. A. Hormel & Company Strike, Austin, Minn., 1985-1986
$0(DLC) sh 89000691$w n1

- Value 'n' in the Leader/05 position for the FAST authority records.

FAST Authority record
Leader /05 'n'
001   [OCLC assigned number]
005   [OCLC assigned date/time stamp]
040   OCoLC $b eng $c OCoLC $f fast
110   Geo. A. Hormel & Company
710 0 Geo. A. Hormel & Company *$0(DLC) n 84082628*

FAST Authority record
Leader /05 'n'
001   [OCLC assigned number]
005   [OCLC assigned date/time stamp]
040   OCoLC $b eng $c OCoLC $f fast
150   Strikes and lockouts
750 0 *Strikes and lockouts $0(DLC) sh 85128731*

FAST Authority record
Leader /05 'n'
001   [OCLC assigned number]
005   [OCLC assigned date/time stamp]
040   OCoLC $b eng $c OCoLC $f fast
043   n-us-mn
151   Minnesota $z Austin
751 0 *Austin (Minn.) $0(DLC) n 79105963*

Other decisions regarding what information from the Library of Congress that should be part of FAST authority records are still under review. Most 4xx fields will be retained, as well as some 5xx fields and selected 6xx note fields. In general, 4xx and 5xx fields are retained if the heading does not cross facets.

Example 1: Geographic
LC Authority record
001   4478097
010   sh 97006510
040   DLC $c DLC $d DLC

005   20010306142236.0
151   Maya Forest
451   Selva Maya
550   Rain forests $z Belize $w g
550   Rain forests $z Guatemala $w g
550   Rain forests $z Mexico $w g

FAST Authority record
001   [OCLC assigned number]
005   [OCLC assigned date/time stamp]
040   OCoLC $b eng $c OCoLC $f fast
043   n
151   North America $z Maya Forest
451   Selva Maya
751 0   Maya Forest $0(DLC) sh 97006510

Example 2: Topical
LC Authority record
001   2000367
010   sh 85000004
040   DLC $c DLC $d DLC
005   19960530131610.0
150   20th Century Limited (Express train)
450   Twentieth Century Limited (Express train)
550   Express trains $z United States $w g
670   Work cat.: Rose, A. 20th Century Limited, 1984.

FAST Authority record
001   [OCLC assigned number]
005   [OCLC assigned date/time stamp]
040   OCoLC $b eng $c OCoLC $f fast
150   20th Century Limited (Express train)
450   Twentieth Century Limited (Express train)
750 0   20th Century Limited (Express train) $0(DLC) sh 85000004

Example 3: Form
LC Authority record
010   sh 99001298
040   DLC $b eng $c DLC $d DLC

005   20010202130538.0
073   H 1095 $z lcsh
185 $v Bibliography of bibliographies
480 $x Bibliography $v Bibliography $w nne
585 $v Bibliography $w g
680   **$i Use as a form subdivision under subjects for works consisting of lists of bibliographies on those subjects.**
681   **$i Reference under the heading $a Bibliography of bibliographies**

FAST Authority record
001   [OCLC assigned number]
, 005   [OCLC assigned date/time stamp]
040   OCoLC $b eng $c OCoLC $f fast
155   Bibliography of bibliographies
555   Bibliography
785 0 $v Bibliography of bibliographies $0(DLC) sh 99001298

CONCLUSIONS

Although much work remains before the FAST authorities files are complete and ready for use, the project has demonstrated that it is viable to derive a new subject schema based on the terminology of the Library of Congress Subject Headings but with simpler syntax and application rules. Upon completion, the FAST authority records will be extensively tested and evaluated. After the evaluation, we will know if we have achieved our goal of creating a new subject schema for metadata that retains the rich vocabulary of LCSH while being easy to maintain, apply, and use.

REFERENCES

Chan, Lois Mai, Eric Childress, Rebecca Dean, Edward T. O'Neill, and Diane Vizine-Goetz. 2001. A Faceted Approach to Subject Data in the Dublin Core Metadata Record. *Journal of Internet Cataloging* 4, No. 1/2: 35-47.
The Future of Subdivisions in the Library of Congress Subject Headings System: Report from the Subject Subdivisions Conference May 9-12, 1991, edited by Martha O'Hara.1992. Washington, D.C.: Library of Congress, Cataloging Distribution Service.

O'Neill, Edward T., Lois Mai Chan, Eric Childress, Rebecca Dean, Lynn El-Hoshy, Kerre Kammerer, and Diane Vizine-Goetz. [Forthcoming] Form Subdivisions: Their Identification and Use in LCSH. *Library Resources & Technical Services* 45, No. 4: 187-197.

Subject Data in the Metadata Record Recommendations and Rationale: A Report from the ALCTS/SAC/Subcommittee on Metadata and Subject Analysis. 1999. http://www.govst.edu/users/gddcasey/sac/MetadataReport.html Accessed 06/26/01.

Semantic Aut*h*ority Control
and the New *Soggettario*

Anna Lucarelli

SUMMARY. The project of the renewal of the *Subject Headings for Italian Library Catalogues* (*Soggettario*), financed by the National Central Library in Florence, proposes a pre-coordinated language, both analytic and synthetic, complying with international rules on vocabulary control and structure, based on category analysis of semantic relationships. It envisages a strict distinction between semantic relationships and syntactic ones, and bases its citation order of subject strings on the analysis model for logical relationships. Thanks to its features, the new *Soggettario* agrees both with the logic of *Guidelines for Subject Authority and Reference Entries* and of *UNIMARC Authorities*, and with *FRBR (Functional Requirements for Bibliographic Records)*. The rigorous structure of the thesaurus will facilitate the transfer of controlled terminology to lists or authority files and archives. The Italian National Bibliography (BNI) will have to play a leading role in the control of coherence of semantic access points. It will validate the strings created by other libraries and control their coherence according to the syntax rules envisaged in the new method. *[Article copies available for a fee from The Haworth Document Delivery Service: 1-800-HAWORTH. E-mail address: <docdelivery@haworthpress.com> Website: <http://www.HaworthPress.com> © 2004 by The Haworth Press, Inc. All rights reserved.]*

Anna Lucarelli is affiliated with Biblioteca nazionale centrale di Firenze.

[Haworth co-indexing entry note]: "Semantic Authority Control and the New *Soggettario*." Lucarelli, Anna. Co-published simultaneously in *Cataloging & Classification Quarterly* (The Haworth Information Press, an imprint of The Haworth Press, Inc.) Vol. 39, No. 1/2, 2004, pp. 353-364; and: *Authority Control in Organizing and Accessing Information: Definition and International Experience* (ed: Arlene G. Taylor, and Barbara B. Tillett) The Haworth Information Press, an imprint of The Haworth Press, Inc., 2004, pp. 353-364. Single or multiple copies of this article are available for a fee from The Haworth Document Delivery Service [1-800-HAWORTH, 9:00 a.m. - 5:00 p.m. (EST). E-mail address: docdelivery@haworthpress.com].

http://www.haworthpress.com/web/CCQ
© 2004 by The Haworth Press, Inc. All rights reserved.
Digital Object Identifier: 10.1300/J104v39n01_04

KEYWORDS. Semantic control, *Soggettario*, thesaurus

I was entrusted with the coordination of the project, financed by the National Central Library in Florence (BNCF), for the Feasibility Study on the New *Soggettario per i cataloghi delle biblioteche italiane* (*Subject Headings for Italian Library Catalogues*), the indexing tool also applied in the Italian National Bibliography.[1] In this capacity I cooperated with the group of experts from IFNET who conducted the study and developed an application project.[2] These experts brought into their task a wealth of experience and collaboration mastered within AIB's (Italian Library Association's) Research Group on Subject Indexing. This enterprise was carried out in observance of international standards and IFLA guidelines. It relied on the contribution of our own traditions and indexing experiences, as well as those different from our own. In 2001 we organized an international seminar to receive opinions and advice coming from Italian and foreign colleagues. We also got in touch with other national libraries, institutions, documentation centres, and corporate bodies involved in cataloguing not exclusively bibliographic materials.

The work was completed in May 2002. Then the project proposals were presented in depth in further professional meetings in order to elucidate the new system and to spread information about its practical implementation from an organizational and management viewpoint. I'll describe its features and potential in relation to what its actual use may imply in the field of authority control.

As Gloria Cerbai said in her paper, until now we have not been able to create national authority files for names of authors, titles, and subjects. However, the Italian National Bibliography (BNI) ensured a form of control with its subject headings. We are going to see how the shift to a new indexing language might facilitate the start of a real system for authority control and how BNI might confirm its role as a frame of reference for Italian bibliographic services.

The *Soggettario*, published in 1956 with BNCF as its editor, is a vocabulary of controlled terms linked by a network of references for various semantic relationships. The language of the *Soggettario* is mostly enumerative (with adaptations of a synthetic nature), pre-coordinated and based on a main heading/subheading structure. It does not create subject strings, but it offers examples for possible combinations of terms. In this sense, the choice of a lead term in the string does not depend on the logical relationship it has with other concepts. The *Soggettario*, obviously a child of the cultural time in which it was devised, has been repeatedly analysed. In the past years, the librarians' interest was centred on its outdated terminology, because such a long lapse of time that saw new disciplines and research fields, made these gaps evident. Only recently has there been an awareness of the need for revision, taking into account the *Soggettario*'s deficiencies in syntax and structure.

The national bibliographic agency constantly applied the *Soggettario* and updated the vocabulary, editing separate lists of new terms used in BNI. These lists were published in 1977, 1982, 1987.[3] The terms in these lists showed no semantic links among themselves or with the ones in the *Soggettario*, no syndetic structure except a few references from rejected forms. More recently, in 1997 and 1999 the Italian National Bibliography published other updates, with different criteria.[4] In fact the terms in these updates are linked to other ones already included in the *Soggettario* or in the lists already published according to ISO 2788/1986. During this first experimental phase, the hierarchical relationship linking the new term to the more general one was favoured. Only in a few, rare cases, when it was impossible to state the broader term, an association relationship was made, indicating the related terms. Besides, each new term was completed with a link to the bibliographic record in which it was first used. This experimental work was a first step towards an overall project for the revision of the *Soggettario* that actually started in 2000.

In the long 1959-2003 period the Italian National Bibliography constantly devoted itself to enriching the vocabulary, applying control strategies and activities much more substantial than they might appear given the simplicity of the published lists. The files for use by staff prove the work behind the introduction of a new term: the cards in the old catalogue for use by library staff, as well as in the current one, continuously refer to used sources and reference works; to references from alternative forms and to relationships with associated terms, to references to the linked bibliographic record and, sometimes, to the relative Dewey number. Reading these "paratexts" we find interesting information that sheds light on the type of issues the cataloguers faced to provide formal consistency of access points.

Observations come to the surface on the form and language of terms, particularly the ones related to personal names, issues on uniformity, standardization, as well as problems dependent upon the evolution of the language, for example, related to the semantic change that some terms may have undergone in time. In short, these "paratexts" demonstrate a well-established methodology in choosing the form of a subject, information however retrievable for future effective authority control.

The fact that BNI has always carried out this type of activity does not mean that contradictory, sometimes not uniform, forms of subject headings cannot be found in the BNI indexes and in the BNCF subject catalogue. On the contrary, there is a lack of uniformity due to various causes. The very language of the *Soggettario*, an exemplifying tool not based on explicit rules with a partly enumerative, partly synthetic structure, leads to incoherent applications both at a syntax and a terminology level. The changes brought by the revision of cataloguing codes and the adoption of new standards, namely the 1981 *Regole italiane di catalogazione per autori* (RICA) (Italian rules for author cataloguing) and the 1984 ISBD (International Standard for Bibliographic Description), did not occur in semantic cataloguing. Yet, some changes brought by RICA involved the form of subjects, too.

The general criterion followed by BNI for subjects that are personal names, was to conform to the form stated in the cataloguing codes for entries in the author catalogue. This caused changes in the form recorded over time. Even when the corresponding (changed) form in the author catalogue was not adopted for a subject heading, as in the well-known case of classical Greek and Latin authors and of Medieval authors, popes, etc., we find variant forms in the subject catalogue, as we can see in the example:

Bonifacio PP. VIII (Benedetto Caetani)	*(Soggettario 1956)*
Bonifacio VIII, papa (Benedetto Caetani)	*(BNI 76–4646)*
Bonifacio VIII, papa	*(BNI 81–2377)*
Bonifacio <papa ; 8.>	*(BNI 2001–2681)*

During the years, further changes were made to meet the requirements of the Servizio bibliotecario nazionale (SBN) software. Some other incongruence in the subject headings is due to a change of strategy and renewed choices in the indexing policy.

Corrections to the *Soggettario* and to its updating lists arose from the control and revision activity carried on by BNI. For example, "Giuoco" became "Gioco," "Diritto sulla propria imagine" became "Diritto all'immagine," "Pianura Padana" became "Val Padana." In these innovations there has not always been retrospective action to amend and renew the file of strings. Links between the new forms and the older, no longer accepted forms have not been provided consistently, so users have not always been adequately informed. Additionally, lack of uniformity was sometimes (and continues to be) caused by simple errors. However, a relevant action for partial renewal took place in 1997, when the bibliographic records created by BNI from 1958 to 1984 were loaded into SBN.

Thanks to the project called Maintenance of Semantic Archives (MARS), headings for personal and corporate bodies' names, for titles, for geographical names and some other categories of subjects were unified. Up to now, this enormous work has benefited only SBN. The corrections were not merged into the BNI CD-ROM where we can find lack of uniform headings, as Gloria Cerbai explained; these problems will be solved with new software.

Presently there is a form of control on indexing terms only at the local, decentralized level, a prerogative of specific SBN nodes that have organized their own subject managing software. In the BNCF node, BNI is responsible for an archive of descriptors where terms, personal names included, can be structured according to semantic relationships. Besides the possibility of keeping information in a "Notes" field, equivalence, association, hierarchy, and syntactic links can be stated (see Figure 1). The equivalence links and, sometimes, the association ones are activated, while as a rule, the hierarchy and syntactic ones are not. BNI creates links to some variant forms, for example, to the form of a name appearing on the title of the document, if it differs from the preferred form for the subject heading. But these references, that both SBN users and BNI users can see, are managed in the archive for descriptors, not, as they should be, in an authority file.[5]

Lacking a real national authority file, long wished for by many people, this is the complex, stratified situation of semantic control by BNI, that has been a frame of reference for Italian libraries that adhere, or don't, to SBN. Lucia Di Geso will discuss the cooperative features in SBN also in relation to the tools implemented.

It is interesting, in this context, to point out how much the new *Soggettario*, besides renewing the indexing language and increasing the system efficiency and effectiveness, will enhance real authority control on the one hand, while on the other hand, will enhance the creation of a national authority file.

Its features are described in the volume *Per un nuovo Soggettario* in which the documents related to the above mentioned feasibility project have been published.[6] The proposed language is pre-coordinated, analytic/synthetic, based on a strict distinction between semantic relationships and syntactic ones, complying with international rules on vocabulary control and structure. It bases its citation order of subject strings on the analysis model for logical roles, and it aims at co-extensiveness (a single, coextensive string), besides specificity.

The system of the new *Soggettario* is organized in four parts: rules, vocabulary, syntax-pragmatics, archive of subject strings. In the new language, the rules will be explicit, organic, and will have to convey both syntactic and semantic principles. The vocabulary, in a thesaurus form, based on the known principles of international standards, will be the backbone of the new system, i.e., a controlled, structured list of terms that can each be used in combination with any other term. The terms will be given a note when necessary to explain how to use them according to the logical roles that the concept conveyed by the term itself may play in the description of the intellectual content of the work. The same term may have a different position in the string (see Figure 2). In some cases a syntactic note will be added to a term to explain how it is to be

FIGURE 1. Administration of Description–SBN BNCF Node

```
┌─────────────────────────────────────────────────┐
│         S B N - Bibl. Nazionale Centrale di Firenze │
│           GESTIONE SOGGETTI - GESTIONE             │
│                   DESCRITTORE                      │
│                                                    │
│                                                    │
│      DESCRITTORE DI PARTENZA:                      │
│      Telefoni cellulari                            │
│                                                    │
│      LEGATO CON:                                   │
│      Telefoni portatili                            │
│                                                    │
│                                   ┌───────────┐    │
│      Usato per:                   │ X         │    │
│                                   └───────────┘    │
│      T.piu'generale:              ┌───────────┐    │
│                                   └───────────┘    │
│      T.piu'specifico:             ┌───────────┐    │
│                                   └───────────┘    │
│      T.correlato:                 ┌───────────┐    │
│                                   └───────────┘    │
│      Ha per sudd. :               ┌───────────┐    │
│                                   └───────────┘    │
│      E' sudd. di:                 └───────────┘    │
│                                                    │
│                             ┌─────────┐            │
│      ALTRI LEGAMI (S/N)?    │ N       │            │
│                             └─────────┘            │
│                       X. USCITA:  ┌───────────┐    │
│                                   └───────────┘    │
└─────────────────────────────────────────────────┘
```

used according to the logical roles the concept embodied in the term may play in the description of the intellectual content of the work.

As shown in the scheme, already presented in the above mentioned volume *Per un nuovo Soggettario* (p. 244), this architecture meets the requirements for semantic control and, by stating the category the term belongs to, and eventually the classification, it allows vocabulary structuring. The historical note, the citation of sources and variant forms, and the thesaurus link it up to the old *Soggettario*. In fact these fields clearly show how the new context of rules will include not only innovative elements, but it will also preserve elements of our cataloguing tradition. The new system will allow the retrieval of terms and relationships from the *Soggettario* and its updating lists, restructuring their terminology according to a better developed model, through a process guided by rules.

As we did in the volume with the results of the Feasibility Study (p. 366), we show an example of heading in which the syntactic note explains possible applications of the term (see Figure 3). Besides the syntactic note, it will be possible to find other accompanying instructions in a manual that will inte-

FIGURE 2. The Structure of Voice (Preferred Term)

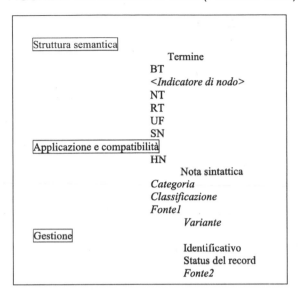

```
┌─────────────────────────────────────────────────────────────┐
│  Struttura semantica                                          │
│                            Termine                            │
│                    BT                                         │
│                    <Indicatore di nodo>                       │
│                    NT                                         │
│                    RT                                         │
│                    UF                                         │
│                    SN                                         │
│  Applicazione e compatibilità                                 │
│                    HN                                         │
│                            Nota sintattica                    │
│                    Categoria                                  │
│                    Classificazione                            │
│                    Fonte1                                     │
│                            Variante                           │
│  Gestione                                                     │
│                            Identificativo                     │
│                            Status del record                  │
│                            Fonte2                             │
└─────────────────────────────────────────────────────────────┘
```

grate the general rules and help the cataloguer to apply them. In the system for the new *Soggettario* we'll have four components: (1) the Rules, a manual of standards; (2) the Vocabulary that is the core component; (3) the Archive of subject strings, created according to the rules; and (4) the Thesaurus, is the final component part of the system (see Figure 4). A system designed in this way is not only compatible and consistent with semantic authority control, it is even potentially functional for the creation of an authority file. As pointed out also by Stefano Tartaglia, the structure of the new language, based on category analysis of semantic relationships, agrees both with the logic of *Guidelines for Subject Authority and Reference Entries* and *UNIMARC Authorities*, and with *FRBR*, which also are mostly based on general semantic categories.[7]

Furthermore, the separation of the syntax and terminology fields at the base of the new *Soggettario* (a separation that finds a junction and a reassembling point through the syntactic note), is in itself an assumption in favour of authority control, since this concerns, *in primis* uniform and consistent terms that can be access points to semantic information.

Of course terminology control cannot be identified with authority control, even less, the terminology control accomplished in a specific language in a specific context with what should be done at a general authority control level. There is no doubt that a tool for a terminology control consistent with interna-

FIGURE 3. Term with Added Syntactic Note

Malattie

BT Processi patologici
NT [Malattie secondo gli organi e parti]
NT [Malattie secondo il modo di
    trasmissione]
NT [Malattie secondo il paziente]
NT [Malattie secondo l'agente]

Nota sintattica: ***Parte/Prop***. *Segue il termine*
che rappresenta il possessore (singoli individui,
gruppi di persone, organismi e loro parti),
p.e., Leopardi, Giacomo - Malattie;
Adolescenti - Malattie; Gatti - Malattie;
Apparato digerente - Malattie;
Bambini - Sistema nervoso - Malattie
[precedent. Sistema nervoso - Malattie - Infanzia];
Laringe - Vasi sanguigni - Malattie

Faccetta: Processi
Classificazione: 616 (DDC21)
Fonte: *Soggettario 1956*

tional rules and standards, based on category analysis, and that fixes relationships among terms on this base, will not only prove apt to be used at various levels in a documentary context but it will also allow sharing already established data in other lists or authority files.

As the IFLA Working Group on Guidelines for Subject Authority Files stated, moving from a subject heading to an authority asks for elaborating a set of relationships and data that partly correspond to what standards require for thesauri, but that, in addition, must guarantee functionality at a wider level than the one required by the specific language used.

The new *Soggettario* was designed exactly to enhance interoperability and to use in quite diverse contexts, proper library contexts, and different ones, such as special collections for media or photos, museums, archives, etc. The relationships among terms in the controlled vocabulary do not necessarily correspond to the relationships stated in the IFLA standard among uniform headings, parallel headings, correlated (i.e., uniform headings bibliographically related to each other) and variant headings. But undoubtedly the thesaurus includes elements and fields that might be used and thus inherited by a structure

FIGURE 4. Components of the New *Soggettario* System

for creating authority records. Besides the fields for equivalence, hierarchy, and association relationships, all the fields related to application and compatibility of the term are significant for authority control, except the syntactic note that might eventually be relevant to guarantee the uniformity of strings and that must not be mistaken for the notes in an authority record.

The 'historical' note "provides indexers with basic data on the use of a term when, during the vocabulary's life span, its role, meaning, structure, or form undergo relevant changes, for whatever reason; for example when a term replaces, fully or in part, another term, or when the meaning of a term becomes wider or more restricted."[8]

The 'Category' (or Facet) brings into the vocabulary a classifying principle similar to the one envisaged by authority control. The same can be said about the classification number that is an element of the information notes area in the *Guidelines*.

The information to be given in 'Source 1' that, in the thesaurus of the new *Soggettario*, denotes the reference works where the term was taken from or checked, is also mandatory for authority control.

The 'Variant form' is where we find "all the variants of a term that are not considered equivalence relationships and that must not necessarily follow the objective term-meaning relationship"[9] (like singular/plural). This allows the creation of a retrospective link with terms in the old *Soggettario* that were not migrated into the new one because, for instance, the old term is now considered linguistically obsolete. The variant form is an atypical component part of semantic control but in this phase where we move from one indexing language to another, it offers the advantage of flexibility and sharing. A single library might retrieve, in this way, a variant, not accepted form and consider it a preferred term for the library's own requirements.

To end, 'Source 2,' where the library or cataloguing agency that presented the new term is cited, is similar to the area in the *Guidelines* where the cataloguing agency responsible for the authority heading, the date of recording, etc., are given (area 1.6).

Various issues are still being studied related to the vocabulary of the new *Soggettario*. If we agree common names will certainly be the object of semantic control, it is still debated whether or not proper names (biographical, geographical, of corporate bodies, etc.) will be included in the thesaurus, and, in case they will be, whether their structure will be the same as for any other heading or not. This issue will be joined by other ones: will the morphology of proper names in the subject catalogue have to be the same as the one in the author catalogue? How must we eventually use qualifiers to disambiguate or identify?

And if we could actually implement an authority control file, complete with all possible links among variant forms of names, would uniform headings still need to be the same in the subject catalogue as in the author catalogue? We all know that the various national bibliographic agencies adopt different solutions on this matter. However, the problem could be solved with the help of software providing automatic links among all possible access points.

These and other choices will be made in the near future, keeping in mind that in many of them it will not be possible to leave out of consideration the politics and resources at disposal. A careful assessment of the cost/benefit ratio will have to produce, if not a real national authority file, at least some lists that will be the result of the new language and, at the same time, useful to those who will adapt the new *Soggettario* to their own requirements. The national bibliographic agency should also be able to validate the subject strings created according to the rules envisaged in the new tool in addition to its control of terms, to which diverse libraries, and the ones specialized in various fields, might cooperate.

A pre-coordinate language, based on consistent but simultaneously flexible rules, is already shareable and a guarantee of a quality catalogue. Authority control, as Tartaglia is going to explain better, pertains to the vocabulary component, the more so in an analytic-synthetic language like the one of the new *Soggettario*.[10] But what can we say about the syntax part since it will be characterized by a revised, standardized syntax? The more the language will be used respecting the rules, the more uniform and coherent will the created strings be. The BNI task will consist in validating the strings and making them controlled access points in this sense. Of course all this will imply rethinking the type of cooperation we now have among libraries and institutions. The cooperation will not be carried on only for the production of new terms for the thesaurus but also on the best and shared use of the new method in all its component parts.

The National Bibliography, directly involved in the Project for a new *Soggettario*, will obviously have to play a leading role on the control of formal coherence of semantic access points. The activity for authority control and implementation of authority files needs resources and investment. New perspectives and new functions at BNI will depend on a real acknowledgment of its role, and a strengthening of its scanty resources. This is the only way for it to confirm itself as a structure for decision-making, study, and in depth investigation of issues related to bibliographic control.

The plan we are dealing with wants to align the new *Soggettario* with present international standards and to redefine choices and solutions with original thinking. BNI will undertake a double function: its headings will be authoritative subjects in themselves, at the same time the bibliographic agency will validate the strings created by other libraries, even if it does not use them, and control their coherence according to the syntax rules envisaged in the new vocabulary.

BNI will provide the model of this new method and will keep in touch with the outside world to make known but also to learn new suggestions and proposals. It will have to try and find out new forms of scientific cooperation, of sharing experimental applications for semantic bibliographic control. For BNI, this will be the occasion to try out new strategies, as well as to build a bridge to new environments where it will learn to dialogue, enlarging the typology of its traditional public.

ENDNOTES

1. *Soggettario per i cataloghi delle biblioteche italiane* / a cura della Biblioteca nazionale centrale di Firenze.–Firenze: Il cenacolo, 1956.
2. The Group of experts, led by Luigi Crocetti, included Alberto Cheti, Daniele Danesi, Massimo Rolle, Stefano Tartaglia. It profited from the collaboration of Carlo Revelli. In addition to myself, Marta Ricci from the National Library in Florence participated in the work. Lucia Di Geso represented ICCU. Diego Maltese brought to the study his scientific contribution.
3. We cite the 1987 edition, cumulating the previous ones: *Bibliografia nazionale italiana : soggetti : liste di aggiornamento 1956-1985.*–Firenze : Biblioteca nazionale centrale, 1987.
4. *Voci di soggetto : aggiornamento 1986-1998 : Bibliografia nazionale italiana.*– Milano : Editrice Bibliografica, [1999].
5. As Paul Weston asserted in *Catalogazione bibliografica : dal formato MARC a FRBR*, "the very existence of links between rejected forms and accepted terms, does

not guarantee in itself coherence in the choice of headings, it does not allow automatic control when data is transferred nor does it provide operators with the set of bibliographic references that are sometimes essential to solve disputed issues and to place in its bibliographic context the access term chosen" (see: http://www.aib.it/aib/boll/2001/01-3-267.htm. Last contact 30th December 2002).

6. *Per un nuovo Soggettario*: *studio di fattibilità sul rinnovamento del Soggettario per i cataloghi delle biblioteche italiane* / commissionato dalla BNCF alla Ifnet, Firenze ; realizzato dal Gruppo di progetto per il rinnovamento del Soggettario.–Milano : Editrice Bibliografica, 2002.

7. *Guidelines for subject authority and reference entries* / Working Group on Guidelines for Subject Authority Files of the Section on Classification and Indexing of the IFLA Division of Bibliographic Control.–München [etc] : Saur, 1993.–(UBCIM publications; n.s., 12). *UNIMARC manual. Authorities format.*–2nd rev. and enlarged ed.–München : Saur, 2001.–(UBCIM publications ; n.s., 22). *Functional Requirements for Bibliographic Records* / IFLA Study Group on the Functional Requirements for Bibliographic Records.–München: Saur, 1998.–(UBCIM publications ; n.s., 19).

8. *Per un nuovo Soggettario,* cit., p. 245, note 8.

9. Ibid., p. 246, note 13.

10. In other national systems for control of terms, both single terms and, sometimes, combinations of them in strings are included in subject authority files, e.g., in: *Notices d'autorité* di RAMEAU (http://noticesautorites.bnf.fr. Last contact: 30th December 2002).

Authority Control
and Subject Indexing Languages

Stefano Tartaglia

SUMMARY. The existence of subject indexing languages does not call for or imply a particular authority control system exclusively dedicated to subject entries. To be really effective and efficient, authority control must be concerned with all categories of entities, and must regard not just the form but also the meaning and the semantic relations of the expressions used to identify the single entities. Thus, it satisfies the lexical needs of all cataloguing languages, including subject indexing languages. It is not correct nor opportune to extend authority control to the syntactic constructions of subject indexing languages, because this reduces the rigor and efficiency of the control process, weighing it down until it becomes unfeasible, and impeding its function as a unifying element between the different cataloguing languages. *[Article copies available for a fee from The Haworth Document Delivery Service: 1-800-HAWORTH. E-mail address: <docdelivery@haworthpress.com> Website: <http://www.HaworthPress.com> © 2004 by The Haworth Press, Inc. All rights reserved.]*

KEYWORDS. Authority control, subject indexing languages, FRBR

Stefano Tartaglia is affiliated with AIB–Gruppo di ricerca sull'indicizzazione per soggetto.

[Haworth co-indexing entry note]: "Authority Control and Subject Indexing Languages." Tartaglia, Stefano. Co-published simultaneously in *Cataloging & Classification Quarterly* (The Haworth Information Press, an imprint of The Haworth Press, Inc.) Vol. 39, No. 1/2, 2004, pp. 365-377; and: *Authority Control in Organizing and Accessing Information: Definition and International Experience* (ed: Arlene G. Taylor, and Barbara B. Tillett) The Haworth Information Press, an imprint of The Haworth Press, Inc., 2004, pp. 365-377. Single or multiple copies of this article are available for a fee from The Haworth Document Delivery Service [1-800-HAWORTH, 9:00 a.m. - 5:00 p.m. (EST). E-mail address: docdelivery@haworthpress.com].

Digital Object Identifier: 10.1300/J104v39n01_05

Artificial languages provide the mediation between a collection of documents and its potential users. As Elaine Svenonius has often explained, in the same way as natural languages, artificial languages are made up of four necessary components:

1. vocabulary, that is, all the elementary expressions used to define individual entities, attributes, and relationships,
2. semantics, that regards the meaning for which a determined expression is included in the vocabulary and used in the language, that is, the relationships which are derived a priori from that meaning and which define it,
3. syntax, that regards the composition, by means of the structure of individual elements taken from the vocabulary, of more complex expressions, and
4. pragmatics, which concerns the conditions and modalities for language application.

Authority control, or the term vocabulary control, which Elaine Svenonius considers to be equivalent, involves the first component: vocabulary, and it takes place in the second: semantics.[1]

This analytical approach to the linguistic systems of "cataloguing" mediation (using "cataloging" in its general sense, not in the librarian's sense only) provides the most correct theoretical reference for a series of considerations that should make the properties and functions of authority control more easily recognizable, consequently clarifying the relationships between authority control and the different cataloguing languages, particularly with regard to subject indexing.

Authority control cannot be identified, nor is it advisable for it to be identified, with a particular cataloguing language, since the syntactic and pragmatic components that characterize and diversify the single languages more than the vocabulary and semantic components are extraneous to authority control. This independence from single cataloguing languages, or from particular types of language, is a basic property and strong element of authority control. Its efficiency must be preserved and widely extended, but specifically must exclude the procedures of vocabulary control that by their nature (being elements and aspects of single languages) produce reciprocally incompatible results and thus do not lead to a single process of control.

The origins of authority control are easily located among the paragraphs of the rules for author and title cataloguing. It is now time to completely abandon the idea that authority control is a phase in the application of a particular cataloguing language, in order to design and implement a system of unique and general authority control that may satisfy not only the needs of systems of real bibliographic mediation, but also of systems of, among others, archival and museum mediation. The more it is general and international, the more vocabulary control is efficient, since it permits the reduction of the waste of resources produced by the repetition of the same practices for control in different places, times, and contexts. This is an asset particularly appreciated in times of full-fledged economic constraints, even for intellectual work. Most of all, however, the more it is unique and general, the more authority control is efficient, since it furnishes the unifying element between different cataloguing systems, essential for the implementation of logic and digital tools that facilitate and give maximum coherence to the research for information in traditionally separated documentary environments, as for example, those of collections in libraries, archives, museums and those in digital formats accessible only by electronic means.[2]

Cataloguing languages distinguish themselves, first of all, because of their diverse pragmatics. That is because they are meant for use in distinct circumstances with discrete functions and modes. However, as mentioned above, authority control does not concern pragmatics. This means that the conditions and relationships which depend upon the material, formal, and substantial characteristics of the single objects to be described and indexed, as well as the various contexts in which such objects are described and indexed, and the particular purposes for their description and indexing that regulate the use of specific cataloguing languages, at any rate, do not bring about a diversification of authority control, either regarding the process or the product of such a process, which will be a unique, normalized/standardized expression inserted in a web of relationships.

Inserting this consideration into the specific theme of this paper, one cannot but observe that the opinion that authority control is distinguishable, and must be distinguished, without further specifications is still widespread, and that it is commonly held regarding "authors." This opinion is unintentionally backed (yet, not to be justified) in the standards activity of IFLA, which published two distinctive guidelines on this subject, one formally presented as relating to "authority records" (formerly "authority entries"),[3] and one formally presented as relating to "subject authority entries."[4] Moreover, it is also easy to establish that such a persistent opinion has determined, although with different consequences, the same organization of two of the most important national systems of vocabulary control, the Library of Congress (LC) one and the Bibliothèque nationale de France (BnF) one.[5]

In the search screens the Library of Congress authorities are divided into subject authority headings, name authority headings, title authority headings and name/title authority headings; nevertheless, a search for the same expression, either as name, title or name/title, or as subject, retrieves the authority. This proves that there is a unique authority file, that the control operations relating to the same expression are carried out only once, and that it is simply considered necessary to adjust the appearance of the control system to the opinion mentioned above, making the "subjects" seem separate from the rest of the entries (and here we are speaking about access to the authority file, not about access to the Library of Congress catalog, where separation of the indexes is obviously appropriate).

The BNF *Notices d'autorité* are analogously presented as separated into *personnes physiques, collectivités, titres uniformes,* and RAMEAU (*Répertoire d'autorité-matière encyclopédique et alphabétique unifié*); but in this case, a search for the same expression, either person, corporate body, title, or subject retrieves two different *notices d'autorité, inside files* (fichiers d'autorité) effectively divided (frBN000 for persons and corporate bodies, frBN002 for titles and frBN001 for subject entries). This means that, at the BNF, all management and control operations for the same expression are duplicated, with a waste of resources that does not match an increase of visible efficiency in the system. It would be sad if it were motivated only by a commitment to keep some slightly justifiable formal difference between expressions which are equivalent. The most evident case is that of the dates of birth and death, not normally stated in the terms given in the *fichier d'autorité personnes physiques*–which proposes, for example, the preferred form Dante Alighieri–but present in the RAMEAU *vedettes*–where the preferred form is Dante Alighieri (1265-1321).

These different solutions and uncertainties in the authority control systems can only induce problems and waste, beginning with the error of considering the "subjects" as semantically distinguishable entities, on the same level as persons, corporate bodies, and works. It is, therefore, indispensable to clarify that it is impossible to identify an entity as a subject if not in relation to the pragmatics, that is, to the concrete circumstances which have implied, in such a case, the use of a subject indexing language in the cataloguing record of a document. However, since authority control does not regard those circumstances, it is not theoretically correct, nor practically useful, to perceive and practice subject authority control as a process in itself.

In the FRBR model,[6] which is actually reflected in the *Guidelines for Authority Records and References* as noted above, *work, expression, manifestation, item, person, corporate body, concept, object, event,* and *place* are classes of entities. These entities "represent the key objects of interest to users of bibliographic data,"[7] and each one, having a formal expression as the primary necessary attribute which designates it (title, identifier, name, or term), can be subjected, and as a norm it is suitable for them all to be subjected, to the authority control procedures. The "subject" is not an entity in the FRBR model, it is a relationship (i.e., the relationship "has as a subject"), that does not strictly correspond to single classes of entities, but that, conversely, can entail entities belonging to each of the classes proposed in the model.

It was certainly not essential for a cataloguer to be reminded by FRBR that the name of a person, of a corporate body, or of the title of a work can be inserted in a cataloguing record in order to fulfill different functions (typically, author or title access and subject access). However, FRBR goes further since it suggests the possibility that even the terms which represent these entities (*concept, object, event,* and *place*), for which only the subject function is indicated, can be linked to a cataloguing record with a diverse function. In fact, if "typically the user will formulate a search query using one or more attributes of the entity for which he or she is searching, and it is through the attribute that the user finds the entity sought,"[8] and if, for example, the second and most important attribute of the work, after the title, is the "form," that is "the class to which the work belongs,"[9] how is it possible to allow an efficient search, using this attribute, of a work concretely expressed in a manifestation, if not by designating this attribute with a controlled term, which cannot but be the same used, in the context of other cataloguing records, for subject access? Putting it very simply, if Walter Scott's *Ivanhoe* is a historic novel, how is it possible to retrieve, by literary genre, the various manifestations of this novel, if not directly or indirectly linking the relative cataloguing records to the term "Historical novel," thus inserting into the search mechanisms of the editions of a work a term presumably also used in the subject indexes, but which, in this case, does not express the subject of the work? It is true that above all, in our catalogs up to now, we did not bother too much to activate retrieval requirements for "genre," but this has been only a convenient default, seeing how Cutter already, over a century before FRBR, had indicated the search by literary genre as one of the requisites of the catalog.[10] If we then move from the bibliographic context to other cataloguing contexts, the use of potentially expressive subject descriptors in order to indicate something else becomes quite prevalent. "Etruscan ceramics" for example, is a term for which the function of a subject is typical in a bibliography, but probably is to be excluded in the catalog of a museum collection, in which "Etruscan ceramics" will indicate what the indexed object is, not its theme. The "form of the work" in FRBR is most relevant, but not the only case where we find the potential use of an entity *concept, object, event,* or *place* for the purpose of indicating not the subject, but another characteristic of the indexed and described document.[11]

Absolutely nothing in the form and the meaning of a term can predetermine the function that the term will play in the single catalogue record and consequently in a particular index, above all if we widen the field from the bibliographic context to other cataloguing contexts. On the other hand, to be efficient, unique, and general, authority control must leave that function out of this consideration. This further confirms that there is no theoretical or practical justification for continuing to distinguish subject authority control in the general activity of vocabulary control. It is not by chance that IFLA, having produced the two guidelines on authority records quoted above, has nevertheless produced an inevitably unique guideline for the codification of authority records in a readable format for the machine, that is to say *UNIMARC Authorities* in which a specific field for all subject entries alone as such does not exist.[12]

Semantics is pertinent in authority control, in the three forms described by Elaine Svenonius:

> referential, relational, category. Referential semantics concerns the uniqueness of meaning (unambiguousness) of each of the elementary expressions included in the vocabulary. It is the task of authority control to guarantee this uniqueness, supplying each strictly indispensable and sufficient expression of all the formal elements to avoid any misunderstanding in use and interpretation.

The potential polysemy of an expression is a frequent phenomenon in natural languages. It has no effect on communication, since normally pragmatic circumstances clarify the meaning for which the polyseme (a word having multiple meanings) is effectively used. But general authority control, although it is functional in most cataloguing contexts, cannot delegate the referential semantics to the clarifying properties of a single context, nor be conditioned by those properties, and must rather satisfy only and fully the needs of unambiguousness of the expressions of the vocabulary in all the cataloguing contexts. In this regard, the case that immediately comes to mind is that of those proper names, often called "geographic," which in common use can indicate both a territory (that is, in a narrow sense, a portion of the earth's surface, e.g., "the climate in Italy"), and the population of that territory ("the economic relations between Italy and France in the 16th century"), as well as the corporate body that holds sovereignty over that territory ("the international relations of Italy in the period after the second World War"). In some contexts these proper names are not polysemes: in the context of author cataloguing "Italy" is not effectively a polyseme, since the meanings of the territory and of the population are not pertinent to the context; while, certainly but not only in other contexts, in the one of the subject indexing, those proper names are real polysemes to the point of sometimes making syntactic relationships ambiguous and the comprehensive meaning of the entries in which they are inserted doubtful. They also often make the search and selection of the cataloguing information fastidiously hard. To be efficient, general authority control must resolve the problems of real polysemy even when not common to all cataloguing contexts, and must guarantee the unambiguousness of the expressions in any context in which they are used.

Relational semantics concerns the relationship of meaning between all of the expressions included in the vocabulary. Among these relationships, one is unquestionably considered pertinent to any form of authority control, and that is the equivalence relationship. If in various cataloguing contexts two or more expressions can be used with the same meaning, that is, if they indicate the same entity, these two or more expressions are correlated in the authority file in such a way to guarantee the identification of that entity by means of any of these expressions. Traditionally, the principle of uniformity was applied to the equivalence relationship, for which one of the expressions was designated as preferred, and became the only one effectively present in the cataloguing records. The informatics management of authority control can offer alternatives to this solution, which allow us to implement a unique and general authority control without imposing the use of the same expression in all contexts, but it must be kept in mind that uniformity has its value as an element of coherence and of predictability in catalogs; therefore, it must be abandoned only in the presence of real and fundamental cataloguing needs.

The control of equivalence relationships, however, does not leave out the needs of semantic correlation of any cataloguing language. Author and title cataloguing imposes control of some cases of associative relationships (between denominations of corporate bodies, distinct bibliographic identities corresponding to the same physical person and works)[13] and of hierarchical relationships (between a corporate body and one of its organs, a work and one of its parts). The opportunity of controlling this type of relationship can only increase with the application of the FRBR model. The control of associative and hierarchical relationships, extended to all categories of entities, represents a fundamental need for the subject indexing languages, but it is presumable that it is essential or useful for any other cataloguing language, too, and certainly advantageous for the interconnection between different languages. Therefore, it is thus appropriate to implement it on the level of general authority control. Obviously, on this level of control, only hierarchical and associative relationships of universal validity may be expressed, that is, those that can be explained by the typical and essential definition of the entity submitted to authority control, and which thus cannot be contradicted in any particular context. Any entity can then be involved in semantic relationships that are not universally valid, but inherent to the context of application of a given language. Such relationships must not be expressed on the level of general authority control, but in specific and discipline vocabulary and classification control instruments, for the elaboration of which the existence of a general semantic control instrument does not necessarily constitute an obstacle, but rather a helpful tool.

Substantially, a semantic relationship structure is a classification structure, and thus needs a primary general criterion of subdivision, upon which further articulations can be based. General bibliographic classifications are based upon a primary articulation by subject, which implies the possibility that the same concept, if pertinent to more than one subject, belongs to several classes. This does not correspond to the needs of characteristic semantic structuring of authority control, since, as has been repeated several times in this paper, such a process must leave out of consideration the single context, even when disciplinary, in which the single entities are concretely quoted. With a view to authority control, it is, therefore, necessary to adopt another general criterion of classification that is independent of single contexts but is valid and useful in all of them and has a secure application. More than a century of studies and of practice in indexing has shown that the criterion of categorical analysis, which consists, as regards semantics, in the individuation of a limited number of general and universal semantic categories, answers these requisites, so that each entity can belong to only one category and in the assigning of each entity, for the single attributes which constitute the typical definition, to one of the located categories.[14] The individuation of semantic categories is necessary to avoid incongruities and contradictions in the identification and expression of semantic relationships, but it is also more generally necessary for the normalization and the informatics management of authority control. It is certainly not a case that upon the citation of general semantic categories is based all of the above mentioned *Guidelines for Subject Authority and Reference Entries*, nor is it a case that every field of *UNIMARC Authorities*, excluding those of the notes and equipment information, correspond to a semantic category. In the exercise of this general category, semantics authority control is, however, not alone. Even in the FRBR model, in order to control other types of cataloguing relationships, some general semantic categories have been individuated (*work* etc., *person, corporate body, object, event,* and *place*) mainly usable even in authority control. This shows a convergence of needs and solutions that supports the hypothesis that full implementation of the FRBR model will make possible a unique and general authority control, but also that a unique and general authority control is indispensable for full implementation of the FRBR model.

Authority control is applied to the single units of vocabulary regarding, a priori, their characteristics and relationships, those which are constantly valid and for which the single unit is admitted in the comprehensively understood linguistic system. That is, authority control concerns the paradigmatic, not the syntagmatic, side of linguistic communication, and does not thus regard a posteriori relationships, the ones depending upon connotations of objects to be described and indexed, and existing among the units of vocabulary only when and because they are both present together in a determined statement. Thus the syntax, the representation of these relationships through the ordering in a sequence of correlated units, and one of the most distinctive elements in the diverse languages, cannot be the object of real authority control, but it can be the object, when necessary, only of a verification of correctness and of substantial uniformity in the area of application of a particular cataloguing language.

Understanding the syntax of authority control involves a series of drawbacks that do not seem to be compensated for by any particular advantage. Above all, it impedes the realization of a unique and general vocabulary control that is a connecting factor between different cataloguing languages. This is because syntax is the element for which less compatibility is shown, not only between typologically distinct languages, but also between kindred languages that could easily share the same vocabulary. The case of subject indexing languages is emblematic. The differences between various languages that express a theme in pre-coordinated form, and those with post-coordinated languages, are not so much differences in terminology, but rather differences in the grade and form of expression of the syntactic relationships that sometimes make it impossible to establish the equivalencies not only between index entries expressed by languages, which draw from different natural languages, as the MACS project[15] has shown, but even between entries expressed by languages which draw from the same natural language.

As an inevitable further consequence, the alleged authority control of syntactic structures makes the entire process more overloaded. Besides this contraction of its own area of efficiency becoming increasingly useless, it does not determine a major expressiveness, as it is virtually unable to contain the whole set of forms submitted to control, thus contradicting the first requisite of controlled vocabulary which is to control its growth, too. The constant expansion of the vocabulary is a need of cataloguing languages, but it has a general limit in the fact that the inclusion of new forms is always motivated by the need to express new unitary concepts, not new concept correlations that can easily be expressed by combining pre-existing forms. To create a new authority record for the string "Hospitals–Administration–Data processing–Evaluation–Computer programs" (*Library of Congress authorities*, sh85062292), when authority records already exist for each of the single terms forming it, is not in any way useful to the expressiveness of the language, but implies at least in theory, the fulfillment for this entry of all of the procedures of control and semantic correlation. Such procedures–particularly articulated and complex, in this case–were not in the least implemented (the entry in question has no link with other entries); this confirms the complete uselessness of this authority record, the creation and management of which has nevertheless absorbed resources. And here is one of the reasons, certainly the most concrete and practical, for avoiding authority control of syntactically structured entries. The creation of authority records for this type of entry determines a waste of resources, which are subtracted from the more qualifying aspects of authority control, making its implementation more difficult, if not impossible. Moreover, the problem is noticed even in the Library of Congress and the Bibliothèque nationale de France since both institutions, in order to avoid the collapse of their vocabulary control systems, are activating a review of the procedures aimed at limiting the application of authority control to only elementary expressions, at least to the extent that they are compatible with the use of indexing languages that remain substantially enumerative. Inverting the preceding procedure, at the Library of Congress a new one has been established to avoid the creation of new phrase headings (for example, the form "Recreation areas–Access for physically handicapped" has been preferred to the form "Access for physically handicapped to recreation areas") and the progressive transformation of many pre-existing phrase headings in entries with subdivisions is in course. At the same time the list of free-floating subdivisions has been notably enlarged, with the attribution of the qualification of free-floating to many subdivisions that were not previously free-floating. This has made quite rare the chance that a new authority record will be produced for a new entry that is a structured combination of pre-existing expressions. Similar action is also taking place in RAMEAU, although it is a more recent language creation (born after 1980), and thus less enumerative that LCSH.[16]

When improperly extended to syntactically structured expressions, authority control becomes quite weakened and inefficient in its semantic component, which loses the necessary exactitude both in the individualization of relationships and in the analysis of categories. To give a simple example, what is the entry immediately above, the BT (broader term) of "Hospitals–Administration"? Hospitals? Administration? Health facilities–Administration? Health facilities–Organization? Hospitals–Organization? And what is the category to which the entry belongs? Is it the category of Hospitals given in the entry in the first position (but this is a merely formal criterion), or that of Administration, which is the focus of the corresponding syntax (administration of hospitals)? Above all, can such uncertain semantics ever satisfy the general needs of authority control? Or, to ask a final question, does it make sense to corrupt authority control to such a point, only to extend, partially and occasionally, syntax to an aspect of cataloguing languages which is not pertinent to it?

In the above paragraphs the sense of the relation between authority control and subject indexing languages is given, but almost hidden behind the closer examination of single problems. It is well to sum them up now. The existence of subject indexing languages certainly does not call for, or imply, the existence of a particular type of authority control exclusively dedicated to subjects. Authority control, being an interconnecting element between different cataloguing languages, must concern all categories of entities, thus satisfying even the lexical needs of subject indexing languages. The use of subject indexing languages, as other cataloguing languages, contributes to the location of new expressions to be submitted to authority control, expressions whose ordinary use cannot predetermine their possible successive uses, and once the control procedures are completed, can be used in any cataloguing context (bibliographic, archival, museums, etc.), either to show a subject or something else. Cataloguing languages that include, among others, subject indexing languages need to be checked for the expressions that are not merely formal but also more completely semantic. This check, insofar as it relates to meanings and relationships of universal validity, is to be effected at the level of general authority control. On the other hand, it is not suitable to extend authority control to syntactic structures, because this reduces the rigor and efficiency of the process, weighing it down until it becomes unfeasible, and impeding its function of being a unifying element between diverse cataloguing languages. Each cataloguing language, and thus each subject indexing language, has its own syntax, and the check of the correctness of its syntax can only be effected in the circumscribed context of the application of each language.

This idea of relationship between authority control and subject indexing languages is born from the meeting, already fertile, but which can become even more so, between technological progress and theoretic thinking. Informatics has made digital interrelation between different documentary contexts, virtually simultaneous access to several contexts and deriving of data from one context to another, not only possible but technologically easy. However, a common logical linguistic instrument is lacking, and this is evident to everyone, but it is not the duty of informatics to furnish it. As concerns subject indexing languages, theory has already identified the principles that are functional in the elaboration of that instrument. In Italy, these principles have already been adapted, disseminated, and often clearly defined by the Gruppo di ricerca sull'indicizzazione per soggetto, and can now find application in the project for renewing the *Soggettario*, promoted by the Biblioteca Nazionale Centrale di Firenze. Among the most important principles are:

- the principle of the subject as relationship entity, a factor of coherence and pertinence in a text and no longer as a pre-existing entity supplied with a name;

- the principle of the separation between semantics and syntax, with the control of semantics, which can exclude the proper formal structures from consideration of the single languages, and thus be potentially unique and general, and the control of the syntax, which is rather the implementation of those structures;
- the principle of the definable relationship, for which the semantic correlation of the vocabulary units is exclusively founded on the essential definition of each unit that is universally valid.

Authority control being unique and general, and thus adequate for the situation created by technological progress, must make use of the most advanced theory on subject indexing languages, and at the same time must satisfy the needs of subject indexing languages much more than it has done until now.

ENDNOTES

1. *The Intellectual Foundation of Information Organization* / Elaine Svenonius.–Cambridge (Mass.); London: MIT Press, c2000.–(Digital libraries and electronic publishing). In particular p. 53-58.

2. P. G. Weston, indicating this cataloguing connection between different collections of documents, uses the quite appropriate expression "interoperability among heterogeneous systems"; in *Il catalogo elettronico: dalla biblioteca cartacea alla biblioteca digitale* / Paul Gabriele Weston.–Rome: Carocci, 2002, p. 28.

3. *Guidelines for Authority Records and References.*–2nd ed. / revised by the IFLA Working Group on GARE Revision.–Munich: Saur, 2001.–(UBCIM publications; n.s., v. 23). Title of the previous edition: *Guidelines for Authority and Reference Entries.*

4. *Guidelines for Subject Authority and Reference Entries* / Working Group on Guidelines for Subject Authority Files of the Section on Classification and Indexing of the IFLA Division of Bibliographic Control.–Munich [etc.]: Saur, 1993.–(UBCIM publications; n.s., v. 12). Already in 1992 the AIB Commissione nazionale per la catalogazione e l'indicizzazione commented on the *draft* of *Guidelines for Subject Authority and Reference Entries* stating: "more than the publication of a specific document, a new edition of GARE including topical subjects would be advisable" (*Comments on the draft 'Guidelines for subject authority and reference entries'*/ AIB Commissione nazionale per la catalogazione e l'indicizzazione, a cura di Andrea Fabrizzi, 1992. Typed document sent to IFLA on June 1st 1992.–p. 2.

5. Respectively accessible at URL http://authorities.loc.gov/ and http://notices autorites.bnf.fr:8095/.

6. *Functional Requirements for Bibliographic Records* / IFLA Study Group on the Functional Requirements for Bibliographic Records.–Munich: Saur, 1998.–(UBCIM publications; n.s., v. 19).

7. *Functional Requirements for Bibliographic Records*, p. 12.

8. *Functional Requirements for Bibliographic Records,* p. 56. Compare on p. 30: "Each of the entities defined in the model has associated with it a set of characteristics

or attributes. The attributes of the entity serve as the means by which users formulate queries and interpret responses when seeking information about a particular entity."

9. *Functional Requirements for Bibliographic Records,* p. 33.

10. Cutter, Charles A. *Rules for a Dictionary Catalogue.*–3rd ed.–Washington: Government Printing Office, 1891, p. 8.

11. For an example of correct structuring of authority control see the version edited by Andrea Fabbrizzi from TECA, archive for catalogue data in CDS-ISIS, in which "access point management is organized not according to their function in the bibliographic records (author and subject indexing), but according to the type of entity they embody and refer to" ("L'applicazione delle norme GRIS in CDS-ISIS TECA" / Andrea Fabbrizzi. In: *L'indicizzazione per soggetto della sezione locale: una applicazione delle norme* GRIS / a cura di Massimo Fedi e Raffaella Marconi, con la collaborazione di Andrea Fabbrizzi, Marta Gori, Paolo Panizza.–Firenze: [s.n.], p. [89]-109. At the head of the title-page: Provincia di Firenze Biblioteca comunale di Bagno a Ripoli, Biblioteca comunale di Fiesole.)

12. UNIMARC *Manual. Authorities Format.*–2nd rev. and enlarged ed.–Munich: Saur, 2001.–(UBCIM publications: n.s., v. 22). Title of the 1st ed.: *UNIMARC. Authorities.*

13. *Guidelines for Authority Records and References,* p. 17-19.

14. *Guida all'indicizzazione per soggetto* / Associazione italiana biblioteche, GRIS Gruppo di ricerca sull'indicizzazione per soggetto.–Reprinted with corrections.– Rome : AIB, 2001, p. 60-63. An examination of the functions and requirements of categorization is also in: *Per un nuovo Soggettario: studio di fattibilità sul rinnovamento del Soggettario per i cataloghi delle biblioteche italiane* / commissioned by the BNCF from IFNET Florence; a study undertaken by the Gruppo di progetto per il rinnovamento del Soggettario.–Milano: Editrice bibliografica, 2002, p. 328-332.

15. *Multilingual ACcess to Subjects,* a project of cooperation among four European national libraries for the construction and management of multilingual subject authority archives in English, French and German; an analysis of this project is in: *Per un nuovo Soggettario,* p. 121-124.

16. The trends of the revision process of the two indexing languages are particularly evident in the respective updating newsletters: *Library of Congress Subject Headings Weekly List* and *RAMEAU. Journal des créations et des modifications.*

Subject Indexing
in the Servizio Bibliotecario Nazionale

Maria Lucia Di Geso

SUMMARY. Over the last ten years, the Servizio Bibliotecario Nazionale (SBN) has become the largest Italian network of bibliographic services. The creation of the SBN Index database and its growth through shared cataloging were the focus of attention during the early phase, and for years, discussion was limited to questions of author cataloging and bibliographic description. Subject cataloging was excluded from the cooperative activity of the member libraries. In 1990 the Working Group on Subject Headings and Classes was established to examine this situation. First, a partial solution was found, to permit the launch of the network itself. This was followed, several years later, by the development of the SBN OPAC and the creation of the file of subject headings and classes in the SBN Index. From an operational perspective, the choice was made to forego managing the subject headings file in accordance with shared cataloging principles, with mixed results.

In order for the subject file to have broader coverage and to further encourage cooperative subject cataloging, the SBN Index Development Program, in which the Istituto Centrale per il Catalogo Unico delle Biblioteche Italiane (ICCU) has been engaged for about two years, aims at enriching services of the database and opening up new and diversi-

---

Maria Lucia Di Geso is affiliated with ICCU.

[Haworth co-indexing entry note]: "Subject Indexing in the Servizio Bibliotecario Nazionale." Di Geso, Maria Lucia. Co-published simultaneously in *Cataloging & Classification Quarterly* (The Haworth Information Press, an imprint of The Haworth Press, Inc.) Vol. 39, No. 1/2, 2004, pp. 379-388; and: *Authority Control in Organizing and Accessing Information: Definition and International Experience* (ed: Arlene G. Taylor, and Barbara B. Tillett) The Haworth Information Press, an imprint of The Haworth Press, Inc., 2004, pp. 379-388. Single or multiple copies of this article are available for a fee from The Haworth Document Delivery Service [1-800-HAWORTH, 9:00 a.m. - 5:00 p.m. (EST). E-mail address: docdelivery@haworthpress.com].

Digital Object Identifier: 10.1300/J104v39n01_06

fied types of usage. Almost simultaneously the Biblioteca Nazionale Centrale di Firenze (BNCF) initiated a feasibility study on the revision of the *Soggettario delle biblioteche italiane (List of Subject Headings in Italian Libraries)* for the catalogs of Italian libraries. Both the BNCF and the ICCU share the goal of building a new, consistent vocabulary for documentation of subject matter. *[Article copies available for a fee from The Haworth Document Delivery Service: 1-800-HAWORTH. E-mail address: <docdelivery@haworthpress.com> Website: <http://www.HaworthPress.com> © 2004 by The Haworth Press, Inc. All rights reserved.]*

KEYWORDS. Subject cataloging, subject access, local nodes, authority files, Servizio Bibliotecario Nazionale (SBN), Working Group on Subject Headings and Classes, OPAC, SBN Index Development Program, Istituto Centrale per il Catalogo Unico delle Biblioteche Italiane (ICCU), Biblioteca Nazionale Centrale di Firenze (BNCF), *Soggettario delle biblioteche italiane (List of Subject Headings in Italian Libraries)*

INTRODUCTION

Over the last ten years, the Servizio Bibliotecario Nazionale (SBN) has become the largest Italian network of bibliographic services; the SBN provides information, holdings details, and item availability, based on cooperative cataloging and the sharing of bibliographic resources among thousands of libraries throughout the country. From the very beginning, these were the objectives envisioned by Angela Vinay, the first director of the Istituto Centrale per il Catalogo Unico delle Biblioteche Italiane (ICCU). In the process leading to the attainment of these objectives–which we still cannot consider to be fully achieved–there was a long period during which the SBN identified itself almost exclusively, at least at the SBN Index level, with the problems of author cataloging and bibliographic description.

The creation of the SBN Index database and its growth through shared cataloging were actually prerequisites for the development of services and of co-operation–and were of necessity the focus of attention during the early phase. Over time, to the objective of bringing the network into being was added that of offering to the library world and its users a database of significance in terms of both quantity and quality, anticipating the development in the SBN Index of data monitoring and "cleansing," elimination of redundancy, and the creation and management of an authority file for authors.

Thus for years, at least at the SBN Index level, discussion was limited to questions of author cataloging; subject cataloging was excluded from the cooperative activity of the member libraries. At a time when the problem of creating a database of consistent quality and without excessive duplication was paramount, it seemed premature to tackle the issue of subject cataloging–especially considering the challenges of achieving in the field of subject cataloging the kinds of uniformity and standardization that can be achieved reasonably, albeit with difficulty, in author cataloging.

THE SBN INDEX

Shared cataloging in the SBN Index initially did not take into account functionality in relation to subject indexing, nor did it foresee the sharing of information relating to the conceptual content of documents. Because of the specificity and different nature of the institutions involved, the decision was made not to oblige the libraries that had joined the network to adopt shared tools. At the stage when the SBN Index was being planned, therefore, the only functions defined as "required" were those relating to the procedures for author and title cataloging (i.e., bibliographic management) and for circulation. In the area of subject indexing, considerable autonomy was left to the various installations of the "Polo" software.[1] This approach has made the practices of subject cataloging and classification appear somewhat aberrant among the various contributing local nodes with regard to both data and functions, and above all the construction of lists of subject terms and the relationships between the terms themselves.

Thus in the early 1990s, when the SBN Index network system became a reality with data migration from the various local nodes, the choice was made to copy to the Index only data relative to descriptive cataloging (authors and associated bibliographic descriptions), and to exclude information such as subject headings and classifications.

THE WORKING GROUP ON SUBJECTS AND CLASSES IN THE SBN

The absence of subject data in the SBN Index and the lack of common directives within the SBN did not, however, prevent a growing consistency from being achieved, even in the area of subject indexing, both through the increasing spread of the *Soggettario delle biblioteche italiane (List of Subject Headings in Italian Libraries)*, and through initiatives aimed at creating opportunities for the librarians working at the local nodes to compare what they were doing.

And so, in February 1990, the Working Group on Subject Headings and Classes was established by the ICCU on the recommendation of the Joint Committee of SBN Experts. The brief of this working group was to compare and establish the effectiveness of the software functions offered by the various information systems in use at the local nodes with regard to the management of subject headings, as well as the adequacy of services offered in relation to user expectations. The members of the Working Group were representative of the various software applications in use and of the various types of libraries involved.

In accordance with the guidelines suggested by the Joint Committee, the Working Group first prepared a survey aimed at collecting information about the use of the various indexing tools among the local nodes. The responses to the survey showed that 80% of the participating libraries were using the *Soggettario* as their main subject indexing tool.

Subsequently, a study was undertaken of the functionalities related to subject headings and classes in the information systems being used at the node level–Bull, Unisys, IBM/ADABAS and IBM/SQL–a study that also made use of a comparative analysis of data relating to the subject heading files in the four types of systems. It was agreed to attempt to define an "SBN standard" for subject heading assignment and classification. On the one hand, this would be the "sum" of the best implementations present in the latest releases of the various software programs, and, on the other, it would take into account the procedures and methods recommended for the control of terminology and for defining the types of relationships between indexing terms recommended by international standards such as ISO 2788 *(Guidelines for the Establishment and Development of Monolingual Thesauri)*.

On the basis of comparison and past experience, the Working Group recommended that a single indexing reference tool should be employed at the local node level, without ruling out the possibility of the local nodes maintaining other tools of a more specialized nature as well. The proposal to share subject headings among the various local nodes, which would undoubtedly foster consistency and standardization in the practice of subject cataloging in the SBN, was, however, deemed to be premature at that stage, which coincided with the launch of the network itself. Putting this proposal into practice would also have had to provide for the creation of centralized controlled lists and a complex organization of authority control for the maintenance and coherence of the whole process. The Working Group therefore proposed a more modest plan, one that envisioned on the one hand the possibility of off-line loading into the SBN Index of subject headings and classes only from the Biblioteca Nazionale Centrale di Firenze (BNCF), with periodic updates; and, on the other hand, the capability of displaying subject headings and classes linked to

BNCF records and the possibility of storing data in a supplementary file to be used subsequently at the local level, with the creation of appropriate links to bibliographic records.

Such a solution, albeit only partial, was intended as a response to continued requests to use the functionality of the SBN Index to capture, along with individual bibliographical records, the linked subject data, with considerable savings in time and costs for the libraries that intended to use the subject headings assigned by the BNCF. Furthermore, the presence of such information in the SBN Index would offer catalogers a form of "cross-check" and a guide to the formulation of subject headings.

THE DEVELOPMENT OF THE OPAC AND THE CREATION OF THE FILE OF SUBJECT HEADINGS AND CLASSES IN THE SBN INDEX

The recommendation of the Working Group on Subjects and Classes could only be put into effect several years later, in 1996/97, thanks to the Accessibility of Databases Residing in the SBN Index project, the goal of which was the creation of the SBN OPAC. The implementation of the SBN OPAC represents an important stage in the evolution of the SBN as a network of services, which is the principal objective of the whole project. The decision to enrich the information residing in the SBN Index with subject data was made by the SBN Management Committee at the suggestion of the ICCU: in relation to the Modern Books database, it was planned to develop functions in the OPAC that would permit subject searching of documents through querying by subject and/or class. To this objective was added that of offering subject cataloging support for library users by copying this information into the management database of the SBN Index. Two phases were identified for this project:

- an initial phase during which the SBN Index database of subject headings and classes would be created through batch loading of subject headings and classes from 11 local nodes;
- a subsequent phase, in which the database of subject headings would be enlarged by means of online procedures to be developed by the same local nodes that participated in the first phase.

To ensure consistency and coherence in the database as it was taking shape, it was decided to include only subject entries created by local nodes that used the *Soggettario*. Once the BNCF node had been given priority, the choice of the other ten local nodes was based on two criteria: quality of data and level of "coverage" in the SBN Index, interpreted as the percentage of records possessed by a local node with respect to the entire national database. This first phase ended in February 1997 with the copying to the SBN Index of approximately one million subject entries covering about 860,000 titles; subsequently the data was loaded into the SBN OPAC. The second phase involved the development of processes at the local node level for both the supply to and the capture of subject data from the SBN Index. Initially, only the Bull software had this functionality; the other systems being used at the node level (Unisys, IBM/ADABAS, and UNIX) later acquired this functionality as well.

The structure of the data and the functions provided for in the SBN Index presented, and still present, characteristics that differ from those in the local nodes. The subject heading is entered as a link to the bibliographic record, like an "appendix" to it. This causes a duplication of identical subject strings, when these are sent to the SBN Index by different local nodes and thus with different identifiers. From an operational perspective, the choice was made to forego managing the subject headings file in accordance with shared cataloging principles, with the following results:

1. There is no subject query function: a subject heading is seen only at the stage of searching/capture, in the context of the bibliographic record to which it is linked.
2. When a record is captured, the local nodes are free to choose whether or not to capture a subject heading that is linked to it.
3. Local nodes that contribute their subject headings to the SBN Index have available to them software that allows them to batch upload data at the end of the day's work; or they may upload directly on line, which also allows catalogers to choose which subject headings they want to contribute.
4. It is not possible to link subject headings or classes coming from more than one local node to the same record: an entry always represents subject headings and classes from a single local node.
5. In the case of "competition" between data from more than one local node, the SBN Index selects one contribution in accordance with a prioritized scale for subject cataloging among local nodes, with the BNCF given top priority.
6. Local nodes receive no updates for corrections to or changes in subject heading strings; therefore a local node that has captured a subject heading that is subsequently modified in the SBN Index may get out of synch with the central database.

THE CURRENT SITUATION

The last complete loading of subject headings and classes into the SBN Index was performed in October 2001; that will probably be the last batch upload, since now almost all SBN software has functionalities that permit real-time uploading of records. At present the SBN Index contains approximately 5,585,000 bibliographic records, of which more than 5,124,000 represent monographs, 3,150,000 published in Italy. Of the total bibliographic records, 1,280,000 have subject headings; some have more than one, which explains the presence of 1,610,000 subject links to records. In absolute terms, the percentage of bibliographic records with subject headings in the SBN Index is less than 23%. If, however, we bear in mind that many publications are not assigned subject headings (for example, fiction, the classics, general encyclopedias, etc.) and that many records that come from retrospective conversions will probably never have subject headings assigned to them, we can perhaps reduce the SBN Index entries that could potentially have subject headings to a figure of between 4.5 and 5 million. In this case, the percentage of records with subject headings would be somewhere between 28.4% and 25.6% of the entire file.[2]

On the other hand, studies show that, as the software applications of the local nodes acquired functions that enabled them to capture the SBN Index's subject data, there was a gradual increase in the activity of subject capture: at present, with about 6,500 records captured daily, between 2,700 and 3,000 transactions are carried out that are subject searches for capture, and from about 1,000 subject captures a day in the early years the present figures show an increase of 270-300%.

Several considerations emerge from even a summary analysis of the data cited above: six years have passed since the first load of subject headings into the SBN Index, which occurred at the beginning of 1997; at that time, the publications represented in the Index amounted to about 2.8 million, and now, as already mentioned, they number 5,585,000; the local nodes, which were then 33 in number, have increased to 51: so we have an Index that has almost doubled in that space of time. It therefore seems obvious that the quantity of records with subject headings is quite small with regard to such a large bibliographic file, in that only about a quarter of the records in the database have been assigned subject headings. On the other hand, we can see that cooperation has certainly taken advantage of the new software functions, in order to facilitate and speed up the cataloging activity of the local nodes, which have shown a great interest in capturing subject headings. Today, about 50% of entries captured are captured with subject headings, and surely this percentage would rise if there were a greater number of subject headings in the SBN Index itself.

If the intention is for the subject file to have broader coverage and to further encourage cooperative subject cataloging, it is necessary to review the initial choices that were made, if possible extending the functionality of subject cataloging in the SBN Index to additional local nodes. The criteria for selection could be the same as those applied to the original eleven participating nodes: use of the *Soggettario* and a well-established, accurate practice in the indexing of items. New participating local nodes could be identified on the basis of their contribution to the subject analysis of items that are not present in the BNI–for example, foreign, highly specialized, or local materials. With reference to the latter type of material, it must be remembered that some publications in the SBN Index will never have subject headings, unless they are assigned by the local node that possesses them.

Furthermore, above all among local nodes that display a greater consistency in their subject work (for instance those of the two national central libraries, and certainly others), we could consider dividing up the publications requiring subject work by type of material or on the basis of other criteria that can emerge only from a comparison among the libraries involved.

THE SBN INDEX DEVELOPMENT PROGRAM

The SBN Index Development Program, in which the ICCU has been engaged for about two years, arose from the need to make the SBN evolve into a new system that would become a general point of reference for the delivery of widespread bibliographic services. To this end, the program provides for an enrichment of services, integrations, and extensions of the database, and opening up to new and diversified types of usage. Beyond guaranteeing maintenance of the rules already in force in the SBN systems currently in existence, the future system will permit:

- an extension of the services provided by the central catalog
- an extension of SBN cooperative cataloging to other types of materials
- a simplification of interactions between the central system and local nodes in the new shared cataloging environment (also via the introduction of mechanisms for copy cataloging)
- an opening towards other library management systems by means of international exchange formats (import-export of bibliographic descriptions).

New functionalities and new data relating to the area of subject cataloging have also been envisioned within the scope of the program. The new database structure will implement files for both subject headings and classes, along with the files for titles and authors. Thus subject headings will no longer be an "appendix" to the bibliographic record–information visible only from the analytic display of a title, as is now the case; rather, they will be an autonomous entity that can be queried separately.

In addition to the existing functions of creation/correction and capture of subject headings and classes in the SBN Index, which are possible with the present SBN protocol, the new structure will need to permit the following new functions to be available to the local nodes, which will be connected via the new SBN MARC protocol:

1. search of the SBN Index by subject headings and classes, used both as access points leading to the files of subject headings and classes, and as access points to the bibliographic records themselves
2. "navigation" from the subject file to the title file and vice versa
3. "monitoring" of the subject file, in order to detect possible duplicates, coding and keyboarding errors, etc.
4. functionalities for "cleansing" the file, which will depend on the results obtained by the monitoring activities and will be directed towards creating a consistent database
5. statistics on the activity and the production of the local nodes with regard to subject indexing
6. extension of subject cataloging operations to new types of non-book materials (e.g., prints, photographs, maps, etc.) that the SBN Index is planning to incorporate.

FEASIBILITY STUDY FOR A NEW SOGGETTARIO FOR ITALIAN LIBRARIES

Almost simultaneously with the SBN Index Development Program, the BNCF initiated a feasibility study on the revision of the *Soggettario* for the catalogs of Italian libraries. The ICCU welcomed with considerable interest the invitation of the BNCF to participate in the working meetings of the group that led the study. Both the BNCF and the ICCU shared the goal of building a new, consistent vocabulary for documentation–an organic vocabulary, constructed on the basis of a few clear, simple and easily applied rules, responding fully to the need for revision often expressed by many in the library world and within the SBN itself. The three principles to which the new vocabulary would aspire–unity, predictability, and specificity–have by now become part of the cultural baggage of anyone involved in indexing. We also saw as valid notions the principle of the co-extension of the string, and the imposition of a citation order no longer founded on the main entry/subdivision heading structure, but on the analysis of syntactic roles. Furthermore, the application of ISO 5963 *(Methods for Selecting Indexing Terms)* for the conceptual analysis of documents and ISO 2788 for the aspect relative to vocabulary control, is a move toward that activity of diffusion of international standards which the ICCU has been urging for years. The realization of such a project seems, then, to be leading towards the creation of an "authority file" for subject cataloging, which would be an invaluable tool for the SBN member nodes.

In my opinion, however, it will be necessary to make one final effort in order to be able to understand whether it will be possible to achieve coordination between the two projects (i.e., the SBN Index Development Program and the creation of a new *Soggettario*). We need to identify the tools, the methods, and the levels of integration of the new *Soggettario* system within the framework of cooperative cataloging in the SBN system.

A great deal of work still lies ahead of us before we can achieve the goals of both projects, but we are optimistic that the two roads upon which we have set out can one day converge. Thus Italy, too, can in the future offer the community of users and librarians not only a large bibliographic database, but also a complex, articulated, open system endowed with qualitatively significant tools such as a subject authority file, as is already the case in other countries that are more advanced in this regard. The ICCU is continuing to work toward this goal.

ENDNOTES

1. The Polo software is installed at the level of the "local nodes," which are territorial aggregations of libraries connected to the same mainframe, which in turn is connected to the SBN Index.

2. The statistics in this section are taken from a report dated 15 December 2002.

AUTHORITY CONTROL EXPERIENCES AND PROJECTS

The Activities for Authority Control in EDIT16: Authors, Publishers/Printers, Devices, and Places

Claudia Leoncini
Rosaria Maria Servello

SUMMARY. This paper presents experiences with authority control within the project *Census of Italian 16th Century Editions* (EDIT16) carried on by ICCU (Istituto Centrale per il Catalogo Unico) with the co-operation of 1,200 library institutions all over Italy. The data elements and structures of the various files in the EDIT16 system are described. *[Article copies available for a fee from The Haworth Document Delivery Service: 1-800-HAWORTH. E-mail address: <docdelivery@haworthpress.com> Website: <http://www.HaworthPress.com> © 2004 by The Haworth Press, Inc. All rights reserved.]*

Claudia Leoncini and Rosaria Maria Servello are both affiliated with ICCU (Istituto Centrale per il Catalogo Unico).

[Haworth co-indexing entry note]: "The Activities for Authority Control in EDIT16: Authors, Publishers/Printers, Devices, and Places." Leoncini, Claudia, and Rosaria Maria Servello. Co-published simultaneously in *Cataloging & Classification Quarterly* (The Haworth Information Press, an imprint of The Haworth Press, Inc.) Vol. 39, No. 1/2, 2004, pp. 389-397; and: *Authority Control in Organizing and Accessing Information: Definition and International Experience* (ed: Arlene G. Taylor, and Barbara B. Tillett) The Haworth Information Press, an imprint of The Haworth Press, Inc., 2004, pp. 389-397. Single or multiple copies of this article are available for a fee from The Haworth Document Delivery Service [1-800-HAWORTH, 9:00 a.m. - 5:00 p.m. (EST). E-mail address: docdelivery@haworthpress.com].

KEYWORDS. EDIT16, *Census of Italian 16th Century Editions*, cooperative authority control project

This paper presents experience about authority control within the project *Census of Italian 16th Century Editions* (EDIT16, http://edit16.iccu.sbn.it) carried on by ICCU (Istituto Centrale per il Catalogo Unico) with the cooperation of 1,200 library institutions all over Italy. It was undertaken with the aim of taking a census of Italian editions printed from 1501 to 1600 in Italy in any language and in Italian abroad. Today the Census is a wide-ranging, live project owing its success to the close network of cooperation that it was able to establish.

The accomplishment of so ambitious a project was due, on the one hand, to the involvement of all state institutions, local, church, and private bodies, in a spirit of cooperation and mutual support. On the other hand, it was due to harvesting the highest possible amount of data in order to have an overview of what exists all over the nation. The difference in types of libraries and in how ready they were to cooperate is at the base of their differentiated involvement in the project.

Within the project, ICCU took the role of scientific advisor and coordinator, not only in the field of standardization, compiling specific rules integrated over the years, but also with respect to the decisions regarding choices and accepted forms or variants of the names of authors and printers.

First of all, we were compelled to define the authority entries in order to create authority control lists in the master file for census taking of the copies of 16th century editions. This was at a time when the possibility of automated management was far in the future, so we had to work in the traditional way, on paper. This led to the definition of a descriptive standard for authority records that had to provide uniformity and consistency, defining in advance the elements to be preferred, the criteria for action, and the hierarchy of the bibliographic sources to be indexed. To this end it was essential to build a catalogue of reference sources arranged by authors, subjects, and standard citations. The variety, complexity, and wealth of entries and the need to allow updating in an environment as highly specialized as the one related to 16th century books led to a constant increase in the number of reference tools, with attention to the literature on the history of printing and to the Italian Renaissance culture.

Even while providing working uniformity, which is essential in teamwork, an organization like this based on paper, did not and could not fully guarantee controlled, unique headings. Therefore, the EDIT16 database, which was completed in 1997 with a LAN built in, served as a focal point for the work on the Census, because it allowed a change in the working procedures and an overall and differentiated management of data that could ensure the formal consistency of all access points to information.

The retrieval of bibliographic information has formed a wide network of relationships in the **Titles File** ranging from traditional elements to the ones characterizing early printed books.

The database was implemented in two stages:

1. the upload of data already at disposal in electronic format;
2. the input of the highly diversified bibliographic material sent by the libraries participating in the Census, which has built up over the years.

This work, together with daily updating, resulted in an always live and constantly growing file of currently 50,000 titles featuring a heterogeneous level of description. That aspect of heterogeneity brought to the fore the issue of management of correlated files for Authors, Printers/Publishers, Places of publication, Printers' devices, and Bibliography. The same issue was present for all these types of files, in spite of their differences, namely, the creation of entries by means of authority control work.

The EDIT16 software is structured to answer the requirements related to the management of data in all the working stages and in various perspectives, playing the basic function of standardization and indexing. In this sense the **Titles File** is connected to all the other files, yet they all keep their autonomy and features. The database grants access to the individual authority files through links and defines their intellectual or material responsibility.

The structure of the record, highly articulated in the master file, looks simplified in the OPAC containing only the elements functional to users' searches. The analysis of the individual files will help us understand their features. The issues related to authority control are present in all of them: uniformity, respect of descriptive standards, organization into structured fields, definition of contents, and descriptive formalization. We anticipate authority control activities in EDIT16 for the elements that need normalization for indexing and research. They are: Authors, Uniform titles, Publishers/Printers, Places, Printers' devices, Bibliography, and Secretariat. In order to start a systematic authority work it was essential to face the management of bibliographic sources first of all.

The **Bibliography File**, currently 1,716 records, meets the double requirement of using bibliographic aids both as source and location of information, and as reference for the definition and documentation of data. This requirement led to the need for a logical subdivision of reference tools into categories for a diversified usage and to the use of subjects for searching. Most of all, the master file had to enable the management of the bibliographic sources starting from the ones owned by the Laboratory for Retrospective Bibliography and the coding of those bibliographic sources by standard citations duly given to them.

The files are structured according to the same logic that mandates descriptive elements and relating elements, as well as coding elements. Specifically, the files for **Authors**, **Printers/Publishers**, and **Titles** show an architecture aimed at meeting the requirements of the *Guidelines for Authority Records and References* (GARR) considered basic in an Authority File: besides the standardized access point, they include notes, information about the entities, and bibliographic sources in separate fields.

As shown in Figure 1, records in the **Authors File** are structured into four areas:

1. Information note, containing bibliographic information;
2. Name in the editions, containing the various forms appearing on the title pages of items found in the database;
3. Sources, containing bibliographic references presented in the form of standard citations based on the **Bibliography File**. Each source citation is followed by the form in which the author's name is presented in it. The bibliographic sources are documented in order to verify the author's identity, the sources for various forms of the name, and the kind of responsibility in relation to the cited source;
4. Cataloguer's note is a free area for use by operators, in which further inquiries or annotations are reported. This is information not contained in the previous fields, used for explanations.

Coded elements are attached to each name:
- Identifier
- Type of name
- Form of name
- SBN number.

The **Authors File** also allows sub-fields:
- Date
- Country
- ISADN (International Standard Authority Data Number)
- Agency
- Rules.

FIGURE 1. An Author Record

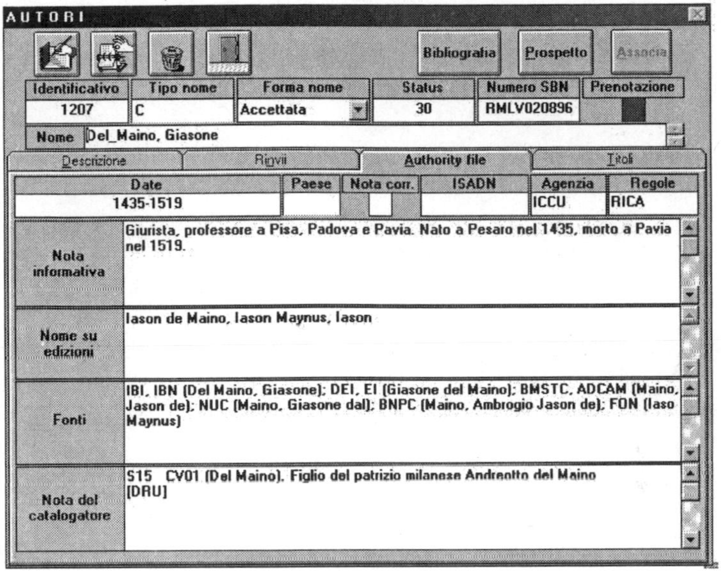

AUTORI

Bibliografia | Prospetto | Associa

Identificativo	Tipo nome	Forma nome	Status	Numero SBN	Prenotazione
1207	C	Accettata	30	RMLV020896	

Nome Del_Maino, Giasone

Descrizione | Rinvii | Authority file | Titoli

Date	Paese	Nota corr.	ISADN	Agenzia	Regole
1435-1519				ICCU	RICA

Nota informativa: Giurista, professore a Pisa, Padova e Pavia. Nato a Pesaro nel 1435, morto a Pavia nel 1519.

Nome su edizioni: Iason de Maino, Iason Maynus, Iason

Fonti: IBI, IBN (Del Maino, Giasone); DEI, EI (Giasone del Maino); BMSTC, ADCAM (Maino, Jason de); NUC (Maino, Giasone dal); BNPC (Maino, Ambrogio Jason de); FON (Iaso Maynus)

Nota del catalogatore: S15 CV01 (Del Maino). Figlio del patrizio milanese Andreotto del Maino [DRU]

The 'Note correction area' offers the operators the opportunity to pose suggestions or to operate on already defined entries for the right revision activities. Elements like "Status" and "Reservation" answer purely managerial needs. Links are provided to variant forms and to titles; future access to the **Bibliography File** is envisioned.

On the Web, the result of a search of **Authors** displays the significant elements in the three first areas and indicates the level of authority of the record; coding of standard citations is guaranteed by pointing. Presently the file holds 15,210 headings (accepted and variant forms), at a high, average, and low level of authorization.

Records in the **Printers/Publishers File** are structured into six areas:

1. Information note, besides providing bibliographic information, describes the printer's or publisher's activity;
2. Insignia, shown with its significant word;
3. Address, documented in the forms presented in the editions;
4. Name in the editions, records the various names by which the printer or publisher is presented in the colophons in the EDIT 16 editions;

5. <u>Sources</u>, documents bibliographic references presented in standard citation form according to the **Bibliography File**. Each citation is followed by the form of name by which the printer/publisher is cited in it. Bibliographic sources are used to verify the printer/publisher's identity, the dates of activity, and, if required, his/her responsibility in the work;
6. <u>Cataloguer's note</u>, is a free area for use by the operators to report further inquiries or annotations, not contained in the previous fields, but to be used for explanations and memoranda.

The **Printers/Publishers** authority file allows the same subfields in the records as does the **Authors File**:

- Dates of activity, for the printer's dates of activity related to the editions in the database
- Country
- ISADN
- Agency
- Rules.

As with **Authors**, a Note correction area offers the operators the opportunity to pose suggestions or to operate on already defined entries for the right revision activities. Coded elements are attached to each name:

- Identifier
- Type (e.g., it shows fictitious printers)
- Form of name
- SBN number.

The same elements like "Status" and "Reservation" are included for purely managerial needs. Links are provided to variant forms of name and titles, places of publication, and printers' devices used. Dates are attached to **Places** and **Devices** combining in various ways the ones in references with the ones in the database. Access to records in the **Places**, **Devices**, and **Bibliography files** is envisioned.

On the Web, the result of a search of **Printers/Publishers** displays the significant elements in the five first areas and data on places related to the dates of activity and the devices used. The level of authority of the record is displayed. Decoding of standard citations is guaranteed by pointing. Presently the EDIT16 Printers file holds 3,339 records (including variant forms), at a high, average and low level of authorization.

The **Places File** is a simplified file. Thesaurus-like, it indexes the names of places of publication and variant forms of those names. At the start the adopted, authorized form was the one in the original national language. Later the Italian form of the name was chosen, conforming to SBN. Coded elements correspond to each name:

- Identifier
- Form of name
- Country
- Type (e.g., it shows fictitious places).

Links are provided to variant forms of names, titles, and active printers. Access to the **Printers/Publishers File** is envisaged. Dates are attached to Places combining in various ways the ones from references with the ones in the titles in the database. The EDIT16 **Places File** amounts to 328 entries, including variant forms.

The **Devices File** is the file for the names of printers'/publishers' devices documented in the editions in EDIT16. It has a special innovative feature, meant to be a model for other similar entities in the database, utilizing image digitization. Coded elements correspond to the name of each printer's device:

- Identifier
- SBN number
- Dates (i.e., it displays the dates of the editions linked to the device)
- Standard citations (i.e., coded reference to the sources)
- Description (i.e., figurative elements in the device)
- Insignia
- Keywords (i.e., words taken from the description).

Each device is given a unique description of its emblematic elements taken from traditional sources for the ones documented, originally compiled by the Laboratory for Retrospective Bibliography for the un-documented ones. There are links, made up of an alphabetic character identifying the source and of digits identifying the device in it, to standard citations from sources reproducing and describing the device. A correspondence table ensures the device can be identified starting from each citation. A **"U"** citation followed by digits has been introduced for devices not in the Census or un-documented devices. Thus the **Devices File** in EDIT16 is the basic "source" for Italian 16th century printers' devices. Links are provided to images, titles, and names of printers to which dates of use are linked. Access to the **Printers' File** is envisioned.

The "Status" element answers purely managerial requirements. The information note and the correction note both give operators the opportunity to insert added information (e.g., size) or correction proposals.

On the Web, the result of a search of the **Devices File** displays the meaningful elements and the level of authority of the record. The **Devices File** currently includes 1,476 descriptions, and as many images are linked to them.

Within the **Titles File** we find the entries for **Uniform titles** or **grouping titles**. Records in this uniform titles authority file have four areas:

1. Information note, where information is provided on the work from the literary-historic perspective of authorship or attribution, particularly for spurious or apocryphal works.
2. Sources, area for bibliographic references presented as standard citations based on the Bibliography file. The bibliographic sources used to verify the traditional title and the various forms in order to establish the authority record.
3. Cataloguer's note, it contains detailed information on the literary and bibliographic tradition of the work and on attribution to possible authors.
4. Correction note, an area to be used by operators to suggest corrections for the entry. Links to authors are provided; access to the Authors, Titles, and Bibliography Files is envisaged.

These records can also have these sub-fields:

- ISADN
- Agency
- Rules.

On the Web, the result of a search of the **Titles File** displays the significant elements in the first two areas and the level of authority of the record, while as with other files, decoding of standard citations is ensured by pointing. There are about 300 authorized titles in EDIT16.

There is also a managerial **Secretariat File** that defines the libraries' names, their codes in EDIT16 (with the equivalent in *Anagrafe Biblioteche Italiane*, http://anagrafe.iccu.sbn.it and SBN, http://www.iccu.sbn.it), and the role played by each library in the cooperation. It also affects some fields in the **Titles File** and **Bibliography File**.

In this paper we have presented the management and organization features of authority control in EDIT16, while the issues related to the definition of the entries have not been exemplified. Obviously, the fact that we had at our disposal archives functional to the requirements of our work has not freed us from difficulties involved in respecting the rules and in reaching consistency in our work, particularly in the far from rare cases in which it proved hard to apply rules that are either too strict or too vague, not constantly inclusive of all the types of names. Suffice it to say the cases involve authors absent in reference tools or whose identity is not defined in bibliographic sources.

The definition of corporate bodies and of uniform titles both pose special problems. The forms of the names for corporate bodies are not always documented in the sources, and only researching of an archival nature allow us to outline their history and discover the forms used in the course of time. An example of problems with names of corporate bodies is 'Brotherhoods and religious Congregations.' For the uniform titles, that include apocryphal works or works not attributed with certainty, etc., we find titles authoritatively documented in reference tools side-by-side with titles transmitted in different forms or that, not being documented, need a grouping title, or titles that recent studies have attributed to an author.

In a project like EDIT16, carried out at the national level and centrally managed, the work of comparison and choice that is basic for the statement of the authoritative form for an author, printer, or uniform title is stressed and emphasized. We trust the experience of authority control within the Census will be fully integrated with the perspectives of the SBN and the National Authority File.

Authority Control in the Field of Music:
Names and Titles

Massimo Gentili-Tedeschi
Federica Riva

SUMMARY. Music is a global and independent language: its main feature is being performed and disseminated far beyond national boundaries. The cataloguing process takes into account all kinds of documents preserving music and information about musical events: printed and manuscript music, sound recordings, librettos and concert programs, music periodicals, and books on music. International repertories, reference tools, and standards were developed by the mid-20th century.

Authority control for music materials focuses on two different groups of problems: common access points like names have to fulfil specific needs, and terms identifying and giving access to the musical content, such as the uniform title, have to be introduced and controlled.

Several issues concerning names need to be faced, varying from the different writings of the same name, to transliteration, to attribution and disambiguation. Specific issues concern music materials: access through generic titles such as "sonata" is often frustrating. There is thus the need

---

Massimo Gentili-Tedeschi is affiliated with Ufficio Ricerca Fondi Musicali, Milano.

Federica Riva is affiliated with Conservatorio di Musica "A. Boito," Parma.

[Haworth co-indexing entry note]: "Authority Control in the Field of Music: Names and Titles." Gentili-Tedeschi, Massimo, and Federica Riva. Co-published simultaneously in *Cataloging & Classification Quarterly* (The Haworth Information Press, an imprint of The Haworth Press, Inc.) Vol. 39, No. 1/2, 2004, pp. 399-412; and: *Authority Control in Organizing and Accessing Information: Definition and International Experience* (ed: Arlene G. Taylor, and Barbara B. Tillett) The Haworth Information Press, an imprint of The Haworth Press, Inc., 2004, pp. 399-412. Single or multiple copies of this article are available for a fee from The Haworth Document Delivery Service [1-800-HAWORTH, 9:00 a.m. - 5:00 p.m. (EST). E-mail address: docdelivery@haworthpress.com].

to create controlled access points through content-related data such as medium of performance, musical form, thematic catalogue number, and music incipit.

Since 1951, the International Association of Music Libraries, Archives and Music Documentation Centres has faced issues of authority control by promoting the publication of an international cataloguing code, through specific working groups (on the structure for uniform titles, on UNIMARC, on the exchange of authority data, and on indexing of music performances), and through international cataloguing projects. *[Article copies available for a fee from The Haworth Document Delivery Service: 1-800-HAWORTH. E-mail address: <docdelivery@haworthpress.com> Website: <http://www.HaworthPress.com> © 2004 by The Haworth Press, Inc. All rights reserved.]*

KEYWORDS. Authority control in music, uniform titles, name authority control, access points for music, multilingual authority control, UNIMARC, IAML activities

MUSIC: A GLOBAL LANGUAGE

Published music (also called musica practica, sheet music, musicalia) are printed works but of a special kind just as are maps, incunabula and art prints. They are printed music and music is an independent language to itself which uses musical notation as its written expression. This independence of music is clearly expressed in writing and printing. (Code international de catalogage de la musique, vol.1, 1957, p. 25) [1]

The independence of music from other languages is self-evident when instrumental music is considered, but is also the case even in the presence of other languages, such as in vocal or operatic music. Music itself is so powerful that the message it carries can be transmitted and understood without any knowledge of the text. Music's main feature is being performed.

While literary works disseminate primarily within the boundaries of a national culture and gain international attention through translations into other national languages, musical works don't need any alteration to spread out from the local dimension to a worldwide one. The history of western music is based essentially on this phenomenon. The expansion of Italian music in the Renaissance, the Baroque, and the Romantic eras spread well over Europe. Operas by Verdi or Puccini are performed in Japan or Latin America as they are in Italy. It is not compulsory to translate the literary sung text from the original language into the local language, as audiences appreciate the music performance as the 'core' event. Ludwig van Beethoven's ninth symphony has just been declared by UNESCO a heritage of all humanity. We all know its hymn to joy by heart, but would the text without music have reached the same popularity?

Parallel to the worldwide dissemination of music is the dissemination of musical documents, presenting some typical characteristics that differentiate it from the dissemination of literary documents. Music notation is a much more complicated and expensive process than text writing. Music manuscripts were widely used until the mid-20th century and many are now preserved in libraries. Written music is the starting point for performance, thus it preserves the original composition as well as adaptations for different performances, as various versions of an opera exemplify clearly: there may be a score and the orchestral parts needed for theatre performances, the vocal score for practising, or the piano arrangement for playing at home.

In any case, the text tells us very little about the performance itself. For a long time, information about performances and performers has been available through secondary sources, like concert programs, newspaper reports, and librettos. With the advent of sound recordings, which became so popular in a short time, we nowadays use the term "music" to intend, generally speaking, primarily a recorded piece of music rather than a musical text.

Thus compelled by the circumstances, by the mid-20th century, music librarianship recognised the need to focus the cataloguing process on all kinds of documents preserving music and information about musical events, regardless of the materials, and developed international repertories, reference tools, and standards.

MUSIC: KIND OF MATERIALS

In addition to collecting and conserving, the music library has the task of making works available. Since music demands hearing, the use of a mute catalogue is not enough. It must be made possible for the work to be heard by means of a musical instrument or machine. Phonograph records and magnetic tape recordings, especially enlarge the field of the music library as their systematic collection, also must be considered. [. . .] The realm of the music library includes the preservation of musical works, research into the origin and the nature of the music and consideration of the problems of performance. Therefore the problems of cataloguing embrace music literature, librettos, program notes, published music and manuscripts, records and magnetic tape recordings, pictorial reproductions, photocopies and microfilms. (Code, vol. 1, p. 13-14)

The list of different kinds of documents involved in the music field quoted here from the *Code International de catalogage de la musique* (1957) may be updated with the addition of electronic resources. A musical text is nowadays available also in digital form, either as a digital text (written with a specific music editor) or as an image file. A sound recording may be analogue or digital and sound itself may be encoded or synthesized in different formats.

In the chapter *Cataloging problems*, the Code divides music related materials into eight classes (A-H), identifying specific issues for each class and recalling in several instances the different national cataloguing traditions. A brief summary may well introduce the authority control issues:

- books on music, as well as manuscript documents and letters, do not require special cataloguing rules for author and subject cataloguing;
- music periodicals also don't require special treatment, and should be abstracted and indexed;
- librettos and concert programs, appearing like books, are primary sources for music performances, local history, and biographic research. They need, therefore, access not only by title and by text author, but also by composer, performers, and other related names that are the subject of the libretto or concert program;
- printed music is usually classified in music libraries by medium of performance and/or musical form, thus authority control on such access points is essential;
- music manuscripts share most issues with printed music, adding the music incipit as a key to identify anonymous works;
- sound recordings cataloguing is peculiar concerning the physical description of these recordings;
- iconographical documents (portraits, music instrument drawings, *mises en scène*, etc.) need access by subject.

FACING THE PROBLEMS OF AUTHORITY CONTROL IN MUSIC

Authority control for music materials focuses on two different groups of problems:

1. common access points like names have to fulfil specific needs of users interested in music;
2. terms identifying and giving access to the musical content, such as the uniform title, have to be introduced and controlled.

Names

The importance of controlled access by names in music is increased by the fact that music titles are often not distinctive. The number of names to be retrieved for each publication, the identification of a person, and the unique form of the name are the main issues related to music bibliographic records.

Names to be retrieved are not only those bearing responsibilities on the publication like authors (composers, lyricists, editors, arrangers) and publishers but also those related to the performance (singers, players, dancers, conductors, ensembles, impresarios, . . .) and even dedicatees. Therefore, the number of names to be linked to each record may be very large. Names of persons active at an international level have different accepted forms in different national authority files and pose issues of transcription and transliteration. The names of sovereigns and nobles, very often dedicatees of musical works, need to be accessible through all the forms of their name and all the associated qualifications they had during their life. The names of persons known to music repertoires may have different accepted forms than those accepted in general repertoires. Professional musicians often belong to the same family, thus the risk of homonymy is very frequent and music sources are not always self-evident. Names of persons active at a local level, or as music amateurs, are seldom documented in local and in music reference tools.

Here follow some practical examples.

Händel–Issue: One Man, More Names

Georg Friedrich Händel (1685-1759), born in Germany, had such a success in London that Anglo-American repertoires consider him an "English composer of German birth"[2] and call him George Frideric Handel, while the German authority files list him as Händel, Georg Friedrich.[3]

The problem is common to musicians and artists of all eras who had international careers, e.g., Giovanni Battista Lulli–Jean-Baptiste Lully (1632-1687), as well as Orlando di Lasso–Roland/Orlande de Lassus (1530/32-1594).

Čajkovskij–Issue: One Name, Different Alphabets

The problem of the transliteration and transcription of names can be well illustrated by the following example, taken from various OPACs and reference tools:

Чайковский, Пётр Ильич
Cajkovski, Petr I.
Čajkovskij, Peter Ilič [Treccani]
Čajkovskij, Pëtr Il'ič [DEUMM, MGG2, Dizionario Treccani]
Chaikovskii, Petr Il'ich
Chaĭkovskiĭ, Petr Il'ich [Unicode, British Library]
Ciaikowski, Pietro [Schmidl, cross reference]
Tchaïkovski, Piotr Ilitch
Tchaïkovsky, Piotr Ilyitch [Encyclopédie de la musique]
Tchaikovsky, Peter
Tjajkovskij, Pjotr
Tschaïkowsky, Peter Iljitsch
Tschaikowsky, Pjotr Iljitsch [MGG]
Tsjaikovskij, Peter Iljitsj [Bibsys].

The number of variants may rise, consistently posing cataloguing and technical issues. Which are the variant forms needed to get all available information and which are the mistakes to be corrected and avoided? How do authority files written in different alphabets dialog? The Unicode standard proposes a solution for the transliteration of non-Latin characters, but, as a paradox, right now the Unicode form used by the British Library gives access to no results in a meta-OPAC search.

Rossini–Issue: One Man, Which Name?

Rossini, Gioachino (1792-1868) is the form of the name chosen by the Italian national database, Musica, within the national library service, SBN. The form was chosen on the basis of updated music reference tools.[4] On the other hand, the authority file of names of the SBN–Libro Moderno–chose the form Rossini, Gioacchino. The discrepancy, therefore, has to be resolved and selection criteria established.

Johann Strauss–Issue: Two Men, One Name?

Composers' names are not always fully indicated in musical sources. The intervention of a specialist having access to a lot of bibliographic material is crucial, as in the case of Johann Strauss, father (1804-1849) and son (1825-1899), or the case of Pietro Carlo (1772-1817) and Pietro Alessandro (1728-1804) Guglielmi, father and son, who wrote music of similar genre and are quite often mentioned on the sources without their second name; not to mention the Bach family who counts some 89 musicians within its members.

Ferdinando IV–Issue: Noble Titles

Sovereigns and nobles, whose titles may vary during their life, were often sponsors, honourees, or dedicatees of musical works. Ferdinando the 1st, king of the Due Sicilie (1751-1825), was previously king of Naples under the name of Ferdinando the 4th, and as such he received dedications of cantatas and operas. Variant forms help in creating appropriate links, in this case Ferdinando <re di Napoli ; 4. ; 1751-1825> as variant form of Ferdinando <re delle Due Sicilie ; 1. ; 1751-1825>.

Pompeo Litta–Issue: One Man, More Activities

"Local" composers, first of all chapel-masters of church music, often have an obscure yet abundant production that does not appear in repertoires. Music amateurs, whose production is often preserved as manuscript music or as self-made/self-financed prints, may be, very occasionally, documented in the music field, but they may be well-known in other scholarly environments. For example, Count Pompeo Litta (1781-1852) is renowned for his studies on genealogy. Is he the same Pompeo Litta who composed or transcribed music and to whom several music works were dedicated? Only local studies or direct investigations sometimes help disambiguating the names.

To summarize the main needs of musicians and music researchers, two issues have to be stressed:

1. an extensive use of dates and qualification is desirable not only to disambiguate recognized homonyms, but also to avoid that the same form of the name refers to different persons in the future;
2. names of persons active in different fields should be uniquely identified through the cooperation of specialists of the different fields.

Music Content-Related Access Points

Music libraries constantly have to fulfil specific searches like the following examples:

- to find music of the 20th century for a group of four wind instruments, including a clarinet and an oboe
- to find German sacred music for soprano, flute, and continuo
- to find the parts of the C major concert for piano and orchestra by Mozart
- to find the original sources (printed or manuscript) of the sonata RV22 for violin and continuo by Antonio Vivaldi

- to know if the scoring of a work by Karlheinz Stockhausen is suitable for a certain ensemble
- to know how many wind instruments are required in order to play Felix Mendelssohn-Bartholdy's first symphony op. 11
- to discover new symphonies for one's ensemble including two oboes, two horns and strings–and what about also adding one flute?
- to find an arrangement of a concert for flute and piano
- to find arrangements for horn and piano of some works by Beethoven
- to find sources of a work of dubious attribution.

It is self-evident that a search by content elements is as crucial as the search by author and title. Since the title on the document does not fully identify the content, music cataloguing uses the uniform title frequently and extensively. Many issues of authority control for music are thus related to the elements of the uniform title: filing title, medium of performance, musical form, opus number, thematic catalogue number, key, and arrangement statement. Studies aiming at an international agreement on uniform titles for music developed since the 1950s.[5]

Titles of instrumental works generally consist of a generic term. The term *Sonata* refers to thousands of works; *Sonata for piano* also thousands; *Sonata for piano in D major* refers certainly to fewer works, but even the addition of the author's name–*Sonata for piano in D major by Wolfgang Amadeus Mozart*–is insufficient to identify a single work. Descriptive cataloguing faced this issue in 1991 in the second revised edition of the ISBD (PM) standard:[6]

> *1.1.2.5 The title proper can include statements about the key, numbering, date of composition, and medium of performance, when the title, exclusive of these statements, consists of a generic term:*
>
> *String quartet no.1, A major, op. 18*
>
> *Sonate en ré majeur, opus 3, pour violon*

Cataloguing rules agree that in the uniform title, generic terms be given in the language of the cataloguing agency. A *symphony* is thus presented as a *symphonie*, or a *sinfonia*. A *violin concert* becomes a *Violinkonzert* or a *Concert für Geige*, a *concerto pour le violon*, a *concerto per violino*, or a *Koncert pre husle*. Dialogue among cataloguing systems and OPACs ought to be organised.

Issues presented by musical forms, medium of performance, and key have resulted in the creation of coded fields in several MARC formats, which overcome the language problem. Ongoing projects focus on the following extant issues:

- to define a more complete, controlled and internationally agreed-upon set of terms for musical forms;
- to establish codes for medium of performance defining, more precisely and at different levels, individual instruments and voices, groups of soloists and ensembles, and the complex relations among them;
- to create specific access points in OPACs to retrieve the stored information;
- to develop an exchange format based on the most detailed existing sets of codes.

The need to have a unique identifier, as a part of the uniform title, is solved by the thematic catalogue number. Opus numbers vary. Titles often differ. The use of different languages will frequently confuse the identification process. Referencing thematic index numbers will solve most problems. Many major libraries have established thematic catalogue numbers as the most useful component of music uniform titles *(Brook-Viano, 1997, xxix)*. This element, however, is available only for those relatively few composers for whom research tools are published.[7]

Music incipit has been recognised in many cases as the unique way to identify works contained in music manuscripts. International guidelines on music incipit cataloguing has been outlined in the *Code International de catalogage de la musique*.[8] Music incipit data can be introduced into an automated system both as an image or as an encoded set of data, but only in the latter case are data available for indexing and searching. Codes such as the *Plaine & easie code* or the *DARMS* code, have been adopted. The largest existing automated catalogues containing music manuscripts, RISM (Répertoire International des Sources Musicales) and SBN, use the *Plaine & easie code*. The interaction between an encoded incipit and the corresponding sound file is the most recent issue of the research in the field, developed by ongoing projects like the Archivio Digitale Musicale Veneto (ADMV), aiming at defining standards and necessary metadata for a meta-OPAC search, involving sound recording, bibliographic and image records.[9]

THE INTERNATIONAL ACTIVITY OF MUSIC LIBRARIANS ON AUTHORITY CONTROL

Authority control issues were first posed in music in the nineteen century with the publication of reference tools like the current international music bibliography, *Handbuch der musikalischen Literatur oder allgemeines systematisch geordnetes Verzeichniss der in Deutschland und in den angrenzenden Ländern erschienen Musikalien* by Whistling and Hofmeister (published 1817-1940, referring to publications of the 1785-1940 period). This first international repertoire was followed by international catalogues of sources: the *Bibliographie der Musik-Sammelwerke des XVI. und XVII. Jahrhunderts* by Robert Eitner (1877); the *Bibliothek der gedruckten weltlichen Vokalmusik Italiens aus den Jahren 1500-1700* by Emil Vogel (1892); and by bio-bibliographical repertoires like the *Biographie universelle des musiciens et bibliographie générale de la musique* by François Joseph Fétis (1835-1844); the *Historisch-biographisches Lexicon der Tonkünstler, welsches Nachrichten von dem Leben und Werken musikalischer Schriftsteller* by Ernst Ludwig Gerber (1890-92), to mention only the most important ones.

The International Association of Music Libraries, Archives and Music Documentation Centres, founded in 1951, supports authority control with its own activities and through projects promoted in cooperation with the International Musicological Society. In 1957, IAML promoted the publication of the *Code international de catalogage de la musique.* Five volumes, published between 1957 and 1983 were devoted to different materials (printed music, music manuscript, sound recordings), as well as to full cataloguing rules.

The international projects, founded in the second half of the 20th century and well known as R-projects, developed research on printed and manuscript historical musical sources (the *Répertoire International des Sources Musicales*, RISM, 1952 onward), on current bibliography of scholarly writings on music and related disciplines (the *Répertoire International de Littérature Musicale*, RILM, 1966 onward), on iconographic materials related to music (the *Répertoire International d'Iconographie Musicale*, RidIM, 1971 onward), and on indexing music periodicals (the *Répertoire International de la Presse Musicale*, RIPM, 1987 onward). Published at first as printed volumes and subsequently in e-format as a CD-ROM,[10] three of the four historical international projects already shifted to the same online platform, making available, for the first time, multiple kinds of information in a single search.[11]

IAML supported authority control research at annual conferences by promoting specific Working groups and by providing information on ongoing projects. Project groups on ISBDs (PM) and (NBM) were active to 1987. The Project group on authority structure for uniform titles was active to 1990. The Working group on uniform titles for music manuscript collections other than liturgical conducted its work from 1991-1995.[12] The following active Working groups met at the 2003 IAML conference in Tallinn, Estonia:

Sub-commission on UNIMARC. Chair: Massimo Gentili-Tedeschi (Ufficio Ricerca Fondi Musicali, Milano). Active as a working group in the 1980s and re-established in 1999, in 2002 undertook the task, which IFLA appointed to IAML, to maintain the lists of UNIMARC codes for the fields relevant to musical forms and on medium of performance.

Working Group on the Exchange of Authority Data. Chair: Brenda Muir (National Library of Canada, Ottawa). At its first meeting in 2002, the Working group stated its aim to consider and evaluate extant and in-progress authority standards. [13]

Working Group on the Indexing of Music Performances. Chair: Rupert Ridgewell (British Library, London). Meeting for the first time at the 2003 annual conference, the working group focused on the co-ordination of projects, organisations and scholars currently indexing performance information and on developing a data structure and online database for indexing performance information found in a variety of primary source documents.

Among the projects presented at the annual conferences, it is worth mentioning here, those which developed multilingual authority control:

Switzerland: Since 1997, the Swiss national sound archive developed a multilingual cataloguing virtual music module in VTLS based on MARC. The module maps music requirements into data structures and implements multilingual authority control allowing the translation of all authority terms, keeping track of the variations of each term in every language. [14]

Japan: A specialised system for music has been more recently developed by Kunitachi College of Music within the LS/1 system. It meets international standardisation of MARC and includes authority databases capable of managing multiple languages and alphabets. A unique tri-layer structure of the record attempts to express the relationships between entities in a catalogue. [15]

International co-operation on music authority control is also advanced by the maintenance of existing standards. In order to allow a fuller exchange of data between specialized cataloguing systems, proposals to update or to create new UNIMARC fields have been submitted recently to the Permanent UNIMARC Committee of IFLA by several countries (Italy, France, Lithuania). Proposals have the aim of allowing more precise access to bibliographic records through controlled codified access fields. Suggested proposals are analytically described in the Appendix.

FUTURE PERSPECTIVES

The aim of this paper is to demonstrate that authority control activities in music require specific competencies, reference tools, and structures. Local level research is as essential as the international coordination of activities. Future needs are to increase available resources to sustain the tasks that have to be faced, and to support cooperation among libraries, research institutes, and scholars. Planning of special projects–the maintenance of one composer's bibliographic records, or the maintenance of relator codes, such as publishers or performers–will be crucial for an efficient deployment of resources and to improve positive feedback from users.

NOTES

1. *Code International de catalogage de la musique* / Association Internationale des bibliothèques musicales. Commission internationale du Code de catalogage.– Frankfurt: C.F. Peters, 1957-1983.–1. Fanz Grasberger, *Der Autoren-Katalog der Musikdrucke,* 1957; 2. *Code restreint* compiled by Yvette Fédoroff, 1961; 3 *Rules for Full Cataloguing* compiled by Virginia Cunningham (1971); 4. *Rules for Cataloguing Music Manuscripts* compiled by Marie Louise Göllner (1975); 5. *Le catalogage des enregistrements sonores* rédigé par Simone Wallon, Kurt Dorfmüller, avec la collaboration de Yvette Fédoroff and Virginia Cunningham (1983).

2. *The New Grove Dictionary of Music and Musicians,* 2nd ed. edited by Stanley Sadie; executive editor John Tyrrell.–London, Macmillan, 2001, sub voce Handel (vol. 10).

3. See the corresponding authority file record of the Deutsches Musikarchiv in Berlin at http://pacifix.ddb.de:7000/SET=2/TTL=1/PPN?PPN=310084954.

4. The Italian reference tool is *Dizionario enciclopedico universale della musica e dei musicisti,* edited by Alberto Basso, Torino, UTET, 1983-1990, in 8 volumes and 1 appendix.

5. *Code international de catalogage de la musique.* vol. 1, 1957, p. 36-45; vol. 2, 1961, p. 45-46; vol. 3, 1971, p. 28-34; vol. 4, 1975, p. 24-26.

6. ISBD(PM): International Standard Bibliographic Description for Printed Music.–2nd rev. ed.–recommended by the Project group on ISBD(PM) of the International Association of Music Libraries, Archives and Documentation Centres (IAML), approved by the Standing Committees of the IFLA Sections on Cataloguing and Information Technology.–München: Saur, 1991.

7. Barry S. Brook and Richard Viano, *Thematic Catalogues in Music.* 2nd ed.–Stuyvesant, NY: Pendragon Press, 1997. (Annotated Reference Tools in Music, 5).

8. *Code international de catalogage de la musique.* vol. 4, *Rules for Cataloguing Music Manuscripts*, 1975, p. 29-31.

9. AMDV see http://www.marciana.venezia.sbn.it/admv.htm.

10. RISM *Musikhandscriften nach 1600: CD-ROM*, 9. ed., München, Saur, 2001. First edited as CD-ROM in 1996; RILM *MuSe: Music Search*, NISC, first edited as CD-ROM in 1996.

11. RILM http://www.rilm.org, RISM http://rism.stub.uni-frankfurt.de and RIPM http://www.nisc.com/ripm/default.htm are available by NISC. RILM is also available in OCLC FirstSearch.

12. Working Group on Uniform Titles for Manuscript Collections other than Liturgical. Reports by Mireille Geering in «Fontes Artis Musicae» v. 40 (1993), no. 1, p. 57; no. 2, p. 151-152; v. 41 (1994), no. 2, p. 207-208; v. 42 (1995), no. 2, p. 184-185.

13. The Working Group on the Exchange of Authority Records was first proposed by Sherry Vellucci.

14. *The Development of the VTLS/Virtual Music Module and Multilingual Cataloguing.* (Stefano Cavaglieri, Swiss National Sound Archive, Lugano, Switzerland), IAML Conference, Genève, 2 September 1997.

15. *Multi-lingual Online Catalogue System: LS/1 Library System at the Kunitachi College of Music.* (Mari Itoh, Aichi Shukutoku University, Nagoya, Japan), IAML Conference, Berkeley, 7 August 2002.

APPENDIX. Table of Proposals Submitted to the Permanent UNIMARC Committee of IFLA (2000-2001)

Field	Name	Proposal description
036	Music incipit	New field for the description and coding of incipit in music manuscripts
105	Coded data field: Language material, monographic	New codes added to include music, religious texts and librettos
125	Coded data field: Sound recordings and music	New codes added to include different formats of music presentation, a subfield added to code multiple formats; field definition extended to include music manuscripts
128	Coded data field: Form of composition and key or mode	Full revision of codes for the form of composition, a subfield added to codify key or mode; subfields for the description of medium of performance moved to a new field (145)
140	Coded data field: Manuscript and antiquarian–general	New positions and codes added to include manuscripts data: watermark, illustrations, and support material
141	Coded data field: Manuscript and antiquarian–copy specific attributes	New positions and codes added to include data related to the manuscript: state of preservation, stitching, composite, copy/autograph, binding
145	Coded data field: Medium of performance	New field allowing a fuller coding of ensembles, instruments, voices, and other performers
210	Publication, distribution, etc.	Field definitions extended to manuscripts
321	External indexes/abstracts/ references note	Field extended to include bibliographic citations in monographs
620	Place and date access	Field modified to allow access by place and date of performance/recording

The CERL Thesaurus File

Claudia Fabian

SUMMARY. The Consortium of European Research Libraries (CERL) builds up a Thesaurus file for place names, printers and publishers, and persons as related to early printing (1450-ca. 1830). The paper explains the creation and logic of the CERL Thesaurus and its function relative to the Hand Press Book Database (HPB) and as a separate information tool for early printing. It also points to the general problem of standardization and authority files and gives indications about further developments of this Thesaurus. *[Article copies available for a fee from The Haworth Document Delivery Service: 1-800-HAWORTH. E-mail address: <docdelivery@haworthpress.com> Website: <http://www.HaworthPress.com> © 2004 by The Haworth Press, Inc. All rights reserved.]*

KEYWORDS. Consortium of European Research Libraries, CERL, Hand Press Book Database, HPB, CERL Thesaurus, authority control in early printing, place names of early printing, printers and publishers in early printing, persons related to early printing, standardization of names in early printing

WHAT IS IT?

The Thesaurus file of the Consortium of European Research Libraries (CERL)[1] has been in existence since 1999 and is freely accessible on the Web.

Claudia Fabian is affiliated with Bayerische Staatsbibliothek.

[Haworth co-indexing entry note]: "The CERL Thesaurus File." Fabian, Claudia. Co-published simultaneously in *Cataloging & Classification Quarterly* (The Haworth Information Press, an imprint of The Haworth Press, Inc.) Vol. 39, No. 1/2, 2004, pp. 413-420; and: *Authority Control in Organizing and Accessing Information: Definition and International Experience* (ed: Arlene G. Taylor, and Barbara B. Tillett) The Haworth Information Press, an imprint of The Haworth Press, Inc., 2004, pp. 413-420. Single or multiple copies of this article are available for a fee from The Haworth Document Delivery Service [1-800-HAWORTH, 9:00 a.m. - 5:00 p.m. (EST). E-mail address: docdelivery@haworthpress.com].

413

It is built up and maintained by the Data Conversion Group in Göttingen. The format is UNIMARC "inspired." It consists of three parts: places, imprint names (printers and publishers), and personal names (authors, editors, translators). As it is still in the process of being built up, more extensions are under discussion, mainly for corporate authors as well as for owners and provenance information.

The CERL Thesaurus exclusively serves–as the choice of these entities indicate–early printing, which in the context of the activities of CERL means printing of the hand press book era, starting from the beginning (1450) until about 1830/40. The Thesaurus is thus closely related to the Consortium's Hand Press Book Database (HPB) containing bibliographic records for early printing coming from different European cataloguing projects in a single and "one stop shopping" database run by RLG. The construction of this database, which contains today 1.5 million records, was undertaken in 1991 with the vision to build up a common database for the printed European cultural heritage, a database that brings together (virtually) holdings and riches dispersed throughout all of Europe. Beyond its value for cataloguing and record reuse, the database is a highly specialised tool for research, allowing a global overview of Europe's printed past. The Thesaurus file is very much in the spirit and methods of this common European database approach, and thus may teach some methodologically important lessons on authority work.

CREATION AND LOGIC OF THE CERL THESAURUS

The name of this file, "Thesaurus," is not arbitrary. It points to a very important fact in European cataloguing and creation of authority files. According to our different national cataloguing rules, but perhaps beyond that, because of our different cultural traditions and, therefore, demands or expectations of our different-language-speaking publics, authority control on a national (or regional or local) level leads to different definitions of standard forms. A traditionally "universal" place, the holy city of Rome, is known by at least three concurrent name forms: Roma (Italian and Latin), Rome (English and French), Rom (German and Swedish). And this is an easy example. You find even more names for this place in the tradition of printing (Romae, etc.). There is no uniformity–not in history, not in language, not in cataloguing, and not in users' expectations. What authority control achieves is to define (again more or less arbitrarily) one of these forms as standard and list all variants as such in one record for this entity. With this modern instrument of cataloguing, in principle, the question of which form is the correct standard form should be overcome. A powerful implementation of any authority file in a cataloguing or better retrieval system should always allow the search under *every* form of name contained in the authority record. The standard form remains however relevant, for example, for display of the authority record or display of the form of the name in the context of a bibliographic record. We cataloguers, however, do not seem able to overcome our national expectations and let go of our "preferred form." The Thesaurus is a clever reaction to this fact. The Thesaurus is not prescriptive on the standard form. The CERL Thesaurus takes in all authority records created by any cataloguing agency and maintains the standard form proposed by each agency, indicating that it is the preferred form chosen by this or that agency. The aim is not to be prescriptive in the choice of the standard form. Therefore, the format of the CERL Thesaurus can be only inspired by UNIMARC, as UNIMARC only allows one standard form, not several parallel standard forms. But, even such an internationally clever policy decision does not overcome all problems. Which form should be displayed first when searching the Thesaurus? The decision was to take the first in alphabet—that is, at least, something on which cataloguers and users can agree. Yet the results are not always convincing: It means Rom for Roma, Parigi for Paris; although Firenze for Florence is the national form. Should we display instead the nationally correct form? For places and for most entities in Europe, this might create other problems for all those who have changed names or national borders. There is no satisfactory answer to this question of multi-language and multi-history. The computers are easier to be satisfied: they need a number which can be standardized, like the ISADN.[2] I am convinced that standard numbers in the field of authority will become inevitable. In principle, CERL would be the right body to assign a standard number to places, printers and publishers, and personal names of early printing.

The CERL Thesaurus brings together authority records created elsewhere. That is the whole philosophy of CERL: merging in one file originally separate files coming from different and independent projects. That is what CERL does in creating the HPB file. For internationally shared authority work, this methodology is interesting, as they experiment elsewhere with search engines, cross file searching, and here with physical merging. I am quite concerned about the rationality and effectiveness of this undertaking. Yet, it is feasible for this limited field of early printing. The difficulties lie less in merging the original files by application of as much machine power as possible than in the maintenance and machine updating of the records that is necessary to bring updated information from the original files into the CERL Thesaurus. In the actual state of the CERL Thesaurus, we can see that machine merging is feasible for entities like place names and we are quite confident on personal names. Still it needs a careful analysis of the original file and a careful mapping and duplication check to the existing file.

For the place name part of the Thesaurus, the file was built up by the file originally created by the Bavarian State Library published in book form.[3] The file was then enhanced by standardized forms from the Stockholm file[4] and it is planned to do the same for the forms of St. Petersburg.[5] These cases are not authority files, but lists of names giving the standardized form and a variant. The machine integration of the Cathedral libraries file[6] and of EDIT16[7] place names was less successful, but as they contain a relatively small number of records, integration will be done manually. In fact, manual updating may be more successful. Machine merging must be complemented by strong manual editing.

As for printers and publishers, the authority files of The Hague,[8] Paris, and Zagreb are already part of the CERL Thesaurus. This part should again be complemented by a file from EDIT16 and the Cathedral libraries. Here huge problems arise because the definitions of the standardized forms differ very much. Printers are sometimes considered as personal names, or sometimes as corporate bodies, and this is reflected in the differing structures of the names.

As for persons, the first imput in the CERL Thesaurus is also from the Royal Library in The Hague, and the authority records from ESTC (52,000 records) have been integrated. Here the next step will be to take in the relevant parts of the German Personennamendatei (PND) which is highly specialized in names of early printing, containing all the classic and medieval authors[9] and all names coming from the German conversion projects of holdings before 1850.

My guess is that the CERL Thesaurus will very quickly become an independent tool for intellectual editing of authority information on early printing. For building it up, all existing files can be helpful, but then it will lead its own life, which again makes sense in this particularly specialised area of cataloguing—whereas this is no solution for ongoing authority work.

FUNCTION OF THE CERL THESAURUS RELATIVE TO HPB

Why did CERL start to build up this Thesaurus file? There are two complementary reasons: one, lots of files arrived for inclusion into HPB, which, in their original context are based on authority files, mostly for names of persons (and corporate authors), and also for printers and publishers. This original link to an authority file is kept in the HPB by maintaining the number for linking, but is of no help in searching as this number lost its linking value. At the same time, all information contained in the authority records referred to is lost for HPB. Only the standardized form is maintained which is just one form. The second reason is HPB itself. This is a highly specialised information tool, and the information contained in the records is carefully maintained, mapped, and thus retrievable in a way that is most adequate for early printing, much better than what our OPACs can do. Still, this sophisticated retrieval cannot overcome, by itself, the different traditions of cataloguing transported in the records. So the Thesaurus was meant to directly help users of HPB to find their way through the multiplicity of cataloguing traditions and to give them the best and most complete results for particular searches without asking them to provide the entire intellectual work (like knowing all variants of a place name).

For the time being, the decision is *not* to implement any new linking structure from the CERL Thesaurus record into the HPB. The CERL Thesaurus remains a completely separate database, even run on a different system and in another continent. The so called "assisted search" takes the user of the HPB into the CERL Thesaurus. The user-identified record and all (relevant) name forms are transported into the HPB to perform a more complete search. At first sight, this is fine and gives better retrieval results. Still, I am not convinced that this is the final answer to the search problems in HPB. Some of them cannot be overcome without a firm linking structure.

Three examples taken from the place names may illustrate my doubts:

- Homonymous names create huge problems and falsify the retrieval results. A simple search with the place name Frankfurt gives 9,265 titles, the assisted search with Frankfurt, Main shows 16,515 titles and with Frankfurt, Oder, 16,515 titles. An assisted search with only Frankfurt gives 20,003 titles.
- Homonymous name variants create the same kind of confusion, e.g., Lugdunum is a variant for Lyon and for Leiden (Lugdunum Batavorum). A simple search with Lyon gives 5,930 titles, the assisted search shows 25,744 titles, among them those for Leiden when a variant form with Lugdunum is used.
- Fictitious place names cannot be used for the assisted search facility. A fictitious name like 'Eleutheropolis' can be used for several real places or fictitious names of the type 'Rom i.e. Schwabach' and would give wrong search results as all imprints published in Rome would be included.[10]

FUNCTION OF THE CERL THESAURUS
AS A SEPARATE INFORMATION TOOL

The true value of the CERL Thesaurus may be found in itself–in a tool that gives us the possibility to bring together and to edit authority information for early printing in a single and authoritative environment and maybe even scientific context. This also allows for unique possibilites of adding value by joining different information tools, all concerned with early printing.

There are already some examples. The place name part of the CERL Thesaurus was built up on the basis of a publication done by the Bavarian State Library in 1991 which needed reediting. The reediting is done inside the CERL Thesaurus and profits from the enhancement through other files. We now try to build up this file systematically. A limited number of entities is to be taken into account and we can do editorial work by using and extracting names from reference sources that do exist and often come from the 19th century (a time where specialised authority work must have also been very much undertaken). Reediting this file means supplementing missing names relevant in the field of early printing, adding about 900 new places. Reediting also means finding alternative name forms, indicating reference sources, and giving other relevant information about the place. A particular concern is to give information on fictitious place names so that the place name Thesaurus file can develop into a precious tool for information on places of early printing. One major aim is to supplement this reedited place name file with the information on geographic coordinates contained in the Getty Thesaurus of Geographic Names. This will be done by machine procedure once our name file is complete enough to include as many relevant names as possible. With these coordinates, we can create an electronic map which would free us from the historically horrible question of country codes and perhaps give a better result to research queries like "French imprints of the 16th century."

Geographic historical information is also provided by other projects not limited to the history of printing. Bavaria, for instance, creates an electronic tool for its regional history.[11] Why not link this information to records in the CERL Thesaurus so that you can switch from one instrument into the next?

One of these adding value methods is already reality inside the CERL Thesaurus. After searching a place name,[12] you may wish to see all printers and publishers working at this place. The tool for that is in place–it is achieved through internal linking between the place name and the printers' and publishers' file. It depends on the fact that a place name is contained in the imprint name record. Not all incoming files have this feature, and manual editing is necessary to provide reliable information.

The imprint name records also allow for further connections. Here we have started to explore the possibility of linking into the rich Italian projects of digitization of printers' or publishers' devices (e.g., in the context of EDIT16). Although this information would not directly lead to the edition in which this device was found (as is done inside the original projects), it would give further information useful in the context of early printing.

Last, but not least, that would be an appropriate place to host or connect the important information of printing characters, which for the time being is contained in very valuable traditional volumes–which may become digitized and thus serve an old need in a new form.

As for personal names, the situation may be different. Here, the national agencies may be much closer to the maintenance of information, but still, why not imagine one of my favorite projects, linking the name records of classical and medieval authors as contained in PAN and PMA, and which really belong to all of Europe (if not beyond), to the digitized copies of those reference sources quoted in the records? It would often help to identify the correct authority record for an author. In this area the allocation of a standard number would also be of great value, because again, the discussion of which entry form is the best will never end, and prescription is not the right method.

In conclusion: presenting a paper on the CERL Thesaurus gave the opportunity to consider a work in progress and to talk about reuse, reorganisation, and adding value to existing work on authority control. I firmly believe that authority work is the way we can better disclose the richness of the bibliographic universe to those who need our services. We must do this in a sensible way, joining our forces, making the best of what exists, and learning from the experiences of each other. For this, this conference gave us an ideal opportunity, which I enjoyed very much.

ENDNOTES

1. For all information about the Consortium and its activities cf. http://www. cerl.org.

2. International Standard Authority Data Number.

3. Druckorte des 16. bis 19. Jahrhunderts: Ansetzungs- und Verweisungsformen / erarb. von der Bayerischen Staatsbibliothek.–Wiesbaden: Reichert, 1991.–XIII, 258 S.

4. Swedish national bibliography for the 17th and 18th century.

5. National Library of Russia, St. Petersburg, early book holdings of the library.

6. Cathedral libraries catalogue: Names of printing towns, cf. http://www.bibsoc. org.uk/cathlibs/towns/.

7. cf. http://www.edit16.iccu.sbn.it.

8. Short-Title Catalogue Netherlands, 1450-1800 (STCN).

9. Personennamen der Antike: PAN; Ansetzungs- und Verweisungsformen gemäß den RAK / Erarbeitet von der Bayerischen Staatsbibliothek. Autorisierte Ausgabe.–Wiesbaden: Reichert, 1993.–XXVI, 613 S.–(Regeln für die alphabetische Katalogisierung; 7) e Personennamen des Mittelalters = Nomina Scriptorum Medii Aevi = Personal Names of the Middle Ages: PMA; Namensformen für 13000 Personen gemäß den Regeln für die Alphabetische Katalogisierung (RAK) / Bayerische Staatsbibliothek.

Redaktionelle Bearbeitung Claudia Fabian.–Zweite erweiterte Ausgabe.–München: Saur, 2000.–XIII, 696 S.

10. In the Thesaurus records these fictitious variants ("other forms of names") are separated from the other variants ("variant forms of names"). For assisted searching, they are not taken into account.

11. Bayerische Landesbibliothek online, Ortsdatenbank.

12. Button: "including imprint names."

The German Name Authority File (PND) in the Bavarian Union Catalogue: Principles, Experiences, and Costs

Gabriele Messmer

SUMMARY. This paper gives a short overview of the library situation in the Bavarian Library Network and the authority files used in German libraries. It deals with the implementation of the authority file for personal names into the Bavarian Union Catalogue and the experiences in using it. Finally, it looks into costs and benefits of the use of authority files in the Bavarian Network Catalogue. *[Article copies available for a fee from The Haworth Document Delivery Service: 1-800-HAWORTH. E-mail address: <docdelivery@haworthpress.com> Website: <http://www.HaworthPress.com> © 2004 by The Haworth Press, Inc. All rights reserved.]*

KEYWORDS. Bavarian Library Network, German name authority files, authority file for personal names, costs and benefits of authority work

First of all, I will give you a short overview of the library situation in the Bavarian Library Network and the authority files used in German libraries. The

Gabriele Messmer is affiliated with Bayerische Staatsbibliothek.

[Haworth co-indexing entry note]: "The German Name Authority File (PND) in the Bavarian Union Catalogue: Principles, Experiences, and Costs." Messmer, Gabriele. Co-published simultaneously in *Cataloging & Classification Quarterly* (The Haworth Information Press, an imprint of The Haworth Press, Inc.) Vol. 39, No. 1/2, 2004, pp. 421-427; and: *Authority Control in Organizing and Accessing Information: Definition and International Experience* (ed: Arlene G. Taylor, and Barbara B. Tillett) The Haworth Information Press, an imprint of The Haworth Press, Inc., 2004, pp. 421-427. Single or multiple copies of this article are available for a fee from The Haworth Document Delivery Service [1-800-HAWORTH, 9:00 a.m. - 5:00 p.m. (EST). E-mail address: docdelivery@haworthpress.com].

next two parts of my presentation deal with the implementation of the authority file for personal names into the Bavarian Union Catalogue and the experiences in using it, and finally, I will look into the costs and the benefits of authority files in the Bavarian Network Catalogue.

THE LIBRARY SITUATION
IN THE BAVARIAN LIBRARY NETWORK

In Germany there are six library networks. Because of the federal system of the country, they are autonomous units and their respective organizational structures vary considerably. One of the oldest and biggest is the Bavarian Library Network. Its beginnings date back to the nineteen-sixties. At the time, several new universities were founded in Bavaria, and they felt the need to cooperate, especially in cataloguing. The off-line union catalogue was started in the seventies, and since 1983, there has been an online catalogue with 95 participating libraries today. In this union catalogue, you find nearly 9.5 million title records with approximately 24 million holding records and about 5.1 million volumes of periodicals.

The largest and most important library is the *Bayerische Staatsbibliothek*, a universal research library with a wide range of special collections such as the Department for Manuscripts and Rare Books, the Music Department, the Department for Eastern European Literature, and the Department for Maps and Photographs. The *Bayerische Staatsbibliothek* holds more than 8.2 million items and adds about 220,000 new items a year to its collection. With its approximately 40,000 current periodicals and newspapers the *Bayerische Staatsbibliothek* is second only to the British Library in Europe. Together with the Deutsche Bibliothek Frankfurt and the State Library in Berlin the *Bayerische Staatsbibliothek* is part of a kind of "virtual" German National Library, and against this background fulfils many tasks for the German library community. So it is the backbone of cataloguing in Bavaria and partner of all the authority files in Germany.

In addition, there are 10 university libraries, 20 libraries of universities of applied sciences and quite a number of special libraries, smaller state and regional libraries, and the libraries of the Bavarian ministries and authorities. All of these libraries together form the Bavarian Library Network, and they all use the Bavarian Union Catalogue. Union Catalogue in this context does not mean a union catalogue in the sense of, for example, OCLC. It is just a catalogue in which all libraries use one and the same title record (including subject headings). They only have to add the local data for their own libraries.

AUTHORITY FILES IN GERMANY

The first authority file used in German libraries was the authority file for corporate bodies. It was initiated in 1973 by the three most important German libraries, the Staatsbibliothek in Berlin, the Deutsche Bibliothek, Frankfurt, and the *Bayerische Staatsbibliothek*, when those three libraries put together their records for corporate bodies and thus formed the "Common Authority File for Corporate Bodies," the so-called *Gemeinsame Körperschaftsdatei* (GKD). The libraries in Berlin, Frankfurt, and Munich still share the central editorial work. In 1997, the Austrian Library Network became the fourth partner of the GKD. Today most of the German libraries use this authority file and constantly add new records.

With the German national journals and serials database (*Zeitschriftendatenbank*, ZDB), another important project was started in 1973. The first task in building up the database was to gather information on all holdings of journals and serials in German libraries. Since 1989, German libraries have created records for journals and serials directly in the ZDB and have downloaded them into their respective union catalogues. Today, most of the libraries of the Bavarian Network are ZDB participants.

The beginnings of the authority file for subject headings (*Schlagwortnormdatei*, SWD) date back to 1988. The SWD contains subject headings in a controlled form and is used by many German and Austrian libraries. Nearly half of the new records are contributed by the Bavarian Library Network.

Creating records for personal names is one of the basic tasks of cataloguing. In the Bavarian Network Catalogue, for about 70% of the records, the main entry is a personal name. Particularly, the names of persons from antiquity, the Middle Ages, and early modern times are often difficult to standardize. Therefore, librarians prefer to have reference books–and nowadays reference databases–where they can find personal names in standardized and reference forms and ideally enriched with data and other information on the person in question.

The creation of an authority file for personal names (*Personennamendatei*, PND) in Germany started in 1989. At first, the Deutsche Bibliothek put together the name headings of two conversion projects, one located in the *Bayerische Staatsbibliothek*, the other in the State and University Library in Goettingen. In the following years, many more names were added to the authority file, for example, all the names of the Deutsche Bibliothek.

In the German Authority File for Personal Names there are two types of records:

- records for non-individualised names, and
- records for persons, e.g., individualised names.

Individualisation in this context means that qualifiers are added to the name, for example, personal dates (birth, death, etc.) or other brief suitable terms. This is necessary to distinguish between identical names or to mark persons with a personal name only. At present, this authority file consists of approximately 2.1 million records. About 630,000 of these are individualised records, 1.5 million are non-individualised. The *Bayerische Staatsbibliothek* is one of the principal editors of the authority file for personal names.

THE IMPLEMENTATION OF THE AUTHORITY FILE FOR PERSONAL NAMES IN THE BAVARIAN NETWORK CATALOGUE

From the beginning of the German Authority File for Personal Names, the Bavarian libraries wished to have an authority file as part of their own union catalogue. They especially wanted to be able to do central corrections in the online database. But it took nearly ten years before an authority file was implemented in the union catalogue of Bavaria.

The Bavarian Network Catalogue is a multi-file database. There is a common file for titles, including the records for journals and serials and subject headings, a second file for the records of corporate bodies, and quite a number of files for the local data of the network libraries. Personal names were part of the title records file, but the standardized and reference forms had to be keyed in manually each time. In 2000, another file was created, the authority file for personal names. A task force of the Bavarian Library Network, including members of its IT Department, started in 1999 to develop a plan and a programme for achieving this goal.

First of all, the new file had to be established in the network database. In a second step, new functions had to be implemented in the union catalogue, allowing the possibility to create new records for personal names or to correct and delete existing records. Then all records of the German Authority File for Personal Names were imported into the Bavarian Authority File. At the same time, the weekly supply with records from the Frankfurt file started.

Next, selected records from the union catalogue of the Library Network of the South-West of Germany *(Südwest-Verbund)* were loaded into the new Bavarian Authority File. In this process, every record was checked. When there was a title with an identical standardized form in the Bavarian Union Catalogue, the respective name record was put into the Bavarian Authority File. All other records were turned away.

At this time the first training took place in the *Bayerische Staatsbibliothek*. All librarians of the Bavarian Network were invited to get to know the new authority file and to learn the new functionalities.

The next step—and I think the most interesting one—was to take the personal names out of the title records and to put them into the Bavarian Authority File. There were intense discussions between librarians and IT specialists as to how to put this into practice. Finally, the following procedure was agreed on:

1. At first, every title was analyzed. Then, the standardized forms of the personal names were compared with the standardized forms in the Bavarian Authority File:

- If there was only one identical name the title was combined with this name.
- If there were several names, the title was combined with a non-individualised name.
- If there was no non-individualised name, a new record was created.

2. If no suitable record was found, an artificial form of the name was generated. In this form, capital letters and diacritics were ignored and the first names were written in one single string. In addition, another form was created: the second forename was shortened and any other forenames were ignored. Then, the name was compared once more with the authority file on the basis of a similar combination method as I explained before.

3. If no name was found, a new record was created in the Bavarian Authority File, and this new record was combined with the title. Thus, nearly 1 million new records were added to the Bavarian Authority File.

Before this procedure started, some more new functions had to be implemented in the network catalogue, for example, the function for putting together two name records. More training took place in order to inform librarians about the new structure of name data.

To build up an authority file was a long-term process and to maintain it takes a lot of time and manpower. It was a long and sometimes straining path from the first visions of a Bavarian Authority File for Personal Names to its realization. Many people had to discuss ideas, to set up plans, to reject those very plans, and to make compromises, but today we have an instrument that is useful for the librarians as well as for the patrons.

EXPERIENCES

The Bavarian Authority File contains records from various sources, controlled records of the German Authority File, and records added by Bavarian libraries. The records of the German Authority File are brought into the Bavarian database weekly and, in certain cases, they replace the Bavarian ones. In addition, records are created automatically when foreign data are put into the Bavarian Network Catalogue. These records are non-individualised ones, of course.

Today the Bavarian Authority File for Personal Names holds more than 4.3 million records, 2.1 million records coming from the German Authority File, and 2.2 million "Bavarian" ones. Like in the German authority file, 630,000 of them have individualising information.

The records can be distinguished according to different marks and grades. The controlled records from the German Authority File, for example, receive grade 8, which means that no librarian in the Bavarian Network can correct or delete them. This must be done in the national authority file itself. Records that were created from titles of the Bavarian Network receive grade 4, which implies that they can be corrected, deleted, or put together with other records.

Today it is no longer possible to simply write a name into a title field, but you have to combine the title with a record in the authority file. To work with the authority file for personal names has become part of the daily routine for Bavarian librarians today. But, there are some problems to be solved in the coming years. In the German cataloguing rules for descriptive cataloguing–called RAK–there are no rules for the individualisation of names like in the Anglo-American cataloguing rules (AACR). There were some efforts to introduce individualisation, but they haven't been successful yet. I think first of all we have to discuss the benefits and disadvantages of the individualisation of all names. Nearly 70% of the names are combined with only one single title. So we have to ask ourselves: Is it really necessary to search for individualising data, because it is very costly. Records without additional data are not any worse, and in many cases they are sufficient.

Another question will be how to combine regional, national, and international authority files and the online communication with these databases. I am sure this will lead to interesting and exciting discussions in the next years.

COSTS AND BENEFITS OF THE AUTHORITY FILE FOR PERSONAL NAMES

The *Bayerische Staatsbibliothek* is one of the backbones of authority control in Germany and the leading editing library in the Bavarian Network. Records from the Bavarian State Library built the foundation of the German Authority File for Personal Names. In addition, the PAN (Personal Names of the Antiquity) and the PMA (Personal Names of the Middle Ages) originated in the *Bayerische Staatsbibliothek*. Today the Munich library is responsible for editing the names of persons who died before 1911 and for names of Eastern European countries. In 2002–as in the years before–a quarter of the new records of the German Authority File were created by librarians of the *Bayerische Staatsbibliothek.*

Though the library is one of the main partners in authority work and has invested a lot of work since the beginning, it cannot ignore the costs of authority work. In times of smaller budgets, it is more and more difficult to give good reasons for expensive tasks like editing authority files. Therefore, we have to ask about the value of authority files for everyday work in libraries. In *Bayerische Staatsbibliothek*, 6 librarians or 1 1/2 full-time equivalents are engaged in the authority file for personal names. A few years ago, a study analyzed costs in *Bayerische Staatsbibliothek.* So we have rather reliable data about the costs of authority work. I would like to illustrate it with the example of the authority records for personal names.

In 2002, 15,502 new authority records for personal names were created–7,817 for the national authority file and 7,685 for the Bavarian one–and 5,929 were corrected. The costs for 1 1/2 persons amounted to about 71,500 Euro. So every new record or correction costs 3.34 Euro.

Creating new records is an expensive task, but it is cheap to re-use records created in a cooperative authority file–especially difficult cases like names of ancient and medieval persons and of princes, kings, etc. In the Bavarian Union Catalogue, there are records from different sources, as I already mentioned, based on different rules (RAK, AACR, and some other special rules) and originally written in different formats (MAB, the German library format, or MARC 21). It is necessary to have controlled access points so that our patrons can find titles in a heterogeneous catalogue too. I don't dare to predict the future of the Authority File for Corporate Bodies, but I am sure that the authority files for personal names will play an important role in future cataloguing. The *Bayerische Staatsbibliothek* will participate in the Virtual International Authority File (VIAF) project, a co-operative project of the Deutsche Bibliothek and the Library of Congress. The aim of the project will be "exploring virtually combining the name authority files of both institutions into a single name authority service."

Project InterParty:
From Library Authority Files
to E-Commerce

Andrew MacEwan

SUMMARY. InterParty is a project that aims to develop a mechanism that will enable the interoperation of identifiers for "parties" or persons (authors, publishers, etc.–persons and corporate bodies in library authority files) across multiple domains. Partners represent the book industry, rights management, libraries, and identifier and technology communities, united by their perception of a common benefit from interoperation in terms of access to "common metadata" held by other members to improve the quality of their own data. The InterParty solution proposes a distributed network of members who provide access to "common metadata," defined as information in the public domain, sufficient to identify and distinguish the "public identity" of a person. At a minimum the InterParty network would provide access to multiple domains of data about persons, including multiple library authority files, author licensing data files, etc. It will also add value by providing a facility for linking records between different data files by means of a "link record." Link records will assert that an identity recorded in one database is the same as

---

Andrew MacEwan is affiliated with the British Library.

[Haworth co-indexing entry note]: "Project InterParty: From Library Authority Files to E-Commerce." MacEwan, Andrew. Co-published simultaneously in *Cataloging & Classification Quarterly* (The Haworth Information Press, an imprint of The Haworth Press, Inc.) Vol. 39, No. 1/2, 2004, pp. 429-442; and: *Authority Control in Organizing and Accessing Information: Definition and International Experience* (ed: Arlene G. Taylor, and Barbara B. Tillett) The Haworth Information Press, an imprint of The Haworth Press, Inc., 2004, pp. 429-442. Single or multiple copies of this article are available for a fee from The Haworth Document Delivery Service [1-800-HAWORTH, 9:00 a.m. - 5:00 p.m. (EST). E-mail address: docdelivery@haworthpress.com].

Digital Object Identifier: 10.1300/J104v39n01_11

another identity recorded in another database. Linked data will be mutually enriching and therefore more reliable and supportive of accurate disambiguation of persons within and between databases. InterParty has potential to develop a common system that supports both the emerging needs of e-commerce and the traditional requirements of library authority control. *[Article copies available for a fee from The Haworth Document Delivery Service: 1-800-HAWORTH. E-mail address: <docdelivery@haworthpress.com> Website: <http://www.HaworthPress.com> © 2004 by The Haworth Press, Inc. All rights reserved.]*

KEYWORDS. InterParty, common metadata, public identities, InterParty links, rights management, book industry, identifiers

ORIGINS AND OVERVIEW OF THE PROJECT

When I was asked to give a presentation on the work of the InterParty project the working title that first occurred to me was "From library authority files to e-commerce." This seemed to capture the thought that we were pushing boundaries by applying the familiar principles and benefits of library authority files to the management of e-content by working in co-operation with publishing and trade sectors for whom authority control is not a familiar notion. On reflection I think it is a more accurate reflection of the key drivers of the project to reverse the caption to read "From e-commerce to library authority files." For in fact this is a project initiated by people working in the trade sector who have identified a "problem" and seen part of the solution as pre-existing in library authority files. I hope to show in this presentation that, although InterParty is not a library-led project, it does offer to open up potential new partnerships that would greatly benefit authority control work in libraries.

What is the InterParty project? It is a project, funded by the European Commission (EC), that aims to develop a mechanism that will enable the interoperation of identifiers for "parties." The term "party" is simply a useful term with which to draw together the disparate types of identities responsible for the creation of intellectual property or "content," such as authors, composers, performers (including groups), producers, directors, publishers, collecting societies, and even libraries. The project brings together partners from the book industry, people involved in rights management, libraries, and identifier and technology communities; all of whom share a common interest in the accurate identification of "parties" in relation to "content" for varying purposes. Specifically the partners are: EDItEUR (the coordinating partner, a European organisation founded by European Federations of Library, Booksellers and

Publishers Associations to coordinate the development, promotion and implementation of EDI in the books and serials sector); the British Library; the Royal Swedish Library; IFLA; Book Data (a leading supplier of bibliographic data to all sectors of the book supply chain in the UK); Kopiosto (a leading copyright agency operating across all the creative media sectors in Finland). U.S.-based partners, not funded by the EC, are: the Library of Congress; OCLC; the International DOI foundation and CNRI (Corporation for National Research Initiatives).

The original idea for the project was an outcome of another EC project <indecs> (Interoperability of Data for eCommerce Systems).[1] <indecs> was similarly concerned with transactions in content and how they can be effectively controlled in a web environment. In its analysis <indecs> proposed that descriptions of content, transactions, and descriptions of rights are all inextricably linked, and recognised that accurate descriptions of content are the core on which the rest is based. Consequently the key outcomes of that project were the definition of a generic data model and the promotion of mapping to that model from specific sector models. The <indecs> model is the foundation for the ONIX Data dictionary that is now the international standard for representing and communicating book industry product information in electronic form.

Central to the <indecs> view on the need for interoperability of metadata about resources was the recognition that a critical part of that metadata is accurate identification of authors, creators, etc. The project left this as unfinished business in the form of a proposal that further work should be undertaken to develop a system for linking existing person identifiers through a Directory of Parties. It is this proposal which InterParty is taking forward and which will complete the picture of interoperable metadata required to support discovery of resources, discovery of rights ownership, negotiation of agreements, payment of royalties and other potential applications. These are substantial goals!

So it is important at this point to emphasise that the InterParty project is aiming at this stage to deliver no more than a working Demonstrator–an Alpha system–not a working network. The project is funded to run for only 12 months and it will effectively aim to provide a proof of concept that can be demonstrated to potential members of a future live network. The key goals for the project are the specification and building of the demonstrator system (this will simulate the interoperation of a network of participating databases); and the development of a business model and governance proposals for a real-world implementation. Supporting these two key goals will be an analysis of existing data models, such as those already underpinning the databases of author licensing agencies and library authority files; the development of an interoperable party metadata model; and an analysis and resolution of any potential privacy and security issues that might arise.

That is the overview of the project in terms of its origins, aims, and goals. It is now time to look in more detail at the path that leads from problems in e-commerce to library authority files.

THE InterParty ANALYSIS

The starting point of the InterParty proposition is the recognition that there are already plenty of existing databases containing metadata about people and organisations and these serve to accurately identify "parties" within their own context. At the present time most of these databases are entirely independent of one another, following different approaches to identification and involving different schemas and formats. Even within sectors, differences in standards are an obstacle to sharing metadata–a problem very familiar to the library sector. We can also appreciate from a library perspective the historical path which has led to independent "data silos." In the past the need for such a level of inter-connectivity was neither apparent nor easy to achieve.

Today the growth of the Web has highlighted the need for metadata which can "travel" across these standards and systems barriers. Again the InterParty analysis concerns barriers to communication across many different sectors with much greater diversity between them than the barriers that exist between libraries internationally, but the arguments are the same. Sharing metadata about parties would improve efficiency, it would improve effectiveness of communication, and it would support navigation between domains and services on the Web. The difference is that the level of barriers that exist between sectors in terms of lack of standardisation is much greater and this in turn links to the different business requirements of different sectors.

From a library perspective the key business requirements are simply an extension of our standard requirements for authority control: access to new sources of metadata with which we can enrich and improve the quality of our own authority files. Ready access to useful additional sources of data already held elsewhere in the wider trade sector would also provide a quicker, potentially more efficient, means of resolving identification problems: is author X the same as author Y? It is easy enough to see that benefits to libraries would be similar in other sectors, for instance in terms of service to end users. A retailer would be able to better support user requests for information on all the recordings of a particular composer, e.g., the recordings of John Williams–but which John Williams? Such requirements are not commercially critical and so from the InterParty perspective they are noted as requiring a reasonable degree of certainty of identification.

By contrast any organisation involved in rights management will require access to sources of metadata that will support business transactions. In the most extreme case this may involve trusting the metadata in an authoritative record for a given "party" with a view to using the data to ensure a payment is made to the right person at the right address. Such requirements involve a very high degree of certainty of identification.

The InterParty proposition is that these disparate business requirements nevertheless converge on a common need for accurate metadata to support the identification of parties. Benefits in terms of quality and efficiency would be gained for members of a cross-sector network because there is a common functional goal in all the databases: the unique identification and disambiguation of parties. Although the goal of unique identification takes on a sharper degree of importance for commercial purposes it remains a common qualitative goal for all sectors.

Having established a common benefit that can be derived from inter-operation, how does InterParty intend to resolve the inherent problems? The fundamental aim of InterParty is to develop mechanisms that will link the existing, disparate databases currently used in different sectors to record and control the identification of parties. InterParty will therefore be a "membership" network of InterParty members or IPMs and these will comprise organisations with metadata to share, and identification schemes to support. Specific membership criteria will need to be defined as part of the Governance model. Members will join InterParty because they perceive a common benefit from interoperation, at the very least in terms of access to "common metadata" held by other members to improve the quality of their own data. Potentially, the development of links between different databases will also support automated machine-to-machine "transaction."

Members will be able to derive new identities on their own databases from other IPMs but InterParty itself will not originate new "party" records. Individuals and organisations ("parties") will only be identified within the Inter-Party network if information about them appears in one or more sets of data created or held by an InterParty member.

The InterParty network or system will provide a "resolution service," a single point of access to the multiple databases on the network. Each database will comprise its own "namespace"–the metadata context within which entities are uniquely identified. Each "namespace" on the network will make available to the network a specified subset of "common metadata" sufficient to disambiguate each identity within its own namespace, excluding where necessary any data that must be restricted for reasons of confidentiality.

To define the "common metadata" required, InterParty draws upon the definition of metadata used in the <indecs> project: "an item of metadata is a relationship that someone claims to exist between two referents." For instance a relationship between a name and a variant form of that name, or between a name and a date of birth. Note that a key part of the definition focuses on who makes the claim of a relationship. In library authority files source of information can give crucial validation to a record, e.g., a letter from the author. Some databases within the InterParty network may be able to provide more of this kind of validation or "authority" than others. All the member databases will already express many such relationships. The InterParty network will add a new layer to these by enabling new relationships to be expressed and recorded as InterParty "Links," e.g., "Person X in Namespace A is the same as Person Y in Namespace B."

Affirming this new level of metadata will require effort and judgement. Although it may be possible to automatically generate or propose many links on the basis of algorithms this is not being developed for the demonstrator system. Potential links will also be identified in the course of each IPM using the network to derive information to confirm or validate the relationships in their own databases. By recording the discovery of relationships between identifiers in different namespaces InterParty will ensure that the effort is not wasted but is made available to all on the network for future reference.

To make this new information available will require a basic format in which an "InterParty Link" can be expressed. In principle the link information could be held locally within IPMs as part of the common metadata set, or it could be held centrally in a separate InterParty Link Database. For the purposes of the demonstrator the project will simulate the latter model. This will require further analysis before confirming the approach best suited to a scaled up working system.

COMMON METADATA AND PUBLIC IDENTITIES

The main task being addressed for the demonstrator is the definition of the metadata required for the InterParty model. It is on this issue that InterParty begins to cover ground familiar to library authority files. The fundamental requirement is that members will need to provide access to sufficient metadata to achieve disambiguation between parties with shared or similar attributes, and also collocation of the same party when they have different attributes, e.g., John Williams the composer is distinct from John Williams the classical guitarist who is the same as the John Williams who formed the group Sky. How much metadata is sufficient will depend on the context. If a given database only contains a record for one John Williams then the name itself is a unique identifier and no other defining metadata is required (although it may be useful to record some in the event of future additions to the database).

Because InterParty is potentially dealing with databases that contain metadata about people that may be commercially sensitive or just private, it has defined the "common metadata set" in terms of information which is in the public domain. By focussing on this subset of information it becomes clear that actually what we are dealing with in identifying parties is, in the case of real individuals, a construct of the real persons underlying them. This construct InterParty has termed the Public Identity.

An individual person may have one or more public identities, most obviously in the case of authors using one or more pseudonyms. The notion of a "public identity" is similar to the concept of a "bibliographic identity" which has been defined as a key entity in the current draft of the FRANAR data model for name authorities. The question of whether someone has more than one "Public ID" is a matter of "functional granularity." Although pseudonyms provide a useful example of the concept a Public ID is not the same as a name since more than one name may be associated with the same public identity. Sometimes, relationships between Public IDs are not public, but become so, for example, Ruth Rendell and Barbara Vine. And sometimes, two or more people may share the same Public ID, for example, Nicci Gerrard and Sean French writing as "Nicci French." This, too, may or may not be publicly known.

KEY DEFINITIONS

To clarify this further, here are some of the key InterParty definitions around the concept of public identity.

- *Party*: An individual or organisation involved in the creation or dissemination of intellectual property
- *Public Identity*: An identity that is associated with and is used publicly by a party (or a group of parties)
- *Public Identity Identifier (PIDI)*: An identifier assigned to a public identity by an IPM and designed to be unique within the domain of that IPM: a PIDI may be a number, or it may be a controlled form of name (e.g., in a library name authority system)
- *InterParty Link*: An assertion about a relationship between two PIDIs in two different IPM domains–i.e., between two public identities

InterParty is concerned with asserting relationships between Public Identities in different namespaces. Within the InterParty network each Public

Identity will require a Public ID Identifier (PIDI) which will comprise a combination of identifier for the namespace and a unique identifier within that namespace. InterParty Links will express relationships between PIDIs in different namespace domains in the InterParty network. Each PIDI will represent a set of "common metadata" which the IPM owner of that namespace is prepared to make publicly available over the network.

What should be provided as "common metadata" will depend on the agreement of the InterParty members and will depend, critically, upon their willingness to share data currently available only to their own users with a wider network of "foreign" users not related to their core business or purposes. The minimal requirement is for a practicable set of data elements that is sufficient for the purposes of disambiguation and which can be regarded as in the public domain. At this stage the project is proposing a set of data attributes for the common metadata set and validating them with potential InterParty members through a combination of questionnaire and workshop sessions.

PROPOSED COMMON METADATA SET

The current list of data elements comprises the following:

PIDI

>The unique ID, comprises Namespace:identifier
>Identifies the IPM and the Public Identity
>Must be persistent, though the associated metadata will typically change

Name

>The name(s) by which a Public Identity is known
>Name types may include: Preferred (standard) form; Known variants; Former names–with dates

Events

>Significant events and their dates, and places where applicable
>e.g., Birth, Death, Incorporation (for a corporate Public Identity)

Works

>Works which with Public Identity is associated, represented by title accompanied by date and role of Public Identity if known

Roles

Roles typically performed by the Public Identity or spheres of activity–not just directly in relation to works
e.g., novelist, conductor, footballer, politician–with dates where appropriate

Relationships

Relationships with other Public Identities
e.g., has collaborated with X, has illustrated books written by Y, in same band as Z

Affiliations

Formal or official positions held by Public Identity
e.g., Professorships, and memberships in organisations, societies, etc.

InterParty Links

Access to the Links is key element of Common Metadata

There are some conceptual difficulties with relating some of these attributes to a Public Identity as defined. Many of the attributes relate more properly to real persons than to public identities as defined. Such attributes may be considered to relate to the public identity insofar as they have been made publicly available in the course of that "identity" releasing a work of intellectual property. This can be problematic with regard to attributing dates of birth, etc., to pseudonyms considered as discrete public identities. Normally the extension of an attribute from the underlying real person to one or more of their public identities will be a simple transference but in extreme cases a pseudonymous identity may take on a life of its own. Nicci French, whom it has already been noted is the Public Identity representing the collaborative output of two real persons, has gathered some real-world attributes in a recent advertisement for their latest thriller: "Nicci French's bestselling novels are The Memory Game, Killing Me Softly, etc. *She lives in Suffolk!*"

Once the Common Metadata set has been agreed upon, we will need to define rules and appropriate format conventions (currently being defined in a draft XML schema). The more standardised the Common Metadata (in terms, for example, of controlled "values") the higher its value–but the higher its cost. The extent to which the "common metadata" will need to adhere to common forms of semantic or syntactical expression will depend on some, as yet undecided, issues concerning a real-world implementation of the system. If the primary use of the network is direct human access and interpretation of data on a case-by-case need, then only limited standardization will be required. If large-scale algorithm-based linking operations are to be run, there may be a requirement for more standardized data.

Finally it cannot be expected that all IPMs will be able to provide metadata for all the proposed categories. Currently, the only mandatory elements are expected to be the PIDI and at least one name. This is the minimal practicable data on which links will need to be based but clearly more data than that will be required to inform either human or algorithmic decisions about links.

INTERPARTY LINKS

Let us now look in more detail at the InterParty Links. As already indicated this is the added-value category of metadata that the InterParty network proposes to offer.

An InterParty Link is the assertion of a relationship between two Public Identities, represented by PIDIs. Any InterParty member (IPM) may propose a Link provided that they own one of the PIDIs that is being established in the Link. The link may then be endorsed or disputed only by the IPM that owns the other PIDI proposed in the Link. Any other IPM may add comments to the record but only the two IPMs that own the namespaces concerned may make or modify the assertion of a relationship. The assertion of a link between two PIDIs is held in a single record. For the purposes of the demonstrator project, the relationships expressed in an Assertion will be restricted to "is," "is complex" and "is not." The record structure is defined so that other relationship values can be added in the future if required. For now other relationships, such as this company is the owner of that company, will be supported only within the databases of individual IPMs.

The relationships are being kept to the level of simple functional equivalence. So PIDI 1 "is" PIDI 2 asserts that PIDI 1 and PIDI 2 have a functional and reciprocal equivalence for the purposes of InterParty.

PIDI 1 "is not" PIDI 2 asserts that PIDI 1 does not have a functional equivalence with PIDI 2 despite appearances.

In order to keep the relationships simple a third type of complex equivalence has been defined to cover a variety of more complex situations that cannot fit into these first two categories.

PIDI 1 "has a complex relationship with" PIDI 2 asserts that PIDI 1 has a partial equivalence or complex relationship with PIDI 2 that is not necessarily reciprocal.

This "is complex" relationship is designed to handle the different ways in which IPMs may hold records for public identities, parties, and names in certain circumstances. For instance, IPM A assigns a single PIDI for Ruth Rendell, with a note that Barbara Vine is a pseudonym of Ruth Rendell; but IPM B assigns separate PIDIs (i.e., separate records) for both Ruth Rendell and Barbara Vine (with or without an internal assertion between them). It cannot be said that IPM A's Ruth Rendell/Barbara Vine "is" IPM B's Ruth Rendell, although there is a relationship. This is expressed as "complex."

There are numerous other circumstances where it cannot be assumed that all IPMs will take the same approach to identification–or even be aware there is an issue. Cases of an author using multiple pseudonyms or two parties combining under the guise of a single pseudonym, as in the Nicci French example, will all tend to fall into this category when different IPMs capture and describe these public identities in different ways. It is not proposed to define all the relationships covered by "Complex" any more precisely at this stage of the project but examples of complex relationships will be included in the demonstrator system.

Since the assertion of these three types of relationship will involve actions by different IPMs over time the Link records will also need to record the current status of the assertion being made. The status of a link will relate to how it is established and to what degree the two IPM owners have been involved. There are 4 status types:

- *"Proposed."* The relationship has been asserted by one IPM owner only.
- *"Authorised."* Concurring assertions have been made by both IPM owners.
- *"Disputed."* Assertions have been made by both IPM owners but they do not concur.
- *"Inferred."* Generated automatically based on inference from "is" relationships only.

Although the primary mode of making and editing links on the demonstrator will be manual it was felt useful to build in a further category of automatically generated links. These are "inferred" links that can be derived from assertions of the type, PIDI 1 "is" PIDI 2. Where a PIDI has become involved in more than one link of this kind it will be possible to infer further relationships. So where PIDI 1 "is" PIDI 2, and PIDI 2 "is" PIDI 3, the system can infer that PIDI 1 "is" PIDI 3.

The current draft outline of the Link record which is proposed for the InterParty demonstrator contains the following elements:

DRAFT OUTLINE OF A LINK RECORD

Link ID

>   Unique identifier for the Link Record

PIDI 1 (Namespace:Identifier)

>   Identifier of Public ID

PIDI 2 (Namespace:Identifier)

>   Identifier of Public ID

Link relationship

>   Code indicating nature of the relationship asserted, i.e., "is," "is not" and "is complex"

Link status

>   Value indicating level of trustworthiness of the link, i.e., "Proposed," "Authorised," "Disputed," "Inferred"

Link method

>   Manual or automatic

Link creation/update timestamp

>   Timestamp indicating when the record was created or last updated

Owner Assertion composite

A group of elements which record each Owner IPM's assertion about the Link, including

- Owner ID
- PIDI owned
- Owner assertion–used to set up/amend Link Relationship type above
- Assertion comment–notes field
- Asserted by–name of individual
- Assertion timestamp

Comment Composite

> A group of elements to allow other IPMs to add further notes/comments
> to the record without directly affecting status of the assertion

Although there are quite a number of data elements listed, the intention in
the functional specification is to make creation of a link as simple and effort-
less as possible, with automated defaults and simple routines for selecting and
entering the PIDIs into the Link Record. Further considerations for processing
links include a facility to automatically alert the IPM owner of the second PIDI
to the presence of a new link whenever an IPM initiates a link. Creating a link
will always trigger the start of a validation process. Only when both owners of
the link have asserted the presence of their PIDI in the link will the status of the
Link become fully authorised. To allow flexibility it will not be mandatory to
complete the validation process but not to do so will weaken the authority or
trustworthiness of the link. It will also be possible to reverse the authorisation
if required, for instance if new information calls it into question.

Finally the links themselves will be retrievable via their record control
numbers (Link IDs) or via the PIDIs within the links. It is assumed the value of
such searches will grow as the universe of proposed and authorised links
grows on the InterParty network. Further uses of such control numbers within
the domains of individual IPMs are a matter for speculation and are not a part
of the InterParty system. But it is possible to imagine InterParty Link IDs gaining a value in their own right as reference points to a network of metadata concerning an individual Public Identity.

CONCLUSION

At the beginning of this paper I emphasised that the InterParty project is a
demonstrator project due to complete on a short timescale–by mid-2003–in
order to offer a proof of concept simulation that will illustrate the potential
value of a real world implementation. The key questions will be answered after the demonstrator is complete. Who will want to join InterParty? If a network is established, will members really want to invest time in creating and
editing links, or will it be seen as just a search service?

It is likely that a real world implementation will have to address the question of automated, large-scale production of links by means of algorithms in
order to provide the InterParty added value as an early benefit. What remains
certain is the level of interest in the problem that InterParty has set out to address. The basic benefits of authority control are clearly perceived as benefits

that are needed outside the library sector. The goal for InterParty is to offer a realisable solution to the problem that is relatively cheap because it is based on interoperation and cooperation, not on the creation of a new standard. I see two main potential benefits to support the engagement of library authority files in an InterParty network. There will certainly be a benefit in terms of access to new realms of metadata that can enrich our own authority work. A further benefit may also derive from content producers and publishers using data (names or IDs) that is already linked to library authority files through the network. In the end, as is the case with all cooperative proposals, success is likely to depend on a few key players coming on board at the outset to make the initial investment.

REFERENCE

1. http:\\www.indecs.org.

Commercial Services
for Providing Authority Control:
Outsourcing the Process

Sherry L. Vellucci

SUMMARY. This paper examines the commercial services available for providing authority control in online catalogs. It identifies common reasons cited by libraries for outsourcing authority control and examines in-depth the types of authority control services. These include retrospective cleanup of the authority and bibliographic files, ongoing authority control work for newly cataloged bibliographic records and previously cataloged records where headings have changed, and periodic file reauthorizations when there was a one-time retrospective authority control database cleanup, but the library did not contract ongoing authority control services. The three phases of the outsourced authority control process are discussed, including pre-processing, machine matching, and manual record review. Finally, reports produced by the vendors are mentioned and challenges for automated international authority control are discussed. *[Article copies available for a fee from The Haworth Document Delivery Service: 1-800-HAWORTH. E-mail address: <docdelivery@haworthpress.com> Website: <http://www.HaworthPress.com> © 2004 by The Haworth Press, Inc. All rights reserved.]*

Sherry L. Vellucci is affiliated with the School of Communication, Information and Library Studies, Rutgers University.

[Haworth co-indexing entry note]: "Commercial Services for Providing Authority Control: Outsourcing the Process." Vellucci, Sherry L. Co-published simultaneously in *Cataloging & Classification Quarterly* (The Haworth Information Press, an imprint of The Haworth Press, Inc.) Vol. 39, No. 1/2, 2004, pp. 443-456; and: *Authority Control in Organizing and Accessing Information: Definition and International Experience* (ed: Arlene G. Taylor, and Barbara B. Tillett) The Haworth Information Press, an imprint of The Haworth Press, Inc., 2004, pp. 443-456. Single or multiple copies of this article are available for a fee from The Haworth Document Delivery Service [1-800-HAWORTH, 9:00 a.m. - 5:00 p.m. (EST). E-mail address: docdelivery@haworthpress.com].

http://www.haworthpress.com/web/CCQ
© 2004 by The Haworth Press, Inc. All rights reserved.
Digital Object Identifier: 10.1300/J104v39n01_12

443

KEYWORDS. Authority control, outsourcing, automated authority control, authority control vendors

INTRODUCTION

Throughout this conference we have discussed the importance of authority control, examined new perspectives, and looked at cutting edge projects for name, title and subject authorities within a variety of information communities. Much of the discussion focused on automated processes and data sharing. This paper will examine another side of automation, the commercial services that are available for providing authority control.

Before I begin, I will say that outsourcing, whether the entire cataloging operation or only specific parts of it, is a controversial issue. A review of the existing literature shows that for every librarian satisfied with the results of outsourcing the cataloging process, there are just as many who believe that outsourcing cataloging will have negative consequences for both the library and the profession. No matter where you stand on this politically-charged spectrum, understanding the authority control services that are currently available from commercial vendors will allow you to make informed decisions.

I'd like to begin with a definition of outsourcing. The American Library Association's Outsourcing Task Force defined outsourcing as "contracting to external companies or organizations, the functions of cataloging that would otherwise be performed by library employees." The ALA Task Force views outsourcing as a useful management tool when the decision to outsource is based on accurate information about the local library's needs (A.L.A. Outsourcing Task Force, p. 23). The Report cites the results of several different surveys that were conducted to discover the extent to which public and academic libraries outsource the cataloging process. One survey conducted in 1998 by the Urban Libraries Council discovered that of the public libraries in metropolitan areas that were surveyed, 61% responded that they outsourced some part of the cataloging process, although none used commercial service providers for more that 50% of the overall process (A.L.A. Outsourcing Task Force, p. 24). This survey, however, did not isolate authority control from the rest of the cataloging process. Another survey, which focused only on academic libraries was conducted by Bénaud and Bordeianu a year earlier. They found that 71% of Association of Research Libraries (ARL) libraries and 56% of the non-ARL medium-sized academic libraries outsourced some portion of the cataloging process. They also discovered that larger libraries outsourced more cataloging than smaller libraries. When authority control was isolated from the overall cataloging process, Bénaud and Bordeianu report that "over half of the libraries surveyed (55%) outsource or have outsourced authority control and of the remaining 45%, an additional 14% plan to do so in the future" (1998, chapter 4). All of this indicates that outsourcing cataloging in general, and the authority control process in particular, has become a common practice in both academic and public libraries in America.

So, why do librarians turn to commercial vendors to perform the authority work for their local catalog? Again, by examining the literature I found a group of core reasons that most libraries held in common.

- Authority control is labor intensive
- Staff efforts better spent elsewhere
- Controlled costs
- Increased efficiency
- Available expertise not otherwise resident in the cataloging unit
- Improved consistency and quality of the catalog database

Many factors influence these rationales, including budget cuts, staff cutbacks and the expanding need for professional librarians to cover other user services in the digital environment. Without the necessary staff, authority control is often neglected. If the required integrity of the catalog is to be maintained, many libraries must look beyond their internal resources. The good news is that this is one area where new computer applications excel in both speed and accuracy and advances made in recent technology make it significantly easier to outsource authority work (Bénaud and Bordeianu, 1998).

As in the rest of the corporate world, there have been startups, buyouts, and mergers among library vendors. The United States currently has at least six agencies that provide authority control services for libraries. These include Library Technologies, Inc., OCLC's WLN MARC Record Service (MARS), MARCIVE, Follett Software, Inc., Autographics, and Internet Systems, Inc. Of these, the primary vendors for large libraries are LTI, MARS, and MARCIVE.

TYPES OF AUTHORITY CONTROL SERVICES

There are several different types of authority control services offered by vendors, most of which are performed after the cataloging process is completed, because the vendor works from the bibliographic record. Vendor-supplied authority work is primarily accomplished using a batch processing method. This requires sending the databases to the vendor and often has a turnaround time of several weeks or months, depending on the size of the database. The vastly superior networking technologies now make it possible to send bibliographic records to vendors using a File Transfer Protocol (FTP). The variety of services offered includes retrospective cleanup; ongoing authority maintenance; and periodic updates.

Retrospective Cleanup

Many libraries turn to vendors to supply their authority control after, or as part of, a retrospective conversion project. Another prime time to outsource authority control is when the library migrates to a different online catalog or integrated library system. This is an ideal time to upgrade bibliographic records, update and correct access points, and provide a richer syndetic structure for the catalog.

When outsourced authority control is part of a retrospective conversion project, the authority control portion of the project is completed after the bibliographic records have been converted to machine-readable form and cleaned up. Because of the limitations of early technology and the expense of computer storage space, many libraries that converted their bibliographic records to MARC format in the early years of migration to online catalogs did not convert and integrate their authority files at that time. In these cases, the process of converting the bibliographic records is already completed and the retrospective authority control cleanup is performed to provide current and accurate headings linked to the authority records with their accompanying references. After the authorization of the bibliographic base file is completed, a copy of the individual library's authority file is retained by the vendor as a master file. This master file can then be used in ongoing authority maintenance.

Ongoing Authority Control

Improved technology has made uploading and downloading records between libraries and vendors an easy process, thus making it possible to provide vendor-processed authority control on an ongoing basis. As everyone knows, authority work never ends–new headings are added, existing headings are updated, changed or deleted and new conflicts between headings can arise. The ongoing aspects of authority control fall into two categories:

- Authority control for newly cataloged bibliographic records
- Authority control of previously cataloged records where headings have changed

Using a File Transfer Protocol (FTP) or a web-based user login, vendor-provided authority control for newly cataloged bibliographic records can be executed on a monthly, weekly or daily basis, depending on the volume of bibliographic records added by the library. Several vendors now offer overnight turnaround time and one vendor (LTI) offers authorities processing using FTP in as little as one hour for files up to 10,000 records. In addition, LTI offers a "Real-Time Authority Control" (RTAC) service based on client-server technology. RTAC allows the cataloger to send a bibliographic record during the cataloging process, have it authorized and returned to the cataloger along with all appropriate authority records almost instantly. However, the RTAC application must be integrated into local system record editors, and vendor systems have been slow to implement this integration.

In addition to ongoing authority control for newly cataloged materials, catalogers need to monitor changes to previously authorized headings. Authority vendors can provide a notification service to help with this process. The vendor tracks the updates and changes made to the national authority files used for the library's catalog and will automatically inform the library when changes are made to a heading that matches an authority record in the library's master file. New authority records for unmatched headings that were previously processed are also obtained. Most vendors allow you the option of deciding which updated authority records are included in your notification (e.g., only changes in 1xx headings, or changes in 4xx and 5xx fields, etc.). This notification can be done on a monthly, quarterly or yearly basis. The vendor will either send a replacement authority record accompanied by updated bibliographic records, or a report that lists which records have been changed, replaced or deleted so that changes can be made in-house by local staff. This will depend on the services that were contracted by the library.

Periodic File Reauthorizations

If the library has completed a one-time retrospective authority control database cleanup, but chooses not to contract immediately for ongoing authority control service and does not have the staff to maintain headings after the initial cleanup, periodic authorization updates for headings may be the way to go (e.g., every few years). This requires the library to export and reauthorize the entire bibliographic database (or a selected portion). The reauthorization process is much like a retrospective cleanup, except that the library does not have to resubmit the existing authority records; only the bibliographic records are required for this process. After the database has been reauthorized, the bibliographic records are reloaded into the local system database, then the new authority records are loaded and new indexes are built.

It should be noted that all of these processes involve not only the authority control vendor, but the integrated library system (ILS) vendor as well. Maintaining good relations with both vendors is important, especially if the ILS vendor must reprogram some software as in the case of LTI's RTAC, which must be integrated into the system record editor. The library should also verify with the ILS vendor that the necessary load tables are in place to allow the processed bibliographic and authority records to be loaded back into the library's local system.

THE VENDED AUTHORITY CONTROL PROCESS

Now that we have looked at the available services that an authorities vendor can offer, let's look more closely at the process itself. The first step is to develop a project profile that lists all of the library's specifications for each step of the processing. The project manager should work closely with the vendor representative to ensure that the specific available options and the pricing structure for each part of the project are understood. Most authority vendors are flexible in customizing the process to the specific needs of the library.

The linkage rate (i.e., matched headings) usually runs from 80% to 95% depending on the libraries conformance with national cataloging standards and the type of material. Pricing structures vary from vendor to vendor and from service to service. Vendors may charge a "per record processed" fee, a "per heading processed" fee, or a flat rate based on database size, with additional charges for customization. It is important to have some idea of the vendor's linkage rate for the library's database before beginning the project, for the costs for manual review and in-house review and cleanup will be affected by the percentage of records that were matched during the batch processing.

Preprocessing

Batch processing involves a series of cleanup operations. Prior to running your database against the national authority files, vendors will preprocess your headings using a variety of software programs to normalize the headings and eliminate common errors and inconsistencies. Several vendors offer the option of cleaning up the entire bibliographic record at this time as well. The library should be able to customize these corrections to take into account local cataloging practices. Some of the most common corrections include:

- Duplicate record resolution
- Abbreviation expansion
- Correction of common errors (typographic)
- Conversion of obsolete MARC subfields

- Deletion of canceled MARC subfields
- Direct-to-indirect geographic subfield conversion (LCSH)
- Pseudonym processing
- Updated General Material Designators (GMD)
- Initial article and filing indicator validation or correction
- Correction of spacing, capitalization, punctuation

A library can elect additional services for this preprocess stage. These might include conversion of non-MARC records to MARC21 format; provision of item level holdings conversion to accommodate local circulation systems; generation of smart bar code numbers and bar code labels; and bibliographic record enrichment such as table of contents and summary enrichment.

Machine Match Against Master Authority Files

Once the preprocessing cleanup is finished and the headings have been normalized, the bibliographic records are run against the master authority files selected by the library, comparing authorized and variant heading forms. The vendor also maintains a supplemental authority file developed from manual review of previous customer files for authorized headings that are not included in the national files. The master authority files commonly include:

- Library of Congress Name Authority File (LCNAF)
- Library of Congress Subject Headings (LCSH)
- National Library of Medicine Medical Subject Headings (MeSH)
- National Library of Canada Canadiana
- Library of Congress Children's Subject Headings (Annotated Card Program)
- Sears Subject Headings
- Genre Headings

When a match occurs, the authority heading record is linked to the bibliographic record heading. If the heading matches a *See* reference (4xx), the authorized heading (1xx) replaces the incorrect heading in the bibliographic record. When all possible headings have been matched to an authority record, they are inserted back into the bibliographic records, replacing the existing headings in each record. The final step in this part of the process is to extract all of the linked authority records and return them along with the processed bibliographic records, to be loaded back into the library's local system. The local system then builds its index tables from the controlled headings in the bibliographic file and the *See* and *See also* references in the authority records.

Libraries have several options for transmitting their files to the vendor. Most vendors can accept and produce output in the following formats:

- 9 track magnetic tape
- 4mm data cartridges
- 8mm data cartridges
- FTP transmission via Internet

Some vendors will also supply records for all levels of a hierarchical heading for which there are matches. For example, the following heading for Beethoven's Kyrie from the Missa Solemnis would generate the following three authority records:

Heading on bibliographic record:

Beethoven, Ludwig van, ǂd 1770-1827. ǂt Missa Solemnis. ǂp Kyrie.

Authority records generated:

Beethoven, Ludwig van, ǂd 1770-1827.
Beethoven, Ludwig van, ǂd 1770-1827. ǂt Missa solemnis.
Beethoven, Ludwig van, ǂd 1770-1827. ǂt Missa solemnis. ǂp Kyrie.

Manual Review and Correction

When the machine match is completed, the library must decide how to handle any remaining unlinked headings, i.e., those headings that did not match an authority record. The vendor will generate a report listing the unmatched headings, which can be used in-house for local manual review, or the library can elect to have a manual review performed by the vendor. A vendor manual review will lengthen the turnaround time for the project and can be very expensive. To determine the cost-benefit of paying for this labor-intensive review, the library should look at the percentage of headings that were linked. If the linkage rate is high and would be increased by only a few percentage points, it is probably not worth the expense (e.g., 94% linked by machine-processing plus 2% linked by manual processing). If the initial linkage rate is low, say 78%, and if an additional 15% can be linked through manual review, then manual review is probably worth the money. Therefore, the library should select a vendor that can give the highest linkage rate (90-95%) through machine processing. No vendor can provide a 100% linkage, so there will always be follow-up review and corrections on any processing project. The library should be prepared to allocate cataloging staff time to this type of clean-up when the records are returned.

Several different types of problems might be discovered by manual review. These include:

- Obvious typographical errors in names and subject headings
- Invalid terms in subject heading subfields
- Incorrect order of multiple surname and corporate heading elements
- Records that match multiple authority records
- Split headings

Mislinked headings will not be picked up by manual review, since linked headings, whether correct or not, are not reviewed manually. When the manual review is completed and corrections made, the bibliographic records with those headings are processed again against the national authority files to generate additional matches.

Reports

The reports provided by the vendor can be customized to the library's needs. They usually include the following lists of information:

- Full match on 1xx field
- Full match on 4xx field
- Unmatched headings
- Partially matched headings
- Headings that match multiple authority records
- Headings that have split
- Incorrectly used headings

Statistical reports can provide a database profile, which analyzes the data and reports on the characteristics of the file. Pre- and post-processing data will give the library information that is useful for predicting future costs and mass storage requirements. Other types of reports can include:

- Frequency counts for each material format type (music, AV, etc.)
- Holding library information
- Average size of a record
- Number of characters in largest and smallest records
- Number of fields per record summary

- Field use summary
  - Number of times a field occurs
  - Average number of times a field is used per record
  - Number and percentage of records in which field appears
  - Average length of each tag

In addition to these common reports the library should be able to request customized reports to meet its specific needs.

FUTURE PROSPECTS

This presentation on commercial services available for authority control provides background information for outsourcing and gives an overview of the process. I have focused on the vendors and processes that are now available in the United States and Canada, but I do not claim to know the state of commercially provided authority control here in Europe and elsewhere in the world. I do know that there are serious issues that must be worked out before authority control vendors can cope with the types of international authority control that we have discussed during this conference. Before we can begin to approach commercial processing using a virtual international authority file, the FRANAR issue needs to be resolved. Many interoperability problems must be solved, including issues of MARC/UNIMARC authority format harmonization, and methods that will allow libraries to use a variety of national authority databases for the matching process, and provide the flexibility to select the authorized form that is appropriate for the local users. Fortunately, interoperability issues are at the forefront of both researchers' and cataloging agencies' concerns and this can only help address many of the authority control issues. It may be that some of the authority control interoperability problems will be handled at the local level, but the commercial vendors must still play a major role. Perhaps the largest hurdle to overcome may be convincing vendors that authority control in an international arena is quite possibly the way of the future. One vendor with whom I spoke said that the concept of an international authority record had a certain "academic appeal," but based on historical and current world events he did not see evidence that a one-world vision was particularly successful. The idea of international authority control was of no concern to him and it was obvious that he was unaware of the work that has been going on among the national libraries and within IFLA. Fortunately, not all vendors feel this way, for they are critical partners in promoting and implementing automated authority control on the international level.

REFERENCES

American Library Association. Outsourcing Task Force. (2000). *Impact of Outsourcing and Privatization on Library Services and Management.* Robert S. Martin, Principal Investigator. Texas Woman's University School of Library and Information Studies. Retrieved January 4, 2003 from http://www.ala.org/alaorg/ors/outsourcing/.

Bénaud, Claire-Lise and Sever Bordeianu. (1998). *Outsourcing Library Operations in Academic Libraries: An Overview of Issues and Outcomes.* Englewood Colo.: Libraries Unlimited.

Lam, Vinh-The. (2001). "Outsourcing Authority Control: Experience of the University of Saskatchewan Libraries." *Cataloging & Classification Quarterly* 34 (2): 53-69.

Tsui, Susan L. and Carole F. Hinders. (1998). "Cost-Effectiveness and Benefits of Outsourcing Authority Control." *Cataloging & Classification Quarterly* 26 (4): 43-61.

APPENDIX 1

Selected Bibliography

"Authority Control Services." *Library Systems Newsletter* 9 (June 1989): 43-45.

Baker, Barry B. "Resource Sharing: Outsourcing and Technical Services." *Technical Services Quarterly* 16 (1998): 35-45.

Bechtel, J.M. "An Authority Control Alternative for Small Colleges." *College & Research Libraries* 53 (November 1992): 485-498.

Bénaud, Claire-Lise, and Sever Bordeianu. *Outsourcing Library Operations in Academic Libraries: An Overview of Issues and Outcomes.* Englewood CO: Libraries Unlimited, 1998.

Block, Rick J. "Cataloging Outsourcing: Issues and Options." *Serials Review* 20 (1994): 73-77.

Bolick, His-Chu. "Problems in the Establishment of Non-Unique Chinese Personal Headings with Special Reference to NACO Guidelines and Vendor-Supplied Authority Control." *Library Resources and Technical Services* 43 (April 1999): 95-105.

Burger, Robert H. *Authority Work: The Creation, Use, Maintenance, and Evaluation of Authority Records and Files.* Littleton, CO: Libraries Unlimited, 1985.

Calhoun, Karen, and Mike Oskins. "Rates and Types of Changes to LC Authority Files." *Information Technology and Libraries* 11 (June 1992): 132-136.

Dalehite, Michele I. "Vendor-Supplied Automated Authority Control: What It Is and How to Get It." *Law Library Journal* 81 (winter 1989): 117-129.

DeGennaro, Richard, D.P. Flecker and K.C. Young. "Positioning Harvard's Libraries for The Electronic Age: A Report on the Harvard Retrospective Catalog Conversion Project." *International Cataloguing and Bibliographic Control* 26 (October/December 1997): 92-94.

Duranceau, Ellen. "Vendors and Librarians Speak on Outsourcing, Cataloging and Acquisitions." *Serials Review* 20 (1994): 69-83.

Johnston, Sara Hager. "Current Offerings in Automated Authority Control: A Survey of Vendors." *Information Technology and Libraries* 8 (September 1989): 236-264.

Kascus, Marie A., and Dawn Hale, eds. *Outsourcing Cataloging, Authority Work, and Physical Processing: A Checklist of Considerations.* Chicago: American Library Association, 1995.

Lam, Vinh-The. "Outsourcing Authority Control: Experience of the University of Saskatchewan Libraries." *Cataloging & Classification Quarterly* 34 (2001): 53-69.

Libby, Katherine A., and Dana M. Caudle. "A Survey on the Outsourcing of Cataloging in Academic Libraries." *College & Research Libraries* 58 (November 1997): 556.

O'Neill, Edward T. "OCLC Authority Control." *OCLC Systems & Services* 10 (winter 1994): 40-58.

Secrest, Angela. "Automated Authority Control: Benefits and Pitfalls." *Iowa Library Quarterly* 26 (1989): 8-17.

Smith, P. "Book Vendor-Supplied Cataloguing: Impacts of Technical Services." *Colorado Libraries* 20 (fall 1994): 14-16.

Smith, Sally Gildea, and Jo Frances M. Calk. "Automated Authority Control <options to discuss with vendors>." *IOLS, Integrated Online Library Systems:* Proceedings 1992, New York, May 6-7, 1992. Medford, NJ: Learned Information, Inc., 1992.

Stone, Alva Theresa. "Vendor Processing and Local Authority File Development." *Law Library Journal* 81 (winter 1989): 131-141.

Taylor, Arlene G., Margaret F. Maxwell and Carolyn O. Frost. "Network and Vendor Authority Systems." *Library Resources and Technical Services* 29 (April/June 1985): 195-205.

Tsui, Susan L., and Carole F. Hinders. "Cost-Effectiveness and Benefits of Outsourcing Authority Control." *Cataloging & Classification Quarterly* 26 (1998): 43-61.

Wilson, Karen A., and Marylou Colver, eds. *Outsourcing Library Technical Services and Operations: Practices in Academic, Public, and Special Libraries.* Chicago: American Library Association, 1997.

Younger, Jennifer A. "After Cutter: Authority Control in the Twenty-first Century." *Library Resources & Technical Services* 39 (April 1995): 133-41.

APPENDIX 2

Authority Control Vendors

Note: The following are examples of authority control vendors. Authority control vendors will accept your bibliographic database on computer tape or FTP, use a computer program to match the access points against Library of Congress and other authority files, and return to you updated MARC bibliographic authority records that can be loaded into your system.

Auto-Graphics, Inc.
3201 Temple Avenue
Pomona, CA 91768
909-595-7204 (voice)
909-595-3509 (fax)
info@auto-graphics.com
http://www.auto-graphics.com/

Library Technologies, Inc. (Authority Express)
2300 Computer Avenue, Suite D-19
Willow Grove, PA 19090
800-795-9504 (voice)
205-830-9422 (fax)
LTI@LibraryTech.com
http://www.librarytech.com/

Marcive, Inc.
P. O. Box 47508
San Antonio, TX 78265
1-800-531-7678 (voice)
1-210-646-0167 (fax)
info@marcive.com
http://www.marcive.com/

OCLC/WLN
P. O. Box 3888
Lacey, WA 98509-3888
1-800-DIALWLN (voice)
360-923-4009 (fax)
info@wln.com
http://www.wln.com/

Internet Systems, Inc.
Division of LSSI (Library Systems and Services, LLC.)
20250 Century Boulevard
Germantown, MA 20874
800-638-8725 (voice)
301-540-5522 (fax)
lssi@lssi.com
http://www.lssi.com/

Follett
1391 Corporate Drive
McHenry, IL 60050-7041
800-323-3397 (voice)
815-344-8774 (fax)
http://www.fsc.follett.com/

Multiple Names

Lucia Sardo

SUMMARY. This paper tries to explain what a multiple name is and how it was and is used. The paper goes on with the examination of the treatment of multiple names in library catalogs, providing some examples from national libraries' OPACs, and with a preliminary analysis of the multiple names using FRBR attributes. *[Article copies available for a fee from The Haworth Document Delivery Service: 1-800-HAWORTH. E-mail address: <docdelivery@haworthpress.com> Website: <http://www.HaworthPress.com> © 2004 by The Haworth Press, Inc. All rights reserved.]*

KEYWORDS. Multiple names, authorship, shared pseudonyms

> Non avrò più nomi, mai più.
> Non legherò la vita al cadavere di un nome.
> Così li avrò tutti.
>
> –Luther Blissett, *Q*

In 1999 the novel *Q* was published, bringing to fame the name of Luther Blissett, already known to a less vast public (see Figure 1).[1] Other preceding

---

Lucia Sardo is affiliated with Università di Udine.

[Haworth co-indexing entry note]: "Multiple Names." Sardo, Lucia. Co-published simultaneously in *Cataloging & Classification Quarterly* (The Haworth Information Press, an imprint of The Haworth Press, Inc.) Vol. 39, No. 1/2, 2004, pp. 457-464; and: *Authority Control in Organizing and Accessing Information: Definition and International Experience* (ed: Arlene G. Taylor, and Barbara B. Tillett) The Haworth Information Press, an imprint of The Haworth Press, Inc., 2004, pp. 457-464. Single or multiple copies of this article are available for a fee from The Haworth Document Delivery Service [1-800-HAWORTH, 9:00 a.m. - 5:00 p.m. (EST). E-mail address: docdelivery@haworthpress.com].

FIGURE 1. Cover of *Q* by Luther Blissett

publications carried the name of Luther Blissett as their author. That name, which seems the name of a real author (and it is a real name, but not that of an author) or a pseudonym, represents instead a more complex reality, that of the so-called 'multiple names.'[2]

WHAT'S A MULTIPLE NAME?

'Multiple names' are tags that the avant-garde of the seventies and eighties proposed for a serial use. They are commonly real or invented personal names, which anyone can take on as an identity; the idea is to create a collective body of artistic works using the invented identity.

The first of these collective identities, was 'Klaos Oldanburg,' used by British male artists in the mid-seventies. A few years later, the American male artist, David Zack, proposed 'Monty Cantsin.' In the mid-eighties emerged the rival names of 'No Cantsin' and 'Karen Eliot.' There have been multiple names for magazines ('Smile,' originating in England in 1984) and pop groups ('White Colours,' first proposed in England in 1982). The idea is to create an open situation for which no one in particular is responsible, to re-examine and break down the western philosophic notions of identity, individuality, value, and truth.

The year 2000 saw the "ritual suicide" of Luther Blissett and the birth of Wu Ming, a new 'multiple name.' In Mandarin *wu ming* means "no name." Unlike the case of 'Pessoa,' where it is the single person who is manifested in a multitude of heteronyms, on the contrary in the case of the 'multiple names,' it is the collectivity, which contains the multitudes, and paradoxically becomes single.

The name is formalized, tending to be unique and uniform, but when we examine the categories for entities outlined in FRBR, we realize that the 'multiple names' do not enter into any of these. They do not belong to personal names nor to corporate names; they approach both of these categories but belong wholly to neither. This uncertain character gives rise above all to the formulation of the name as being in a direct or inverted form. With some timely reference work, obviously of a practical nature, the problem can be resolved (assigning as one wishes from the codification of a MARC field); the lack of uniformity of choice made initially by the BNI (National Library of Italy, Rome) and the BNCF (National Central Library, Florence) can only emphasize the uncertainty of the situation: BNI indexed it in direct form, BNCF both in direct and inverted form. Neither gave, nor do they today give qualifications. Luther Blissett is also the name, the real name, of a person; a qualification would not be inopportune, so as to avoid cases of homonymy. But what kind of qualification might be used?

A second problem emerges with the publication of the new novel *54* by Wu Ming (see Figure 2). (Who knows why the problem of the title *Havana Glam*, published as if by Wu Ming 5, and of *Asce di guerra*, was noticed or discussed by only a few?) The problem is one of cross-referencing between two 'multiple names.' Certainly it should be done, as the authors themselves maintain, but have the preceding problems been resolved? In my opinion, no.

Let us see the results of a research study undertaken this year in various OPACs.[3]

FIGURE 2. Cover for Wu Ming, *54*

MULTIPLE NAMES AND LIBRARY CATALOGS:
A FEW EXAMPLES

For the most part we can say that after an initial uncertainty, all too understandable, the inverted form is the form preferred by all the bibliographical agencies, with some deviations. I find irritating the fact that Luther Blissett Project is also accepted as an access point (some works were published with this name on the title page), even if one supposes that there are cross-references between this form and that of Blissett, Luther. So far we have not found cases of cross-referencing between Wu Ming and Luther Blissett. In Italy, the title *Havana Glam* has not been linked to Wu Ming 5, but only Wu Ming, which is not true in other countries (Bayerische Staatsbibliothek (BSB) and the Library of Congress (LC), for example). I remain perplexed, and I admit this reluctantly, upon seeing three authority records created by LC, as shown in Figures 3-5 (one of them is clearly wrong, but this is due to some false information to be seen on some works by Luther Blissett). On the other hand, LC's authority record for Wu Ming 5 is very accurate and informative (see Figure 6), even if, personally, I do not find the use of the term 'collective pseudonym' satisfactory for the case of Luther Blissett and Wu Ming. The Bibliothèque national de France (BnF) uses the form Blisset, with just one t, and this leaves us in doubt, since the usual form is generally with two t's, and BnF defines the nationality and language of the author as Italian. I maintain that that is a bit lim-

FIGURE 3. Authority Record from the Library of Congress Web Authorities for Luther Blissett, Author of *Q*

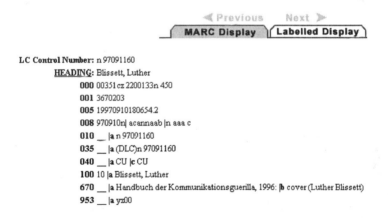

FIGURE 4. Authority Record from the Library of Congress Web Authorities for Luther Blissett, Author of *Handbuch der Kommunikationsguerilla*

ited for its possible use as an access point. It is banal to say this, but it is easier to criticize afterwards than to make the decisions at the time of operation.

Qualifications are lacking in all the examples analyzed.

What form has been chosen? 'Luther Blissett,' or 'Blissett, Luther,' or 'Luther Blissett Project' (some texts present this latter as author). In any case, has the form chosen been qualified, and if so, how? And 'Wu Ming,' 'Wu, Ming,' 'Wu Ming 5'? Shall we pretend we did not see the number? But the home page of the *Wu Ming Foundation* is explicit in the necessity of indicating more than

FIGURE 5. Authority Record from the Library of Congress Web Authorities for Luther Blissett Project

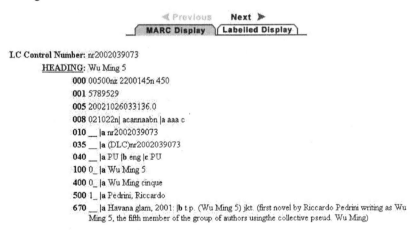

MARC Display | Labelled Display

LC Control Number: no 00001441
    HEADING: Luther Blissett Project
        000 00336nz 2200121n 450
        001 5010994
        005 20000108070145.0
        008 000107n| acannaabn |n ana c
        010 __ |a no 00001441
        035 __ |a (OCoLC)oca05132035
        040 __ |a ICU |b eng |c ICU
        110 2_ |a Luther Blissett Project
        670 __ |a Nemici dello Stato, 1999: |b t.p. (Luther Blissett Project)

FIGURE 6. Authority Record from the Library of Congress Web Authorities for Wu Ming 5

◄ Previous   Next ►
MARC Display | Labelled Display

LC Control Number: nr2002039073
    HEADING: Wu Ming 5
        000 00500nz 2200145n 450
        001 5789529
        005 20021026033136.0
        008 021022n| acannaabn |a aaa c
        010 __ |a nr2002039073
        035 __ |a (DLC)nr2002039073
        040 __ |a PU |b eng |c PU
        100 0_ |a Wu Ming 5
        400 0_ |a Wu Ming cinque
        500 1_ |a Pedrini, Riccardo
        670 __ |a Havana glam, 2001: |b t.p. (Wu Ming 5) jkt. (first novel by Riccardo Pedrini writing as Wu
            Ming 5, the fifth member of the group of authors using the collective pseud. Wu Ming)

one Wu Ming (considering the meaning of the name, the discussion seems paradoxical!). The Library of Congress presents 'Wu Ming 5' as author of *Havana Glam*, with a reference to the real name, but without connections to Wu Ming (see Figure 6). The Bayerische Staatsbibliothek does the same thing, without, however, a reference to the real name. Texts are available online of Wu Ming 1, Wu Ming 2, and Wu Ming 4, of which the real names are known. Cross references between all of the forms and with all of the real names? A new Ming dynasty?

PERSONAL OR CORPORATE AUTHOR?

Returning to the first problem cited, and that is, to the "hybrid" nature of 'multiple names,' we can make an analysis of the attributes of the personal entity and the corporate name presented in FRBR, while awaiting the results of the Working Group on FRANAR to verify which of these can be considered as valid. Above all, we see the attributes of the person as outlined in FRBR:

Name of person

Personal name heading–name sub-elements

Dates of person

Additions to the name–dates of birth, death, etc.

Title of person

Additions to the name–title of nobility, honor, address, etc.

Other designation associated with the person

Additions to the name–other additions

Only the first of these attributes, name, can be applied to 'multiple names.' The second, dates, can be applied only in the wider sense and only with reference to the date of "birth." The title or other designations are obviously so generic as to be almost universal in application.

The attributes of a corporate name, however, are the following:

Name of corporate body

Corporate name heading–name sub-elements

Number associated with the corporate body

Qualifier–number [of meeting, etc.]

Place associated with the corporate body

Qualifier–geographic name [place of meeting, etc.]

Date associated with the corporate body

Qualifier–date [of meeting, etc.]

Other designation associated with the corporate body

Qualifier–type of body [etc.]

In this case, beyond the attribute "name," only the place is partially applicable to 'multiple names.' One could indicate the place on a general level: nation, region, or more specific city in which the 'multiple name' is operative (for example, the country where the name is most used, or the locality where the name was first used, as far as this is possible to determine). We can consider them personal names as such, inasmuch as they are expressly declared to be that way (an oversimplified explanation, perhaps, but corresponding to the concept of the promulgators). Moreover, they do not have the specific characteristics of the definitions of corporate names. The fact that they deal with more than a single individual can approach the idea of a corporate name, but the results of the activity of the multiple name do not necessarily represent the aims of a corporate name, due to the obvious fact that there is no single corporate body with clearly defined aims; there is a basic philosophy which regulates the use of the name, but it would be more correct to say that the name is identified with a defined personality and ideas, that anyone can assume, and that anyone can alter. The works can be of performance, theater, works of literature, art, music, writings, journals; the absence of copyright means they can be freely reproduced and transformed by anyone who cares to. It would not be incorrect to allow for the conceptual insertion of a new entity, definable as a 'multiple name.' Its existence is documented. The difficulties it imposes are evident. It is almost impossible as things stand now, to make a realistic assessment of the growing visibility and popularity of such names.

ENDNOTES

1. It is of secondary importance that the names of the "real" authors of the novel were revealed later.

2. [*Editor's note: In AACR2, a 'multiple name' in this sense is considered a shared pseudonym (AACR2 rule 21.6D) and treated as if it represents a "person" entity, in FRBR terms.*]

3. This paper is based on some of the findings of my ongoing project about personal authorship. During 2003, I searched the OPACs of several European and North American national libraries and present here only the most significant results of that research.

Chinese Name Authority Control in Asia: An Overview

Lily Hu
Owen Tam
Patrick Lo

SUMMARY. This research paper provides an overview on the latest developments of Chinese authority control work implemented in Mainland China, Taiwan, Japan, and Hong Kong. In this research, a variety of authority databases developed by different national libraries and leading academic institutions are featured, together with detailed statistical data on coverage, size, and subscription rates of individual databases. Authority record samples collected from individual databases are also documented. This research study provides materials for discussions that can generate an increased understanding of the practical manifestations of authority control works carried out by different libraries among the regions of East Asia. It is hoped that the research findings documented in this paper can facilitate better cooperative cataloguing and resource sharing of Chinese/Japanese/Korean (CJK) materials among libraries on a global scale. *[Article copies available for a fee from The Haworth Document Delivery Service: 1-800-HAWORTH. E-mail address: <docdelivery@haworthpress.com> Website: <http://www.HaworthPress. com> © 2004 by The Haworth Press, Inc. All rights reserved.]*

Lily Hu, Owen Tam, and Patrick Lo are all affiliated with Lingnan University Library, Hong Kong.

[Haworth co-indexing entry note]: "Chinese Name Authority Control in Asia: An Overview." Hu, Lily, Owen Tam, and Patrick Lo. Co-published simultaneously in *Cataloging & Classification Quarterly* (The Haworth Information Press, an imprint of The Haworth Press, Inc.) Vol. 39, No. 1/2, 2004, pp. 465-488; and: *Authority Control in Organizing and Accessing Information: Definition and International Experience* (ed: Arlene G. Taylor, and Barbara B. Tillett) The Haworth Information Press, an imprint of The Haworth Press, Inc., 2004, pp. 465-488. Single or multiple copies of this article are available for a fee from The Haworth Document Delivery Service [1-800-HAWORTH, 9:00 a.m. - 5:00 p.m. (EST). E-mail address: docdelivery@haworthpress.com].

Digital Object Identifier: 10.1300/J104v39n01_14

KEYWORDS. HKCAN, NACSIS-CAT, Authority control work–Asia, Authority control work–Japan, Authority control work–Hong Kong, Authority control work–China, Authority control work–Taiwan, CNMARC, CMARC

INTRODUCTION

This research paper consists of five parts. Part I and II feature the Chinese authority files created by the National Library of China, as well as the "Chinese Authority Database" set up jointly by the National Central Library and the National Taiwan University Library. Part III is dedicated to the different authority control works and their latest developments implemented by the National Diet Library (Japan), "Toshokan Ryustu Centre," NACSIS-CAT operated by the National Institute of Informatics (Japan), and the MARC formats currently being used by the Waseda University Library (Tokyo). Part IV focuses on the working relations between "China Academic Library & Information System" and NACSIS-CAT. Part V is devoted to the "JULAC-Hong Kong Chinese Authority, Name (HKCAN)" Database established by the academic libraries in Hong Kong in 1999.

MAINLAND CHINA

In order to enhance precision in bibliographic retrieval and to meet the demands raised by document indexing, the National Library of China has recently compiled and created the following.[1]

- *"Chinese Classification Subject Thesaurus"* based on the *"Chinese Library Classification"*;
- *"Chinese Subject Thesaurus"*;
- *"Subject Thesaurus to Classification Corresponding List"*;
- *"Chinese Classification Subject Thesaurus Database"* compiled 120,000 subject authority records based on 800,000 keywords, synonyms, etc., collected from journal articles and bibliographic databases.

In order to provide standardization and format for authority control, the National Library of China also compiled the *"Chinese MARC Authority Format"* (trial edition) and *"Description Rules for Entries of Authority Data,"* on which to base the compilation of the authority databases.

"Chinese Ancient Author Database" has collected Chinese ancient individual authors and corporate bodies,[2] whose works have been handed down for

generations, from ancient times to 1911, and contains more than 40,000 entries. In recent years, the National Library of China's Rare Book and Special Collection Departments have also compiled a total of 11,000 records. Each record includes author's name, dates of birth and death, dynasty, place of birth, style and assumed name, family relations, imperial examination's position, official position, major accomplishments,[3] and representative works, etc.

A *"Modern Author Authority Database"* was also set up by the National Library of China. It mainly collects authority records of authors who had expanded works and corporate bodies since 1912. The records include authors' names (original names, writing names), dates of birth and death, nationalities, titles of works, authors' genders, birthplace, and position, etc. There are now more than 325,900 records in the database, featuring mainly personal names, corporate names, and title names. About 40,000 records were compiled in year 2001 (see Figure 1).

TAIWAN

In 1990, the National Central Library (NCL) and the National Taiwan University (NTU) Library jointly established a Chinese authority taskforce for tackling Chinese authority control in Taiwan.

Initial Setup. In June 1996, after having collected a total of 180,000 personal name authority records, and 10,000 corporate name records from NCL, plus another 30,000 personal names from NTU, the Authority Taskforce then began combining all of the collected records into a single authority file.

FIGURE 1. Authority Record Example of Author "白楊" from National Library of China (CNMARC)[4]

Control #	001		A9400245
Fixed-length data	100		$a19940205achiy0120#####ea
	152		$aBDM
Heading (Personal Name)	200	0	$a 白楊$c(女, $f1920~1996)
			$7ba$abai yang
General Public note	300	0	$a 著名電影演員. 湖南湘陽人. 主演劇目甚多, 主要有《十字街頭》,·《一江春水向東流》,·《祝福》等. 建國後任中國電影家協會副主席. 著有《落入滿天霞》,·《電影表演探索》等.
See From	400	0	$0 對於這個著者的著作, 見他的藝名: $6a05$a 楊成芳
	400	0	$6a05$7ba$ayang cheng fang
Cat. Source	801	0	$6CN$b 北圖$c19940205
Source Data found	810		$a 文化辭典

This authority file was later named the *"Chinese Name Authority Database"* (CNAD). The NCL records are created using the Chinese authority MARC (CMARC) format set out by Chinese libraries in Taiwan, whereas the NTU files use MARC 21 format for their authority data.[5] Once the database consolidation is completed, the new authority file will be made available on NBINet, with data searching and downloading functionalities provided via remote login. Such a setup will allow libraries around the world to share and make maximum use of this helpful cataloguing reference tool in the most convenient and speedy fashion.

Size of Existing Database. While CNAD's consolidation work still continues, the current Database contains slightly more than 420,000 authority records, featuring mainly personal names, plus a small number of group/corporate names.

Record Format/Standards. In order to ensure consistency of authority data, as well as retrieval precision, only one unique entry is created for each individual author. Authority records are built upon the CMARC originated in Taiwan, with other guidelines and principles set out by the CNAD Workgroup (see Figure 2).

Capabilities of Software System. The initial setup of the Database Software was completed in May 2001, and was officially entitled, *"Chinese Name Authority Database Workgroup (Taiwan)."* The CNAD Software is

FIGURE 2. Record Example of Author "賈恩紱" from CNAD

Control #	001	31834
Fixed-length data	100	$a19950621achiy09 ea
	152	$aCCR
Heading (Personal Name)	200 1	$a賈$b恩紱$f1866-1945?
See From	400 0	$aP'ei-ch'ing,$f1866-1945?
	400 0	$aSsu-i-ts'ao-lu,$f1866-1945?
	400 0	$aSsu-i-ts'ao-t'ang,$f1866-1945?
	400 0	$a思易草堂$f1866-1945?
	400 0	$a思易草廬$f1866-1945?
	400 0	$a佩卿$f1866-1945?
	400 1	$aChia,$bEn-fu, $f1866-1945?
	400 1	$aChia,$bP'ei-ch'ing,$f1866-1945?
	400 1	$aJia,$bEnfu, $f1866-1945?
	400 1	$a賈$b佩卿$f1866-1945?
Cat. Source	801 0	acwb中圖$c199506
Source Data found	810	$a中國近現代人物名號大辭典, 民82 :$b面 718
	810	$a定縣志. 台北市: 成文, 民58
	810	$aHis Tsao-Ch'ang hsien chih, 1987 :$bcaption (Chia En-fu)
General Cataloguer's note	830	$a天津人, 字佩卿; 室名思易草堂, 一作思易草廬

now equipped with basic capabilities, such as data searching/data retrieval, record maintenance, and downloading, etc. The CNAD Software also provides different internal codes and MARC formats which users can choose during record display and downloading. Trial use is also available for other collaborating or participating libraries. They may simply apply to NCL and seek permission for accessing the CNAD Database.

User Manual. In April 2002, both the *"CNAD User Manual,"* and the *"CNAD Software Maintenance Manual"* were made available in electronic format for the participating libraries' reference.

JAPAN

Currently, there are three different types of MARC formats being used throughout different libraries and research institutes in Japan, and they are as follows:

- JAPAN/MARC–provided by the National Diet Library (Japan).
- TRC/MARC–based on enhanced JAPAN/MARC format, and is provided by *"Toshokan Ryustu Centre,"* a commercial company in Japan. TRC/MARC is used mainly by public libraries.
- NACSIS-CAT (National Centre for Science Information Systems Cataloguing System)–a Japanese bibliographic utility developed by the National Institute of Informatics (Japan) (NII) whose data is used widely and mainly by academic libraries in Japan.

Further descriptions of the different MARC Formats used in Japan follow.

JAPAN/MARC (A)

The existing JAPAN/MARC Authority File (JAPAN/MARC (A)) was created and maintained by the National Diet Library (Japan), with coverage restricted to name headings only (see Figure 3). For exchange of records, the UNIMARC format is used. The current JAPAN/MARC (A) is available for sale in magnetic tape from the Japan Library Association or in CD-ROM format from Kinokuniya Co. Ltd. The latest version of CD-ROM is the year 2000 edition. The actual use statistics on NDL's JAPAN/MARC (A) are unknown.

TRC/MARC

According to the TRC corporate profile, TRC/MARC has been adopted by 70% of Japanese Libraries, and NACSIS-CAT also stores TRC/MARC in

FIGURE 3. Record Example in *Existing* JAPAN/MARC (A) Format from NDL[6]

```
001 00281976
005 19980130132800.0
100 $a19930726ajpny0112    da
152 $aNCR
210 02$6a01$a早稲田大学図書館
210 02$6a01$7dc$aワセダ ダイガク トショカン
210 02$6a01$7ba$aWaseda daigaku tosyokan
801 0$aJP$bNDL$c20001122
810 $a早稲田大学図書館和漢図書分類目録 11 東京 早稲田大学図書館 昭和16
911 $ag$ba
```

their referral database. The TRC Name Authority File is updated on a daily basis. The file is available in FTP, magnetic tape, and CD-ROM format, and is delivered to customers on a weekly basis. In addition to the TRC Name Authority file, TRC also uses a different type of MARC format, TRC/MARC, which is supposed to be an enhanced version of the original JAPAN/MARC format (see Figure 4).

NACSIS-CAT

NACSIS-CAT is the online cataloging system, which the National Institute of Informatics (Japan) provides.[7] The main purpose of the NACSIS-CAT is to construct a union catalogue of books and serials covering the whole country through cooperative data entry (shared cataloging) from the participating university libraries. This union database, complemented with useful authority data, prevents duplicate cataloguing work in libraries and facilitates the saving of labour and quicker processing. NACSIS-CAT can be accessed on the World Wide Web through the Webcat service.

Unique Characteristics of NACSIS-CAT and Its Authority Data

To be free from the restrictions posed by MARC structure, NACSIS-CAT provides both bibliographic and authority data in non-MARC format (raw data only). Member libraries may simply download or extract data from NACSIS-CAT and manipulate it according to their own in-house cataloguing practices afterwards. For members, authority data will be free of charge when downloading from NACSIS-CAT. However, in order to be compatible with NACSIS-CAT, participating institutes must first install the CAT-P (their own communication protocol) client software for cataloguing. Furthermore, NII also provides various in-house and overseas training programmes or work-

FIGURE 4. Authority Record Example from TRC/MARC

```
001      :110000737940000
005      :19920427
100    A :19920427AJPNY
152    A :NCR
200  1 7 :DB
       A :夏目
       B :漱石
       F :1 8 6 7~1 9 1 6
200  1 7 :DC
       A :ナツメ
       B :ソウセキ
320    A :小説家，英文学者
801  0 A :JPN
       B :TRC
802    A :国立国会図書館著者名典拠録，　Ｊ－Ｂｉｓｃ
825    A :MARC No. 74003058 夏目漱石全集 1 筑摩書房
```

shops for participating libraries on the specialized, latest developments related to NASIS-CAT's operations.

The coverage of NACSIS-CAT includes author names (see Figure 5) and uniform title authority files. In addition to Japanese and Western name headings, NACSIS-CAT also includes a large number of name headings of Chinese authors. Recently, they have also begun to introduce Korean headings with original script into this union database.

NACSIS-CAT Services on an International Scale

In order to raise the standard of science research, and to promote the distribution of science information on a global scale, NII is developing a number of international projects and co-operations to improve access to information processed by overseas universities and research institutes. Currently, 31 universities and research institutes in Europe and Asia participate in NII's Cataloging Systems project and provide access to the NACSIS-CAT services. These include major research libraries that have collections of Japanese language materials, such as the British Library, and other institutes devoted to research on Japan and East Asia. They have registered more than 270,000 books and serials (August 2002). In addition, the *"Science Information Exchange Project with China"* was initiated in 1998. NII has been assisting computerization of the catalogue records of the Beijing Center for Japanese Studies with the assistance of the Japan Foundation. For a full list of participants of NACSIS-CAT see Appendix IV.

FIGURE 5. Example of NACSIS-CAT's Name Authority in Non-MARC Format

```
<DA00151899>
HDNG:夏目,漱石(1867-1916)||ナツメ,ソウセキ
LCAID:DA00151899
TYPE:p
PLACE:牛込(東京)
DATE:1867-1916
SF:夏目,金之助||ナツメ,キンノスケ
SF:*Natsume, Siseki, 1867-1916
SF:Natsume, Sôseki
SF:Natume, Sôseki
SF:Natsume, Kinnosuke, 1867-1916
SF:Haruykos, Cocsxar
SF:Sôseki
SF:Nitsimah, Sisahki
NOTE:文化人名録による。
NOTE:EDSRC:夏目漱石 ; 寺田寅彦 ; 鈴木三重吉 ; 内田百間(筑摩書房, 1968)
NOTE:EDSRC:La porte : roman / Sôseki ; traduit du japonais par Corinne Atlan(Philippe Picquier, c1992)
NOTE:夏目漱石集(河出書房新社, 1965.8)
NOTE:切抜帖より / 夏目漱石著(春陽堂,1926.1)
```

Overall Statistics and Participating Institutes

More than 95% of Japanese colleges/universities are currently using NACSIS-CAT. As of March 1999, a total of 670 libraries had connected online to NACSIS-CAT for the sharing of bibliographic and authority data. And in September 2002, the total number of institutions using NACSIS-CAT reached 995 (see Figures 6, 7).

CJK Authority Control at Waseda University Library (Tokyo)

Currently, two different types of authority record are being used at Waseda University Library (Tokyo). In order to support data retrieval in original Japanese script, Waseda University Library has created its own unique authority record structure by executing the concept of repeating regular tags for non-roman data, as suggested in MARBI Discussion Paper no. 111. In fact, they are currently using triple 1xxs to represent different forms of Japanese data in both their bibliographic and authority records:

- 1st 1xx–Vernacular
- 2nd 1xx–Katakana transliteration
- 3rd 1xx–Japanese Romanization (Hepburn)

Meanwhile, Waseda University Library also subscribes to OCLC authority services for headings in romanized/Western-language form. For CJK authors, in order to facilitate easy identification, original Japanese script is introduced

FIGURE 6. Overall Statistics on NACSIS-CAT Participating Institutes[8]

Member Libraries/Types	Number
National Universities	97
Local Public Universities	73
Private Universities	461
Inter-University Research Institutes	14
Junior Colleges and Colleges of Technology	176
Others	174
Total	**995**

FIGURE 7. Statistics on NASIS-CAT Member Libraries

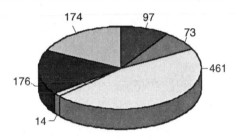

97 ■ National Universities
73 ▨ Local Public Universities
461 ☐ Private Universities
14 ☐ Inter-University Research Institutes
176 ■ Junior Colleges and Colleges of Technology
174 ▨ Others

in tag 667 for cataloguers' references. Currently, Waseda University Library is trying to merge these two different types of authority format into a single one, with the aim of facilitating comprehensive and concurrent retrieval of bibliographic records by the same author under one single search (see Figure 8).

CALIS AND NACSIS-CAT

Relationship between CALIS and NACSIS-CAT

A networked environment has greatly enhanced resource sharing and cataloguing of works between different libraries of various regions. CALIS (China

FIGURE 8. Examples of Chinese Authority Records Provided by Waseda University Library

```
A10022065              Last updated: 99-11-10 Created: 99-11-10 Revision: 1
01 ACODE1:  n        02 ACODE2:  -       03 ASUPPRESS:  -
04 005     19991028135143.0
05 008     991028      abb                           nnz n
06 100     |811|a林 語堂.|d1895-1978
07 100     |812|aリン．ユイタン.|d1895-1976
08 100     |813|arin, yuitan.|d1895-1976
09 400     |811|a林 語堂
10 400     |812|aリン．ゴドウ
11 400     |813|arin, godo

A10253804              Last updated: 02-08-21 Created: 01-11-15 Revision: 6
01 ACODE1:  n        02 ACODE2:  -       03 ASUPPRESS:  -
04 001     oca00379079
05 003     OCoLC
06 005     20011115111244.0
07 008     800226n| acannaabn          |a aaa ||| cz n
08 010     n  79147999
09 040     DLC|cDLC|dDLC|dNJP
10 053     PL2781.N2|cChinese
11 053     PR9470.9.L5|cEnglish
12 100   1 Lin, Yutang.|d1895-1976.
13 400   1 Yutang, Lin.|d1895-1976
14 400   1 Lin, Y[232]u-t[176]ang.|d1895-1976
15 400   1 Im, [280]0-dang.|d1895-1976
16 400   1 L[227]am, Ng[228][189] [163][189][225][188]ng.|d1895-1976
17 667     Tag 400 の Rin, God[229]o.|d1895-1976 (は和書の典拠レコード(Tag
           400)とバッティングするため削除．
18 670     Hu, S. China's own critics ... 1931.
19 670     His Igyodo es[230]o Kidokkyodoro, 1977.
20 670     His S[226][227]ong [179][242]ep. 1993: |bt.p. (L[227]am Ng[228][189]
           [163][189][225][188]ng (Lin Yutang))
21 670     Lun y[232]u shih ch[176]i ti Lin Y[232]u-t[176]ang yen chiu, 1993.
22 670     Lin Y[232]u-t[176]ang p[176]ing chuan, 1994:|bp. 7, 3rd group (Lin
           Yu Tang [in rom.]) p. 1, 5th group, etc. (b. 10-10-1895, Lung-hsi
           hsien, Fukien; d. 3-26-1976, Hong Kong)
```

Academic Library & Information System) now has more than 100 members subscribing to its various services. Within CALIS, there are a total of fourteen member institutions in China taking part in this joint cataloguing project on Japanese language materials. Each of these individual fourteen member libraries can also gain direct access to NII (Japan)'s NACSIS-CAT independently, as they are also required to contribute their own cataloguing data to NACSIS-CAT in return, via the use of CAT-P Protocol.

Currently, there are more than 22,000 bibliographic records in the Japanese language being held in CALIS. More than 90% of these Japanese bibliographic records originate from NACSIS-CAT. Japanese language records are downloaded from NACSIS-CAT at no cost to a member. The Peking University Library is one of the fourteen members of CALIS participating in this joint cataloguing project, and did not become a member until October 2000.

Until now, CALIS has only bibliographic records, and does not come with an authority database. However, the Japanese authority data is maintained while the corresponding bibliographic record is being downloaded, in order to facilitate CALIS in building its own authority database to complement the existing bibliographic data.

Although NACSIS-CAT contains cataloguing data in many different languages, Peking University Library currently downloads only Japanese language data from NACSIS-CAT, while relying on other databases for the cataloguing of foreign language materials. NII also provides training workshops for their NACSIS-CAT members at no cost. However, at Peking University Library, Japanese data cannot be uploaded directly onto their database, as it needs to go through a MARC conversion programme. Hence, NII's training workshops are not applicable in this case.

For both CALIS and NACSIS-CAT, flowcharts on the overall workflow for MARC format conversion are documented in Appendix V.

HONG KONG

In June 1998, Lingnan University Library (Hong Kong) organized jointly with the Department of Library and Information Science, Zhongshan University (China), the *"Joint Symposium on Library & Information Services"* in commemoration of the University's 30th Anniversary. The Symposium attracted over 200 scholars, librarians and library vendors from Mainland China, Taiwan, Singapore, North America and local institutions, etc. At the Symposium, there was a consensus that a regional network should be formed to enable cooperation and resources sharing among the four Chinese-speaking areas, i.e., Mainland China, Taiwan, Hong Kong and Macau. It was proposed that a Chinese Resource Sharing Workgroup (consisting of nine different member libraries from four regions) be formed to coordinate the development of the cooperative projects. Three cooperative projects were then proposed for consideration:

- Chinese Name Authority Database
- Multimedia Database on Dr. Sun Yat-sen
- Union Catalogue of Chinese Rare Books

HKCAN Project[9]

In January 1999, a group of academic libraries in Hong Kong agreed to set up among themselves the *"H*ong *K*ong *C*hinese *A*uthority, *N*ame (HKCAN)" Workgroup for establishing an authority database that would reflect the unique characteristics of Chinese authors and organizational names.[10] This project was spearheaded by both the Lingnan and Chinese University Libraries of Hong Kong, and aimed to build a Chinese name authority database with CJK scripts, with the goal modeled after the Programme for Cooperative Cataloguing: to improve and streamline authority-control operations in order to make them *"Better," "Faster,"* and *"Cheaper"* while producing *"More."*[11] At the 2nd HKCAN Meeting in May 1999, it was agreed that Lingnan University Library would serve as Convenor of the HKCAN Workgroup, while the Chinese University of Hong Kong Library would take up the responsibility of hosting the database itself (see Figure 9).

The establishment of the HKCAN Project was carried out in the following three parts/stages:

- Design of the HKCAN Authority Record Model
- Indexing and Display of Authority Records in the OPAC and its Linkage with the Bibliographic Database
- Setup of the HKCAN Database: development and maintenance of software and hardware.

After four years of intensive hard work, the HKCAN Workgroup finally completed the initial phase of database building, and its success has attracted international attention and recognition. The Project finally became a JULAC (Joint University Libraries Advisory Committee)[12] Project in the year 2001, and was officially renamed as the JULAC-HKCAN Database in the same year. The JULAC-HKCAN Database now contains over 100,000 authority records with original Chinese scripts, and the number of records is increasing at about 1,000 a month. On October 4, 2002, a one-day Opening Seminar was launched at the Host Institution (Chinese University of Hong Kong Library), to celebrate this special occasion with internationally acclaimed guest speakers from the United States, including representatives from the Library of Congress (U.S.), RLG, and the MARBI Multilingual Taskforce.[13]

Design of HKCAN Authority Record Model

Hong Kong is a bilingual society with both Chinese and English as the official languages. Many local authors publish in English, in addition to their first language, Chinese. Therefore, the biggest challenge for the Workgroup lay in identifying a solution that would support the comprehensive retrieval of bilingual publications under the same authors in a concurrent fashion under our OPAC system. After two years of planning and with valuable advice from various Chinese authority control experts, the existing 7xx Authority model was agreed upon with the recommendation from the Library of Congress (U.S.) in May 2000 (see Figure 10).

In early 1999, representatives of Lingnan University Library visited various libraries in Mainland China, as well as Taiwan, with the aim of learning

FIGURE 9. JULAC-HKCAN Project Homepage (http://hkcan.ln.edu.hk)

more about the overall operations of Chinese authority control works being implemented in these two places. Meanwhile, several Chinese cataloguing experts from the National Library of China and Peking University Library were invited to visit Hong Kong by Lingnan University Library to conduct several small-scale workgroups and seminars on Chinese authority works–to share with the Hong Kong cataloguers their own valuable experiences and expertise.

In 2001, HKCAN member libraries were busy with Pinyin conversion. As soon as the Pinyin conversion project was completed, member libraries began to contribute their records to the database starting in January, 2002. The de-duplication and merging of nearly 150,000 contributed records was completed in July 2002. At the moment, the database has about 100,000 records, mainly personal names, all with Chinese script provided in the 7xx field. In 2000, representatives of HKCAN first presented the HKCAN project at the CEAL (Council on East Asian Libraries) Annual conference and received overwhelming response. In the past year, trial access was granted to the National Library of Africa, National Library of Australia, East Asian Library of Columbia University (NYC), Waseda University Library (Tokyo), and some other local libraries.

In order to facilitate the sharing and exchange of information and resources among the library communities in Asia, the HKCAN Workgroup also initiated

FIGURE 10. 7xx Authority Record Example of Author "劉若愚"

Ctrl. # Identifier	003		HkCAN
Date & Time - Latest Transaction	005		19990127162938.0
Fixed-length Data	008		801020n| acannaab |a aaa
LC Ctrl. #	010		$an 50062079
System Ctrl. #	035		$a(OCoLC#)oca00096472
Cata. Source	040		$aDLC$cDLC$dDLC$dDLC-R$dHKIEd$dHkCAN
Character Sets	066		c1
Heading--Personal Name	100	1	$aLiu, James J. Y
	400	1	$aLiu, Jo-yü
See From	400	1	$aRyu, Jakugu
	400	1	$aYu, Yag-u
	670		$aHis Elizabethan and Yuan ... 1955
Source Data Found	670		$aHis Yu yen yu shih, c1988:$bt.p. (James J.Y. Liu) pref., etc. (b. 1924; d. May 1986; was pro. of Chinese and chairman of the Dept. of Asian Languages at Stanford Univ.)
	670		$aHis Chungguk sihak, 1984:$bp. 5 (James J.Y. Liu : Yu Yag-u)
	670		$a 其中國的文學理論, 1987:$bt.p. (劉若愚)
Historical data	678		$ab. 1926
Heading Linking Entry	700	1	$a 劉若愚

programmes to strengthen their liaison. In addition to fulfilling the special cataloguing needs of the bilingual community in Hong Kong, the database also aims at providing a more comprehensive coverage of Chinese names in the Asian Pacific Region. In October 1999, the HKCAN Workgroup also acquired the authority file on CD-ROM from the National Library of China (Beijing), which would be inserted into the HKCAN Database at a later stage. In November 1999, a memorandum of agreement was signed between representatives of the National Central Library (Taipei) and the HKCAN Workgroup, to the effect that the NCL (Taipei) would, in the future, share and exchange its enhanced authority control software as well as its authority data with the HKCAN Workgroup. Near the end of database consolidation, trial access was granted to the following overseas libraries beginning in 1999:

- East Asian Library of Columbia University (NYC)
- National Library of Australia
- Waseda University Library (Tokyo)

In 2001, the HKCAN Workgroup invited two Chinese cataloguing librarians from Peking University Library to come to Hong Kong to assist in the database consolidation for five months.

Indexing and Display of Authority Records in the OPAC
and Its Linkage with the Bibliographic Database

While setting up the authority database, the Workgroup also worked closely with the library system vendor, Innovative Interfaces Inc. (III), to find a software solution to support the 7xx authority model, and fortunately, all of the existing contributing HKCAN Members happen to employ the same library system. In August 2001, a remote 7xx Beta-Test site was installed by III for Members' testing of its actual functionality. The linkages of 1xx English/ romanized headings and 7xx CJK headings greatly enhanced OPAC searching. The progress is encouraging, and the new software to support 7xx will be in operation in mid-2003 (see Figure 11). In 2002, two of the existing HKCAN members installed 7xx Beta-Test software on their own library systems for further testing.[14]

Setup of the HKCAN Database: Development and Maintenance
of Software and Hardware

At the end of 1999, a software vendor in Taiwan, *"Transmission Information System Co., Ltd."* (TISC) was contracted to upgrade the NCL's authority control software for the HKCAN database. (The future development and ongoing maintenance of HKCAN Software was taken over by "大鐸資訊股份有限公司"/TTS Co., Ltd. in August 2002 (see Figure 12).)

Current Status of the HKCAN Database

Presently, the HKCAN Project's staffing and operational costs are shared among the six participating libraries:

* Chinese University of Hong Kong Library (Host Institution)
* Hong Kong Baptist University Library
* Hong Kong Institute of Education Library
* Hong Kong Polytechnic University Library
* Lingnan University Library
* University of Hong Kong Libraries

In addition to cost-sharing, the above academic libraries also contributed a large amount of authority records to the HKCAN Database. As an observer, the City University of Hong Kong Library also contributed more than 60,000 authority records to the HKCAN Database in January 2001.

FIGURE 11. Screenshot of a 7xx Beta-Test[15]

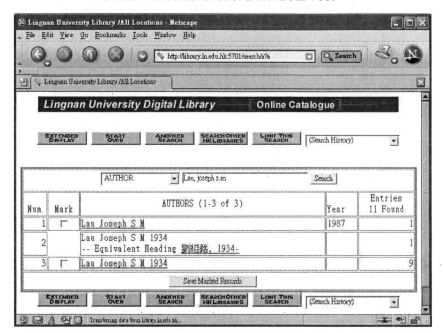

In addition, there are also a number of local, as well as overseas, libraries that have already expressed interest in using the HKCAN Database including:

Hong Kong

- Hong Kong Academy of Performing Arts Library
- Hong Kong Central Library
- Hong Kong Hospital Authority Library
- Hong Kong Legislative Council Library
- Hong Kong Monetary Authority Library
- The Open University of Hong Kong Library

Mainland China, Taiwan and Macau

- Biblioteca Central de Macau
- National Library of China
- Peking University Library

Overseas

* East Asian Library, Columbia University (NYC)
* Library of Congress
* Macquarie University Library
* University of New South Wales Library
* Waseda University Library

Based on recent statistics, the HKCAN database has collected more than 142,000 authority records from seven local JULAC libraries. During database consolidation, over 8,400 records were updated/amended. More than 15,600 records were removed during the de-duplication process. Upon completion of de-duplication, the database contained more than 100,000 unique records, including:

* 73,000 personal names
* 14,000 entries for group name
* 1,000 conference/meeting names
* 17,000 uniform titles

FIGURE 12. HKCAN Database User Interface Screenshot

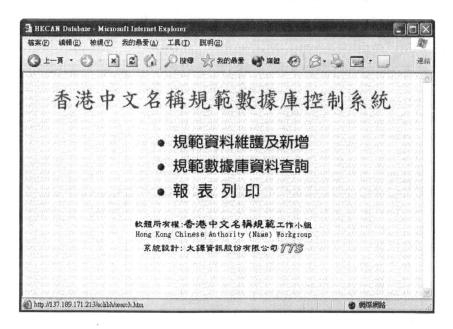

After four years of intensive hard work, a one-day Joint University Librarians Advisory Committee-HKCAN Opening and Seminar was launched at the Host Institution (The Chinese University of Hong Kong Library), in October 2002, to celebrate the meaningful collaboration among academic libraries.

CONCLUSION

No one can deny that authority control work is an indispensable part of the daily cataloguing routine. However, when it comes to the treatment of non-Roman/non-Western authority data, many libraries are still using merely Romanized forms. The JULAC-HKCAN model has been developed specifically to tackle this problem. JULAC-HKCAN not only made original Chinese scripts available in their authority records in MARC 21 format, they also managed to identify a software solution, which enabled the concurrent and yet comprehensive retrieval of bilingual publications by the same author under a single search. This practice has already proven to be successful and has attracted international attention, and some overseas libraries have already expressed their interest in participating in this project.

Hong Kong has always carried a harmonious blend of things both ancient and modern, and of Western influences and ethnic Chinese traditions, creating an irresistible mix of cultures and heritages. As an international city, and as the Special Administrative Region of China, Hong Kong has a special role to play. Not only is it the living fusion of East and West, Hong Kong also lives to promote East-West cultural and resource exchanges, as well as understanding. It also serves as a gateway to the immeasurable resources in China, and JULAC-HKCAN is one of the very best examples.

With a mission modeled closely after the city of Hong Kong, the HKCAN Database is set up to infuse authentic Asian contents and perspectives into the readily available and yet widely accepted data and format introduced from the West–and through members' active participation, the HKCAN Database can look forward to better cooperative cataloguing and resource sharing of oriental Asian materials among all libraries on a global scale.

ACKNOWLEDGMENTS

The authors take this opportunity to thank Peking University Library and Waseda University Library (Tokyo) for providing the Chinese and Japanese authority record examples as well as other information on authority control works.

Special thanks are due to the following library colleagues for their immeasurable support and contribution to this research paper:

Ms. Kazuko Matsui (National Diet Library)
Mr. Haruo Asoshina (National Institute of Informatics)
Mr. Yoshiaki Taikoh (TRC)
Mr. Masayuki Shoji, Mr. Rikuo Takagi, and Ms. Mitsuko Kanazawa (Waseda University Library (Tokyo))
Ms. Lijing Liu and Ms. Yun Pan (Peking University Library)

ENDNOTES

1. Sun, Beixin. "The Development of Authority Database in National Library of China." Paper presented at *Workshop on Authority Control Among Chinese, Korean, and Japanese Languages (CJK Authority 3)*, Karuizawa, Tokyo, Kyoto, 24th-28th March 2002.
2. Sun calls these "group authors."
3. Sun calls this category "major behavior."
4. MARC 21 versus CNMARC format comparison documented in Appendix I. Overall statistical data on Chinese Authority File (by National Library of China) is documented in Appendix II. Authority record example on "William Shakespeare" in CNMARC format (supplied by Peking University Library) is documented in Appendix III.
5. "NCL and NTU to Jointly Establish Database of Chinese Authority Files" *National Central Library Newsletter,* Vol. 30, No. 4, February, 1999, pp. 1.
6. (Will be replaced by UNIMARC in 2003.)
7. NII (Japan) is a government-funded institute, and was founded in April 2000 as an Inter-University Research Institute, to implement comprehensive research in the field of Information science. This involves the reorganization of NACSIS (National Centre for Science Information Systems) and assumption of its functions.
8. National Institute of Informatics (Japan) Homepage–Statistics. Available from: http://www.nii.ac.jp/CAT-ILL/INFO/sanka-kikan.html.
9. The acronym of "HKCAN" is purposely designed to encourage each of the Workgroup participants that "Hong Kong can!"
10. Hu, Lily, Kylie Chan and Patrick Lo "中文名稱規範合作_香港的提議" presented at the Conference on Chinese Libraries in the 21st Century at the Chinese University of Hong Kong on 4th November 1999.
11. Hu, Lily, Kylie Chan and Patrick Lo "A Collaborative Project on Chinese Name Authority Control: the HKCAN Model," *Journal of East Asian Libraries,* no. 120, February, 2000. Articles also presented at Council on East Asian Librarian (CEAL) Annual Meeting in San Diego in March 2000.
12. The *Joint University Librarians Advisory Committee (JULAC)* was first established in 1967 by the Heads of University Committee (HUCOM). It is a forum to discuss, coordinate, and collaborate on library information resources and services among the libraries of the eight tertiary education institutions funded by the University Grants Committee (UGC) of the Hong Kong SAR Government.
13. Overall statistical data on JULAC-HKCAN versus Chinese Authority File by (National Library of China) is documented in Appendix II. HKCAN (MARC 21) vs CNMARC–format comparison documented in Appendix I.
14. Lingnan University Library and The Hong Kong Polytechnic University Pao Yue-kong Library.

15. Special feature of 7xx authority enhancement–allowing concurrent and comprehensive bibliographic retrieval of bilingual publications by the same author under a single search in WebPAC. For example, to search for author *"Lau, Joseph"* in English form, the system will also prompt all equivalent headings in original Chinese script.

REFERENCES

Hu, Lily, Kylie Chan and Patrick Lo "中文名稱規範合作–香港的提議" presented at the Conference on Chinese Libraries in the 21st Century at the Chinese University of Hong Kong on 4th November 1999.

Hu, Lily, Kylie Chan and Patrick Lo "A Collaborative Project on Chinese Name Authority Control: the HKCAN Model," *Journal of East Asian Libraries*, no. 120, February, 2000. Articles also presented at Council on East Asian Librarian (CEAL) Annual Meeting in San Diego in March 2000.

"NCL and NTU to Jointly Establish Database of Chinese Authority Files" *National Central Library Newsletter,* Vol. 30, No. 4, February, 1999, pp. 1.

Sun, Beixin. "The Development of Authority Database in National Library of China." Paper presented at *Workshop on Authority Control among Chinese, Korean, and Japanese Languages (CJK Authority 3)*, Karuizawa, Tokyo, Kyoto, 24th-28th March 2002.

National Institute of Informatics (Japan) Homepage–Statistics. Available from: http://www.nii.ac.jp/CAT-ILL/INFO/sanka-kikan.html.

APPENDIX I. Comparison of MARC 21 and CNMARC

		MARC 21 used by (HKCAN)		CNMARC used by (National Library of China)			CNMARC used by CNAD	
Ctrl.#	001	000042412	001		A9401245	001		31834
Ctrl.# Identifier	003	HkCAN						
Date & Time-Latest Transaction	005	20001027121223.0						
Fixed-length Data	008	810810nc acannaabn a aaa ‖	100	0	$a19940205achiy0120 ea	100		$a19950621achiy09 ea
LC Ctrl. #	010	$an 81047202	152		$aDM	152		$aCCR
System Ctrl.#	035	$a(CDLC#)n 81047202a						
Cata. Source	040	$aDLC$beng$cDLC$dOCoLC$dHkCU$dHkCaN	801	0	$6CN$b 北圖$c19940205	801	0	acwb中國$c199506
Character Sets	066	c1						
Heading-Personal Name	100 1	$aBai, Xianyong,$d1937-	200	0	$a白樺$c(文, $f1920-1996)	200	1	$a賈$b思慈$f1866-1945?
			200	0	$7b$a白海 yang			
Public General Note			300	0	$a著名電影演員 湖南籍個人、主演劇目甚多，《紅旗》等，建國後在中國電影家協會副主席、審有《落入凡天霞》，《電影藝術探索》等			
See From	400 1	$wnnea$aPai, Hsien-yung,$d1937-	400	0	$0於一連個審看者的著作，見他的筆名 $6a05$a楊成芳	400	1	$aP'ei-ch'ing,$f1866-1945?
						400	‖	$aSsu-ts'ao-lu,$f1866-1945?
			400	0	$6a0D$7b$a$ayang cheng fang	400	1	$aSsu-ts'ao-t'ang,$f1866-1945?
						400	1	$a思慈草堂$f1866-1945?
Source Data Found	670	$aAuthor's Tie hsim cha (鐵仙札), 1967.				810		$a中國近現代人物名號大辭典, 民82 $b面 718
Found	670	$a劉俊 悲閔情懷 [1995] $btp. (白先勇)	810		$a文化辭典	810		$a定盦志 台北市: 成文, 民58
						810		$aHis Tsao-Ch'ang hsien chih, 1987. $bcaption (Chia En-fu).
Heading Linking Entry	700 1	$a白先勇,$d1937-						
General Cataloguer's Note						830		$a天津人, 字隅卿, 室名見曼室, 一作見曼廬

485

APPENDIX II

Overall Statistics
HKCAN vs Chinese Authority File by (National Library of China)

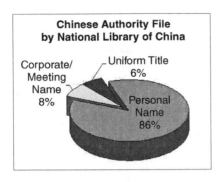

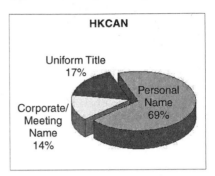

Authority Database/File	HKCAN		Chinese Authority File by (National Library of China)	
Personal Name	73,372	69%	285,000	86%
Group/Meeting Name	14,449	14%	25,000	8%
Uniform Title	17,667	17%	20,000	6%
Total	105,488	100%	330,000	100%

APPENDIX III

Authority Record Example on Shakespeare, William in CNMARC

200	1	$a 莎士比亞.$bW.$g(Shakespeare, William),$f1564-1616
200	1	$7ec$aSha Shi Bi Ya$g(Shakespeare, William),$f1564-1616
700	1	$aShakespeare,$bWilliam,$f1564-1616
801	0	aCNbPUL$c19940307
810		$aEB(V.15 p. 248)
810		$aCH(1989 ; p.1552)
830		$a英國文藝復興時期戲劇家、詩人。代表作品有: 《羅密歐與茱麗葉》、《哈姆雷特》等。

APPENDIX IV

Participating Institutes of NACIS-CAT

(1)	Beijing Center for Japanese Studies
(2)	Bodleian Library, University of Oxford
(3)	Cambridge University Library
(4)	China Agricultural University Library
(5)	Dalian University of Technology Library / (大連理工大学圖書館)
(6)	Dept. of Japanese Antiquities, The British Museum
(7)	Dept. of Japanese Studies, University of Heidelberg
(8)	East Asian Institute, Japan Center, University of Munchen
(9)	East Asian Library, University of Zurich
(10)	East-Asien Library, Katholieke Universiteit Leuven
(11)	Geophysical Institute, University of Alaska
(12)	Institute of East Asian Studies, Duisburg University
(13)	Institute of Japanese Studies, Hallym Academy of Sciences, Hallym University
(14)	Japan Center Library, University of Marburg
(15)	Japan Cultural Center, Bangkok, The Japan Foundation
(16)	Japan Cultural Center, Koln, The Japan Foundation
(17)	Japanese-German Center Berlin
(18)	Ji Lin University Library / (吉林大學圖書館)
(19)	Nanjing University Library / (南京大學圖書館)
(20)	Oriental and India Office Collections, The British Library
(21)	Peking University Library / (北京大學圖書館)
(22)	School of East Asian Studies Library, University of Sheffield
(23)	School of Oriental and African Studies, University of London
(24)	Scottish Centre for Japanese Studies, University of Stirling
(25)	Society for Buddhist Understanding, Germany
(26)	Sun Yat-Sen University Libraries / (中山大學圖書館)
(27)	Teachers College, Columbia University Japan
(28)	The Asia Library, Stockholm University
(29)	The Japan Foundation London Language Centre
(30)	Tianjin Library / (天津圖書館)
(31)	Wuhan University / (武漢大學圖書館)

The following libraries will participate in NACSIS-CAT soon:

(32)	Centre for Documentation and Information, Chinese Academy of Social Sciences / (中國社會科學院文獻信息中心)
(33)	Dalian University of Foreign Languages / (大連外國語學院圖書電教館)
(34)	East China Normal University Library / (華東師範大學圖書館)
(35)	Fudan University Library / (復旦大學圖書館)
(36)	JETRO London Center
(37)	LiaoNing Provincial Library / (遼寧省圖書館)
(38)	Northeastern University Library / (東北大學圖書館)
(39)	Shanghai Jiaotong University / (上海交通大學圖書館)
(40)	The Library of Renmin University of China / (中國人民大學圖書館)
(41)	Tsinghua University Library / (清華大學圖書館)
(42)	Xiamen University Library / (厦門大學圖書館)

APPENDIX V

Flow Chart[1]

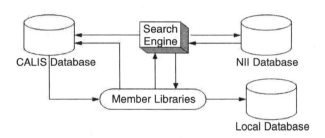

Overall Workflow

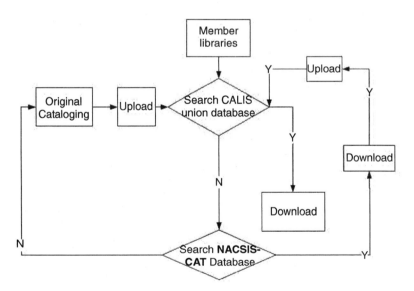

[1]This flowchart documents in detail how member libraries contribute and download data from NACSIS-CAT via CALIS, including steps for MARC and data conversion.

Progetto Lombardo Archivi
in INternet–PLAIN
(Lombardy Project for Archives
on the Internet):
Identification, Retrieval, and Display
of Creators of Archives
and of Archival Fonds

Maurizio Savoja
Paul Gabriele Weston

SUMMARY. The Progetto Lombardo Archivi in INternet (PLAIN[1]), which is coordinated by the University of Pavia, on the basis of an agreement with the Regione Lombardia, an agreement in which the State Archives of Milan is also represented, intends to create an environment

---

Maurizio Savoja is affiliated with Archivo di Stato di Milano.
Paul Gabriele Weston is affiliated with Università di Pavia.

This text, which was previously discussed and later revised together with Paul Gabriele Weston, was written by Maurizio Savoja with the help of Saverio Almini and Daniela Bondielli (see note 3), who contributed by helpfully including some technical documentation regarding this project.

[Haworth co-indexing entry note]: "Progetto Lombardo Archivi in INternet–PLAIN (Lombardy Project for Archives on the Internet): Identification, Retrieval, and Display of Creators of Archives and of Archival Fonds." Savoja, Maurizio, and Paul Gabriele Weston. Co-published simultaneously in *Cataloging & Classification Quarterly* (The Haworth Information Press, an imprint of The Haworth Press, Inc.) Vol. 39, No. 1/2, 2004, pp. 489-503; and: *Authority Control in Organizing and Accessing Information: Definition and International Experience* (ed: Arlene G. Taylor, and Barbara B. Tillett) The Haworth Information Press, an imprint of The Haworth Press, Inc., 2004, pp. 489-503. Single or multiple copies of this article are available for a fee from The Haworth Document Delivery Service [1-800-HAWORTH, 9:00 a.m. - 5:00 p.m. (EST). E-mail address: docdelivery@haworthpress.com].

enabling easy public access to the wide heritage of descriptions in electronic format of historical archives preserved in Lombardy. Databases produced over the years that include a remarkable quantity of descriptive records are made available for consultation as a whole, while the system is implemented by the inclusion of further descriptive records processed within ongoing archival inventory and census projects. In addition, PLAIN should provide a structure able to receive, organize and display on the Web the descriptive records created from 1997 onwards within the project *Civita*, also promoted by the Regional Authorities. More evolved instruments of integration will therefore be provided in order to enable integrated searching.

This paper is focused on some of the problems concerning the organization and presentation of archival descriptions, with particular reference to the creation of a system of *lists* referring to archival collections and the creators of archives described in the system. The conclusions indicate how the adopted solutions foreshadow further integration between the whole body of archival descriptions and the historical-institutional profiles of the *Civita* project, and how they open up promising perspectives of communication with other external systems. *[Article copies available for a fee from The Haworth Document Delivery Service: 1-800-HAWORTH. E-mail address: <docdelivery@haworthpress.com> Website: <http://www.HaworthPress.com> © 2004 by The Haworth Press, Inc. All rights reserved.]*

KEYWORDS. Historical Archives on the Web Project, archival descriptions, archival fonds, archival repositories, Lombardy cultural heritage, PLAIN Project (Progetto Lombardo Archivi in Internet), archival information system architecture, management of concurrent descriptive records, list entry headings

PROGETTO LOMBARDO ARCHIVI IN INTERNET

The Progetto Lombardo Archivi in INternet (PLAIN) intends to create an environment that enables easy public access to the wide heritage of descriptions, already existing in electronic format, of historical archives preserved in the region.[2]

The project is coordinated by the University of Pavia, on the basis of an agreement with the Regione Lombardia, an agreement in which the State Archives of Milan is also represented.[3] The project is being developed within the wider project *Archivi storici sul web (Historical Archives on the Web)*, in which the Regione Lombardia and the State Archives of Milan are collaborating in the context of the *Accordo di Programma Quadro in materia di beni culturali* (Framework Program Agreement for cultural heritage).[4]

Within the region, several archival inventory and survey projects have been active for over a decade, mostly developed using one of the successive releases of the *Sesamo* software, which have been being developed by the Regione Lombardia since 1992, or by software related to it: *Nautilus*, for the survey of archives, and *Mens*, for the inventory of personal archives.

Over the years such projects, mostly developed with the direct contribution of the Regione Lombardia, have produced databases with a remarkable quantity of descriptive records, which are about to be made accessible in a single information system. The descriptions derived from the previous inventory and census projects will enter the new system and will be available for consultation as a whole. Naturally, the system will be capable of expansion through the inclusion of further descriptive records processed within new archival inventory and census projects.

The creation of a single system will make searching speedier and more rewarding within the individual sets of descriptive records, retrieval of which could otherwise be difficult, and it will further enrich the information system, thanks to the global overview it offers of projects and archival descriptions. Another enhancement will be achieved through direct interventions into the cumulative system, by the linking of individual descriptive records to records with a common "context," and by the explicit highlighting of the relationships between descriptive records originally created during different projects and with different aims, as will be explained below.

Another rich heritage of descriptions, available in electronic format but so far not publicly accessible to Internet searchers, is that related to archival collections preserved in the State Archive of Milan, for all of which summary descriptions were prepared in the *Anagrafe* Project.[5] The PLAIN Project also aims to make these descriptions accessible within the same environment, with further and more notable advantages: a broader and richer information base, the possibility of cross-searching, and the opportunity to highlight relationships between the archives described and the entities (organizations, persons, families) linked to them.

Beyond the creation of tools for management of, and access to, archival descriptions, from its very first phase, the project has been built to provide a structure able to receive the descriptive records created from 1997 onwards within the project *Civita,* promoted by the Regione Lombardia, in order to integrate their processing and display them on the Web. These records refer to historical institutions with local political and administrative functions, and to institutions of the central and peripheral state administration which succeeded one another on the current Lombard territory, starting from the first regional state (14th century) up to the creation of today's statutory regions (1971), as well as, in a further phase of the project still under development, to the territorial ecclesiastical institutions of Lombard dioceses (13th-20th centuries).[6]

Integration between the two information resource units mentioned above–archival descriptions and institutional descriptions of the *Civita* project–is at the moment limited to common access and the uniform presentation of information. With time, more evolved instruments of integration will be provided in order to enable integrated searching.

Further developments of the system will see the analysis and the creation of new ways of integration with other somewhat contiguous projects, such as the *Codice diplomatico della Lombardia Medievale* (*Diplomatic Codex of Medieval Lombardy*[7]), and of further units of information resources, such as a *Normative historical Lombardy corpus*, at present still in the planning stages.

This paper is focused on some of the problems concerning the organization and presentation of archival descriptions, with particular reference to the creation of a system of *lists* referring to archival collections and the creators of archives described in the system. The conclusions will indicate how the adopted solutions foreshadow further integration between the whole body of archival descriptions and the historical-institutional profiles of the *Civita* project, and how they open up promising perspectives of communication with other external systems.

THE ARCHITECTURE
OF THE ARCHIVAL INFORMATION SYSTEM

The architecture of the archival system PLAIN mostly follows that of SIUSA (United Information System of Archival Superintendences),[8] of which it should become one of the local centers.[9] In the system are descriptive records referring to: (a) actual *archival fonds,* organized on different levels, in the manner provided for by international standards and archival descriptive practice; (b) *archives' creators;* (c) *archival repositories,* as well as additional records referring to *bibliography* and *sources* and to archival *finding aids.*

Concise Diagram of the SIUSA Conceptual Model[10]

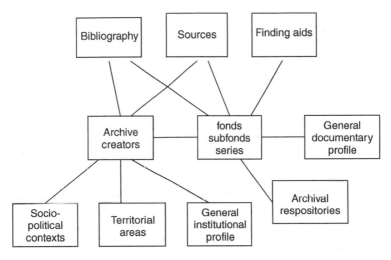

The databases of archival descriptions loaded into the PLAIN system contain information mostly concerning *archival fonds* and *archives' creators*. In the original databases, besides, are usually to be found all data concerning *finding aids* and *bibliography*. In the process of importing descriptive records into the system, however, for each *fonds*, references to the pertinent *repository* are inserted, even when such information is not present in the original database. Additionally, in the PLAIN system, records are provided for *archival files* and *items*, the description of which is a fundamental component of inventory databases.

Descriptions of *socio-political contexts*, of *general institutional profiles*, of *territorial areas* and of *general documentary profiles*, which are available in the system as well as in the SIUSA conceptual framework, are not generally to be found in the original databases of descriptions, at least not as structured records. The mentioned descriptive profiles actually provide a more general level of information than the specific historical context represented in the inventory of a *fonds*–information relative to:

- institutional context (*socio-political contexts*: for instance, Kingdom of Italy, *1805-1814*);
- common features of institutions of the same kind (*general institutional profiles*: for instance, the *Comune* in the Kingdom of Italy after unification);

- information concerning distinctive common features of documentary series of the same type in different archives (*general documentary profiles*: for instance, *Registri dello stato civile*);
- information with reference to historical-geographical determinations (*territorial areas*: for instance, *Triangolo Lariano*).

Such descriptive records introduce into the system some general information that can be very valuable to the user, whether a professional researcher or a simple inquirer. It is to be emphasized, with regard to this subject, that any record in the system permits the introduction of a link to other information resources existing within and outside of the system itself, as well as the direct insertion of descriptive information.

Besides the descriptive records already existing in the SIUSA model, PLAIN's distinctive features provide for further kinds of records, referring both to *projects* (that is, to the operations by which the descriptions introduced into the system were generated), and to *lists*, that will be dealt with later, and which are the main focus of attention here.

The informative core of the PLAIN system, obviously, consists of the descriptive records related to *archival fonds* and their *creators*, which are at its heart from both a conceptual and a functional viewpoint. Also as far as searching by users is carried out, records for *fonds* and *creators* form the main access points to the system (of course, apart from access via the name of the repository, which, however, is the result of a different approach). The same descriptive records for *items*, which in their turn carry information of great detail on archival documentation, are initially accessible via the records referring to the *fonds* to which they belong). The main search keys the system puts at the users' disposal are, therefore, access to descriptions of *creators*, or to those of *fonds*, through searches on the text of the descriptions themselves or through the display of lists of all *fonds* or *creators* present in the system (in alphabetical or chronological order, etc.) or a subset of them (selected on the basis of type, place or other criteria).

The Uploading of Archival Descriptions

Archival descriptions, as indicated in the introductory remarks, enter the system from a series of databases created over the years using different software applications. In phase 1 of the project, it is planned to load inventory databases created using the *Sesamo* software, prepared by the Regione Lombardia from its first version in 1992 as an aid to archive operators. This software has gradually become a vehicle for standardization among descriptive data organizing formats. Version 4[11] of this software was completed in the last months and its distribution should take place shortly. This new version was developed taking into account the SIUSA conceptual model, so as to facilitate export of descriptions within a system built in keeping with that architecture, such as PLAIN.

Procedures for importing inventory databases built with earlier versions of *Sesamo* into the PLAIN system will make use of the existing provisions for conversion of data between different versions of the Sesamo application, by carrying out the transfer in two stages. A further procedure is planned for the intake of archival descriptions relating to documentation preserved in the State Archive of Milan.

In a following phase, intake procedures will be introduced for importing into PLAIN the results of census operations carried out within the region using *Nautilus* software, and bodies of descriptions produced with other software, among it the abovementioned *Mens*, which also belongs to the *Sesamo* family and is intended specifically for the inventory of personal archives.

DESCRIPTIVE RECORDS FOR THE PROJECTS

Operations for the intake of descriptive records into the system generally concern whole sets of interrelated records referred to one or more specific *fonds* and to their *creators* (and to the other mentioned types of record, if appropriate). These come from individual databases, each of which is the result of a specific project of archival inventory or survey.

On the other hand, it is well-known that an archival description is characteristically not made up of a simple accumulation of records referring to individual "pieces," but of the identification and representation of a complex network of relationships that brings the descriptive records together in a kind of hierarchy–such as items within a series, series within a fonds–and correlations between different types of record–such as a collection with its own *creator*, one *creator* with another that has taken over its functions upon its termination, and so on.

In this setting it is particularly important to have in the information system a record in which identifying information can be recorded on each specific project[12] that can be linked to the relevant descriptive records. In this way the information about the original context in which each description was prepared comes up side by side with the information, provided for each record, about the author and about successive updates and revisions; furthermore, information is preserved to show which records have a common origin from a particular database resulting from a specific project.

Operations to load inventory databases into the system, however, require preliminary verification and rearrangement of the original descriptive records.[13] The range of intervention potentially required is vast, even considering–for the moment–only uploads from *Sesamo* software applications. It ranges from simple reformatting of data arranged differently in the source software (as happens, for instance, with *finding aids* which, before version 4 of *Sesamo*, were described in a field of the record referring to the *fonds*) to the need to render explicit the links between records for *fonds* and those for *creators*. Sometimes these are simply juxtaposed in the source database, to arrive at the necessary creation of a link between the *fonds* and its own *repository entry*, the record for which was not provided for in the original *Sesamo* source software. Further, as indicated, there is the possibility of creating new inquiry possibilities from specific descriptive records in the PLAIN system, such as, for example, *general documentary profile* records, or of generating links between imported descriptive records and those already existing in the system.

In all cases, however, there are limits to the amount of intervention possible on records being loaded into PLAIN. Rarely can there be any substantial review of the description, in particular for records that refer to entities of particular significance, such as a *creator* or a *fonds* which has a detailed and carefully worded description. The intervention undergone by the individual record in the course of the process, in any case, is specified in the appropriate area of the descriptive record (reference to the compiler). The link with the original project from which the record came, and hence with the other descriptive records produced in the same operation (and imported from the same original database), remains information to be protected.[14]

LISTS AS A TOOL FOR THE MANAGEMENT
OF CONCURRENT DESCRIPTIVE RECORDS

The uploading of whole files of interrelated descriptive records, each the product of a specific project, into a cumulative system such as PLAIN, brings with it the need to be able to handle concurrently different descriptive records referring to the same "object," whether *fonds* or *creator*. Actually, the same subject may have been catalogued in the course of different projects, perhaps because it turns out to be *creator* of different *fonds* (for instance there are family or personal archives that have gone to different repositories, or even into different fonds). Likewise, a *fonds* may have been described within an inventory operation and, on another occasion (and with different criteria) within a survey project. It will not always be appropriate to delete one descriptive record and merge its data into another: for one thing, this is an inherently difficult operation, which could end up as a complete revision; but also, there are implications for the relationships between the original record and others connected to the same project.

In PLAIN, this problem is faced with the creation of two *lists*, referring to *creators* and *fonds*, respectively. Each *creator* record in PLAIN is linked to a *list entry*; every entry of the relevant list can be linked to one or more descriptive records, thus developing an immediate linking function. For *fonds* and its component parts, on the other hand, in general, only the records "of first level," that usually correspond to the *fonds* itself, are assigned a *list entry*).[15]

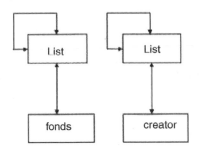

The entries present in both *lists* perform the following functions: uniquely identifying each "object" described (*fonds* or *creator*); linking descriptive records to this same "object," if there is more than one such in the system, and identifying from among these, one record to be proposed as "preferred" for users of the system; and forming a kind of meta-index of the descriptive records present, which is displayed to users at the site where they access the system. In addition to the element (database field) for the *heading,* every *list entry* contains elements for description, notes and editorial notes.

The system permits production of *references* between *list entries* of the type *See* and *See also*, the latter in a reciprocal and symmetrical relationship. The *See* reference is unidirectional, from a non-preferred to a preferred heading (from which all headings referring to it are traceable). *List entries* that refer to other entries by means of *See* references have no direct connection with descriptive records (*fonds* or *creator* records), but refer solely to other list entries; furthermore, each of these headings will have a *See* relationship with only one other heading.

See also relationships between records are reciprocal relationships; each of the *list entries* correlated thus is connected to one or more descriptive records. Such reciprocal relationships can be generated within the system, occasioned by an upload; or they can be generated as a consequence of the presence, in an imported descriptive record, of several alternative headings; or, again, to represent, also at list level, relationships expressed between several imported records (for example, to correlate the entries referring to two *creator* records that in their original inventory are connected by a *Succeeds* relationship, such as occurs these days in the relationship between a former *Ufficio del Registro* and a present-day *Ufficio Locale dell'Agenzia delle Entrate*).

LIST ENTRY HEADINGS

Every list entry has a heading as its identifying element, which is displayed to users in the directories set up as access to the system for **specific searches and browsing**. The heading is assigned by PLAIN managers in accordance with the principles that are being defined by the *Gruppo di studio per le intestazioni di autorità* (Study Group on Authority Headings), set up by the Servizio V of the *Direzione Generale per gli Archivi*.[16]

In general, each heading for a body comprises its name (which can be, or can include, a typological specification, such as *Prefettura*), name of place (usually the location, which is sometimes conveyed by the name itself), a range of dates or an open date (for duration) and, if necessary, an indication of the context (for instance, if needed to express the immediate context, in the case of subordinate bodies such as the 'Ministry of Culture and the Environment, Administrative Affairs, and Personnel Directorate'). The order of elements presently envisaged for the system is: location in first position, followed by full names and inclusive dates, e.g.:

> Ardesio, Asilo Bari Maninetti (1908-)
> Ardesio, Quadra di Ardesio (1610-sec. XVIII)
> Serina, Comunità della Valle Brembana superiore (sec. XV-sec. XVIII)
> Serina, Comune di Serina (sec. XV-)

For persons, the heading generally consists of surname, forename, and dates of birth and death qualified by place if known, e.g.:

> Cavarocchi Franco (Lucca, 1911-1996)
> Garovaglio Alfonso (Cantù, 1820-Milano, 1905)

For families, the heading includes surname, relevant dates, place if available and further qualifications or titles, e.g.:

> Martinengo Colleoni, Bergamo (sec. XV-)

In the list of archival fonds, the heading for each list entry is composed of the archive's name and inclusive dates, e.g.:

Fondo Franco Cavarocchi (sec. XV-1996)
Fondo Martinengo Colleoni (883-1912)

THE ROLE OF LISTS IN CONTROLLING ACCESS POINTS FOR SEARCHING AND BROWSING BY USERS

The user basically gets access to the system in the following ways:

- directory of *archival repositories* (a list of all records present, which can be screened and searched in various ways);[17]
- **list** of *creators*
- **list** of *fonds*;
- searching of descriptive records (on single fields by type of record, or in full text)

Selection of a *list heading* entails accessing a directory of all records linked to it, with the "preferred" record highlighted and an indication of the *project* from which the records are derived, and with the possibility of accessing the descriptive record for the project itself.

Access to one of the proposed records then leads the user to consultation of the record itself with its descriptive fields and expressed relationships. If, for instance, a user reaches one of the records in the system that refers to an archival fonds, he/she will have access to the hierarchy of descriptions related solely to this particular descriptive record, with the possibility of accessing any related records for series, subseries, items, etc. The same applies to a *creator* record, which will give access to links to other records of that kind and to descriptive records for *fonds* only if related to the selected record. It will be the concern of those in charge of the system in the location where the databases are loaded and checked, to ensure the consistency of the relationships presented in the various cases.

LISTS AS INTERFACE WITH OTHER SYSTEMS

The lists built up in the system also serve to provide an immediately available interface to link descriptions present within the system with those in other systems, whether or not including descriptions of archives.

Actually, the lists also serve, as has been emphasized, to identify "objects" for which descriptive records exist in the system (the *fonds* actually preserved, in their physical entirety, within a *repository*, and their *creators*). Hence, the *list entries* lend themselves to the development of linking functions between systems, such links being founded on the presence in both, of descriptions of the same object. Of particular interest and practicality is the possibility of a link between *creators,* who–as actual persons or legal persons–can easily have carried out activities in other contexts and have been described within the scope of other information systems, from different points of view.

An initial area of investigation in this direction will take place in the next phase of the project's development, by using the lists to correlate the descriptions of *creators* in PLAIN and the descriptions of civil and ecclesiastical institutions described in the database of the Civita project.

In the present phase of the PLAIN project, a consistent and compatible interface is being developed for access to the two systems (the cumulative database of archival data and the Civita database). These, however, remain quite separate with regard to searching and general access to descriptive records. In many cases the *institutional subjects*–civil and ecclesiastical–described in Civita are also among those described as *creators*: *comuni* and parishes described as institutional subjects in Civita, are also, in many cases, described as *creators* in archival databases. In the two systems, descriptions are prepared according to different criteria, sometimes even with a different "time extension" of the subject. For instance, in the abovementioned example, *Comune di Serina (15th century-)* (an *archives' creator*, for which a specific descriptive record exists in the archival descriptive system), there are nine different descriptive records in Civita, referring to different time-spans in the life of the *comune*, corresponding to an equal number of institutional changes.[18] Nevertheless, a link between the lists can permit the possibility of a combined search, while maintaining the unique character of the separate information contexts, notwithstanding any dissimilarity in formulating descriptions, or any inconsistency in software formats. In a following phase of PLAIN development, it is thought that similar mechanisms will allow linking with other systems, firstly, the abovementioned *Codice Diplomatico della Lombardia Medievale*, or directly to information systems referring to different sectors of cultural heritage.

ENDNOTES

1. We're using here the acronym that was temporarily adopted to identify the project, and particularly, to indicate the publishing environment of information resources relevant to archives.

2. For a first draft of the project (in some respects more exhaustive, although referring to a preceding phase), see M. Savoja, *L'archivista in rete: primi cenni ad un*

progetto in corso, "Archivi per la Storia", a. XIV, n. 1-2 Jan.-Dec. 2001, pp. 341-354; see also D. Bondielli, *I sistemi informativi arc*▓*istici in rapporto alle risorse telematiche: nuovi progetti a confronto*, which is about to be published in "Archivi e Computer."

3. The project, which started when the convention between the Regione Lombardia and the University of Pavia signed the agreement on January 30, 2002, is directed by Saverio Almini, while Daniela Bondielli is responsible for its technical aspects. It is managed by a technical scientific committee chaired by Ezio Barbieri (University of Pavia) and made up of Michele Ansani and Paul Gabriele Weston (University of Pavia), Roberto Grassi (Regione Lombardia), Maurizio Savoja (AS Milano).

4. The Framework Program Agreement was drawn up by the Ministry of Cultural heritage and the Regione Lombardia in 1999. See http://www.cultura.regione. lombardia.it/proScheda.cfm?id=69 (all links quoted here were checked in December 2002).

5. The *Anagrafe* Project was financed, following law n. 84/90, for archives controlled by some of the *Soprintendenze Archivistiche* and was later carried on and extended to some State Archives with the financial help of the law n. 145/92. It aimed to create a central database at the Ministero per i Beni Culturali by putting together in a single central database the descriptions gathered with a specifical data-entry software: see E. Ormanni, *Progetto per una anagrafe informatizzata degli archivi italiani*, "Bollettino d'Informazioni–Centro Ricerche Informatiche per i Beni Culturali–Scuola Normale Superiore, Pisa," 1991, pp. 11-30, and by the same author, *La normalizzazione della descrizione archivistica nei progetti di informatica dell'Amministrazione degli Archivi di Stato in Italia*, in *Storia e multimedia, Atti del VII congresso internazionale dell'Association for History and Computing*, Bologna 1994, pp. 21-27. During recent years, the Archival Administration has been actively engaged in making accessible to the public all data gathered during the *Anagrafe* Project: see (among others) *Riprogettare "Anagrafe." elementi per un nuovo sistema archivistico nazionale. Relazione del gruppo di lavoro per la revisione e la reingegnerizzazione del sistema informativo nazionale "Anagrafe informatizzata degli archivi italiani,"* "Rassegna degli Archivi di Stato" LX (2000), n. 2, pp. 373-454, and the project *SIUSA–Sistema Informativo Unificato per le Soprintendenze Archivistiche*, mentioned in the text, which is in the process of recovering all data gathered through *Anagrafe*: see Giuseppe Mesoraca, *Recupero delle banche dati di Anagrafe in SIUSA,* "Bollettino d'Informazioni–Centro Ricerche Informatiche per i Beni Culturali–Scuola Normale Superiore, Pisa," XI, 2001, n. 2 (a monographic number of the Bulletin, devoted entirely to the SIUSA project).

At the State Arvchive of Milan, the Anagrafe Project was realized between 1998 and 2000. The descriptions which were gathered referring to all archival fonds preserved in the Institute, are for the moment accessible to the public, but only on site and with the help of specialized staff.

6. Regione Lombardia, Direzione generale cultura, Servizio biblioteche e sistemi culturali integrati, *Progetto CIVITA. Le istituzioni storiche del territorio lombardo. XIV-XIX secolo, Milano 1999-2000* (general supervsion: Roberto Grassi; archival advice and final editing: Mario Signori; technical design and operational direction: Michele Giordano; organization: Consorzio Archidata, Milano). The volumes, out of print and partly out of stock, were published in the following order: *Sondrio* (April 1999); *Bergamo, Brescia, Mantova, Milano–la provincia* (December 1999); *Lecco, Como, Lodi, Cremona* (February 2000); *Pavia, Varese, Milano–la città* (June 2000).

The volumes were also published in PDF format, in CD-ROM (a temporary edition) in February 2000. In May 2000 the volume devoted to *Fonti. Criteri. Metodi* was published. About the CIVITA Project, see also: Roberto Grassi, *Il Progetto CIVITA*, and M. Giordano, *Il censimento delle istituzioni lombarde dal XIV al XIX secolo*, in *Archivi & Computer*, n. 4/97. In 2001 two books concerning civil institutions created after 1861 up to the beginning of the 1970s were published: *Le istituzioni storiche del territorio lombardo. 1859-1971*. Milano, October 2001 (in two volumes).

In 2001 the project was extended to ecclesiastical institutions and was coordinated by the University of Pavia: Regione Lombardia, Direzione generale Culture, Identità e Autonomie della Lombardia–Università degli Studi di Pavia, Dipartimento di scienze storiche e geografiche "Carlo M. Cipolla," *Progetto CIVITA. Le istituzioni storiche del territorio lombardo. Le istituzioni ecclesiastiche. XIII-XX secolo,* (general supervision: Roberto Grassi; scientific direction: Saverio Almini, Ezio Barbieri; operational supervision: Saverio Almini; technical realization: Michele Giordano; organization: Università degli Studi di Pavia, Dipartimento di scienze storiche e geografiche "Carlo M. Cipolla"). In March 2002 two volumes devoted to the ecclesiastical institutions of the Diocese of Milan were presented in a temporary edition: Regione Lombardia, Direzione generale Culture, Identità e Autonomie della Lombardia–Università degli Studi di Pavia, Dipartimento di scienze storiche e geografiche "Carlo M. Cipolla," *Progetto CIVITA. Le istituzioni storiche del territorio lombardo. Le istituzioni ecclesiastiche. XIII-XX secolo. Diocesi di Milano*, Milano, March 2002 (in two volumes), which were followed by: Regione Lombardia, Direzione generale Culture, Identità e Autonomie della Lombardia–Università degli Studi di Pavia, Dipartimento di scienze storiche e geografiche "Carlo M. Cipolla," *Progetto CIVITA. Le istituzioni storiche del territorio lombardo. Le istituzioni ecclesiastiche. XIII-XX secolo. Diocesi di Vigevano*, Milan, December 2002. Books about the Dioceses of Crema, Lodi, Pavia, Tortona (Lombard territory), Mantova and Como are about to be published.

7. The project, coordinated by M. Ansani (University of Pavia), refers to the systematic edition of documentary sources of the Lombard area preceding the XIII century: see http://cdlm.unipv.it/.

8. About the SIUSA system, see the already mentioned monographic number of the "Bollettino d'Informazioni–Centro Ricerche Informatiche per i Beni Culturali–Scuola Normale Superiore, Pisa" (XI, 2001, n. 2).

9. On the basis of an agreement between the Regione Lombardia, Servizio III della Direzione Generale per gli Archivi, and the Centro Ricerche Informatiche Beni Culturali della Scuola Normale Superiore di Pisa, one of the software modules of SIUSA (with which the software modules created *ad hoc* for the PLAIN system itself interact) is used within the PLAIN project for collecting and managing archival descriptions.

10. D. Bondielli, *Il Sistema Informativo Unificato per le Soprintendenze Archivistiche: elaborazione, sviluppo, descrizione del progetto*, "Bollettino d'Informazioni . . . ," *cit.,* pp. 43-71; the diagram translated here is on p. 51.

11. The first version of the software was written for the Macintosh; from version 2 it has run on Windows, using Access DBMS software. From version 3 the system has been modelled on the separate descriptions of *fonds* and *creators*. For *Sesamo* and its development see R. Grassi, *Le scelte di Sesamo*, "Rassegna degli Archivi di Stato," LIX (1999), n. 1-2-3, pp. 104-109, and by the same author, *Il futuro di Sesamo*, "Archivi e Computer," 2/2000, pp. 176-178.

12. For thoughts on these questions see also M. Savoja, *Lo standard ISAAR come riferimento per la messa a punto di sistemi informativi archivistici*, intervento al Convegno *Arianna. Un software per archivisti* (Pisa, 30-31 maggio 2000), "Bollettino d'Informazioni–Centro Ricerche Informatiche per i Beni Culturali–Scuola Normale Superiore, Pisa," IX (1999), n. 2, pp. 31-49.

13. Achievable by means of operations to be completed in the PLAIN system and operations realized in the software of origin, or if possible, by employing the latest version of *Sesamo* if used for an intermediate upload.

14. Employing terminology and referring to a concept which, in recent times, has received a great deal of attention, one could say that information with regard to *projects* is an essential ingredient of *metadata* of the descriptive records imported into the system.

15. In certain cases it can happen that lower level records also are linked to list entries.

16. *Cf.* "Il Mondo degli Archivi," a. X–N. S. n. 1/2002, ANAI p. 28 e DGA pp. 34-37.

17. In the system one cannot have more than one record for the same *archival repository*, in contrast to *creators*, given that the information on the repository has the eminently practical purpose of indicating how to gain physical access to the documentation.

18. Comune di Serina (sec. XIII-1797); comune di Serina (1797-1798); comune di Serina con Lepreno e Frerola (1798-1804); comune di Serina (1804-1810); comune di Serina (1810-1812); comune di Serina (1812-1816); comune di Serina (1816-1818); comune di Serina con Lepreno e Bagnella (1818-1859); comune di Serina (1859-1971).

Modeling Authority Data
for Libraries, Archives and Museums:
A Project in Progress at AFNOR

Françoise Bourdon

SUMMARY. To give a national basis to the considerations developed at IFLA with FRANAR, a working group devoted to modelling authority data was created in the framework of the French Organization for Standardization (AFNOR) in 2000. The Working Group aims at developing interoperability among libraries, archives and museums. Composition, goals, and the working plan of this Group are presented. *[Article copies available for a fee from The Haworth Document Delivery Service: 1-800-HAWORTH. E-mail address: <docdelivery@haworthpress.com> Website: <http://www.HaworthPress.com> © 2004 by The Haworth Press, Inc. All rights reserved.]*

KEYWORDS. Modelling authority data, libraries, archives, museums, interoperability, AFNOR

The Bibliothèque nationale de France (BnF) *authority files*, created in 1985, were the first in digital format in France. Designed at first as simple tools at the cataloguers' disposal for the management of access points to the

Françoise Bourdon is affiliated with Bibliothèque nationale de France.

[Haworth co-indexing entry note]: "Modeling Authority Data for Libraries, Archives and Museums: A Project in Progress at AFNOR." Bourdon, Françoise. Co-published simultaneously in *Cataloging & Classification Quarterly* (The Haworth Information Press, an imprint of The Haworth Press, Inc.) Vol. 39, No. 1/2, 2004, pp. 505-516; and: *Authority Control in Organizing and Accessing Information: Definition and International Experience* (ed: Arlene G. Taylor, and Barbara B. Tillett) The Haworth Information Press, an imprint of The Haworth Press, Inc., 2004, pp. 505-516. Single or multiple copies of this article are available for a fee from The Haworth Document Delivery Service [1-800-HAWORTH, 9:00 a.m. - 5:00 p.m. (EST). E-mail address: docdelivery@haworthpress.com].

Digital Object Identifier: 10.1300/J104v39n01_16

505

catalogue, they were promptly adopted by other libraries that used them in their own catalogues. But because in the catalogue there are digital links, both among authority files and between bibliographic descriptions and authority files, users quickly realized that authority records are a valuable aid to define research and a means to enrich the bibliographic information retrieved.

Now that large bibliographic databases are expected to provide easy, relevant access, not only libraries, but also archives and museums are interested in authority files as tools for managing and providing consistent access points and also as means to better place a search in context.

In 2000, French professionals were ready for a detailed check of authority data in order to establish which authority data they needed as well as to improve interoperability among the different cultural sectors: libraries, archives and museums. AFNOR (Association française de normalisation) offered an adequate environment for this consideration.

THE CREATION OF THE AFNOR WORKING-GROUP ON AUTHORITY DATA

Why Was an AFNOR Working-Group on Authority Data Created in 2000?

To Give a National Basis to the Considerations Developed at IFLA with FRANAR

In 1999, a working-group on authority data was created at IFLA, with the acronym FRANAR (Functional Requirements And Numbering of Authority Records). I chaired FRANAR for three years (1999-2001), and I deemed it necessary to share the considerations developed at an international level with some French experts.

To Develop Interoperability Among Libraries, Archives and Museums

The BnF authority files were issued on microfiches (in a display format observing GARE recommendations) from 1989 to 1998 and on CD-ROM since 1991 (permitting display and download in INTERMARC, and starting in 1999, in UNIMARC). Since its publication, the CD-ROM has been at users' disposal both at the national library and at other institutions, and it has quickly become popular. From 1998, the authority records have been accessible online via the BN-OPALE Plus catalogue, in local and remote mode. The diffusion of the BnF authority files has played a central role in awakening French librarians' attention to the issue of authority control in public and academic libraries.

Since the early 1990s, the idea of developing a single catalogue for all types of documents for the future *"Très grande bibliothèque"* has required the development of a new format, an "integrated" INTERMARC format for bibliographic and authority records. To bring this project to a satisfying conclusion, a thorough check has been made of all the needs of every department of the national library, including printed and audio-visual documents and also special documents (engravings, medals, ancient and modern manuscripts, etc.), similar to documents preserved in archives and museums. This blend of ideas and needs led to the creation of new types of authority records and to new types of links among authority records and between these and bibliographic records. This was a first step towards taking into account the needs voiced in archives and museums.

It then looked feasible to widen the application field of authority records. Managers of authority files devoted themselves to finding out what was done in other libraries and cultural sectors. As regards libraries, the guide of the AUTHOR European project (1995-1998) by BnF was a first attempt at achieving interoperability. The creation of the AFNOR Authority Metadata group in 2000 was another step.

Why AFNOR Is a Privileged Meeting Ground for the Three Interested Communities

Within AFNOR we have the General Commission 46 "Information and documentation," corresponding to ISO Technical Committee 46, responsible for the sector on rules for libraries, archives, and museums. After several years, CG46 is presently aware that we no longer need to state particular rules for the library and documentation sector only, but we also must develop a multi-sector normative process to avoid any sector being left marginal. That's why CG46 recommends adopting general, open rules.

Within CG46 we have the Commission of standardization 357 called "Modelling, production and access to documents," comprising the Group of experts "Authority metadata." AFNOR/CG46/CN357 is the French equivalent to subcommittee SC4 "Computerization in documentation," and, in part, to ISO/TC46/SC9 "Presentation, identification and description of documents." At the end of 1999, CN347 decided to defer, for at least three years, revising traditional cataloguing rules, and instead, fixed new priorities:

- introduction to the SGML/XML encoding of documents, proceeding to the translation into French of DTD EAD (Encoded Archival Description) to code finding aids in archives and libraries.

- definition of the descriptive metadata automatically retrievable starting from electronic versions of theses and academic works, on the basis of Dublin Core Elements.
- training in techniques of modelling and study of existing models.
- draft of an authority data model based on the international projects now in progress.

The Group of experts "Authority metadata" was created in June 2000 and I agreed to chair it.

The Group's Objectives

The Group aims at examining in depth, from a multi-disciplinary perspective, the treatment of authority data to build up a dictionary of elements of these data. To accomplish such work one must control the authority data needed for managing databases of bibliographic, archival, and museum data, and assess the needs related to the management of intellectual copyrights.

The Group finds inspiration in the international activities in progress in the field of modelling within IFLA (its work on FRANAR), ISO (its work on CRM by CIDOC/ICOM) and in the European projects INDECS, INTERPARTY, and LEAF, on which some papers have been presented at this conference.

The Group's Composition

The Authority metadata group, that meets a full day a month, on average, is made up of about thirty participants of diverse origins :

- librarians and documentation experts representing: the Agence bibliographique de l'enseignement supérieur (ABES), the Bibliothèque nationale de France, the Bibliothèque universitaire de Nice, the École nationale supérieure des sciences de l'information et des bibliothèques (ENSSIB), the Bibliothèque de la Fondation nationale des sciences politiques, the Institut national des techniques de la documentation (INTD), the Médiathèque de la Cité des sciences et de l'industrie;
- some archivists representing the Direction des Archives de France and the Centre historique des Archives nationales;
- some members responsible for the museum databases of the Direction des musées de France, the Département des Estampes of the BnF, the Bibliography of the history of art;

- some experts in audio-visual materials representing the Institut national de l'audiovisuel (INA), and, more precisely, its research and development department and its Département Inathèque;
- some managers of intellectual property rights for the Société des auteurs et compositeurs dramatiques.

This well diversified composition is of great importance for the Group that aims at implementing an assessment of authority data on a multi-disciplinary level.

A THREE-PHASE WORK PROJECT

The work methodology for these ambitious aims is based on alternating what we might call "reports from experience" and some "theoretical considerations."

Acquiring a Common Culture

Within the Group the "reports from experience" are an aid to acquire a common culture about authority data. What are the practices in the different sectors of activity represented in the Group? What have we in common? What are each sector's specific features? In order to identify convergence and divergence points, each participant has been questioned on various themes such as:

- *authority files* as tools for managing library catalogues: the BN-OPALE Plus authority files <www.bnf.fr>, the university system for documentation authority files <http://www.sudoc.abes.fr>, the role played by authority files in the management of OCLC, particularly in the CORC program (Cooperative Online Resource Catalog) <www.oclc.org>;
- the vocabularies and authority lists in museum and iconographical databases were the subject of various papers on practices applied in the JOCONDE documentary database <http://www.culture.fr/documentation/joconde/pres.htm>, operated by the Ministère de la Culture et de la Communication, on the functioning and work organization on the thesaurus and authority files of the Bibliography of the history of art (BHA), on the management of the BnF Département des estampes et de la photographie (BN-OPALINE/Estampes base) iconographical database <www.bnf.fr>;
- the reference sources of the databases of the Institut national de l'audiovisuel <http://www.ina.fr/inatheque>;

- the role of authority data in archival description, presentation of ISAAR (CPF) and ISAD(G) and demonstration of the digital images ARCHIM databank <http://www.culture.fr/caran/archim/>;
- authority data have been examined from two perspectives: the principles of thesaurus creation and the index languages as aids to help multi-language subject searching thanks to a presentation of the European project MACS (Multilingual ACces to Subjects) <http://infolab.kub.nl/prj/macs/>;
- authority data useful for managing intellectual copyrights have been described by the representatives of the Société des auteurs et compositeurs dramatiques (SACD) <http://www.sacd.fr>;
- the presentation of the conceptual models of data, not confined to authority data, but bringing in a management of information, helping the Group get familiar with the particular modelling technique:

  - the FRANAR model in course of definition (see Glenn Patton's paper);
  - the *Functional Requirements for Bibliographic Records*, "entity/relation" model elaborated between 1992 and 1997 by IFLA, better known as FRBR;
  - The conceptual reference model elaborated by the Groupe de normalisation documentaire du Comité international pour la documentation du Conseil international des musées (ICOM-CIDOC), better known as CRM (Conceptual Reference Model) <http://cidoc.ics.forth.gr/>. CRM is an "object-oriented" model approved at the end of 2002 as ISO/CD 21127 under the title "A reference ontology for the exchange of data related to cultural heritage."

All of these papers permitted us to know the objectives, the practices and the tools applied in the various fields of activity represented in the Group. Each one raised real interest and led to lively debates on the management praxis and on the terminology employed: referential, thesaurus, vocabulary, authority list, authority file, etc. This training about what others are doing is an investment that will yield fruit when the Group goes on from "reports from experience" to "theoretical considerations."

Defining the Elements of Authority Data

The fact that the group of experts spends half of its monthly meeting being informed about what is going on in the field of authority data on a national and international level does not mean it is a permanent training course! The Group works in this way to establish a vocabulary of authority data that enumerates, denominates, and defines each one of the information elements that contribute to identification of an entity, and may eventually specify the sources to be used. An unambiguous definition must be proposed for each term, and agreement must always be sought among the representatives of the various sectors of activity (libraries, archives, museums, managers of copyrights).

The Group decided to devote itself, first of all, to defining the main entities met in the "reports from experience" sessions, that is, Body, Person, Place, Medium, Material, Work, Technique, Object, Concept, Group, Temporary manifestation and Event. The identification card of each entity is compiled and the file includes the following sections: definition of entity, specification of what is not entity or of what must be excluded from the application field of entity, some examples, a list of unsolved questions, the reference documents used as definition sources, and the text of definitions found in these diverse reference documents.

The main sources used to compile the definitions of entities are the ones found in:

- ISO 5127: Oct. 2001 Information and documentation–Vocabulary
- ISAD(G): general and international rule for archival description <http://www.ica.org/>
- ISAAR(CPF): International rule on archival authority records for bodies, persons and families <http://www.ica.org/>
- FRBR
- FRANAR
- The Dublin Core Element Set (ISO/DIS 15836 being voted at present)
- CRM <http://cidoc.ics.forth.gr/>
- Getty vocabulary and rules <http://www.getty.edu/research/institute/standards>
- AFNOR cataloguing rules
- INTERMARC, MARC 21 and UNIMARC formats (rather poor in their definitions!)

Just as an example, the cards for identifying PLACE, MEDIUM and MATERIAL entities are included (see Appendix). The definitions found in the reference documents cited there are not reproduced, but these identification cards give an idea of the issues faced by the working group.

Debates are often lively! The more so since, collateral to this *stricto sensu* definition work, the Group tries to put at stake all data elements it wants to treat and meets serious difficulty in rendering all the wealth of information to be considered. The Group has tried many ways:

- to state immediately a hierarchy of identifying elements: e.g., for the PERSON identity we can subdivide some "biographical data" into "affiliation," "filiation," "artistic influences," etc.; affiliation, in turn, can be subdivided into affiliation "to a family," "to a corporate body," "to a school of thought," etc.
- to limit itself to an alphabetical list of identifying elements: "artistic influences," "initials," "inventions," "jingle," etc.
- to cross the identifying data elements and the above defined entities in order to point out the elements common to more than one entity. . . .

None of these methods were wholly satisfying; so the Group went on to the third phase in its program: to get familiar with modelling techniques.

Organizing Data Elements: Modelling

Modelling is the last phase, the one in which entities are identified as well as their attributes, and we can form the network of relationships among data elements. Some prerequisites are imperative that require training the Group in modelling. This training must be progressive, even reiterated. Modelling techniques are usually addressed to informatics students; so the main problem was finding a trainer capable of understanding the information specialists' preoccupations and to present material within their range of knowledge.

A first awareness course was proposed to the Group in October 2001 by a doctor in engineering from the Centre national de la recherche scientifique. The aim of this first half-day course was to measure the contributions of a modelling method in the development of a project, to understand how analysis methods evolved, to discover the different approaches in the field of modelling, and to master the principles of object-oriented modelling. Since it was presented in this course as an aid for modelling and structuring ideas, as a help for reasoning and simulations, and as a means for communication among different persons, the Group quickly became convinced they really had to make this effort.

The second phase of training took place in November 2002, for a whole day, during a Seminar on the startup of data standardization in UML [Unified Modeling Language], run specifically for the AFNOR Group by a professor from Institut national des sciences appliquées de Lyon (INSA-Lyon). The basic notions dealing with models and practical modelling were mentioned, but the essential part of the presentation was based on UML diagrams and mainly on structure diagrams and the concepts of "class," "heritage," "properties" and on diagrams of usage cases. This second phase was less interesting for the participants; yet it should help the Group to choose a tool to give form to the results of its considerations. An assessment of this seminar was scheduled for the meeting in January 2003.

CONCLUSION

At the end of 2002, the Group is at a turning point in its existence. Sharing experiences on the treatment of authorities in various cultural sectors has been definitely fruitful, an asset for the future. Librarians have come to know ISAAR(CPF) and CRM. Archivists and professionals from museums have come to know FRANAR and learned a lot about normative tools at librarians' disposal. Each one was made richer by the other's point of view and has acquired new knowledge on modelling. Then, are we ready to meet our commitment and propose a common conceptual model? The Group must again examine its primary objective that meant proposing a general model for authority data in order to allow interoperability among libraries, museums, and archives. It must measure its actual ability to fulfil this task within a reasonable lapse of time, eventually curtail its aspirations identifying some more manageable subgroups, and choose the type of model to develop: entity/relation model, object-oriented model, or semantic model. The Group's next meetings will be decisive ones.

APPENDIX

ENTITY n°3 : **PLACE**

- Definition:

  Real or fictitious part of space

- Examples:

- place where Nelson died: it is on a ship, but what are the precise coordinates of the place? On the ship, but somewhere on the Ocean. (CRM)
- place of abode of a person, a family. (Archives–ISAAR(CPF))
- seat: place where the body acts. (Archives–ISAAR(CPF))
- places of existence: place of foundation, of expiration, of birth, of death. (Archives–ISAAR(CPF))
- location of a municipality, a city, a congress. (FRBR, Getty Thesaurus of geographical names)

- geographical attribute: continent, rivers, mountains (Getty Thesaurus of geographical names)
- oil platform (example made by the Group of experts)
- the 140 altitude (example made by the Group of experts)
- the 52nd parallel (example made by the Group of experts)
- the Atlantis (example made by the Group of experts)
- the isle of Avalon (king Arhur cycle) (example made by the Group of experts)

- Remarks

- This part of space can be taken into consideration in order to locate another entity or in itself.
- CRM differentiates "place" as mere topographic indication and "site," a place whose boundaries are vague and that can be represented on an iconographical object. Place is used to qualify something else (an event, a body, etc.). Site can be defined in relation to a place.
- ISAAR(CPF) specifies that it is necessary "to qualify the place name with a word or an expression specifying its context and use."
- The Thesaurus of geographical names (Getty) defines "place" but the Guide for the description of architectural drawings (Getty) defines "location."
- FRBR similarly differentiates "place" and "location."
- Corporate bodies are excluded (e.g., the Louvre Museum as a corporate body).
- The horizon is not a place.

- Unsolved issues:

- confusion, sometimes, between a place and a building, or a body, e.g., n°10 Downing Street. How can we distinguish them? It depends on points of view . . .
- difficulty in differentiating body and place: e.g., "Paris"; the "Louvre" (building, place, body); the Picasso Museum at Antibes is located in the Grimaldi castle.

ENTITY n°4 : **MEDIUM**

- Definition:

Concrete element designed to contain written, sound, electromagnetic, numeric, graphic information

- Examples:

- audio-cassette, video-disc, microfilm, slide (FRBR)
- archival medium, recording medium, magnetic medium, optical medium, physical medium, primary or secondary medium, chemical photosensitive medium (Vocabulaire de la documentation)
- papyrus, paper, metal, parchment, fabric, wood, film, magnetic tape (Archives)
- canvas
- parchment (see also material)
- movie film (FRBR)

- Remarks:

- CRM: the concept of medium is not dealt with by CRM, perhaps because the English term for "medium" is "material." Therefore, is the concept dealt with under that class? Also the English term "format" designates the medium.
- Archives: medium is defined as material but there is no definition for material.
- FRBR: the concept of "medium" implies the concept of "dimension," "medium," and "material" are not differentiated.
- The Vocabulaire de la documentation: associates medium and process (a technique, then?)

- Unsolved issues:
- to create a Physical features entity including "medium" and "material"?

ENTITY n°5 : **MATERIAL**

- Definition:

Material an object is made of or part of its components

- Examples:

- ink
- microfilm (medium) silver or diazo (material)
- parchment (medium and material): calf or goat
- painting, oil
- plastic (Vocabulaire de la documentation)
- glass (Vocabulaire de la documentation)

- <u>Remarks</u>:

– Except the case of sculpture in which medium and material cannot be distinguished, the material is what we put on the medium. Concept of "injective" and "subjective" (!)
– All media need a material, conversely, we may have a material without medium (e.g., a sculpture).
– Archives: medium is defined as material but there is no definition for material.
– Vocabulaire de la documentation: it uses the term "substratum."

- <u>Unsolved issues</u>:

– to create a Physical features entity including "medium" and "material"?

A First Contribution
in the Field of Religion:
The ACOLIT Project

Fausto Ruggeri

SUMMARY. This paper presents a description of ACOLIT, an authority list of names of persons, corporate bodies, and works associated with the Catholic Church. *[Article copies available for a fee from The Haworth Document Delivery Service: 1-800-HAWORTH. E-mail address: <docdelivery@haworthpress.com> Website: <http://www.HaworthPress.com> © 2004 by The Haworth Press, Inc. All rights reserved.]*

KEYWORDS. ACOLIT, authority list, Catholic Church, liturgical works, Catholic authors

The idea of an authority list in the Catholic religious field arose in 1995 in Assisi, during the Congress of the Associazione Bibliotecari Ecclesiastici Italiani (Italian Catholic Librarian Association). This idea was immediately

---

Fausto Ruggeri is affiliated with Associazione Bibliotecari Ecclesiastici Italiani (ABEI).

[Haworth co-indexing entry note]: "A First Contribution in the Field of Religion: The ACOLIT Project." Ruggeri, Fausto. Co-published simultaneously in *Cataloging & Classification Quarterly* (The Haworth Information Press, an imprint of The Haworth Press, Inc.) Vol. 39, No. 1/2, 2004, pp. 517-522; and: *Authority Control in Organizing and Accessing Information: Definition and International Experience* (ed: Arlene G. Taylor, and Barbara B. Tillett) The Haworth Information Press, an imprint of The Haworth Press, Inc., 2004, pp. 517-522. Single or multiple copies of this article are available for a fee from The Haworth Document Delivery Service [1-800-HAWORTH, 9:00 a.m. - 5:00 p.m. (EST). E-mail address: docdelivery@haworthpress.com].

realized by the constitution of a Work Group directed by Mauro Guerrini. The director also proposed the title of the work: ACOLIT, an acronym of liturgical savour, *Autori cattolici e opere liturgiche in italiano* (*Catholic Authors and Liturgical Works, in Italian: an Authority List*). After seven years, one half of the plan has been realized. Two volumes have already been published:

1. Bible, Catholic Church, Roman Curia, Papal State, Vatican, Popes and Antipopes / editorial staff: Mauro Guerrini, Paola Pieri, Fausto Ruggeri, Luciano Tempestini (1998). lxi, 385 p.
2. Religious Orders / editorial staff: Silvana Chistè and Giorgio Mocatti (2000). 1102 p.

The third volume, concerning liturgical works, will follow before the end of this year.

THE AIMS OF ACOLIT

First, ACOLIT tries to offer a reliable authority list in the religious field; it tries to completely cover all the aspects, past and present, of history and life of the Catholic Church: two thousand years of culture and civilization, continuously evolving and leaving deep traces in culture, in literature, and art. ACOLIT fills a large gap in the professional literature.

Another aim of ACOLIT is to help the cataloguer in the choice of the form of the name. It does not tackle the problem of the distinct bibliographic identity, a concept allowed by the *Paris Principles* under point 6.2, excluded from *RICA* (Italian cataloguing rules), but considered by AACR 42B, note 5 and by AACR2 22.2B2. The scope of ACOLIT is limited to listing the standard form the names and equivalent forms of names by which an author or a title are known. Libraries will adopt the form they consider most suitable for their catalogue (e.g., the Latin or the vernacular form of a pope's name;[1] one order of citation rather than another) and–if they prefer to do so–will adopt more than one name to index groups of works written by the same author under different names (principle of plurality of headings or distinct identity). ACOLIT, for example, uses blind entries to cross-reference the civil name of the popes to their papal name, under which the variant forms of both are listed.

This authority list has been made especially for librarians and tries to improve their professional ability. It tries to bring the catalogues of libraries into harmony by providing:

1. authoritative uniform headings;
2. cross-references between entries and their variants in order to facilitate research;
3. periodical lists of revision, according to the evolution of the ecclesiastical world, which in the course of the ages was closely connected with the civil one, in harmony or in contrast with it, and which has always showed a continuous and sometimes surprising sprightliness. The first lists of revision and their means of publication are being planned.

ACOLIT has been made for all libraries, not only for the religious ones, but also for all which have religious books. It covers the well-known vicissitudes, sometimes dramatic, of Italian religious institutions (and of their libraries) in two thousand years of history. It is intended as an instrument of standardization in cataloguing religious works.

ACOLIT also includes proposals aimed at contributing to the present debate about the revision of *RICA* and about the construction of national authority lists. It is a list of controlled names, and so it can also be an introduction to a list of subject headings in the field of religion.

This is the general plan of the work (each volume concerns one or more sections of the Catholic religious world):

1. the *Bible* and its partial editions;
2. the Catholic Church, comprising the names of institutions, departments, and commissions of the Roman Curia (Holy See); the names of the offices for the civil administration of the Papal State, of Vatican City State and of the institutions dependent on it;
3. the names of all the Popes (from Linus to John Paul II) and of the Antipopes;
4. the names of religious communities, institutes, congregations, and orders, with the exclusion of military orders, orders of knighthood, and charitable associations of diocesan right;
5. the titles of liturgical works;
6. the names of authors whose activities or whose works are connected with Christianity, with particular attention to authors who lived in the medieval period (e.g., Fathers of the Church, saints, theologians, bishops);
7. the names of Italian Catholic institutions and a listing of the main international Catholic institutions: associations, agencies, groups, movements, confraternities, universities and educational institutes, seminaries, colleges, bishops' conferences (national and regional), dioceses;

For religious orders, ACOLIT presents the most complete list of religious orders ever realized out of library science. Such an exhaustive list had never been seen, neither by the Congregation for Religious Orders of the Holy See (which is put at the head of the present religious orders, not of the extinguished ones that ACOLIT has tried to list completely) nor by the "Annuario pontificio."

There are two lists in the appendix. One gives the initials of the religious orders (e.g., S.I. for Jesuits), while the other gives the names of the cities where the female institutions have their main house. The second list is particularly useful as it helps to identify the institution more easily. The name of the institution often contains the name of the city either of origin or of the seat of the mother house.

Obviously, such a list as ACOLIT can be used outside of the specific field of libraries for which it has been made. It can also be, for example, a sort of guide for some aspects of the Catholic religious world.

Finally, let me present the Agency which has taken it upon itself to do this work: the Associazione dei bibliotecari ecclesiastici italiani (ABEI). It was founded in 1978, and it currently has about 300 members (persons and different types of libraries from every part of Italy). It is the association of Catholic librarians that has the major number of members in Europe. Among its main activities are the following: two censuses of the Italian Catholic libraries, whose data are contained in two volumes (published in 1990 and1995); an electronic union catalogue of the Italian Catholic libraries on CD-ROM: first edition published in 2001 with 550,000 records from 40 religious libraries; second edition published in 2002 with 1,000,000 records from 66 libraries. ABEI periodically organizes courses of training for librarians, congresses, and seminars and publishes their proceedings, and additionally publishes the "Bollettino di informazione" (1981- ; new series 1992-). It has a website (www.abei.it), which presents all the news useful for learning about the association.

ENDNOTES

1. There was a time when French research libraries adopted the Latin form for the names of classical authors and the public libraries used the French form.

2. *AACR2R* is also available in an Italian edition: *Regole di catalogazione anglo-americane, Seconda edizione, Revisione del 1988* / redatte sotto la direzione del Joint Steering Committee for Revision of AACR; a cura di Michael Gorman e Paul W. Winkler.–Edizione italiana / a cura di Rossella Dini e Luigi Crocetti.–Milano: Editrice bibliografica, c1997.–xxii, 712 p.–ISBN 88-7075-469-3.

French Official Corporate Bodies of the Ancient Regime (COPAR) and Religious Corporate Bodies (CORELI): Two Operations in Creating Authority Records in Order to Standardise the Entries of Bibliographic Records in Bibliothèque Nationale de France Retrospective Conversion

Nadine Boddaert

SUMMARY. During the retrospective conversion of its printed and card catalogues, the Bibliothèque nationale de France was confronted with the existence of old bibliographic records without corporate body headings, because this concept was unknown when the books were catalogued. The Library launched two programs aimed at creating authority records for specific fields important for access to the national bibliographic heritage, respectively named COPAR–for the official corporate bodies, mainly national and preceding the French Revolution–

Nadine Boddaert is affiliated with Bibliothèque nationale de France.

[Haworth co-indexing entry note]: "French Official Corporate Bodies of the Ancient Regime (COPAR) and Religious Corporate Bodies (CORELI): Two Operations in Creating Authority Records in Order to Standardise the Entries of Bibliographic Records in Bibliothèque Nationale de France Retrospective Conversion." Boddaert, Nadine. Co-published simultaneously in *Cataloging & Classification Quarterly* (The Haworth Information Press, an imprint of The Haworth Press, Inc.) Vol. 39, No. 1/2, 2004, pp. 523-531; and: *Authority Control in Organizing and Accessing Information: Definition and International Experience* (ed: Arlene G. Taylor, and Barbara B. Tillett) The Haworth Information Press, an imprint of The Haworth Press, Inc., 2004, pp. 523-531. Single or multiple copies of this article are available for a fee from The Haworth Document Delivery Service [1-800-HAWORTH, 9:00 a.m. - 5:00 p.m. (EST). E-mail address: docdelivery@haworthpress.com].

and CORELI–for the religious corporate bodies (parishes, dioceses, confraternities, orders and congregations, etc.). The 2,550 records created by the COFAR and CORELI programs have been included in the authority file of BN-OPALE PLUS; so they are visible either via the online catalogue or separately with other authority records. They give librarians an extra tool for identifying entities. They also represent a valuable source of information accessible to anyone who takes an interest in the history of French government institutions or religious entities.
[Article copies available for a fee from The Haworth Document Delivery Service: 1-800-HAWORTH. E-mail address: <docdelivery@haworthpress.com> Website: <http://www.HaworthPress.com> © 2004 by The Haworth Press, Inc. All rights reserved.]

KEYWORDS. Authority files (cataloging), France, corporate headings (cataloging), Catholic Church, government headings (cataloging), French administrative and political divisions, 1500-1800

During the retrospective conversion of its printed and card catalogues,[1] the Bibliothèque nationale de France (BnF) was confronted with the existence of old bibliographic records without corporate body headings, because this concept was unknown when the books were catalogued.

The intellectual process behind systematic classifications was used at the Bibliotheque nationale at the time to facilitate research by readers. In particular, cataloguers of past centuries made the classification outline visible to users by indicating names of corporate bodies on index cards (i.e., guide cards) in some specialized classified catalogues. Relying partly on this information and partly on statements of responsibility found in bibliographic records, we were able to create headings allowing us to index corporate bodies during the preparatory work to the retrospective conversion. However, for lack of time, we could not plan the creation of corresponding authority records.[2] This is why the BnF later launched two research programs aimed at creating authority records for specific fields–specific but very important for access to the national bibliographic heritage. These two programs were respectively named COFAR and CORELI.

COFAR
(COLLECTIVITÉS OFFICIELLES FRANÇAISES D'ANCIEN RÉGIME/ FRENCH OFFICIAL CORPORATE BODIES OF THE ANCIENT REGIME)

The COFAR Program was approved in February 1995. Its purpose was to enrich the authority file of the bibliographic database–BN-OPALE–with a corpus of official corporate bodies, mainly national and preceding the French Revolution. To carry out this program, we relied on a list of access points to Administrative acts of the Ancient Regime descriptions drawn up by the retrospective conversion team. Between November 1995 and March 1996, the program was managed by the Bureau des autorités collectivités (Corporate body Section) of the Service de cordination bibliographic (Bibliographic coordinating Division) of the BnF.[3]

The very old catalogue of Administrative acts of the Ancient Regime was a handwritten card catalogue, organised systematically into 9 categories:

1. Actes administratifs
2. Actes judiciaires
3. Actes des corporations
4. Actes des universités et collèges
5. Actes des hôpitaux et hospices
6. Actes des maisons princières
7. Actes des provinces annexées
8. Actes des pays étrangers
9. Actes postérieurs à 1789

Each category of the acts was subdivided according to the types of act and the corporate bodies which produced them, that is, not according to alphabetical order but to the way the Ancient Regime was organised. For example:

Administrations centrales
    Chancellerie
        Chancelier
        Chancellerie du palais
        Chancellerie des secrétaires du roi
        Commissions de la Chancellerie
        Tarifs du sceau

or

        Actes judiciaires
            Juridictions ordinaires
                Grand conseil
                Requêtes

> Parlement de Paris
> Généralités
> Recueils d'actes généraux
> Recueils par matières
> Cour des pairs
> Avocats et procureurs
> Basoche du palais
> Procureur général
> Requêtes du palais
> Grands jours
> Arrêts isolés

When the COFAR project started, we estimated that we would have to create or update about 500 authority records for corporate bodies. We ended up with 850 authority records.

We created our headings according to the NF Z 44-060 standard–*Forme et structure des vedettes collectivité-auteurs*[4]–which is the version by AFNOR (French association for standardisation) of the IFLA international recommendations *Form and structure of corporate headings*.[5] The main characteristic of these authority records is that a great number of them include a note on the history of the item.

Example of COFAR record:

France. Chambre de l'édit de Castres   *forme internationale*

Nationalité : France   Langue : français
Naissance : 1595-....

   Du ressort du parlement de Toulouse, elle siège d'abord à Castres puis à Castelnaudary ; elle est composée d'un nombre égal de catholiques et de protestants

Source(s) : Marion. - Zeller

   < France. Chambre de l'édit de Languedoc

Notice n° : FRBNF12502875   1996/02/26

Whenever necessary, we made links with other authority records. In general, these are chronological links to different forms of name due to political and/or administrative changes.

France. Intendance (Lille)   *forme internationale*

Nationalité : France   Langue : français
Naissance : 1691-....

   Cette intendance de pays d'Etats réunit la Flandre et l'Artois et comprend 8 baillages et une gouvernance. Le comté de Flandre entre dans le royaume au cours du règne de Louis XIV. Une intendance est d'abord établie dans chacune des deux régions naturelles (Flandre wallonne, Flandre maritime). En 1715, les deux Flandre sont réunies en une seule intendance dont la capitale est Lille. A partir de 1754, l'Artois relève également de cette intendance

Source(s) : Marion. - Lex. adm. de la France d'anc. rég.

   >> << Avant 1715, voir : Intendance de Flandre wallonne
   >> << Avant 1715, voir : France. Intendance de Flandre maritime

Notice n° : FRBNF12491748   1995/11/28

France. Assemblée nationale constituante (1789-1791)   *forme internationale*

Nationalité : France   Langue : français
Naissance : 1789-06-17   Mort : 1791-09-30

Les États généraux se transforment en Assemblée constituante, proclamée le 17 juin 1789 (Assemblée nationale) et définitivement constituée le 9 juillet ; la Constitution solennellement acceptée par le roi le 14 septembre 1791, la Constituante laisse la place à l'Assemblée législative le 30 septembre

Forme(s) rejetée(s) :
< France. Assemblée nationale (1789-1791)
< France. États généraux (1789)

Forme(s) associée(s) :
>> << Regroupé par : France. Assemblée nationale

Source(s) : GDEL. – Lalane

Notice n° : FRBNF11863837   2002/07/19

This corpus of authority records, which identifies the official corporate bodies of the Ancient Regime, is a new working tool which is now at the disposal of libraries for cataloguing old collections, and particularly for those libraries which contain books coming from French Revolution confiscations. It also represents a valuable source of information accessible to any one who takes an interest in the history of French government institutions.

After the conclusion of the COFAR program, the BnF Service de coordination bibliographique started a similar project for religious corporate bodies.

CORELI (COLLECTIVITÉS RELIGIEUSES/ RELIGIOUS CORPORATE BODIES)

CORELI is a much more ambitious project because its aim is to create authority records for all kinds of religious corporate bodies (parishes, dioceses, confraternities, orders and congregations, etc.) which appear in bibliographic descriptions of monographs in three ancient specialised catalogues which are now retrospectively converted: i.e., Ecclesiastical acts catalogue, CORDA (or statements of judicial causes prior to 1791) catalogue, and French history catalogue, totalling about 3,000 corporate bodies.

Whereas the COFAR program was entirely carried out by the BnF, the CORELI program, on the other hand, is a collaboration between several institutions which have large collections of religious books–BnF, Bibliothèque du Saulchoir, Bibliothèque de Fels de l'Institut catholique de Paris, Bibliothèque du Centre national de pastorale liturgique–or are expert in the field, as Ecole pratique des hautes études en sciences sociales. An agreement was signed between BnF and each institution in order to give an official basis to the partnership. The division of the field was decided according to the specialisation of each of them. For example, all corporate bodies connected with Dominican spirituality were taken up by the Dominican Bibliothèque du Saulchoir.

Each partner supplies information on a form, which all parties developed at the beginning of the project. The main items are: date of creation, date of foundation, date of approval, dates of activities, accurate juridical statute, official name, other forms of the name (such as old/obsolete names, common denomination, abbreviations, nicknames, etc.), hierarchical links, chronological data about merging or partition of the entity, some information about history, address, and sources of all these data. The BnF has the responsibility for the control of the data, the eventual verifications, the harmonisation and conformity with national cataloguing rules and IFLA recommendations. The BnF enters the records in its database–formerly BN-OPALE, now BN-OPALE PLUS–in INTERMARC format. All the data supplied in the forms by the partners are not present in the authority records; part of the information is used to identify the entity without ambiguity, to distinguish one from another, or to establish links.

It is the official name of the corporate body which is the heading chosen. For an abbey, a convent or a monastery, for example, headings are:

* *Abbazia di Montecassino*
* *Abbaye de Saint-Guilhem-le-Désert*
* *Carmel royal de Sainte-Thérèse (Paris)*
* *Couvent Saint-Jacques (Paris)*

- *Monastère de Fontaine-lès-Dijon (1614-1790)*
- *Prieuré Notre-Dame de Verdelais (1627-177.)*[6]

For a religious order, a congregation, a confraternity:

- *Confraternità di santa Maria della Carità (Bologne, Italie)*
- *Confrérie de Saint Ferreol et Saint Ferjeux (Besançon)*
- *Congrégation des soeurs de Sainte-Clotilde*
- *Frères agricoles et hospitaliers du vénérable Géronimo*
- *Ordre des Frères mineurs*
- *Suore salesiane dei Sacri Cuori*

Some of the partners did not agree with these headings:

- on the one hand, some would prefer the common name and not the official one (Franciscans, Jesuits, Dominicans, etc.)
- on the other hand, hierarchical structured headings were preferred in order to gather the spiritual families.

As the BnF did not want to introduce inconsistencies in its authority file, and in order to answer to the particular needs of some libraries and the future users of the authority records, we proposed to enter common names and hierarchical forms as additional variants. For instance:

- *Congrégation de Solesmes. Abbaye Sainte-Anne de Kergonan*
- *Ordre des frères prêcheurs. Province de France. Couvent Saint-Jacques (Paris).*

This way we would make it easier for all kinds of users to search the catalogue whatever their expertise in the field.

As with the authority records created by the COFAR program, the CORELI records also contain historical notes.

Collège de Boissy (Paris)   *forme internationale*

Nationalité : France   **Langue :** français
Naissance : 1358   **Mort :** 1763

Collège fondé en 1358 par le chanoine Geoffroi Vidé et le chanoine Etienne Vidé, son neveu, originaires de Boissy-le-Sec (diocèse de Chartres), pour des étudiants pauvres de cette ville, ou, à défaut, de la paroisse Saint-André-des-Arts de Paris. Il fut réuni au collège Louis-le-Grand en 1763 et ses bâtiments vendus en 1764

Source(s) : Dictionnaire historique des rues de Paris / Jacques Hillairet, 1985

Notice n° : FRBNF13756731   2001/12/14

In this corpus of religious entities are present not only famous orders and congregations but also local communities of diocesan law, groups which had a very short life and, consequently, are difficult to identify.

Frères agricoles et hospitaliers du vénérable Géronimo   *forme internationale*

Nationalité : France   **Langue** : français
Naissance : 1869   **Mort** : 1872

Fondé en 1869 par Mgr Lavigerie, évêque d'Alger, cet institut (du nom d'un Arabe converti, martyrisé au XVIe siècle) avait pour but de soutenir financièrement par le travail de ses membres les oeuvres fondées en Algérie. Il ne connut guère de succès, et les quelques membres recrutés furent incorporés à partir de 1872 dans la Société des Missionnaires d'Afrique (fondée en 1868 par Lavigerie)

Sources : D.H.G.E., t. 18, col. 1351-1352

Notice n° : FRBNF13618172   2001/05/29

When it was necessary, links were established between religious communities which had united them, for example:

Soeurs du Saint-Enfant-Jésus d'Aurillac   *forme internationale*

Nationalité : France   **Langue** : français
Naissance : 1804   **Mort** : 1957

Congrégation fondée en 1804 par Marie Maisonobe (qui venait du Puy). En 1957 elle fit fusion avec les Béates de l'instruction chrétienne du Puy et les Sœurs de la Sainte-Enfance de Jésus de Rambouillet pour former la Congrégation de l'Enfant-Jésus de Versailles, transférée à Paris en 1999

Forme(s) rejetée(s) :
< Congrégation du Saint-Enfant-Jésus d'Aurillac
< Religieuses du Saint-Enfant-Jésus d'Aurillac
< Saint-Enfant-Jésus d'Aurillac

>> << Après 1957, voir : Congrégation des Soeurs de l'Enfant-Jésus (Paris)

Source(s) : Guide des sources de l'histoire des congrégations féminines françaises de vie active / Charles Molette, 1974. – Histoire de la Congrégation du Saint-Enfant-Jésus d'Aurillac, 1927

Notice n° :FRBNF13574950   2003/02/04

The CORELI program is still in progress. At the end of November 2002, 1,127 records had been created. They give users an extra tool for identifying entities. But, unfortunately, lack of resources devoted to this task do not allow a quicker progress. On the other hand, new agreements with other institutions will be necessary in order to cover all the areas of the project.

CONCLUSION

All of the records created by COFAR and CORELI programs have been included in the authority file of BN-OPALE PLUS, so they are visible either via the online catalogue (URL: http://catalogue.bnf.fr), or separately (by the following steps: http://bnf.fr, then choosing "Informations pour les professionnels," "Consulter les notices d'autorité").

The authority records proceeding from the COFAR and CORELI programs are not yet linked to bibliographic records from the retrospective conversion. This linking will be another stage of the immense task aimed at improving the coherence of the online catalogue. It should be programmed as one of the BnF's numerous correction projects. It will be up to the newly created Catalogue Committee[7] to determine priorities.

NOTES

1. Twenty-nine catalogues of printed documents were retrospectively converted between 1988 et 1999. Cf. Beaudiquez, Marcelle. *Le chantier de conversion rétrospective à la Bibliothèque nationale,* In «Bulletin des bibliothèques de France», t. 38, n°3, 1993, p. 10; Beaudiquez, Marcelle et Beaugendre, Anne-Marie. *Du tiroir à l'écran: les opérations de conversion rétrospective de la Bibliothèque nationale de France*: Workshop on retrospective conversion, IFLA, Beijing, 29 August 1996.

2. During the retrospective conversion it was impossible to introduce authority control for the 6,000,000 records of monographs. Originally it was planned as a four-year program. Cf. *Bilan du chantier de conversion rétrospective des imprimés, CRI: 1988-1999* / Bibliothèque nationale de France, Agence bibliographique nationale; [réd. par A.-M. Beaugendre], 2001, p. 48.

3. *DDSR: Programme COFAR,* In «Trajectoire en bref: lettre interne de la Bibliothèque nationale de France», n° 12, 31 mai 1996.

4. *Catalogue d'auteurs et d'anonymes: forme et structure des vedettes de collectivités-auteurs: NF Z 44-060 décembre 1996.*–Paris: AFNOR, 1996.

5. *Form and structure of corporate headings: recommendations of the Working group on corporate headings* / approved by the Standing committees of the IFLA Section on cataloguing and the IFLA Section on official publications.–London: IFLA International office for UBC, 1980. *Report from the Review group on form and structure of corporate headings,* In «ICBC», oct-dec. 1992.

6. [Editor's note: A period is a convention used in this authority file for showing an unknown exact date. In this case, a note in the authority record tells us that the entity closed between 1774 and 1780.]

7. Created in March 2002, within the framework of a reorganization of the National Bibliographic Agency.

The Project *Authority File*
for Names Relating to Perugia and Its Area

Claudia Parmeggiani

SUMMARY. The project *Authority File* by Biblioteca Augusta, the State Archives of Perugia, and the Archive Superintendence of Umbria aims at the creation of an experimental aid for reference and bibliographic control addressed to librarians, keepers of archives, and historians interested in the study of the Perugian area in the period prior to the nineteenth century. This paper describes the project to build this authority file. *[Article copies available for a fee from The Haworth Document Delivery Service: 1-800-HAWORTH. E-mail address: <docdelivery@haworthpress.com> Website: <http://www.HaworthPress.com> © 2004 by The Haworth Press, Inc. All rights reserved.]*

KEYWORDS. Perugia, Italy, Umbria, authority file, archives

The project *Authority File* by Biblioteca Augusta (hereafter referred to as Augusta), the State Archives of Perugia, and the Archive Superintendence of Umbria aims at the creation of an experimental aid for reference and biblio-

---

Claudia Parmeggiani is affiliated with Biblioteca Augusta, Perugia.

[Haworth co-indexing entry note]: "The Project *Authority File* for Names Relating to Perugia and Its Area." Parmeggiani, Claudia. Co-published simultaneously in *Cataloging & Classification Quarterly* (The Haworth Information Press, an imprint of The Haworth Press, Inc.) Vol. 39, No. 1/2, 2004, pp. 533-541; and: *Authority Control in Organizing and Accessing Information: Definition and International Experience* (ed: Arlene G. Taylor, and Barbara B. Tillett) The Haworth Information Press, an imprint of The Haworth Press, Inc., 2004, pp. 533-541. Single or multiple copies of this article are available for a fee from The Haworth Document Delivery Service [1-800-HAWORTH, 9:00 a.m. - 5:00 p.m. (EST). E-mail address: docdelivery@haworthpress.com].

http://www.haworthpress.com/web/CCQ
© 2004 by The Haworth Press, Inc. All rights reserved.
Digital Object Identifier: 10.1300/J104v39n01_19

graphic control addressed to librarians, keepers of archives, and historians interested in the study of the Perugian area in the period prior to the nineteenth century.

Augusta aims at giving wide publicity about the project and, for that purpose, a text on the Web is regularly updated both in Italian and in English entitled, "Authority file of names of Perugia and its region." The text has the following components:

- origins of the project
- working group
- identified categories and catalogues
- stage of work in progress
- dictionary of data.

The text is available at http://augusta.comune.perugia.it, which is a sub-section "Projects" of the Biblioteca Augusta Web site.

THE PROJECT

In the course of recent research initiatives that have been realized by Augusta with the National State Archives in Perugia and other cultural institutions interested in local history, we felt we needed an authority file of names of Perugia and its region. Such an authority file would integrate with existing indexes, to facilitate cataloguing modern and antiquarian documents that were included in SBN (Servizio bibiotecario nazionale, Italy's national bibliography service) since 1994, as additions from the regional node of Umbria. Augusta also needed this authority file for three initiatives: a bibliographic exhibition on the registers of the arts and crafts in Perugia, a meeting on the scholar Annibale Mariotti, and a workshop on cataloguing manuscript items of cultural heritage value.

The exhibition "Per buono stato della citade: le matricole delle arti di Perugia"[1] was held from June 20 to September 15, 2001 at Penna Palace in the City of Perugia, and was organized with the support of the Senate of the Republic, by Augusta in collaboration with the National Archives and Deputazione di Storia Patria for Umbria. On that occasion, we created a catalogue of the manuscripts containing the statutes and registers of the arts preserved in their originals at Augusta, and we standardized the existing descriptions relating to manuscripts no longer present in Perugia, but a copy of which was available in electronic format. The creation of bibliographic descriptions made according to national and international standards, as stated by the national census of manuscripts (MANUS), involved some problems in identifying the names cited in the documents and in their inclusion in the authority file.

Also in 2001, in the context of the conference on Annibale Mariotti, Augusta started cataloguing the fond of the Perugian scholar. The fond, consisting of about 250 units dating from the seventeenth century, is of extreme importance for the cultural history of Perugia. There is no detailed index of its papers. It was donated to the City in 1867 and includes the autograph manuscript 1230, titled "Index of registers of the arts." In this case too, MANUS was used. The MANUS system provides software created for medieval and humanist manuscripts, which allows the surveying of data for classical codices but that also can be used for modern manuscripts.

Thanks to the assistance of ICCU (Istituto Centrale per il Catalogo Unico), the use of MANUS for cataloguing of modern manuscripts or document-like items produced excellent results in the Biblioteca Augusta. We treated not only texts that can be identified as works, but also annotations, notes, drafts, fragments, and also archival documents, acts, in original or copy, and official documentation of bodies and persons. These documents, when preserved in libraries, are usually separated from their original collection and consequently deprived of the archival bond which is part of their nature; therefore, they are catalogued as bibliographic documents.

In January 2002, Augusta organized a one-day workshop about cataloguing of the manuscript cultural heritage in order to discuss in depth the issues related to modern manuscripts. In this context, a roundtable, "The cultural heritage in archives and libraries: aspects of cataloguing and access," was coordinated by Giovanna Merola, president of the permanent Commission for the revision of *RICA*.[2] It was in the context of the roundtable that we decided to create a Working Group made up of experts from Augusta, the State Archives, and the Archive Superintendence of Umbria. The use of catalogues of national relevance does not always meet the requirements of scholars, since names which are mainly of local interest are not often cited and can, on the contrary, be more easily identified by bibliographic and archival research made on site. Today, archives and libraries can easily share the results of their research using computer technologies, but in order to create shared working tools, they first must discuss the technologies and standards to be adopted. Conforming to standards is a process presently evolving at the international level.[3] It aims at reaching common objectives. From its start, the Perugia project was planned as a useful place for experimentation.

The project Working Group[4] had the following objectives:

1. analysis of recent cataloguing experiences at the local level, implemented with computer technologies
2. comparison of existing standards, at the national and international level, for authority control of catalogue headings
3. comparison with normalization choices adopted in the project for a national authority file in Italy
4. planning an implementation of a model for the *Authority File* able to manage the names cited in the documents held by institutions that are members of the Working Group.

SELECTION OF LOCAL PROJECTS

The Working Group identified a set of projects of high historical interest, whose conformation to cataloguing rules has been verified by the State Archives and Biblioteca Augusta, but also by other important national institutions interested in Umbria and its cultural documents. The four selected projects provide an electronic version of the results of their research:

- Inventory of the notaries' fonds in the State Archives of Perugia (ASP), Notarial Deeds
- List of notaries of the registers of the arts in Perugia, derived from the MANUS database created by Biblioteca Augusta
- Inventory of the names of people of Perugia Studiorum taken from the database "Maestri e scolari a Siena e Perugia 125-1500," created by the University of Siena and published on the Internet at: http://www.unisi.it/docentes/
- List of Perugian publishers, taken from the EDIT16 database created by ICCU and published on the Internet at: http://edit.16.1ccu.sbn.it/.

The Working Group also selected the following printed texts and manuscripts that were agreed upon as reliable reference sources to start the project for Perugia and its area:

- Vermiglioli, G. B. *Biografia degli scrittori perugini e notizie delle opere loro.* Perugia: Bertelli e Giovanni Costantini, 1829.
- Arrighi, A. *Notizie di famiglie perugine*. (Mss. BAP 1548-57)
- Alessi, C. *Elogia civium perusinorum.* (Mss. BAP 1202 1205; idem ed. Fulginae, apud Augustinum Alterium, 1635).

COMPARISON BETWEEN NATIONAL
AND INTERNATIONAL CATALOGUING RULES

Following the suggestions that emerged at the roundtable in January in Perugia, the Working Group decided to concentrate its analysis on the issues related to name entries in catalogues. The first stage consisted of compiling a reference list of rules adopted by libraries and archives that the group had recognized as authoritative sources for transcription of name in the authority file to be created in Perugia. The following is that list of rules:

- *Regole italiane di catalogazione per autori.* Roma: ICCU, 1979. (known as *RICA*)
- *Guida alla catalogazione in SBN. Pubblicazioni monografiche e in serie.* Roma: ICCU, 1995.
- *Guida alla catalogazione in SBN, Libro Antico.* Roma: ICCU, 1995.
- *Guida a una descrizione uniforme dei manoscritti e al loro censimento.* Roma: ICCU, 1990.
- *ISAD(G): norme generale et internationale de description archivistique.* Ottawa, 2000.
- *ISAAR(CPF) International Standard Archival Authority Record for Corporate Bodies, Persons and Families.* Final version approved by the International Archives Council, Paris, 1995.[5]

RICA was considered a useful set of rules for forms of names, also for the ones cited in archival documents or manuscripts, though some of their criteria are difficult to apply in this context, such as the rules for the preferred form of names:

- the name "mainly identified in the editions of his works in the original text,"
- "the name usually used in publications is to be preferred even though it is not the real name or the name in the original form."

As examples, the names of many famous people cited by C. Alessi appear in manuscripts and printed texts with different forms; a person is named with different forms in a single manuscript; or there are no reference works or printed texts that could be a valuable reference.

The SBN *Guides* published by ICCU were considered a good reference for punctuation, characters, and codes to assign to authority records.

The study of archival rules for documentary materials (i.e., ISAD) and for description of creators (i.e., ISAAR) showed, also in this context, the importance of authoritative identification as a tool of control of the entries in a collection.

International rules that were taken into consideration are:

- IFLA. *Direttive per le voci di autorità,* ed. it. A cura di ICCU. Roma: ICCU, 1993.
- IFLA. *Guidelines for Authority Records and References.* München: K.G. Saur, 2001. (Also known as *GARR; updates the 1993 Guidelines for Authority and Reference Entries (GARE)*)
- *UNIMARC Manual, Authorities Format.* 2nd revised and enlarged ed. München: K. G. Saur, 2001.

The 1993 *GARE* and 2001 *GARR* were analysed for the division of authority entries and cross-references into areas and were chosen as a reference for elements to be included in authority records of names cited in archives, manuscripts, and printed documents, and for conventional punctuation to be adopted in the transcription.

The *UNIMARC Authorities Manual* provided extremely interesting hints for the treatment of 'families' as types of additional entry different from personal names and corporate bodies and not present in the international rules for treatment of authors.

NORMALIZED CHOICES ADOPTED IN THE PROJECT AS CONTRASTED WITH THE CREATION OF A NATIONAL AUTHORITY FILE

The SBN Authority File[6] was studied through both documentation and direct research in the database hosted by SBN Index for the functions of query, creation, correction, and deletion of data.[7] ICCU's Laboratory for Bibliographic Control offered its help to answer questions from the Perugian group, mostly derived from new problems emerging from treatment of names cited in archival documents and manuscripts.

It is known that ICCU, with its Project for exploitation of the SBN Index, started in March 2001 and finished at the end of 2002. They activated an experimental stage of SBN's National Authority File in conformity with current national rules that, however, are still under revision by the Permanent Commission for revision of *RICA*.[8] In contrast, the Perugian project, being an experiment, has implemented a model where some solutions are not always in complete conformity with national standards, but which are believed to be useful at this stage to solve problems of identification of a name cited in documents but not present in authoritative catalogues or other known published documents.

STRUCTURE AND REALIZATION
OF THE AUTHORITY FILE DATABASE

On the basis of analysed documentation and of national projects already carried out, the Working Group has defined the dictionary of data that compose an authority record in the prototypal database. We recognize three types of entry record:

- Personal name
- Name of corporate body
- Family name.

Every record comprises the following elements:

- *identification number*: identifies without ambiguity the record
- *date of cataloguing*: states the date of creation of the record in the database
- *country code*: is based on the ISO standard 3166-1993 used also in SBN
- *agency*: states whether a national agency is responsible for entry
- *type of name*: is based on SBN codes
- *form code*: states, as in SBN, whether a form is accepted or is a variant form
- **level of control**: states the level of control applied to the record, with the values minimum, medium (checked by Augusta and State Archive), high (checked by the whole Working Group), maximum (entry made by a national agency)
- *source*: of cataloguing, states the rules applied to the record: *RICA*, SBN *Guides, ISAD(G), ISAAR(CPF)*
- *name*: identifies the authoritative entry following punctuation stated by SBN
- *dates*: includes chronological specifications and are always provided, even when dates to solve homonymy are present in the authoritative entry
- *informative notes*: give information following the guidelines in *GARR* in a syntactic form

- *cataloguing notes*: give information following the guidelines in *GARR*
- *bibliography*: provides citations of catalogues and other published and unpublished sources from which the form of name has been derived. The complete list of catalogues used by the Working Group and structured into categories is published on the Web pages of the Project that Augusta keeps up-to-date. The bibliography must be given in a syntactic form.
- *relation code*: states the primary area of activity and helps in the identification of a name. A list of categories is under construction.
- *link name*: codifies links between an accepted form and a variant form, but also an inclusion link (includes, is part of) and an historical link, very useful in the treatment of family entries.

Inclusion codes and historical codes at present are not active and such information is now given in the informative notes.

Data indicated in **bold** above are still under discussion by the Working Group and differ from current choices by SBN's National Authority File. In particular, link codes have been recently introduced and a network of links used by Bibliothèque nationale de France is being studied.[9]

The Biblioteca Augusta implemented the access database and started the input of names using an online function for the creation of records and automatic creation of tables in electronic format. At the moment, over 2,000 names have been added, taken from G. B. Vermiglioni's *Biografia degli scrittori perugini e notizie delle opere loro*, Perugina, 1829, A. Arrighi's *Notizie di famiglie perugine*, "mss. BAP 1548-57," A. Alessi's *Elogia civium perusinorum*," mss. BAP 1202 e 1205; Idem ed. Fulginia Alterium, 1635" and derived from the EDIT16 database, "Maestri e scolari a Siena e Perugina 1250-1500" and MANUS for the notary registers and names of the arts. The State Archives is preparing a table consisting of 3,000 citations of Perugian Notaries, that will be soon imported into the database.

A Web version of the *Authority File* is at an advanced stage of realization. It allows free access for query to all Internet users who visit our site at http://augusta.comune.perugia.it. The Web version of the *Authority File* also has a function for creating records that will be available to authorized users of Augusta. In fact, the Working Group plans to extend the project to cultural institutions of the town that will adopt the defined rules and cooperate in the management of the File, creating new records and maintaining and using the existing records to make this instrument a service for historic research, as well as a project for shared cataloguing.

ENDNOTES

1. *Per buono stato de la citade: le matricole delle arti di Perugia.* Perugia: Volumnia, 2001. Note that 'arti' relates to the arts and crafts of medieval guilds of artisans.

2. Texts of the papers presented at the workshop are published in the section "Attività" at the Web site http://augusta.comune.perugia.it.

3. Tillett, Barbara. "AACR2's Strategic Plan and IFLA Work towards an International Cataloguing Code," available at: http://www.iccu.sbn.it/ricaaf.html or http://www.iccu.sbn.it/Tillett.ppt.

4. Members of the working group are: Pier Maurizio della Porta (Archivio di Stato), Giovanna Giubbini (Soprintendenza Archivistica), Francesca Grauso, Fabrizia Rossi, Claudia Parmeggiani, Paolo Renzi (Biblioteca Augusta). The Group profited by cooperation from Alessandra Zanasi at Augusta who is responsible for the "Master on studies on early printed books and training of librarians who will manage historical collections," University of Siena–CISLAB of Arezzo.

5. The document in Rich Text Format (rtf) is available at: http://archivi.beniculturali.it/Divisione_V/isaar/isaar_cpf.htm.

6. See Bonanni, Laura. *La progettazione e l'avvio dell'Authority file nazionale nell'Indice SBN,* available at: http://www.iccu.sbn.it/ricaaf.html.

7. ICCU. *Progetto di valorizzazione dell'Indice SBN,* 2002.

8. Magliano, Cristina. *La Commissione RICA e la sua attività,* available at: http://www.iccu.sbn.it/ricaaf.htm.

9. Bourdon, Françoise. *Les fichiers d'autorité de la Bibliothèque nationale de France: structure, mise à jour, diffusion,* available at: http://www.iccu.sbn.it/ricaaf.html.

The Catalogue as Language,
Quality in Terms of Service:
An Experience at the University of Florence

Luciana Sabini

SUMMARY. This contribution gives an account of the experience at the University of Florence, where a common language for its numerous libraries and collections was found, at the end of the eighties, in the Servizio Bibliotecario Nazionale, by assuming common cataloguing practices. These years were important years for academic libraries, defining their position in the growth of information needs and orienting their mission to service management and customer satisfaction. So at the Florentine library system a new concept was adopted: a *client-centred library* with a *user-oriented catalogue*, able to communicate and retrieve information. The key concept of the whole process was *the catalogue as a service*. To realize this, it was necessary to provide a permanent training plan for the library staff and a common working method based on quality. The Work Group for the Management and Maintenance of the Catalogue was formed, and entrusted with tasks related to the control of access points and the ordinary management of the SBN catalogue. *[Article copies available for a fee from The Haworth Document Delivery Service: 1-800-HAWORTH. E-mail address: <docdelivery@haworthpress.com> Website: <http://www.HaworthPress.com> © 2004 by The Haworth Press, Inc. All rights reserved.]*

Luciana Sabini is affiliated with Università di Firenze.

[Haworth co-indexing entry note]: "The Catalogue as Language, Quality in Terms of Service: An Experience at the University of Florence." Sabini, Luciana. Co-published simultaneously in *Cataloging & Classification Quarterly* (The Haworth Information Press, an imprint of The Haworth Press, Inc.) Vol. 39, No. 1/2, 2004, pp. 543-550; and: *Authority Control in Organizing and Accessing Information: Definition and International Experience* (ed: Arlene G. Taylor, and Barbara B. Tillett) The Haworth Information Press, an imprint of The Haworth Press, Inc., 2004, pp. 543-550. Single or multiple copies of this article are available for a fee from The Haworth Document Delivery Service [1-800-HAWORTH, 9:00 a.m. - 5:00 p.m. (EST). E-mail address: docdelivery@haworthpress.com].

KEYWORDS. Academic library, client-centred library, user-oriented catalogue, University of Florence, Servizio Bibliotecario Nazionale

A GLANCE BEHIND THE SCENES

Once upon a time . . . .

This contribution, aiming at giving an account of our experience at the University of Florence, might well begin with these words. In a not too distant past, at the end of the eighties, the University of Florence included 21 libraries and 77 collections, some greatly valuable for their completeness, currentness, and constant growth, but isolated, closed in themselves, in their way of conceiving services and offering them, in their cataloguing and management procedures.[1]

The common language in this "little Babel" was found in the Servizio Bibliotecario Nazionale (SBN), which was put into effect with two aims, one of a "pedagogic nature," i.e., the training of librarians aware of the importance of adopting common cataloguing practices respecting international standards,[2] the other of an "organizational nature," i.e., assuming a working method centred on cooperation and resource sharing. A third, perhaps the most meaningful, aspect was to be found within the Servizio Bibliotecario Nazionale in the choice of its name: developing a sense of service.

The SBN's Library Service, a central administrative office, was assisted by the Work Coordination Group (GRO), a technical organization made up of librarians responsible for the various applications of SBN in the libraries, with the task of identifying operative, homogeneous standards and playing the role of tutors in each unit.

It is in this context that the issue of the control of access points to the catalogue was faced for the first time, trying to envisage a set of controlled terms by means of developing an authority list for Greek, Latin, ancient Eastern, Medieval and Renaissance authors, for uniform titles of works by classical authors and anonymous works, and for subject headings. The limited dimensions of the catalogue allowed, even without automatic control, an *a posteriori* analysis of the information thus created, as well as the possibility of dialogue with single librarians on specific issues.

Furthermore, the presence of the notes field in the link between the rejected forms and the accepted terms allowed brief *apparatus* and explanatory notes. Lacking a national authority file, the GRO took on the role of identifying, choosing, and indicating national and international reference material for each linguistic and disciplinary field. They were supported in this work by the librarians' personal competence, by the development of common experience, and by innovative interaction with the academic staff.

THE STAGE

The years in which this activity was carried out were important years for academic libraries. They felt that, in a global context, they were asked to play a new and basic role in the growth of information needs, in terms of both quality and quantity, as well as in the development of the demand for more and more refined documentation. In fact, in those years, there was a shift from the *"age of collection building"* to the *"age of service."*[3] A new mentality of organization moved the *focus* of the library mission from the mere implementation of book collections to providing access to the information owned, indeed to offer proposals that the library be a provider of services for its users.[4]

Service management, then, is the new organization model, which directs attention from the product to the market and evaluates quality in terms not of results but of customer satisfaction. This gives the user, with his/her information needs, behaviour, and expectations, a central role taken directly from the business world.

The new concept of a client-centred library[5] became one of the building blocks for the new library system at the University of Florence that had as its primary aim to improve its information service while preserving its bibliographic collections. This was directed at better use of its collections and constant, assessable promotion of the quality of its services.[6] The University Library System presented itself as a workshop for the development of organization methods directed to satisfying its users.

It is in this context that new services were created, such as reference, ILL (interlibrary loan), and DD (document delivery), that strengthen traditional ones such as lending, time open to public, and space for studying.

"MADAMINA, IL CATALOGO È QUESTO "

–W. A. Mozart, *Don Giovanni, atto 1., scena 4*

What about the catalogue? Actually, the catalogue had been user-oriented since its inception, having as its objective *"the connection between book A and user B"* condensed in a vividly clear formula by Gorman.[7] However, Cutter,[8] too, was very clear when he put the public's "convenience" before the cataloguer's when applying rules, even to the detriment of the systematic nature of the catalogue.

Anyway, in the everyday activities in documentation centres, the methodologies put into effect to organize collections as well as the indexes to provide access to them, even though designed to meet the information needs of users consulting them, have sometimes become a hindrance for finding a document. Thus, it may happen that the catalogue is felt by the user as an intrusive infrastructure, and that it fails in its institutional objective: to communicate and retrieve information.

The fact that the user's central role had long been neglected in the cataloguing process did not help in overcoming these difficulties. The catalogue had been considered, for a long time, in terms of the quality of the recorded bibliographic data–accuracy, adherence to rules, and rule interpretation–with little attention to readability and clarity, and, most of all, with no check on how effective users' searches resulted.[9]

The electronic catalogue, "revolutionizing" the user's approach, according to a stimulating image devised by Weston and Pernigotti,[10] made it even more evident that a tool not designed as user-centred was inadequate as a new and more effective tool in the organization of knowledge. The old-style catalogue, "no longer linked to the user's needs" nor "to the ways the information process is organized and made clear in it" abdicated its chief task to be the "historically formed tool"[11] and was running the risk of being confined to the overcrowded *limbo* of procedures for their own sake.

The belief that the catalogue should be rooted in its environment, that the creation of a different correlation in the communication between user and document was necessary, that new services designed to disseminate information were needed was the element that quickened the process for a change in the library system of the University of Florence. It was no longer seen only as a bibliography, property and management tool, but rather, as a service, a user-centred catalogue, which takes form while it is consulted, conditioned if not determined by its users, a catalogue interacting with its environmental and cultural context, the more effective the more it is known and understood.

Implementing the catalogue as a service meant the adoption of two assumptions that contained two novelties for the library world:

a. shifting attention from the product to the client, i.e., moving from the quality–or expected as such–of the catalogue to the quality of the information, functional to its targeted public;

b. creating a new relationship between the cataloguer and the user, enhancing their interaction.

To meet assumption (b) we opted for a permanent training plan for the library staff, with the aim of steering it towards developing of a sense of service, allowing, at the same time, for professional growth, as a reward for being involved in more than one activity, developing and maintaining competence and specialisation required in a rapidly evolving context.[12] To meet assumption (a) we looked for a solution by promoting a common working method based on quality.

THE TROUPE AT ITS DÉBUT: "NOTTE E GIORNO A FATICAR"

–W. A. Mozart, *Don Giovanni, atto 1., introduzione*

At this point we need to detour briefly from the point, to relate how, concomitant with the reorganization of services, a migration of the catalogue from the University of Florence to the National Index took place. The downloading of the records of 240,000 titles and 110,000 authors into a not-integrated, cumulated union catalogue[13] caused considerable havoc in everyday catalogue management and confused users rather than helping them.

In order to follow the post-migration activities, the Work Group for the Management and Maintenance of the Catalogue was formed, according to the organization model employed at the Florence library system. It was entrusted with tasks related to the ordinary management of the SBN catalogue, such as adjustments, proposals for corrections, etc., plus the additional steps, both urgent and necessary, to prevent the duplication of serial and monographic titles and of authors. All this was, and is, possible thanks to a cooperation protocol with the National Central Library in Florence that let us use its software for unifying titles and authors and correcting them.

The next choice was based on the belief that substantial changes were needed in the quality of the catalogue to enable people to use current and historical collections more effectively and to have access to electronic resources, which have been integrated into OPAC. This Group would provide the technical-organizing reference structure and be in charge of the coordination of cataloguing activities and the promotion of the cataloguers' knowledge, particularly of professional technological developments and their impact on service.

The organization model of the Work Group was characterized by an open, cooperative, and motivated spirit, relying on individual capabilities and qualifications. This turned out to be beneficial for the cataloguer, redesigning his/her professional profile and facilitating the development of interaction with the public.[14]

THE ACTORS ON THE STAGE: "IN QUESTA FORMA, DUNQUE"
–W. A. Mozart, *Don Giovanni, atto primo scena 6*

Once the scope of action had been defined and directed at correcting, avoiding duplicates, and standardizing, and after analyzing the situation, the Work Group started planning its activities, based on its specific professional capabilities, identifying objectives, and defining priorities.

The first area of work was the creation and dissemination of common standards through a clear and uniform implementation of cataloguing rules, partly in view of the lack of a single code, as well as lack of possession and access to the related documentation. Besides the training courses and tutor activities, we attempted to remedy the problem during the development of the project by putting a case-book at disposal online that treats dubious cases and lists solutions, integrating them with rules and official updates.[15]

The second action area of work, as a necessary activity particularly in a global communication and hybrid library context, was the need to promote the control of access points, starting from the assumption that "without authority control the referential and syndetic structures of the catalogue have feet of clay."[16]

Even within the limits of the SBN operational context we tried to obtain the formal homogeneity of terms chosen as access points, names of authors and corporate bodies, uniform titles and titles of series, all conforming to the standard form of the relative authority lists of the Italian National Bibliography. It is from this viewpoint that a list, subdivided by discipline, that indicates the reference sources for the formulation of headings is in a phase of redefinition and updating. With regard to access control in semantic indexes, a re-qualification process is taking place, based on authority file maintenance to review subject strings for coherence according to the requirements of the Subject Index of Florence, to control of descriptive terminology and to determine the suitability of new subject headings.

The great disciplinary range offered by an academic library requires specialized competence for determining the choice of the standard form and the indication of the reference sources; all this makes professional updating a constant condition for the librarian.

The third activity area of work regards continuous catalogue monitoring and approval operations. The experience gathered through the years has made us well aware of how onerous and inadequate *a posteriori* control and corrections are–as we are still forced to do with the erasing of duplicate cataloguing data. Conversely, it has convinced us that we need a strong commitment to shared knowledge and decentralized capacities. Also, we are confident that the key to success lies in the even too simple determination "to make fewer mistakes in order to correct less."

For this reason, much attention must be given to continuous training and tutoring, an easy activity that includes everyday training and assistance. This model of decentralized responsibility–at least one Group member for each area library–has been repeated also in the procedure for channelling the requests for correction, duplication, differences, or for simple clarification and comparison requests received by the Group.

A chain of actions is typical of the systemic perspective in which libraries operate. Wherever the quality of the catalogue is easily measured in terms of effective overall services, you will find a coherent archive, selected and updated working tools, logically planned management procedures, and librarians conscious of their task to guarantee quickly accessible documents. This is another element of a quality user-oriented catalogue.[17]

THE CURTAIN IS LOWERED

Thus, if the quality catalogue is user-oriented, it is apt to manage a more effective dissemination of information, speaking in the different languages of the personal and subjective search strategies. The experience reported in this paper describes attempts to fulfil the mission of producing personalized, quality services as a prerequisite of a solid, long-lasting relationship with library users.

NOTES

1. Citroni, M. "L'applicazione di SBN nell'Università di Firenze: situazione attuale e prospettive di sviluppo," in *La cooperazione interbibliotecaria: livelli istituzionali e politiche: atti del convegno regionale, Firenze, 27-29 novembre 1989 /* a cura di Susanna Peruginelli, Anna Marie Speno.–Firenze: Giunta regionale toscana; Milano: Bibliografica, 1990, p. 153-159.

2. Weston, P.G. "Catalogazione bibliografica: dal formato MARC a FRBR," in *Bollettino AIB*, 41 (2001), 3, p. 267-286.

3. Gorman, M. "Avoiding the seven deadly sins, or technology and the future of library service in academic libraries," in *People Come First: User-Centered Academic Library Service /* edited by Dale S. Montanelli and Patricia F. Stenstrom.–Chicago: Association of College and Research Libraries, 1999, p. 1-12. (ACRL Publications in Librarianship; 53).

4. Brophy, P. *The Academic Library.*–London: Library Association Publishing, 2000, p. 41ff.

5. Martell, C. *The Client-Centered Academic Library: an Organizational Model.*–Westport, Conn.: Greenwood Press, 1983, cited in M. Gorman, *op. cit.*, p. 4.

6. See <http://www.unifi.it/universita/biblioteche/progetto/progetto.htm>, cited: 16 April 2003. See also Vannucci, L. "Cambiare la gestione e gestire il cambiamento: il caso dell'Università di Firenze," in *Biblioteche oggi*, 17 (1999), 7, p. 14-22.

7. Gorman M., *op. cit.*, p. 6.

8. Cutter, C.A. *Rules for a Dictionary Catalog.*–4th ed. rev.–Washington, D.C.: Government Printing Office, 1904.

9. Stenstrom, P.F. "Cataloging: a Case Study of Self-imposed Obsolescence," in *People Come First: User-Centered Academic Library Service*, edited by Dale S. Montanelli and Patricia F. Stenstrom.–Chicago: Association of College and Research Libraries, 1999, p. 65-78. (ACRL Publications in Librarianship; 53).

10. Weston, P.G. and A. Pernigotti, *La biblioteca nel computer: come automatizzare?*–Città del Vaticano: Biblioteca apostolica vaticana, 1990, p. 41ff. (La casa dei libri; 1).

11. Crocetti, L. and R. Dini, *ISBD(M). Introduzione ed esercizi.*–3. ed.–Milano: Bibliografica, 1995, p. 11. (Bibliografia e biblioteconomia; 38).

12. Vannucci, L. "La formazione continua del personale nei sistemi bibliotecari: il caso dell'Università di Firenze," in *Bollettino AIB*, 40 (2000), 1, p. 61-74.

13. Weston, P.G. "Catalogazione bibliografica: dal formato MARC a FRBR," in *Bollettino AIB*, 41 (2001), 3, p. 269, and, more generally Guerrini, M. "Il catalogo di qualità: che vi sia, ciascun lo dice, dove sia, nessun lo sa," in Guerrini, M. *Il catalogo di qualità.*–Firenze: Pagnini e Martinelli: Regione toscana, 2002, p. 44.

14. Quaglino, G.P., S. Casagrande, and A. M. Castellano, *Gruppo di lavoro, lavoro di gruppo: un modello di lettura nella dinamica di gruppo, una proposta di intervento nelle organizzazioni.*–Milano: Cortina, 1992, *passim*.

15. <http://www.unifi.it/universita/biblioteche/af/libretto2002.pdf >. Cited: 16 April 2003.

16. Guerrini, M. *op. cit.*, p. 35.

17. Guerrini, M. *op. cit.*, p. 39-40.

Authority Control in the Academic Context: A Hobson's Choice

Guido Badalamenti

SUMMARY. This paper presents a case study of a shared authority control system in Tuscany, Italy, involving academic libraries, the Central National Library of Florence, and civic and provincial libraries. *[Article copies available for a fee from The Haworth Document Delivery Service: 1-800-HAWORTH. E-mail address: <docdelivery@haworthpress.com> Website: <http://www.HaworthPress.com> © 2004 by The Haworth Press, Inc. All rights reserved.]*

KEYWORDS. Shared authority control, Tuscany, Italy, LACoBit, LAIT, BNI, SBS

THE ACADEMIC CONTEXT

Control and standardization of cataloging access is a subject that has always been present in academic libraries' services organization. This control has been apparent in both the cataloging context and in the setting up of OPAC tools that are coherent and adequate for the users, enabling students and re-

---

Guido Badalamenti is affiliated with Università di Siena.

[Haworth co-indexing entry note]: "Authority Control in the Academic Context: A Hobson's Choice." Badalamenti, Guido. Co-published simultaneously in *Cataloging & Classification Quarterly* (The Haworth Information Press, an imprint of The Haworth Press, Inc.) Vol. 39, No. 1/2, 2004, pp. 551-576; and: *Authority Control in Organizing and Accessing Information: Definition and International Experience* (ed: Arlene G. Taylor, and Barbara B. Tillett) The Haworth Information Press, an imprint of The Haworth Press, Inc., 2004, pp. 551-576. Single or multiple copies of this article are available for a fee from The Haworth Document Delivery Service [1-800-HAWORTH, 9:00 a.m. - 5:00 p.m. (EST). E-mail address: docdelivery@haworthpress.com].

Digital Object Identifier: 10.1300/J104v39n01_21

searchers to conduct easy and thorough searches of the bibliographic collection.

As Liv Aasa Holm [1] states, the problem of authority control is more apparent in larger libraries than in those of smaller size as it is easier to "control" the search results in smaller libraries. However the increased use of the Internet has highlighted the need to improve the quality of the results of bibliographic researches.

In the last few years this need has been felt more strongly because of the introduction of important projects involved in the conversion of card catalogs and retrospective cataloging into newer information mediums. In whatever way these projects have been conducted, through the use of optical scanning or retyping or through the derivation from other databases, and also through the evolution of cataloging rules for the choice of headings, a need for standardization has been identified. The integration of the acquisition and cataloging functions, coupled with the chance to involve staff with less specific training in cataloging has sharpened this need.

'Derived' cataloging (or copy cataloging) is by now a habit of many of our libraries, with a retrieval match percentage in the humanities field of between 80 and 90 percent of the searched data. The retrieved records come from a variety of sources, both nationally and internationally, that often have different cataloging standards. The headings in the retrieved records vary according to the different standards. The ability to rapidly correct cataloging access points and to standardize important data in a manner that is compatible with the catalog's structure, is a need strongly felt both in terms of maintaining the catalog's consistency and as a tool to shorten the cataloging time, thereby raising the overall quality of the catalogs.

Authority control, as Guerrini points out [2], must be considered as the first of the ten indicators (parameters) for measuring the catalog's quality. The user doesn't have to "guess" the right form, but must be capable of using well-known terms, in order to rely on an automated system of translation of the search into a more appropriate form. Until recently this kind of need could only be carried out by the checking, cleaning, and the *a posteriori* merging of the access points, but recent library automation systems allow the configuration of authority databases to be integrated with bibliographic databases, which has considerably changed the work's perspective. However, this technological development is hindered by the absence of important existing authority archives in the national environment or the absence of an authoritative centre with specific duties that enable retrieving authority records that are consistent with national cataloging codes and with international standards. Universities and other libraries therefore need to face this task internally and to commit considerable resources to this field, because a high level of specialization is required for the maintenance and updating of authority records.

Of course, important bibliographic catalogs exist, among these SBN (Servizio bibiotecario nazionale or "National Library Service"), and constitute a precious resource for cooperation and for 'derived cataloging'–especially in the humanities field–even if different levels of cataloging expertise exist in these shared catalogs. In fact, sometimes the addition and substitution of old and new records can obliterate records made by centers of excellence. SBN's creation of an authority file with UNIMARC/Authorities formatted output, will surely be an important answer to the needs of the Italian libraries.

Some specialized libraries offer important national resources by introducing databases with authority headings on specific subjects, structured according to international standards. In particular, think about the work on the medieval authors in progress at the Library Franceschini of the Galluzzo (Florence) or the work in progress at the Museum of Science of Florence for authors of the historical-scientific field.[1] The major problems that remain are 'critical mass' and the online availability of these tools. They are the primary source of information for the other libraries, so it is necessary to save the resources and to avoid duplication of efforts.

AUTHORITY CONTROL AS A SEARCH TOOL

Many factors have contributed to the serious problems that exist in the organization of the cataloging offices in academic libraries, especially in the context of a general reduction in economic resources. These include the growth of services offered by libraries, their growing complexity, the need to adequately reserve human resources for the integration of traditional library's services with those offered by electronic resources, and the installation of the digital library. In re-organizing the library's workflow, academic libraries raise doubt about the possibility of maintaining adequate resources for cataloging and for the control of catalog access points, which brings the added risk of a progressive decline in the quality of catalogs.

However, it has become evident that as the instruments for assisting searches are set up (such as the introduction of a controlled list of authors and thesaurus) even if it is time-consuming due to the high training level required by cataloging staff, these controlled vocabularies constitute an important tool not only for consulting the bibliographic catalogs, but also as support for searches in the digital library and to help users search the Internet more thoroughly.

The main function of the authority file will move from cataloging towards searching [3]. It is widely recognized that there is a need to have tools that help users follow customized and controlled search paths, which normally escape the commercial policy of big editors or of the search engines. The search engines are always more powerful, but their results are influenced by the mechanism of information promotion, which is linked to the practice of highlighting and emphasizing some electronic resources rather than others. Gori and Witten [4] have analyzed the mechanism through which it is possible to arbitrarily increase the visibility of a Web site in a search engine like Google, with the deliberate construction of a number of artificial pages. There is also talk of the danger of a speculative bubble similar to those experienced by the Stock Exchange. The only way to avoid this danger is by the setting up of tools which allow a semantic analysis of the Web [5, 6].

Barbara Tillett [7] suggests the idea that, given the existence of international authority files that are real or virtual, whereby versions of every entity with parallel forms in different languages and in different alphabets are recorded, it could be possible to develop a level of software interface suitable to the specific needs of each user. She also points out that the national and international cooperation, whereby institutions have the chance to benefit from the survey and investigation work done by other colleagues, can be the only valid solution to the economic problems that arise from an activity that is strongly dependent on the use of human resources. Academic libraries can have an important role in this context because of the wide variety of collections that interest their institution's users, which includes the works of local, national, and international authors covering a variety of subjects. However the major problem that arises is that of the general work's organization, which needs to succeed in combining the availability of internal resources with the ability to use general external resources online in order to create an authority file compatible with the needs of the specific users' search and that can simultaneously create a common entry. At the moment, even in the international context, there are not many authority files available online and accessible through the Z39.50 protocol.

From a recent survey [8] in which 568 libraries and archives from different nationalities participated, it was found that barely a quarter of them load authority records from external sources, while most of the structures work with local archives.

An important project in this context, which should be able to provide answers to unsolved problems, is the European Union project LEAF (Linking and Exploring Authority Files),[2] which has as its aim the creation of a centralized system that will house localized records concerning personal and corporate authors existing in the databases of both small and large libraries in different countries. These records will be gathered through recurrent procedures of "harvesting" in the different databases, in order to assure a constant upgrade of data. The project provides an aggregation of records, which refer to the same entity, though preserving the identity of the sources from which the records originate and the specifics of each database. Data would be easily accessible not only for professional staff, but also for the end user.

LACoBiT: A PILOT PROJECT

The Siena Bibliographic Service–as in other universities–has tried to compensate for the lack of references and an authority structure by creating a database of personal and corporate authors' headings derived from its own bibliographic catalogs.[3] However large the catalog is, built from the cataloging activity of an entire library system, it could hardly answer–alone–to the demands of the current cataloging system. In this context and in that of the Tuscany Committee SBN–to which the representatives of the Tuscany libraries participate independently from the automation system that is used–a database has been built as a regional initiative to pilot a project which could be of use in setting up an archive of controlled headings that can be consulted in the context of the regional *Metaopac*,[4] namely LACoBiT (Integrated List of Controlled Authors in Tuscany Libraries).

LACoBiT will integrate and merge into one database data created by a center of excellence, namely the Central National Library of Florence (that produces the Italian National Bibliography) with data from two specialized archives: the Siena Bibliographic Service (that gathers data produced by the academic libraries and municipal libraries) and the database LAIT (Libri antichi in Toscana, 'Ancient books in Tuscany') produced by the municipal library of Pistoia, in which data is collected during the survey of ancient books in Tuscany libraries. One aim is to create a consistent working tool that builds on the daily cataloging activity of the libraries involved. The system will connect the similar and the different forms of the names of a personal or corporate author in records that adhere to the standard UNIMARC/Authorities. The database will be limited to personal and corporate authors' names.

The participating institutions will determine their preferences for selecting among variant forms to merge the structured records for the list of authors. Being a *work in progress*, the database could present records with different levels of analysis, with varying degrees of control, answering to different rules of choice. So another aim is to provide a numerically substantial online tool of comparison and analysis from which each library can access information that is useful for the organization of its own database, answering the cataloging needs of each library. LACoBiT will provide an opportunity to reflect on the problems of integrating records of headings of controlled names of authors (personal or corporate) built from the collections of libraries with different structures and aims.

Barbara Tillett [9] has pointed out the importance of moving the emphasis to "access control" rather than to "authority control" and of the necessity of building structures that are flexible and adherent to the users' demands. Linda Barnhart [10] who defines the access control record as a "super authority record" has suggested various hypotheses in the configuration of the authority records (also using local fields to classify an author from a biographic point of view) in order to fully utilize the data gathered from external partners and then making adjustments according to the internal demands of each catalog.

The LACoBiT project has limited resources, mainly from the human resource contributions of the participating institutions, as well as through the support of the Tuscany region and the technological contribution and know-how of the University of Siena. As Alan Danskin [11] highlights, in his attentive analysis on the relationship between costs and benefits linked to the management of authority control, massive investments don't automatically translate to massive results. Instead, it is necessary to pay major attention to the standardization of cataloguing codes, to the use of standard exchange formats, and to making the data easily accessible online. With this in mind, we believe that we can offer everybody a huge archive of data through the Internet, even if it is incomplete and has internal inconsistencies due to the stratification of catalogs. Even so, being structured according to the major national and international standards, it can still make a large contribution to the development of common requisites for cooperation in a uniform cultural context, such as the Italian national context.

In a limited amount of time, we propose to build a central database which will collect data from the catalogs of three libraries in the Tuscany area, and which will then be open to contributions from other libraries. In this database, which has originated from the integration of three catalogs, it is necessary to guard the identity of each of the libraries that supply the catalog with their data.

OPERATIVE/FUNCTIONAL MODEL

The project involves loading and searching of all data through the software ALEPH500,[5] currently in use at the University of Siena, through which a specific database for the management of authority control has been defined. Starting from the information in the bibliographic records, the system will create records for controlled authors' names to include their variant forms using specific conversion programs. Such records will keep the system number of the original entry on the basis of which they have been created; this will allow the periodic addition of new records and the transfer of updated records from the original archives.

Through a Web interface, it will be possible to separately consult the three archives of controlled authors created and maintained individually by the Italian National Bibliography (BNI), LAIT, and Siena Bibliographic Service (SBS). There will be a fourth integrated archive that enables users to search the three integrated catalogs: LACoBiT.

Records referring to the same entry and that present the same variants, even if a discrepancy between the accepted form and the variant form exists, will be gathered and represented in one single record, with reference to the database from which these records have been created.

In the absence of an ISADN number for the unique identification of the entry, this identification with all the complexities of the case, will be made according to the author's name. The decision is not to reduce the complexity of each individual record (flatten or squeezing of records) as the choice of variants will depend on different perspectives, especially when considering the specificity of each library user. But it will be made possible at any time to verify the record in the context of the catalog where it has been produced.

A suitable link will enable a user to move automatically from the record included in the integrated catalog directly to the original record contained in the single database. Indeed, the link will include a reference to the original database, as well as the source record's system number in the specific original database, and it will indicate the level of completeness of the record. All the other records, which present a structure with a wider number of variants or which include different interpretations of the heading or that cross-reference to other connected headings, will at this stage be kept as independent records.

A second group of *links* will permit the navigation from the record that is currently being examined to other records that are marked as "to be checked" and included in the same shared catalog:

- some of these can be records related to the same entity but that contain further variants to the form of the name; once the system is running regularly, these records will have no reason to exist as, from the inception, all the variants of an entity would be gathered in a single record [12]. But in this initial stage, when much work still has to be done, we believe they can be useful as a warning for catalogs and end users.
- other links can enable navigation among records that relate to different entities and can present a variant of the author's name similar to a record

that has already been examined, or it could even present the same name's form when there isn't any qualification to permit the differentiation between authors.

This is shown in the example described below where, besides the variant forms of Latin, Italian, and French names, the classical philosopher Plato remains ambiguous from the present-day author.

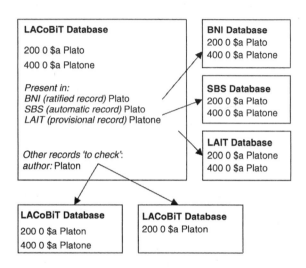

When the records in question are controlled and integrated by the staff of the local database, we will no longer have the second group of navigation links at the level of the shared database. We will only have the first group, which will allow navigation from the record of all the variant forms of the name to the linked database.

The second record will now be unambiguous so it will not be part of the records "to check." For example:

001000334496
100 $a 20020329aitay0103----ba0
106 $a 0
120 $a bb
152 $a RICA
200 0 $8 italat $a Plato
340 $a Filosofo grcco
400 0 $8 itaita $a Platone
400 0 $8 itafre $a Platon

400 0 $8 itager $a Platon
001000110011
100 $a 20020929aitay0103----ba0
106 $a 0
120 $a ba
152 $a RICA
200 0 $8 itafre $a Platon $c karuna $f 1932-
340 $a Autore francese di opere esoteriche nato il 07.03.1932, il titolo karuna significa 'compassione divina'
400 1 $8 itafre $a Platon, $b Karuna $f 1932-

Obviously this does not take into account that in one or more local databases, records can appear with other variants:

100 $a 20020329aitay0103----ba0
106 $a 0
120 $a bb
200 0 $8 itaita $a Platone
400 0 $8 italat $a Plato

Interventions of revision and integration of the records of controlled authors will take place in a peripheral manner, in the various native databases: BNI, SBS, LAIT, while the shared database will reflect the adjustments done to these archives. This procedure ensures the autonomy and the coherence of each of the data's source databases, without any danger of reducing the complexity of the record (flattening). Interventions made on a single database can be evaluated and considered in the context of other databases, because each subsequent amendment to a record after its initial loading, will be redistributed to the other libraries. In this way the changes done on a BNI record (that is, for instance, the object of merging a single record with a record coming from SBS) will be highlighted in an electronic way to the users of SBS. The same will also happen for the other catalogs, and it will therefore be an optional choice to align with changes that have been done in a database different from their own.

This aspect is particularly delicate as authority records, unlike bibliographical records that have a kind of stability, are subject to continuous change due to the necessity of modification in the variant forms, to the introduction of new bibliographic sources, to the necessity to construct clear and related forms, to the change of an author's name, or simply the necessity of amending the biographic information to reflect dates of death, etc. These are all elements that obviously considerably complicate the problem of the catalogs' alignment and of the exchange of records; problems that cannot however be solved with the "flattening" of data.

It will be possible to consult the four catalogs via Z39.50, through one's own client or through those available online. This will allow the configuration of the cataloging interface by the staff of any library, so that it will be possible to consult one's own database of authority first and of those at its disposal through the Z39.50 server of the University of Siena, in addition to those available online.

During the cataloguing phase, the cataloger could firstly search the local authority database to link the heading chosen to the bibliographic record. If unsuccessful, the cataloger could do the search through Z39.50 on the integrated catalog LACoBiT or singularly on the three catalogs that form it. The records found could be exported and loaded into the local database of authority records, in order to integrate or modify it coherently with the cataloging choices that are internal to each institution and to be later linked to the records of the bibliographic database.

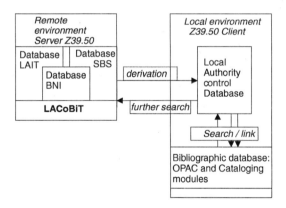

THE STANDARDS

The standards for the creation of records within the databases are the rules of RICA [13] for the form of the authority's headings, GARR [14] and ISAAR (CPF) [15]. In the analysis and discussion of the rules, time has been devoted specifically to the training and updating of cataloging staff. The work done by the Working Group in charge of the revision of RICA has been considered, and we have been faced with the themes concerning the choice of heading and the coherence of the catalogs, which have been also recently subject of a wide discussion [16]. The comparison between different positions and the analysis of specific surveys has been particularly significant in the comprehension of the complexity of the choices that must be made by the catalogers and for the organization of future work.

In particular, the preliminary work of analysis has served to instill in the operators the belief of the necessity, often recalled by Gorman [17] and Tillett [18], to focus on the concept of the authority record as an organized structure of variants of a name, rather than as a relation between accepted and rejected forms of a name. By following this viewpoint, the result was to easily acquire the principle—when in doubt opting for the first of the variants of an author or corporate body's name to insert in a record—of abiding to the choices set by BNI and to follow the type of work, which has been developed in that context.

Obviously, this can't be immediately reflected on all the databases that, as we have mentioned, are in the first phase of execution and are based on the automatic creation of author's records derived from bibliographic catalogs. These catalogs are the result of a stratification of ages. It will only be through the progressive work of refinement and the increase of human resources that it will be possible to address the major internal coherence of the databases.

For the records format the standard is UNIMARC/Authorities. One of the first tasks with colleague Dina Pasqualetti from the National Central Library of Florence has been to fix a subset of data elements according to what has been defined by the IFLA's Working Group, which has established the minimum level of the authority records for international exchange.[6]

Obviously, the adopted scheme—that could be eventually reviewed during the application phase—serves as a reference for the creation of new records, but it cannot be applied in full to the automatic generation of records from bibliographic databases, because the lack of a detailed analysis of the original data means that sketchy information could be automatically integrated instead of the more careful manual revision of records (scheme in Appendix).

SBS DATABASE

The first database on which we have worked is that of the Servizio Bibliotecario Senese, for which the database SBS10 has been created and is now available online at the Web address http://sbs2.unisi.it/ALEPH/. The principle choice has been to use elaborate records for the authority control starting both from the shared database of the academic and civic libraries and from the cumulative database formed by the catalogs of the public libraries of Siena's Province. In these catalogs numerous duplications were present, in comparison with the main catalog, but there were also many authors linked to local production and to children's literature.

A total of 1,200,000 bibliographic records have been processed, from which all of the tags 70X and 71X have been extracted to make a total of 1,328,278 entries for personal or corporate authors. Routine de-duplication created 460,168 records in the authority database, enriched with the tags fore-seen from the requested subset for UNIMARC/Authorities. The new records will retain, in an 810 tag, the indication of the source document held in the bib-liographic database, according to which the authors' names have been created.

Programs of de-duplication have permitted the exclusion of strings that are an exact copy. They also use a subsequent "normalization" of characters in-side the strings following a table of equivalence between the ISO set of charac-ters and the basic ones, concerning punctuation marks, special characters, abbreviations, and capitals and small letters. An algorithm has been defined for the selection of strings that have a bigger "weight" according to the criteria of complexity of the string: form (capital, small letter), numbers of subfields, majority of accents, chronology, staff's experience, level of completeness of the bibliographic record of origin, etc. As a result, the rejected forms of the name have been used to clean up the respective bibliographic catalogs. The authority database, which is linked to the bibliographic database, is constantly updated, modified, and integrated according to the daily cataloging that takes place.

BNI DATABASE

The second step of the project, currently in progress, consists in the creation of an authority database, SBS11, where records from the database BNI will be loaded and immediately made available online. The first part of the work con-sisted of setting up and developing, together with colleagues at the Central Na-tional Library of Florence, the control tests for downloading data with the UTF8 character set.

From the SBN database, all the records have been extracted for authors of whatever type of an accepted form, to which a record from BNI has been linked. The result has been 495,479 author records with these aforementioned features.

From the initial file (containing the identifying author's name, identifica-tion number for the bibliographic record, and BNI number) only the author records linked to BNI records from 1958-2002 have been selected, as in that range of time the standards RICA and ISBD were used. The result is 247,740 author records in which, barring mistakes, there would be no duplications. For each author with an accepted form the process generates a UNIMARC record which includes the label, indicator, tag 7XX, 300, 9XX, as well as the date of the creation of the data in order to allow the staff who have to use the record to contextualize them historically. The structure of the record follows ISO2709.

Now there are going to be defined programs for the conversion of tags 9XX to the correct tags 4XX/5XX and for the integration of data extracted from BNI with tags dictated by the subset of data elements from UNIMARC/Authorities [19].

LAIT DATABASE

The LAIT[7] database includes around 90,000 descriptions of ancient books edited between 1501 and 1885, the result of five years of work by forty-two Tuscan libraries. The descriptions and in particular the names of 35,298 authors have been checked and normalized by the Forteguerriana Library of Pistoia.

The third phase of the project consists of the exportation of the names of the authors and the variants forms of names in ISO2709 format by the Library of Pistoia. A specific program will be used to convert to UNIMARC tags, and they can be integrated with the tags dictated by the subset for UNIMARC/Authorities. The records that are obtained will be uploaded to the database SBS12.

THE INTEGRATED DATABASE

The fourth part of the project consists in setting up a central catalog (SBS19) where records will be gathered from the three databases of controlled headings, and, if successful, also with those from the other libraries throughout the regional area. The day-to-day activity of cataloging, involving the cleaning up and integration of the existing records, remains at a local level, and it is reflected in the central catalog through the batch loading of data.

The most complex aspect is the process of de-duplication and setting up an algorithm that will allow the "weighting" of records in order to fix which, among similar records, will be displayed in the catalog as a guideline for grouping the other records. We are thinking about a dynamic process that also reflects the evolution of records in the native database. We need to take into account that a record can be simply the result of automatic generation or can be a provisional/preliminary entry or can be a record controlled by qualified staff.

This dynamic process will also allow the user immediate clarification of the status of the record, because it will be possible to establish in which order the links for the navigation to the native database must be created: from the most controlled record towards the less controlled one. Besides the definition of the criteria of equivalence of characters and strings explained earlier (4.2) the following need to be taken into consideration:

- the authoritativeness of the source;
- the bare automatic generation or the manual revision of the record;
- the level of completeness of the record;
- the presence of a bibliography (citations to bibliographic sources) starting from when the entry has been checked;
- the date of creation or subsequent updating of the record.

CD-ROM

As we have mentioned, the project should be perceived as a *work in progress* that can be used as assistance for libraries during the process of original or 'derived' cataloging, to assist in their choice of headings for bibliographic records. It is assumed that there will be a publication of a CD-ROM with periodical updating to allow *off-line* queries of the databases, particularly for libraries with major problems of accessibility to the Internet.

PROJECT DEVELOPMENT

The presence of three libraries together in a specific geographic area makes it easier for contact among institutions but especially among staff in charge of cataloging and the maintenance of catalogs. In fact it is important in this kind of operation to arrange collective training times, providing constant coordination of the involved resources and the formalization of working in a group.

This model for progressive aggregation on a regional or thematic base of a self-generated authors' database could also have significant implications for the future in setting up national or international integrated databases, such as the LEAF project.

WORK GROUP

The management of the project has been undertaken by eminent figures from the libraries in the surrounding region,[8] but an important development has been the constitution of an inter-institutional Work Group in which experienced librarians comment on all the structures involved. Besides the work of normalization done on the respective catalogs, continuous common activities are scheduled, aimed at defining a shared methodology of work, to make an analysis of the different levels of intervention, to make a precise evaluation of the resources necessary to the cleaning up of the archives, to set up a schedule and a controlled procedure of intervention. It is not sufficient to define operation manuals to give to staff. The complexity of the clean up operation, the need for wide documentation, the discussion of the priority of the sources of reference, but also the discussion on specific cases, requires a closer involvement with relevant staff.

We strongly believe that this kind of approach can have significant positive effects from the point of view of the homogeneity of the catalogs that will be created, because they will progressively generate a common inheritance of knowledge.

DOCUMENTATION

It has been shown that one of the major problems that is met in authority control work is that of the identification of bibliographic sources to consult. The Working Group has started to set up a bibliographic archive, purposefully built, where the main bibliographies present in the involved libraries and the bibliographies available online are recorded. This will draw attention to those bibliographic sources that–for scope and authoritativeness–are appropriate to consult. This will allow each cataloger to easily identify and locate bibliographic sources and to be able to cooperate in an electronic way with their colleagues who hold the original material.

The bibliographic database has been structured in such a way that, with the progressive use of the bibliographies, it is possible to record guideline notes about the characteristics of each source, on their usefulness from the point of view of the form and structure of headings, but also on their integration or superimposition with other paper bibliographies; and more impressively, with those available online that can be easily accessible from any library. A key will be defined for the abbreviation of bibliographic sources, to be used in the notes of authority records.

Manuals about the use of the catalogs, the UNIMARC standard and the subset of UNIMARC/Authorities data elements defined within the project will be available online in a special section.

Another tool of great utility, on which we are working, and which has already been widely used for other operational modules, is the database of FAQs (frequently asked questions). It records questions that have arisen during the routine cataloging activities of librarians in the different institutions and records the explanations of the experienced librarians who are involved in the Working Group.

This bibliographic archive has already been built and is filling up with data that will be accessible online through a Web interface.

TRAINING

The process of training and updating is certainly one of the more important aspects of the project. It must involve not only the staff who generate and update the records in the authority database, but also those who perform a normal activity of cataloging or pre-cataloging in the bibliographical databases, as it is from their preferences that authority records will be generated. A first step in training at the Siena Bibliographic Service has involved all the staff from the academic and the provincial libraries (a total of 120 people), as well as some colleagues from the Central National Library of Florence who are involved in the Working Group.

The training has been accomplished with the contribution of local staff, but has also turned to qualified external experts: Mauro Guerrini from University of Florence and Gloria Cerbai Ammannati from the Central National Library of Florence. Topics have included authority control, the analysis of the principal experiences of the work, the analysis of sources, the choice and form of headings, the evolution of the national cataloging code, the structure of UNIMARC/Authorities, and the management and implementation of the authority database. From this first step, others must surely follow, devoted to the staff in all of the libraries, differing according to the individual training needs: to the induction of new staff, as a moment of control of the work done and of the knowledge acquired by those who are already involved in the work.

INTERNAL ORGANIZATION

The different participating information organizations determine the different procedures for the generation of records. The LAIT database, specializing in antiques books, is the result of a regional project, which has staff contributed from numerous libraries who control the bibliographic sources from the first phase of cataloging documents. After this step the process of the control of headings is done at the Library of Pistoia with the generation of authority records.

For the Italian National Bibliography, produced by the Central National Library of Florence (BNCF), the daily activity of the description of monographs is given to a specific section and connected to that of the revision, done by a group that controls headings and conducts frequent checks and validations. A new database, UNIMARC/BNI, will soon be available and will be independent from the bibliographic database, where structured records will be connected to names of authors and titles according to the principle of authority control.[10] At this stage, records of the controlled authors will be created with a specific procedure originating with the bibliographic records.

Within the Siena Bibliographic Service, a database for the authority control has been separately set up next to several bibliographic databases, but remains strongly connected with those bibliographic databases, which are updated daily by the cataloging activities of the different libraries. In the organization of daily work, in order to guarantee a certain control on the quality of catalogs, a different password has been designed for the staff who work on the bibliographical database:

- the first level only allows them to derive and capture the headings from the authority database, to import them into the bibliographic catalogs, and to create a link between the controlled heading and the bibliographic record;
- the second level–besides the derivation of records–allows the automatic generation of a record in the authority database according to tags that contain the name of the author included in the bibliographic record. Records automatically created in the authority database must be checked, as they will have a low level of completeness and they must be controlled and validated by the staff with a password of level four;
- the third level allows access to the database of authority for adjustments, but only on the accepted form and for the creation of bibliographic notes;
- the fourth level permits the operation of adjustment, amendment, and validation of the authority records, including the introduction of the variants of the authors' name and allows the cataloging of the record as "complete." This password is reserved for those cataloging staff of each library whose work is primarily cataloging;
- with the password of the fifth level there is no limitation, and it is reserved for the staff of the inter-institutional Working Group, who will operate the whole database. Besides authority records, they can generate

cross-reference records for complex variants of the accepted form or records containing general notes about the use of some terms within the authority database.

Cataloging staff and the Working Group will be kept informed of developments through a procedure that arranges the automatic creation of electronic messages starting from the contents page of the authority record. This will facilitate the exchange of information and will keep people informed of any problems that have reported. Messages can be addressed to a specific person or to a group, and they can include descriptive notes or alerts on changes to be done on records. Librarians in charge of the authority work will find on their desk, at the opening of the system, information on how to deal with problems and any suggestions proposed. These records can be extracted and controlled at any time.

ENDNOTES

1. Ezio Franceschini foundation (S.I.S.M.E.L.), Library of Medieval Culture: http://www.sismelfirenze.it/, Library of the History of Science, Institute of Florence: http://galileo.imss.firenze.it/biblio/icat.html.
2. Linking and Exploring Authority Files (LEAF), http://xml.coverpages.org/leaf. html.
3. All the libraries of the University of Siena, the principal public and private and research libraries of the town of Siena, and the libraries of the Municipality of Siena Province that are part of the net ReDoS (Siena Provincial documentary net): http://redos.unisi.it/ALEPH/-/start/sbs02 participate in the network of the Siena Bibliographic Service (SBS), http://www.unisi.it/servizi/sab/welcome.html.
4. Metaopac of the Tuscany Region allows users to consult all of the calalogs of all the libraries of the region that have a Z39.50 server. See: http://www.cultura.toscana. it/bibl/metaopac.htm.
5. The software produced by ExLibris, http://www.aleph.co.il, allows the creation of databases of authority files consistent with the MARC standards, independent and integrated with the bibliographic database.
6. Mandatory Data Elements for Internationally Shared Resource Authority Records, Report of the IFLA UBCIM Working Group on Minimal Level Authority Records and ISADN: http://www.ifla.org/VI/3/p1996-2/mlar.htm.
7. The database, wanted by the Tuscany Region, has been created at the Forteguerriana Library using ISIS/EDAN, and it has been reproduced on CD-ROM. Cfr. *Avvertenza tecnica* and *Bibliografia* in [20].
8. Gloria Cerbai Ammannati (National Central Library of Florence), Guido Badalamenti (University of Siena), Mario Moretti (National Central Library of Florence), Dina Pasqualetti (National Central Library of Florence), Gian Bruno Ravenni (Tuscany Region), Paola Ricciardi (Tuscany Region), Maurizio Vivarelli (Forteguerriana Library of Pistoia).
9. As Gloria Cerbai Ammannati has explained in: *La Bibliografia nazionale italiana e il controllo dei punti di accesso.*

BIBLIOGRAPHY

[1] Liv Aasa Holm, "Authority Control in an International Context in the New Environment," *International Cataloging and Bibliographic Control,* 28, no. 1 (1999): 11-13.

[2] Mauro Guerrini, *Il catalogo di qualità* (Firenze: Regione Toscana, Pagnini e Martinelli, 2002), p. 35.

[3] Paul Gabriel Weston, *Il catalogo elettronico: dalla biblioteca cartacea alla biblioteca digitale* (Roma: Carocci, 2002), p. 138.

[4] Marco Gori, Ian Witten, *The Bubble of Web Visibility*, Working papers (Siena: Università degli studi di Siena, Facoltà di Ingegneria). In press in: *Communications of the ACM*, (2003). Available online at http://www.acm.org/cacm/.

[5] Tim Berners-Lee, James Hendler, and Ora Lassila, "The Semantic Web," *Scientific American,* 284, no. 5 (2001):28-37.

[6] Terrence A. Brooks, "The Semantic Web, Universalist Ambition and Some Lessons from Librarianship," Information research, 7, no. 4 (2002). Available online at http://InformationR.net/ir/7-4/paper136.html.

[7] Barbara Tillett, *International Shared Resource Record for Controlled Access.* In: *Authority Control in the 21st Century: an Invitational Conference, March 31-April 1, 1996.* Available online at http://www.oclc.org/oclc/man/authconf/tillett.htm.

[8] Max Kaiser, "LEAF User Survey," *LEAF Newsletter,* 1, no. 1 (2002). Available online at http://www.crxnet.com/leaf/news_online.html.

[9] Barbara Tillett, "International Shared Resource Record for Controlled Access," *ALCTS Newsletter,* 10, no. 1 (1998). Available online at http://www.ala.org/alcts/alcts_news/v10n1/gateway.html.

[10] Linda Barnhart, *Access Control Record: Prospects and Challenger.* In: *Authority Control in the 21st Century: an Invitational Conference, March 31-April 1, 1996.* Available online at http://www.oclc.org/oclc/man/authconf/barnhart.htm.

[11] Alan Danskin, "International Standards in Authority Data Control: Costs and Benefits," *International Cataloging and Bibliographic Control,* 26 (1997), n. 2, p. 33.

[12] Alfredo Serrai, *Biblioteche e cataloghi* (Firenze: Sansoni, 1983), p. 85.

[13] *RICA: Regole italiane di catalogazione per autori* (Roma: Istituto centrale per il catalogo unico delle biblioteche italiane e per le informazioni bibliografiche, 1979).

[14] International Federation of Library Associations and Institutions, *Guidelines for Authority Records and References,* 2nd ed., revised by the IFLA Working Group on GARE Revision (München: Saur, 2001).

[15] *ISAAR (CPF): International Standard Archival Authority Record for Corporate Bodies, Persons and Families, Final ICA approved version,* prepared by the Ad Hoc Commission on Descriptive Standards, Paris, 15-20 November 1995 (Ottawa, 1996).

[16] Guerrini, *Il catalogo di qualità,* p. 79 and next.

[17] Michael Gorman, *Cataloging and the New Technologies.* In: *The Nature and Future of the Catalog: Proceedings of the ALA's Information Science and Automation Division's 1975 and 1977 Institutes on the Catalog,* edited by Maurice J. Freedman and S. Michael Malinconico (Phoenix, AZ: Oryx, 1979):127-136.

[18]   Barbara Tillett, *Access Control: A Model for Descriptive, Holding and Control Record.* In: *Convergence: Proceedings of the Second National Library and Information Technology Association, October 2-6, 1988, Boston, Massachusetts* (Chicago: American Library Association, 1990): 48-56.

[19]   International Federation of Library Associations and Institutions, *UNIMARC Manual: Authorities Format*, 2nd ed. rev., enlarged ed. (München: Saur, 2001).

[20]   Angela Bargellini et al., *LAIT, Libri antichi in Toscana 1501-1885*, ed. by Biblioteca Forteguerriana di Pistoia (Firenze: Regione Toscana, [2001]).

APPENDIX 1. Project Schema

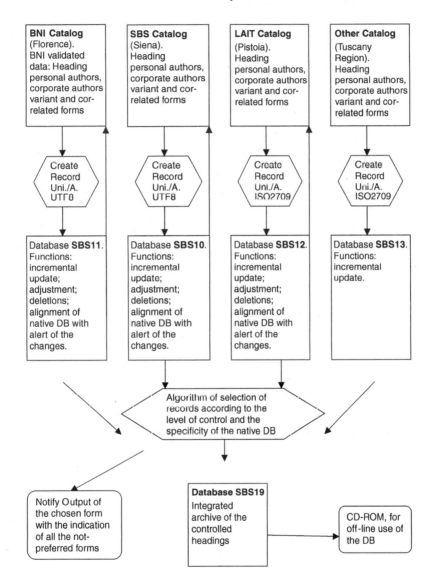

APPENDIX 2. Subset of the UNIMARC Authorities Standard Defined for the LACoBiT Project[1]

Data	Definition	UNIMARC/A	Mandatory Repeatability	Notes for the Automatic Generation of Authority Records
Status of the record – c = corrected – d = deleted – n = new	New or corrected record. The value 'd' in the exchange of data means 'has to be deleted'	Position 5 of the Label	Yes Not repeatable	Automatic records will have value 'n'
Type of record – x = authority entry – y = reference entry – z = general explanatory entry		Position 6 of the Label	Yes Not repeatable	Automatic records will be only authority entry records, value 'x'
Type of entity – a = personal name – b = corporate name	The code indicates the type of entity identified in the 2XX fields	Position 9 of the Label	Yes Not repeatable	In the automatic creation of records the value could be defined because of the type of 2XX tags
Encoding level – # = complete – 3 = partial	Show the degree of completeness of all the record	Position 17 of the Label	Yes Not repeatable	Automatic records will have value '3', it could be changed to # when it is checked manually
Record identifier	Record control number	Tag 001 No indicators	Yes Not repeatable	Assigned by the system when the data will be loaded in the LACoBiT Database
Last update	Date and time of the latest record transaction	Tag 005 No indicators	Yes Not repeatable	Automatically done by the system
ISADN	International Standard Authority Number	Tag 015		Reserved for ISADN
Other system control numbers	System number of the Agency where the record originated	Tag 035 Indicators: ## $a, $z	Yes Repeatable	A code for the Agency in parentheses will precede the system number
Date entered on file	Date of loaded records in the LACoBiT database	Tag 100 No indicators $a positions 0-7	Yes Not repeatable	Historical data, not to be changed. (ISO8601) yyyymmdd
Status of authority heading code – a = established – c = provisional – x = not applicable	Show if a deeper investigation is necessary to establish the heading, when it is next used	Tag 100 $a position 8	Yes Not repeatable	Automatic records will have value 'a'
Language of cataloging	Code of the language used in cataloging	Tag 100 $a positions 9-11	Yes Not repeatable	Value 'ita' automatically assigned by the system

572

Field	Description	Tag	Repeatable	Notes
Transliteration code — a = ISO scheme — y = no transliteration scheme	Show if and which transliteration scheme has been used	Tag 100 $a position 12	Yes / Not repeatable	Automatic records will have value 'y'
Character Set	Codes related to the character sets used in the record	Tag 100 $a positions 13-16 and 17-20	Yes / Not repeatable	Character set Unicode: 50-----, used by the Agency that maintains the records
Script of cataloging		Tag 100 $a positions 21-22	Yes / Not repeatable	Value 'ba' assigned by the system
Direction of script — 0 = left to right — 1 = right to left		Tag 100 $a position 23	Yes / Not repeatable	Value '0' assigned by the system
Language of the entity	The field contains indication of the language/s used by the entity	Tag 101 Indicators: ## $a (repeatable)	Yes / Not repeatable	Automatic records will have tree fillers '|||' in subfield $a. Value to be completed.
Nationality of the entity	The field contains the nationality of person, corporate body	Tag 102 Indicators: ## $a $b	No / Not repeatable	Automatic records will have value 'XX' in subfield $a. Value to be completed.
Coded data fields: heading used as subject heading	Show if the 2XX heading could or couldn't be used as subject heading	Tag 106 Indicators: ## $a	Yes / Not repeatable	Automatic records will have value 0 (more frequent), it could be changed when it is checked manually
Coded data field: personal name	Show if the name is differentiated or not and what is the gender of the entity	Tag 120 Indicators: ## $a position 0 (a,b,c,u,x) position 1 (a,b)	Yes / Not repeatable	Position 0 = filler automatically assigned by the system. Position 1 = if there is a subfield $c, $f or $g in the 2XX tag, the default value is 'a', in the other circumstance the default is 'b'
Coded data field: corporate name	Codes for the level of the government organization	Tag 150 Indicators: ## $a position 0 (a,b,c,d,e,f,g,h,u,y,z)	Yes / Not repeatable	Position 0 = filler, automatically assigned by the system
Rules $a cataloging rules $b subject system	Rules used to formulate the heading/reference structure	Tag 152 Indicators: ## $a	Yes / Not repeatable	Code 'RICA'. Automatically assigned by the system for the subfield $a
Heading—Personal name	Heading chosen according to the RICA rules	Tag 200 Indicator 1: #; Indicator 2: 0,1 $a,$b,$c,$f,$g,$8	Yes / Repeatable	In the Automatic generation of the record, the control subfield will have the value: $8ita|||. Value to be completed

Data	Definition	UNIMARC/A	Mandatory Repeatability	Notes for the Automatic Generation of Authority Records
Heading–Corporate name	Heading chosen according to the RICA rules	Tag 210 Indicator 1: 0,1 Indicator 2: 0,1,2 $a,$b,$c,$d,$e,$f,$g, $h,$8	Yes Repeatable	In the Automatic generation of the record, the control subfield will have the value: $8ita||. Value to be completed
Information note	Explain the relationship between the 2XX heading and the other entities	Tag 300 Indicator 1: 0,1; Indicator 2: # $a	No Repeatable	The first indicator will have the value '0'
Textual see also reference note	Explain in detail the relationship between the 2XX heading and the 5XX headings	Tag 305 Indicator 1: 0,1; Indicator 2: # $a,$b	No Repeatable	The first indicator will have the value '0'
Biography and activity note	It records biographical details or activity notes about the entity	Tag 340 Indicators: ## $a	No Repeatable	
See reference tracing–personal name	The field records the variant form of a heading–personal name	Tag 400 Indicator 1: #; Indicator 2: 0,1 $a,$b,$c,$f,$g,$8	No Repeatable	In the Automatic generation of the record, the control subfield will have the value: $8ita||. Value to be completed
See reference tracing–corporate body name	The field records the variant form of a heading–corporate body name	Tag 410 Indicator 1: 0,1 Indicator 2: 0,1,2 $a,$b,$c,$d,$e,$f,$g, $h,$8	No Repeatable	In the Automatic generation of the record, the control subfield will have the value: $8ita||. Value to be completed
See also reference tracing–personal name	The field records the correlated form of a heading–personal name	Tag 500 Indicator 1: #; Indicator 2: 0,1 $a,$b,$c,$f,$g,$8	No Repeatable	In the Automatic generation of the record, the control subfield will have the value: $8ita||. Value to be completed
See also reference tracing–corporate body name	The field records the correlated form of a heading–corporate body name	Tag 510 Indicator 1: 0,1 Indicator 2: 0,1,2 $a,$b,$c,$d,$e,$f,$g, $h,$8	No Repeatable	In the Automatic generation of the record, the control subfield will have the value: $8ita||. Value to be completed

Parallel heading–personal name	Parallel form of the heading in a language other than the language of the 2XX chosen according to RICA	Tag 700 Indicator 1: #; Indicator 2: 0,1 $a, $b, $c, $f, $g, $8	No Repeatable	At the moment it is not planned to have headings in alternative scripts, that demand the use of the subfield $7
Parallel heading–corporate body name	Parallel form of the heading in a language other than the language of the 2XX chosen according to the RICA	Tag 710 Indicator 1: 0,1 Indicator 2: 0,1,2 $a, $b, $c, $d, $e, $f, $g, $h, $8	No Repeatable	At the moment it is not planned to have headings in alternative scripts, that demand the use of the subfield $7
Originating source	The field identifies the agency responsible for the creation of the record and the date of the entry. Repeatable for transcribing, modifying or issuing agency	Tag 801 Indicator 1: # Indicator 2: 0,1,2,3 $a, $b, $c, $9	Yes Repeatable	**–801 0** name of the agency originating the record **–801 3** name of the agency issuing the record $9 used for the BNI number of the record where the heading was last used.
Source data found	Reference sources containing useful information about the heading. The first 810 field usually contains the citation of the bibliographic work for the cataloging of where the heading was established	Tag 810 Indicators: ## $a, $b, $9	No Repeatable	The first 810 will have a subfield $9 containing the BID of the record in the SBN-BNCF database (or in the other databases) related to the bibliographic work for the cataloging of where the heading was established.
Source data not found	Consulted reference sources in which no information about the heading was found	Tag 815 Indicators: ## $a	No Not repeatable	
Usage or scope information	Information for differentiating persons or bodies with similar names	Tag 820 Indicators: ## $a	No Repeatable	
Example under note	To highlight that the heading has been used as an example in another record	Tag 825 Indicators: ## $a	No Repeatable	

APPENDIX 2 (continued)

Data	Definition	UNIMARC/A	Mandatory Repeatability	Notes for the Automatic Generation of Authority Records
General cataloger's note	Biographical, historical or other information about the heading	Tag 830 Indicators: ## $a	No Repeatable	
Deleted heading information	It records why the heading in 2XX is being deleted from the authority file	Tag 835 Indicators: ## $a,$b,$d	No Repeatable	
Replaced heading information	It records why the heading in the 2XX is being replaced by an authority file	Tag 836 Indicators: ## $b,$d	No Repeatable	It appears in a record with value 'c' or 'n' in position 5 of the Label
Electronic location and access	It contains information available electronically about the entity for which the record was created	Tag 856 Indicator 1: 4 Indicator 2: # $a,$g,$u,$z	No Repeatable	It contains information required to locate an electronic item via HTTP
Data not converted from source format	It contains data (of the source format) for which there is no specific UNIMARC field	Tag 886 Indicator 1: 0,1,2 Indicator 2: # $a,$b,$2	No Repeatable	

NOTE

1. The LACoBiT project is limited to headings for personal names and corporate body names. Accordingly, the subset is limited to the related fields. So the scheme is not complete and specifically we did not include—for the moment—family name, place name, uniform title, subject, etc.

In the fourth column, the choice of mandatory and repeatable fields for the LACoBiT project is explained. In the fifth column we specially give notes about the automatic generation of the authority records from the bibliographic records and the related default value. During the manual check of the records, the default values of the mandatory fields have to be completed by librarians.

Ancient Italian States:
An Authority List Project

Annarita Sansò

SUMMARY. The project to create an authority list of the Italian states arises from the lack of such a list in Italy. The standardization of headings for the ancient states has taken into account all of the problems and difficulties arising from the nineteenth-century concept of 'state,' as we mean it today. That concept is quite difficult to apply to Italian states established before that time. This paper describes making this list. *[Article copies available for a fee from The Haworth Document Delivery Service: 1-800-HAWORTH. E-mail address: <docdelivery@haworthpress.com> Website: <http://www.HaworthPress.com> © 2004 by The Haworth Press, Inc. All rights reserved.]*

KEYWORDS. Authority lists, Italian states

The project to create an authority list of the Italian states arises from the lack of such a list in Italy. The standardization of headings for the ancient

Annarita Sansò is affiliated with Senato della Repubblica.

This paper summarizes some ideas from the author's PhD dissertation defended at the Scuola speciale per archivisti e bibliotecari, Università La Sapienza di Roma (academic year 2000-2001), with thanks to Professor Mauro Guerrini for his valuable suggestions.

[Haworth co-indexing entry note]: "Ancient Italian States: An Authority List Project." Sansò, Annarita. Co-published simultaneously in *Cataloging & Classification Quarterly* (The Haworth Information Press, an imprint of The Haworth Press, Inc.) Vol. 39, No. 1/2, 2004, pp. 577-584; and: *Authority Control in Organizing and Accessing Information: Definition and International Experience* (ed: Arlene G. Taylor, and Barbara B. Tillett) The Haworth Information Press, an imprint of The Haworth Press, Inc., 2004, pp. 577-584. Single or multiple copies of this article are available for a fee from The Haworth Document Delivery Service [1-800-HAWORTH, 9:00 a.m. - 5:00 p.m. (EST). E-mail address: docdelivery@haworthpress.com].

http://www.haworthpress.com/web/CCQ
© 2004 by The Haworth Press, Inc. All rights reserved.
Digital Object Identifier: 10.1300/J104v39n01_22

states has taken into account all of the problems and difficulties arising from the nineteenth-century concept of 'state,' as we mean it today. That concept is quite difficult to apply to Italian states established before that time.

The creation of the authority list is mainly based on two sources: the *Raccolta di statuti, consuetudini, leggi, decreti, ordini e privilegi dei comuni, delle associazioni e degli enti locali italiani dal Medioevo alla fine del secolo XVIII* and the *Fondo delle leggi degli antichi Stati italiani*, both of which are held in the Senate Library.[1] The documents about administration and legislation (including communal, seigniorial, urban, rural, and maritime statutes, customary laws, privileges, and seigniory decrees) have been examined from the *Raccolta di statuti* (771 manuscripts, 39 incunabula, 3,626 editions printed between the 16th and 17th centuries and partially reissued since the 19th century). The statutes concern all the areas within the borders of the ancient Italian states, including those under foreign domination, possession and colonies, the local administration and legislation, and the statues of the towns later changed into states.

In the introduction to the first volume of the Biblioteca del Senato del Regno's *Catalogue*, Corrado Chelazzi defines the real meaning of 'statute.' The term refers to "a specific concept of the law-history but is used generically to designate a set of documents not belonging to the *ius statuendi* which governed certain social relations in the place of imperial, ecclesiastic or individual state legislation."[2] Therefore, it appears that some documents of a different kind and laws promulgated by different entities were often named 'statutes.'

The *Fondo delle leggi degli antichi Stati italiani* (670 works in several volumes), probably constituted when the Senate Library was founded in 1848, has been fully examined. The classification of the first core, dating back to 1865, is clear and easy to understand. It includes those States consecrated after the Restoration and "the Napoleonic states, including the French Republic, Piemonte, Liguria and Parma."[3] The acquisition of older sources has enlarged the fond but made it more difficult to identify States and their successor entities. At the end of the era of the City-State, the statutes were dependent on sovereign ratification, which confirmed them as laws of the new State. In 1934, on the occasion of the renovation of the library, all collections were examined, grouped together and finally classified. In the preface to the catalogue of 1986, the compiler points out that the catalogue has no scientific or bibliographic pretensions and should be considered as an inventory of the archival holdings, an instrument of access to the printed library indexes. The compiler also warned of the potential problems in the identification of the thirty-five headings[4]–referring to the modern states–and the alphabetical index, including spurious names and groups of headings.

Both fonds have been studied in order to identify cataloging errors or mistakes in location and dating problems of documents and the Italian legal and political system. The working method has involved the study of the historical events and government transformations in the Italian states in order to clarify the main changes reflected in the authority list. Regarding the establishment and development of modern states in the nineteenth century, historians turned their attention more closely to national monarchies than to Italy, considering a disordered group of political entities difficult to define. For a considerable period of time, Italian historiographers considered our peninsula a confused and fragmented mosaic of little backward states, often unsuccessful in comparison with other European entities. Recently, the nineteenth-century concept of 'state' has come under discussion, because it does not appear to refer either to the ancient or modern states.[5]

The modern concept of 'state' does not apply to the ancient territorial entities, and the lack of sources and documents from available sources has caused problems in dating the establishment of those states. In the past, laws were issued in the name of the King or Lord who often exercised power over several territories. This makes identification of state entities difficult, and the authority file will need to be revised and augmented after further investigation in other libraries and archives.

The authority list includes those Italian States established between 1400 and 1850 and States established before the 12th century that were still in existence in the reference period. The list includes only those States within the present Italian boundaries. Each entity has been given a preferred title in bold face, followed by dates in italics, and unauthorized terms linked to authorized headings in regular script. For those States whose names have changed over time, an authorized term is linked to the authorized headings via cross-references. Each variant form of geographical names in the documents consulted– for example, Venexia instead of Venezia (i.e., Venice in English)–is shown as linked to the terms actually used. The headings are listed in alphabetical order:

1. Name of the place, followed by specification (e.g., the Italian words for duchy, provisional government, grand duchy, marquisate, princedom, regency, kingdom, and republic) in parentheses;
2. Compound name or expression found in publications or already used in SBN (Servizio bibiotecario nazionale, Italy's "National Library Service"), for example, Repubblica ligure, Repubblica romana, Regno d'Italia, Stato dei Presidi.

In case of coincidence of two authorized forms being the same, they have been sorted chronologically by date of the establishment of the State in ascending date order. The differences of names due to the use of capital and small case letters have been disregarded; Latin headings use uppercase letters also for the adjectives, which are usually lowercase in Italian.

Foreign expressions, as drawn from consulted sources, have not been compared to those of national libraries' OPACs. As soon as possible, the authority list will be supplemented with relative headings in the most common foreign languages.

Authorized headings usually take a short form, although problems were encountered in a number of cases, which we illustrate hereafter:

- The authorized heading is **Brescia** (Governo provvisorio) *1797*: in SBN the *Manifesto del governo provvisorio rappresentante il sovrano popolo bresciano (. . .)* is entered under **Brescia**, but the *Raccolta dei decreti del governo provvisorio bresciano (. . .)* under **Brescia** <Governo provvisorio; 1797>;
- The authorized term for the Regno delle Due Sicilie is **Due Sicilie** (Regno), in SBN we find **Due Sicilie**; in SBN the *Codice civile di Napoleone il Grande tradotto nella lingua italiana d'ordine di Giuseppe Napoleone re delle Due Sicilie* (published in 1808) is entered under **Francia** <Impero>; the *Traité de paix entre S.M. le Roi des Deux Siciles et la Republique française* of 1801 under **Napoli** <Regno>. The matter could be controversial because the headword "Regno delle Due Sicilie" has been in use before 1808 and used since that time;
- In SBN, the *Statuta (. . .) civitatis Ferrariae del 1534* and the *Statuta urbis Ferrariae (. . .) of 1567* are entered under **Ferrara**; *Capitoli et ordini del ser.mo D. Alfonso II Duca di Ferrara, & c. (. . .)* and the *Statuta prouisiones, et decreta gabellarum ciuitatis Ferrariae (. . .) of 1624* under **Ferrara** <Ducato>; in our authority list the authorized term is **Ferrara, Modena e Reggio** (Ducato) because the State of the Estensi, founded when Borso d'Este was made a duke in 1471, included the above mentioned territories;
- The authorized heading for Regno lombardo-veneto is **Lombardo-Veneto** (Regno) by analogy with SBN;
- Some authorized headings for Lucca are:
  - **Lucca** (Repubblica), *116?-1799;* in SBN the heading **Lucca** <Repubblica> is also referred to the Repubblica lucchese of 1801, instead in our authority list the state entities of 1799 and 1801-1805 are distinguished from the Repubblica di Lucca–previously established–by the headword **Repubblica lucchese**;
  - **Lucca** (Principato), *1805-1814*, by analogy with the heading in SBN: the Principato di Felice and Elisa Baciocchi, Napoleon's sister, in-

cluded the Repubblica lucchese territories in addition to Piombino, Massa, Carrara, and Garfagnana; in the documents examined the headword most commonly found is "Principato lucchese";

- **Lucca** (Provincia), *1815-1817,* for the Provincia lucchese of 1815-1817, including the territories of Lucca and Piombino for a few months in 1815, and the former feudal territories of the Lunigiana under Austrian domination; in SBN the *Bollettino delle leggi della Provincia lucchese* is entered under **Austria**;
- **Lucca** (Ducato), *1817-1847* for the Ducato lucchese, the same heading in SBN;
- In SBN (Ancient Books section), all the records relating to Modena–part of the Duchy of Ferrara, Modena and Reggio–and a document sent to the commander of Modena from general La Poype (commander of the Cisalpina) are entered under **Modena**; some statutes of Modena, published in 1547 and the documents concerning the Duchy of Modena, Reggio and Mirandola (1814-1829) are entered under **Modena** <Ducato>; the authorized terms in our *authority list* are:

Modena (Consulta), *1734-1736*
Modena (Governo provvisorio), *1831*
Modena e Reggio (Ducato), *1452-1471; 1598-1734, 1736-1796*
Modena e Reggio (Governo provvisorio), *1848*
Modena e Reggio (Reggenza), *1848*
Modena e Reggio, Mirandola (Ducato), *1814-1829*
Modena e Reggio, Mirandola, Massa e Carrara (Ducato), *1829-1847*
Modena e Reggio, Mirandola, Massa e Carrara, e Guastalla (Ducato), *1847-1859*

- The chosen heading for Padova–state entity established in 1797–is **Padova** (Municipalità); in SBN (Ancient books section) the *Annali della libertà padovana* (published in 1797) are entered under the generic heading **Padova**;
- **Parma** (Ducato), **Parma e Piacenza** (Ducato), **Parma, Piacenza e Guastalla** (Ducato) are authorized terms; in SBN the relative documents are entered under the headings **Parma e Piacenza** <Ducato> (including the *Codice penale per gli stati di Parma Piacenza e Guastalla*), or **Parma, Piacenza e Guastalla** <Ducato> (for instance, the *Codice civile per gli stati di Parma, Piacenza e Guastalla*), with the exception of the *Cerimoniale per la ducal corte di Parma*, published in 1824 and entered under **Parma** <Ducato>;

- In SBN, we find both the headings **Regno italico** and **Regno d'Italia** (the latter is more commonly used) for the Italian Kingdom of Bonaparte (1805-1814); in our *authority file*, the chosen heading is **Regno d'Italia** because this is commonly used in the official documents;
- The authorized and preferred heading is **Repubblica anconitana**, denomination used in the official documents for that state-entity; in SBN, we find the generic heading **Ancona**;
- The authorized term is **Repubblica bergamasca** for the same reasons as above; in SBN, the *Raccolta di avvisi, editti, ordini ec. pubblicati in nome della Repubblica bergamasca (. . .)* is entered under **Bergamo**;
- The authorized heading for the Republic established in Genoa, during the Napoleonic age, is **Repubblica ligure** (heading most used in the official documents); in SBN, we find three different headings: **Repubblica Ligure, Genova** <Repubblica, 1797>, and **Liguria** <Repubblica>, the first of which is the most commonly used.
- For the Napolitan Republic of the 1799, the authorized heading is **Repubblica napoletana**, instead of **Repubblica partenopea** (both of them are used in SBN);
- For the Roman Republic ruled by Mazzini, Saffi, and Armellini, the chosen heading is **Repubblica romana**, *1849*; it is mainly used in SBN where we find **Roma** <Repubblica> and **Roma** <Repubblica, 1849> as well;
- The authorized heading for the State of San Marino is **San Marino** (Repubblica), in SBN, we find both **San Marino** <Repubblica> and **Repubblica di San Marino**;
- In SBN, we find both **Regno di Sardegna** <1717-1861> and **Sardegna** <Regno> (the second one is used most); we have chosen the short form **Sardegna** (Regno);
- For the Papal States, the temporal power was declared lost in both 1798 and 1849, and in Napoleonic age the territory was divided with the annexation of Marche to the Kingdom of Italy and the transformation of Lazio and Umbria into French districts. Therefore, it is necessary to verify the headings used for the Papal States of the time by reference to pontifical documents not found in the Senate Library collections;
- The authorized heading for Siena is **Siena** (Repubblica): in SBN, we find **Siena, Siena** <Repubblica> and **Siena** <Stato>;
- In SBN, we find both **Toscana** <Granducato> and **Toscana** <Ducato>: in our authority list, the two forms are referred to as **Toscana** (Granducato) and **Firenze** (Ducato), respectively.

Here is an example of the authority list for Repubblica bresciana of 1797:[6]

Legend
> = see (link to the authorized heading)
< = from (cross-referenced from unauthorized term to authorized term)
> = see also (cross-reference among variant forms)

Abbreviations
? = unknown
cent. = century
in. = ineunte (first half/beginning of the century)
ex. = exeuntc (sccond half/end of the century)

Brescia (Governo provvisorio), 1797
    < Governo provvisorio di Brescia, 1797
    < Governo provvisorio bresciano, 1797
    < Municipalità di Brescia, 1797
    < Municipalità provvisionale di Brcscia, 1797
    < Municipalità provvisionale del Sovrano popolo bresciano, 1797
    < Municipalità provvisoria di Brescia, 1797
    < Repubblica bresciana, 1797
        > **Repubblica cisalpina**, *1797-1802*
        > **Venezia** (Repubblica), *sec. 8. in.-1796*

Governo provvisorio di Brescia, 1797
    > **Brescia** (Governo provvisorio), *1797*

Govcrno provvisorio bresciano, 1797
    > **Brescia** (Governo provvisorio), *1797*

Municipalità di Brescia, 1797
    > **Brescia** (Governo provvisorio), *1797*

Municipalità provvisionale di Brescia, 1797
    > **Brescia** (Governo provvisorio), *1797*

Municipalità provvisionale del Sovrano popolo bresciano, 1797
    > **Brescia** (Governo provvisorio), *1797*

Municipalità provvisoria di Brescia, 1797
    > **Brescia** (Governo provvisorio), *1797*

Repubblica bresciana, 1797
    > **Brescia** (Governo provvisorio), *1797*

The suggested authority list is not a final solution but should, hopefully, lead to further investigation and discovery. The librarian should not limit his/her activities just to the disciplines proper to Library Science but needs to be skilled in many subjects (e.g., history, law, information technology, etc.), avoiding the paradox of the polymorphous and utopian librarian (Née de la Rochelle, Peignot) who loses sight of his goal, which should be to provide instruments for searching and widening human knowledge.

ENDNOTES

1. The *Raccolta degli statuti* and the *Fondo delle leggi degli antichi Stati italiani* are available to selected readers in the reading rooms (Italian law history section) of the new building of the Italian Senate Library.

2. Biblioteca del Senato del Regno. *Catalogo della raccolta di statuti, consuetudini, leggi, decreti, ordini e privilegi dei comuni, delle associazioni e degli enti locali italiani, dal Medioevo alla fine del secolo XVIII,* Volume I, A-B. Roma: tip. del Senato, 1943, p. xviii.

3. Senato della Repubblica. Biblioteca. *Le leggi degli antichi Stati italiani. Catalogo della Raccolta di fonti possedute dalla Biblioteca del Senato,* edited by W. Montorsi. Roma: Tipografia del Senato, 1986, p. 17.

4. The thirty-five headings are: Adige *vel* Tirolo meridionale, Bergamo, Bologna, Brescia, Chioggia, Dalmazia e Illiria, Due Sicilie, Emilia, Ferrara, Genova, Italia, Liguria, Lombardia, Lucca, Milano, Modena, Napoli, Padova, Parma, Piemonte, Roma, Romagna, San Marino, Sardegna, Savoia, Sicilia, Siena, Stato pontificio, Ticino, Toscana, Treviso, Venezia, Venezia Giulia e Tridentina, Verona, Vicenza.

5. For a thorough analysis of this problem, see E. Fasano-Guarini. "'Etat moderne' et anciens Etats italiens. Elements d'histoire comparée," *Revue d'Histoire moderne et contemporaine*, 45 (1998) n. 1, pp. 15-41; and C. Casanova. *L'Italia moderna. Temi e orientamenti storiografici.* Roma: Carocci, 2001.

6. The complete authority list is available in the libraries of the Scuola speciale per archivisti e bibliotecari (Università La Sapienza of Rome) and of the Italian Senate, depositary of a copy of the dissertation from which this paper has been abstracted.

The *Authority File*
of the Biblioteca di Cultura Medievale

Maria Teresa Donati

SUMMARY. The A*uthority File* of the Biblioteca di Cultura Medievale is an archive of personal name forms and uniform titles (about 34,000 entries of authors' names and subjects) that have been indexed while producing a catalog for a substantial specialized bibliographic collection. It covers the classical and late-antique periods through the humanistic period, and comprises all literary genres, disciplines, and texts relevant to the institutional history of the time. Considering the complexity and multiform nature of the entries registered in the library, and due to the international character of its use, a large number of analytics were created for works from the classical period through the sixteenth century (about 5,300 entries).

The development of the *Authority File* has been completed thanks to the automated tools and particularly favorable circumstances that have enriched it, making it useful both to librarians and students who want to consult the catalog. The collaboration of BISLAM, for example, besides ensuring the scientific character of the archive's content and assisting in the research of relevant repertories, has helped to distinguish the characteristics of the respective products and, consequently, the diversity of methodological approaches, as well as other choices. The choice of the

---

Maria Teresa Donati is affiliated with Fondazione Ezio Franceschini, S.I.S.M.E.L.

[Haworth co-indexing entry note]: "The *Authority File* of the Biblioteca di Cultura Medievale." Donati, Maria Teresa. Co-published simultaneously in *Cataloging & Classification Quarterly* (The Haworth Information Press, an imprint of The Haworth Press, Inc.) Vol. 39, No. 1/2, 2004, pp. 585-596; and: *Authority Control in Organizing and Accessing Information: Definition and International Experience* (ed: Arlene G. Taylor, and Barbara B. Tillett) The Haworth Information Press, an imprint of The Haworth Press, Inc., 2004, pp. 585-596. Single or multiple copies of this article are available for a fee from The Haworth Document Delivery Service [1-800-HAWORTH, 9:00 a.m. - 5:00 p.m. (EST). E-mail address: docdelivery@haworthpress.com].

585

ALEPH500 software, a program which effectively and completely supports the format UNIMARC, has led the Biblioteca not only to discover and resolve the problems connected with the structure and content of the archive, mainly through the use of *UNIMARC/Authorities*, but also to search for every possible interaction with the bibliographic catalog. Moreover, the specificity of the proper names and titles selected by us, in addition to the international profile of our users, has required us to consider, from the first phases of the *Authority File*, the rules of national and international catalogs and other issues concerned with them, such as the language of the catalog itself, the standard formulation of the proper names and uniform titles for all cases of ambiguous or pseudo-epigraphic works, and the cross-references between them. *[Article copies available for a fee from The Haworth Document Delivery Service: 1-800-HAWORTH. E-mail address: <docdelivery@haworthpress.com> Website: <http://www.HaworthPress.com> © 2004 by The Haworth Press, Inc. All rights reserved.]*

KEYWORDS. Authority file, Biblioteca di Cultura Medievale, analytics

WHY CREATE AN AUTHORITY FILE? THE CIRCUMSTANCES, THE PLANNING

The 'Biblioteca di Cultura Medievale' is a joint organization of the Fondazione Ezio Franceschini and S.I.S.M.E.L. (Società Internazionale per lo Studio del Medioevo Latino). Its *Authority File* is a database of proper names and uniform titles (about 34,000 entries) built from the cataloging of a specialized bibliographic collection with more than 110,000 units. It covers a period from the classical to the humanistic age and includes literary genres, disciplines, and texts that belong to the institutional history of the age in either Latin or vernacular. The bibliography relative to such a period is extremely rich. Each year new critical editions of works and new studies enlarge our catalog with further information, proposing first editions of uncertain or sometimes multiple attribution, or new attributions for works that have already been published. It is not simple to assign unique access points. The examination stage that precedes the catalog registration of a bibliographic description has proven to be indispensable, for both historical-philological problems and problems related to the standardization of access points.

Given the complexity and multiple forms of the entries registered, the library has chosen an analytical approach, taking advantage of the syndetic and informative apparatus of the authority records related to about 5,300 authors and anonymous classic texts of the period. Moreover, an update of records of about 25,000 headings related to modern scholars of medieval studies (individuals and scientific institutions) is now underway.

Automated tools and favorable circumstances rendered a systematic approach possible from the planning stage of the *Authority File*, in particular with reference to the advent of new software for the library (ALEPH500), which was bought, among other reasons, using two criteria: to support, effectively and completely, the UNIMARC format and to allow automatic interaction between the authority records in the *Authority File* and the bibliographic records in the catalog. The software enables the display of 'see' and 'see also' references and allows optimized searching.

This *Authority File* project was also conducted in reference, moreover, to the collaboration with BISLAM (Bibliotheca Scriptorum Latinorum Medii Recentiorisque Aevi), as well as to the availability of a significant collection of specialized consulting materials integrated with a systematic policy of bibliographical updating (230 reference works, 90 encyclopedias, 24 incipits, several hundred manuscript catalogs, manuals, and the most authoritative critical editions).

The *Authority File* was drawn up following a suitable staff training program based on *GARE*,[1] *GARR*,[2] *GSARE*,[3] *UNIMARC/Authorities*,[4] and *RICA* (*Regole italiane di catalogazione per autori*, the Italian cataloging rules) for the choice and form of headings on entries, without disregarding the cataloging uses of other linguistic realities.

The authority records are constructed in four areas: (1) an area for the coded elements and for identification, (2) an area for the references (see and see also), (3) an area for the sources, and (4) an area for notes, in the *UNIMARC/Authorities* format (see Figure 1).

CHOICES AND CRITERIA

One of the primary criteria in the creation of the *Authority File* was the choice of the language[5] together with a correct interpretation of cataloging standards. Bearing in mind the international nature of the library users and the multilingualism of the bibliographic collection, the Latin language was preferred following the standards of *RICA*, with some necessary exceptions for consistency and uniformity. This choice was believed to be not only functional in the present situation, but also to conform to what was agreed to in the Paris Principles, the ISBD recommendations of the IFLA Meeting in Copenhagen in 1969, as well as the orientation expressed by the IFLA Working

FIGURE 1. From the *Authority File*: Latin Author from Late Classical Antiquity

```
┌─────────────────────────────────────────────────────────────────────┐
│                [1. Area of Codified and Identified Elements]          │
│                                                                       │
│  N. sistema 0000404                                                   │
│  Codice autore AC [=Autore classico e tardo-antico]                   │
│  Status della notizia BCMD [=notizia controllata e aggiornata]        │
│  Regole di catalogazione: R.I.C.A.                                    │
│  Fonte del record IT Biblioteca di Cultura Medievale                  │
│                                                                       │
│      [2. Area of the Heading, of References such as 'see' and 'see also'] │
│                                                                       │
│  Autore Persona        Augustinus, Aurelius, santo                    │
│                                                                       │
│  Rinvio        Augustinus Hipponensis                                 │
│  Rinvio        Agostino, Aurelio, santo                               │
│  Rinvio        Augustin d'Hippone                                     │
│  Rinvio        Augustin, saint                                        │
│  Rinvio        Agostino, santo                                        │
│  Rinvio        Augustinus, sanctus                                    │
│  Rinvio        Augustin, saint                                        │
│  Rinvio        Augustín, san                                          │
│  Rinvio        Aurelius Augustinus                                    │
│  Rinvio        Aurelio Agostino                                       │
│  Rinvio        Augustine of Hippo, saint                              │
│  Rinvio        Augustinus van Hippo                                   │
│  Vedi anche    Augustinus, Aurelius, santo, pseudo                    │
│                                                                       │
│                        [3. Area of the Sources]                       │
│                                                                       │
│  Fonte intest.  BNI; PAN                                              │
│  Fonte rinvii   CPL ; PAN (rinvio) (Augustinus episcopus Hipponensis) │
│  Fonte rinvii   DEI ; BS ; BNI (soggetto)                             │
│  Fonte rinvii   Bibliografia                                          │
│                                                                       │
│                        [4. Area of the Notes]                         │
│                                                                       │
│  Nota guida relativa all'intestazione e ai rinvii: Questa voce comprende anche le opere di attribuzione │
│  incerta. Per tutte le opere pseudepigrafe e spurie vedi la voce "Augustinus, Aurelius, santo, pseudo"  │
│                                                                       │
│  Datazione 354-430                                                    │
│                                                                       │
│  Nota informativa Per quanto riguarda la "Regola" di Agostino sembra accertato che la "Regula ad │
│  servos Dei" ("Praeceptum" o "Regula tertia") sia autentica e che la sua primitiva versione sia quella │
│  maschile. Per una panoramica sul problema cfr. A. Trapè, La regola di Sant'Agostino, 1986 │
└─────────────────────────────────────────────────────────────────────┘
```

Group on Minimal Level Authority Records to respect the linguistic and cultural needs of the user.

In this way, there was no doubt on the choice of 'Thomas de Aquino, santo' as the preferred form among the variety of linguistic forms provided by the editions owned by the library and potentially accessible for an initial research by the library users. In fact, it seemed that the only possible form was the one most used in the original editions of the published works (RICA 50.1), or, better still, the form found in the more attested and recent critical editions, which is often that commonly quoted in the specialized reference works.

A similar choice was adopted for authors who wrote both in Latin and vernacular, at least until the middle of the fourteenth century, for authors who only produced a 'technical' form of literature (notaries, canonists, draftsmen of the law, etc.), and for authors who only wrote one work in Latin: in the latter two cases, the chronological limit for the use of the Latin language has been moved to the fifteenth century, and sometimes to the sixteenth century. Following the same chronological criteria for the biographical subjects, Latin is the chosen linguistic form. Furthermore (for the same author) the subject entry is the same as the heading (as shown in Figure 2). In contrast, Latin has not been used for authors who are universally quoted in the vernacular style such as 'Alighieri, Dante.'

However, the most significant decision made possible by the *Authority File*'s syndetic apparatus was to provide a high degree of analytics in the catalog. Among other things, this allows the authority record to capture the transcribed forms present on the frontispiece or in other significant parts of the volume along with those proposed by the national bibliographies related to the place of origin of the author or of the texts described. Through the authority record, all these forms can be used for retrieval. The same level of analytics is applied to the description in the bibliographic record of complete or partial works contained in the volume and not declared on the frontispiece with the main text, as shown in Figure 3.

Our experience as *Authority File* users and compilers has shown, in fact, that the authoritativeness of an *Authority File* is assured not only by the form chosen, but also by the richness of the syndetic apparatus, the sources and the informative notes present in each record, as well as by the links that connect the headings to each other.

With regard to this we should consider works falsely-attributed to an author and pseudo-epigraphic works. The cataloging of works of controversial attribution (a frequent event in our catalog) has a non-uniform character in *RICA*, which foresees an optional secondary heading for the author indicated in any given cataloged edition, both in the common form and with the prefix 'pseudo' (if present on a given frontispiece) (*RICA* 6). Moreover, this latter one is only admitted by *RICA* to express conventional onomastic forms identifying one unique entity, such as in the case of pseudo-Dionysius. In answer to this problem, the optional secondary heading, providing pseudo-epigraphic names for authors of given texts, may help to distinguish many 'onomastic entities' from the genuine authors to whom works have been erroneously attributed.

The solution suggested by *RICA* for bibliographic catalogs and to answer the question as to whether the library possesses a certain publication, as noted

FIGURE 2. From the Bibliographic Catalog: Record Relative to a Monograph

> Felder, Hilarin
>   Die mitteldeutsche Legendendichtung Passional (um 1240) und ihr Leben von Sante Francisco
> und Sante Elizabet / Hilarin von Luzern. - P. 481-517
>   In: Collectanea franciscana, 3 (1933), 4. - L'estratto presenta anche paginazione propria
>
>   1. **Franciscus Assisiensis, santo** - Vita - Fonti altotedesche - Sec. XIII 2. Elisabeth Thuringiae,
> santa - Vita - Fonti altotedesche - Sec. XIII

FIGURE 3. From the Bibliographic Catalog: File Related to One Excerpt (Analytical Cataloging of the Textual Context of Each Document)

> Wielockx, Robert
> Poetry and Theology in the "Adoro te devote": Thomas Aquinas on the Eucharist and Christ's
> Uniqueness / Robert Wielockx. – P. 157-174
>
> In: Christ among the medieval dominicans, Notre Dame, [1998]. - In appendice: Adoro te devote
> /Thomas Aquinas ; Super Dionysium De ecclesiastica hierarchia / Albertus Magnus (cap. 3;
> Napoli, Biblioteca Nazionale, ms. I.B.54, fols. 51r-51v)
> I. Thomas de Aquino, santo II. Albertus Magnus, santo

above, is to provide both forms, but this is not suitable for an *Authority File* where each authority record for these attributed authors of anonymous works must be connected in a uniform, unique way to one or more anonymous works present in the bibliography. Moreover, works of controversial authorship often have multiple attributions, for which it is necessary to assign a uniform, possibly conventional, title to define the work in a unique way.

For all of these cases, both a unique authorized form for the proper name and many uniform, possibly conventional, titles were fixed. They connect up through reciprocal cross-references to the one authorized heading and to all the proper names to which the work is attributed. A numerical specification was introduced for works without a sufficiently identifiable title, obtained from the corresponding specialized reference work. Where this is not possible, appropriate notes in the 'pseudo-author' file help in the consultation of the catalog. An analogous procedure was followed for the headings and subjects related to complex literary genre (such as liturgy or hagiology), which often present difficulties of unique identification. Figures 4 and 5 show the records related to pseudo-Augustinus and one of St. Augustine's ambiguous or pseudo-epigraphic works.

Other complexities for anonymous classics occur as shown in Figures 6 and 7 for the French "Sept sages de Rome" that is a conventional title used also as

FIGURE 4. From the *Authority File*: Record of Pseudo Latin Author from Late Classical Antiquity

```
N. sistema 0021945
Codice autore ACP [=Autore classico e tardo antico pseudo]
Status della notizia BCMD [=notizia controllata e aggiornata]

Autore Persona  Augustinus, Aurelius, santo, pseudo

Rinvio  Pseudo-Augustinus
Rinvio  Pseudo-Agostino
Vedi anche      De assumptione Beatae Mariae Virginis
Vedi anche      Solutiones diversarum quaestionum ab haereticis obiectarum
Vedi anche      Testimonia divinae Scripturae et Patrum
Vedi anche      Speculum peccatoris
Vedi anche      Contra Varimadum Arianum
Vedi anche      Testimonia de Patre et Filio et Spiritu Sancto
Vedi anche      De altercatione Ecclesiae et Synagogae
```

FIGURE 5. From the *Authority File*: Record of Uniform Title of a Work Falsely Attributed to More Than One Author

```
Numero sist.    0032894
Codice TC [=Titolo Uniforme testo di epoca classica e tardo-antica]
Status notizia   BCMD

Titolo uniforme   Speculum peccatoris

Rinvio  Speculum peccatorum
Rinvio  Speculum amatorum mundi
Rinvio  Speculum mortis
Rinvio  Manipulus curatorum
Rinvio  Specchio dei peccatori
Vedi anche      Augustinus, Aurelius, santo, pseudo
Vedi anche      Bernardus Claraevallensis, santo, pseudo
Vedi anche      Richardus Rollus
Vedi anche      Hieronymus Stridonius, santo, pseudo

Fonte intestazione     CPPM IIB 3076
Fonte intestestazione   DS (sotto la voce Augustin)
Fonte rinvii   CPPM IIB 3076 (altre forme)
Fonte rinvii   bibliografia

Datazione 1116-1141 ca

Nota informativa Trattato sulla morte del peccatore falsamente attribuito ad Agostino, Gerolamo e a
San Bernardo. L'opera è stata attribuita anche a Riccardo Rolle. La datazione risale all'epoca in cui fu
scritto il "De modo orandi" di Ugo da San Vittore, cui si ispira

Nota informativa L'opera è anche uno pseudoepigrafo di Agostino (CCPM IIA 163)
```

FIGURE 6. From the Bibliographic Catalog: Record Related to an Edition of *Dolopathos* (French Version, in Verses)

Herbert
   Le roman de Dolopathos : edition du manuscrit H 436 de la Bibliothèque de l'École de Médécine de Montpellier / Herbert ; publiée par Jean-Luc Leclanche. - Paris : Honoré Champion Éditeur, 1997. - 3 v. - (Les classiques français du Moyen Age ; 124-126)

Si tratta della traduzione versificata del "Dolopathos" di Giovanni d'Alta Selva
MEL 19

Altri autori: I. Iohannes de Alta Silva II. Leclanche, Jean-Luc
Tit. un. sec.: I. Sept sages de Rome

FIGURE 7. From the *Authority File*: Uniform Heading of a Work Subject to Translations and Rewriting

N. sistema 0030999
Codice titolo TUM (Titolo uniforme medievale)
Status della notizia BCMD

Titolo uniforme   Sept sages de Rome

Rinvio	Roman des sept sages
Rinvio	Livre des sept sages
Rinvio	Sette Savi
Rinvio	Libro dei Sette Savi di Roma
Rinvio	Dolopathos
Rinvio	Roman de Dolopathos
Vedi anche	Historia septem sapientum
Vedi anche	Iohannes de Alta Silva
Vedi anche	Herbert
Vedi anche	Roman de Laurin

Fonte intest <u>ACl</u>
Fonte intest <u>BNF</u>
Fonte intest <u>BNI</u>
Fonte rinvii <u>DLF</u>
Fonte rinvii <u>DEI</u> (Sette Savi, Libro dei)
Fonte rinvii <u>DizBiobibl. Einaudi</u>
Fonte rinvii <u>ACl</u> (rinvio)
Fonte rinvii <u>BNF</u> (rinvio)

Datazione   1155 ca.

Nota informativa Romanzo francese in versi ispirato all'opera indiana nota come "Sindbad" o "Libro di Sindbad"

Nota informativa Il rifacimento latino in prosa dal tit. "Dolopathos" è di Iohannes de Alta Silva del XII sec. La versione francese versificata del "Dolopathos" è di un certo Herbert del XIII sec. ed ha conosciuto una fortuna autonoma, anche se non comparabile al "Roman des sept sages" an access point for an excerpt that was translated and put to verse by Herbert (Figure 6).

Equally complex problems are posed for the headings of works of literary genres such as, to quote only a few, hagiography or liturgy. It should be mentioned that for liturgical works prior to the Concilio of Trento, for example, it does not seem suitable to apply the *RICA* cataloging rule 39, nor are authority lists with uniform headings available. It proves very difficult, moreover, to identify such works with suitable unique headings which respect the historical-philological connotations of this kind of literature. To avoid the dispersion of the cataloging uniformity of this collection, the choice of conventional headings has proven necessary, even if of a classifying type, as they are useful in grouping together different entities.

COLLABORATION WITH BISLAM

Collaboration with BISLAM provided an important opportunity both when it was necessary to distinguish between the characteristics of the respective products and different methodologies and in the compilation stage of the *Authority File*. The chart in Figure 8 compares the two projects.

If the author examined during the cataloging is treated also in BISLAM's database (considered the primary authoritative source for the library), the editorial staff of BISLAM is notified to create or update the authority list record. From this updated record, it shall then be possible to automatically extract both the heading and associated references useful for consultation of the library catalog. The library is, in fact, capable of consulting the BISLAM database directly, and viewing the sources linked to the headings and associated references. Subsequent intervention, with respect to the chosen form of BISLAM (which generally coincides with that of the library), may consist of the simplification of overly-complex entries, translation of terms into Italian, or translation of Latinized attributions into their respective vernacular forms, following *RICA* guidelines. The *Authority File* presents, for example: 'Agnellus Ravennas' for 'Agnellus qui et Andreas Ravennas'; 'Adalbero Laudunensis' for 'Adalbero Laudunensis episcopus'; 'Augustinus Aurelius, Santo'; or 'Henry VII, King of England' for 'Henricus VII, Angliae et Franciae rex ac dominus Hiberniae.'

CONCLUSIONS

In the international scenario of interaction between different authority files that have been emerging since the mid-nineties, it seems that a point has been

FIGURE 8. A Comparison in Methodology and Content Between BISLAM and the *Authority File* of the Library

---

Methodology

BISLAM   prearranged, systematic, complete as far as regards the number of the authors and cross-references dealt with. Opens with a methodological examination of reference works and bibliographical sources, which have been systematically pre-selected and quoted.

AUTH. FILE   occasional, even if set up with predefined criteria, only includes the entries present in the bibliographic catalog, is selective in cross-references, and dynamic. The examination of the reference works and bibliographical sources is functional when choosing a heading.
Sources examined include national bibliographies (based on the place of origin, and the occupation of the authors or the texts described) and cataloged bibliographies: the form drawn from the latter (corresponding to the linguistic form of the various countries) is quoted methodically to ease research.

Content

BISLAM   deals with a survey of authors which have been predetermined using linguistic and chronological criteria, and by the typology of the documents they produced.

AUTH. FILE   considers all the onomastic entries and uniform titles which represent an access key to the catalog (headings and subjects), even if the analytics criteria was limited to a specific sphere (ancient times - 16th century). Includes the following categories of authors that are absent in BISLAM:

- Greek and Byzantine authors
- Latin authors up to 479
- Medieval vernacular authors
- Anonyms identified by a toponym or meaningful conventional expression
- Pseudo-epigraphs
- Signatory authors of documents drawn up for legislative or administrative purposes
   - Uniform titles
- Saints, sovereigns, historical characters who are not authors but who represent an access key as a subject

---

Consultation

BISLAM   is an autonomous file which can be consulted using various supports.

AUTH. FILE   is a file which can be consulted online, and is connected to the bibliographic catalog: the more specialized, wide-ranging and up-to-date the latter, the more authoritative will be the result of the linked consultation between the two files, as well as in the richness of information and of connections present in the authority file.

---

reached where the role and contribution of specialized bibliographic catalogs has to be defined, together with that of national libraries or other authoritative bodies, such as a universities, which have general catalogs. On the one hand, this is equivalent to acknowledging a particular institutional character (such as the collection, the users, the operative methodology) of these library situations, analogous to what has been recently done (with regard to the authority files) in the rich and specialized environments of archives and museums. On the other hand, it should perhaps be emphasized that the nationality and original language of authors and works, prominent tools for classification in national library collections, are not always the criteria that adequately discriminate or define the authoritativeness of records for other cataloging agencies. With regard to this, people working in the specialized field of medieval studies can find a stimulating cause for reflection on the question recently posed by Pino Buizza and Mauro Guerrini concerning pre-national entries on which 'no-one is competent, and, if the criteria of the original language is dropped, the oscillation remains between the adoption of the local form or the adoption of the form traditionally agreed on.'[6]

An evaluation of the national panorama in Italy reveals the scarcity of libraries with significant authority files (that are not only the result of an indiscriminate duplication of bibliographic data): the EDIT16 file, for example, is held to be one of the richest and most authoritative. Even more limited is the number of files that are accessible online through the Z39.50 protocol. As far as regards our situation, we hope that our records will be available online within a short period of time, as soon as a significant number of records are edited and reliable. Another authority file project, conducted by the Istituto Centrale per il Catalogo Unico delle Biblioteche Italiane e per le Informazioni Bibliografiche (ICCU), provides interesting results with its *UNIMARC/Authorities* output format. The LEAF Project (at an international level) and the LACoBiT Project (at a national level), and the recent hypothesis of potential internal collaboration within these projects, can be noted with interest among the projects under development discussed in other papers in this volume. Apart from the technical specificities and the partners involved, ICCU participates as the external partner for Italy in the first case, while the "Bibliografia Nazionale Italiana" (BNI) is among those foreseen in the second case. It is interesting to emphasize here the necessary attention paid to optimizing the richness and the distinctiveness of content in the various databases, without 'squashing' research results carried out in local situations or allowing single, shared databases to be overly-influenced by special interests and operating requirements of individual entities, yet at the same time allowing users the freedom to choose the context of research and the collection of information.

It is to be hoped that an evaluation of available authority files can be achieved in this manner as soon as possible, at least at a national level, with the aim of improving operating links between different disciplinary and institutional sectors, while starting a solid collaboration which will prove truly functional for each kind of library. It will become indispensable in the short term, if we consider that the impact of the application of the FRBR model on authority files will involve a loss of resources, at least in its initial stage. This latter problem seems resolvable if we consider the distribution of competence among the cataloging agencies: looking into the not too distant future, the different but equally important functions of authority files, which are now already outlined, will be realized. On the one hand, the function of the *Authority File* is to control correct access from a philological, historical or bibliographical point of view, while also developing as an autonomous file for consultation and navigation. On the other hand, the function of file management is to supervise automatic operations linked to the registration and pre-coordination of access points: above all, this is a function which demands good cataloging, bibliographical and 'bibliological' skills–most relevant for the principle national cataloging entities that share richer resources.

ENDNOTES

1. *Guidelines for Authority and Reference Entries*, recommended by the Working Group on an International Authority System, approved by the Standing Committees of the IFLA Section on Cataloguing and the IFLA Section on Information Technology. London: IFLA International Office for UBC, 1984.

2. *Guidelines for Authority Records and References*. 2nd ed., rev. by the IFLA Working Group on GARE Revision. München: Saur, 2001. http://www.ifla.org/V/saur.htm#UBCIMnew.

3. *Guidelines for Subject Authority and Reference Entries*. Working Group on Guidelines for Subject Authority Files of the Section on Classification and Indexing of the IFLA Division of Bibliographic Control. München: Saur, 1993.

4. *UNIMARC/Authorities: Universal Format for Authorities*. Recommended by the IFLA Steering Group on a UNIMARC Format for Authorities, approved by the Standing Committees of the IFLA Sections on Cataloguing and Information Technology. München: Saur, 2001.

5. This argument was expressed by Mauro Guerrini in "La lingua del catalogo: gli autori greci, latini, dell'Oriente antico, del periodo medievale e umanistico, i papi: forma Latina o forma italiana?" *Accademie e biblioteche d'Italia* 67 (1999), no. 3, p. 21-48. Also see Mauro Guerrini. *Il catalogo di qualità*. Firenze: Regione Toscana, Pagnini e Martinelli, 2002.

6. Cfr. Pino Buizza and Mauro Guerrini. *Il controllo del punto di accesso alla registrazione per autore e titolo: riflessioni sul comportamento delle principali agenzie bibliografiche nazionali a quarant'anni dai Principi di Parigi*, relazione alle Giornate di studio "Catalogazione e controllo di autorità," Roma, 21-22 novembre 2002. http://www.iccu.sbn.it/BuizzaGuerrini.doc.

The Compilation of an Authority List of Medieval Latin Authors: Objectives, Methodological Issues, and Results

Roberto Gamberini

SUMMARY. A census of the authors of the Middle Ages and the creation of an authority list for them pose various methodological problems. In developing such a program, it is necessary to consider–in addition to the diverse needs of its users–the specific type of proper names in question, the peculiarities of Medieval Latin philology, the relative lack of such specialized programs, and the historic literary tradition. The project BISLAM, which studies onomastic sciences for SISMEL, has developed a program entitled *Authors in "Medioevo latino,"* available both in print and on CD-ROM, which is comprised of an authority list of nearly 5,300 entries for about 12,500 nominal forms. The research criteria and the development of this program are the results of a collaboration between the Bibliographic and Onomastic divisions of the Società Internazionale per lo Studio del Medioevo Latino and the Biblioteca di Cultura Medievale, which serves the Società and the

---

Roberto Gamberini is affiliated with Società Internazionale per lo Studio del Medioevo Latino (S.I.S.M.E.L.).

[Haworth co-indexing entry note]: "The Compilation of an Authority List of Medieval Latin Authors: Objectives, Methodological Issues, and Results." Gamberini, Roberto. Co-published simultaneously in *Cataloging & Classification Quarterly* (The Haworth Information Press, an imprint of The Haworth Press, Inc.) Vol. 39, No. 1/2, 2004, pp. 597-606; and: *Authority Control in Organizing and Accessing Information: Definition and International Experience* (ed: Arlene G. Taylor, and Barbara B. Tillett) The Haworth Information Press, an imprint of The Haworth Press, Inc., 2004, pp. 597-606. Single or multiple copies of this article are available for a fee from The Haworth Document Delivery Service [1-800-HAWORTH, 9:00 a.m. - 5:00 p.m. (EST). E-mail address: docdelivery@haworthpress.com].

Fondazione Franceschini. The purpose of such a joint project is to offer a program useful both to scholars of medieval Latin literature and to specialists in bibliographic catalogs and repertories. *[Article copies available for a fee from The Haworth Document Delivery Service: 1-800-HAWORTH. E-mail address: <docdelivery@haworthpress.com> Website: <http://www. HaworthPress.com> © 2004 by The Haworth Press, Inc. All rights reserved.]*

KEYWORDS. BISLAM, authority list, medieval authors, Middle Ages, medieval Latin, authority control, personal names

The authority control for Medieval Latin literature presents a particularly delicate and complex problem for many reasons. A vast literary production has reached us, in fact, from the thousand years which form the Medieval Age: over ten thousand authors and a formidable number of anonymous works are known.[1] As is recognized, a large part of this literature is still unpublished and much is even entirely unknown, since a complete census of the manuscript collections of the European libraries is still far from being finished. The lack of editions inevitably results in a shortage of historical-literary studies; nevertheless, discoveries of new authors and attribution of anonymous works to previously recognized authors follow closely one after another every year. In this way, the large reference works get older with discouraging speed, obliging those who edit them to chase after a constantly increasing quantity of material using a science where insistent, substantial progress renders both insufficient and inadequate every attempt to obtain a definitive order of the knowledge attained. The first necessity, which continues to be hard to satisfy for the person who is compiling a biographical, bibliographical, or historical reference work in the field of medieval literature, is to be able to depend on a reliable author list, a list which forms a solid starting point for the planning of the work and a help in resolving some of the frequent identification problems. Such a requirement is obviously shared by those who work with the cataloging of printed books and manuscripts, as well as by scholars who occasionally have to measure themselves against extremely varied and uncertain forms of names found in individual manuscripts or in modern bibliographical repertories.

The most important authority lists of medieval authors that have been carried out and made available to the public, even in a printed format, were done by the Bayerische Staatsbibliothek (*Personennamen des Mittelalters*) and by Vittorio Volpi (*Dizionario delle opere classiche*).[2] The German work is particularly important in that it developed directly from the work of bibliography cataloging and from the application of rules of name standardization studied specifically for medieval authors. In this way, the express requirement of John Francis Macey to regulate the medieval onomastic disorder, in order to facilitate the validation of the completed authority list, becomes fulfilled.[3] The prevalently formalistic orientation of the instruments compiled by Volpi and Fabian results, however, in an unavoidable weakness in the historical and philological level of research, and finishes in limiting their function to that of simple files with standardized nominal forms.[4] The identification problems, therefore, remain to be faced and resolved, to allow the compilation of a full, reliable catalog of those who wrote in Latin during the medieval period.

Since there is no reliable census of authors, the authority control for medieval Latinity often requires original research, which in turn demands qualified competence. As a result, the idea of creating a new authority list developed within the "Società Internazionale per lo Studio del Medioevo Latino" (SISMEL) and the "Fondazione Franceschini." The list includes all authors who wrote in Latin between 500 and 1500. For these institutions the problem in authority control is present on several fronts: the production of bibliographical tools (the *Medioevo latino* newsletter[5] and the *C.A.L.M.A.* reference work[6]), manuscript cataloging (the *Codex* project[7]), and the production of the library catalog for these two bodies, highly specialized in medieval Latin literature.[8] Therefore, bearing in mind the different users and taking advantage of their collaboration for definitions of research criteria and standards for its implementation, the BISLAM Project (*Bibliotheca Scriptorum Latinorum Medii Recentiorisque Aevi*) was launched, with the aim of producing useful tools for authority control in the field of Latin literature.

The first of these tools, called *Authors in "Medioevo latino"* (available in CD-ROM and a printed volume[9]), includes about 12,500 names, referring to over 5,300 authors. To obtain results that were consistent with the most recent acquisitions in medieval Latin philology, the authors chosen for the first volume of BISLAM were those listed in the *Medioevo latino* volumes between 1980-2000, that is, those authors who have been the subject of the most recent studies. Using such a bibliographical base (made up of about 140,000 essays and editions shown with back reference to the *Medioevo latino* entry number) as well as more up-to-date and reliable reference works, a group of eleven medievalists examined each single name, standardizing the names according to prearranged standards and recording the main variants in Latin, and in the case of bilingual authors, in vernacular. Since this dealt with a list of Latin authors, the Latin form of the name was chosen as the main heading, with the eventual vernacular forms listed among the variants. The uniformity of the data is guaranteed by appropriate standards, drawn up to start from philological and historical practice, as well as from the bibliographical usages applied in *Medioevo latino*. Such a choice has allowed the necessary independence to be maintained both from Italian cataloging rules (RICA, *Regole italiane di catalogazione per autori.* Roma: ICCU, 1979), and from different national and international cataloging standards.

The compilation did not only have a pragmatic and formalistic scope, but attempted to supply a scientific answer to the identification of problems related to many authors. Homonyms which are often confused, as, for example, the two *Iohannes de Garlandia* (see Figure 1), or the seven *Iohannes Diaconus* (see Figure 2), have been distinguished by not only linking the secondary forms given to their name to each entry, but also by referring to the most recent bibliography on each author.

Apart from homonymy, one of the principle identification difficulties is the variety of names testified by the handwritten tradition, which could be the mistaken cause of different headings for the same author. Such situations have been resolved through a series of historical-literary controls sometimes associated with an examination of the contents of the manuscripts. In some situations, it was necessary to select from the variants of the author's name, as with *Iohannes de Hauvilla*, traditionally named in more than thirty different ways, but only three of which are acceptable from a historical, linguistic, or philological point of view[10] (see Figures 3 and 4).

Historical research has sometimes been necessary to be able to define primary and secondary headings, as with the jurist *Irnerius* (see Figure 5), who was always called *Irnerius* in the tradition of glosses and law history, but when undersigning acts as a judge, he always signed in a different way (*Wernerus, Gernerius, Garnerius*, etc.).[11]

If the instability of the forms and the variations in spelling are common in all Medieval Latin, the standardization process is never commonplace. Historical criteria were followed in the above-mentioned situation, but on other occasions, historical-linguistic factors can have more weight, or it might be necessary to reconstruct the variable courses of the transmission of the author's name, which can vary considerably from one to another. The name can, in fact, come from autographic documents or be compiled under the author's supervision, it can come from works copied in outside *scriptoria*, from quotations made by other authors, from archive documents, from choices made by ancient and modern editors, from reference work entries, and so on. Extreme importance, therefore, is assumed not only by the standardization, but also by the availability of those graphic variations, which represent well-established, traditional exceptions to such regularization. For such cases, the electronic edition of the database, linked together with the printed version, allows a greater versatility in searching functions and offers an additional tool for the identification of the author, as it allows results to be obtained not only starting from nominal forms, or parts of these, but also from bibliographical entries published in *Medioevo latino*, that is to say, from publications about the author himself.

An authority list of medieval Latin literature which, like BISLAM, aims for reliable results from a historical as well as philological point of view, which follows a scientific method appropriate to medieval Latin disciplines, and which avails of the contribution of specialized scholars, finishes, therefore, in not being a simple list of name headings, but a complete onomastic, historical-literary, and bibliographical reference work.

As previously stated, the rapid evolution of Medieval Latin philology means that any reference work ages quickly, and, as such, the first volume of BISLAM does not claim to be a definitive instrument, but only the first stage of a research that will continue towards a constantly increasing knowledge of Medieval Latin authors.

ENDNOTES

1. The overall number of authors results from an approximate estimate based on the BISLAM project database (*Bibliotheca Scriptorum Latinorum Medii Recentiorisque Aevi*), made up of 5,300 authors from the first volume (BISLAM. Bibliotheca Scriptorum Latinorum Medii Recentiorisque Aevi. Repertory of Medieval and Renaissance Latin Authors. I, Gli Autori in "Medioevo latino." Authors in "Medioevo latino," cur. R. Gamberini, dir. M. Donnini, C. Leonardi. Firenze: SISMEL–Edizioni del Galluzzo, 2003), and of the authors who are still being researched will be included in the second volume.

2. *Personennamen des Mittelalters. PMA. Ansetzungs- und Verweisungsformen gemäß den RAK*, erarbeitet von der Bayerischen Staatsbibliothek. Regeln für die alphabetische Katalogisierung. RAK, 6. Wiesbaden: Reichert, 1989. The 1989 edition has been followed by a second edition, which has been enlarged in the number of authors, and supplied with some bibliographical information: *Personennamen des Mittelalters. Nomina Scriptorum Medii Aevi. PMA. Namensformen für 13000 Personen gemäß den Regeln für die Alphabetische Katalogisierung (RAK)*, redaktionelle Bearbeitung C. Fabian, zweite erweiterte Ausgabe. München: Saur, 2000. Volpi, V. *DOC. Dizionario delle opere classiche. Intestazioni uniformi degli autori, elenco delle opere e delle parti componenti, indici degli autori, dei titoli e delle parole chiave della letteratura classica, medievale e bizantina.* Milano: Editrice Bibliografica, 1994.

3. Macey, J. F. *The Cataloging of Medieval Names: A Definition of the Problem and a Proposed Solution.* Diss., University of Pittsburgh, 1974, p. 156; Fabian, C. "Personennamen des Mittelalters–PMA. Reflexionen zu einem langjährigen Normdateiprojekt der Bayerischen Staatsbibliothek," *Bibliotheksforum Bayern* 28 (2000): 33-54, in particular p. 33.

4. Cfr. C. Fabian, art. cit., p. 53: "Es muss auch festgehalten werden, dass eine Normdatei keine Enzyklopädie und kein Lexikon ist und keineswegs mit demselben Aufwand erstellt werden darf."

5. *Medioevo latino. Bollettino bibliografico della cultura europea da Boezio a Erasmo (secoli VI-XV)* 1 (1980)-.

6. *C.A.L.M.A. Compendium Auctorum Latinorum Medii Aevi (500-1500)*, I, cur. G.C. Garfagnini, C. Leonardi, M. Lapidge, adiuv. L. Lanza, R.C. Love, and S. Polidori. Firenze: SISMEL–Edizioni del Galluzzo, 2000-.

7. The *Codex* project deals with an inventory of medieval manuscripts in private and public collections in Tuscany, and publishes the catalogs in the series: "Biblioteche e Archivi" by SISMEL–Edizioni del Galluzzo, Firenze.

8. The catalog of the library is available at: http://www.sismelfirenze.it.

9. BISLAM. Bibliotheca Scriptorum Latinorum Medii Recentiorisque Aevi. Repertory of Medieval and Renaissance Latin Authors. I, Gli Autori in "Medioevo latino." Authors in "Medioevo latino," op. cit.

10. Cfr. Johannes de Hauvilla, *Architrenius*, ed. comm. P.G. Schmidt. München: Fink, 1974, pp. 18-20.

11. Cfr. Spagnesi, E. *Wernerius Bononiensis iudex. La figura storica d'Irnerio.* Accademia toscana di scienze e lettere "La Colombaria." Studi, 16. Firenze: Olschki, 1970, passim.

BIBLIOGRAPHY

BISLAM. Bibliotheca Scriptorum Latinorum Medii Recentiorisque Aevi. Repertory of Medieval and Renaissance Latin Authors. I, Gli Autori in "Medioevo latino." Authors in "Medioevo latino," cur. R. Gamberini, dir. M. Donnini, C. Leonardi. Firenze: SISMEL–Edizioni del Galluzzo, 2003.

C.A.L.M.A. Compendium Auctorum Latinorum Medii Aevi (500-1500), I, cur. G.C. Garfagnini, C. Leonardi, M. Lapidge, adiuv. L. Lanza, R.C. Love, and S. Polidori. Firenze: SISMEL–Edizioni del Galluzzo, 2000-.

Fabian, C. "Personennamen des Mittelalters–PMA. Reflexionen zu einem langjährigen Normdateiprojekt der Bayerischen Staatsbibliothek," Bibliotheksforum Bayern 28 (2000): 33-54.

Johannes de Hauvilla, Architrenius, ed. comm. P.G. Schmidt. München: Fink, 1974.

Macey, J.F. The Cataloging of Medieval Names: A Definition of the Problem and a Proposed Solution. Diss., University of Pittsburgh, 1974.

Medioevo latino. Bollettino bibliografico della cultura europea da Boezio a Erasmo (secoli VI-XV) 1 (1980-).

Personennamen des Mittelalters. PMA. Ansetzungs- und Verweisungsformen gemäß den RAK, erarbeitet von der Bayerischen Staatsbibliothek. Regeln für die alphabetische Katalogisierung. RAK, 6. Wiesbaden: Reichert, 1989.

Personennamen des Mittelalters. Nomina Scriptorum Medii Aevi. PMA. Namensformen für 13000 Personen gemäß den Regeln für die Alphabetische Katalogisierung (RAK), redaktionelle Bearbeitung C. Fabian, zweite erweiterte Ausgabe. München: Saur, 2000.

Spagnesi, E. Wernerius Bononiensis iudex. La figura storica d'Irnerio. Accademia toscana di scienze e lettere "La Colombaria." Studi,16. Firenze: Olschki, 1970.

Volpi, V. DOC. Dizionario delle opere classiche. Intestazioni uniformi degli autori, elenco delle opere e delle parti componenti, indici degli autori, dei titoli e delle parole chiave della letteratura classica, medievale e bizantina. Milano: Editrice Bibliografica, 1994.

APPENDIX

FIGURE 1. BISLAM Authority Records for Iohannes de Garlandia

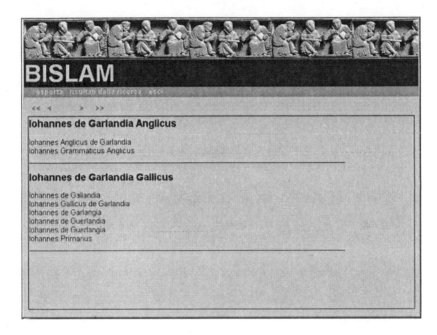

APPENDIX (continued)

FIGURE 2. BISLAM Records for Iohannes Diaconus

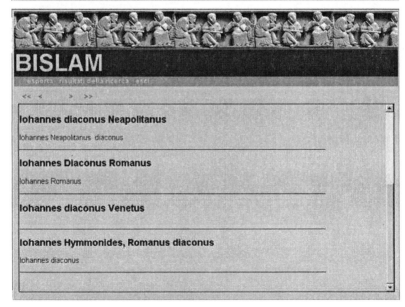

FIGURE 3. Variant Proper Names for Iohannes de Hauvilla

Iohannes de Hauvilla		
Iohannes	Iohannes de Anville	Iohannes Hanuwillensis
Iohannes magister	Iohannes Anwillanus	Iohannes de Hauteville
Iohannes de Alta Villa	Iohannes de Auville	Iohannes de Hautivilla
Iohannes de Altavilla	Iohannes de Hainvyle	Iohannes Hautvillensis
Iohannes de Alvilla	Iohannes de Hanteville	Iohannes de Hauviteville
Iohannes de Annavilla	Iohannes de Hantivill	Iohannes Hautwillus
Iohannes Annaevillanus	Iohannes de Hantvill	Iohannes de Hawyll
Iohannes Annaevislanus	Iohannes Hantwillensis	Iohannes Magnavillanus
Iohannes de Anneville	Iohannes de Hanvill	Iohannes de Nantville
Iohannes Antivillensis	Iohannes de Hanville	Iohannes Neustrius
Iohannes de Anvilla	Iohannes de Hanwill	Johannes af Havilla

FIGURE 4. BISLAM Record for Iohannes de Hauvilla

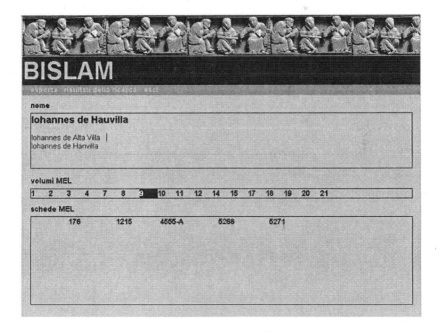

APPENDIX (continued)

FIGURE 5. BISLAM Record for Irnerius

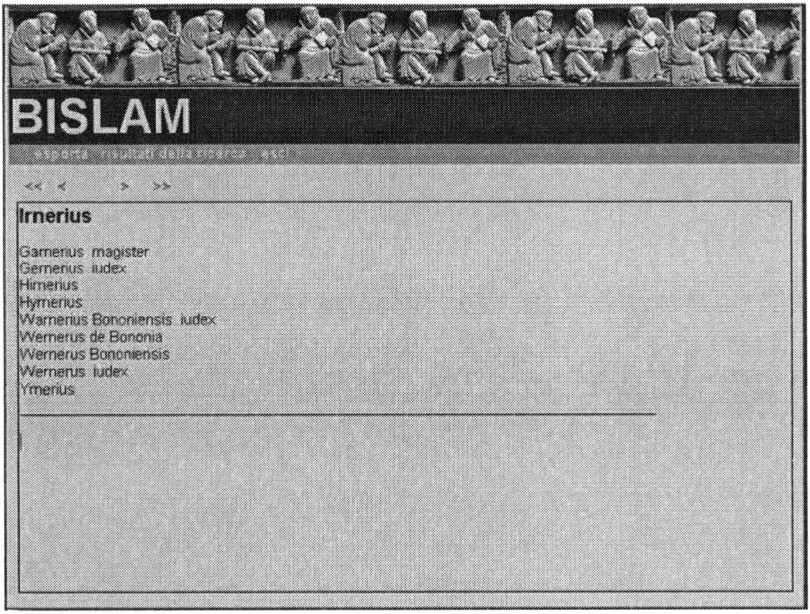

Congedo

Luigi Crocetti

SUMMARY. This paper provides a conclusion to the International Conference on Authority Control: Definitions and International Experiences, held in Florence, 10-12 February 2003, stressing the importance of authority work in Italy and internationally, and offering a tribute to Mauro Guerrini, the conference organizer. *[Article copies available for a fee from The Haworth Document Delivery Service: 1-800-HAWORTH. E-mail address: <docdelivery@haworthpress.com> Website: <http://www.HaworthPress.com> © 2004 by The Haworth Press, Inc. All rights reserved.]*

KEYWORDS. Authority control, international cooperation, Mauro Guerrini

Dear colleagues, dear friends,

I was entrusted to close this conference and express final greetings in the name of all (and they are many) who have worked for its organization. I feel very honored, despite my various incompetencies, and probably right for this. These were three very intense days, and very rich in contributions: with the structure given to the conference, we could find large overviews of theoretical and technical updates refreshing, as well as a very large exemplification (practical, sometimes also with theoretical aspects) of different experiences.

Luigi Crocetti is past President of Associazione italiana biblioteche (AIB).

[Haworth co-indexing entry note]: "Congedo." Crocetti, Luigi. Co-published simultaneously in *Cataloging & Classification Quarterly* (The Haworth Information Press, an imprint of The Haworth Press, Inc.) Vol. 39, No. 1/2, 2004, pp. 607-609; and: *Authority Control in Organizing and Accessing Information: Definition and International Experience* (ed: Arlene G. Taylor, and Barbara B. Tillett) The Haworth Information Press, an imprint of The Haworth Press, Inc., 2004, pp. 607-609. Single or multiple copies of this article are available for a fee from The Haworth Document Delivery Service [1-800-HAWORTH, 9:00 a.m. - 5:00 p.m. (EST). E-mail address: docdelivery@haworthpress.com].

The result was a sort of large mosaic; and, as in mosaics, every tessera is necessary and has its own function. I think–and I hope you will agree–that final results are extremely important: a widening of the world horizon, a better knowledge of what is going on or what is in project, a deepening of perspectives and possibilities of international cooperation.

After first hesitations and first doubts, in times of the accession of computers, *authority work* has attested more and more as the foundation of the whole library work of recording and creating access. I think that the present stage is a significant and useful one in the way to an increasingly better elaboration of this tool. Florence is pleased and proud to have hosted this meeting.

Certainly this stage is helpful for my country, Italy, where practice and knowledge of *authority files* have, for a long time, been ignored or neglected. Our conference is evidence, in reference to this, of a lively interest that has been developing for many years now, and finally, I think, is mature enough to undertake concrete realizations. Work, here, seems particularly difficult because of little or no agreement between library science and cultural needs in general. If, as it appears more and more clearly even from the works of our conference, authority control is, among library activities, probably the one most closely linked to general culture, at least in the fact that decisions have to be taken on the basis of contemporary historical, literary, and social studies, we must remember that this is the country where the most important and best biographic reference work (I refer to *Dizionario biografico degli italiani*, published by Istituto per l'Enciclopedia Italiana, whose 59th volume contains the letter G) has chosen for its entries the so-called 'private name' (and almost without cross references!). The result, quite ironically, is that some scholars, e.g., Poliziano or Jacopone da Todi, have been ignored for some time, without suspecting that Poliziano could be under the improbable *Ambrogini* and Jacopone under the absurd *Benedetti*.

The fact is that the principal determining element in establishing the form of a name (or a subject) cannot be other than that used by the respective insiders (for example, for a writer or philologists and literary critics). Therefore, the example brought by Michael Gorman in his fine introduction in the opening of our conference, about Giuseppe Tomasi di Lampedusa (unexceptionable according to ordinary sources), should be, in my opinion, reversed, because all historians and literary critics name *Lampedusa* the author of *Gattopardo*; and it will be enough to recall that monograph titled *Ricordo di Lampedusa*, which is not a memory of the island, but of the writer, or the current adjective *lampedusiano*. Also in this case, indexes, dictionaries, and encyclopedias prefer *Tomasi*. But reference works are important and essential to our work only when they do not adopt criteria that are not acceptable for whatever reason to our purposes (and this, unfortunately, is the case for most of the Italian ones). The truth does not lie in this kind of reference work but in actual use.

Much has to be done, as we can see; but we do not doubt that, included in a context of international cooperation, Italian libraries can achieve the goal. Whether Italian or not, work is hard and long-lasting for everybody; it is perpetual in itself. I did not hear anyone complain about this. Librarians' work is all difficult and many things we do are never-ending.

We really hope that, for all of you, your Florentine days have been pleasant. Our greetings and our wish for good work is addressed to all of you, with particular emphasis on those who came from very far.

Finally—as a participant in the audience of the conference—let me thank and greet all to whom we owe these three nice days, and hail the person who has been the soul of the event: Mauro Guerrini.

OCLC's MARS
and Innovative's Millennium:
Authority Control Procedures

Lihong Zhu

SUMMARY. Discusses the three major facets of authority control and provides guidelines on authority control procedures for libraries that use OCLC MARC Record Service (MARS) as their authority control vendor and Innovative Millennium as their local automated system. *[Article copies available for a fee from The Haworth Document Delivery Service: 1-800-HAWORTH. E-mail address: <docdelivery@haworthpress.com> Website: <http://www.HaworthPress.com> © 2004 by The Haworth Press, Inc. All rights reserved.]*

KEYWORDS. Authority control, database maintenance, cataloging, OCLC MARS, Innovative Millennium

INTRODUCTION

Authority control is a set of procedures to update the authority database and to maintain consistency in the form of the headings used in a library catalog.

Lihong Zhu is Head, Bibliographic Control Department, User Support Services Division, Holland Library, Washington State University Libraries, Pullman, WA USA.

[Haworth co-indexing entry note]: "OCLC's MARS and Innovative's Millennium: Authority Control Procedures." Zhu, Lihong. Co-published simultaneously in *Cataloging & Classification Quarterly* (The Haworth Information Press, an imprint of The Haworth Press, Inc.) Vol. 39, No. 1/2, 2004, pp. 611-619; and: *Authority Control in Organizing and Accessing Information: Definition and International Experience* (ed: Arlene G. Taylor, and Barbara B. Tillett) The Haworth Information Press, an imprint of The Haworth Press, Inc., 2004, pp. 611-619. Single or multiple copies of this article are available for a fee from The Haworth Document Delivery Service [1-800-HAWORTH, 9:00 a.m. - 5:00 p.m. (EST). E-mail address: docdelivery@haworthpress.com].

When a library embarks on authority control, it should create procedures to cover the following facets:

- Bring the existing bibliographic database up to current authority standards and build a new authority database;
- Bring the newly added bibliographic records up to current authority standards;
- Keep the newly created authority database up-to-date as external authority structure evolves, and, at the same time, keep the existing bibliographic records up to current authority standards.

OCLC MARC Record Service (MARS) provides authority control services that "automatically examine each heading in your library's bibliographic database, compare each heading to the national authority files selected by your library, verify and/or upgrade all headings to current forms, and supply a complete and accurate set of MARC 21 authority records, including notes and cross-references" [1]. A library that has Millennium (by Innovative Interfaces, Inc.) as its local automated system can use MARS, together with Millennium Automatic Authorities Processing, Millennium reports, and Millennium Global Update, to develop a set of procedures to cover the above three facets of authority control with minimum manual power. In this article, I will discuss the key elements in authority control procedures for a library that uses Millennium as its local automated system and MARS as its authority control vendor.

GETTING READY FOR MARS AUTHORITY PROCESSING

The first step, when a library decides to use MARS as its authority control vendor, is to fill out nine profiles for customizing MARS authority control services according to the *OCLC MARS Authority Control Planning Guide*. This is a very crucial step since it will determine what authority control procedures you will use later. Several issues have to be considered in this step:

- What data exchange format do you prefer?
  Though MARS accepts a wide choice of media, File Transfer Protocol (FTP) is the most common data exchange format and it is supported by Millennium.
- How do you want MARS to distribute authority files?
  Since the authority records in Millennium are divided into two files: name and subject, the library should have MARS distribute authority rec-

ords in two files: Names/Series/Titles in one file and subjects in another file.

- What MARS reports do you want to order?
  MARS includes reports for gathering statistics and catching headings that might need change but cannot be easily decided by MARS software. Deciding which MARS report to order depends on the nine MARS profiles you filled out, as well as on the local procedures that are created based on the chosen profiles.
- Do you want to subscribe to MARS Authority Notification Service?
  MARS Authority Notification Service keeps your authority database up-to-date by notifying you when the authority records in your local system need to be updated, replaced, or deleted.
- Do you want to subscribe to MARS Current Cataloging Service'?
  MARS Current Cataloging Service keeps your newly added bibliographic records up to current authority standards and provides you with new authority records.

The second step in getting ready for MARS is to make sure everything is ready on your local Millennium system. The following issues have to be decided:

- What kind of bibliographic records do you want to send out for authority work? For example, do you want to include brief records like circ-on-the-fly or on-order records?
- Are your output tables up-to-date? Do you need to set up special load tables just for MARS authority control? What overlay parameters should be protected?

THE FACETS OF AUTHORITY CONTROL

Bring the Existing Bibliographic Database Up to Current Authority Standards and Create a New Authority Database

This facet of authority control can be accomplished in the initial authority processing of MARS. The library sends its whole bibliographic database to MARS. MARS processes it according to the profiles the library chose and returns it to the library updated to current authority standards. Together with the returned bibliographic database, the library also gets a file of up-to-date authority records. The "washed" bibliographic database and the file of authority records are then loaded into the local system. If the library had an old local authority database, it should be removed before the file of authority records from MARS is loaded. This initial authority "wash" will bring the existing bibliographic database up to current authority practices and create a brand-new authority database. MARS will also provide the library with various MARS reports that the library has ordered. The authority control librarian should go through those reports and take appropriate actions in the local system.

Bring the Newly Added Bibliographic Records Up to Current Authority Standards

This facet of authority control is an ongoing process that can be achieved by MARS Current Cataloging Service. After the initial database "wash," the library can send newly added bibliographic records to MARS at a frequency it prefers for authority processing. With the returned file of updated bibliographic records, the library also gets a file of new authority records that match the headings in the updated bibliographic records. The library can request that only the bibliographic records that have been changed by MARS processing be returned. Both files are loaded into the local system. Reports ordered by the library detailing changes made or noting records suspected of being in need of change are also delivered. The authority control librarian goes through those reports and makes appropriate changes in the local system.

In addition to MARS Current Cataloging Service, the library can also use Millennium reports such as First Time Use Headings and Invalid Headings to monitor newly added headings. This depends on how frequently the library sends its newly added bibliographic records to MARS. One point to remember is that the library should have the MARS software do as much as possible to save manpower. For example, if the library decides to take advantage of the First Time Use Headings, it should not have the authority control librarian check each heading in the authority database since MARS will do the work later. Instead, the authority control librarian can just browse the report and correct obvious mistakes, such as misspellings, wrong tags, or wrong indicators.

Keep the Newly Created Authority Database Up-to-Date as External Authority Structure Changes, and, at the Same Time, Keep the Existing Bibliographic Records Up to Current Authority Standards

This facet of authority control is ongoing, also. This can be done through MARS Authority Notification Service, Millennium Automatic Authorities Processing, Millennium Global Update, and Millennium reports, among other services.

MARS Authority Notification Service notifies the library of updated, replaced, or deleted authority records at a frequency picked by the library. It delivers a file of replacement authority records which get loaded into the local system. At the same time, the existing bibliographic records in the local system get updated through the Millennium Automatic Authorities Processing.

Millennium Automatic Authorities Processing updates headings under authority control in MARC 21 bibliographic records. Whenever an authority record is edited or downloaded, it is written to a system file. At a time designated by the library, the system file is processed. For each *see from* heading (MARC 4XX) in an authority record, the Millennium Automatic Authorities Processing software searches for a matching bibliographic heading in the same index. If it finds a match, it updates the bibliographic heading based on the valid form of the heading (MARC 1XX) in the authority record.

Several issues need to be monitored when using Millennium Automatic Authorities Processing:

- If an authority record is used both as name and subject headings in bibliographic records, the authority record has to go through the system transaction file twice, once as the name heading and once as the subject heading.
- This function does not update free floating subdivisions (MARC 180, 181, 182, or 185 fields). The library needs special procedures for this situation. One possibility is to use *Library of Congress Cataloging Service Bulletin* to monitor the changes in free floating subdivisions and then use Millennium Global Update to update them.
- This function does not update subfield z of a 6XX field. The library needs special procedures for this situation, too. The library can also use *Library of Congress Cataloging Service Bulletin* to monitor the changes in geographical subject headings and then use Millennium Global Update to update the subfield z.
- This function is triggered strictly by the existence of 4XX references in authority records. Unfortunately, updated authority records do not always have 4XX references to their former headings. This happens frequently with name authority headings. For example, when a death date is added to a name authority heading, the former heading which is without the death date is not added as a 4XX reference in the updated authority record. Thus, after a file of MARS authority records gets loaded into the local Millennium system, the library will often get a much larger than normal blind reference list. The authority control librarian has to be very careful when dealing with the blind reference list after a MARS authority record load because most of the entries on that blind reference list are

authority records provided by MARS. They show up on the blind reference list because Millennium Automatic Authorities Processing fails to update the bibliographic records due to the lack of 4XX to their former headings in the authority records. The authority control librarian has to update the headings in the bibliographic records manually with the help of Millennium Global Update.

With the returned file of replacement authority records, MARS Authority Notification Service also delivers a list or file of deleted authority records if the library orders it. This list is crucial for deleting the obsolete authority records from the local authority database.

In addition, reports generated by Millennium are very useful in this facet. One important report is Blind References. Blind references are generated by 4XX or 5XX entries in authority records to which no bibliographic records are linked. The authority records that cause blind references should be deleted since they will confuse library users. The authority control librarian should review the blind reference lists carefully instead of deleting them without checking the nearby headings because some of the entries, by the standards of the library, might not be blind at all.

For example:

```
01 ACODE1: -    02 ACODE2: -    03 ASUPPRESS: -
04 001    sh 85114460
05 003    DLC
06 005    19920422083755.1
07 008    860211i| anannbab|         |a ana ||| cz n
08 010    sh 85114460
09 040    DLC|cDLC|dDLC
10 053    HD9717.5.R6|bHD9717.5.R64
11 150   0 Road construction equipment industry
12 550   0 |wg|aConstruction equipment industry
```

The above authority record for "Road construction equipment industry" appears on the blind reference list. But, after checking the catalog, it is found that, though there is not any bibliographic record using "Road construction equipment industry" itself as a subject heading, there are bibliographic records using the heading "Road construction equipment industry |z United States." In this case, "Road construction equipment industry" might not be blind by the standpoint of the library because it provides reference pointers for "Road construction equipment industry |z United States." For instance, if a library user searches for "Construction equipment industry" (the 550 in the above authority record), he will get "Construction Equipment Industry--See also--<u>Road Construction Equipment Industry</u>" in the WebPAC. Click on the hotlink "<u>Road Construction Equipment Industry,</u>" it will lead to the bibliographic record using the heading "Road construction equipment industry |z United States." Similar cases happen to title and name headings. Thus, deleting blind references using the Millennium blind reference lists alone, without the inspection of the nearby headings, would not be recommended.

Another important report is Invalid Headings. Invalid headings should be checked against the OCLC authority database to ensure that they are indeed invalid. Invalid headings will be caught by MARS processing. If a library chooses to have MARS authority processing on an infrequent basis, the authority control librarian can use Invalid Headings to update authority records more timely.

Besides Blind Reference and Invalid Heading reports, Bibliographic Updates, NON-Unique 4XX, Cross-Thesaurus Matches, Near Matches, and Busy Matches can be very helpful too, depending on the setup in the local system.

Special Issues

- Staffing

  The library should designate an authority control librarian to oversee the whole process of authority control and deal with reports from MARS and Millennium. That librarian should work closely with the library's Millennium systems administrator or whomever is responsible for outputting records to MARS and loading returned records back into the local system. Authority control will constitute only a certain percentage of the work of an authority control librarian since the MARS processing does not happen on a daily basis. How much of a percentage authority control will amount to in the job description of an authority control librarian depends on how large the local bibliographic database is and how frequently the library sends its newly added bibliographic records to MARS for processing.

- MARS master authority profile

  MARS keeps a master "authority profile" of a library's authority database, which governs the delivery of new and updated authority records to the library. If authority records get deleted or added without notifying MARS, the reality of the library's local authority database will differ further and further from its master profile at MARS. To prevent this from happening, the library should submit to MARS lists of authority records added or deleted in its local authority database at a frequency coordinated with MARS.

• Split headings

Split headings are headings replaced by two or more new headings. In the MARS profile, there are two choices for dealing with split headings. The library can choose either to let MARS replace the obsolete headings with all replacement headings or leave obsolete headings intact.

If the library chooses to replace obsolete split headings blindly with all replacement headings, it will create inaccurate subject headings in some bibliographic records. This can be solved by ordering relevant MARS reports and doing a manual review of those reports. If the library chooses to have MARS leave the obsolete split headings intact, it can order relevant MARS reports and deal with them later, manually, with the help of Millennium Global Update.

• Normalization

According to "Authority File Comparison Rules (NACO Normalization)," "a field 4XX may normalize to the same string as another 4XX in the same or another record" [2].

This presents the potential for incorrect heading replacement in the MARS automatic authority processing. The authority control librarian has to be aware of this problem and notify MARS when it occurs.

• Gap time policy

The gap time begins when bibliographic records are sent to MARS for processing and it ends when returned bibliographic records are loaded into the local system. The library might want to have special cataloging policies for gap time periods since some of the changes made in the database during the gap time could be wiped out by the reloaded records.

CONCLUSION

This article provides general guidelines on authority control procedures for Millennium users that choose to outsource authority control to MARS. It could also be useful to Millennium users that choose to use other authority control vendors. It is important to remember that authority control does not exist in an abstract universe. It always exists in a specific environment which involves local systems and/or authority control vendors. Decisions on authority control procedures should be based on the context of a specific local environment.

AUTHOR NOTE

The author wishes to thank Mike Nelson, the bibliographic control librarian at Eastern Washington University, for his invaluable insight and extensive trouble-shooting work in the WSU-EWU shared authority control project (2001-2003) which inspired the writing of this article. Special thanks go to Janet Chisman, Mark Jacobs, Mike Nelson, Marilyn Von Seggern, Elisabeth Spanhoff, and Sharon Walbridge for reading a draft of the article and for their helpful comments.

ENDNOTES

[1] "OCLC MARS." Available http://www.oclc.org/western/products/mars/authorityprocessing.htm (viewed June 5, 2003).

[2] "Authority File Comparison Rules (NACO Normalization)." Available http://www.loc.gov/catdir/pcc/naco/normrule.html (viewed June 5, 2003).

Index

621

BOOK ORDER FORM!

Order a copy of this book with this form or online at:
http://www.haworthpress.com/store/product.asp?sku=5444

Authority Control in Organizing and Accessing Information
Definition and International Experience

____ in softbound at $34.95 (ISBN: 0-7890-2716-X)
____ in hardbound at $59.95 (ISBN: 0-7890-2715-1)

COST OF BOOKS _____

POSTAGE & HANDLING _____
US: $4.00 for first book & $1.50
for each additional book
Outside US: $5.00 for first book
& $2.00 for each additional book.

SUBTOTAL _____

In Canada: add 7% GST. _____

STATE TAX _____
CA, IL, IN, MN, NJ, NY, OH & SD residents
please add appropriate local sales tax.

FINAL TOTAL _____
If paying in Canadian funds, convert
using the current exchange rate,
UNESCO coupons welcome.

❑ BILL ME LATER:
Bill-me option is good on US/Canada/
Mexico orders only; not good to jobbers,
wholesalers, or subscription agencies.

❑ Signature _____

❑ Payment Enclosed: $ _____

❑ PLEASE CHARGE TO MY CREDIT CARD:

❑ Visa ❑ MasterCard ❑ AmEx ❑ Discover
❑ Diner's Club ❑ Eurocard ❑ JCB

Account # _____

Exp Date _____

Signature _____
(Prices in US dollars and subject to change without notice.)

PLEASE PRINT ALL INFORMATION OR ATTACH YOUR BUSINESS CARD

Name

Address

City   State/Province   Zip/Postal Code

Country

Tel   Fax

E-Mail

May we use your e-mail address for confirmations and other types of information? ❑ Yes ❑ No We appreciate receiving
your e-mail address. Haworth would like to e-mail special discount offers to you, as a preferred customer.
We will never share, rent, or exchange your e-mail address. We regard such actions as an invasion of your privacy.

Order From Your **Local Bookstore** or Directly From
The Haworth Press, Inc. 10 Alice Street, Binghamton, New York 13904-1580 • USA
Call Our toll-free number (1-800-429-6784) / Outside US/Canada: (607) 722-5857
Fax: 1-800-895-0582 / Outside US/Canada: (607) 771-0012
E-mail your order to us: orders@haworthpress.com

For orders outside US and Canada, you may wish to order through your local
sales representative, distributor, or bookseller.
For information, see http://haworthpress.com/distributors

(Discounts are available for individual orders in US and Canada only, not booksellers/distributors.)

Please photocopy this form for your personal use.
www.HaworthPress.com

BOF04